Lecture Notes in Computer Science 9677

Commenced Publication in 1973
Founding and Former Series Editors:
Gerhard Goos, Juris Hartmanis, and Jan van Leeuwen

More information about this series at http://www.springer.com/series/7409

Carl K. Chang · Lorenzo Chiari · Yu Cao
Hai Jin · Mounir Mokhtari · Hamdi Aloulou (Eds.)

Inclusive Smart Cities and Digital Health

14th International Conference
on Smart Homes and Health Telematics, ICOST 2016
Wuhan, China, May 25–27, 2016
Proceedings

 Springer

Editors
Carl K. Chang
Iowa State University
Ames, IA
USA

Lorenzo Chiari
University of Bologna
Bologna
Italy

Yu Cao
The University of Massachusetts
Lowell, MA
USA

Hai Jin
Huazhong University of Science
  and Technology
Wuhan
China

Mounir Mokhtari
Institut Mines Télécom Paris/CNRS
Paris
France

Hamdi Aloulou
Institut Mines Télécom
Paris
France

ISSN 0302-9743   ISSN 1611-3349   (electronic)
Lecture Notes in Computer Science
ISBN 978-3-319-39600-2   ISBN 978-3-319-39601-9   (eBook)
DOI 10.1007/978-3-319-39601-9

Library of Congress Control Number: 2016940103

LNCS Sublibrary: SL3 – Information Systems and Applications, incl. Internet/Web, and HCI

Printed on acid-free paper

This Springer imprint is published by Springer Nature
The registered company is Springer International Publishing AG Switzerland

Preface

After 13 very successful conferences held annually in Europe, Asia, and North America—ICOST was inaugurated in France (2003), and was subsequently hosted in Singapore (2004), Canada (2005), Northern Ireland (2006), Japan (2007), USA (2008), France (2009), Korea (2010), Canada (2011), Italy (2012), Singapore (2013), USA (2014) and Switzerland (2015)—the 14th International Conference on Smart Homes and Health Telematics (ICOST 2016) was hosted for the first time in China by Huazhong University of Science and Technology (HUST).

ICOST provides a premier venue for the presentation and exchange of research in the design, development, deployment, and evaluation of smart environments, assistive technologies, robotics and health telematics systems. ICOST brings together stakeholders from clinical, academic, and industrial perspectives along with end users and family caregivers to explore how to utilize technologies to foster independent living and offer an enhanced quality of life. ICOST 2016 invited participants from around the world to present and discuss their experience in the design, development, deployment, and evaluation of assistive and telehealth systems, as well as ethical, professional practice, and governmental policy issues. The conference featured a dynamic program incorporating a range of technical, clinical, and industrial keynote speakers, oral and poster presentations, along with demonstrations and technical exhibits.

The theme of the conference this year was "Inclusive Smart Cities and Digital Health" focusing on the quality of life of dependent people not only in their homes, but also in outdoor living environments, with the aim of improving mobility and social interaction in the city. Extending the living space with suitable ICT support in term of smart transportation, mobility, interaction, and socialization is the scientific challenge and promising innovation that ICOST community decided to tackle. ICTs are not limited only to end-users with special needs, but also to providers, caregivers and family members in charge of taking care of dependent and elderly people. To be more effective and impactful, technologies in different areas, such as Internet of Things (IoT), big data analytics, smart mobility etc., should target all the stakeholders.

ICOST 2016 and the organizing team and host in the famous city of Wuhan were proud to extend their hospitality to the participants from the international community from major universities and research centers as well as representatives of industry and users from more than 20 countries. This year we selected 38 full papers out of 83 submissions following a double-blind review, which were presented during the conference as oral presentations and regular posters sessions. A demonstration session was also planned so that academic and industry representatives could share their prototypes and future devices with the participants.

We were very pleased to host several world-renowned keynote speakers from the USA and France. We were extremely honored for the confidence of the sponsors and particularly the active support of the French Embassy in China and Renault, the industrial Gold Sponsor, who accepted to contribute actively to ICOST 2016.

April 2016

Carl K. Chang
Lorenzo Chiari
Yu Cao
Hai Jin
Mounir Mokhtari
Hamdi Aloulou

Organization

Honorary Chair

Shu Wang   Huazhong University of Science and Technology, China

General Chairs

Carl K. Chang   Iowa State University, USA
Hai Jin   Huazhong University of Science and Technology, China

Advisory Board

Jian Lv   Academician and Vice President, Nanjing University, China
Hong Mei   Academician and Vice President, Shanghai Jiaotong University, China
Kwang-Hwa Lii   Vice President, National Central University, Taiwan
Ling Liu   Professor and Editor-in-Chief of IEEE TSC, Georgia Institute of Technology, USA
Peter Martin   Professor and Fulbright Scholar, Iowa State University, USA
Liang-Jie Zhang   Chief Scientist, Kingdee, China
Qinghua Zheng   Vice President, Xi'an Jiaotong University, China

Scientific Committee

Chair

Sumi Helal   University of Florida, USA

Members

Bessam Abdulrazak   Université de Sherbrooke, Canada
Z. Zenn Bien   Korea Advanced Institute of Science and Technology, South Korea
Carl K. Chang   Iowa State University, USA
William Cheng-Chung Chu   Tunghai University, Taiwan
Jean-Louis Coatrieux   Université de Rennes 1, France

Sylvain Giroux	Université de Sherbrooke, Canada
Nick Hine	University of Dundee, UK
Ismail Khalil	Johannes Kepler University, Austria
Yeunsook Lee	Yonsei University/The Korean Gerontological Society, South Korea
Mounir Mokhtari	Institut Mines Télécom, CNRS IPAL, Singapore/ CNRS LIRMM, France
Chris Nugent	University of Ulster, UK
Cristiano Paggetti	I+ S.r.l, Italy
Christian Roux	Institut Mines Télécom, École des Mines de St. Etienne, France
Tatsuya Yamazaki	National Institute of Information and Communications Technology, Japan
Daqing Zhang	Institut Mines Télécom/Télécom SudParis, France

Program Committee

Chairs

Lorenzo Chiari	University of Bologna, Italy
Sunyoung Lee	Kyung Hee University, South Korea

Vice Chair

Yu Cao	The University of Massachusetts Lowell, USA

Members

Iyad Abuhadrous	Palestine Technical College, Palestine
Jehad Aljaam	Qatar University, Qatar
Hamdi Aloulou	Institut Mines Télécom, France
Sameer Antani	National Library of Medicine, National Institutes of Health (NIH), USA
Guohua Bai	Blekinge Institute of Technology, Sweden
Lucia Ballerini	University of Dundee, UK
Yu Cao	The University of Massachusetts Lowell, USA
Filippo Cavallo	The BioRobotics Institute, Scuola Superiore Sant'Anna, Italy
Carl K.Chang	Iowa State University, USA
Lorenzo Chiari	DEI, University of Bologna, Italy
Belkacem Chikhaoui	Prospectus Laboratory, University of Sherbrooke, Canada
Paolo Ciampolini	University of Parma, Italy
Juan Corchado	University of Salamanca, Spain
Pepijn Van de Ven	University of Limerick, Ireland
Mark Donnelly	University of Ulster, UK

Romain Endelin	Institut Mines Télécom, France
Bjoern Eskofier	Friedrich-Alexander-Universität Erlangen-Nürnberg, Germany
Elisabetta Farella	Bruno Kessler Foundation, Italy
Babak A. Farshchian	SINTEF ICT, Norway
Siang Fook Victor Foo	Institute for Infocomm Research, Singapore
Xiaohong Gao	Middlesex University London, UK
Hayit Greenspan	Tel Aviv University, Israel
Kasper Hallenborg	The Maersk Mc-Kinney Moller Institute, Denmark
Sanqing Hu	Hangzhou Dianzi University, China
Weimin Huang	Institute for Infocomm Research, Singapore
Byeong-Ho Kang	University of Tasmania, Australia
Victor Kaptelinin	University of Bergen, Norway
Hisato Kobayashi	Hosei University Tokyo, Japan
Duckki Lee	University of Florida, USA
Jae-Woong Lee	University of Central Missouri, USA
Ji-Hyun Lee	GSCT, KAIST, South Korea
Sunyoung Lee	Kyung Hee University, South Korea
Yan Liu	Advanced Digital Sciences Center of Illinois at Singapore, Singapore
Martina Mancini	Oregon Health & Science University, USA
Fulvio Mastrogiovanni	DIBRIS, University of Genoa, Italy
Sabato Mellone	DEI, University of Bologna, Italy
Abdallah M'Hamed	Telecom SudParis - Evry, France
Pino Mincolelli	University of Ferrara, Italy
Hongbo Ni	Northwestern Polytechnical University, Xi'an, China
Chris Nugent	Computer Science Research Institute, University of Ulster, UK
Cristiano Paggetti	I+, Italy
Patrice C. Roy	NICHE Research Group, Dalhousie University, Canada
Michael Schwenk	Robert Bosch Hospital Stuttgart, Germany
Daby Sow	IBM Research, USA
Thibaut Tiberghien	Image & Pervasive Access Lab (IPAL), UMI CNRS, France
Ramiro Velazquez	Universidad Panamericana, Mexico
Jiayin Wang	Xi'an Jiaotong University, China
Manfred Wojciechowski	University of Applied Sciences, Düsseldorf, Germany
Philip Yap-Lin-Kiat	Khoo Teck Puat Hospital, Singapore
Rami Yared	University of Sherbrooke, Canada
Yueting Zhang	Chinese University of Hong Kong (CUHK), Hong Kong, SAR China
Tatjana Zrimec	University New South Wales, Australia

Organizing Committee

Chair

Tian Xia   Huazhong University of Science and Technology, China

Members

Hongbo Jiang   Huazhong University of Science and Technology, China

Ke Ma   Huazhong University of Science and Technology, China

Gui Liu   Huazhong University of Science and Technology, China

Wenping Liu   Hubei University of Economics, China

Qinghua Lu   China University of Petroleum, China

Panel Chair

Daqing Zhang   Peking University, China

Workshop Chair

Mu-Chun Su   National Central University, Taiwan

Proceedings Chair

Hamdi Aloulou   Institut Mines Télécom, CNRS LIRMM, France

Community Networking Chair

Bessam Abdulrazak   Université de Sherbrooke, Canada

Web Chairs

Ke Ma   Huazhong University of Science and Technology, China

Gui Liu   Huazhong University of Science and Technology, China

Finance Chair

Ying Cai   Iowa State University, USA

Registration Chairs

Sangbo Nam   Iowa State University, USA
Gui Liu   Huazhong University of Science and Technology,
                            China

Sponsors (Alphabetical Order)

French Embassy in China, France
French National Centre for Scientific Research, France
Huazhong University of Science and Technology, China
IEEE Computer Magazine
IEEE Transactions on Services Computing
Image and Pervasive Access Lab, CNRSUMI 2955, Singapore
Institut Mines Télécom, France
Iowa State University, USA
National Central University, Taiwan
Peking University Medical Informatics Center, China
Renault (Beijing) Automotive Co. Lt., France
University of Florida, USA

Contents

Home Networks and Residential Gateways

Middleware Support for Smart Homes and Health Telematic Services

E-Health and Chronic Disease Management

E-Health Technology Assessment and Impact Analysis

Tele-Assistance and Tele-Rehabilitation

Modeling of Physical and Conceptual Information in Intelligent Environments

Medical Big Data Collection, Processing, and Analysis

Human Machine Interfaces

Wearable Sensors and Continuous Health Monitoring

Social, Privacy, and Security Issues

Workshop 1: Mobile Health Services

Workshop 2: Smart Rehabilitation Technologies

Smart Homes, Smart Urban Spaces and New Assistive Living Space Concepts in the Smart City

Multi-resident Location Tracking in Smart Home through Non-wearable Unobtrusive Sensors

Jie Yin, Meng Fang, Ghassem Mokhtari, and Qing Zhang[✉]

CSIRO, Herston, QLD, Australia
{jie.yin,meng.fang,ghassem.mokhtari,qing.zhang}@csiro.au

Abstract. Tracking indoor locations of residents is a prerequisite of accurate monitoring and advanced understanding of human activities in smart homes. Without using any indoor video surveillance devices in terms of preserving privacy and security, majority of existing approaches often utilise wearable BLE/RFID sensor tags to track locations of residents through analysing variations of received signal strength and angle of sensor tags. In a multi-residential environment, these tags can also be used as unique identifiers to help distinguish individuals. However, the extra burdens of remembering and wearing sensor tags all day along restrict them to be widely accepted by senior communities, let alone by people with neurodegenerative diseases. In this study, we propose a novel indoor tracking technique for smart homes with multiple residents, through relying only on non-wearable, environmentally deployed sensors such as passive infrared motion sensors. We design a multi-tracker system that uses multiple, independent probabilistic models, such as Naive Bayes and hidden Markov model, to track different residents' movements separately. We evaluate our tracking technique on real sensor data acquired from a dual-occupancy smart home in our clinical trials. The experiment results, through comparing with location details acquired by wearable tags, demonstrate that our proposed technique is a simple yet feasible solution to tracking multi-residents' indoor movements.

Keywords: Smart home · Indoor localisation · Multiple residents · Motion sensors

1 Introduction

The original Smart Home concept was proposed in 1980s and found its wide application in health and ageing to support independent livings of elderly people [11]. Over the last two decades, along with the emerging of new technology in mobile computing, smart sensor and Internet of Things, smart home has been a hot topic and is poised for strong growth in assistance in health and wellbeing. Communicating with in-home deployed sensors, a Smart Home monitors changes of its residents' health and wellbeing status through understanding their circadian rhythms of indoor activities and behaviour, such as sleeping patterns,

© Springer International Publishing Switzerland 2016
C.K. Chang et al. (Eds.): ICOST 2016, LNCS 9677, pp. 3–13, 2016.
DOI: 10.1007/978-3-319-39601-9_1

activities of daily living (ADL), to provide timely interventions when necessary. Since many indoor activities happen at certain locations, such as preparing meal and eating usually in kitchen and lounge, showering in bathroom, sleeping in bedroom, tracking indoor locations of smart home residents with room-level granularity patently becomes a prerequisite of many if not all smart home monitoring and assistive functions.

For a smart home only targeting residents living alone, indoor localisation can be easily achieved through passive infrared (PIR) motion sensors deployed in each room, assuming they can only be triggered by this only resident [5,9]. However, for smart homes with multiple residents, indoor localisation and tracking for separate individuals becomes very challenging. A naive approach is to install video cameras in each room which is intrusive and raises considerable concerns on privacy. Thus we do not consider using cameras in this study. Another commonly adopted approach in smart home is to ask residents to carry RF tags, such as RFID, BLE, or even their own mobile phones. These tags communicate with base stations to report their ID and distance frequently, which can be then used to accurately pinpoint their locations. Nevertheless these tags, or wearable sensors, share a common problem, i.e. adding extra burdens by requiring residents to always remember wearing those tags, which could become over-demanding requirements especially to seniors with neurodegenerative diseases. Motivated by these, we provide a tag-free indoor tracking solution that aims at reporting individuals' real-time locations with room-level granularity in a multi-occupancy smart home through only environmentally deployed sensors such as PIR motion sensors.

There exist some tag/device-free indoor localisation methods, such as through pressure mat, ultrasound, electric field, etc., that have been witnessed in literature, [6,10]. However, these solutions are either too costly in terms of price and installation efforts, or focus solely on localisation without differentiating identities of residents. In our work, we propose the use of passive infrared motion sensors to track individuals' locations in multi-occupancy smart homes. To differentiate residents, we design a multi-tracker system that employs multiple, independent probabilistic models, such as Naive Bayes and hidden Markov model, to track different residents' movements separately. We believe the multi-tracker system proposed in this paper can provide a low-cost but practical solution to multi-resident indoor tracking based on PIR motion sensors only.

In order to track locations of smart home residents to an acceptable level, we need to train our multi-tracker system that requires accurately labeled data, i.e. ground truth, for learning. However, one of the major challenges in this paradigm is the collection of reliable ground truth. Previous work has deployed intrusive devices such as video cameras to record residents' whereabouts [1], or relied on residents themselves to manually log their movements over a period of time [3]. These solutions either invariably invoke privacy issues or result in incomplete, error-prone annotations for learning. In this work, to collect quality ground truth without intrusive sensor deployment or residents' manual logging, we borrow the idea of tag-based localisation to propose a semi-automatic approach that utilises wearable Bluetooth Low Energy (BLE) tags to assist with the training of our multi-tracker system. Initial experimental results on real sensor data collected from a dual-occupancy smart home has demonstrated that our proposed technique is a low-cost yet promising solution to tracking multi-residents' indoor movements.

The rest of this paper is structured as follows. In Sect. 2, we introduce our Smart Home platform and ground truth collection from a dual-occupancy smart home in our clinical trials. Section 3 details our probabilistic model for multi-resident location tracking. This is followed by experimental results and discussions in Sect. 4. Section 5 concludes this paper with some future works.

2 Smarter Safer Home Platform

To test the proposed multi-resident location tracking method, we use real sensor data collected through the Smarter Safer Home (SSH) platform. In the following, we first give an overview of the SSH platform, and then discuss the bluetooth localisation approach we take to collect ground truth for multi-resident location tracking.

2.1 Overview of SSH Platform

The SSH platform aims at developing an innovative wireless sensor based in-home monitoring and data analytics platform, which seeks to support and extend independence and improve quality of life for aged residents through the use of cutting edge pervasive computing and wireless communication technologies. The potential benefits of these technologies are multiplied where distance separates families and adds substantial costs to delivery of health and other services.

The core principle of the SSH platform is to infer health and wellbeing status of residents through wireless sensor based in-home monitoring system [12]. This system consists of approximately 20 sensors positioned discretely throughout the home to detect motion, temperature, humidity, appliance usage, door open/close and sleep restlessness, as an example shown in Fig. 1.

Almost all sensors, except power sensor, are battery powered to increase installation flexibility and decrease maintenance requirements. Each of the sensor gathers data about a different aspect of resident lifestyle and activities contributing to functional independence. For instance, a motion sensor detects movements within its vicinity and reports to an in-home gateway using Zigbee communication protocols. These data will be then analysed to track locations of smart home residents to understand their mobility performance. To simplify installation and ensure continuously high quality sensor data, we use only quality proofed off-the-shelf sensors in our smart homes. The motion sensor is a passive infrared one, having up to five meters detection range with 100° angle. It has one second delay before firing when a movement is first detected, with 20 s delay when no movements are detected. So even for a smart home with an independent living

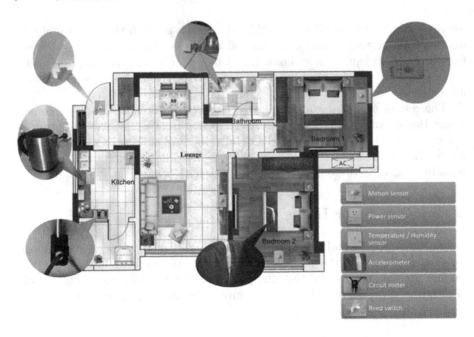

Fig. 1. A smart home with various types of wireless sensors.

resident, it is not surprising that two motion sensors fire simultaneously by signalling movements detected, let alone smart home with multiple residents. This patently complicates the location and tracking problem and poses a big challenge for indoor localisation through only environmentally deployed motion sensors.

2.2 Ground Truth Collection Through Bluetooth Localisation

To gather ground truth of individual movements in home, we install Bluetooth Low Energy scanners in SSH and detect Received Signal Strength Indicator (RSSI) of wearable sensors through BLE scanners. Figure 2 shows the floor map of a dual-occupancy smart home, with positions of motion sensors and BLE scanners. For each room, we deploy one motion sensor to sufficiently cover room/interesting zone level movements.

We also deploy six scanners that listen to BLE broadcasts from two tags attached to in-home residents separately. Each tag has a unique ID to be considered as the identity of the resident wearing it. Tags advertise their IDs in a fixed time interval (*advertising interval*). On each scanner, we developed a mobile application to scan and receive tag advertisements with their signal strength values. Similar to BLE advertisement, BLE scanning scans all BLE signals in a fixed time interval (*scanning interval*). The information of scanned tags is uploaded to a centralized server by scanners, and will be collectively computed to determine the location of tag bearers by the server. Figure 3 shows the framework of our BLE RSSI localisation approach.

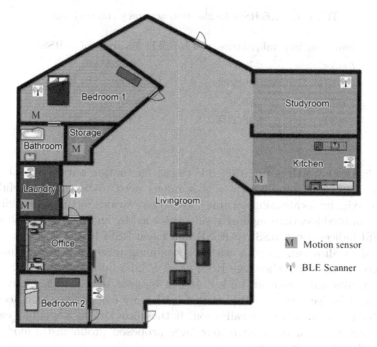

Fig. 2. A dual occupancy smart home with motion sensors and BLE scanners

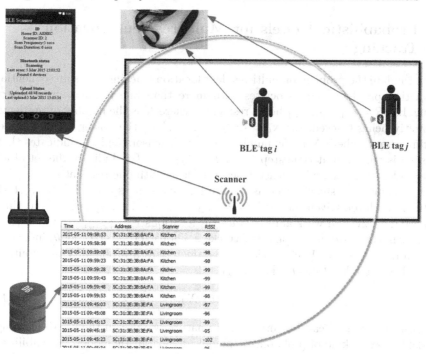

Fig. 3. An indoor localisation system based on BLE RSSI scanning

Table 1. BLE RSSI localisation accuracy comparisons

Sampling interval	Accuracy of p-RSSI	Accuracy of m-RSSI
$t = 5\,\mathrm{s}$	79.17 %	88.61 %
$t = 10\,\mathrm{s}$	80.56 %	92.22 %
$t = 15\,\mathrm{s}$	80 %	96.67 %
$t = 30\,\mathrm{s}$	78.33 %	100 %

It is however worth noting that due to the fluctuation nature of BLE RSSI signal strength, the sampling rates of scanners need to be tuned carefully to achieve maximum localisation accuracy. We tested various settings through comparing computed locations against results recorded by an independent observer. Two RSSI indices, peak RSSI (p-RSSI) and mean RSSI (m-RSSI), are used for residential localisation. That is within a sampling interval t, p-RSSI/m-RSSI represents the maximum/average RSSI of all RSSI values within t. Our experimental results are shown in Table 1. It can be seen that in this smart home environment, by selecting m-RSSI with $t \geq 15\,s$, we can achieve high accuracy (above 95 %) for room-level localisation. It thus provides us a reliable, easy to acquire ground truth to evaluate our later proposed probabilistic models for multi-resident location tracking.

3   Probabilistic Models for Multi-resident Location Tracking

We formulate the problem of multi-resident location tracking as a sum sequential prediction problem that associates with more than one residents in a smart home. Let $R = \{r_1, \cdots, r_K\}$ be all residents, where K is the number of residents currently being tracked. Let $\mathbf{x}_t = \{x_{1,t}, \cdots, x_{N,t}\}$ be the sensor data collected at time step t, where N is the number of motion sensors and $x_{i,t}$ indicates that sensor i is triggered at time step t. Let $F = \{f_1, \cdots, f_K\}$ indicate the set of all independent trackers, where each tracker f_i deals with one resident i.

Let us model a smart home as a finite location-state space $\mathbb{L} = \{l_1, \ldots, l_M\}$ at the room level. Given sensor data $X_{t:t+\Delta} = \{\mathbf{x}_t, \cdots, \mathbf{x}_{t+\Delta}\}$ collected at time interval $[t, t+\Delta)$, our work aims to track the locations $Y = \{\mathbf{y}_{1,t}, \cdots, \mathbf{y}_{K,t+\Delta}\}$ of K residents that are the output of K trackers. For each tracker f_j, let θ_j indicates the parameter vector. Each tracker f_j parameterizes a probability distribution over all possible locations $l \in \mathbb{L}$, that is,

$$\mathbf{y}_j = f_j(\theta_j, X). \tag{1}$$

Because sensor data can be very noisy in nature, we design the above learning model to be any kind of probabilistic models. Probabilistic models have abilities to capture the uncertainty of sensor data and can calculate the likelihood of residents being at possible locations accordingly.

There are some advantages using the multi-tracker algorithm discussed above. First, the state space of multi-resident location tracking is very large, making the process of model learning intractable. By simply assuming independence between different trackers, the state space can be largely reduced and the learning algorithm can be efficiently implemented. Second, each tracker can model different preferences and behaviour of individual residents in the context of the multi-resident spaces [7], so that locations of different residents can be estimated accurately.

In our work, we primarily investigate the use of two probabilistic models, including a Naive Bayes classifier and a hidden Markov model (HMM). The two probabilistic models have been demonstrated with good performance in other smart home research projects [3,4]. The two models are both trained using the results of bluetooth localisation as ground truth and make inferences to perform room-level location tracking.

3.1   Multi-tracker with Naive Bayes

A Naive Bayes classifier is first used in our multi-tracker algorithm to estimate the locations of residents. It falls into a family of simple probabilistic methods by applying Bayes' theorem with independence assumption between the features. In our location tracking problem, let each state indicate possible locations of residents and motion sensors provide observations about the state. A Naive Bayes classifier can directly estimate the likelihood of residents being at specific locations from the data collected from motion sensors.

Specifically, given the sensor data $\mathbf{x}_t = \{x_{1,t}, \cdots, x_{N,t}\}$ collected from N motion sensors at each time step t, for each resident j, the Naive Bayes classifier computes the posterior probability by applying Bayes' theorem as follows:

$$p(y_{j,t}|\mathbf{x}_t) \propto p(y_{j,t}) \prod_{i=1}^{N} p(x_{i,t}|y_{j,t}), \tag{2}$$

which indicates the likelihood of resident j being at possible locations. Based on this, we can estimate the location $y_{j,t}$ of resident j at time step t as

$$y_{j,t}^* = \arg\max_{y_{j,t}} p(y_{j,t}|\mathbf{x}_t). \tag{3}$$

In our problem, since location tracking should provide sequential predictions about a resident' locations. Thus, by assuming a resident's locations are independent at different time steps, we have

$$\mathbf{y}_j = \{y_{j,t}^*, \cdots, y_{j,t+\Delta}^*\}. \tag{4}$$

Then for all residents, we have

$$Y = \{\mathbf{y}_1, \cdots, \mathbf{y}_K\}. \tag{5}$$

3.2   Multi-tracker with Hidden Markov Models

The Naive Bayes classifier assumes that residents' locations at different time steps are independent of each other. This assumption may not hold in practice, because when residents move around at home, their locations possibly exhibit certain temporal dependency over time. Therefore, we adopt a hidden Markov model in our multi-tracker algorithm. An HMM is proved to be a powerful statistical tool for sequence modeling in different application domains.

The HMM is a generative probabilistic model characterised by an underlying Markov process that generates an observation sequence from the hidden state sequence. In our problem, let the location of residents y be the hidden state variable and the sensor data $\mathbf{x}$ be the observable variable. There are two dependence assumptions in HMM modeling. First, the motion model $p(y_t|y_{t-1})$ represents the likelihood of transition from the previous state y_{t-1} to the current state y_t. That means the current state is dependent only upon the previous state. Second, the current observation $\mathbf{x}_t$ depends only on the current state y_t. Given the observation sequence $X = \{\mathbf{x}_1, \cdots, \mathbf{x}_t\}$, we would like to find the most likely sequence of hidden states $\mathbf{y} = \{y_1, \cdots, y_t\}$, which indicates the most probable sequence of a resident's locations.

Formally, for each resident j, we use an HMM to model the joint probability as follows:

$$p(X, \mathbf{y}_j) = \prod_{t=1}^{T} p(y_{j,t}|y_{j,t-1})p(\mathbf{x}_t|y_{j,t}). \tag{6}$$

where, simply, we write the initial data distribution $p(y_1)$ as $p(y_1|y_0)$. Here $\mathbf{y}_j$ is the inferred sequence of locations for resident j.

Given the observation sequence X, the Viterbi algorithm can be used to compute the most likely sequence of locations for resident j, and we have

$$\mathbf{y}_j^* = \arg\max_{\mathbf{y}_j} p(X, \mathbf{y}_j). \tag{7}$$

Then for K residents, we construct a HMM-based tracker for each resident. Thus, we have

$$Y = \{\mathbf{y}_1, \cdots, \mathbf{y}_K\}. \tag{8}$$

4   Experiments

In our experiments, we used the dual-occupancy smart home shown in Fig. 2 as the testbed. This smart home consists of six rooms, including living room, kitchen, bathroom, laundry and two bedrooms. The data that we used in the experiments was generated by a couple of elder residents in a 12-month trial. During the trail, residents followed their normal daily routines such as making meals, watching TV, without wearing any tags/devices. We also installed five motion sensors that simply generated binary values when triggered by residents' movements within their vicinities. Our aim is to track the locations of these two residents only using the data collected from all motion sensors.

We evaluate the performance of our location tracking algorithms using the data collected over a period of seven days. During this period, two residents were requested to wear BLE tags, and six BLE scanners were deployed in the testbed that listen to BLE RSSI signals broadcast from two tags attached to residents. The locations of two residents at different time were estimated using the BLE localisation approach proposed in [8], which served as ground truth in our experiments. As a result, there are 2,880 records generated every day during which we had a location label every 30 s. Thus, we had a total of 20,160 records. For evaluation, we trained the models using the motion sensor data collected over the first four days, for which location labels estimated using the BLE localisation approach were treated as ground truth. The data collected at the rest of days were used for testing, in which location labels were kept hidden at first and then revealed for evaluation.

In our experiments, we focus on answering two research questions. First, is it feasible to track multiple residents' locations by using motion sensors only? Second, are there strong temporal dependencies among elderly people's movements at home?

We ran experiments to validate the localisation accuracy using both Naive Bayes and hidden Markov models with different settings. Because hidden Markov models capture temporal dependencies among consecutive states, we partitioned sequences of daily sensor data into segments and varied segment length from two to six. The results are reported in Table 2. We can see that, Naive Bayes and hidden Markov model can achieve about 73 % localisation accuracy. The performance of two models is comparable in regard to localisation accuracy, while hidden Markov models perform slightly better than Naive Bayes. We also observe that, hidden Markov models achieve the best localisation accuracy of 73.70 % when segment length is set to be four.

Table 2. Localisation accuracy using motion sensors

Naive bayes	Hidden Markov model
73.01 %	73.10 % (len = 2)
	73.20 % (len = 3)
	73.70 % (len = 4)
	73.34 % (len = 5)
	73.26 % (len = 6)

Our experimental results on room-level location tracking confirm findings found in previous studies (e.g., [2,7]) that multi-occupant activities can be better recognised if individual models for the residents are learned. Yet, using probabilistic sequence models for multi-resident location tracking, like hidden Markov models, does not lead to significant improvement over Naive Bayes, as it does for activity recognition. This is because, in-home activities, with a finer time granularity, such as cooking, tend to exhibit strong temporal dependencies among decomposed subtasks. The local temporal dependencies enforced by hidden Markov models can therefore place a strong emphasis on proper orderings of subtasks to improve recognition performance. In contrast, such strong dependencies do not exist for room-level location tracking, especially for the elderly people. For example, in this smart home testbed, one resident usually spends most of his time in the living room watching TV and seldom makes transitions to other rooms. This leads to weak dependencies among his movements at home, which can not be leveraged by probabilistic sequence models to boost the localisation accuracy.

5 Conclusion and Future Work

This paper addressed the problem of tracking indoor locations of multiple residents in smart home environments. We argued that, due to privacy and burden concerns, previous approaches to indoor location tracking that rely on wearable devices are not suitable as a practical solution in multi-resident smart homes. Thus, we proposed a new indoor tracking technique through non-wearable, environmentally deployed sensors such as motion sensors. To distinguish multi-residents' movements, we designed a multi-tracker system that uses multiple, independent probabilistic models, such as Naive Bayes and hidden Markov models. To aid in the collection of ground truth to learn such probabilistic models, we also presented a semi-automatic approach that makes use of Bluetooth Low Energy scanners to estimate locations in a less labor-intensive manner. Our tracking technique was evaluated on real sensor data collected from a dual-occupancy smart home in our clinical trials. The experimental results, through comparing with locations acquired by our BLE localisation approach, showed that our proposed technique could be a feasible solution to assist indoor tracking of multiple residents in real smart home systems.

The proposed work in this paper lays the groundwork for follow-on research on multi-resident location tracking and activity recognition. First, we will investigate how to improve localisation accuracy of our proposed tracking technique based on our deployed SSH platform. Second, we will evaluate the performance of the proposed tracking technique through larger-scale datasets collected from more multi-occupancy smart home testbeds in our clinical trials. Third, we will further examine temporal/spatial dependencies that are possibly present in room-level location tracking and other advanced probabilistic models, and investigate their potential to improve localisation accuracy.

References

1. Ayuningtyas, C., Leitner, G., Hitz, M., Funk, M., Hu, J., Rauterberg, M.: Activity Monitoring for Multi-inhabitant Smart Homes. SPIE Newsroom, Den Haag (2014)

2. Chiang, Y.-T., Hsu, J.Y.-J., Lu, C.-H., Fu, L.-C., Hsu, J.Y.-J.: Interaction models for multiple-resident activity recognition in a smart home. In: Proceedings of the 2010 IEEE/RSJ International Conference on Intelligent Robots and Systems (IROS), pp. 3753–3758. IEEE (2010)

3. Crandall, A.S., Cook, D.J.: Resident and caregiver: handling multiple people in a smart care facility. In: Proceedings of AAAI Fall Symposium 2008 – AI in Eldercare: New Solutions to Old Problems, pp. 39–47. AAAI Press (2008)

4. Crandall, A.S., Cook., D.J.: Using a hidden Markov model for resident identification. In: Proceedings of the Sixth International Conference on Intelligent Environments (IE), pp. 74–79. IEEE (2010)

5. Kim, H.H., Ha, K.N., Lee, S., Chang, K.: Resident location-recognition algorithm using a Bayesian classifier in the PIR sensor-based indoor location-aware system. IEEE Trans. Syst. Man Cybern. Part C Appl. Rev. **39**(2), 240–245 (2009)

6. Kivimäki, T., Vuorela, T., Peltola, P., Vanhala, J.: A review on device-free passive indoor positioning methods. Int. J. Smart. Home **8**(1), 71 (2014)

7. Lin, Z.-H., Fu, L.-C.: Multi-user preference model and service providion in a smart home environment. In: Proceedings of the IEEE Internatinal Conference on Automation Science and Engineering, pp. 759–764. IEEE (2007)

8. Mokhtari, G., Zhang, Q., Karunanithi, M.: Modeling of human movement monitoring using bluetooth low energy technology. In: Proceedings of the 37th Annual International Conference of the IEEE Engineering in Medicine and Biology Society (EMBC), pp. 5066–5069. IEEE (2015)

9. Narayana, S., Venkatesha Prasad, R., Rao, V.S., Prabhakar, T.V., Kowshik, S.S., Iyer, M.S.: PIR sensors: characterization and novel localization technique. In: Proceedings of the 14th International Conference on Information Processing in Sensor Networks, pp. 142–153. ACM (2015)

10. Pirttikangas, S., Suutala, J., Riekki, J., Rning, J.: Footstep identification from pressure signals using hidden Markov models. In: Proceedings of the Finnish Signal Processing Symposium, pp. 124–128 (2003)

11. Togawa, T., Tamura, T., Zhou, J., kMizukami, H., Ishijima, M.: Physiological monitoring systems attached to the bed, sanitary equipments. In: Proceedings of the 11th Annual International Conference of the IEEE Engineering in Medicine, Biology Society (EMBC), pp. 1461–1463. IEEE (1989)

12. Zhang, Q., Karunanithi, M., Bradford, D., van Kasteren, Y.: Activity of daily living assessment through wireless sensor data. In: Proceedings of the 36th Annual International Conference of the IEEE Engineering in Medicine and Biology Society (EMBC), pp. 1752–1755. IEEE (2014)

People Tracking in Ambient Assisted Living Environments Using Low-Cost Thermal Image Cameras

Christian Mandel$^{(\boxtimes)}$ and Serge Autexier

German Research Center for Artificial Intelligence,
Cyber Physical Systems Cartesium {0.51/1.49}, Enrique-Schmidt-Str. 5,
28359 Bremen, Germany
{Christian.Mandel,Serge.Autexier}@dfki.de

Abstract. In this paper we propose the use of low-cost thermal imaging sensors for the application of people tracking in Ambient Assisted Living environments. We describe background subtraction and segmentation on low-resolution thermal images as the necessary preprocessing steps to derive suitable percepts. Extensive data association to samples of a set of Monte-Carlo particle filters is realized by circle-circle intersection tests between percepts and pose hypotheses. Experimental evaluation conducted in the Bremen Ambient Assisted Living Lab proves the precision of the proposed system by comparing the tracking results against ground truth data coming from an ARTTRACK optical tracking system.

Keywords: Tracking system · Thermal camera · Data association · Particle filter · Ambient assisted living

1 Introduction

Age-appropriate assistance systems for self-determined living is a key focus of the *Bremen Ambient Assisted Living Lab* (BAALL) [2]. People with mobility impairments are supported by providing intelligent mobility devices that are embedded in the apartment [10]. Appliances such as lights, doors, height-adjustable cabinets, and mirrors are becoming intelligent through mutual interconnection and control. All of these applications depend on, or benefit from, the knowledge about the spatial location of their users. For instance, a wheelchair can be sent to a goal to pickup a person if the person's initial location is known, and ceiling lights can be controlled such that only the direct surrounding of a person's location is lit at a time.

While the aforementioned mobility devices, i.e. wheelchairs and walkers, localize themselves and their users by matching readings from on board laser range finders against map data (cf. the *GMapping* approach in [8]), pure people localization should be realized without instrumenting the persons to be tracked.

© Springer International Publishing Switzerland 2016
C.K. Chang et al. (Eds.): ICOST 2016, LNCS 9677, pp. 14–26, 2016.
DOI: 10.1007/978-3-319-39601-9_2

Fig. 1. Illustration of essential methods used in this work: a thermal camera mounted at the ceiling of the depicted kitchen area perceives the superimposed video image. The blue area contrasts to the thermal signature of a person rendered by a red pixel cluster. This cluster is abstracted by the yellow circular-shaped percept, and fed into a Monte-Carlo particle filter that tracks the green colored trajectory of the Subject. (Color figure online)

Initial experiments in this direction solely required the user to carry a smart-phone that received signals from *Bluetooth Low Energy*-beacons mounted in the BAALL, in order to realize fingerprinting-based localization (cf. [13]).

Therefore, this paper proposes the use of downward facing thermal cameras mounted at the ceiling of the apartment. We will show that the stream of low-resolution (80 × 60 pixels) thermal images can be utilized to successfully track people in the BAALL by feeding them into a set of multi-hypotheses *Monte-Carlo* particle filters (cf. Fig. 1 for the application scenario). Please note that tracking does not imply to recognize individual persons from a trained set.

The remainder of this article is structured as follows: Sect. 2 gives an overview on state of the art approaches in visual people tracking, including thermal camera-based solutions. Section 3 overviews our solution of a Monte-Carlo particle filter-based tracking system that works on thermal camera percepts. Section 4 details the methods proposed by our work, namely thermal camera image preprocessing, data association between image percepts and particle filter hypotheses, and the actual tracking algorithm. In Sect. 5 we describe the experimental evaluation, including a comparison of tracking results between our proposed method and the gold standard, an *ARTTRACK* optical tracking solution. The latter tracks retroreflective markers fixed on the subjects. We finally conclude with Sect. 6 by discussing the achieved results and future work.

2   Related Work

A good starting point for dealing with people localization services in Ambient Assisted Linving environments is given by Eisa and Moreira. In [4] they define requirements and metrics for AAL related localization techniques.

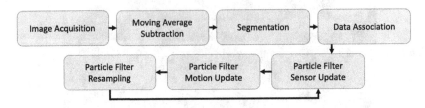

Fig. 2. Flowchart diagram of the people tracking system described in this paper. The software is structured into image acquisition and preprocessing steps (blue), data association (green), and the particle filter cycle (red). (Color figure online)

In [9], Hevesi et al. describe a system that makes use of cheap arrays of infrared sensors (8×8 pixels) for people localization with an accuracy of 1 m in home and office environments. By classifying time series of temperature feature vectors, it is also possible to monitor household appliances such as water cookers. Tracking of multiple sources of heat while recognizing their identity is not described.

Kumar et al. [11] also use a low resolution thermal sensor consisting of 32 single infrared receivers for people tracking in indoor environments. By rotating the linear system about $140°$ in 94 discrete steps, they construct a 2-dimensional image in one minute. After fusing blobs from the infrared image with a 640×480 pixel wide RGB image, the results of pure RGB-based template tracking can be improved. Since track identity is not handled by the system, this work is more about estimating the location of people in image frames.

A performance comparison between Kalman filter and particle filter-based optical people tracking approaches is given by Bazzani et al. in [3]. Although working on RGB-image datasets and not on monochromatic thermal images, and thus dealing with different strategies for background subtraction and percept modeling, this work motivates the application of the particle filter method since it shows a better *tracking success rate*.

Beside the research perspective, people localization and tracking in ambient assisted living environments is already a commercial issue. Therefore, actual research and developments have to prevail against already available solutions, e.g. the people tracking flooring material *SensFloor* [7].

The contribution of our own work is straightforward. We describe a particle-filter-based tracking system with an accuracy that is well-suited for security and convenience appliances in ambient assisted living environments. In spite of the low resolution sensorial input, we can prove a mean error of $< 12\,\mathrm{cm}$ compared to a sophisticated marker-based optical tracking system that served as our ground truth. From this perspective, we can enhance the performance of available thermal sensor-based tracking solutions.

3   System Overview

The thermal imaging sensor setup as shown in Fig. 3 is mounted in a height of 4.4 m under the ceiling of the BAALL, but over a suspended ceiling made of textile that is opaque for the human eye, but transparent for the infrared spectrum of electromagnetic radiation. Hardly noticeable for visitors of the flat, the thermal camera observes approximately 6m² of the kitchen area. According to Fig. 2, image acquisition is the first step of our proposed tracking system (see Sect. 4.1). Running as a C++ application on a Raspberry Pi, this step reads out the thermal images from the sensor, and forwards the video stream to a PC running the next steps under the robotics framework *SimRobot* [12].

Thermal images are now preprocessed by first increasing contrast through static background subtraction (cf. Sect. 4.2). The following segmentation process outputs blobs that are candidates for people silhouettes. Abstracted by encompassing circles, these percepts are associated to hypotheses of particle filters that each track a single person. The data association described in Sect. 4.3 builds on the assumption that a given percept better explains a sample if the area of intersection between the two circles is large. Since even multiple percepts can explain a single hypothesis about the position of a person, the particle filter's sensor update step (cf. Sect. 4.4) computes the sample's weight by summing up the total area of intersection with all percepts associated to this sample.

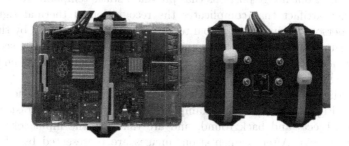

Fig. 3. The experimental sensor setup includes a boxed *FLiR Lepton* longwave imaging module (right), and a connected *Raspberry Pi 2 Model B* (left) for initial data acquisition. The Pi is also used for forwarding the video stream to a computer running the preprocessing and tracking algorithms.

4   Detailed System Description

4.1   Sensorial Equipment

For acquiring thermal images, we use a *FLiR Lepton* longwave infrared imaging module that connects via a breakout board to a *Raspberry Pi 2 Model B*.

The Lepton (cf. [5] for a more detailed description) is based on a microbolometer focal plane array, and is capable of outputting 80 × 60 pixels with a thermal sensitivity of < 50 mK. Given the sensor's 51° wide horizontal, and 63.5° wide diagonal field of view, our application scenario asks for a sufficiently high mounting position in order to cover a preferably large area on the ground plane of the room observed. Please note that the camera doesn't output absolute temperature values per pixel. Instead, the sensor maps the observed temperature spectrum to a 14 bit wide range, and sets each pixel to a value within this interval. After basic image data collection is performed by the Raspberry Pi, the video stream is transfered to a PC via a TCP/IP stream. We have selected this multi-host solution for the reason of convenience, i.e. the Raspberry Pi and the camera module can stay online mounted on the ceiling, while code changes in the preprocessing and filtering part is done on a development PC.

4.2   Preprocessing of Raw Images

A typical raw image coming from the thermal camera can be seen in Fig. 4 (left). Beside the desired information, raw images contain undesirable properties that are tackled during the preprocessing steps.

The first major drawback of raw images is given by picture fragments that depict sources of heat different from the human body, e.g. the upper left pixel blob in Fig. 4 (left) that is caused by the motor of a fridge. Although we cannot decide the question which one of the two image fragments equal in shape and temperature is originating from a person's silhouette, and which one not, it is possible to filter out image portions that present a static temperature over time.

A further artifact that complicates the recognition of thermal signatures caused by persons is given by a global temperature gradient caused by the camera or the sun's thermal radiation passing through windows into the scene. An exemplary situation is shown in Fig. 4 (left), where the gradient extends from the upper right corner to the lower left corner.

Both artifacts described are tackled by background subtraction. The resulting images (see Fig. 4 (centre) for an example) show an increased contrast between foreground objects and background, and are taken as the input for the segmentation process. After segmentation, images are represented by blobs, i.e. pixel-groups sharing the same flattened temperature value (cf. Fig. 4 (right)).

Background Subtraction. By subtracting the moving average temperature of a given pixel, from the current temperature reading of the same pixel, we obtain values that tend towards 0 for static background pixel, and values $\neq 0$ for foreground pixels. The moving average filter is implemented as in (1), and (2). Here, $ma_{x,y}^t$ denotes the moving average of the pixel located at position (x, y), at time t. The current reading at the same location is given by $p_{x,y}^t$ and $bsp_{x,y}^t$ is the value after background subtraction. The parameter $c \in [0..1]$ describes how strong the actual reading influences the moving average.

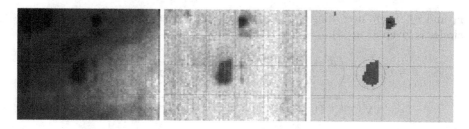

Fig. 4. Illustration of thermal image preprocessing pipeline - *Left*: Raw image as outputted from the sensor. Warm areas render dark, while colder areas render light. This image depicts two persons, one in the center and one to the upper right. The dark area to the upper left originates from a static source of heat. *Centre*: After background subtraction, the static source of heat, as well as an image wide thermal gradient, caused by sensor miss-calibration, disappears. *Right*: Segmentation yields two blobs describing the persons observed by center coordinates and a maximal radius.

$$ma_{x,y}^t = c\, p_{x,y}^t + (1-c)\, ma_{x,y}^{t-1} \tag{1}$$

$$bsp_{x,y}^t = \left| p_{x,y}^t - ma_{x,y}^t \right| \tag{2}$$

Segmentation. This step is implemented by recursively processing each pixel via an 8-neighbor connectedness. A neighboring pixel is assigned to the center pixel's blob, if it has not been visited so far, and if its temperature value differs from the blob's mean temperature no more than a given threshold. After including a new pixel into an existing blob, the temperature values of all of the blob's pixels are set to the blob's mean temperature. If an unvisited pixel is not recorded into the currently processed blob, a new blob is opened by that pixel.

4.3 Data Association

The key task of data association is to assign percepts generated from preprocessed images to pose hypotheses of the tracking filters (cf. Sect. 4.4) for validation. Basically a percept is given by a pixel blob that might correspond to a person's silhouette, i.e. it matches in size and mean temperature the expected values. We abstract a percept by the smallest circle that contains all blob pixels. Thus, we define the structure of a percept as follows:

$$\mathcal{P}_t = [(x_t, y_t), r_t, t_t, \mathcal{S}_t] \tag{3}$$

In (3), $\mathcal{S}_t$ denotes the set of blob-pixels the percept is generated from, (x_t, y_t) and r_t the center and radius of a circle that encompasses $\mathcal{S}_t$, and t_t the mean temperature of $\mathcal{S}_t$. Our basic strategy for judging whether or not a given percept supports a pose hypothesis of a tracked person, that is modeled by a circle as well, is to calculate the overlapping area between the circles involved. According to that, let d be the distance between the midpoints of two circles with radii

r_1 and r_2. Then, according to [14], the area of intersection A between the two circles is given as in (4).

$$A = r_1^2 \cos^{-1}\left(\frac{d^2 + r_1^2 - r_2^2}{2dr_1}\right) + r_2^2 \cos^{-1}\left(\frac{d^2 + r_2^2 - r_1^2}{2dr_2}\right)$$
$$-\frac{1}{2}\sqrt{(-d + r_1 + r_2)(d + r_1 - r_2)(d - r_1 + r_2)(d + r_1 + r_2)} \qquad (4)$$

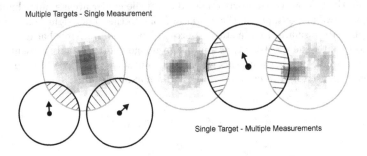

Fig. 5. Illustration of two cases where image segmentation fails to produce suitable percepts for the given situation. The red area describes the intersection between the percepts modeled by green circles, and the pose hypotheses modeled by black circles. (Color figure online)

Beside the trivial case in which one percept overlaps with exactly one hypothesis of an already existing filter, data association handles the following situations:

1. Multiple Targets - Single Measurement: This case (cf. Fig. 5 (left)) typically occurs in situations where two persons that are already tracked by their individual filter move close together. Image segmentation produces a single blob that describes the merged shape of both individuals.
2. Single Target - Multiple Measurements: In this situation (cf. Fig. 5 (right)) image segmentation has failed to produce a single blob for the silhouette of a person. Instead, two separate blobs explain a pose hypothesis.
3. No Match: Since there is no filter with at least one hypothesis that explains the given percept $\mathcal{P}_t$, a new filter is instantiated. The samples of the new particle filter are initialized at (x_t, y_t) of the given percept $\mathcal{P}_t$.

Occlusion Handling. A special case for *single target - multiple measurements* data association is given by partly occluded silhouettes. Because of the suspended ceiling's beams in-between the camera and the persons to be tracked (cf. Fig. 7 (right)), pixel blobs describing a single target are split sometimes (cf. Fig. 6 for an illustration). Since the general rule of data association requires an overlap between the percept's and the sample's circles, which is obviously not given in this situation, a different strategy is necessary. Therefore, we model the static beams of the suspended ceiling by rectangles in world space. After also transforming the image percepts into world space, we check for the number of intersections between a line that connects a sample's position with a percept's position, and the beam rectangle's lines. If we can conclude that both circles are located on different sides of the beam, and if they are no more separated than a given threshold, the percept is attached to the sample and adds to its weighting.

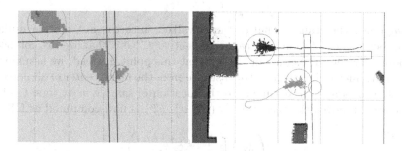

Fig. 6. Illustration of percepts that are partly occluded by beams of the suspended ceiling in-between the camera and the person to be tracked. Red colored rectangles model the beams that can also be seen in Fig. 7(right). (Color figure online)

4.4 Monte-Carlo Particle Filter Tracking

We chose the Monte-Carlo particle filter approach [6] to track people's trajectories, since this algorithm is able to deal with the non-linear motion model involved, and its ability to handle multiple hypotheses. Let a single hypothesis about the position and orientation of a tracked person at point of time t be described by the sample $s_t = [(x_t, y_t), \theta_t, r_t, \omega_t]$. The vector (x_t, y_t) denotes the cartesian position in the ground-parallel plane, and θ_t the direction of movement, which we interprete as the person's orientation w.r.t. the global x-coordinate axis. Furthermore, r_t represents the mean radius of all circular percepts that confirmed s_t, and ω_t the weighting, or probability that s_t describes a person respectively. A single particle filter is now defined as $PF_t = [S_t, P_t]$, with $S_t = \{s_t^1, ..., s_t^m\}$ describing the discrete probability distribution about the position and orientation of a tracked person by m samples, and $P_t = \{p_{t-n}, ..., p_t\}$ describing the path of this filter, i.e. the list of the mean positions over all samples during the last n cycles of *sensor update*, *motion update*, and *resampling*. Above, the parameter n is chosen freely for informational purposes only.

Sensor Update. Since data association has already assigned the set of percepts $\{\mathcal{P}_t^1, ..., \mathcal{P}_t^i\}$ that overlap with the sample under scope, computing the sample's weight ω_t^m is straightforward given the following formula:

$$\omega_t^m = \mathcal{N}(0, \sigma^2) \left(1 - \min\left(1, \frac{\sum_{i=1}^n A(s_t^m) \cap A(\mathcal{P}_t^i)}{A(s_t^m)}\right)\right) \tag{5}$$

In (5), the inner fraction describes the relative area of the sample's circle that is covered by all of the percepts attached. By adjusting σ, one can let even small overlaps produce a good weighting, or favor only extensive overlaps respectively.

Motion Update. A sample's state transition through motion is given by

$$u_t^m \models \langle d_t, h_t \rangle \tag{6}$$

with d_t being the translational distance walked since the last motion update, and h_t being the rotational distance respectively. Note that we do not use a real odometry sensor, e.g. a gait detector, at this point. Instead, we assume the traveled distance to be given by the distance from the mean center of all percepts associated to sample m at time t, to the location of sample m at time $t-1$. A 3-dimensional movement vector $v^m = (v_x^m, v_y^m, v_\theta^m)$ is now computed as follows:

$$v^m = \left(M_\theta^m \begin{pmatrix} d_t + a_1 n_x^m (d_t) \\ a_2 n_y^m (d_t) \\ a_3 n_\theta^m (h_t) \end{pmatrix} \right) \tag{7}$$

In (7), M_θ^m denotes a rotation matrix that describes the sample's orientation θ^m, $n_{x,y,\theta}^m$ noise functions sampled from a triangular distribution, and a_1, a_2, a_3 three different scalars for the generated noise.

$$x_t^m = x_{t-1}^m + v_x^m \tag{8}$$

$$y_t^m = y_{t-1}^m + v_y^m \tag{9}$$

$$\theta_t^m = \theta_{t-1}^m + v_\theta^m \tag{10}$$

With the movement vector v^m described in (7), a sample's new position and orientation is computed according to (8), (9), and (10).

Resampling. Samples from each particle filter are carried over to the next cycle of computation according to their weighting. This means, that hypotheses with a high weighting are cloned, while hypotheses with a low weighting disappear.

5 Experimental Evaluation

In order to prove the accuracy of the tracking system proposed in this work, we compared its results from an experimental evaluation with the output of an *A.R.T. DTrack2* reference tracking system [1]. The DTrack2 tracking system configuration consisted of two cameras actively sending out infrared light at 880 nm wavelength, which is well reflected by retro reflective markers. The spherical markers that were used had a diameter of 30 mm, and were fixed on top of a cap worn by the tracked person. After calibration of the DTrack2 system, three-dimensional marker positions were outputted at 60 Hz.

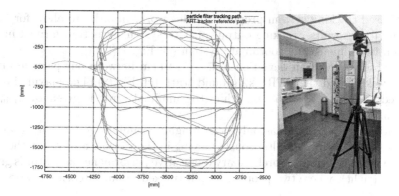

Fig. 7. Comparison of paths tracked by the thermal image percepts driven particle filter, and a DTrack2 optical tracking system (left). The evaluation took place in the kitchen area of the BAALL (right). Here, one person walked clockwise and counterclockwise rounds between the table and the kitchen bench.

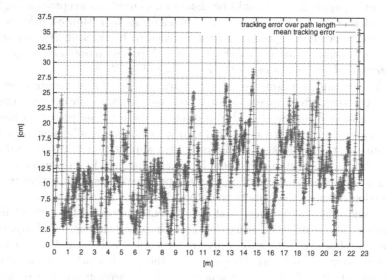

Fig. 8. Error plot indicating the performance of the tracking system proposed in this work. The red curve depicts the distance between associated points along the paths outputted by the A.R.T. DTrack2 system, and our approach (cf. Fig. 7(left)). Given the DTrack2 ground truth, we observed a minimal, maximal, and mean error of $\varepsilon_{min} \approx$ 1.94 mm, $\varepsilon_{max} \approx$ 35.58 cm, and $\bar{\varepsilon} \approx$ 11.91 cm, along the $d \approx$ 23 m long path. (Color figure online)

Starting at the kitchen table, the test person walked approximately 23 m in two clock-wise and two counter-clockwise oriented circles located in-between the table and the kitchen bench (cf. Fig. 7 (right)). During that walk, the probandee was observed by the DTRack2 system described above, and the thermal image-based tracking system proposed in this work. In order to allow for comparison of the results, tracking output of both systems was transformed into a common two-dimensional coordinate system (cf. Fig. 7 (left)).

We observed a mean deviation of $\bar{\varepsilon} \approx 11.91\,\mathrm{cm}$ between our particle filter-based tracking and the DTRack2 ground truth (cf. Fig. 8). The maximal error observed was $\varepsilon_{max} \approx 35.58\,\mathrm{cm}$, while the minimal error is given by $\varepsilon_{min} \approx 1.94\,\mathrm{mm}$.

Multi people tracking has only been roughly examined so far, with a maximum of three subjects simultaneously moving in the viewing area of the thermal camera tracking system. A preliminary qualitative performance indicator is given in Fig. 6 (right), where two people are well tracked in our kitchen scenario.

6   Conclusions and Future Work

We have presented a people tracking system that is embedded into an ambient assisted living apartment. It could be shown that circular percepts coming from segmented thermal camera images are sufficient to *feed* Monte-Carlo particle filters for estimating the position of the persons to be tracked. A comparative experiment contrasted our approach with an high-precision optical marker tracking system, and revealed a mean tracking error of $\approx 12\,\mathrm{cm}$.

To develop this promising approach towards a real solution requires redesign of the thermal camera to have wide angle to allow for low mounting positions, for instance. This is future work and also discussed below. The presented method already handles occlusions due to fixed infrastructure such as beams; using wide angle cameras, this could also be pillars or high appliances in the observed area. It is certainly not reasonable to manually specify the positions of such objects in the camera image as has been done in our experimental setup. It rather requires a calibration phase of the camera to detect these, but is conceivable.

That said, the results show that a sufficiently accurate tracking of multiple persons can be achieved using low-cost thermal cameras. For instance, in museums or shops, it allows to easily track peoples walking paths and length of stays at points of interests. By combining the people tracking with information about actuators in the environment allows to develop pro-active environment assistance, such as to automatically adjust the illumination. Finally, it can be used to realize safety mechanisms, such as to detect unconscious persons, which is a side-effect of the background subtraction: the blob tracking a person losing consciousness vanishes over time due to the background subtraction. Hence, vanishing blobs, which are in the middle of a camera image, can be used as indicators. To avoid false-positives requires to adjust the parameter used in background subtraction such that common durations of immobility do not lead to blob disappearance, and to combine tracking information with information over the environment, to exclude areas where people typically rest, such as sofas or beds.

Since the overall tracking system proposed in this paper involves various methods, future work is manifold. Starting with the preprocessing of thermal images, segmentation could be improved by integrating dynamic adjustment of the segmentation threshold. Applying a shape-based classifier for pixel-blobs, instead of abstracting to circular percepts, would enable us to better discriminate not only persons from other sources of heat, but also persons in different postures, e.g. standing vs. sitting. Because of the thermal camera's narrow field of view, a tracking system covering the whole apartment asks for integrating multiple cameras. This extension will require a new layer of abstraction that allows single particles from instantiated filters to *move* from one camera view to another. In this context, we want to keep in mind that the unusual high mounting position of the thermal camera system used, is due to its quite low field of view. For lower mounting positions, not only wide angle lenses are necessary, but also a perspective correction of raw images, which could be neglected in this work.

Acknowledgement. Special thanks go to Felix Wenk and Jan Janssen who supported us in setting up the A.R.T. DTrack2 tracking system for evaluation.

References

1. Advanced Realtime Tracking GmbH. ARTTRACK System (2015). http://www.ar-tracking.com/products/tracking-systems/arttrack-system/
2. Autexier, S., Hutter, D., Mandel, C., Stahl, C.: SHIP-tool live: orchestrating the activities in the bremen ambient assisted living lab. In: Augusto, J.C., Wichert, R., Collier, R., Keyson, D., Salah, A.A., Tan, A.-H. (eds.) AmI 2013. LNCS, vol. 8309, pp. 269–274. Springer, Heidelberg (2013)
3. Bazzani, L., Bloisi, D., Murino, V.: A Comparison of multi hypothesis kalman filter and particle filter for multi-target tracking. In: Performance Evaluation of Tracking and Surveillance workshop at CVPR, pp. 47–54, Miami, Florida (2009)
4. Eisa, S., Moreira, A.: Requirements and metrics for location and tracking for ambient assisted living. In: 2012 International Conference on Indoor Positioning and Indoor Navigation (IPIN), pp. 1–7, November 2012
5. FLIR Systems Inc. FLIR LEPTON Long Wave Infrared (LWIR) Datasheet (2015). http://cvs.flir.com/lepton-data-brief?_ga=1.148414963.572252733.1449483173
6. Fox, D., Burgard, W., Dellaert, F., Thrun, S.: Monte carlo localization: efficient position estimation for mobile robots. In: Proceedings of the National Conference on Artificial Intelligence (AAAI), pp. 343–349 (1999)
7. Future-Shape GmbH. SensFloor large-area sensor system (2015). http://www.future-shape.com/en/technologies/23/sensfloor-large-area-sensor-system
8. Grisetti, G., Stachniss, C., Burgard, W.: Improved techniques for grid mapping with rao-blackwellized particle filters. IEEE Trans. Rob. **23**(1), 34–46 (2007)
9. Hevesi, P., Wille, S., Pirkl, G., Wehn, N., Lukowicz, P.: Monitoring household activities and user location with a cheap, unobtrusive thermal sensor array. In: Proceedings of the 2014 ACM International Joint Conference on Pervasive and Ubiquitous Computing, UbiComp 2014, pp. 141–145. ACM, New York (2014)
10. Krieg-Brückner, B., Röfer, T., Shi, H., Gersdorf, B.: Mobility assistance in the bremen ambient assisted living lab. GeroPsych J. Gerontopsychology Geriatr. Psychiatry **23**(2), 121–130 (2010)

11. Kumar, S., Marks, T.K., Jones, M.: Improving person tracking using an inexpensive thermal infrared sensor. In: 2014 IEEE Conference on Computer Vision and Pattern Recognition Workshops (CVPRW), pp. 217–224, June 2014
12. Röfer, T., Laue, T.: On B-human's code releases in the standard platform league – software architecture and impact. In: Behnke, S., Veloso, M., Visser, A., Xiong, R. (eds.) RoboCup 2013. LNCS, vol. 8371, pp. 648–655. Springer, Heidelberg (2014)
13. Voigt, M.: Monte-Carlo Lokalisierung im Innenraum mittels Bluetooth Low Energy basiertem Fingerprinting. Master's thesis, University of Bremen, May 2015
14. Wolfram MathWorld - the web's most extensive mathematics resource. Circle-Circle Intersection 2015. http://mathworld.wolfram.com/Circle-CircleIntersection.html

A Preprocessing Algorithm to Increase OCR Performance on Application Processor-Centric FPGA Architectures

César Crovato[1], Delfim Torok[1], Regina Heidrich[2],
Bernardo de Cerqueira[3(✉)], and Eduardo Velho[3]

[1] Institute of Technology and Exact Sciences, Feevale University, Novo Hamburgo, Brazil
{cesarc,delfimLT}@feevale.br
[2] Feevale University, Novo Hamburgo, Brazil
rheidrich@feevale.br
[3] Scientific Improvement Researcher, Feevale University, Novo Hamburgo, Brazil
{bcerqueira,velho}@feevale.br

Abstract. The aim of this research is to build up a fully automatic preprocessing algorithm capable of binarize and dewarping digitized documents, embedded in an application processor-centric Field Programmable Gate Array (FPGA), in order to develop an autonomous voice scanner for blind and visually impaired. Providing for blind the ability of hearing books without further assistance is the main purpose of this work overall. This is a part of a larger project, called "The Vocalizer Project", emerged due to a demand by Brazil's Ministry of Culture and Education for utilization in schools and public libraries, and is addressed for having more inclusive and intelligent cities. Furthermore, it is destined for the inclusion of blind and visually impaired people to the vast bibliographic material existent.

Keywords: OCR · Application Processor-Centric FPGA · Visually impaired · Voice scanner for blind people · Social inclusion

1 Introduction

This work is a part of the Vocalizer Project, which was developed due to a demand by the Ministry of Culture and Education of Brazil for the application in schools and public libraries, and its goal is to create more inclusive and intelligent cities. It is funded by Finep – a Brazilian agency which finances projects on research and innovation.

The project objective is to develop a flatbed scanner that can be manipulated by blind as well as visually impaired people. The aim of this paper is to develop a pre-process capable of scanning books [1] and automatically turn its data into a digital and audible experience afterwards. This technique consists of taking digital pictures of each page of the book through mechanical process assisted by an automated electronic system [2]. It is not easy to capture an analog image and turn it into software readable digital data, hence to the natural distortion caused by the specification of the device used to capture the image [3], the ambient variables such as light exposure [4, 5], the kind and format of the captured object and its characteristics [6], and the overall deformations that the software must be able to read [1, 5, 6] and reinterpret in a way that the other further necessary software should be able to understand it [3, 7].

© Springer International Publishing Switzerland 2016
C.K. Chang et al. (Eds.): ICOST 2016, LNCS 9677, pp. 27–34, 2016.
DOI: 10.1007/978-3-319-39601-9_3

In order for making the software reading easier, it is possible to run gathered digital data by an algorithm capable of preprocess and dewarping each captured image, correcting possible nonlinear scanning issues [6, 8], which is the main purpose of this paper. Afterwards, identifying words in this preprocessed digital image is necessary, and can be achieved through specialized software such as Optical Character Recognition (OCR) [2–4, 8], which is capable of reading and decoding patterns to recognize characters and words within images, then transferring these identified patterns into a new, digitally written document [1, 7]. Through this process, another software is necessary to transform these words into spoken language, known as text-to-speech software, so the output of this operation provide for blind people the ability of hearing books without further assistance [1, 3, 7]. It's known that there are two ways to turn a bound document into digital data: using a straight-line device such as a flatbed scanner, or nonlinear device such as a digital camera [9]. The main difference between these methods consists on the geometry distortion caused in the captured image [3, 9], resulting in invalidation of OCR process as a whole, due to lack of information [6]. We investigate in this paper how to assure proper recognition of gathered data, enhancing picture quality through preprocessing of the images [2, 9].

The algorithm proposed in this paper operates in the preprocessing of the captured image, and then the output is run through open source OCR, Tesseract [10], in order to study the possibility of handling better and reliable results to the final user [2, 3].

2   Related Works

In book camera capturing there are issues related to non-planar/non-linear scanning, which results in heavier page curling and warp than linear scan [2, 3]. Many techniques exist in order to overcome the distortion generated by the camera image, which can be classified into two categories: 2D image processing [8] and 3D document shape discovery [6, 9]. These techniques have in common the objective of restoring each line of the document as the original form, and in this case, so the OCR can be applied with lesser error range [6].

From the best of this research, there weren't found similar works that are the confluence of OCR techniques and preprocessing in reconfigurable hardware with high-level synthesis, in the sense of blind people usability and benefit. The abrangency of the presented preprocessing method is tested within OCR results on unprocessed and preprocessed image on the next pages.

Methods like line-by-line dewarping through a 3D model based on each character position and orientation [9], is not applicable to this presented method due to superior hardware, processing and time consumption compared to binarization [8, 9]. 2D Grayscale document segmentation through threshold varying [4, 5, 9] is a way to acquire depth information from image's shading, and it's used in this algorithm so it can identify the center of the open page and compare horizontal and vertical character information for further dewarping, gathering a sum of columns. This 2D image dewarping consists into transforming each character into a rectangular model [6, 8, 9], then identify its respective line and column, placing them correspondingly.

3   The Specification

This work was driven by the need to develop low-cost voice scanner for blind people, to vocalize open books up to A3 size. It has set up a multidisciplinary team so this could be achieved effectively. The overall system has some important mechanical and electronic specification, but the most important concerns are about the usability. For blind people, the usage of this equipment is to be "most natural as possible", in the sense of "the reading" experience. In order to do this, the handling must be simple and the processing must be quick. It was proposed a high configurable model able to use either smartphones or specialized platform as well and, hence to this, studies on the warping phenomena and the computational effort to dewarping the captured image suggested that a mechanical approach could minimize this effect. It was studied the Android Tesseract [10] OCR performance and error rate for a 12 Mpx image and around 250dpi. But in order to parallelize the overall process, it was developed an algorithm for character position identification and line identification presented in this paper. For a first approach, much earlier than working on a specific hardware platform, all routines were developed on desktop personal computer core i5, 4 GB Ram, using Matlab and HDLcoder [11] in combination with Vivado [12] as synthesis platform.

To acquire the image, a smartphone Samsung Galaxy SII (with 8Mpx camera) was used, without any kind of special treatment. The image (no compressed jpg) was downloaded to the PC using a simple USB cable. At this stage there was no real-time requirement. The distance from the camera to the open book was around 15 cm in order to guarantee the desired 250dpi. Several photographs are taken in non-controlled illumination environment.

4   The Algorithm

From the RGB image, a simple average of R, G and B are performed to obtain a gray scale image. Then, with the gray scale image, a 50×50 "one's" kernel are used in order to estimate a "illumination mask", which will be remove from the original gray scale image, resulting in a more uniform illumination gray scale image. The binarization [5] is treated as simply thresholding operation [4]. From the binary image, it was identified

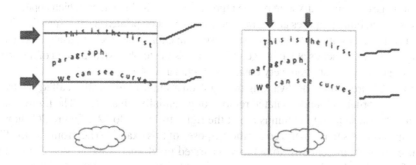

Fig. 1. Cumulative sum of pixel at rows and columns.

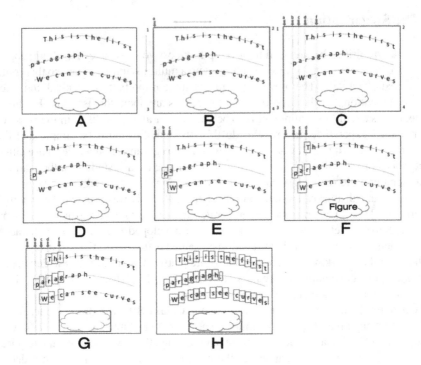

Fig. 2. Some important steps in order to identify islanding regions and chains of regions. (Color figure online)

the center of the open book performing the cumulative sum of columns, and comparing this cumulative sum with a trigger level. Each page is treated separately. In fact, in addition to columns cumulative sum, the cumulative sum of lines is also performed. This was done for later version of algorithm can be extracted horizontal and vertical histogram of each character, as depicted in Fig. 1, and with this, it will be possible to extract unique features to each letter that allow to identify them.

The Fig. 2 shows some important steps in the detection of lines of text, called here for convenience: "isolated regions chains". Figure 2A shows the left page of a book, which was placed at the base of a structure previously mentioned.

This page contains a curvature profile represented by solid blue lines, which appear here only for highlighting purposes and in fact there is no exist on printed sheet in question. This curvature and the position of the camera are responsible for some level of misalignment and distortion of the characters at the image. It is also possible to observe at the end of the sheet a kind of graphical illustration, very common in scholar books.

In Fig. 2B are shown the "walking through" on a single column slice called "a" from "1" to "3" in order to found "isolated region" or potentially, characters. The figure show too, that the subsequently columns are at the right, from "1" to "2". Figure 2C show 5 important columns to be analyzed for the purposes of this example (i.e. from "a" to "f"), because all of them contains non-empty binarized pixel, that is mean, that can by the start of an isolated region (a character, a figure, a table, or a more complex shape).

Figure 2D it is possible to analyze the first column ("b") in which exist a start of an isolated region, in this case, the letter "p" of "paragraph". For every isolated region, there are some properties saved for pos-processing in order to identify if the region is a character, or, in order to determine which line in text the character belongs. The properties are shown in Fig. 3A. Ci, Cf, Li, Lf (Initial and Final Column, Initial and Final Line; on BinaryImage), also height (h) and width (w).

The Fig. 3B shows that for two letters are regarded as belonging to the same line in the text, there must be an area of intersection between their parallel bottom and top lines, and the distance between them must be less than h/3 pixels.

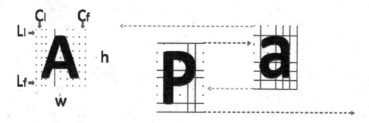

Fig. 3. **A.** Properties of single character. **B.** Rules for determining two consecutive characters on the same line.

In order to recognize the boundaries of the region, a simple algorithm shown in Fig. 4 can be run; in fact, this algorithm can be detect all isolated regions in binary image, putting all, coordinates and sizes of all these "objects" in a collection called isolated regions chain. The subsequent figures, from Fig. 2E to H shows the evolution of the process, from just 3 regions until all region detected.

It's important to say that atypical isolated region like the "cloud" at the bottom of the sheet (Fig. 2) are removed, because are too big to be a character. Similarly, small regions are removed, but before that, an algorithm of unification of small regions are running, to join two or more region belonging the same character, like "j", ";", ":", "i", and others. In the column "walking through" process describe through Fig. 2B and subsequent, the first isolated region founded starts a "new line" object that contains properties like: This Line #, Next Line #, Previous Line #, Char Chain (the text on the line) and First char distance from Top. For example, in Fig. 2D, we have the first line object with contains the Char Chain: "p", like depicted in Fig. 5. For every new isolated region founded at the beginning, a new line object is started, and will be inserted in a binary tree in coherent manner with its previous and next line, modifying the entire relationship between lines, as depicted in Fig. 6.

The described approach above combines procedural and object oriented routines, and because that the hybrid FPGA and centric processor like Zynq from Xilinx was chose.

For the ARM embedded processor the Android Operational System was chosen in order to run Tesseract OCR inside. For the FPGA side, an entire Matlab m-script, that implement the complete algorithm describe above, was created in attempt to pass through the HDLcoder later, but when writing the m-script code, the programmer chooses techniques aiming the productivity, reuse of previously developed high-level functions and the fast validation. However, the use of m-scripts jointly with HDLcoder

(MATLAB 2015) becomes more restrictive because there are several unsupported data types, non-synthesizable functions and best practice required by HDLcoder. Therefore, this makes the use of code written not fully compatible and for this work rewrite some parts of the code is necessary and will by subject on next paper.

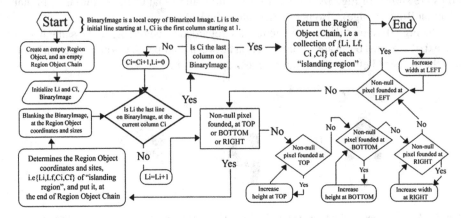

Fig. 4. Algorithm for recognize isolated regions in all BinaryImage.

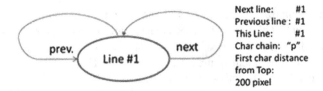

Fig. 5. First "line object" referenced itself as "previous" and "next", corresponding at status of Fig. 4D.

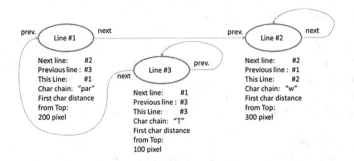

Fig. 6. Binary tree of line objects, corresponding at status of Fig. 2F.

Other high level synthesis tool like HLS/SDSoc from Xilinx is based on C/C++ language but also have some limitations: No dynamic memory (all need to be static), no system calls (std, file i/o, etc.), avoid recursive functions and function must be more atomic as possible; HDLcoder makes stand-alone ip-cores. In other hand SDSoc makes improved co-processor ip-cores for the Zynq Accelerator Coherency Port (ACP). For existing source-code like Tesseract, it becomes necessary to perform profiling tests in order to identify some candidate functions to become synthetizable using SDSoc. This also will be subject on next paper.

5   Results

For testing purposes, the same image was used with and without the presented prepro-cessing technique. Comparison criteria are the average execution time and the perform-ance of OCR. For the execution time, the Tesseract was performed using an image already pre-processed to isolate the time that used to prepare the image. To obtain the execution time, Tesseract was executed utilizing a preprocessed image, aiming to isolate time consumption on preparing the image. The execution time was obtained from the average of five executions. For the performance of OCR, it was measured the amount of hits and misses. It was considered an error when Tesseract:

(a) Detected a character wrongly;
(b) Didn't detect a character;
(c) Detected an inexistent character (soil).

A hit is characterized when Tesseract detects the respective character on image. To perform the comparison, the Google Diff Match [13] software was used. This serves to compare texts in character level. Still, all spaces, special characters and line breaks was removed.

The exact text of the image being used in the tests was obtained by transcribing the text of the image to a text file. A person transcribed text and revised it twice and another person revised the text once again. The results of hits and error obtained using the DiffMatch are shown in Table 1. Other similar image gives similar results.

Table 1. Preliminary Results

	With preprocessing	Without preprocessing
Well identified chars	1602	1568
Wrong or not identified chars	378	412
Non-chars identified as chars	329	451
Execution Time (in seconds)	18,5662	11,9318

6   Conclusion

This work is a contribution to Vocalizer Project. It is a tool for blind people, proposing a preprocessing technique which aims at the acceleration and/or increasing the performance of OCR algorithm on the Tesseract routines, predicting the increased of parallelism afforded by the future conversion of m-script Matlab code to VHDL using HDLcoder from Math-works. The preliminary results as shown in Table 1 are satisfactory.

Future work also points to development of an entire self-contained system independent from Tesseract; preliminary tests show that with the simple measurement of euclidean distance from each character to all database font pattern characters, the algorithm presents good and very quick results in OCR.

Acknowledgement. We would like to thank FINEP and CNPq for the financial support. And a special acknowledgment to Pináculo company and also the multi-disciplinary team whose worked through the stages of this project.

References

1. Xiu, P., Baird, H.: Scaling up whole-book recognition. In: 10th International Conference on Document Analysis and Recognition, pp. 698–702. IEEE Press, Barcelona (2009)
2. Ulges, A., Lampert, C., Breuel, T.: Document image dewarping using robust estimation of curled text lines. In: 8th International Conference on Document Analysis and Recognition, pp. 1001–1005. IEEE Press, Seoul (2005)
3. Kakumanu, P., Bourbakis, N., Black, J., Panchanathan, S.: Document image dewarping based on line estimation for visually impaired. In: 18th IEEE International Conference on Tools with Artificial Intelligence, pp. 625–631. IEEE Press, Arlington (2006)
4. Otsu, N.: A threshold selection method from gray-level histogram. In: IEEESMC, pp. 62–66 (1979)
5. Sauvola, J., Seppänen, T., Haapakoski, S., Pietikäinen, M.: Adaptive document binarization. In: Proceedings of the 4th International Conference on Document Analysis and Recognition, pp. 147–152. IEEE Press, Ulm (1997)
6. Shamqoli, M., Khosravi, H.: Warped document restoration by recovering shape of the surface. In: 8th Iranian Conference on Machine Vision and Image Processing, pp. 262–265. IEEE Press, Zanjan (2013)
7. Panchanathan, S., Black, J., Rush, M., Iyer, V.: iCare - a user centric approach to the development of assistive devices for the blind and visually impaired. In: 15th IEEE International Conference on Tools with Artificial Intelligence, pp. 641–648. IEEE Press, Sacramento (2003)
8. Stamatopoulos, N. Gatos, B., Pratikakis, I., Perantonis, S.: A two-step dewarping of camera document images. In: The 8th IAPR International Workshop on Document Analysis Systems, pp. 209–216. IEEE Press, Nara (2008)
9. Song, L., Wu, Y., Sun, B.: A robust and fast dewarping method of document images. In: International Conference on E-Product E-Service and E-Entertainment, pp. 1–4. IEEE Press, Henan (2010)
10. Tesseract, version 3.03 (rc1), computer software, Google Inc., Mountain View, California (2014)
11. MATLAB, version R2015b, computer software, The MathWorks Inc., Natick, Massachusetts (2015)
12. Vivado, version 2015.2, computer software, Xilinx Inc. San José, California (2015)
13. DiffMatch, version 20121119, computer software, Google Inc., Mountain View, California (2012)

E-Health for Future Smart Cities

DeepFood: Deep Learning-Based Food Image Recognition for Computer-Aided Dietary Assessment

Chang Liu[1], Yu Cao[1(✉)], Yan Luo[1], Guanling Chen[1],
Vinod Vokkarane[1], and Yunsheng Ma[2]

[1] The University of Massachusetts Lowell,
One University Ave,
Lowell, MA 01854, USA
ycao@cs.uml.edu
[2] The University of Massachusetts Medical School,
419 Belmont Street,
Worcester, MA 01605, USA
Yunsheng.Ma@umassmed.edu

Abstract. Worldwide, in 2014, more than 1.9 billion adults, 18 years and older, were overweight. Of these, over 600 million were obese. Accurately documenting dietary caloric intake is crucial to manage weight loss, but also presents challenges because most of the current methods for dietary assessment must rely on memory to recall foods eaten. The ultimate goal of our research is to develop computer-aided technical solutions to enhance and improve the accuracy of current measurements of dietary intake. Our proposed system in this paper aims to improve the accuracy of dietary assessment by analyzing the food images captured by mobile devices (e.g., smartphone). The key technique innovation in this paper is the deep learning-based food image recognition algorithms. Substantial research has demonstrated that digital imaging accurately estimates dietary intake in many environments and it has many advantages over other methods. However, how to derive the food information (e.g., food type and portion size) from food image effectively and efficiently remains a challenging and open research problem. We propose a new Convolutional Neural Network (CNN)-based food image recognition algorithm to address this problem. We applied our proposed approach to two real-world food image data sets (UEC-256 and Food-101) and achieved impressive results. To the best of our knowledge, these results outperformed all other reported work using these two data sets. Our experiments have demonstrated that the proposed approach is a promising solution for addressing the food image recognition problem. Our future work includes further improving the performance of the algorithms and integrating our system into a real-world mobile and cloud computing-based system to enhance the accuracy of current measurements of dietary intake.

Keywords: Deep learning · Food image recognition · Dietary assessment

© Springer International Publishing Switzerland 2016
C.K. Chang et al. (Eds.): ICOST 2016, LNCS 9677, pp. 37–48, 2016.
DOI: 10.1007/978-3-319-39601-9_4

1 Introduction

Accurate estimation of dietary caloric intake is important for assessing the effectiveness of weight loss interventions. Current methods for dietary assessment rely on self-report and manually recorded instruments (e.g., 24 h dietary recall [1] and food frequency questionnaires [2]). Though the 24 h dietary recall is the gold standard for reporting, this method still experiences bias as the participant is required to estimate their dietary intake (short and long term). Assessment of dietary intake by the participant can result in underreporting and underestimating of food intake [3, 4]. In order to reduce participant bias and increase the accuracy of self-report, enhancements are needed to supplement the current dietary recalls. One of the potential solutions is a mobile cloud computing system, which is to employ mobile computing devices (e.g., smartphone) to capture the dietary information in natural living environments and to employ the computing capacity in the cloud to analyze the dietary information automatically for objective dietary assessment [5–15]. Among the large selection of mobile cloud computing software for health, many have proposed to improve dietary estimates [13–15]. While these apps have features to track food intake, exercise, and save data in the cloud, the user has to manually enter all their information. To overcome these barriers, some research and development efforts have been made over the last few years for visual-based dietary information analysis [5–12]. While progresses have been made, how to derive the food information (e.g., food type) from food image effectively and efficiently remains a challenging and open research problem.

In this paper, we propose new deep learning-based [16] food image recognition algorithm to address this challenge. The proposed approach is based on Convolutional Neural Network (CNN) with a few major optimizations. The experimental results of applying the proposed approach to two real-world datasets have demonstrated the effectiveness of our solution.

The rest of the paper is organized as follows. Section 2 introduces related work in computer-aided dietary assessment and visual-based food recognition. Section 3 presents the proposed deep learning-based approach for food image recognition. Section 4 describes the implementation details and the evaluation results of our proposed algorithms. We make concluding remarks in Sect. 5.

2 Related Work

The first related research area is technology solutions for enhancing the accuracy of dietary measurement. As we have introduced before, the ubiquitous nature of mobile cloud computing invites an unprecedented opportunity to discover early predictors and novel biomarkers to support and enable smart care decision making in connection with health scenarios, including that of dietary assessment. There are thousands of mobile cloud health software (e.g., mobile health Apps available for iPhone, iPad, and Android) and many mobile health hardware options (e.g., activity tracker, wireless heart rate monitors). Among this huge selection, many have proposed to improve dietary estimates [13–15]. While these Apps have features to track food intake, exercise, and save data in the cloud, the user still has to manually enter everything they ate. Several apps have an improved level of automation. For example, Meal Snap [17] estimates the calorie content by asking the user to take a picture, dial in data such as whether you are eating breakfast or lunch, and add a quick text label. However, the accuracy of calorie estimation is unstable and is heavily dependent upon the accuracy of manually entered text input from users. Another App named "Eatly" [18] simply rates the food into one of the three categories ("very healthy", "it's O.K.", and "unhealthy") using the food image taken by the user. However, the rating is actually manually performed by the app's community of users, instead of by automated computer algorithms.

The second related research area is visual-based dietary information analysis [5–12]. Yang et al. [6] proposed a method to recognize fast food using the relative spatial relationships of local features of the ingredients followed by a feature fusion method. This method only works for a small number of food categories (61 foods) and is difficult to extend to composite or homemade food. Matsuda et al. [7] proposed an approach for multiple food recognition using a manifold ranking-based approach and co-occurrence statistics between food items, which were combined to address the multiple food recognition issue. However, this type of solution is computationally intensive and may not be practical for deployment within the mobile cloud-computing platform. A sequence of papers [8–10] from Purdue University TADA project [11] covered food item identification, food volume estimation, as well as other aspects of dietary assessment, such as mobile interface design and food image database development. The majority of their techniques for food recognition are based on traditional signal processing techniques with hand-engineered features. Recently, due to the occurrence of large annotated dataset like ImageNet [19], Microsoft COCO [20], and the development of powerful machine equipped with GPU, it is plausible to train large and complex CNN models for accurate recognition, which surpassed most of the methods adopted using hand-crafted features [21]. In this paper, we employ machine-learned features with deep learning based method, rather than the hand engineered features, to achieve a much higher accuracy.

3 Proposed Approach

In this paper, we propose a new deep learning-based approach to address the food image recognition problem. Specifically, we propose Convolutional Neural Network (CNN)-based algorithms with a few major optimizations, such as an optimized model and an optimized convolution technique. In the following sub-sections, we will first introduce the background and motivations of the proposed approach, follows with the detailed introduction of the proposed approach.

3.1 Deep Learning, Convolutional Neural Network (CNN), and Their Applications to Visual-Based Food Image Recognition

Deep learning [16, 22], aims to learn multiple levels of representation and abstraction that help infer knowledge from data such as images, videos, audio, and text, is making astonishing gains in computer vision, speech recognition, multimedia analysis, and drug designing [23]. Briefly speaking, there are two main classes of deep learning techniques: purely supervised learning algorithms (e.g., Deep Convolutional Network [21]), unsupervised and semi-supervised learning algorithms (e.g., Denoising Autoencoders [24], Restricted Boltzmann Machines, and Deep Boltzmann Machines [25]). Our proposed approach belongs to the first category (supervised learning algorithms). With the help of large-scale and well-annotated dataset like ImageNet [19], it's now feasible to perform large scale supervised learning using Convolutional Neural Network(CNN). The issue of convergence has been addressed by Hinton's work in 2006 [22]. Subsequent theoretical proof and experimental results both shows that large scale pre-trained models in large domain, with specific small scale unlabeled data in another domain, will give excellent result in image recognition and object detection [26]. To address the issue of limited abilities of feature representation, many researchers have proposed more complex CNN network structure, like VGG [27], ZFNet [28], GoogLeNet [29] and so on. On the other hand, ReLU [30] is also proposed to make it converge faster and also gains a better accuracy. Most of current researchers have put efforts in making the network deeper and avoid saturation problem [21, 27].

Inspired by the advances of deep learning technique, some researchers have applied deep learning for visual-based food image recognition. In a paper by Kawano et al. [31], the researchers developed an Android application to collect and label food image. They also created a food image database named "UEC-256 food image data set". With this data set, they first conducted some experiments using SIFT features and SVM, and shows much better result comparing with PFID [32]. Then, they used AlexNet [21] to the same data sets and showed much better result than SIFT-SVM-based method [33].

3.2   Proposed CNN-Based Approach for Visual-Based Food Image Recognition

Our proposed approach was directly inspired by and rooted from LeNet-5 [34], AlexNet [21], and GoogleNet [29]. The original idea of CNN was inspired by the neuroscience model of primate visual cortex [35]. The key insights from paper [35] is how to make the machine learning with multiple level neurons like human mind. In human brain, it's known that different neurons control different perception functionality, how to make the computer recognize and think in human-like way has long been a topic for many artificial intelligence experts. In [34] the article by LeCun et al., they proposed the initial structure of LeNet-5, which is considered to the first successful trial in deep learning. In their paper, a 7-layer network structure is proposed to represent human-written digital characters and used for digits recognition. The input of the network is 32×32 grey-scale image, after several layers of convolution and sub-sampling, a feature map is generated and feed into the two fully-connected layers. After the fully-connected layer's computation, a 10-class output is generated, representing the digital 0 to 9.

This network shows the basic components of convolutional neural networks (CNN). It's consisted of three convolutional layers marked as C1, C3 and C5, sub-sampling layers marked as S2, S4 and fully connected layers as F6 and output layer. For convolutional layer, a receptive field (we call it fixed-size patch or kernel) is chosen to compute convolution with the same size patch in the input. A stride is set to make sure every pixel in the original image or feature map is covered and generates the corresponding output in the output feature map. After the operation of convolution, a sub-sampling is done within the feature map to reduce the dimension and avoid repeat computation. Finally, fully connected layers are used to concatenate the multi-dimension feature maps and to map the feature into fix-size category as a classifier. All these layers have trainable parameters (weights) adjusted when it's training using character sample images. According to some of the latest research, researchers are putting more efforts in strengthening the capabilities of the representing image features using more complex model. In the article [21], a 7-layer model called AlexNet, consisting 5 convolutional layers and 2 fully-connected layers is used with large scale labeled image dataset ImageNet. Since then, more and more work is done to increase the number of layers and layer size, while using Dropout, ReLU to address the problem of overfitting and saturating. In the following years, ZFNet, VGG, GoogLeNet are developed using more complex neurons, computation units and layer structures.

Similar to GoogleNet, we employed an Inception module to increase the representation power of neural network. This work is motivated by the Network-in-Network approach proposed by Lin et al. [36]. In this module, additional 1×1 convolutional layers are added to the network, increasing the depth of overall network structure. On the other hand, this additional module can reduce the dimension of feature map, thus removing the computation bottlenecks. Normally, an Inception module takes the feature map as the input, followed with several convolutional layers varying from *1×1* convolutions, to *3×3* and *5×5* convolutions, and max-pooling layers like *3×3* pooling. Each layer generates different output and then these filters are concatenated into one feature map as the output. The outputs of the Inception module are used for next layer's convolution or pooling.

Based on the aforementioned inception modules, an optimized convolution is used to conduct dimension reduction and depth increasing. The input is not fed directly into the *3×3* and *5×5* convolutional layer. Instead, an additional *1×1* convolutional layer is added to reduce the input dimension. Furthermore, after the *3×3* max-pooling layer, the output is fed into an additional *1×1* convolutional layer. This way the Inception module is adjusted with more depth and less dimension. Similar to GooglNet, experiment shows that this network enhances the capturing of more visual information under constrained computational complexity. The improved inception module is illustrated in Fig. 1. The dotted rectangle shows the added *1×1* convolution layer. In this Figure, we used dotted convolutional layer called convLayer to represent the layers that we added in the Inception module. Unlike the previous network structure that doesn't contain the dotted layer, which is only

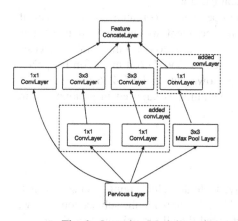

Fig. 1. Inception Module

three layers: previous layer, conv/max-pool layer and concateLayer, after adding these convLayers, we have four layers: previous layer, conv/max-pool layer, conv layer and concateLayer. In this way, a feature map contains much more information than before.

After the Inception module is formed, we use multiple modules to form the GoogLeNet, as shown in Fig. 2, the two modules are connected via an additional max pooling layer, each module takes the input of another module, after concatenation and pooling, the output is feed into another Inception module as the input. In this way, the network forms a hierarchical level step by step. In [37], Kaiming et al. gives the general guidance for modifying models considering the influence of different depth, number of filters and filter size. In our experiment, we inherit the 22-layer network structure in GoogLeNet, run the experiment multiple times using different kernel size and stride. In our experiment, an input size of 224×224 taking RGB channels, with "1×1", "3×3" and "5×5" convolutions, yield the best result. Other parameters are the same as the proposed GoogLeNet, Sect. 4 gives the detailed parameters when training on different data.

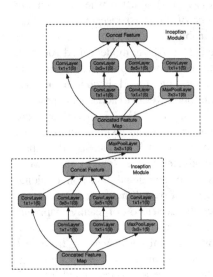

Fig. 2. Module connection

The network has 22 layers in depth, if only counting the layers with parameters. The average pooling layer is 5×5 filter size, and 1×1 convolutional layer is equipped with 128 filters and rectified linear activation (ReLU). In addition, the fully-connected layers are bound to 1024-dimension for feature mapping, and it's mapped into 1000-class output using ImageNet data set. A 70 % dropout rate is used to reduce over fitting, and the final classifier uses Softmax loss. Given different datasets, the output class number may vary according to the actual categories.

Due to the efficacy and popularity among open source community, we implement the proposed approach using Caffe [38]. In our experiment, we choose Ubuntu 14.04 as our host system. Four NVidia Tesla K40 GPUs were used to boost the training process. According to the model zoo, we used the pre-trained GoogLeNet model on ImageNet dataset with 1000 class, then fine-tuned on our own dataset UEC-256 and Food-101 with 256 classes or 101 classes. The model definition is adjusted in prototxt file in Caffe.

4   Experimental Results

In our experiments, we used two publicly available and challenging data sets, which were UEC-100/UEC-256 [31] and Food-101 [39]. As shown in the sub-sections below, the results of our proposed approach outperformed the all the existing techniques.

4.1 Experimental Results on UEC-256

The first datasets we used is called UEC dataset [31], which includes two sub-data sets: UEC-100 and UEC-256 [31]. This dataset was developed by DeepFoodCam project [33]. This dataset includes a large volume of food categories with textual annotation. We note that most of the foods in the dataset are Asian foods (i.e., Japanese foods). For UEC-100, there are 100 categories with a total of 8643 images, each category has roughly 90 images. For UEC-256, there are 256 categories with a total of 28375 images; each category has roughly 110 images. All of these images are correctly label with food category and bounding-box coordinates indicating the positions of the label food partition. In our experiment, because of the requirement of large-scale training data, we chose UEC-256 as the baseline dataset. All these images are divided into 5 folds, and 3 folds were used for training while the remaining 2 folds were used for testing.

In our experiment, we first used the pre-trained model with 1000-class category from ImageNet dataset. This model is publicly available in model zoo from Caffe's community. The pre-trained model was trained using 1.2 million images for training and 100,000 images for testing. Based on the pre-trained model, we further fine-tune the model using the UEC-256 dataset whose output category number is 256. The model was fine-tuned (ft) with a base-learning rate at 0.01, a momentum of 0.9 and 100,000 iterations. The results are shown below in Table 1.

Table 1. Comparison of accuracy on UEC-256 at different iterations using UEC-256)

# of Iterations	Top-1 accuracy	Top-5 accuracy
4,000	45.0 %	76.9 %
16,000	50.4 %	78.7 %
32,000	51.2 %	79.3 %
48,000	53.1 %	80.3 %
64,000	52.5 %	80.3 %
72,000	**54.7 %**	**81.5 %**
80,000	53.6 %	80.1 %
92,000	54.0 %	81.0 %
100,000	53.7 %	80.7 %

We also compared our result with the original results from the DeepFoodCam papers [31, 33]. To make a fair comparison, we used the same dataset as original papers, which is UEC-100, as well as the same strategy of dividing image dataset, the result is shown in the Table 2. From this table, we can tell that our proposed method outperformed all existing methods using the same dataset:

4.2 Experimental Results on Food-101

The second data set we used is Food-101 by Lukas et al. [39]. This dataset consists of 101 categories and each category has around 1000 images. Among the 1,000 images,

Table 2. Comparison of accuracy between our proposed approach and existing approaches using the same data set (UEC-100)

Method	top-1	top-5
SURF-BoF + ColorHistogram	42.0 %	68.3 %
HOG Patch-FV + Color Patch-FV	49.7 %	77.6 %
HOG Patch-FV + Color Patch-FV(flip)	51.9 %	79.2 %
MKL	51.6 %	76.8 %
Extended HOG Patch-FV + Color Patch-FV(flip)	59.6 %	82.9 %
DeepFoodCam(ft) [33]	72.26 %	92.00 %
Proposed Approach in this Paper	**76.3 %**	**94.6 %**

around 75 % of them were used for training and the rest 25 % were used for testing. There are 101,000 images in total in this dataset. However, since all these data were collected by food sharing websites, images do not contain any bounding box information indicating the food location. Each image only contains the label information indicating the food type. Most of the images are popular western food images.

The implementation of our algorithm for this dataset is similar to the one used in Sect. 4.1. We did adjust the parameters to fit for 101 food categories, and then used a base learning rate of 0.01, a momentum of 0.9 and (up to) 300,000 iterations. Based on the 1000-class pre-trained model on ImageNet dataset, we fine-tuned the model on Food-101 dataset, the accuracy is shown as the following table, and we have achieved a **77.4 %** top-1 accuracy and **93.7 %** top-5 accuracy (Table 3).

Table 3. Comparison of accuracy on Food-101 at different iterations

# of Iterations	Top-1 accuracy	Top-5 accuracy
10,000	70.2 %	91.0 %
30,000	74.7 %	93.0 %
50,000	75.1 %	93.0 %
70,000	74.0 %	92.1 %
90,000	76.3 %	93.4 %
160,000	76.6 %	93.4 %
180,000	77.2 %	93.3 %
200,000	76.9 %	93.4 %
250,000	**77.4 %**	**93.7 %**
300,000	76.4 %	93.0 %

We also compared our experiment with the state of the art techniques using the Food-101 datasets for evaluation. As shown in Table 4, our proposed method is better than all existing work using the same dataset and division.

From the above table, we can see that pre-trained model with domain specific fine-tuning can boost the classification accuracy significantly. And fine-tuning strategy improves the accuracy comparing with non-fine-tuning method. In this table, we use "ft" to represent the method using fine-tuning, otherwise "no ft" means that we don't

Table 4. Comparison of accuracy using different method on Food-101

Method	top-1	top-5
CNN-based Approach from Lukas et al. [39]	56.40 %	NA
RFDC-based Approach from Lukas et al. [39]	50.76 %	NA
Proposed Approach in this Paper	**77.4 %**	**93.7 %**

use fine-tuning and directly train the CNN model using designed architecture. The "NA" value in the "top-5" column means "not available", as we used the original experiment data from their paper [39], and they don't provide the top-5 result in it.

4.3 The Employment of Bounding Box

In the above experiment, we have shown that our proposed approach outperformed all existing approach. One further improvement is to add a pre-processing step with bounding box before fine-tuning. Specifically, based on the original image dataset, we first used the bounding box to crop the raw image. After this processing, only the food image part is remained for training and testing. We then conducted similar experiment on UEC dataset as shown Sects. 4.1 and 4.2 (Table 5).

Table 5. Comparison of accuracy of proposed approach using bounding box on UEC-256

Method	Top-1 Accuracy	Top-5 Accuracy
Proposed Approach without Bounding Box	54.7 %	81.5 %
Proposed Approach with Bounding Box	**63.8 %**	**87.2 %**

We also conducted the experiment on UEC-100, as follows:

Table 6. Comparison of accuracy of proposed approach using bounding box on UEC-100

Method	Top-1 Accuracy	Top-5 Accuracy
Proposed Approach without Bounding Box	57.0 %	83.4 %
Proposed Approach with Bounding Box	**77.2 %**	**94.8 %**

Food-101 was not used as it does not contain bounding box information and we cannot preprocess the image. Our experiment in these two subsets on UEC dataset shows that using bounding box information will significantly boost the classification accuracy. One intuitive explanation for this result is that the cropped image using bounding-box eliminates the abundant information in the raw image and forms a more accurate and clear image candidate for training, which yields a more accurate model for classification during the testing (Table 6).

4.4   Running Time

Training a large model requires a large amount of time. On a K40 machine, it takes 2 to 3 s per image for forward-backward pass using GoogLeNet. Since large dataset like ImageNet, Microsoft COCO contains so many images, it's a bit waste of time to train the model from scratch. One practical strategy is to use the pre-trained model in model zoo, which is public for all researchers. In our real experiment, the training time is influenced by how powerful the machine or GPU is, how large the image candidate is, how many iterations we choose, and what value we choose for learning rate etc. According to the rough estimation, if we use the pre-trained GoogLeNet model, then fine-tune on the UEC-100, UEC-256, Food-101 dataset, it roughly takes 2 to 3 days nonstop for a server equipped with Nvidia K40 GPU to train the model. After we have trained the model, we directly apply the model for classifying the image. It takes less than 1 min to test one image.

5   Conclusion

Obesity is a disorder involving excessive body fat that increases the risk of type 2 diabetes and cardiovascular diseases. In 2014, about 13 % of the world's adult population (11 % of men and 15 % of women) were obese. Accurate estimation of dietary intake is important for assessing the effectiveness of weight loss interventions. In order to reduce bias and improve the accuracy of self-report, we proposed new algorithms to analyze the food images captured by mobile devices (e.g., smartphone). The key technique innovation in this paper is the deep learning-based food image recognition algorithms. Our proposed algorithms are based on Convolutional Neural Network (CNN). Our experimental results on two challenging data sets using our proposed approach exceed the results from all existing approaches. In the future, we plan to improve performance of the algorithms and integrate our system into a real-word mobile devices and cloud computing-based system to enhance the accuracy of current measurements of dietary caloric intake.

Acknowledgments. This project is supported in partial by National Science Foundation of the United States (Award No. 1547428, 1541434, 1440737, and 1229213). Points of view or opinions in this document are those of the authors and do not represent the official position or policies of the U.S. NSF.

References

1. Beaton, G.H., Milner, J., Corey, P., McGuire, V., Cousins, M., Stewart, E., et al.: Sources of variance in 24-hour dietary recall data: implications for nutrition study design and interpretation. Am. J. Clin. Nutr. (USA) **32**, 2546–2559 (1979)
2. Willett, W.C., Sampson, L., Stampfer, M.J., Rosner, B., Bain, C., Witschi, J., et al.: Reproducibility and validity of a semiquantitative food frequency questionnaire. Am. J. Epidemiol. **122**, 51–65 (1985)

3. Buzzard, M.: 24-hour dietary recall and food record methods. Monogr. Epidemiol. Biostatistics **1**, 50–73 (1998)
4. Poslusna, K., Ruprich, J., de Vries, J.H., Jakubikova, M., van't Veer, P.: Misreporting of energy and micronutrient intake estimated by food records and 24 hour recalls, control and adjustment methods in practice. Br. J. Nutr. **101**, S73–S85 (2009)
5. Steele, R.: An overview of the state of the art of automated capture of dietary intake information. Crit. Rev. Food Sci. Nutr. **55**, 1929–1938 (2013)
6. Yang, S., Chen, M., Pomerleau, D., Sukthankar, R.: Food recognition using statistics of pairwise local features. In: 2010 IEEE Conference on Computer Vision and Pattern Recognition (CVPR), pp. 2249–2256 (2010)
7. Matsuda, Y., Yanai, K.: Multiple-food recognition considering co-occurrence employing manifold ranking. In: 2012 21st International Conference on Pattern Recognition (ICPR), pp. 2017–2020 (2012)
8. Zhu, F., Bosch, M., Woo, I., Kim, S., Boushey, C.J., Ebert, D.S., et al.: The use of mobile devices in aiding dietary assessment and evaluation. IEEE J. Sel. Top. Sig. Process. **4**, 756–766 (2010)
9. Daugherty, B.L., Schap, T.E., Ettienne-Gittens, R., Zhu, F.M., Bosch, M., Delp, E.J., et al.: Novel technologies for assessing dietary intake: evaluating the usability of a mobile telephone food record among adults and adolescents. J. Med. Internet Res. **14**, e58 (2012)
10. Xu, C., He, Y., Khannan, N., Parra, A., Boushey, C., Delp, E.: Image-based food volume estimation. In: Proceedings of the 5th International Workshop on Multimedia for Cooking & Eating Activities, pp. 75–80 (2013)
11. TADA: Technology Assisted Dietary Assessment at Purdue University, West Lafayette, Indiana, USA. http://www.tadaproject.org/
12. Martin, C.K., Nicklas, T., Gunturk, B., Correa, J.B., Allen, H.R., Champagne, C.: Measuring food intake with digital photography. J. Hum. Nutr. Diet. **27**(Suppl 1), 72–81 (2014)
13. MyFitnessPal.com: Free Calorie Counter, Diet & Exercise Tracker. http://www.myfitnesspal.com/
14. MyNetDiary: the easiest and smartest free calorie counter and free food diary for iPhone, iPad, Android, and BlackBerry applications. http://www.mynetdiary.com/
15. FatSecret: All Things Food and Diet. http://www.fatsecret.com/
16. Bengio, Y.: Learning deep architectures for AI. Found. Trends®. Mach. Learn. **2**, 1–127 (2009)
17. Meal Snap: Magical Meal Logging for iPhone. http://mealsnap.com/
18. Eatly: Eat Smart (Snap a photo of your meal and get health ratings). https://itunes.apple.com/us/app/eatly-eat-smart-snap-photo/id661113749
19. Deng, J., Dong, W., Socher, R., Li, L.-J., Li, K., Fei-Fei, L.: ImageNet: a large-scale hierarchical image database. In: Proceedings of IEEE Computer Vision and Pattern Recognition (CVPR), Miami, Florida, USA (2009)
20. Lin, T.Y., Maire, M., Belongie, S., Hays, J., Perona, P., Ramanan, D., Dollár, P., Zitnick, C. L.: Microsoft COCO: common objects in context. In: Fleet, D., Pajdla, T., Schiele, B., Tuytelaars, T. (eds.) ECCV 2014, Part V. LNCS, vol. 8693, pp. 740–755. Springer, Heidelberg (2014)
21. Krizhevsky, A., Sutskever, I., Hinton, G.E.: ImageNet classification with deep convolutional neural networks. In: NIPS, p. 4 (2012)
22. Hinton, G.E., Osindero, S., Teh, Y.-W.: A fast learning algorithm for deep belief nets. Neural Comput. **18**, 1527–1554 (2006)
23. Scientists See Promise in Deep-Learning Programs, by John Markoff, New York Times (2012). http://www.nytimes.com/2012/11/24/science/scientists-see-advances-in-deep-learning-a-part-of-artificial-intelligence.html

24. Bengio, Y., Yao, L., Alain, G., Vincent, P.: Generalized denoising auto-encoders as generative models. In: Advances in Neural Information Processing Systems, pp. 899–907 (2013)
25. Salakhutdinov, R., Hinton, G.E.: Deep boltzmann machines. In: International Conference on Artificial Intelligence and Statistics, pp. 448–455 (2009)
26. Girshick, R., Donahue, J., Darrell, T., Malik, J.: Rich feature hierarchies for accurate object detection and semantic segmentation. In: 2014 IEEE Conference on Computer Vision and Pattern Recognition (CVPR), pp. 580–587 (2014)
27. Simonyan, K., Zisserman, A.: Very deep convolutional networks for large-scale image recognition, arXiv preprint arXiv:1409.1556 (2014)
28. Zeiler, M.D., Fergus, R.: Visualizing and understanding convolutional networks. In: Fleet, D., Pajdla, T., Schiele, B., Tuytelaars, T. (eds.) ECCV 2014, Part I. LNCS, vol. 8689, pp. 818–833. Springer, Heidelberg (2014)
29. Szegedy, C., Liu, W., Jia, Y., Sermanet, P., Reed, S., Anguelov, D., et al.: Going deeper with convolutions. In: Proceedings of the IEEE Conference on Computer Vision and Pattern Recognition (CVPR), pp. 1–9 (2015)
30. Nair, V., Hinton, G.E.: Rectified linear units improve restricted boltzmann machines. In: Proceedings of the 27th International Conference on Machine Learning (ICML 2010), pp. 807–814 (2010)
31. Kawano, Y., Yanai, K.: Foodcam: a real-time food recognition system on a smartphone. Multimedia Tools Appl. **74**, 5263–5287 (2015)
32. Chen, M., Dhingra, K., Wu, W., Yang, L., Sukthankar, R.: PFID: pittsburgh fast-food image dataset. In: 2009 16th IEEE International Conference on Image Processing (ICIP), pp. 289–292 (2009)
33. Kawano,Y., Yanai, K.: Food image recognition with deep convolutional features. In: Proceedings of the 2014 ACM International Joint Conference on Pervasive and Ubiquitous Computing, pp. 589–593. Adjunct Publication (2014)
34. LeCun, Y., Bottou, L., Bengio, Y., Haffner, P.: Gradient-based learning applied to document recognition. Proc. IEEE **86**, 2278–2324 (1998)
35. Hubel, D.H., Wiesel, T.N.: Receptive fields, binocular interaction and functional architecture in the cat's visual cortex. J. Physiol. **160**, 106–154 (1962)
36. Lin, M., Chen, Q., Yan, S.: Network in network, arXiv preprint arXiv:1312.4400 (2013)
37. He, K., Sun, J.: Convolutional neural networks at constrained time cost. In: Proceedings of the IEEE Conference on Computer Vision and Pattern Recognition, pp. 5353–5360 (2015)
38. Jia, Y., Shelhamer, E., Donahue, J., Karayev, S., Long, J., Girshick, R., et al.: Caffe: convolutional architecture for fast feature embedding. In: Proceedings of the ACM International Conference on Multimedia, pp. 675–678 (2014)
39. Bossard, L., Guillaumin, M., Van Gool, L.: Food-101 – Mining discriminative components with random forests. In: Fleet, D., Pajdla, T., Schiele, B., Tuytelaars, T. (eds.) ECCV 2014, Part VI. LNCS, vol. 8694, pp. 446–461. Springer, Heidelberg (2014)

Deep Learning Based Emotion Recognition from Chinese Speech

Weishan Zhang[1]([✉]), Dehai Zhao[1], Xiufeng Chen[2], and Yuanjie Zhang[1]

[1] Department of Software Engineering, China University of Petroleum,
No.66 Changjiang West Road, Qingdao 266580, China
zhangws@upc.edu.cn, {525044691,307304660}@qq.com
[2] Hisense TransTech Co., Ltd., No.16 Shandong Road, Qingdao, China
chenxiufeng@hisense.com

Abstract. Emotion Recognition is challenging for understanding people and enhance human computer interaction experiences. In this paper, we explore deep belief networks (DBN) to classify six emotion status: anger, fear, joy, neutral status, sadness and surprise using different features fusion. Several kinds of speech features such as Mel frequency cepstrum coefficient (MFCC), pitch, formant, et al., were extracted and combined in different ways to reflect the relationship between feature combinations and emotion recognition performance. We adjusted different parameters in DBN to achieve the best performance when solving different emotions. Both gender dependent and gender independent experiments were conducted on the Chinese Academy of Sciences emotional speech database. The highest accuracy was 94.6 %, which was achieved using multi-feature fusion. The experiment results show that DBN based approach has good potential for practical usage of emotion recognition, and suitable multi-feature fusion will improve the performance of speech emotion recognition.

1 Introduction

Emotion status is an outward manifestation of people's inner thoughts, which plays an important role in rational actions of human beings. There is a desirable requirement for intelligent human-machine interfaces for better human-machine communication and decision making [4]. However, there are still many problems existing in the process, such as limited range of application, low recognition rate, etc.

It is generally believed that emotion is quite a complex reaction that even human cannot distinguish perfectly. It is also a useful data for human-computer interaction. Therefore, finding an effective way to recognize hidden emotion efficiently and accurately is really meaningful work. This has introduced a relatively new research field named emotion recognition, which is defined as detecting the emotion status of a person. Four decades ago, Williams and Stevens [16] presented an early attempt to analyze vocal emotion, which takes the first step on emotion recognition. Since two decades ago when Picard put forward affective

© Springer International Publishing Switzerland 2016
C.K. Chang et al. (Eds.): ICOST 2016, LNCS 9677, pp. 49–58, 2016.
DOI: 10.1007/978-3-319-39601-9_5

computing [12], emotion recognition became a hot topic and great efforts has been made in this field. Researchers have tried to predict high-level affective content from low-level human-centred signal cues by using every possible features extracted from the whole body such as speech, facial expression, heart rate, etc.

Emotion recognition is particularly useful for applications which require a natural man-machine interaction where the response to a user depends on the detected emotion. For example, if computers are able to give real-time response depend on users' affect, it will be more life-like than conventional systems which operate according to rigid rules. In addition, if some important posts such as car, aircraft and workshop where the mental status of the workers may affect the working status seriously can be monitored and get the information of tiredness or stressfulness out in advance, it's possible to guarantee workers' safety and avoid the accident [5]. What's more, it will be helpful for doctors to make the right diagnosis and it can also be employed as a diagnostic tool for therapists [13].

However, emotion recognition is a complex task that is furthermore complicated because there is no unambiguous answer to what the correct emotion is for a given sample [15]. Emotion recognition is still a challenging task because of the following reasons. First, it is difficult to decide which feature should be chosen for the recognition system. For speech emotion recognition, the acoustic variability introduced by the existence of different sentences, speakers, speaking styles, and speaking rates adds another obstacle because these properties directly affect most of the common extracted speech features such as pitch, and energy contours [2]. Moreover, there may be more than one perceived emotion in one sample and it is difficult to determine the boundaries between different portions.

In this paper, we apply DBN to conduct speech emotion recognition. In addition, we compare and analyze different feature combinations. In fact, our work is more challenging than those who use Berlin emotion database or USC-IEMOCAP database because we use Chinese emotion database. The Chinese language's prosodic features are complex, which makes Chinese vocal emotion recognition more difficult. Thus, we try to extract more feature from speech samples and combine them in a suitable way to solve this problem.

The rest of the paper is organized as follows. Section two describes some features that used widely in speech emotion analyzation. Section three introduces the classifier we use. Section four is the evaluation of our methods. Conclusion and future work end the paper.

2   Background Knowledge of Speech Emotion Feature Extraction

It is known that any emotion from the speaker is represented by a large number of parameters which are contained in the speech signals and the changes in these parameters will result in corresponding change in emotions. Thus, an important step in the design of speech emotion recognition system is extracting suitable features that efficiently characterize different emotions. Many researches have shown that effective parameters to distinguish a particular emotion status with high efficiency are spectral features such as Mel frequency cepstrum coefficient (MFCC), linear prediction cepstrum coefficient (LPCC) and prosodic features such as pitch frequency, formant, short-term energy, short-term zero-crossing rate, and so on [14]. Each speech signal is divided into small intervals of 20 ms to 30 ms, which are known as frames [14], and features are extracted from every frame respectively. All the extracted features have its own unique significances to the speech emotion recognition and they are described as follows:

1. Pitch frequency. Generally, pitch frequency is related with the length, thickness, toughness of one's vocal cords and reflect personal characteristics to a large degree. As one of the most important parameter of describing excitation source in speech signal processing filed, pitch frequency is used widely to solve speaker identification problem, especially for Chinese. Because Chinese has intonation, which is very helpful to Chinese semantic comprehension, accurate pitch detection plays outstanding role in Chinese speech emotion recognition.
2. Short-term energy. Short-term energy can be used to distinguish voice and noise because voice has more energy than noise. If the environment noise and the input noise is low enough, voice and noise can be separated easily by computing short-term energy of the input speech signal. Besides, short-term energy based algorithm performs well when detecting voiced sound because the energy of voiced sound is much more than voiceless sound. But it's hard to get a good performance for voiceless sound perception.
3. Short-term zero-crossing rate. Short-term zero-crossing rate indicates the times of speech signal wave crossing horizontal axis in each frame. It can be used to distinguish voiced sound and voiceless sound because the high band of speech signal has a high zero-crossing rate since low band has a low zero-crossing rate. In addition, short-term zero-crossing rate and short-term energy are complementary approximately because high short-term energy corresponds low short-term zero-crossing rate while low short-term energy corresponds high short-term zero-crossing rate.
4. Formant. Formant is an important parameter for reflecting vocal track information, which carries speech identity attribute like an ID card. The position of formant varies with different emotion because the pronunciation with different emotion can make vocal track change accordingly.
5. MFCC. MFCC is extracted based on the human ears' hearing characteristics, which is the most common kind of characteristic parameter of speech emotion recognition. Work on human auditory systems show that the response of human ears to different frequency is nonlinear but logarithmic. Human auditory system is good enough that it can not only extract semantic information but also emotion information. MFCC is extracted by imitating human auditory system, which is helpful for improving accuracy. The process of extracting MFCC is shown in Fig. 1.

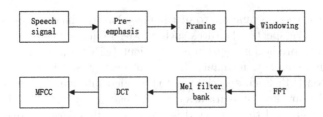

Fig. 1. The process of extracting MFCC

3   Deep Belief Networks

Deep learning has been used widely in multi-classification problems and it performs well. The characteristic of self-learning reduces the heavy work of feature selection, which makes classification more effective. Supposing that there is a bipartite graph, in which one layer is visible layer and the other layer is hidden layer. The nodes in the same layer are unconnected and all the nodes in the bipartite structure are random binary variables. Meanwhile, the probability distribution is Boltzmann distribution. This structure is known as Restricted Boltzmann Machine (RBM). Deep belief networks (DBN) is constituted by many RBM. Comparing with conventional neural networks with discrimination model, DBN is a probability generation model, which is a joint distribution of observation and labels [6]. That is to say, the probability generation model estimates P(Observation|Label) and P(Label|Observation) since the discrimination model only estimates P(Label|Observation). There may exist some problems when using DBN. For example, a labeled dataset is needed for training, the speed of learning process is slow and the learning results may converge to local optimal solution because of unsuitable parameter.

A typical DBN model is shown in Fig. 2. The networks contain only one visible layer and one hidden layer. All the layer connects with each other but nodes in the same layer is unconnected. The hidden layer is trained to catch the correlation between high level data expressed by the visible layer. The connection of DBN is determined by top-down weights generation and RBMs constitute the whole structure like building blocks. Comparing with sigmoid belief networks, DBN performs well in weights connection learning.

Ignoring the complex work on feature representation and selection, DBN can effectively generate discriminative features that approximate the complex non-linear dependencies between features in the original set. So it has been widely applied to speech processing as well as emotion recognition tasks [11]. In our work, we present a DBN model to investigate audio feature learning in emotion domain, which is a three-layer model. The audio features from the input layer are learned in the hidden layer. The learned features from the hidden layer are used as the input to the output layer. Finally, a binary list which represents the emotion category of the speech sample is obtained.

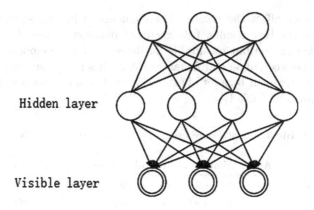

Fig. 2. A simple structure of DBN

4 Evaluation

4.1 Database

The database we use in the experiments is Chinese Academy of Sciences emotional speech database[1], which is provided by the Chinese Academy of Sciences Institute of Automation State Key Laboratory of Pattern Recognition Research Group. The corpus is recorded by four processional announcers, including two males and two females. The total 1200 sentences contains 6 kinds of emotion status: anger, fear, joy, sadness, surprise and neural status, and each emotion status has 50 recording scripts. Pitch frequency, short-term energy, short-term zero-crossing rate, formant and MFCC are extracted from speech segments and the corresponding statistic characteristics such as minimum, maximum, mean, variance and standard deviation are calculated at the same time. Finally, a feature dataset with 74 dimension is obtained.

4.2 Experiments with DBN

Allowing for the difference between male and female, whose vocal characteristics are so disparate that will influence speech analyzation greatly, we divide the dataset into two groups, the male group and the female group. Each group contains 500 training samples and 100 testing samples. And MFCC is the most widely used feature for speech emotion recognition because it can simulate human auditory system in a large degree. So the first group of experiment used MFCC to train with DBN. After loading one group of dataset with labels added by ourselves, We adjusted the parameters of DBN to get a good model. Then we evaluated the trained model with the rest of speech samples. During the training process, we found that this four parameters of *numpochs*, *bachsize*, *momentum*

---

[1] http://www.datatang.com/data/39277.

and *alpha* mainly affect the results. The challenge is finding suitable parameters to achieve the best results. One group of parameters may be suitable for detecting male emotion but unsuitable for detecting female emotion because of the difference between male and female voice. So it's important to find the rule of parameter adjustment by a lot of experiments. The final true positive of using MFCC are shown in Table 1.

Table 1. Results only using MFCC features with DBN

Emotion	Anger	Fear	Joy	Neutral	Sadness	Surprise	Average
Male (%)	86	88	94	88	90	94	90
Female (%)	98	82	94	98	88	82	90.3

As other features also play the important role of reflecting speech emotion, three group of experiments were conducted. We choose the most representative feature combinations in the experiments. Table 2 shows the true positive using MFCC and pitch. Table 3 shows the true positive using MFCC and formant. And Table 4 are the true positive using all features we extracted

Table 2. Results using MFCC and pitch features with DBN

Emotion	Anger	Fear	Joy	Neutral	Sadness	Surprise	Average
Male (%)	92	90	94	88	94	92	91.6
Female (%)	94	90	90	90	92	90	91

Table 3. Results using MFCC and formant features with DBN

Emotion	Anger	Fear	Joy	Neutral	Sadness	Surprise	Average
Male (%)	92	88	94	94	94	94	92.6
Female (%)	94	92	94	90	94	90	92.3

Though the results of each group are very similar, we can find some characteristics of different feature combinations. For example, when using MFCC and pitch, neutral status has the lowest accuracy. But when using MFCC and formant, fear performs badly. What's more, the fusion of all features interaction decreases the contingency of single feature, leads to similar results of male group and female group and at the same time, achieves a higher accuracy. It's necessary to note that the fusion features are not simple series of different features and they need adjusted weights for every feature. The weights of one feature can be adjusted according to its contribution to reflect emotion or the dimension of it. For example, the dimension of MFCC is higher than pitch, so we give pitch a larger weight than MFCC. All the adjustments should be changed by the practical applications.

Table 4. Results using all features with DBN

Emotion	Anger	Fear	Joy	Neutral	Sadness	Surprise	Average
Male (%)	92	94	90	98	98	96	94.6
Female (%)	94	96	96	96	90	96	94.6

4.3 Experiments with SVM

Additionally, we conducted the experiment using SVM as a comparison of DBN. Three kinds of SVM multi-classification methods, one versus one, one versus rest and minimum output coding (MOC) are evaluated. Meanwhile, the conventional dichotomous method is implemented. The true positive of male emotion recognition are shown in Table 5.

Table 5. Results of male emotion recognition with SVM

Emotion	Anger	Fear	Joy	Neutral	Sadness	Surprise
OneVsAll (%)	36	92	18	94	80	26
MOC (%)	86	100	84	94	98	98
OneVsOne (%)	74	98	10	100	94	18
Dichotomy (%)	84	96	74	98	74	96

As we can see from Table 5, when using one versus one method to deal with male dataset, fear, neutral status and sadness have a higher accuracy of 92 %, 94 % and 80 % respectively. Similarly, these three emotions have a higher accuracy when using one versus one method. Since all the emotions have the highest accuracy when using MOC method. We can see obviously that the three methods perform better than conventional dichotomous method.

The true positive of female emotion recognition are shown in Table 6.

Table 6. Results of female emotion recognition with SVM

Emotion	Anger	Fear	Joy	Neutral	Sadness	Surprise
OneVsAll (%)	94	96	66	86	100	84
MOC (%)	96	100	100	86	98	98
OneVsOne (%)	98	98	86	96	100	94
Dichotomy(%)	90	72	98	86	100	98

From Table 6 we can see that when using one versus rest method, only joy has a low recognition of 66 % since the rest five emotions have a high accuracy.

And one versus one method can get a good result for all the emotions. MOC method performs better than other methods, which is same with the result of male emotion recognition. We can also see that conventional dichotomous method can't get a good result.

As shown in the experiments above, the highest accuracy of DBN is 94.6 %, which is higher than SVM method of 84.54 %. That is to say, when applying DBN, the performance of speech emotion recognition is better than SVM, which satisfies the expected result.

4.4   Related Work

Prashant Aher et al. [1] put forward a noise robust speech emotion recognition system. They find that MFCC is good in clean environment but degrades when there exists data mismatch between training and testing phase. Features extracted from input speech samples are fed into SVM with RBF kernel function and get an accuracy of 89 % on Berlin emotion database. We also extracted MFCC as the main feature but we fused other speech features to achieve a better performance.

In [7], the authors generated feature representations from both acoustic and lexical levels. They extracted both low-level acoustic features and lexical features. And they also used the traditional Bag-of Words (BOF) features. Their work was evaluated on USC-IEMOCAP database and achieved an accuracy of 69.2 %. The experimental results showed that late fusion of both acoustic and lexical features were suitable for speech emotion recognition task. Though they used both acoustic and lexical feature, they didn't use deep learning method.

In [17], the authors proposed modulation spectral features for the automatic recognition of human affective information from speech. The features were obtained using an auditory filter bank and a modulation filter bank for speech analysis. They evaluated their system on Berlin emotion database and Vera am Mittag database with SVM and achieved an overall recognition rate of 91.6 %, which was a good performance.

Yelin Kim et al. [9] focused on deep learning techniques which can overcome the limitations of complicated feature selection by explicitly capturing complex non-linear feature interactions in multi-modal data. They proposed and evaluated a suite of deep belief networks models and demonstrate that these models show improvement in emotion classification performance. An accuracy of 62.42 % has been achieved on the Interactive Emotional Dyadic Motion Capture Database. We also used deep learning method but we applied some artificial assistance of selecting suitable feature fusion, which leaded to a better performance.

In [3], the authors removed the gaussian white noise with the adaptive filter. Then the Mel Frequency Cepstrum Coefficients (MFCC) based on Empirical Mode Decomposition (EMD) was extracted and with its difference parameter to improve. At last they presented an effective method for speech emotion recognition based on Fuzzy Least Squares Support Vector Machines (FLSSVM) so as to realize the speech recognition of four main emotions. The experiment results showed that this method has the better anti-noise effect when compared with traditional Support Vector Machines. However, deep learning method that we used has been confirmed to have a robust performance when facing noisy speech.

Chi-Chun Lee et al. [10] proposed a hierarchical binary decision tree approach to realize emotion recognition. They performed feature selection on the 384 features including pitch frequency, short-term energy, MFCC, etc. using the software SPSS and obtained a reduced feature set which was in a range of 40-60. The results show that comparing with SVM baseline model, this approach has an improved accuracy of 3.37 % and 7.44 % on the AIBO database and the USC-IEMOCAP database respectively. The features they extracted was more than ours but not all the features are helpful.

Akshay S. Utane et al. [15] handled five emotion status (joy, sadness, surprise, anger and neutral status) using two different classifier, SVM and GMM. Prosodic features such as pitch frequency and spectral features such as MFCC were extracted. And the system was evaluated on Berlin emotion database and achieved an accuracy of 12.18 %–74.37 % among different emotion status. They found that both SVM and HMM provide relatively similar accuracy for classification. The accuracy they achieved had a large range between various emotions, which represented that it was an unstable method.

In [8], the authors proposed a speech emotion recognition system using multi-algorithm, i.e., the MFCC and Discrete Wavelet Transform based algorithm have been successfully used to extract emotional information from speech signal. Similarly, they used SVM as the classifier, but the speech database they use is created by themselves. An accuracy of 11 %–89 % is achieved among different emotion status, which is also a large range.

5 Conclusions and Future Work

In this work, we investigate the utility of single feature and fusion features for speech emotion recognition. The results show that fusion features can improve the performance of DBN. However, the combination is not a simple series process and it needs suitable weights for different features according to the practical applications. Moreover, both SVM and DBN can be used for multi-classification well. But the evaluation of DBN shows that deep learning method can make the best of low-level features to complete high-level emotion detection. That is to say, deep learning method has advantage over the SVM method when facing multi-dimensional features, because it avoids artificial selection of complex features.

In the future, we will collect more speech data to train DBN and generalize the network model. What's more, lexical feature is a very important part of speech. If we combine lexical feature with audio feature, the system will work better. Besides, the single speech feature is too few to reflect one's real emotion. The combination of various features from the whole body is the biggest challenge.

Acknowledgement. This research was supported by the International S&T Cooperation Program of China (ISTCP, 2013DFA10980).

References

1. Aher, P., Cheeran, A.: Auditory processing of speech signals for speech emotion recognition (2014)
2. Banse, R., Scherer, K.R.: Acoustic profiles in vocal emotion expression. J. Pers. Soc. Psychol. **70**(3), 614 (1996)
3. Chu, Y.Y., Xiong, W.H., Chen, W.: Speech emotion recognition based on EMD in noisy environments. In: Advanced Materials Research, vol. 831, pp. 460–464. Trans Tech Publication (2014)
4. El Ayadi, M., Kamel, M.S., Karray, F.: Survey on speech emotion recognition: features, classification schemes, and databases. Pattern Recogn. **44**(3), 572–587 (2011)
5. France, D.J., Shiavi, R.G., Silverman, S., Silverman, M., Wilkes, D.M.: Acoustical properties of speech as indicators of depression and suicidal risk. IEEE Trans. Biomed. Eng. **47**(7), 829–837 (2000)
6. Hinton, G.E.: Deep belief networks. Scholarpedia **4**(5), 5947 (2009)
7. Jin, Q., Li, C., Chen, S., Wu, H.: Speech emotion recognition with acoustic and lexical features. In: 2015 IEEE International Conference on Acoustics, Speech and Signal Processing (ICASSP), pp. 4749–4753. IEEE (2015)
8. Joshi, D.D., Zalte, M.: Recognition of emotion from marathi speech using MFCC and DWT algorithms (2013)
9. Kim, Y., Lee, H., Provost, E.M.: Deep learning for robust feature generation in audiovisual emotion recognition. In: 2013 IEEE International Conference on Acoustics, Speech and Signal Processing (ICASSP), pp. 3687–3691. IEEE (2013)
10. Lee, C.C., Mower, E., Busso, C., Lee, S., Narayanan, S.: Emotion recognition using a hierarchical binary decision tree approach. Speech Commun. **53**(9), 1162–1171 (2011)
11. Mohamed, A.R., Dahl, G.E., Hinton, G.: Acoustic modeling using deep belief networks. IEEE Trans. Audio Speech Lang. Process. **20**(1), 14–22 (2012)
12. Picard, R.W., Picard, R.: Affective Computing, vol. 252. MIT Press, Cambridge (1997)
13. Schuller, B., Rigoll, G., Lang, M.: Speech emotion recognition combining acoustic features and linguistic information in a hybrid support vector machine-belief network architecture. In: Proceedings of IEEE International Conference on Acoustics, Speech, and Signal Processing (ICASSP 2004), vol. 1, pp. I-577. IEEE (2004)
14. Shen, P., Changjun, Z., Chen, X.: Automatic speech emotion recognition using support vector machine. In: 2011 International Conference on Electronic and Mechanical Engineering and Information Technology (EMEIT), vol. 2, pp. 621–625. IEEE (2011)
15. Utane, A.S., Nalbalwar, S.: Emotion recognition through speech using gaussian mixture model and support vector machine. Emotion **2**, 8 (2013)
16. Williams, C.E., Stevens, K.N.: Emotions and speech: some acoustical correlates. J. Acoust. Soc. Am. **52**(4B), 1238–1250 (1972)
17. Wu, S., Falk, T.H., Chan, W.Y.: Automatic speech emotion recognition using modulation spectral features. Speech Commun. **53**(5), 768–785 (2011)

SVM Based Predictive Model for SGA Detection

Haowen Mo[1,2], Jianqiang Li[1,2], Shi Chen[3], Hui Pan[3],
Ji-Jiang Yang[4(✉)], Qing Wang[4], and Rui Mao[2]

[1] School of Software Engineering, Beijing University of Technology, Beijing, China
[2] Guangdong Key Laboratory of Popular High Performance Computers,
Shenzhen Key Laboratory of Service Computing and Applications, Shenzhen, China
lijianqiang@bjut.edu.cn
[3] Department of Endocrinology, Peking Union Medical College Hospital, Beijing, China
[4] Tsinghua National Laboratory for Information Science and Technology,
Tsinghua University, Beijing, China
yangjijiang@tsinghua.edu.cn

Abstract. The medical diagnosis process can be interpreted as a decision making
process, which doctors determine whether a person is suffering from a disease
based on the medical examination. This process can also be computerized in order
to present medical diagnostic procedures in an accurate, objective, rational, and
fast way. This paper presents a detection model for small for gestational age
(SGA) based on support vector machine (SVM). For this purpose, a dataset was
adopted from pregnancy eugenic investigation to train the classification model.
Then empirical experiments were conducted for SGA detection. The results indicate that support vector machine is considerably effective to detect SGA to help
doctors make the final diagnosis.

Keywords: Small for gestational age · Support vector machine · Classification ·
Healthcare

1 Introduction

Small for gestational age (SGA) refers to a fetus that has failed to achieve a specific
biometric or estimated weight threshold by a specific gestational age. SGA is a compli-
cation of pregnancy. It's the main reason of fetal mortality and morbidity in the perinatal
period. It can cause perinatal complications such as acute fetal distress, meconium aspi-
ration, neonatal asphyxia, polycythemia increase and neonatal hypoglycemia. SGA
often represents placental pathology, and it may precede the clinical manifestations of
preeclampsia, preterm labour and placental abruption. More seriously, SGA fetus may
cause intrapartum complications or stillbirth [1, 2]. After the birth, SGA babies are
known to that they are at increased risk for a wide range of difficulties [3]. Some studies
have shown that, in preschool and school age populations, SGA children present minor
neurological signs, poor school performance, fine motor coordination abnormalities,
spatial relation deficits and poor visual-motor integration [4, 5]. Compared to those
detected after birth, these risks may be substantially reduced in case of SGA antenatal
identified, which helps reduce the incidence using medical intervention [6].

© Springer International Publishing Switzerland 2016
C.K. Chang et al. (Eds.): ICOST 2016, LNCS 9677, pp. 59–68, 2016.
DOI: 10.1007/978-3-319-39601-9_6

Early prediction and treatment for SGA is of great significance to improve children's health and ensure their safety to grow. Improved identification of infants at risk for SGA could help pediatrician draw up customized care plans to those infants. In past, pediatrician needed to weigh newborns manually in the delivery room to determine whether the newborn was SGA. This approach isn't fit for large-scale SGA detection. In addition, doctors can only check out SGA infants but not reduce the incidence of SGA. However, recently studies have found that parents' lifestyle and psychological factors may be relevant with incidence of SGA [7, 8]. Using of these factors from parents would make it possible for us to predict SGA and then help pediatrician be more focus on the care of at-risk infants. But how to use risk factors to construct a predictive model for SGA and simultaneously improve the predictive accuracy as high as possible? The objective of this study was to develop an algorithm using machine learning to predict infants at high risk of SGA.

1.1 Related Work

Studies on SGA prediction have been made for years. Doppler Umbilical Artery Waveform Analysis [9] has been used. Based on this technique, one real-time ultrasonography was used to measure the respective abdominal circumferences. Doppler recordings of the umbilical blood flow velocity waveforms were taken immediately after the real-time probe was removed from the abdomen. By abdominal circumferences to judge whether infant develops to a reasonable size. Meanwhile measuring the umbilical blood flow velocity to check out how much nutrients fetus gets from mother and whether metabolism is normal. For abnormal infants, they need further examination to make the final diagnosis. Researchers are also trying to apply to predict SGA infants in twin pregnancies. But the results indicated that was not of much value. This research is relevant but not closely related to the work in this paper since our research is to use machine learning to build a classifier for SGA detection. The main objective of the study is to construct an automatic classification model to quickly and accurately predict SGA before infant were born.

From the angle of large-scale of SGA detection, the work in [10] is closely related to this paper. In [10], George Karagiannis et al. used maternal characteristic, fetal nuchal translucency thickness, serum pregnancy-associated plasma protein-A and free β-human chorionic gonadotropin from biophysical and biochemical makers to develop a regression model for prediction of SGA. The work in this paper is different from both these two pieces of work since we adopt the machine learning framework for large-scale SGA detection, where more fast and accurate prediction on the SGA classification.

1.2 Machine Learning Based SGA Classification

Machine learning (ML) is studying how the computer to simulate or to realize the study behavior of human being. The aim is to obtain the new knowledge or the skill, organize the knowledge structure, which can make progressive improvement of its own performance. Any machine learning method consists of two steps [11], i.e., selecting a candidate model, and then, estimating the parameters of the model using a learning algorithm and available data. Support Vector Machine (SVM) is a machine learning algorithm which is developed from the statistical learning theory of Vapnik-Chervonenkis (VC) dimension structural and risk minimization principle [12], which shows generalization errors to be bounded by the sum of training errors and a term depending on the VC dimension of the learning systems. By minimizing this upper bound, high generalization performance can be achieved. In recent years, SVM has been applied to broad areas, including handwritten digit recognition, face detection in images, pattern recognition and function regression [13, 14]. SVM has important research value for system identification and disease diagnosis [15, 16]. A SVM approach for detection of Pima Indian Diabetes had achieved 82 % for the diagnosis success [17]. It also had been applied to Lymph diseases detection and reached 83.1 % for accuracy [18].

SVM has high performance in classification. So we selected it to detect SGA. It was developed to classify data points of linear separable data sets. The target result after finished training is separated into 2 groups which divided set by a separating hyperplane. The distance between the separated hyperplane and closest data points of dataset is called "the margin" [19]. SGA positive samples are on one side of the hyperplane and the negative samples are on the other side.

2 Method

2.1 Support Vector Machine

Based on the structural risk minimization principle from statistic learning theory, SVM is originally introduced for solving the two-class pattern recognition problem. Its main idea is to build a hyperplane classifier that separates the positive and negative examples while maximizing the smallest margin (i.e., has the largest margin from two classes of data).

A separating hyperplane can be written as,

$$f(\mathbf{x}) = W^T \mathbf{x} + b \tag{1}$$

Where W is a weight vector and b is a bias.

Thus any point that lies above the separating hyperplane satisfies

$$W^T \mathbf{x} + b > 0 \tag{2}$$

Similarly, any point that lies under the separating hyperplane satisfies

$$W^T \mathbf{x} + b < 0 \tag{3}$$

Assume $\{(x_1, y_1), (x_2, y_2), \ldots (x_n, y_n)\}$ is a set of training data, where x_i is an input vector and y_i is its class label, $y_i\{1, -1\}$. The function yields $f(x_i) > 0$ for $y_i = 1$, and $f(x_i) < 0$ for $y_i = -1$.

For a given training set, while there may exist many hyperplanes that separate the two classes, the SVM classifier is based on the hyperplane that maximizes the separating margin between the two classes. We use the soft margin SVM to find the hyperplane between positive and negative training data, through which the problem that the training data are not linearly separable can be solved. Formally, it can be stated as the optimization problem:

$$\text{Minimize:} \frac{1}{2}||\omega||^2 + C\sum_i \xi_i \qquad (4)$$

Such that:

$$c_i(wx_i - b) \geq 1 - \xi_i, \, i = 1, 2, 3, \ldots, n \qquad (5)$$

C is a user-specified, positive, regularization parameter. In (4), the variable is a vector containing all the slack variables $\xi_i, i = 1, 2, \ldots, $ n.

As a discriminative classifier that learns from both positive and negative data, SVM models posterior class probabilities $P(c_j|d_i)$ for all classes directly and learn mapping from d_i to c_j. SVM has two important advantages: (1) it is fairly robust to overfitting and can scale up to high dimensionalities; (2) no efforts in parameter tuning is needed, since the theoretically derived "default" choice of parameters setting has been shown to provide the best effectiveness. It has been recognized as one of the best classification algorithms for many classification tasks [20].

2.2 Feature Selection

In this paper, all of the data was obtained from Peking Union Medical College Hospital (PUMCH) pregnancy eugenic database. 400 kinds of attributes were obtained in database including parents' family history, medical history, lifestyle, physical examination, laboratory examinations etc. We gave up the records that missed more than 20 %, and then we selected 147 attributes as SGA risk features that may have clinical significance. But the features are still too many for large-scale and rapid SGA detection. We need to estimate the influence that each feature makes on the pathogenesis of SGA. Based on the impact to the SGA we select an appropriate feature subset to reduce the data dimension thus speeding up the succeeding learning algorithms as well as improving predicting accuracy.

In feature selection, the wrapper approach is deemed as a search problem: the importance of features is evaluated by their contribution to the final prediction accuracy. Statistical tests (χ^2 test, T-test) are popular wrapper method in the feature selection. The core idea is to compare the difference between observations and theoretical value to determine whether the hypothesis is established.

T-test is one methodology for testing the degree of difference between two means in sample; it uses T distribution theory to infer the probability when disparity happens, then judge whether the disparity between two means is significant. So it's fit for continuous variable statistical deduction. For χ^2 test, it seeks to determine whether there's a well fit between the frequencies of the observed data and the frequencies of the expected or theoretical data. It uses the chi-square statistic to compare the two frequency distributions and test the hypothesis that the observations come from the same probability distribution. So it's fit for continuous variable statistical deduction. P-value is defined by its critical region which is determined by the significance level α ($0 < \alpha < 1$). The significance level α is found under the constraint of the degree of confidence, which is used to estimate the reliability of an estimator. It's is a diminishing indicator of confidence level. The greater the P-value, the more we cannot think that the variables associated with the sample to be reliable indicators of population variables associated.

Each selected features had been conducted to the statistical test to validate relevance with SGA. For continuous features, we make a T-test to them, i.e. serum creatinine (SC), the SGA infants' maternal mean SC is 71.5 while not SGA infants' is 71.8. The P-value is 0.026. As platelet (PLT), the SGA infants' maternal mean PLT is 202.46*10^9/L while not SGA infants' is 201.62*10^9/L. The P-value is 0.165. The rest of continuous features are conducted to the same T-test and got the P-values. For the non-continuous features, we validate relevance with SGA by χ^2 test.

We rank the features with respect to the P-value from small to large after statistical test. Suppose the features are independent, we can select the top 50 features as the subset we want to predict SGA in this research, which includes 10 continuous features and 40 non-continuous features.

2.3 Classifier Construction

The aim of this paper was to use a Support Vector Machine approach for early detection of SGA. In the first step, we used the 50 features for classifier training. According to the definition of SGA, we marked to different infants as SGA group or not SGA group. In this paper, we use SGA^+ and SGA^- to denote SGA positive sample and SGA negative sample. According to the present medical statistics, the morbidity of SGA is 5 %–10 %. In this range, data set was randomly split into subset for training, testing and validation for SVM development. In preprocessing, difference between features' value field made some features had big impact to others. In order to prevent a few dimensions making too large effect on the data, meanwhile speed up the convergence of the training process. All features were normalized in [−1, 1]. After that, randomly select subset of data for training.

The kernel function in an SVM plays the central role of implicitly mapping the input vector (through an inner product) into a high-dimensional feature space. In this paper, we selected Gaussian RBF kernel. It's defined as follows.

$$K(\mathrm{x}, \mathrm{y}) = \exp\left(-\frac{||\mathrm{x} - \mathrm{y}||^2}{2\sigma^2}\right) \tag{6}$$

Where $\sigma > 0$ is a constant that defines the kernel width.

The Gaussian RBF kernel function in (6) assumes its maximum when and are identical. The associated parameters σ is determined during the training phase. When the results of training meet the Aarush-Kuhn-Tucker (KKT) optimality conditions, Training completed and got a model file. Next step, we used the model to predict and validate the test sets. In order to make the results more accurate, we used different sizes of training and test sets and predicted with cross-validation.

3   Experiment

3.1   Dataset

Data on 248501 infants were obtained from pregnancy eugenic database [18]. This database includes 200 pilot counties' pregnancy eugenic data. It recorded 1737718 evaluated family archives. All information involved the infants is as follows: 230,190 live births account for 92.6 %; 18311 were miscarriage, abortion, stillbirth or other ending accounting for 7.4 %. 222449 infants with weight were recorded in the database. According to the definition of SGA, 11629 infants belong to SGA^+ and 210820 belong to SGA^-.

3.2   Task and Evaluation Criteria

The main task is defined based on the real-world medical requirement for SGA detection. It needs the classifier to determine whether an infant is high risk of SGA or not, which is a two-class classification; the goal of this task is to apply to large-scale SGA detection before infants' birth. For the target, the performance of SVM classifier was evaluated by using performance indices such as accuracy, sensitivity, specificity. Main formulations are as follows:

$$\text{Accuracy} = \frac{TP + TN}{TP + FP + TN + FN} * 100\% \tag{7}$$

$$\text{Sensitivity} = \frac{TP}{TP + FN} * 100\% \tag{8}$$

$$\text{Specificity} = \frac{TN}{FP + TN} * 100\% \tag{9}$$

Where TP, FP, TN and FN and are true positive, false negative, true negative and false negative. Sensitivity is the proportion of positive test results that are true positives. Specificity is the proportion of negative test results that are true negative.

3.3   Performance of Classifier

In this research of 222449 infants, their mean gestational age was 39.1 weeks, and mean birth weight was 3306.6 ± 527.1 grams, which is basically consistent with the WHO recommended standard birth weight. The mean weight of SGA group was 2099.9 grams, and it was 3374.5 grams for not SGA group. Figure 1 gives the experiments results of different trends percentile for gestational age. In this study, SGA was defined as standard of 3rd centiles below the population average weight.

From Fig. 1 we can know that the baby's weight is gradually increased with the increase of time, which indicates that the fetus continues to get nutrients from the mother to develop completely. However, the fetus under 3rd and 10th centiles is greater fluctuations in weight during development. This reflects a greater likelihood of SGA infants with

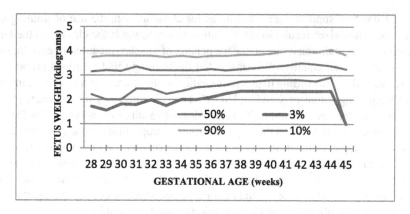

Fig. 1. Different weight trends percentile for gestational age

complications throughout the development process. It is noteworthy that 50th and 90th centiles fetus is a slight decrease in weight while 3rd and 10th centiles fetus is a sharp decline from 44 to 45 weeks. This is because a normal fetus can grow to a normal weight, and there is no problem with placental function. The decline of mature placental function will be very slow. So there will be no significant decrease in body weight. On the contrary, there will be the phenomenon of excessive placental maturity for a SGA fetus, which may cause insufficient blood supplies leading to get less and less nutrients and oxygen from the mother. In order to maintain their own growth, fetuses have to consume the substance already stored. Thus it will be significantly decreased with body weight.

Over the same proportion between SGA$^+$ and SGA$^-$, the size of training set would effect in the performance of classification. Through the combination of feature sets, four independent classifiers were built. For example, training set including 5000 SGA$^+$ and 75000 SGA$^-$ derived the classifier which presented the classification sensitivity on the test set was 81.19 %. However, training set including 3000 SGA$^+$ and 45000 SGA$^-$ derived the classifier which only reached 74.96 % on sensitivity. The main cause is that imbalance data results in insufficient classifier training. Similarity, the experimental results of the four classifiers for the SGA detection based on different size of training sets are illustrated in Table 1. From the table we can find that the greater scale training set is, the higher sensitivity classifier gets. And the specificity is far beyond sensitivity. It's mainly caused by the relatively low morbidity of SGA.

Table 1. Classification accuracy based on different sizes of training sets

	3000 SGA$^+$ 45000 SGA$^-$	5000 SGA$^+$ 75000 SGA$^-$	7000 SGA$^+$ 105000 SGA$^-$	9000 SGA$^+$ 135000 SGA$^-$
Sensitivity (%)	74.96	81.19	83.80	85.67
Specificity (%)	99.87	99.82	99.81	99.79
Accuracy (%)	98.71	98.96	99.06	99.13

In the standard support vector machines for classification, the use of training sets with uneven class sizes results in classification biases towards the class with the large training size. The main causes lie in that the penalty of misclassification for each training sample is considered equally. We constructed the training sets by various proportions of SGA$^+$ and SGA$^-$. According to precious medical statistics, we built three training sets with different proportions of SGA$^+$ and SGA$^-$. Then classification was conducted to the same test set by the new classifiers. The classification results were presented by Table 2. From the table we can find that the larger the sample proportion for one class, the larger it's corresponding classification accuracy, while the smaller the sample proportion, the smaller the classification accuracy. This suggests that we can reconstruct data sets to increase the number of minority class in order to reduce the degree of imbalance data. Class boundary can offset more to the minority class. Thus the corresponding classifier improves accuracy obviously on the prediction to positive samples.

Table 2. Classification accuracy based on different proportions of training sets

	7000 SGA$^+$ 70000 SGA$^-$	7000 SGA$^+$ 105000 SGA$^-$	7000 SGA$^+$ 140000 SGA$^-$
Sensitivity (%)	86.66	83.80	81.60
Specificity (%)	99.77	99.81	99.83
Accuracy (%)	99.15	98.06	99.98

Some cases may both exist in the training and the test sets when them were built randomly. To avoid self-validation in classification, we adopted 10-fold cross-validation method to evaluate the performance of the classifier. One data set including SGA$^+$ and SGA$^-$ was equally divided into ten subsets, nine of them were the training sets to derive a new classifier, and the other one was classified. Each data set was conducted to classification once by cycling that step. Average accuracy was the final cross-validation accuracy. Cross-validation accuracy to different size of data set was presented by Table 3. We can find that the accuracy is very high after eliminating the effects of self-validation. That is to say, it's believable to apply SVM as a predictor to detect a risk SGA.

Table 3. Cross-validation on different size data set

	3000 SGA$^+$ 45000 SGA$^-$	5000 SGA$^+$ 75000 SGA$^-$	7000 SGA$^+$ 105000 SGA$^-$	9000 SGA$^+$ 135000 SGA$^-$
Accuracy for Cross Validation (%)	99.93	99.74	99.93	99.11

4 Discussion

Even though SGA is considered as a complex disease, physiological and psychological factors of both parents used by Support Vector Machine appeared to be important in the prediction of SGA. Only two steps, small for age risk factors were being artificially selected as first. Second, we can predict SGA in the data set after we use Support Vector

Machine approach to train a classifier. To evaluate its applicability and performance in real detection of SGA, several real medical datasets have been built to compare its accuracy base on SVM. The experiment results suggest that SVM is a powerful predictor for small for gestational age. However, due to the complexity of SGA, SVM with only few, and e.g. in this study's 50 risk factors cannot be expected to outperform experienced clinicians in predicting which infant is likely to develop SGA. To make SVM stronger performance in the classification, more extensive SGA factors need to be taken into consideration because SVM's final computational complexity depends on the number of support vectors, rather than the dimension of the sample space, which can avoid the "curse of dimensionality". Using large scale SGA risk factors as SVM feature vectors will likely lead to higher accuracy for the prediction of SGA, which in turn should lead to better acceptance of the SVM methodology by clinicians.

5 Conclusion

This paper proposes an optimization approach to the medical application. We present a predictive model that utilizes machine learning with risk factors from parents. Support Vector Machine as an effective predictive tools help podiatrist detect high risk infants of SGA. It makes it possible to reduce the morbidity of SGA by early intervention to the risk factors. Although there is still much improvement for the accuracy of the classifier, it has a very broad application prospect on community doctors' diagnosis and large-scale detection of SGA. The feature work is that clustering SGA sample makes each class generates the corresponding subset of SGA recognition, and then we would use heterogeneous integrated learning via some special voting strategy, which may lead to a higher accuracy to further the reliable prediction of SGA in risk infants or other disease detection.

Acknowledgments. This work is supported by Beijing Natural Science Foundation (4152007), China National Key Technology Research and Development Program project with no. 2013BAH19F01 and Guangdong Key Laboratory of Popular High Performance Computers, Shenzhen Key Laboratory of Service Computing and Applications.

References

1. Gardosi, J.O.: Prematurity and fetal growth restriction. Early Hum. Dev. **81**, 43–49 (2005)
2. Gardosi, J., Kady, S.M., McGeown, P., Francis, A., Tonks, A.: Classification of stillbirth by relevant condition at death (ReCoDe): population based cohort study. BMJ **331**, 1113–1117 (2005)
3. Basso, O., Frydenberg, M., Olsen, S.F., Olsen, J.: Two definitions of "small size at birth" as predictors of motor development at sixmonths. Epidemiology **16**(5), 657–663 (2005)
4. Ounsted, M., Moar, V.A., Scott, A.: Small-for-dates babies, gestationalage, and developmental ability at 7 years. Early Hum. Dev. **19**(2), 77–86 (1989)
5. Sommerfelt, K., Sonnander, K., Skranes, J., Andersson, H.W., Ahlsten, G., Ellertsen, B., et al.: Neuropsychologic and motor function in small-for-gestation preschoolers. Pediatr. Neurol. **26**(3), 186–191 (2002)

6. Lindqvist, P.G., Molin, J.: Does antenatal identification of small-for-gestational age fetuses significantly improve their outcome? Ultrasound Obstet. Gynecol. **25**, 258–264 (2005)

7. Li, J., Liu, C., Liu, B., Mao, R., Wang, Y., Chen, S., Pan, H., Wang, Q.: Diversity-aware retrieval of medical records. Comput. Ind. **69**(1), 30–39 (2015)

8. Yang, J.J., Li, J., Mulder, J., Wang, Y., Wang, Q.: Emerging Information Technologies for Enhanced Healthcare. Comput. Ind. **69**(1), 3–11 (2015)

9. Hastie, S.J., Danskin, F., Neilson, J.P., Whittle, M.J.: Prediction of the small for gestational age twin fetus by doppler umbilical artery waveform analysis. Obstet. Gynecol. **5**, 730–733 (1989)

10. Karagianis, G., Akolekar, R.: Prediction of small-for-gestation neonates from biophysical and biochemical markers at 11–13 weeks. Fetal Diagn. Ther. **29**(2), 148–154 (2011)

11. Yang, J.J., Li, J., Shen, R., Zeng, Y., Wang, Q.: Exploiting ensemble learning for automatic cataract detection and grading. Comput. Methods Program. Biomed. **124**, 45–57 (2016)

12. Vapnik, V.N.: The Nature of Statistical Learning Theory. Springer, New York (1995)

13. Boser, B.E., Guyon, I.M., Vapnik, V.N.: A training algorithm for optimal margin classifiers. In: Proceedings of Fifth Annual Workshop Computing Learning Theory, pp. 144–152 (1995)

14. Vapnik, V.N.: An overview of statistical learning theory. IEEE Trans. Neural Netw. **10**(5), 988–999 (1999)

15. Jianguo, X.: A Study on Application of Support Vector Machine in GPC with Real Test Analysis [D]. Master's degree thesis, Zhejiang University (2006)

16. Fung, G.M., Mangasarian, O.L.: A feature selection newton method support vector machine classification. Comput. Optim. Appl. **28**(2), 185–202 (2004)

17. Karatsiolis, S., Schizas, C.N.: Region based support vector machine algorithm for medical diagnosis on Pima Indian Diabetes dataset. In: Proceedings of the BIBE, Larnaca, Cyprus, 11–13 November 2012 (2012)

18. Elshazly, H.I., Elkorany, A.M., Hassanien, A.E.: Lymph diseases diagnosis approach based on support vector machines with different kernel functions. In: 2014 9th International Computer Engineering & Systems (ICCES), 22–23 December 2014, pp. 198–203 (2014)

19. Bentley, P.M., McDonnell, J.T.E.: Wavelet transforms: an introduction. IEEE J. Electron. Commun. Eng. **40**, 175–185 (1992)

20. Liu, M., Wang, Q., et al.: Status assessment of preconception health risk exposure in Chinese reproductive women during 2010-2012. Natl. Med. J. China **95**(3), 172–175 (2015)

Context Awareness and Autonomous Computing

Situation-Aware Decision Making in Smart Homes

Hoda Gholami[✉] and Carl K. Chang[✉]

Iowa State University, 226 Atanasof Hall, Ames, IA 50011, USA
{hgholami,chang}@iastate.edu

Abstract. The ability to efficiently predict the elderly's future situations and make the right decision accordingly is a necessity in developing smart homes. In this paper, we propose a hybrid and dynamic predictive model which utilizes higher order Markov models integrated with a situation ranking technique. More specifically, we employ a revised version of PageRank algorithm to take the properties of the situation-graph (structure and semantics) into account and dynamically rank the situations considering the user's mental state. Then we apply rankings as prior probabilities in order to build the corresponding Markov model. Also, we utilize rankings to identify milestone situations and transitions in order to compress the representation model. Experiments show that the predictions obtained by this approach are more efficient and effective than the ones produced from the pure predictive graphical model-based approaches.

Keywords: Smart home · Situation-aware decision making · Situation prediction · Markov models · Big data · Page ranking

1 Introduction

As the population is aging, the number of older adults who have difficulties doing daily tasks is also expected to increase. This changing demographic has created an increasing need for developing efficient and effective technologies that help individuals live independently with the least burden placed on caregivers. The development of smart homes is one of the promising research areas in this context.

According to [19], a smart home is "an augmented environment with miniaturized processors, software (agents) communicating between each other, and multi-modal sensors that are embedded in any kind of common everyday objects, making them effectively invisible to the resident". Smart Home monitors inhabitant's behavior using sensors and improves the elderly's comfort, safety by predicting the inhabitant's situations and making the right decisions. For example, when an inhabitant forgets to take medicine or to turn off the oven, the smart home can predict the danger and take a suitable action such as turning off the oven automatically or making an automatic phone call to the caregiver to inform her about the potential medical issue.

Over the past decade, the problem of predicting user's situations in smart homes has attracted many research interests due to: (1) It is vital to dynamically predict the user's next situation and make a right decision to, for example avoid any danger. (2) In order to personalize the user's daily activity experience (i.e. recommending the most

© Springer International Publishing Switzerland 2016
C.K. Chang et al. (Eds.): ICOST 2016, LNCS 9677, pp. 71–82, 2016.
DOI: 10.1007/978-3-319-39601-9_7

efficient and effective plans to fulfill the personal goal), there is a need to understand the user's mental state.

In this study, the solution proposed to the above problem is first to construct a situation graph from the sensor data. In this graph, nodes represent situations and links represents transitions between situations. Weights on the links show the frequency of traversals on the transitions and they can be interpreted as the user's implicit feedback of her preferences in the situation transitions [3]. Second, we employ a revised version of PageRank algorithm [16] to rank the nodes based on their importance w.r.t. user's current desire. Third, we use the rankings as the prior probabilities to create the corresponding Markov model [3].

More specifically, these are the contributions of our research represented in this paper:

- A new hybrid and dynamic situation-aware decision-making model combining predictive graphical models and page ranking techniques.
- A desire-oriented situation ranking algorithm to rank situations considering the user's current mental state.
- Predicting not only the individual's next situation but also the plans to reach the goal.
- Identifying milestone situations and transitions in order to compress the representation model and provide more objective predictions.

2 Related Work

Developing of smart homes has attracted much attention among researchers from diverse areas such as gerontology, computer science, architecture and design, etc. Usually, a smart home has multiple rooms which are equipped with sensors and actuators. In the area of healthcare, smart homes are mainly designed to support daily life of people with lack of autonomy by making situation-aware decisions [1]. Although many studies have been done on activity recognition in designing smart homes [20, 21], less work has been accomplished on the activity prediction problem in smart homes [22]. As smart home technologies have gotten attention for health monitoring and assistance, it is important to have highly adaptive system that is able to make the most informed decision based on the context and predict some specific situations emerging in the near future to prevent any hazards by choosing the right actions to do (e.g. home safety concern).

In [23], an activity prediction component is used to prevent accidents by interacting with the user as a reminder. In [24], the authors utilize clustering techniques and association mining rules to discover temporal relations of activities. Also, the authors in [25] present a multi-agent architecture for activity prediction in order to detect emergencies in smart homes. Furthermore, in [26], soft computing techniques have been employed for prediction of an older adult's behavior in a smart home. The authors of [26] examine different neural networks and show that frequent neural networks will be capable of finding the temporal relationships of input patterns.

Over the past decade, many researchers have explored probabilistic graphical models to detect and predict user activities. For example, the authors in [27] use Hierarchical Hidden Semi-Markov Models (HHSMMs) to predict the inhabitant activity. In [28], Hidden Markov Models (HMMs) have been employed to model the residents' behavior in order to detect abnormal activities. Furthermore, in [29], the authors present an activity prediction model based on Markov models and partial matching in the context of smart homes. The authors in [1, 14] propose an approach based on Markov Logic Networks for decision making in smart homes. They assume that the user interacts with the system through voice and explicitly express her demand.

The approach presented in this study can be distinguished from the existing probabilistic graphical model-based efforts in three main ways. First, this study presents a new hybrid and dynamic situation-aware decision-making model combining predictive graphical models and page ranking techniques to predict not only the user's next situation but also the path to the goal. Second, in situation[1] prediction, the proposed model takes into account the user's activities and environmental context values together with her mental state which leads to more accurate and objective predictions with less user intervention. And, the third distinction is that we address one of the big data issues in the context of smart homes (i.e. state space complexity and huge amount of sensor data) by compressing the representation model through identifying *milestone* situations and transitions.

2.1 Markov Models

Markov models [2] have been used for studying and understanding stochastic processes and shown to be well suited for modeling and predicting a user's next action on a graph-based model of user's sequential behavior. In these problems, the input usually is the sequence of observations and the goal is to build Markov models in order to predict the next state of the system. For example, in the problem of web surfing, the input is sequence of web pages accessed by a user, and the output is the web page which is most likely to be accessed by the user next. In the context of smart homes, the next situation of an inhabitant relies not only on the current situation but also on the history of her milestone activities in the past. The reason is that it is more likely to observe stochastic behavior of the elderly. For instance, the user might get distracted with something else while she is doing her daily activities (i.e. transition to a random situation) and forgets her previous situation. Therefore, a predictive graphical model which keeps the history of user's activities and support randomness and uncertainty is needed.

Higher-order Markov models have been widely used in predicting user's behavior since lower-order models do not look far into the past in order to predict user's next step. By taking into account the sequence of user behavior, the model would be able to correctly recognize differences between observed patterns and make the most accurate prediction [6, 8]. In these studies, the initial probabilities of nodes have a uniform

---

[1] According to definition proposed in [6], situation is defined as a 3-tuple=<desire, behavioral-context, environmental-context>.

distribution leading to a less accurate prediction results. To address this issue, some other studies [3, 4, 9, 11, 13] have defined different priors in Markov models. For instance, in [3] the authors used a revised version of PageRank algorithm and in [4, 13] the authors utilized link and citation analysis to assign prior probabilities to nodes based on their importance in the graph to obtain more objective predictions. Furthermore, some studies have proposed methods to improve the accuracy or reduce state complexity of Markov models in the context of predicting the system's next state [4, 10, 11]. However, the authors in these studies presented methods to address the problem of m-path prediction (prediction of user behavior in m steps), and such methods have high computational cost [9, 12]. Our study is based on the Markov models, and other predictive models are out of the scope of this paper.

2.2 Situation Analytics

This study employed the definition proposed in [5] for "situation". In [5], the authors introduce a framework called *Situ* for modeling and predicting human intentions as an integrated part of software development and evolution. In order to model and detect human intentions, *Situ* defines a new concept called "situation" which is a time-stamped triplet including user's desire, user's behavior and environmental context values. In [5], user's actions can be seen as the observable consequence of the user's unobservable mental state (desire). Besides, user's behavior may change some context values. Some approaches [5, 7] have been proposed to infer the user's desire using the user's actions and context values. Based on [5] a user's intention is a path of situations with the same desire for achieving a goal. Formally, situation at a time t is defined as a triple S = $\{d, A, E\}$, here d is the user's desire, A is a set of actions to satisfy desire d and E is a set of observed context values. Intention I is expressed as $I = (S_1, S_2, \ldots, S_k)$ such that $S_1, S_2, \ldots, S_k$ is a temporal sequence of situations with the same desire d. Although many other existing works in this area ask the user to interact with the system and express their needs explicitly, the proposed approach in [7] does not need any interaction with a user in run time.

2.3 Page Ranking

PageRank [17] is the most popular link analysis algorithm, used broadly for ranking web documents in a web graph based on their importance. The rank of a page is defined as the probability of being at this page after k steps and the importance of it is defined by evaluating the importance of other pages connected to this one. In a directed graph G with N nodes representing system states and the edges representing the transition between them, a random walk creates a Markov Chain in which S is the set of states (nodes in G), and M is the stochastic transition matrix with mij indicating the one-step transition probability from state sj to state si [16]. For each j : $\sum_{i=1}^{N} mij$. PageRank is guaranteed to converge to a matrix with one column which shows the unique stationary distribution independent of the initial distribution if and only if M is irreducible and aperiodic [16].

Even though Markov models and page ranking techniques have been mostly used in the context of web surfing, they have gotten much attention in other applications such as predicting the next command-typed by the user on a word processor based on her history of commands, or the alarm state of telephone switches based on its past states. In this study, we construct a situation-graph from sensor data which is a directed and strongly connected graph G. Each node represents one situation and the edges show the transition between situations. Since each situation is a 3-tuple <desire, behavioral-context, environmental-context>, the situation graph can be seen as a semantic graph where each node has knowledge about the inhabitant's desire and actions in specific environmental context (i.e. location, time), and each edge has knowledge about the changes in any elements of the user's current situation. In order to extract this knowledge, we associate each pair of adjacent situation nodes with a weight that shows the frequency of transition between the pair. The new graph is a weighted, directed and strongly connected graph G with adjacency matrix M. In order to assign weights to nodes, we take the properties of the weighted situation-graph structure into account by employing a PageRank-style algorithm [16]. This algorithm takes a graph with irreducible and aperiodic transition matrix as input and returns the ranks of each node as output. The adjacency matrix M corresponding to graph G is an irreducible[2], aperiodic[3] matrix which represents a situational stochastic behavior of the user during a period of time in a smart home. We employ the algorithm in [16] to assign weights to the situation nodes based on their importance in the situation graph. PageRank can be used in its original form which assumes that the user chooses one of the outgoing links with equal probabilities, or uniformly, go to a random node or consider a range of probabilities in a personalized form [3, 16] by adjusting the personalization vector to favor certain nodes. We employ its personalized form to bias the ranking based on the behavior of the elderly in the context of personalized situation predictions in smart homes.

3 Proposed Approach

In this section, we present our approach for the prediction of user's future situations in smart homes. We assume the domain of our study is a single-user domain. The user is believed to be rational and has only one desire at a time instant. That is, the user no concurrent desires and they are sequential so that user is executing one desire at a time). The other important assumption is that the user's actions and context values are visible and can be observed by sensors. On the other hand, the user's current desire may or may not be visible; if not, we can employ the method proposed in [7] to infer the current desire. Besides, in this study we consider time, location and temperature as environmental context parameters however other context values can be applied to our model too. In the rest of this section, first we define some concepts used in our approach, then we explain each component of our model which is illustrated in Fig. 1.

---

[2] The adjacency matrix of a directed graph is irreducible if and only if the graph is strongly connected.

[3] A square matrix M such that the matrix power $M^{K+1} = M^K$ for k a positive integer is called a periodic matrix. A matrix which is not periodic, will be considered aperiodic.

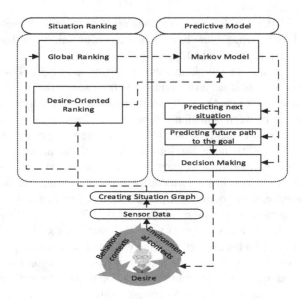

Fig. 1. The proposed approach diagram

Situation Session. A situation session is a sequence of the user's situations in chronological order during a specific period of time. During the construction of situation sessions, the start and end of the sessions can be determined either without or with user intervention. In the former case, sessions can internally be defined by the system. For instance, when there is a transition from a goal situation to another situation with different desires or after a certain time of inactivity of the user. Because we want to minimize the user's intervention, we consider being inactive for a while[4] as a differentiating indicator to separate situation sessions.

Global Situation Ranking. It is a PageRank-style algorithm [16] which can be applied to a directed, weighted, strongly connected graph in order to rank its nodes based on its link structure and the paths followed by the user in the past. This process gives the "global" ranking of situation nodes in the graph.

Desire-Oriented Situation Ranking. It is a PageRank-style algorithm [16] to rank the situations considering the user's current desire, i.e. providing a "desire-oriented" ranking. We employed the Localized-PageRank-style algorithm [16] to do desire-oriented ranking. The only difference is that in [16], the algorithm considers the location and the path that user has followed so far; but in this study, we localize the ranking based on the user's desire.

---

[4] In the context of user's web surfing, if user remains inactive for 25.5 min, it means a new session will starts [15].

Milestone Situations. We define milestone situations as "significant" situations which are more likely to be observed to reach the goal g w.r.t. desire d. milestone situations are obtained from applying the desire-oriented situation ranking technique.

Milestone Transitions. We define milestone transitions as "significant" transition of milestone situations which are more likely to be observed in order to reach the goal g w.r.t. desire d. milestone transitions are the ones with higher weights compared to other transitions w.r.t. desire d. The weights can be obtained from either employing the algorithm proposed in [3], or using the association rules mining techniques.

Table 1. Situation sessions for three days w.r.t. desire of "taking a shower"

ID	Day	Desire	Session	Milestone situations	Milestone transitions
1	1	Taking a shower	grab towel → turn on the hot water → turn off the water → put on clothes	turn on the hot water, turn off the water	turn on the hot water → turn off the water
3	2	Taking a shower	turn on the hot water → brush the teeth → open the fridge → close the fridge → put the food in the microwave → open the microwave	turn on the hot water	–
3	3	Taking shower	grab towel → turn on the hot water → turn off the water → put on clothes	turn on the hot water, turn off the water	turn on the hot water → turn off the water

For example, in Table 1, three situation sessions and corresponding milestone situations and milestone transitions are listed w.r.t. desire of "taking a shower". Here, "turning on the water" and "turning off the water" are milestone situations because they have higher ranks compared to other situations. Also, "turn on the hot water → turn off the water" is a milestone transition since both situations involved are milestone situations and the weight of this transition is more than that of others w.r.t. desire of "taking a shower".

The proposed model has two main components: situation ranking, predictive modeling. The description of these components follows.

Situation Ranking: There are two different types of situation ranking: global ranking and desire-oriented ranking. We employ the algorithm proposed in [16] to rank the situations. The input of this step is the weighted, directed, strongly connected situation graph and the output includes global and desire-oriented rankings. We apply the results of global ranking to Markov model as prior probabilities to bias the prediction in favor of the user's past situational behavior. Also we utilize the desire-oriented ranking to identify milestone situations and provide more objective decisions in runtime.

Probabilistic Modeling: In order to predict the user's next and future situations, and make the right decision a higher order Markov model that encodes the users' known behavior patterns need to be built. However, using higher order Markov models would be very expensive in terms of computation cost. To address this issue, in this study, we build a predictive model based on milestone situations and milestone transitions in order to compress the transition matrix. When the model is built based on training data, it can be used to predict the user's next situation by matching the current user's situational path to the model's paths, and recommending the most likely one. Also, the model can predict the future path by utilizing desire-oriented ranking and providing the path including the high-ranked milestone situations. After predicting the elderly's future situations, the system can make the right decision in case of any concerns.

4   Experimental Evaluations

To evaluate our approach, we employed one data set called Aruba [18] which contains sensor data that was collected in a smart home for two years. The situations are recorded in terms of sensor status (3 types of sensors: motion, door, temperature) annotated with the desire of user (11 categories). We evaluated our approach in three different setups of the prediction model. The first setup is pure Markov model and the second one is Markov model extended with global situation ranking. The third setup is the one with both global and desire-oriented situation rankings.

   As the reader can observe from Fig. 2, the proposed approach provides an improvement over the other two setups in terms of accuracy of prediction[5]. The reason is that pure Markov model assigns equal prior probabilities to all nodes but in the two other setups, Markov model is extended with ranking process which uses the ranks as prior probabilities. In the proposed approach, two different levels of ranking have been applied, global and desire-oriented. Desire-oriented ranking provides more objective and accurate predictions because it utilizes the user's current desire to filter out all the possible paths which do not match the desire. Therefore, by removing the unrelated nodes from the state space, the prediction will return more effective and objective results. Figure 3 depicts the OSim[6] similarity for the top 3, 5, 8 rankings of Aruba dataset w.r.t. d = "Meal-Preparation". The top-n rankings from desire-oriented ranking are more similar to actual user's behavior compared to global ranking because it takes into account the user's current desire in ranking situations. Figure 4 shows the comparison of three setups in terms of complexity. However our proposed approach utilizes higher order Markov models to look far into the past in order to provide more accurate user's situation and next path prediction, it only considers milestone situations and transitions to compress the model. As a result, as Fig. 4 shows, our approach has lower complexity and prediction time compare to two other setups.

---

[5] Precision = $\dfrac{\text{Number of correct predictions retrieved (TP)}}{\text{Number of correct predictions retrieved (TP)} + \text{Number of wrong predictions retrieved (FP)}}$

[6] OSim(T1, T2) indicates the degree of overlap between the top n situations of two rankings, T1 and T2. OSim(τ1, τ2)=$\dfrac{|\tau 1 \cap \tau 2|}{n}$ [3].

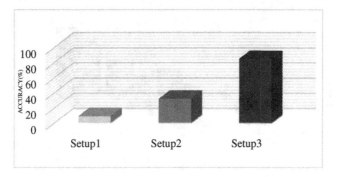

Fig. 2. Comparison of setup1 (pure Markov model), setup2 (Markov model extended with global ranking) and setup3 (proposed model) in terms of accuracy of prediction

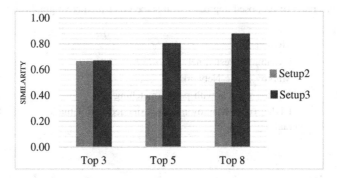

Fig. 3. Comparison of setup2 (Markov model extended with global ranking) and setup3 (proposed model) in terms of similarity of top-n (n = 3, 5, 8) rankings to the user's actual data w. r.t. desire = Meal-Preparation

In Table 2, we compare our approach with some other probabilistic graphical model-based approaches [1, 22, 29] in terms of prediction accuracy. Please note that the dataset used in [22] was not available and the datasets used in [1, 29] were not annotated with the user's desires so they are not applicable to this paper. Nevertheless, we employed Aruba dataset to evaluate our model. According to the authors of [22], Aruba is closer to dataset used in [22] with same assumptions and features compared to other available smart home datasets. Also, Aruba dataset includes user's activity data collected for two years; however, the dataset used in [29], includes user's activity data for only two months. Considering the fact that Aruba has much more data than dataset used in [29], our approach has comparable (i.e. against SPEED [29] that was validated for only two-month data) accuracy while keeping the complexity low which is an improvement over that of [1, 22, 29]. We speculate the reason that our approach outperforms the other three approaches is because it ranks the situations dynamically based on the user's current desire. Also, it compresses the representation model by identifying milestone situations and milestone transitions.

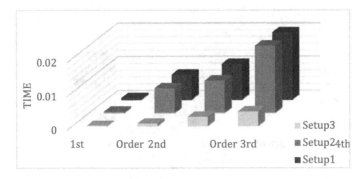

Fig. 4. Comparison of setup1 (pure Markov model), setup2 (Markov model extended with global ranking) and setup3 (proposed model) in terms of prediction time

Table 2. Comparison of proposed approach with some other predictive graphical model-based approaches

Name	Method	Accuracy
CRAFFT [22]	Dynamic bayesian network	74.75 %
[1]	Markov Logic Networks	65 %
SPEED [29]	Markov models with partial matching	88.3 %
Proposed approach	Higher order Markov models extended with situation ranking	84.84 %

5 Conclusions

In this paper, we proposed a novel hybrid probabilistic predictive model, which deals with uncertainty and large amounts of sensor data in run time and make the situation-aware decisions in an efficient and effective way. The presented model utilizes higher Markov models together with a link analysis techniques (i.e. PageRank algorithm) to handle priori knowledge using the structure of the graph. Although the focus of this study was on the situation-aware decision making in smart homes, the application of the proposed model is not limited to this domain and it should be applicable to other domains as well.

In order to predict the elderly's situation efficiently and make effective decisions, we employed a desire-oriented situation ranking algorithm to rank the situations based on their importance and identify milestone situations and transitions accordingly. Then, we built the Markov model based on milestone situations and transitions to provide more accurate and objective predictions while keeping the complexity low. We evaluated the proposed approach using a real open-source dataset collected based on observing an inhabitant's daily activities in smart homes for two years. The experimental results suggest the superior performance of our model over the other related predictive approaches. The reason of outperformance of our model lies in the idea that it employs a ranking process to identify milestone situations (i.e. high-ranked) and transitions with respect to the user's current mental state in order to compress the transition matrix while keeping the accuracy high.

In the future, we plan to integrate our ranking process with other probabilistic graphical models and validate it against other datasets. Also, we aim to extend the proposed approach to address the big data issues as we believe that our compression technique will outperform many other approaches when the datasets are huge.

References

1. Chahuara, P., Portet, F., Vacher, M.: Making context aware decision from uncertain information in a smart home: a markov logic network approach. In: Augusto, J.C., Wichert, R., Collier, R., Keyson, D., Salah, A.A., Tan, A.-H. (eds.) AmI 2013. LNCS, vol. 8309, pp. 78–93. Springer, Heidelberg (2013)
2. Papoulis, A., Pillai, S.U.: Probability, Random Variables and Stochastic Processes. McGraw Hill, New York (2002)
3. Eirinaki, M., Vazirgiannis, M., Kapogiannis, D.: Web path recommendations based on page ranking and markov models. In: Proceedings of the 7th Annual ACM International Workshop on Web Information and Data Management, pp. 2–9. ACM, New York (2005)
4. Zhu, J., Hong, J., Hughes, J.G.: Using markov chains for link prediction in adaptive web sites. In: Bustard, D.W., Liu, W., Sterritt, R. (eds.) Soft-Ware 2002. LNCS, vol. 2311, pp. 60–73. Springer, Heidelberg (2002)
5. Chang, C.K., Jiang, H., Ming, H., Oyama, K.: Situ: a situation-theoretic approach to context-aware service evolution. IEEE Trans. Serv. Comput. **2**, 261–275 (2009)
6. Deshpande, M., Karypis, G.: Selective markov models for predicting web page accesses. ACM Trans. Internet Technol. **4**, 163–184 (2004)
7. Xie, H., Chang, C.K.: Detection of new intentions from users using the CRF method for software service evolution in context-aware environments. In: 2015 IEEE 39th Annual Computer Software and Applications Conference (COMPSAC), pp. 71–76 (2015)
8. Pitkow, J., Pirolli, P.: Mining longest repeating subsequences to predict world wide web surfing. In: Proceedings of the 2nd Conference on USENIX Symposium on Internet Technologies and Systems - Volume 2, p. 13. USENIX Association, Berkeley, CA, USA (1999)
9. Rituparna Sen, M.H.H.: Predicting web users' next access based on log data. J. Comput. Graph. Stat. **12**, 143–155 (2003)
10. Sarukkai, R.R.: Link prediction and path analysis using markov chains. Comput. Netw. **33**, 377–386 (2000)
11. Borges, J.A., Levene, M.: Data mining of user navigation patterns. In: Masand, B., Spiliopoulou, M. (eds.) WebKDD 1999. LNCS (LNAI), vol. 1836, pp. 92–112. Springer, Heidelberg (2000)
12. Cadez, I.V., Gaffney, S., Smyth, P.: A general probabilistic framework for clustering individuals and objects. In: Proceedings of the Sixth ACM SIGKDD International Conference on Knowledge Discovery and Data Mining, pp. 140–149. ACM, New York (2000)
13. Wang, J., Chen, Z., Tao, L., Ma, W.-Y., Wenyin, L.: Ranking user's relevance to a topic through link analysis on web logs. In: Proceedings of the 4th International Workshop on Web Information and Data Management, pp. 49–54. ACM, New York (2002)

14. Chahuara, P., Fleury, A., Portet, F., Vacher, M.: Using markov logic network for on-line activity recognition from non-visual home automation sensors. In: Paternò, F., de Ruyter, B., Markopoulos, P., Santoro, C., van Loenen, E., Luyten, K. (eds.) AmI 2012. LNCS, vol. 7683, pp. 177–192. Springer, Heidelberg (2012)
15. Papadakis, G., Kawase, R., Herder, E., Nejdl, W.: Methods for web revisitation prediction: survey and experimentation. User Model. User-Adap. Inter. **25**, 331–369 (2015)
16. Eirinaki, M., Vazirgiannis, M.: Usage-based PageRank for web personalization. In: Fifth IEEE International Conference on Data Mining, p. 8 (2005)
17. Brin, S., Page, L.: Reprint of: the anatomy of a large-scale hypertextual web search engine. Comput. Netw. **56**, 3825–3833 (2012)
18. Cook, D.J.: Learning setting-generalized activity models for smart spaces. IEEE Intell. Syst. **27**, 32–38 (2012)
19. Giroux, S., Pigot, H.: From smart homes to smart care: ICOST 2005. In: 3rd International Conference on Smart Homes and Health Telematics. IOS Press (2005)
20. Duong, T.V., Bui, H.H., Phung, D.Q., Venkatesh, S.: Activity recognition and abnormality detection with the switching hidden semi-markov model. In: IEEE Computer Society Conference on Computer Vision and Pattern Recognition, CVPR 2005, vol. 1, pp. 838–845 (2005)
21. Liao, L., Fox, D., Kautz, H.: Location-based activity recognition using relational markov networks. In: Proceedings of the 19th International Joint Conference on Artificial Intelligence, pp. 773–778. Morgan Kaufmann Publishers Inc., San Francisco (2005)
22. Nazerfard, E., Cook, D.J.: CRAFFT: an activity prediction model based on bayesian networks. J. Ambient Intell. Humanized Comput. **6**, 193–205 (2015)
23. Dante, I., Tapia, A.A.: Agents and ambient intelligence: case studies. J. Ambient Intell. Humanized Comput. **1**, 85–93 (2010)
24. Nazerfard, E., Rashidi, P., Cook, D.J.: Using association rule mining to discover temporal relations of daily activities. In: Abdulrazak, B., Giroux, S., Bouchard, B., Pigot, H., Mokhtari, M. (eds.) ICOST 2011. LNCS, vol. 6719, pp. 49–56. Springer, Heidelberg (2011)
25. Mocanu, I., Florea, A.M.: A multi-agent supervising system for smart environments. In: Proceedings of the 2nd International Conference on Web Intelligence, Mining and Semantics, pp. 55:1–55:4. ACM, New York (2012)
26. Mahmoud, S., Lotfi, A., Langensiepen, C.: Behavioural pattern identification and prediction in intelligent environments. Appl. Soft Comput. **13**, 1813–1822 (2013)
27. Kautz, H., Etzioni, O., Fox, D., Weld, D.: Foundations of assisted cognition systems (2003)
28. Monekosso, D.N., Remagnino, P.: Anomalous behavior detection: supporting independent living. In: Monekosso, D., Remagnino, P., Kuno, Y. (eds.) Ambient Intelligence Techniques and Applications. Advanced Information and Knowledge Processing, pp. 35–50. Springer, London (2009)
29. Alam, M.R., Reaz, M.B.I., Mohd Ali, M.A.: SPEED: an inhabitant activity prediction algorithm for smart homes. IEEE Trans. Syst. Man Cybern. Part A Syst. Hum. **42**, 985–990 (2012)

Towards an Adaptation Model for Smart Homes

Yannick Francillette[✉], Sébastien Gaboury, Abdenour Bouzouane,
and Bruno Bouchard

Université du Québec à Chicoutimi, Chicoutimi, Canada
{yannick.francillette1,Sebastien_Gaboury,abdenour.bouzouane,
Bruno_Bouchard}@uqac.ca

Abstract. Smart buildings have to provide occupants with a good
experience in order to encourage people to use them. To reach this goal, a
smart building must always perform an appropriate behavior and select
its actions according to the user's environment (context) and preferences.
However, due to its dynamic nature, the context can change; smart building designers need to make these systems able to adapt by themselves.
In this paper, we present our on-going research on an adaptive model
which aims to help smart building designers to make systems able to
adapt their behavior by themselves. Our approach is based on behavior trees in order to structure behaviors of smart homes and a generic
adaptive strategy.

1 Introduction

The advances in domains such as sensors network, electronic and ambient intelligence allow us to create *"smart homes"* [4]. This expression defines homes
with technological features which aim to make occupants' lives more comfortable. It is important to make the difference between *"smart home"* and *"home
automation"*. The latter expression defines the fact of allowing the control of all
components of a home through a central access. Occupants can control heating,
lighting and locking of windows and doors through a mobile device for instance.
Conversely, a smart home can act autonomously on several elements in order to
satisfy a need. In other words, it can trigger actions without an explicit request
from an occupant.

These systems realize vision of Marc Weiser. The computing is everywhere in
the service of people, instead of being just a computer in a room which is used
by few persons [19].

Smart homes can significantly impact the quality of life. Indeed, people spend
a most of their life in their respective home. Consequently, it is very interesting
to enhance life at home [12].

Fundamentally, we can use smart homes to reduce energy consumption,
through an intelligent managing of lighting and heating for instance. They
can also provide an assistance to impaired or frail persons by giving an assistance, warnings or guidance. This could decrease the necessary for caregivers
and enhance the quality of life of elderly people [2].

© Springer International Publishing Switzerland 2016
C.K. Chang et al. (Eds.): ICOST 2016, LNCS 9677, pp. 83–94, 2016.
DOI: 10.1007/978-3-319-39601-9_8

However, we need to overcome some challenge in order to increase the use of smart homes. One of the main issues is to reduce building costs. Designers can reach this objective by using models and approaches which do not require expensive devices [14]. Moreover, advances in electronic components will decrease the cost of these devices. Another main issue is to provide occupants of building with a pleasant and good experience. For example, a smart home designed for an impaired person should encourage him to live inside, reassure his family and increase his autonomy.

We have to notice the fact that several elements contribute to user's experience. For example, the aesthetic of a building affects this experience. However, in this study we focus on one element: smart home behavior. Indeed, actions done by the system have a great impact on occupants' experience. Ideally, it should perform the right action at the right time.

However, it is important to notice that homes are not static places. Indeed, internal state evolves according to time and activities that are conducted by occupants. Consequently, the impact of each action depends on the state of the environment. In fact, the system needs to adapt to the state of the environment in order to maintain a good experience.

Let us take a simple example to highlight these considerations. We can imagine a smart home designed to help a person who suffers from memory troubles and a physical disability. Consequently, the home monitors its occupant at every moment. When he is cooking, it opens and closes drawers and cupboards automatically according to his progressing. When he receives mail or some visitors, it uses the best way to notify him. It uses a visual signal if he is in a room which provides this kind of signal. Otherwise, it uses an audible signal because the occupant prefer the first solution. When he is with his family, the system proposes less assistance in order to promote interaction between them. Finally, when he has free time, it proposes an appropriate memory game in order to help him to train his memory.

However, designing adaptive systems is a problematic task. Basically, when designers want to build adaptive systems, they must define when, what and how to adapt? Moreover, they have to do these tasks for each system because objectives and behaviors can be different.

In this paper, we present our on-going research about a generic approach for building adaptive smart home. It is composed by a generic model of smart home behavior, a model of the context and an adaptation strategy.

The structure of this document is the following. Next section presents main concepts of our research. Section 3 presents the related works. Section 4 presents the proposition we develop. We conclude and present future works in Sect. 5.

2   Background

2.1   Context-Aware Systems

In order to define context-aware systems, we first need to define context information. For this, we use definition given by Dey in [5]: "*context is any information that can be used to characterize the situation of an entity. An entity is a person, place, or object that is considered relevant to the interaction between a user and an application, including the user and applications themselves"*.

The expression "context-aware system" is used to define systems that use context information. For example, without context-awareness, a smart home will use audible notifications for guidance regardless if the environment is noisy or not. In contrast, with context-awareness, it will use an audible notification if the environment is quiet or a visible notification if it is noisy.

2.2 Adaptation

Cybernetic and control theory have introduced the adaptation concept in computer science [20]. In this domain, we can describe the adaptation, as an ability for a system to maintain equilibrium of a set of parameters despite external perturbations. So, it has to be able to detect changes into these parameters and act in order to reduce the difference.

According to the kind of action, two categories of adaptation can be distinguished:

1. Passive adaptation, if actions affect only internal state of the system.
2. Active adaptation, where two systems interact with different roles. One is the controller and the second is the target [6]. The target provides an interface to perceive and modify parameters.

It is interesting to note that a smart home should perform both kinds of adaptations. Indeed, according to the context, it could not be able to act on the environment. For example, if several persons are cooking and it has to assist one. It cannot force the others to leave the kitchen. For the active adaptation, it can act on lights and alter the global lighting in order to provide a better guidance.

3 Related Works

Several solutions are proposed in order to make easier the building of smart homes. The projects *"Eclipse Smart Home"* [10] and *"Open HAB"* [18] propose frameworks that simplify the managing of sensors and effectors. In fact, these frameworks propose a homogenized environment for implementation. Consequently, designers can focus on the defining of smart home behaviors. However, these frameworks do not provide an adaptation model.

Real Games proposes *"Home I/O"* [7] and *"Connect I/O"* [8] which are respectively a smart home simulator and a visual programming environment. *"Connect I/O"* simplifies the defining of the system behavior thanks to visual programming. With this software, designers use a node-based interface to define how the system must react. By using these two softwares, designers can quickly prototype a set of behaviors and experiment how do these behaviors affect the user's experience. However, this framework does not provide an adaptation model.

Kadouche et al. [11] propose an approach to build a smart home which is able to perform personalization. This approach has been developed in the domain of smart homes for disable people. In this study, they aim to implement smart homes which can adapt to users' profile. Basically, the proposition uses an inference engine with a semantic model to deduce a handicap situation from a user's profile and an environment description. According to the inference engine, the system provides the appropriate service.

Gouin-Vallerand et al. [9] propose a solution to build smart environments with context-aware capacity. Functionally, authors use fuzzy logic to compute the matching between a service and context. When a service needs to be deployed, their engine computes a score (called Device Capabilities Quotients) for each devices. Then, the system selects the device with the higher score.

To summarize the related works, we can classify the different contributions in two categories. In the first one, we can regroup the projects *Eclipse Smart Home*, *Open HAB* and *Connect I/O* which aims to make easier the development of smart home behaviors. These tools are very useful in smart-home development. Indeed, developers do not need to manage the software integration of smart home electronic devices. However, we can notice that these tools provide a lower abstraction level. In fact, they do not propose an explicit model for smart home behaviors. Consequently, each behavior is developed from an ad hoc way. An explicit model could promote the reusing of elements which come from previous development.

In the second one, we can group works of Kadouche et al. and Gouin-Vallerand et al. These works focus on the adaptation. They provide a good solution to manage adaptation of smart homes. Indeed, their adaptation models propose a simple way for designers to define the comportment of the system according to the context. However, as works in the first group, they do not propose an explicit model to design a smart home behavior.

In conclusion to this section, we can notice that a generic model of smart home behavior, a generic model to define the context and a generic adaptation strategy are mandatory to propose a generic framework for building self-adaptive smart homes. Without a generic framework, smart home designers need to use ad hoc solutions for designing their systems.

4   Proposition

We propose a design approach allowing a simpler way to develop the behaviors of smart homes. We build this approach on two main components:

- A generic model of smart home behavior. Basically, this model splits the running of a smart home into several components.
- A generic adaptive approach with a simple method for defining contexts that are compatible with a component.

The overview of our proposition is illustrated by the Fig. 1. The main steps are the following:

1. At the beginning, activity detection and guidance modules are developed by the community.
2. Smart home designers use these modules to define the behaviors of the smart home.
3. During the running of the home, a process collects pieces of information about the context.
4. A process control if current smart home activities fit with the current context and perform an adaptation process if an activity does not fit.

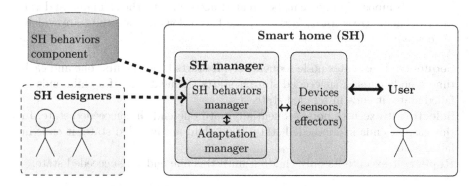

Fig. 1. Scheme giving a overview of the system

4.1   Smart Home Activities Model

We use behavior trees as a tool to model smart home behaviors. This model is interesting for smart home design because it is not a simple analytic tool. It can have a direct application in smart-home development. Indeed this concept is already used in domains such as video games, robotic and unmanned aerial vehicles (UVA) [1,3,16,17]. Before introducing how we use behavior trees in smart home design, we will first introduce their main principles.

Behavior Tree Principle. Basically, a behavior tree is a formalism used in planning. More precisely, it is a rooted tree which hierarchies the executions of tasks that are performed by an entity. In this tree, leaf nodes represent an atomic task that can be directly executed. Control the state of an entity for instance. Intermediate nodes that can be called composite node control how their children evolve. Composite nodes are described below.

When the behavior tree is executed, nodes can be in one of the following states:

– **Not Running:** The node has never been started.
– **Running:** The node has been started but is not finished yet.

– **Succeeded:** The node is finished in success.
– **Failed:** The node finished in failure.

It is important to notice that in this model, failed does not mean an error. For example, if the task consists of controlling that the entity has performed a particular action before the end of a timer. The succeeded state means that the action has been done. The failure state that the action has not been done and the action cannot be done in the future. Basically, succeeded and failed state represent two ending state for the node. The parent of a node will act according to the ending state of their child and its nature.

Several composite nodes can be created according to the domains and the need of behavior trees users. However, the two following composite are widely implemented:

– **Sequence:** it executes node sequentially. It starts from the first one and each time a node ends in succeeded state it starts the next one. If a child ends in failed state, it ends in a failed state.
– **Selector:** it executes node sequentially until one ends in succeeded state. In this case, it ends in succeeded state. If all child are in failed state, it ends in failed state.
– **Repeat:** it execute its only children until this one ends in succeeded state.

It is important to notice that in behavior trees, order of children has a meaning. Children are aligned horizontally and the first node is the leftmost.

Application in Smart Home Design. One advantage of behavior tree is the ability to compose complex behaviors from a set of simple elements. Additionally, it allows a smart home designers to define the behavior of a home without worrying about how simple tasks work. In our approach, we call leaf nodes behavior components. A behavior component is the entity that interacts with devices (sensors and effectors) in order to reach one objective. Detect if the user while he is cooking is an example of a behavior component objective. Giving assistance to a user who is cooking is another example. Fundamentally, we implement behavior components by defining a function that interact with sensors or/and effectors and that return succeeded when the objective is accomplished.

Example. Let us use a design scenario to show the use of behavior trees for smart home design. We use the example given in the introduction. However, we will not consider adaptation issue. In this scenario, we need six behavior components which are the following:

– **Cooking detection:** it interacts with a subset of sensors in order to detect when the occupant starts a cooking activity.
– **Cooking guidance:** it interact with a subset of sensors and effector in order to help the occupant while he is cooking.

- **Visitor monitoring:** it interacts with a set of sensors which are outside in order to detect if somebody come to visit the occupant.
- **Visitor notification:** it actions effectors which are dedicated to alert the occupant about a visitor.
- **Exercice monitoring:** it compute time since the last exercise in order to detect if the occupant needs to train his memory.
- **Exercise 1:** it performs one memory game that trains the occupant.
- **Exercise 2:** it performs another memory game which uses other devices to play.

The behavior trees for the smart home of this scenario are shown in Figs. 2 and 3. In our model, each behavior tree is computed in parallel. Consequently, with this design, this smart home performs three activities at the same time.

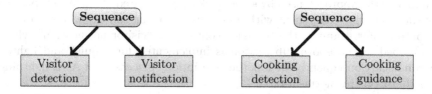

Fig. 2. Behavior trees that manage cooking assistance and visitors notification

The Fig. 2 shows the behavior trees of cooking assistance and visitor notification. Modeling of these behaviors is simple with behavior trees. It is a sequence of two behavior components. Broadly, the first behavior component uses sensors and artificial intelligence models to detect a pattern. Once this pattern is detected, it finishes with a succeeded state. Then the parent starts the next behavior component which has to perform the guidance.

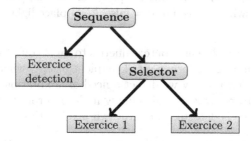

Fig. 3. Behavior tree that manages user's exercises

The Fig. 3 shows the behavior tree of exercise management. The overall principle is the same as the Fig. 2. A behavior component checks when the exercise should start and notify its parent. The main difference with previous trees is the use of "Selector" node. The main idea in this tree is to try the exercise 1. If the user fails this exercise, the system proposes the exercise 2. In this context, we consider that the exercise 2 is easier and the user will always succeed.

4.2   Adaptation Model

The previous model allows us to define smart home behavior. During the execution the behavior tree evolve according to interactions with occupants. In order to support adaptation to context, we propose to allow the system to adapt the behavior tree according to context state. Our approach is the following: each time a behavior component is started or the context state changes, the system checks if behavior components are adapted to the current context. If one does not fit, it reacts by changing the behavior tree or acting on the context. This approach is built from the two main concepts: (i) context query; (ii) an adaptation strategy.

Context Query. The context query is the element that allows our system to identify if a behavior component fits to the current context or not. The principle is similar to the approach used by some works in the related work. We propose to link each behavior component with a description of the context where they are compatible. For example, the behavior component "visitor notification" which is described in the above sub section is implemented for a quiet and lighted environment. Consequently, we link the description "place is quiet AND lightning is good" to "visitor notification".

Or context queries are also similar to the media query concept [13] from responsive web design [15]. From a technical point of view, a context query is a predicate on some context characteristics. The evaluation of the predicate must return *true* value in order to consider that the linked component is compatible.

In order to define and evaluate context queries, we define a model of the context. We use an object oriented approach to define this model. The main advantage of the oriented approach is to allow us to extend it easily. In fact, the goal of this model is not to be exhaustive and to provide enough information to define and evaluate our queries. The Fig. 4 show our current model.

According to this model the context query for the component "visitor notification" is the following "place.noise = false AND place.light = hight".

Adaptation Strategy. We use context queries to tag a collection of component $A = \{b_1, b_2, .., b_n\}$ in order to form a set of couple $< b_i, c_i >$ where c_i is the query. The Algorithm 1 describes how we detect a need of adaptation.

Basically, the process traverse all running nodes in order to evaluate context queries. When a issue is detected, we have two possibilities:

- to act on the environment in order to create an appropriated context for running.
- to act on behavior trees in order to run only components which fit.

We will first introduce our approach for the second possibility. The Algorithm 2 describes how we process in order to act on the behavior trees. Fundamentally, our approach requires several methods for reaching an objective. Moreover, we group all components according to their objectives. Our process selects the approach that can be applied according to its context query.

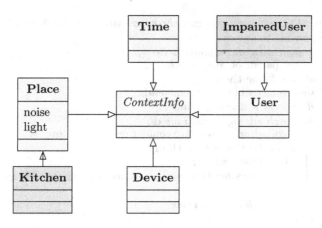

Fig. 4. Our class diagram for the context. On this diagram, yellow classes represent the core of our modelization. Blue classes show how we can extends these objects to add new elements. (Color figure online)

Data: *context* : the current context, *shcomponents* : list of running behavior
       components
for *each* *component* **in** *shcomponents* **do**
    evaluation ← evaluate context query of *component*
    if *evaluation* =*false* **then**
        is_environment_adapted ← try to act on the environment
        if *is_environment_adapted* = *false* **then**
           | adapt behavior trees
        end
    end
end

Algorithm 1. Detect need for adaptation

We can notice that our algorithm act on the behavior tree according to the nature of intermediate nodes. Basically, the semantic of the node *"Selector"* means that at least one of the children must be compatible. Consequently, we verify in the set of current children if one child is compatible before acting on the tree.

In order to allow the system to act on the environment, we use a naive approach. We add for each entity of our context model a boolean variable that indicate if this system contains a way to act on the entity. For example, for lighting, the variable is true because the system has an access to the light. However, for the number of people in a room the variable is false because the system cannot force people to leave. If it exists the system can get from a service the future state of the context according to the different actions. Then, the system can verify if one of the proposition can fit and valid. The Algorithm 3 describes our approach.

Data: *context* : the current context, *shcomponents* : list of behavior components to switch

```
for each component in shcomponents do
    parent ← get parent of component
    if parent is selector then
        siblings ← get sibling of component
        if siblings is not empty then
            for each sibling in siblings do
                evaluation ← evaluate context query of sibling
                if evaluation =true then
                    activate sibling
                    // we start this component and we stop its siblings
                end
                find_subtitute ← true
            end
        else
            find_subtitute ← true
        end
    else
        find_subtitute ← true
    end
    if find_subtitute= true then
        subtitute ← find in component library a subtitute activate subtitute
        // if no subtitute is found, we stop the component until a current
        context is created
    end
end
```

Algorithm 2. Adaptation of the behavior trees

Data: *shcomponents* : list of running behavior components, *shcomponentstoswitch* : list of running behavior components that do not fit

```
correct ← false
while correct ≠ true do
    for each component in shcomponentstoswitch : do
        context ← get ideal context for component if context is applicable and
        context is compatible with shcomponents then
            correct ← true apply context
        else
            find subtitute for component
        end
    end
end
```

Algorithm 3. Adaptation of the environment

5   Conclusion and Future Works

In this paper, we have presented our on-going research about a generic model for smart home with adaptive behavior. Our proposition is built from three main concepts: (i) a model for the smart home behavior; (ii) a model for the context; (iii) an adaptive strategy.

As future work, we have objectives for both short and long terms. Our short-term objective is to experience the adaptation of smart home behaviors on users in order to measure the impact on the user's experience. For the long-term, we aim to enhance this model in order to deal with adaptation to users' preferences. Indeed, activities of our model should be activated according to these preferences in order to maximize the user's experience.

Furthermore, our adaptation strategy has been designed in case of smart home designed to help one main users. Our approach needs to be enhanced in order to deal with multi-user context.

References

1. Andrew Bagnell, J., Cavalcanti, F., Cui, L., Galluzzo, T., Hebert, M., Kazemi, M., Klingensmith, M., Libby, J., Liu, T.Y., Pollard, N., et al.: An integrated system for autonomous robotics manipulation. In: 2012 IEEE/RSJ International Conference on Intelligent Robots and Systems (IROS), pp. 2955–2962. IEEE (2012)
2. Bouchard, K., Bouchard, B., Bouzouanea, A.: Practical guidelines to build smart homes: lessons learned. In: Opportunistic Networking, Smart Home, Smart City, Smart Systems (Book Chapter), pp. 1–37 (2014)
3. Champandard, A.J., Dawe, M., Hernandez-Cerpa, D.: Behavior trees: three ways of cultivating game AI. In: Game Developers Conference, AI Summit (2010)
4. Das, S.K., Cook, D.J.: Designing smart environments: a paradigm based on learning and prediction. In: Pal, S.K., Bandyopadhyay, S., Biswas, S. (eds.) PReMI 2005. LNCS, vol. 3776, pp. 80–90. Springer, Heidelberg (2005)
5. Dey, A.K., Abowd, G.D.: Towards a better understanding of context and context-awareness. In: Workshop on The What, Who, Where, When, and How of Context-Awareness, Conference on Human Factors in Computing Systems 2000 (2000)
6. Franklin, G.F., Powell, D.J., Emami-Naeini, A.: Feedback Control of Dynamic Systems, 4th edn. Prentice Hall PTR, Upper Saddle River (2001)
7. Real Games. Smart house simulation software for stem (2016). www.realgames.pt/connect-io. Accessed April 2016
8. Real Games. Visual programming environment freeware (2016). www.realgames.pt/connect-io. Accessed April 2016
9. Gouin-Vallerand, C., Abdulrazak, B., Giroux, S., Dey, A.K.: A context-aware service provision system for smart environments based on the user interaction modalities. J. Ambient Intell. Smart Environ. 5(1), 47–64 (2013)
10. Eclipse IOT. Eclipse smart home (2014). www.eclipse.org/smarthome. Accessed April 2016
11. Kadouche, R., Abdulrazak, B., Mokhtari, M., Giroux, S., Pigot, H.: Personalization and multi-user management in smart homes for disabled people. Int. J. Smart Home 3(1), 39–48 (2009)
12. Leitner, G.: The Future Home is Wise, Not Smart. Springer, Heidelberg (2015)
13. Lie, H.W.: Cascading html style sheets - a proposal (1994). http://www.w3.org/People/howcome/p/cascade.html
14. Maitre, J., Glon, G., Gaboury, S., Bouchard, B., Bouzouane, A.: Efficient appliances recognition in smart homes based on active and reactive power, fast fourier

transform and decision trees. In: Workshops at the Twenty-Ninth AAAI Conference on Artificial Intelligence (2015)

15. Ethan Marcotte. Responsive web design (2010). http://alistapart.com/article/responsive-web-design
16. Marzinotto, A., Colledanchise, M., Smith, C., Ogren, P.: Towards a unified behavior trees framework for robot control. In: 2014 IEEE International Conference on Robotics and Automation (ICRA), pp. 5420–5427. IEEE (2014)
17. Ogren, P.: Increasing modularity of uav control systems using computer game behavior trees. In: AIAA Guidance, Navigation and Control Conference, Minneapolis, MN (2012)
18. open HAB: open hab (2014). www.openhab.org. Accessed April 2016
19. Weiser, M.: The computer for the 21st century. Sci. Am. **265**(3), 94–104 (1991). Communications, Computers, and Network
20. Wiener, N.: Cybernetics Or Control and Communication in the Animal and the Machine. M.I.T. Paperback Series. Wiley, New York (1965)

Design and Implementation of a Prototype System for Automatic Obstacle Avoidance Information Collection Vehicle

Yan Zhang$^{(\boxtimes)}$, Xuying Zhao, Ri Xu, Jianjin Jiang, and Kejun Zhang

Department of Computer Science and Technology, Beijing Electronic Science and Technology Institute, Beijing 100070, People's Republic of China
{zhangyan,xyzhao,xrhp,jiangjj,zkj}@besti.edu.cn

Abstract. For acquiring information about an environment under which people cannot work, a prototype system of autonomous information collection is designed and implemented. The prototype system consists of a vehicle and a mobile terminal. The vehicle can autonomously move in a horizontal two-dimensional space and not collide with any obstacle under the control of a build-in obstacle-avoidance algorithm. By an information collection subsystem that includes a camera, a video server and some sensors mounted on the vehicle, and a communication subsystem, the vehicle sends acquired environment information, namely video, by wireless signal, to the mobile terminal in real time. The mobile terminal, with a client application deployed on it, can receive the environment information. In the implemented prototype system, we use pcDuino to integrate the dynamic control module based on obstacle-avoidance algorithm and Pulse-Width Modulation (PWM), the information collection module based on infrared sensors and USB camera, the video server based on mjpg-streamer with the 3G communication module. An Android App that can be installed on a smart phone is developed for receiving the video sent by the vehicle. Using "Port Mapping (PM) + Dynamic Domain Name Server (DDNS)" mode, we implement the interconnection based on 3G between the vehicle and the mobile terminal, i.e., a smart phone. We test the implemented prototype system in some scenario and the result shows that it can be applied to smart home or city, service for dangerous task and unmanned exploration.

Keywords: Obstacle avoidance · Autonomous information collection · pcDuino · 3G · Smart home

1 Introduction

Today, no matter for urban management or family life, it is necessary to learn about an environment that people cannot enter into. For example, we need to look at the damage under nuclear leaks or to search something in a very narrow space. Thus, it is required that an equipment can autonomously move, gather and return environment information.

© Springer International Publishing Switzerland 2016
C.K. Chang et al. (Eds.): ICOST 2016, LNCS 9677, pp. 95–106, 2016.
DOI: 10.1007/978-3-319-39601-9_9

Accordingly, we design and implement a prototype system of automatic obstacle avoidance information collection vehicle (AOAICV) by the interoperation of pcDuino [1] and Android [2] based on 3G communication. The prototype consists of a car model and a smart phone. A set of infrared sensors and a USB camera built on the car model detects obstacles and captures video about the environment where the car model run. The video can be sent to the smart phone by 3G signal. An obstacle avoidance program, which controls the car model to bypass obstacles, and a video server, which controls video capture and transmission are built in a pcDuino mainboard that integrates all hardware and software. The smart phone can send a request for collecting information to car model, receive and display the video by an Android application deployed on it.

There are two main contributions of this work. Firstly, we solve point-to-point communication between two terminal devices in 3G network. Since 3G network only assigns a dynamic IP address to any access device, two access devices cannot exchange messages based on IP in 3G network. We adopt Port Mapping (PM) [3] and Dynamic Domain Name Server (DDNS) [4], called PM+DDNS mode, to tackle this problem. Secondly, by building lightweight video server on pcDuino, we solve video transmission with limited network bandwidth and storage space. The video server can encode video into continuous photographs and push them to a client based on HTTP protocol.

The remainder of this paper is organized as follows. Section 2 gives the architecture of the prototype system and describe the function of every component in it. Section 3 presents the implementation of the prototype system in detail. Section 4 explains an experiment for validating our implementation, especially, the function of automatic obstacle avoidance and video transmission. Section 5 considers related works. Finally, we conclude this paper in Sect. 6.

2   Design of Prototype System

The prototype system of AOAICV comprises two parts: an information collection vehicle and a mobile terminal, which is shown in Fig. 1. The information collection vehicle autonomously runs in an environment without collision with any obstacle, and collects information about the environment after receiving an request from the mobile terminal. At the same time, the information collection vehicle can sends collected information to the mobile terminal. The mobile terminal, only for remotely incepting environment information in real time, can send a request for collecting the environment information and display the information sent by the information collection vehicle. All interaction between the information collection vehicle and the mobile terminal bases on wireless signal.

2.1   Information Collection Vehicle

The information collection vehicle is composed of an information collector, a dynamic controller, a computing center and a communication module.

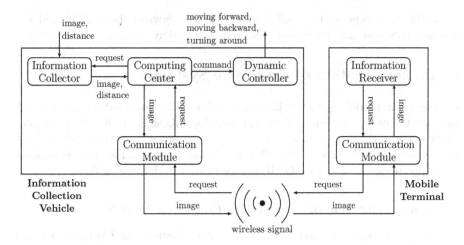

Fig. 1. The architecture of the prototype system for automatic obstacle avoidance information collection vehicle.

The information collector gathers the environment information, such as the distance between the vehicle and an obstacle, and a landscape around the vehicle. The collector sends all of this information to computing center.

The computing center is the kernel of the vehicle. It commands the vehicle to move, such as going forward, backward and turning round, according to the distance to obstacles output by the information collector. At the same time, it also takes charge of sending the landscape gotten from the information collector to mobile terminal. Moreover, it transfers a request for collecting information, sent by the mobile terminal, to the information collector. This component determines whether the vehicle would collide with a obstacle or not, and the collected information would be successfully sent to the mobile terminal.

The dynamic controller drives the vehicle in terms of the command sent by the computing center. The communication module with the counterpart in the mobile terminal builds a channel for message exchange between the vehicle and the terminal.

2.2 Mobile Terminal

In the smart city or smart home, mobile devices are widely used. For facilitating remote reception of the environment information in real time, a mobile terminal is adopted. It has two components: an information receiver and a communication module. The function of the latter is same as the counterpart in the information collection vehicle. The information receiver is mainly responsible for receiving the environment information sent from the information collection vehicle and displaying the information. Additionally, it also initials a request for collecting environment information.

In the prototype system, all communication between the vehicle and the terminal uses wireless signal that can broadcast widely enough.

3   Implementation of Prototype System

We use a car model to realize the information collection vehicle and a smart phone to the mobile terminal. Moreover, we adopt 3G signal to remotely communicate between the car model and the smart phone, since 3G signal can broadcast more widely than WiFi or Bluetooth with the same quality. The implementation of the prototype system for AOAICV is presented in detail as follows.

3.1   Implementation of Information Collection Vehicle

Two Direct-current (DC) motors that drive two wheels of the car model to turn are the dynamic controller in the information collection vehicle. Infrared sensors and USB camera, which detect obstacles and capture image of an environment respectively, are the information collector. At the same time, some software, i.e., obstacle-avoidance algorithm and video server — mjpg-streamer, plays the role of computing center, which controls the car model running and transmit the captured video. A 3G router fulfils the wireless communication based on 3G signal. All this hardware and software are integrated in the car model by a pcDuino — a mini PC platform. Figure 2 sketches the implementation of the information collection vehicle.

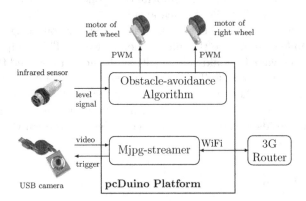

Fig. 2. The implementation of the information collection vehicle.

Dynamic Controller and Information Collector. The body of the car model is a 2-wheel-drive electric vehicle (2WD EV), which uses two DC motors to independently drive the car. Compared with a 4WD EV, the 2WD EV have more powerful detouring and climbing capacity. Furthermore, the power dissipation of 2WD EV is less than the 4WD. In our 2WD EV, two LFF 130 DC motors are used. The rotation speed of the two motors is 10000 revolutions per minute (RPM) with rated voltage from 4.5 V to 6 V. The maximum velocity might meet to 68 cm/s. The reduction ratio of the reducer is 1 : 120.

We can control the rotation direction of the DC motors by the direction of current, and the rotation speed by the intensity of current. When the two DC motors rotate clockwise, the two wheels of the car model will turn forward and the car model will run forward. On the contrary, when the two DC motors rotate anticlockwise, the car model will run backward. If the rotation speed of the right motor that drive the right wheel is faster than the left one, the car mode will turn left. On the contrary, if the rotation speed of the left one is faster than the right one, the car mode will turn right. Thus, the dynamic of the car model can be controlled by the current of the two motors.

An infrared sensor E18-D80NK is used to measure the distance to an obstacle. The sensor can detect a range from 3 cm to 80 cm with a sensitive angle no more than 15°. It can work under 10000 lux (sunlight) or 3000 lux (incandescent light). Its response time is no more than 2 ms and current consumption no more than 25 mA. The sensor can directly output level signal without analog-to-digital conversion, namely, it will output a high-level signal when an obstacle is detected, or a low-level one when no obstacle. We use three E18-D80NKs to respectively detect obstacles at the front, right front and left front.

An USB Video Class (UVC) camera is used to capture a video about the environment where the car mode run. The camera owns 300000 pixel. Its frame rate is 30 fps and maximum resolution 640×480 dpi. The operating distance of the camera is no less than 3 cm.

The infrared sensors and the USB camera together compose the information collector.

Computing Center. Software undertakes the computing task. A program based on an obstacle-avoidance algorithm controls the travel direction of the car model according to the distances to obstacles output from infrared sensors. A video server drive USB camera to capture images about the environment, and transmits these images to the smart phone.

Obstacle-Avoidance Algorithm. The obstacle avoidance has three steps. When infrared sensors detect some obstacle, the system enter the first step of obstacle avoidance. In this step, the vehicle runs backward for a certain distance. The reason of this step is to escape from some dead space in which vehicle cannot turn round. The second step is to bypass. If the obstacle exists at front or left front of the vehicle, the vehicle turns right. If the obstacle exists at right of the vehicle, the vehicle turns left. If there are obstacles at front and left front of the vehicle, it turns right. If there are obstacles at front and right front, or at left and right of the vehicle, it turns left. If there are three obstacles at front, left front and right front of the vehicle respectively, the vehicle also turns left. Finally, if there is not any obstacle, the vehicle run forward all the time.

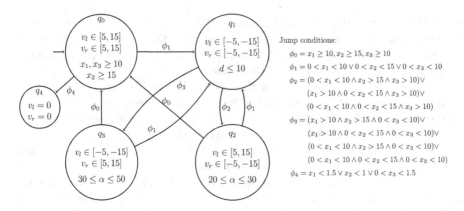

Fig. 3. The hybrid automaton of the obstacle-avoidance algorithm.

In Fig. 3, a hybrid automaton [5] is used to describe the obstacle-avoidance algorithm. q_0 is the initial control mode in which vehicle keeps moving forward with velocity from 5 to 15 cm/s, where v_l and v_r are the velocity of left and right wheel respectively, and positive (resp. negative) represents move forward (resp. backward). The control mode q_1 corresponds to the first step of the obstacle avoidance, i.e., moving backward. q_2 is turning right and q_3 turning left. The control mode q_4 means collision with some obstacle. In Fig. 3, x_1, x_2, x_3 are the distance between an obstacle and the left, middle and right infrared sensor respectively; α is the angle of rotation; d is the distance of retreat. $1 < x_1 < 10$ means that the left sensor finds an obstacle and $1 < x_2 < 15$ means that the middle sensor finds an obstacle.

Video Server. Mjpg-streamer, a command line-based application, is used to build a light weight video server. By IP-based network, it transmits images, captured by USB camera, in stream mode to a client browser on the smart phone. Mjpg-streamer is plugin-based. In mjpg-streamer, the input and output of plugins and the connection among plugins have be predefined. Hence, for building our video server, we only need to choose plugins according to our requirements. "input_uvc" and "output_http" are two important plugins used in the video server. The former is responsible for inputs and the latter outputs. Moreover, data obtained from single input plugin can be send to multiple output plugins.

Figure 4 shows interactions among mjpg-streamer, client and USB camera. When mjpg-streamer gets the request for collecting environment information, the input_uvc plugin starts up the USB camera, and repeatedly reads images in Joint Photographic Experts Group (JPEG) format from the camera and writes them to a buffer in mjpg-streamer. At the same time, output_http repeatedly reads images from the buffer and sends them to the client.

Since the size of data captured by the camera is too big to transmit with limited network bandwidth and storage space, the data must be compressed. In the video server, we adopt Motion Joint Photographic Experts Group (MJPEG)

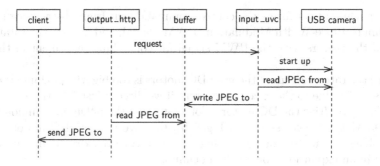

Fig. 4. The sequence diagram of mjpg-streamer working.

that splits a dynamic video into a sequence of static photographs to compress video. Firstly, a video is encoded to a set of continuous JPEG images and the video server sends them to the client. Secondly, the client restores the video by decoding.

Integration of Hardware and Software. We use a pcDuino platform, shown in Fig. 5(a), to integrate all hardware and software mentioned above. A pcDuino that combines mini personal computer (PC) based on Advanced RISC Machine (ARM) architecture and Arduino is an open source hardware platform with many I/O interface (e.g., USB, HDMI and RJ45) and a suite of program development environment. Since Linux run on the pcDuino, we can use different programs to control different I/O interfaces at the same time only if these I/O could not conflict with each other. Therefore, a pcDuino can be used as many Arduino — connecting with and controlling many devices such as sensors and motors.

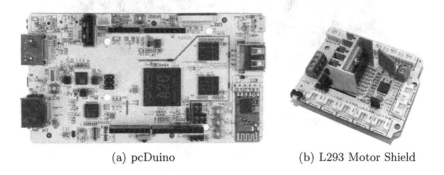

(a) pcDuino   (b) L293 Motor Shield

Fig. 5. The platform for integrating hardware and software.

Our pcDuino owns a 1 GHz ARM Cortex A20 CPU, a Mali-400 GPU, 1 GB DRAM, 32 GB Micro SD card and an USB. At the communication aspect, it supports wireless networking by WiFi and wired by RJ45.

The pcDuino transforms the control command sent from obstacle-avoidance algorithm to Pulse-Width Modulation (PWM) signal, and adjusts the rotational speed of the motors with the PWM signal for controlling movement of the car model.

Since the rated current of the used DC motors is too big, the pcDuino is easily to be damaged due to the excessive current if we directly use PWM output from the pcDuino to drive the DC motors. For protecting the pcDuino mainboard, we use L293 Motor Shield, shown in Fig. 5(b), to drive the two DC motors. L293 Motor Shield is a motor control module based on H-bridge driver chip. It can be plugged in an expansion slot on the pcDuino.

The pcDuino only support WiFi wireless networking. Since we are attempt to use 3G network that broadcasts more widely than WiFi, a HUAWEI E355 3G router is installed on the car model. The router can send out at most five WiFi signals. The pcDuino can connect 3G network by WiFi.

We adopt two sets of power supply. One set, six 1.2 V batteries (AA size), services for the DC motors. The other, 5 V/2 A power bank, services for the pcDuino, infrared sensors, USB camera and 3G router. Since the DC motors are big consumers of electricity, we allot a independent set of power for them.

The physical facade of the implemented information collection vehicle is given in Fig. 6.

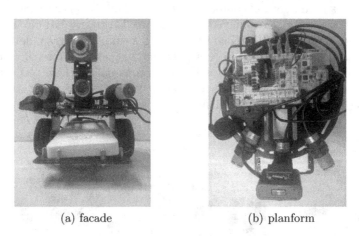

(a) facade   (b) planform

Fig. 6. The appearance of the information collection vehicle.

3.2   Implementation of Mobile Terminal

We use a smart phone based on Android platform to realize the mobile terminal. Then, the communication module in the mobile terminal can reuse the communication component in the smart phone.

A client application that sends request for information collection to the video server, receives video sent by the server and displays it is deployed on Android platform.

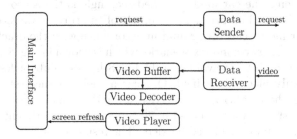

Fig. 7. The architecture of the client application on Android.

The client uses HTTP protocol to connect with the video server, i.e., mjpg-streamer. Firstly, by using Apache interface, the client sends a HTTP request to mjpg-streamer. After responding to the client, the mjpg-streamer sends encoded JPEG images to the client by HTTP protocol. Secondly, the client repeatedly receives JPEG images from the mjpg-streamer and puts them in a buffer. By decoding the data in buffer, the video about environment can be restored and be displayed on the screen of the smart phone. The architecture of the client is given in Fig. 7.

3.3   Implementation of Wireless Communication

All messages between the car model (i.e., the information collection vehicle) and the smart phone (i.e., the mobile terminal) are transmitted by 3G signal. Since a terminal only obtain an dynamic IP address rather than a static IP address when it accesses the Chinese 3G network, two devices in 3G network cannot communicate in point-to-point mode. As a result, we use PM+DDNS mode to realize 3G-based communication between the car model and the smart phone.

The process has two steps. In the first step, we set up a forwarding rule by PM in the management page of the 3G router. For example, we can mapping a video port, say 8090, into an IP of the pcDuino, say 192.168.0.101. As a result, any access to 8090 port from internet will be forwarded to 192.168.0.101. The second step is to configure dynamic domain name. Oray DDNS is used. We firstly apply a dynamic domain name from Oray. Then, we bind the intranet IP (i.e., 192.168.0.101) of the pcDuino with the dynamic domain name. Henceforth, whenever the pcDuino gets a new dynamic IP, the new IP will be sent to Oray DDNS by a dynamic domain name program installed on the pcDuino, and the database for domain name server is updated. If anyone accesses the dynamic domain name, Oray DDNS can return the right IP to him.

4   Experiment

For testing the automatic obstacle avoidance of the implemented prototype, we design a series of experiments that are shown in Fig. 8(a) to (g), where a hollow rectangle represents the car model, a filled rectangle is the sensor, a hatchures means an obstacle, and an arrow is the oracle of the turning direction. In these scenario our car model can turn round in accordance with the oracles.

We also conducts two complex scenario, which is shown in Fig. 8(h) and (i), to test the automatic obstacle avoidance. In Fig. 8(h), some obstacles in different shape is randomly placed in a field. Our car model can successfully run from the entrance to the exit with the success rate 95 %, which means that only 1 collision with obstacles was observed in 20 times of the experiment. In Fig. 8(i), the obstacles are randomly placed barriers. The result of the experiments shows that our car model may not successfully get through if the diameters of the obstacles are too small.

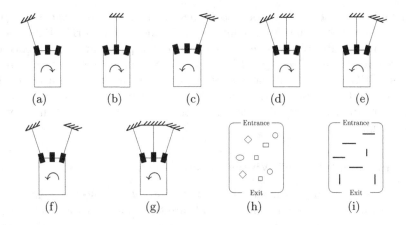

Fig. 8. The scenario for testing obstacle avoidance.

For testing the video transmission of the implemented prototype, we conduct an experiment in the scenario that is shown in Fig. 9. Under good 3G signal, the smart phone can smoothly display the video sent by the car model. When the 3G signal is weak, frame skipping frequently happen.

5   Related Works

In our early work [6], we had designed and implemented an autonomous collision avoidance vehicle that was remotely controlled by a smart phone. There are many differences between the prototype in [6] (say the old prototype) and the current one. Firstly, the old prototype realizes the collision avoidance by stopping at the font of obstacles rather than bypassing. Secondly, in the old prototype, the

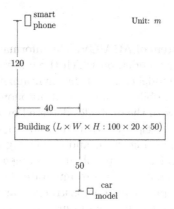

Fig. 9. The scenario for testing video transmission.

vehicle cannot send massive data, such as video, to the smart phone. In fact, in the old prototype, exchanged messages between the vehicle and the smart phone is simple control command such as movement or stop. Finally, the computing center is built on the smart phone in the old prototype rather than on the vehicle. In current prototype, if we put computing center in the smart phone, the control program must run concurrently with the video reception on the Android OS and the performance would be degraded by the reason of Android. Therefore, we move the computing center to the vehicle in the current prototype.

The other relevant work is Xu et al. [7]. They built a remote control system for a mobile object. The system was deployed on Android platform. By the interaction between Android and Arduino, the mobile object can be controlled not to collide with some obstacle. Authors did not show their real system, and not explain the implementation of the mobile object in detail, such as the integration of Android and Arduino on the mobile object and the way of driving motors by Arduino. In our implementation, we adopt pcDuino to integrate Android with Arduino on the car model.

In [8], author designed an Arduino intelligent vehicle, which was controlled by Android platform and can measure distance, move under control, and transfer image wirelessly. However, their control is based on WiFi rather than 3G. Thus, the control range of their system is limited.

In the aspect of automatic obstacle avoidance, [9,10] gave methods that derived spatial data of obstacles from images about an environment and bypassed obstacles in accordance with these data. Compared with them, our prototype cannot deal with some obstacles such as deep pits and steep slopes, but our obstacle avoidance algorithm requires the computing resources less than them.

In the aspect of video transmission, hitherto, we do not find any better proposal that can realize point-to-point data exchange between two mobile devices by 3G signal than ours in literatures.

6 Conclusion

We design a prototype system of AOAICV. The information collection vehicle is implemented by a 2WD car model, on which three infrared sensors and a USB camera are fixed. The car model can send the environment information collected by the USB camera to a mobile terminal, and autonomously bypass obstacles according to the distance with the obstacles detected by the sensors. The mobile terminal is realized by a smart phone with Android OS, on which a client application is deployed for requesting video and displaying it. The communication between the car model and the smart phone is implemented by HTTP based on 3G signal. We use pcDuino platform to integrate the hardware and software on the car model. Some experiments demonstrates that the prototype is sound. The implemented prototype can be used in urban management or family life.

References

1. LinkSprite technologies, Inc. http://www.linksprite.com
2. Meier, R.: Professional Android 4 Application Development. Wrox Press, UK (2012)
3. Port forwarding. https://en.wikipedia.org/wiki/Port_forwarding
4. Dynamic DNS. https://en.wikipedia.org/wiki/Dynamic_DNS
5. Henzingert, T.A.: The theory of hybrid automata. In: Proceedings of the 11th Annual IEEE Symposium on Logic in Computer Science (LICS 1996), pp. 278–292. IEEE Computer Society, Los Alamitos (1996)
6. Zhang, Y., Zhao, X.Y., Zhang, K.J., Li, J.W., Yang, Z.Z.: Design and implementation of remote control-based autonomous collision avoidance system prototype. In: Proceedings of the 2015 Second International Conference on Computer, Intelligent and Education Technology (CICET 2015), pp. 77–80. CRC Press, UK (2015)
7. Xu, R., Liang, J.C., Yang, H., Teng, J.W.: Design and implementation of remote control system for mobile platform based on interoperation of android and arduino. Int. J. Smart Home 8(4), 105–112 (2014)
8. Xin, G.: Arduino intelligent vehicle design based on andriod. Comput. Telecommun. 3(1), 62–64 (2014)
9. Samanta, D., Ghosh, A.: Automatic obstacle detection based on gaussian function in robocar. J. Res. Eng. Appl. Sci. 2(2), 354–363 (2012)
10. Galibraith, J.: Vision-based obstacle avoidance. United States Patent Application Publication. US 2004/0093122 A1 (2004)

Home Networks and Residential Gateways

An Empirical Study of the Design Space of Smart Home Routers

Tausif Zahid, Fouad Yousuf Dar, Xiaojun Hei$^{(\boxtimes)}$, and Wenqing Cheng

School of Electronic Information and Communications,
Huazhong University of Science and Technology, Wuhan 430074, China
{tausif,fouad,heixj,chengwq}@hust.edu.cn

Abstract. Home networks are becoming increasingly complex with the rising number of networked smart appliances with communication and control capabilities. These smart devices alongside diverse user applications usually share a single broadband access link via a router to access the Internet. The traffic streams competing for bandwidth on a best-effort basis may lead to poor quality-of-experience for users or malfunctioning of smart devices. Home routers used to only serve as dumb networking devices. Nevertheless, we expect that these routers will play a central role in communicating, networking and controlling emerging smart-home appliances. They should be programmable in a cost-effective way to efficiently transmit the real-time data, flexible in aggregating resources and convenient in providing management interfaces to upper-layer applications. The emerging software defined networking (SDN) offers a high degree of flexibility for implementing novel networking solutions to improve performances of distributed systems such as smart homes. The switching performance of the programmable switches is important for the forwarding service of the data plane after the traffic policies are deployed by the controller. In this paper, we conducted a measurement-based empirical study of the design space of different Open-Flow switches in multiple scenarios of a smart home network. Our testbed includes the performance of off-the-shelf commercial switches and FPGA-based networking boards. Our results demonstrate the trade-off between performance and flexibility for the OpenFlow switches. This empirical study focused on the throughput performance which is measured for different software-based OpenFlow switches. Zynq-based FPGA boards with networking capabilities demonstrate good potentials to facilitate the experimentation and implementation with high flexibility and sufficiently good performance. Our experiment results may provide insights into constructing evolvable and cost-effective software defined smart home routers with enhanced performance under budget constraints.

1   Introduction

Home networks are becoming increasingly complex with the rise of an era of smart devices. Not only the user held devices like tablets, smart phones and PCs but also many smart devices like media gateways, smart TVs, smart refrigerators

© Springer International Publishing Switzerland 2016
C.K. Chang et al. (Eds.): ICOST 2016, LNCS 9677, pp. 109–120, 2016.
DOI: 10.1007/978-3-319-39601-9_10

and washing machines are available leading towards a network of smart home devices. Those smart devices alongside diverse user applications like browsing, peer-to-peer, VoIP and gaming share the single broadband access link. The traffic streams competing for bandwidth on a best effort basis may result in poor quality of experience for users or malfunctioning of a smart device. The home network must be programmable enough to efficiently and reliably transmitting the real-time data, scalable and flexible in aggregating resources, secured and convenient in providing management interfaces to upper-layer applications.

A smart home is functionally categorized into two main networks: the broadband access network mainly for devices associated with personal needs such as entertainment, study, home, office etc., whereas the control network is envisioned for the control and management of appliances like refrigerator, air conditioning system and light switches etc. Both the broadband communication network and the control network converge at the household service gateway, which bridges the single home network to the outside network in a wired or wireless way. The broadband communication network is mostly attached to devices such as a laptop/desktop, digital TV and telephones etc. Most network traffic are generated from heterogeneous multimedia applications which indicates potential expectations of high bandwidth without stringent constraints on the reliability and consistency in data flows. The control network mainly administers the regular operations for all kinds of home devices such as the switching-on/off for lamps and curtains, the start-up and stop of the air-conditioner along with the adjustment of temperature and velocity of wind, the signal collection and execution in security and surveillance system, indoor data measurement through wired or wireless sensors located at different places of the house as well as the adjustment of power usage based on the data indication on electrical meters. Therefore, the control network is loaded with short data used for control and sampling in length which are featured with relatively low signal frequency and accordingly low transmission rate in order to meet their requirements. On the other hand, the expectation of reliability is higher. It is unacceptable that excessive errors or loss of control information occur in the network, which likely leads to the malfunction or even breakdown of target devices.

The emerging software defined networking (SDN) provides a new paradigm for controlling network behaviors in a unified framework [16]. SDN offers a high degree of flexibility for implementing novel networking solutions to improve performances of distributed systems. SDN turns the whole platform of the network in the control of programmable entities. Software-based OpenFlow switches are flexible but this flexibility is often achieved at the cost of performance degradation [9]. This programmable network is one of the techniques that can help in the above scenario of home network. By the identification of some common features in the flow tables of the simple commodity switches, the researchers provide a standardized protocol to control the flow table of a switch through software. OpenFlow has become the de facto south-bound protocol implementation of software defined networks. OpenFlow provides a practical approach to control a switch without requiring the vendors to expose the code of their devices [12]. The performance evaluation and the limitation of these OpenFlow-enabled switches is a prerequisite for using them for experimentation and implementation in smart-home networks which require high performance in terms of flow labeling and traffic slicing. The evaluation of these OpenFlow-enabled switches is the first step towards understanding the data plane performance. Although there have been growing interests on the data plane performance while most of the research contributes towards the control planes. In this paper, we use the programmable hardware enabled with SDN to implement smart home network environments and compare the performance of FPGA-based networking boards including ONetSwitch20, ONetSwitch45 and NetGear WNDR3700 commodity programmable hardware with the off-the-shelve commercial but non-programmable TP-Link TL-SG1024DT switch. To the best of our knowledge, we are the first to conduct the performance comparison between software and hardware based implementation of flow table in the smart home environment. Our results may provide insights into utilizing low-cost Zynq-based devices in smart home networks to achieve the balance between cost, functionality and programmability of the network.

The outline of the paper is as follows. In Sect. 2, we discuss the related work. Section 3 provides some background on different OpenFlow switches used in our testbed for performance evaluation. In Sect. 4, we report the settings of our experimental testbed. In Sect. 5, our measurement results are analyzed. Finally, we conclude this paper in Sect. 6.

2   Related Work

With the increasing complexity of home networks, research interests have been arising on home network management issues [7,17]. There is still limited research on commercial hardware that address the interface gap between home networking devices and users. Home network management should either be made easier for the user to configure or the responsibility taken away from users altogether. One early system was presented in [7], which is an OpenFlow-based universal logging platform which supports diagnostics and troubleshooting problems in home networks. Calvert et al. pointed out that the major difficulty on home network troubleshooting is due to lacking of ability to identify what changed in the network at the moment of failures.

A few research and commercial prototypes have been built utilizing SDN for home networks. Brush et al. reviewed various home networking problems on addressing the needs of home users [6]. There conducted studies shows that high cost of hardware, insufficient flexibility to configure and poor manageability are the main barriers towards samrt homes. Martin and Feamster studied dynamic traffic prioritization for home networks to better suit immediate needs for users [15]. They propose an interaction between the home router and user activity associated with different traffic flows. Using this approach, the prioritization of traffic for different flows is achieved in the home router. In [8], Fratczak et al. implemented an OpenFlow-based home network to achieve configurability and automation. The authors argued to slice the home network and centralize the control outside of the home network. This approach provides ISPs or third parties to efficiently manage the home network remotely so that new business models may be invented to meet the needs of smart home users. In [13], Lee et al. proposed an auto-configuration mechanism for home networks using SDN without middleware and home gateways. In [20], Wang et al. proposed slicing strategies to differentiate home network flows for performance enhancement based on application requirements. In [5] Boussard et al. proposed a software-based approach to interconnect devices of smart environments using the virtualization framework based on virtual objects. This provides the end-user with a centralized control and management of the smart home devices by device and network programmability.

Performance evaluation studies have been conducted quite extensively on the control plane while our study focused on the data plane. In [4], Bianco et al. compared the performance of OpenFlow switching, the link layer Ethernet switching and network layer IP routing with different types of rules and packet sizes. Throughput and packet latency are measured at different network conditions. In [14], Lu et al. proposed to use CPU in the switch to handle not only the control plane but also the data plane. The authors pointed out two limitations of current switches: a limited size forwarding table for flow-based forwarding scheme and a limited size packet buffer. In [9], Gelberger et al. evaluated the performance of two SDN architectures including OpenFlow and the programmable generic forwarding element (ProGFE) in terms of the flexibility and performance. The authors claimed that the SDN flexibility can be achieved at the cost of tolerated performance degradation although the exact degradation also depends on the SDN implementation. In that study, the impact of the controllers was not considered in the tested scenarios. In [21], Shijie et al. designed and implemented an OpenFlow-based switch on a Xilinx Zynq ZC706 board. In [11], Hu et al. designed and implemented a family of OpenFlow-based switches, namely ONetSwitch, on Xilinx Zynq SoCs. ONetSwitch has been further utilized to construct a data center networking testbed on a desk in [10].

3   Background

An OpenFlow switch has two important components: (1) a flow table, used for packet look up and forwarding; (2) a secure channel connects the remote controller and the switches for coordination. A flow table consists of flow entries, activity counters and more actions to apply to matched packets. Every packet is compared against the flow table and processed by the switch. If a matched entry is found, then a specified action is performed to process the packets. If there is no match, then the packet is forwarded to the controller for further processing. The responsibility of a controller is to deal with those packets which don't have valid flow entries in the switch. For processing each packet, switches may utilize the Ternary Content Addressable Memory (TCAM) and the Random Access Memory (RAM) for efficient packet forwarding.

There are two types of OpenFlow switches: hardware-based and software-based flow table switches. The hardware flow table is hardware accelerated Open-Flow switch, using multiple stages of FPGA-implemented hardware flow tables, which are cascaded with software flow tables inside the virtual Switch running in the CPU. Hardware based flow table pipeline has fixed number of flow tables and entries. Besides this, hybrid openflow switches also available which take advantages of both technologies. Hardware-based OpenFlow switches use TCAM and vendor-specific operating systems. Since they are implemented in hardware ASIC chips, they have high processing and switching speed. Software-based OpenFlow switches commonly use open source operating systems such as Linux. The packet processing is accomplished in software-based approaches hence the switch performance is often constrained. An OpenFlow reference switch implementation can be divided into two categories: user space and kernel space. For the encryption of communication, the user space communicates with the OpenFlow control plane architecture through SSL. Messages from the controller to switches and vice versa are exchanged between the user space and the kernel space [18]. The responsibility of the kernel module is the maintenance of the flow table, packet processing and statistics update.

4   Testbed

In this section, we report the experiment setup to evaluate the switching performance of OpenFlow switches. We have implemented a smart-home network testbed with different network topologies using programmable switches and SDN controllers. The performance comparisons have been conducted between the FPGA-based networking boards against the off-the-shelf commodity TP-LINK TL-SG1024DT switch. Our testbed consists of three parts: OpenFlow switches implemented on Xilinx Zynq boards, a SDN controller and traffic generators/receivers. As shown in Fig. 1, our testbed utilized three standard PCs: one with 2.8 GHz processor for the controller and the other two PCs with core i3 processors for the traffic sender and the receiver. All PCs have 4 GB of RAM, 1 Gbit/s NIC card and are running Ubuntu 14.04 operating systems.

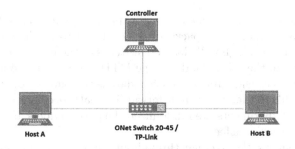

Fig. 1. Testbed setup

The FPGA-based programmable switches under test are ONetSwitch20 and ONet-Switch45 against NetGear 3700v4 router. ONetSwitch20 is a quick programmable solution for the OpenFlow switch based on the Xilinx Zynq TM-7000 as CPU and Avnet/Digilent ZedBoard as motherboard. ONetSwitch20 utilizes the MeshSr FMC4GE card to extent four Gigabit Ethernet interface. The processing software components makes ONetSwitch20 software programmable. ONetSwitch45 has an ARM architecture, all-programmability in both software and hardware. It also have four Gigabit Ethernet ports [2]. The third switch is NetGear WNDR 3700v4. It uses Atheros AR8327 switch, 560 MHz CPU and 128 MB of RAM.

The ONetSwitch20, ONetSwitch45 and NetGear OpenWRT-based switches are deployed with the RYU controller [3]. Ryu is an open-source SDN controller fully written in Python. These switches can also be configured with the usage of OpenFlow datapath configuration tool called Data Path Control (dpctl). dpctl provides command-line utilities to configure these switches as OpenFlow switches without an external controller.

The Mausezahn [1] traffic generator is used to generate packets with different sizes for the experiments. Mausezahn allows to send packets with arbitrary configurations in the interactive mode in our experiments. In these experiments, one PC acts as a traffic sender and the other acts as a receiver. In the interactive mode, both end-hosts establish a connection through telnet. In our experiments, one constant bit rate traffic session consists of 200,000 UDP packets with different types of packet sizes such as 128, 256, 512, 1024 and 1500 bytes.

5 Results

In this section, we examined the switching performance of OpenFlow switches with different packet sizes and flow table sizes. The major performance criteria is the average and maximum throughput of the network with different number of entries and table sizes. The performance analysis focused on hardware-based and software-based table implementations in the programmable switches.

5.1 Packet Size

The throughput performance increases as the packet size increases. With a small packet size, a large number of packets are generated to reach the same traffic load and they impose a high CPU load on switches as the number of flows is substantially large. On the other hand, a large MTU size may introduce additional delay. This effect is considerably large when data is transmitted over slower links. Therefore, it is likely that the switch forwarding path becomes the bottleneck. Note that in our experiments, we randomized the port numbers and IP addresses to minimize the caching effect.

Figure 2(a) shows the average throughput performance of three switches: ONetSwitch20, ONetSwitch45 and NetGear-OpenWRT against TP-Link TL-SG1024DT. In Fig. 2(a), the average throughput of the TP-Link switch and

ONetSwicth20/ONetSwicth45 with the hardware flow table achieve the same performance level. In this case the average performance of commodity hardware is slightly better than the FPGA boards. Note that the performance of ONetSwitches with software flow tables is almost same in this scenario.

Figure 2(b) shows the maximum throughput performance of ONetSwitch20, ONetSwitch45, NetGear-OpenWRT and TP-Link TL-SG1024DT. Note that the maximum throughput performance of ONetSwitch20/45 with the hardware flow table is better than all the switching cases for large packet sizes (1024 and 1500 bytes) reaching to 900 Mbps. ONetSwitch45 achieves even higher throughput of 1 Gbps as compared to TP-Link TL-SG1024DT by taking advantages of TCAM. These high average and maximum throughput rates are due to the fact that hardware tables of these switches are implemented in ASIC which has the capability to perform switching at line rate.

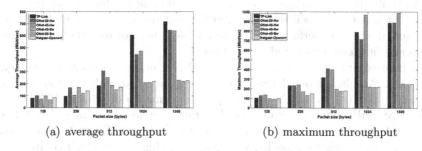

(a) average throughput   (b) maximum throughput

Fig. 2. Performance comparison with different flow entries

Figure 3(a) shows the maximum achievable throughput of the NetGear-OpenWRT router, ONetSwitch20 and ONetSwitch45 with the software table implementation. In this case, ONetSwitches with software flow table configuration behave almost same as NetGear-OpenWRT. Note that all the three switches use cPqD as the soft switch which is implemented as a user-space module in the Linux kernel.

Figure 3(b) shows the comparison of maximum throughput of TP-Link TL-SG1024DT with ONetSwitch20 and ONetSwitch45 enabled with hardware based flow table. It shows that the maximum throughput of ONetSwitch45 is slightly better than TP-link TL-SG1024DT with the packet size of 1500 bytes. With large packet sizes, the flow table lookups will be reduced as the total number of packets will be less as compared to the cases with smaller MTU sizes of 128 and 256 bytes packets.

5.2   Flow Table Size

In this subsection, we take a closer look at the impact of the flow table sizes on the throughput performance with different number of flow entries and number of tables. The flow table consists of number of flow entries each with its own priority.

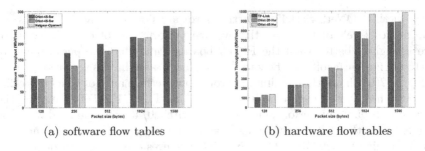

(a) software flow tables   (b) hardware flow tables

Fig. 3. Performance comparison: maximum throughput

A packet can match multiple entries so priority based mechanism is designed. When a packet enters the data plane, the parser extracts its related objects and forms a tuple. Then, this tuple is processed to lookup flow tables. When the final decision of lookup is obtained the counter for that specific entry is updated and the required action is performed. The flow table generates record of active flow entries and flow counters are also maintained.

In these experiments, we have inserted different number of entries in a single flow table. We also changed the criteria from single to multiple flow tables. Figure 4(a) and (b) shows the throughput performance of 64 and 1500 bytes packet sizes with different number of flow table entries in a single flow table. Figure 5 shows the dropping trend of performance with different table sizes. This performance degradation is likely due to the higher switching complexity. For the case of large flow tables, the switching on these FPGA board is more challenging for optimizing resource utilization [19]. In this case we compare the performance with different table sizes. In these experiments, in order to fill up forwarding tables we use bash scripts to generate random class C IP addresses.

The throughput performance shows a dropping trend with the increasing size of the tables. The throughput of switches with the hardware flow tables shows slightly better performance as compared to the cases with software flow tables. This trend is due to the fact that the lookup entry time for a flow in a flow table with large number of entries, increases exponentially. Hence, the performance degradation effect is similar for both hardware and software flow tables.

Each programmable switch has the capability to have multiple flow tables to be configured. For ONetSwitches 20/45 flow tables can be configured with each having maximum of 4096 flow entries. The throughput performance is depicted in Fig. 5. The programmable switches are configured with different number of flow tables ranging from 1 to 64 tables. The performance of highly programmable switches ONetSwitch20 and ONetSwitch45 is comparatively higher for hardware flow tables as compared to software flow tables. The reason is the impeccable forwarding ASIC logic of hardware flow tables.

Figure 6 shows the delay comparison of three programmable devices with software and hardware table implementation. We have populated different number of entries in flow tables of ONetSwitches to test the latency performance of

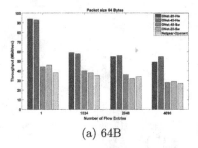
(a) 64B

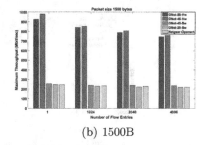
(b) 1500B

Fig. 4. Performance comparison: maximum throughput with different flow entries

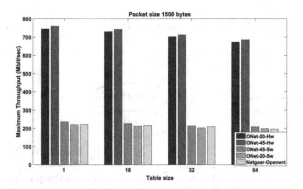

Fig. 5. Throughput with different flow table sizes

switching devices. Host A sends ping requests to host B. The time consumed by these devices under different number of flow entries in tables is used to calculate the delay. Figure 6 demonstrates that the programmable devices with hardware flow tables with small number of flow entries in the table introduces very low latency that is up to 50 ms. The reason is the line switching rate of the ASIC implementation of the hardware table. When the size of flow table increases, the delay increases. This is due to the fact that now the switch has to run more table lookups as compared to previous scenarios. With a flow table of more than 0.2 million flow entries the delay is still in an acceptable range, that is less than 300 ms. This demonstrates that these programmable devices with hardware flow tables are capable enough to handle latency sensitive application flows like VoIP.

On the other hand, the ONetSwitch 20/45 switch and the NetGear-OpenWRT switch with software table implementation introduce low delay for small flow tables but as the tables become larger than 0.1 million entries, the delay becomes significantly large up to 500 ms, make them unsuitable for latency sensitive flows. As for home networks, the flow table entries is not likely to exceed from these upper limits of 4096 entries, these devices with software table are very suitable for real world deployments as they provide high programmability and flexibility to control and manage the network.

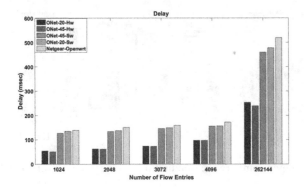

Fig. 6. Delay with different number of flow entries in the flow tables

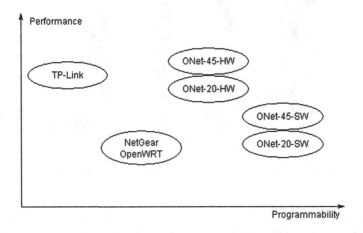

Fig. 7. Device comparison: performance vs programmability

Figure 7 shows the trade-off between programmability and performance of utilized devices. The programmable devices with hardware flow tables have high switching performance comparable to TP-link non-programmable switch. The hardware tables are low in memory but being implemented in ASIC, gives them the edge to switch at line rate. On the other hand, the devices with software flow tables have relatively lower throughput performance but they provide similar programmability capabilities. Hence, they are suitable for smart home networks where higher network programmability is required for flow prioritization. The degradation on the throughput performance is tolerable for home networks as the throughput is still sufficiency high.

6   Conclusion

Software defined networks can be of great potentials to achieve measurable, manageable and controllable smart homes. In this paper, we conducted an evaluation study on the performance of OpenFlow-enabled switches in an SDN testbed tailored for home networks including Xilinx Zynq boards and commodity switches. Our results demonstrate that FPGA-based networking boards show good potential to facilitate the experimentation and implementation of new ideas with good flexibility and sufficiently high performance for smart home network scenarios. The Zynq-based OpenFlow switches, ONetSwitches, can perform as well as commodity switches at various different conditions. This flexibility does not degrade the performance of the network with large packet sizes. For small packet sizes, commodity switches outperforms ONetSwitches while with large packet sizes the performance of TCAM-based OpenFlow switches outperform other forwarding devices in case of limited flow entries. This performance comparison indicates that there exists room for improving the implementations of Zynq-based switches to fully utilize the hardware capability.

Acknowledgement. This work was supported in part by the National Natural Science Foundation of China (no. 61370231) and in part by the Fundamental Research Funds for the Central Universities under Grant HUST:2014QN156.

References

1. Mausezahn (2015). http://www.perihel.at/sec/mz/mops.html
2. MeshSr (2015). http://www.meshsr.com
3. Ryu (2015). http://osrg.github.com/ryu/
4. Bianco, A., Birke, R., Giraudo, L., Palacin, M.: OpenFlow switching: data plane performance. In: IEEE ICC, May 2010
5. Boussard, M.E.: Software-defined LANs for interconnected smart environment. In: 27th International Teletraffic Congress (ITC), pp. 219–227 (2015)
6. Brush, A., Lee, B., Mahajan, R., Agarwal, S., Saroiu, S., Dixon, C.: Home automation in the wild: challenges and opportunities. In: Proceedings of the SIGCHI Conference on Human Factors in Computing Systems, pp. 2115–2124 (2011)
7. Calvert, K.L., Edwards, W.K., Feamster, N., Grinter, R.E., Deng, Y., Zhou, X.: Instrumenting home networks. SIGCOMM Comput. Commun. Rev. **41**(1), 84–89 (2011)
8. Fratczak, T., Broadbent, M., Georgopoulos, P., Race, N.: HomeVisor: adapting home network environments. In: Second European Workshop on Software Defined Networks (EWSDN), pp. 32–37, October 2013
9. Gelberger, A., Yemini, N., Giladi, R.: Performance analysis of software-defined networking (SDN). In: IEEE MASCOTS, pp. 389–393, August 2013
10. Hu, C., Yang, J., Gong, Z., Deng, S., Zhao, H.: DesktopDC: setting all programmable data center networking testbed on desk. In: Proceedings of the 2014 ACM Conference on SIGCOMM, pp. 593–594 (2014)
11. Hu, C., Yang, J., Zhao, H., Lu, J.: Design of all programmable innovation platform for software defined networking. In: Open Networking Summit, Santa Clara, CA, US (2014)
12. Lara, A., Kolasani, A., Ramamurthy, B.: Network innovation using OpenFlow: a survey. IEEE Commun. Surv. Tutorials **16**(1), 493–512 (2014)

13. Lee, M., Kim, Y., Lee, Y.: A home cloud-based home network auto-configuration using SDN. In: IEEE 12th International Conference on Networking, Sensing and Control (ICNSC), pp. 444–449 (2015)
14. Lu, G., Miao, R., Xiong, Y., Guo, C.: Using CPU as a traffic co-processing unit in commodity switches. In: Proceedings of the First Workshop on Hot Topics in Software Defined Networks, pp. 31–36 (2012)
15. Martin, J., Feamster, N.: User-driven dynamic traffic prioritization for home networks. In: ACM SIGCOMM Workshop on Measurements Up the Stack (2012)
16. McKeown, N., Anderson, T., Balakrishnan, H., Parulkar, G., Peterson, L., Rexford, J., Shenker, S., Turner, J.: OpenFlow: enabling innovation in campus networks. SIGCOMM Comput. Commun. Rev. **38**(2), 69–74 (2008)
17. Mortier, R., Rodden, T., Tolmie, P., Lodge, T., Spencer, R., Crabtree, A., Sventek, J., Koliousis, A.: Homework: putting interaction into the infrastructure. In: Proceedings of the 25th Annual ACM Symposium on User Interface Software and Technology, pp. 197–206 (2012)
18. Naous, J., Erickson, D., Covington, G.A., Appenzeller, G., McKeown, N.: Implementing an OpenFlow switch on the NetFPGA platform. In: ACM/IEEE Symposium on Architectures for Networking and Communications Systems (2008)
19. Qu, Y.R., Zhou, S., Prasanna, V.K.: High-performance architecture for dynamically updatable packet classification on FPGA. In: ACM/IEEE Symposium on Architectures for Networking and Communications Systems (ANCS) (2013)
20. Wang, S., Wu, X., Chen, H., Wang, Y., Li, D.: An optimal slicing strategy for SDN based smart home network. In: International Conference on Smart Computing (SMARTCOMP), pp. 118–122 (2014)
21. Zhou, S., Jiang, W., Prasanna, V.: A flexible and scalable high-performance OpenFlow switch on heterogeneous SoC platforms. In: IEEE International Performance Computing and Communications Conference (IPCCC), pp. 1–8, December 2014

Simplifying Installation and Maintenance of Ambient Intelligent Solutions Toward Large Scale Deployment

Hamdi Aloulou[1,2(✉)], Bessam Abdulrazak[2,3], Romain Endelin[1,2],
João Bentes[4,5], Thibaut Tiberghien[1,4], and Joaquim Bellmunt[1,4]

[1] Institut Mines Telecom, Paris, France
{hamdi.aloulou,romain.endelin,thibaut.tiberghien,
bellmunt}@mines-telecom.fr
[2] Laboratory of Informatics, Robotics and Microelectronics, Montpellier, France
[3] University of Sherbrooke, Sherbrooke, Canada
bessam.abdulrazak@usherbrooke.ca
[4] Image and Pervasive Access Laboratory, Singapore, Singapore
[5] School of Information Technology, Halmstad University, Halmstad, Sweden
joao.bentes@hh.se

Abstract. Simplify deployment and maintenance of Ambient Intelligence solutions is important to enable large-scale deployment and maximize the use/benefit of these solutions. More mature Ambient Intelligence solutions emerge on the market as a result of an intensive investment in research. This research targets mainly the accuracy, usefulness, and usability aspects of the solutions. Still, possibility to adapt to different environments, ease of deployment and maintenance are ongoing problems of Ambient Intelligence. Existing solutions require an expert to move on-site in order to install or maintain systems. Therefore, we present in this paper our attempt to enable quick large scale deployment. We discuss lessons learned from our approach for automating the deployment process in order to be performed by ordinary people. We also introduce a solution for simplifying the monitoring and maintenance of installed systems.

Keywords: Ambient Assisted Living · Large-scale deployment · Automation · Maintenance · Monitoring

1 Introduction

Simplifying the installation and maintenance of Ambient Intelligence (AmI) solutions is nowadays an important need, given recent progress in this domain. In fact, AmI maturity has increased over the years. As a consequence, a number of AmI applications would target large-scale deployment in a near future. A survey from Memon et al. [8] shows that research projects are gradually shifting towards real-world deployments. The existing real deployment of AmI solutions

© Springer International Publishing Switzerland 2016
C.K. Chang et al. (Eds.): ICOST 2016, LNCS 9677, pp. 121–132, 2016.
DOI: 10.1007/978-3-319-39601-9_11

had great impact in highlighting the benefit of AmI. Still, difficulties exist during the process of installation and maintenance of AmI systems. The process tends to be tedious and time-consuming. Usually, technicians are required to move in site and perform the installation and maintenance, as these tasks typically involve manual configuration and expert knowledge. Typically, the installation process requires to prepare the AmI system off-site (e.g., pre-program, wiring), configure the system manually, move on-site and set up the system. Once the system is deployed, frequent errors may occur. These errors can be caused by hardware failures, network issues or unpredictable behaviors from the end-users (e.g., unplugging the system by mistake). These errors have to be consistently monitored, and occasionally require to move on-site for maintenance. This process may be acceptable for small scale real-world deployment (e.g., couple of houses), but it is not suitable for large-scale deployments. This issue of installation and maintenance was addressed for the first time in 2005 by Elzabadani [6] but surprisingly, only few research works have been conducted since that time.

We have experienced several successes, and a number of frustrations during our real-world deployment experiences [4]. Thus, the deployment enabled us to be aware of several technical issues related to in-situ deployment (e.g., networking, ease of deployment, maintenance). It also helped us to identify the challenges linked to the large-scale deployment. For example, customization is a major challenge that needs to be addressed as each AmI deployment is specific to an environment and to the needs of one end-user. Therefore, customization should be made simple and easy to perform in order to sweet large number of end-users. The second challenge is the need for remote maintenance to ensure good continuous performance of the system. Knowing that the maintenance of an AmI system is a tedious process, the human and logistic cost associated to maintenance should be minimized.

Following, we present our approach for the improvement of the installation and maintenance process of AmI systems. Section 2 positions our contribution within the literature. Section 3 presents our vision for the large-scale deployment of AmI systems and discusses the architecture we propose to enable smooth installation and maintenance. Section 4 describes our proposed process for simplifying installation of a new deployment. Section 5 details our proposed monitoring and maintenance process. Section 6 discusses the step-by-step installation procedure. Section 7 presents the validation of our approach. Section 8 concludes the paper.

2   Related Work

Early researches on adaptable deployments for AmI are those of Helal et al. [7] who proposed a programmable spaces, Elzabadani et al. [6] who proposed a device Plug & Play, and Ranganathan et al. [10] who proposed an application polymorphism similar to today's cloud computing. These three papers, all published in 2005, carry the vision of a customizable and extensible ecosystem for

AmI, from hardware to software. Since 2005, a number of researches have been published about automatic sensor discovery using Service-Oriented Architecture (SOA) architectures [3] and the integration of sensors into a knowledge-base for the reasoning [1]. SOA is a popular architecture in AmI, as it helps to create Plug & Play integration of sensors/actuators (S/A) into the system. Similarly, a large number of AmI solutions rely on ontological models using the semantic web technologies, as these models can easily integrate new S/A into the knowledge-base. Pathan et al. [9] propose a complete approach ranging from sensor discovery to a semantic-based automatic configuration of the system.

The problematic of deployment simplicity in AmI was originally introduced by Abdulrazak et al. [2] in 2006, whom introduced for the first time the term "smart-home in a box." In this paper, the authors mention their goal of minimizing engineering expertise and lowering the costs of deployments.

To our knowledge, only few researches have been published since 2006 on simplicity of deployment. In the last couple of years, industrial solutions such as Resin.io[1] propose to automate the deployment, provisioning and maintenance of Internet of Things (IoT) solutions, using technologies like Docker. This solution is interesting, but it mainly target IoT, and does not include dynamic integration of sensors in knowledge-bases, communication between gateway and server, nor specific aspects related to AmI. In addition, to our knowledge, the maintenance of AmI deployments has not yet been addressed in the literature.

3   Our Vision for Deployment of AmI Solution

In this paper, we propose a practical approach for the installation and maintenance of AmI systems. Our goal is to provide end-users with a "smart-home in a box" solution that would be delivered to and installed by an end-user, and remotely maintained by technicians. The parcel would include a gateway and S/A to be placed in an end-user environment. The gateway is in charge of the collection of data from sensors, the communication between S/A and a remote server, as well as forwarding the collected data to a cloud-based framework hosted on the remote server (Fig. 1). This framework includes a reasoning engine in charge of context understanding and service provisioning.

In order to achieve this goal, different measures need to be adopted. First, the installation and customization process should be made simple and easy to perform. Therefore, we propose an approach including an automatic S/A discovery and integration into the system. Thus, we prefer the use of a configuration interface rather than manually modifying files. This enable to generate the configuration file automatically and minimize syntactic and semantic errors. Second, the maintenance should be performed remotely as much as possible. In order to reduce the technician's workload and the unnecessarily move in-situ, the system should automatically detect problems and send notifications.

Technically, we propose to extend the regular AmI architecture in order to facilitate the installation, deployment and maintenance process. We propose

---

[1] https://resin.io.

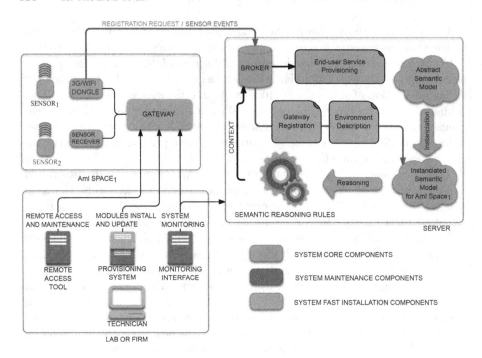

Fig. 1. Extended AmI architecture

to provide technicians with a provisioning system that enable smooth install, remote maintenance and update of gateways. We recommend to integrate dedicated user-interfaces into the framework to facilitate the deployment by non-experts (e.g., regular end-users). In addition, we propose the use of a monitoring interface that allow technicians check the system status and be notified in case of problems. Remote access tools should also be provided to grant access to deployed gateways when needed.

Following we will start by presenting our solution to simplify the installation process.

4   Simplifying Installation Process

We aim in our deployment process to make the installation as easy as possible, so an expert is not anymore required for set up. We propose a process based on three following major tasks: (1) serial provisioning for quick gateway installation, (2) Gateway & S/A discovery, and (3) Semantic Plug & Play of gateway and S/A.

4.1   Serial Provisioning

Preparing a gateway for a deployment is very tedious and time-consuming task. It requires installing the appropriate operating system, configuring the network in order to enable remote connection with the server, installing the different modules needed for the communication between S/A and server, and make sure that software dependencies are fulfilled. This installation is also a repetitive task as the same gateway installation process will be performed for each new deployment.

In order to deal with this issue, we propose a two-step installation process. First, a guided installation along with a script automatize the setup of the operating system on gateways. Second, a provisioning tool automatize the installation of the gateway modules on the operating system. We recommend for this aim "Ansible"[2]. "Ansible" includes playbooks[3] that allow to configure and automatize the installation of the different modules. "Ansible" also handle parallel installation and deployment process on multiple gateways. In order to speed the installation process even further, a new distribution (i.e., a collection of software applications built on top of the operating system) with all the required modules and dependencies could optionally be generated based on a newly installed gateway, and then used for the subsequent installation of other gateways.

4.2 Enable Gateway & S/A Discovery

Deployed gateways and sensors need to be recognized and integrated into the server framework in order to receive events, perform context understanding and provide appropriate services to end-users. Usually, gateways and sensors are manually integrated into the framework and linked to specific spaces and objects. This manipulation requires an expert of the framework details to make the required changes and configurations. We propose a communication protocol between the gateway and the framework in order to automatize this process and ease the deployment of AmI solutions.

Once a gateway is deployed, it only has the IP address of the framework's server. Since the gateway configuration file doesn't have information needed to exchange with the framework on switch-on, the gateway uses a secured communication protocol (HTTPS) to send basic information (e.g., mac address and local IP address) to the server and ask for registration in the framework. The registration request is sent repetitively until approval by an installer (e.g., end-user, technician) through a dedicated user interface. Once approved, a virtual AmI space is generated in the framework and linked to the newly approved gateway. The framework therefore generates and sends credentials to the gateway. The gateway uses these credentials to connect to the framework and ask for its configuration file.

The configuration file contains the ID and the name associated to the gateway. It also have a blank list of sensors which will be updated progressively upon detection, approval and integration of new sensors into the framework.

---

[2] "Ansible" is a free provisioning and application deployment platform. http://www.ansible.com/.

[3] http://docs.ansible.com/ansible/playbooks.html.

As mentioned earlier, part of the gateway configuration concerns sensors plugged in the AmI space and registered with that gateway. Another list concerns blacklisted sensors representing undesirable sensors (e.g., noise sensors, malfunctioning sensors or neighborhood sensors). Registered sensors' events are sent to the server for processing (i.e., context awareness and service provisioning) while blacklisted sensors' events are ignored. New sensors' events are sent for registration to the server on a dedicated handler. A configuration interface is provided by the framework for the description of a given space (i.e., rooms' names, rooms' types, objects' names, objects' types) and the approval or blacklisting of sensors discovered previously (record) or in real time.

4.3   Semantic Plug & Play

The discovery task, described in the previous section, allows the framework to discover and identify gateways and S/A deployed in AmI spaces. Still, S/A need to be integrated into the reasoning process in order to use events from/to these devices. At this stage, there is a semantic gap which prevents the integration of events received from the sensors in the AmI reasoning process. Therefore, our semantic Plug & Play approach aims at filling this gap by providing a simple user-interface to let users define the semantics of S/A. For example, type of sensor, kind of events provided and their meaning, bindings relatively to the space such as the kind of room it is deployed in or object it is attached to.

In order to be included in the framework reasoning process, all these information need to be integrated in the AmI solution's knowledge base. The knowledge base allows description of an AmI spaces (e.g., rooms, objects, sensors, persons) and the relations between its entities. We have chosen to use semantic web, through ontologies, for the definition of AmI solution knowledge bases. This choice is justified by the fact that semantic modeling satisfies the constraints of context aware systems for adaptability and flexibility in dynamic and changing environments [4]. It allows to define an *a priori* knowledge, separate human profile and environment representation from the system logic, and reuse and share of common knowledge among several applications [5]. Using ontologies, it is possible to define an abstract model common to divers AmI spaces, that will be instantiated with information related to each new environment in which the system will be deployed.

Typically, an AmI solution's knowledge base is manually alimented with information about the newly deployed space (e.g., rooms, objects, sensors). Changes need also to be made on the reasoning part in order to include the new entities in the context awareness and service provisioning process. This task requires an expert to go deep into the framework code and make the required changes. We chose to automatize all this process in our semantic Plug & Play approach. The framework is in charge of instantiating the abstract semantic model related to the newly deployed AmI space once the gateway and the new deployed sensors are approved by the installer. It uses the information provided by the installer through the dedicated user-interface to feed the instantiated semantic model with the new environment elements and the bindings between these elements. In order to make the integration of the new sensors into the reasoning process straightforward, the reasoning rules should be highly declared and abstracted. In this case, there is no need for manual modification to be made. At this level, an expert is not required to integrate the newly discovered sensors in the AmI space. The semantic reasoning offers such ability to declare abstract reasoning rules. As an example, the rule below infers the location of the end-user based on events received from motion sensors. As you can see, the rules is applied to all motion sensors deployed in the AmI space without specifying concretely these sensors.

$$\forall \ Sensor \ se; \ SensorState \ st; \ Room \ r; \ User \ u$$
$$(se, \ hasCurrentState, \ st) \wedge (se, \ hasType, \ PIR) \wedge (st, \ indicateLocation, \ true)$$
$$\wedge \ (se, \ deployedIn, \ r) \wedge (u, \ liveIn, \ r) \Rightarrow (u, \ detectedIn, \ r)$$

5   Maintenance

The maintenance is another key point for a real deployment. It becomes important for large-scale deployment. It is hard to perform, time consuming and economically expensive if essential procedures have not been adopted. In fact, in-situ maintenance should be minimized and limited to critical situations hard to solve remotely. Also the time of detection and intervention is very crucial, and can have a strong impact in specific AmI solutions (e.g., failure in dependent people assistive AmI solutions). Solutions need to be developed in order to automatically detect and alert on system strange behaviors. A remote intervention should also be possible in order to investigate and solve the detected problems.

Based on our real world deployment feedback, the three key issues that need to be addressed for any future large scale deployment are (1) Remote access to gateways, (2) Remote monitoring of the gateways, and (3) Failure handling.

5.1   Gateway Remote Access

A large scale deployment of AmI solutions raises the problem of remote access, maintenance and update of these systems. In fact, thousands copies of an AmI solution might be installed on a large area in a city, country or even all over the world. Moving in-situ to solve problems or update these systems at this scale becomes virtually unaffordable.

Different technical problems could arise unexpectedly after the installation of an AmI solution. In addition, new versions of modules installed on the gateway could appear and therefore these modules need to be updated. Moreover, new modules could be required on the gateway to integrate new sensors' types and protocols. Therefore, a mechanism of remote access need to be established to reach the gateway from distance (i.e., in laboratory or in firm) even if the gateway is installed in a private network behind a Network Address Translation (NAT) router of firewall.

Several technical solutions can be adapted to overcome this issue, without the need for specific hacking tricks such as port forwarding, static IP addresses or dynamic DNS. As an example we can use SSH reverse proxy or commercial solutions such as Weaved[4].

5.2   Ambient Intelligence Monitoring System

To automatically detect problems that could arise unexpectedly after the installation, the availability and performance of the gateways has to be continuously monitored. Additionally, technicians should be informed about the occurrence of abnormal events.

In order to address those requirements, a monitoring solution should be putted in place. A set of agents should be installed on gateways. These agents collect data (e.g., CPU, memory and network usage) from the gateways and sent it periodically to a monitoring server. The monitoring server stores, analyzes and exposes the data collected. It also provides mechanisms to notify technicians about the occurrence of strange events and to require the execution of remote commands on gateways. Also, some commands can be automatically sent from the server to be run on the gateway, such as restart system services, enable/disable a network port.

Monitoring tools should also provide strategies to easily set up a huge number of gateways. One strategy could be providing the concept of set-up templates. Since gateways have the same operational system and needs of monitoring, creating a template can facilitate the configuration and update of our monitoring system. For example, a template would be created with the items to check: (i) usage of resources like CPU and memory; (ii) availability of services like SSH and NTP; (iii) monitoring string patterns in log files. Then, when a new gateway is registered, it is added on the monitoring system by creating a new host based on the template. Commercial solutions such as "Zabbix"[5] could be integrated in AmI solutions in order to address the monitoring and maintenance issues.

5.3   Automatic Failure Handling

We have identified numerous cases of failure issues related to the gateway during our experience with real deployment. An example is the gateway shutdown, whether accidentally by the user or due to power cut. Another issue is related to possible software bugs that break the gateway modules operation. In addition, the network is one major problem that affect the normal behavior of the system. Internet disconnection causes loss of sensor events, and therefore stops all the reasoning and the service provision process. Either case, a human intervention should not be required to re-operate the system. We propose different techniques to handle the discussed failures: First, every module in the gateway should be running as a background process (i.e., daemon). The gateway ensures that the required processes are running. Second, a script should permanently check the

---

[4] https://www.weaved.com.
[5] "Zabbix" is an open source high performance real-time monitoring solution. http://www.zabbix.com/.

gateway internet connection (through LAN or 3G) to detect disconnections and reconnect consequently. Finally, a process should be integrated on the server side to notify the gateway to restart its faulty services when they are unreachable.

6   Installation & Maintenance Procedure

Based on our five years experience in real world deployment of AmI solutions, we conclude on a four step-by-step procedure that we believe suites the best large scale deployment. Following the details of this installation procedure:

1. Prepare Gateway & S/A. We choose to use small size single-board computer as a gateway (for our deployment: Raspberry Pi). Using a script, we install the default operating system on the gateway (for our deployment: Raspbian, the most widespread Linux distribution for Raspberry Pi), we register the gateway's IP into the serial provisioning (for our deployment: Ansible) and run it. The gateway is therefore provisioned. As a final step to be performed off-site, S/A have be selected and prepared (e.g., placing batteries, setting up unique code). S/A receiver modules also have to be plugged into the gateway.

2. Deploy Gateway & S/A. We start by plugging-in the gateway to an electric plug and placing the sensors into the environment. We then edit the serial provisioning system, to finalize the network configuration (for our deployment: replace the gateway's initial IP address with the permanent one).

3. Configure the System. The gateway and sensors must be coupled with our cloud-based framework. The gateway is regularly sending registration requests to the server, so that the installer can view and accept the registration using a web interface as shown in Fig. 2.

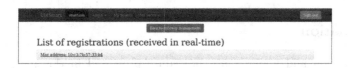

List of registrations (received in real-time)

Mac address: 10:c3:7b:57:33:b4

Fig. 2. Registration request web interface

Once the installer accepts the gateway registration, he is redirected towards the space description interface as shown in Fig. 3. In this page, he can define relevant rooms and items present in the environments, as well as the sensors deployed. To assist the installer in defining sensors, newly received sensor events appear automatically on the interface, so that the installer can accept the sensor, and attach it to an object/room.

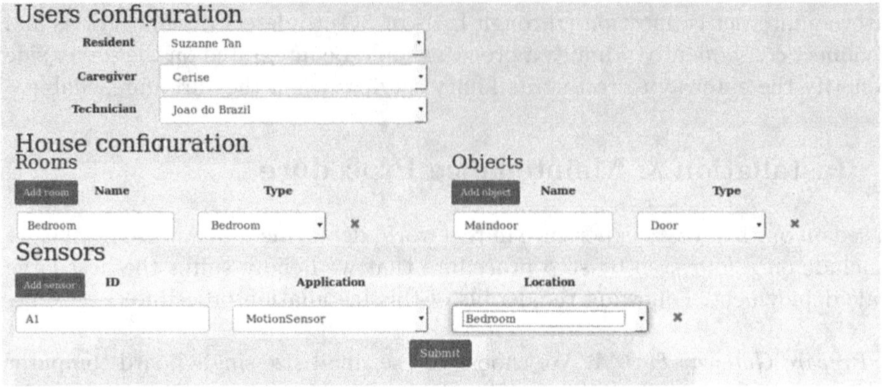

Fig. 3. Space description user interface

4. Maintain the System. The gateway modules upgrade is guaranteed by a routine which makes a request on the remote repository (for our deployment: Ansible), looking for updates, every 24 h. If new versions are available, the gateways will download the new provisioning file, and upgrade itself automatically, with no need for human intervention. The monitoring system (for our deployment: Zabbix), continuously receives reports on the gateways current state. If it detects an error that can be fixed automatically, the monitoring system launches a remote procedure on the gateway. If the error cannot be fixed automatically, a technician will remotely log-in to the gateway using our remote access procedure, and solve the problem manually. In case the technician cannot fix the problem remotely (e.g., connection lost, hardware problem), he will move on-site, and replace the faulty system by a new one. This procedure was recently adopted in our deployment in a nursing home and three individual houses. The validation of this procedure is detailed in the next section.

7   Validation

The installation and maintenance procedure presented in this paper has the potential to boost a large scale deployment of AmI solutions. We have validated this approach for the installation and maintenance of our Ambient Assisted Living (AAL) solution *UbiSmart* [4]. Following we highlight the benefits of our approach through the validations of three main features:

Validating Improvements on the Installation Process: We have installed and configured our own AAL solution with and without the approach presented in this paper. Without our proposed approach, a expert technician needs an average of 45 min of active work to install and configure the system, diluted in a total 1 h and 45 min (including 1 h of background process). However, when using our approach, the technician only needs less than five minutes of active work to run the process. The process will execute in background for approximately 1 h.

Furthermore, installing the system with our proposed approach requires only little technical skills, compared to the manual approach.

(5 min + 1 h + non expert installer compared to 45 min + 1 h + expert installer)

Empirically, our recent deployments have required 20 min in-situ, using the configuration interface provided by our framework, whereas earlier deployments required up to 4 h. The in-situ deployment now consists only in placing the sensors, plugging the gateway, configuring and testing the system.

(20 min + non expert installer compared to 4 h + expert installer)

Validating Improvements on the Upgrade Process: A manual upgrade of the gateway, assuming it is performed remotely, requires between 5 min and 20 min per gateway. The total duration of the upgrade scales poorly as the number of gateways increases, and would be as high as several hours if considering 50 gateways. Using our approach, the upgrade process is now fully automated, and requires no involvement from a technician.

(0 min compared to 5 to 20 min required from a technician)

Validating Improvements on the Maintenance Process: In order to measure the impact of our approach during the maintenance stage, we introduce Eqs. 1 and 2, which estimates respectively the daily maintenance duration of AmI systems, and the expected downtime in case of failure.

$$\text{Daily Maintenance Duration} = N \times (C + R \times (1 - A) \times T) \qquad (1)$$

$$\text{Expected Downtime} = D + (1 - A) \times T \qquad (2)$$

where: N the number of houses deployed — C the time required to check one house manually — R the daily probability of having a failure in a house — A the probability that a house can be fixed automatically after a failure — T the time required to manually fix a house — D the expected duration until a faulty house is noticed.

When using our approach, it is reasonable to assign $C = 0$ (i.e., no need to check houses manually), $A = 0.8$ (i.e., 80 % of the failures can be fixed automatically) and $T = 30$ min (i.e., we need in average 30 min to solve a failure manually). Without our approach, we may assign $C = 1$ min, $A = 0$ and $T = 30$ min. With these assumptions, the expected downtime of a house would be 6 min with our approach, and 12 h without.

On a deployment of 5 houses, and given $R = 0.05$ (i.e., there will be a failure every 20 days in average for a given house), $D = 10$ s if using our approach (i.e., the monitoring system checking frequency), and $D = 12$ h without our approach. The Daily Maintenance Duration of the deployment is 1:30 min with our approach, and 12:30 min without. On a deployment of 50 houses, the Daily Maintenance Duration of the deployment becomes 15 min with our approach, and more than 2 h without.

8 Conclusion

We have presented in this paper our approach to optimize the installation and maintenance of AmI solutions, as well as reduce the human involvement and expertise required in these tasks. We also introduce the related lessons learned from our real world deployment. A dedicated installation and maintenance procedure for real world deployment based on installation and maintenance techniques are also discussed in this paper. The paper include a validation section that highlight the importance and the significant impact of our proposed approach. We are working on leveraging the work presented in this paper towards a real large-scale deployment in smart city project.

Acknowledgments. This research project is supported by the Quality Of Life Chair formed by Foundation Telecom of the Institut Mines-Telecom in France, La Mutuelle Generale and AG2R La Mondiale. The work is also supported by the grand emprunt VHP inter@ctive project. We also wish to acknowledge the support of the Saint-Vincent-de-Paul nursing home and its director Brigitte Choquet, who kindly let us deploy our system within their environment.

References

1. Abdulrazak, B., Chikhaoui, B., Gouin-Vallerand, C., Fraikin, B.: A standard ontology for smart spaces. Int. J. Web Grid Serv. **6**(3), 244–268 (2010)
2. Abdulrazak, B., Helal, A.: Enabling a plug-and-play integration of smart environments. In: Information and Communication Technologies, 2006, ICTTA 2006, 2nd vol. 1, pp. 820–825. IEEE (2006)
3. Alonso, R.S., Tapia, D.I., Bajo, J., García, Ó., de Paz, J.F., Corchado, J.M.: Implementing a hardware-embedded reactive agents platform based on a service-oriented architecture over heterogeneous wireless sensor networks. Ad Hoc Netw. **11**(1), 151–166 (2013)
4. Aloulou, H., Mokhtari, M., Tiberghien, T., Biswas, J., Yap, P.: An adaptable and flexible framework for assistive living of cognitively impaired people. IEEE J. Biomed. Health Inform. **18**(1), 353–360 (2014)
5. Aloulou, H., Mokhtari, M., Tiberghien, T., Endelin, R., Biswas, J.: Uncertainty handling in semantic reasoning for accurate context understanding. Knowl. Based Syst. **77**, 16–28 (2015)
6. Elzabadani, H., Helal, A., Abdulrazak, B., Jansen, E.: Self-sensing spaces: smart plugs for smart environments. In: Proceedings of the 3rd International Conference on Smart Nomes and Health Telematics, pp. 91–98 (2005)
7. Helal, S.: Programming pervasive spaces. IEEE Pervasive Comput. **4**(1), 84–87 (2005)
8. Memon, M., Wagner, S.R., Pedersen, C.F., Beevi, F.H.A., Hansen, F.O.: Ambient assisted living healthcare frameworks, platforms, standards, and quality attributes. Sensors **14**(3), 4312–4341 (2014)
9. Pathan, M., Taylor, K., Compton, M.: Semantics-based plug-and-play configuration of sensor network services. In: Proceedings of the 3rd International Conference on Semantic Sensor Networks, vol. 668, pp. 17–32, CEUR-WS. org (2010)
10. Ranganathan, A., Shankar, C., Campbell, R.: Application polymorphism for autonomic ubiquitous computing. Multiagent Grid Syst. **1**(2), 109–129 (2005)

Middleware Support for Smart Homes and Health Telematic Services

A Distributed VCG-Like Multi-resource Allocation Algorithm for Multimedia Systems

Junjie Chen[✉], Hui Zhou, and Xiaomei Zhang

School of Electronics and Information, Nantong University, Nantong, China
cjjcy@ntu.edu.cn

Abstract. In this paper, we study the multi-resource allocation problem for multimedia systems, which aims at maximizing the total system utility under the resource capacity constraints. We model the resource allocation problem as a convex optimization problem and propose a pricing mechanism based resource allocation algorithm. This paper considers the strategic behaviors of the tasks. To prevent the tasks from manipulating the resource allocation, a distributed resource allocation algorithm based on VCG mechanism is proposed, which combines the pricing mechanism based algorithm with the VCG payments. Simulation results show that the proposed algorithm can achieve an approximately optimal resource allocation in polynomial time and it is robust against strategic manipulation from the tasks.

Keywords: Multi-resource allocation · Pricing mechanism · Strategic behavior · VCG mechanism

1 Introduction

Recently, the resource allocation problem for multitask systems attracts more and more attentions in many fields, such as networking, multimedia systems, real-time systems and distributed systems. In multitask systems, multiple elastic tasks share the system resources. Using the allocated resources, the tasks are executed and achieve the corresponding utilities. The resource allocation problem for multimedia systems studies how to optimally allocate the limited system resources to multiple multimedia tasks.

Rajkumar et al. proposed a QoS-based resource allocation model called Q-RAM, which aims to maximize the total system utility under the constraint that each task can meet the minimal resource requirements [1]. There are several approaches that can be used to compute optimal solutions, such as dynamic programming or mixed integer programming. However, these approaches are not suitable for real-time systems due to computational complexity. Lee et al. proposed several heuristic algorithms which can yield near-optimal solutions in polynomial time [2, 3].

Traditional resource allocation algorithms depend upon each task declaring its utility function truthfully. However, the tasks are often thought to be strategic and they may report their utility functions untruthfully to achieve as much resources as possible. The VCG mechanism is the most well-known method to prevent strategic manipulation, which incentivizes each task to report its utility function truthfully by introducing the VCG payments [4–6]. The standard VCG mechanism is a direct mechanism and

© Springer International Publishing Switzerland 2016
C.K. Chang et al. (Eds.): ICOST 2016, LNCS 9677, pp. 135–147, 2016.
DOI: 10.1007/978-3-319-39601-9_12

requires each task to report the entire utility function. To address this problem, Lazar and Semret proposed the progressive second price auction mechanism [7]. Subsequently, Maillé and Tuffin proposed a one-shot version of the PSP auction [8]. Since a direct mechanism requires centralized decision-making, it is not suitable for large-scale systems. To overcome this drawback, Parkes and Shneidman introduced the distributed implementations of VCG mechanisms [9, 10] and Tanaka et al. proposed a faithful implementation of dual decomposition [11].

This paper explicitly considers the strategic behaviors of the tasks, which may degrade the system performance significantly. We show that the resource allocation scheme based on VCG mechanism is robust against the strategic manipulation from the tasks. However, the centralized resource allocation scheme has some drawbacks. In this paper, we model the resource allocation problem as a convex optimization problem and propose a pricing mechanism based resource allocation algorithm. To prevent the tasks from manipulating the resource allocation, we combines the pricing mechanism based algorithm with the VCG payments and propose a distributed resource allocation algorithm based on VCG mechanism.

This paper is organized as follows. Section 2 presents the system model of the resource allocation problem. In Sect. 3, we analyze the impact of the strategic behaviors of the tasks on the resource allocation problem. In Sect. 4, we propose a distributed resource allocation algorithm based on VCG mechanism, which combines the pricing mechanism based algorithm with the VCG payments. Section 5 gives the simulation results of the proposed algorithm. Finally, the conclusions are presented in Sect. 6.

2 System Model

Consider a system consisting of n tasks $\{\tau_1, \tau_2, \ldots, \tau_n\}$ and m resources $\{\mathcal{R}_1, \mathcal{R}_2, \ldots, \mathcal{R}_m\}$. Each resource $\mathcal{R}_j$ has a finite capacity R_j and can be shared by n tasks, either temporally or spatially.

Let $r_{ij}(\in R_+)$ be the portion of resource $\mathcal{R}_j$ allocated to task τ_i. The task is executed using the allocated resources and obtains a utility u_i. The utility is improved by the allocation of additional resources.

The relationship between the utility and the requirement of a resource is described by a monotonically increasing resource consumption function ϕ_{ij}, where $\phi_{ij}(u_i)$ represents the amount of resource $\mathcal{R}_j$ required for the utility u_i. Hence, for a specified resource allocation $r_i = (r_{i1}, r_{i2}, \ldots, r_{im})$, the utility achieved by task τ_i is determined as follows,

$$u_i(r_i) = \underset{1 \leq j \leq m}{\text{minimize}} \quad \phi_{ij}^{-1}(r_{ij})$$

Each task τ_i has a weight w_i denoting its relative importance. The total system utility is defined as the weighted sum of the utilities, $U = \sum_{i=1}^{n} w_i * u_i$. For convenience, we denote the weighted utility of τ_i by u_i and then the total system utility is the sum of the weighted utilities, $U = \sum_{i=1}^{n} u_i$.

The objective of the resource allocation problem is to maximize the total system utility and satisfy the resource capacity constraints. The resource allocation problem is defined as follows,

$$\underset{r \geq 0}{\text{maximize}} \quad U = \sum_{i=1}^{n} u_i(r_i)$$
$$\text{subject to} \quad \sum_{i=1}^{n} r_{ij} \leq R_j, \forall j \tag{P}$$

It is easy to show that the problem (P) can be reduced to the following problem,

$$\underset{u \geq 0}{\text{maximize}} \quad U = \sum_{i=1}^{n} u_i$$
$$\text{subject to} \quad \sum_{i=1}^{n} \phi_{ij}(u_i) \leq R_j, \forall j \tag{P1}$$

3   Resource Allocation Based on VCG Mechanism

3.1   A Resource Allocation Game

From the above analysis, the resource allocation framework can be depicted by Fig. 1. The framework has two types of nodes, where the resource manager is in charge of allocating the resources to the tasks and the tasks provide information for determining the resource allocation.

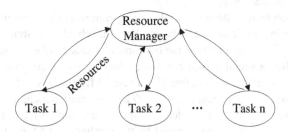

Fig. 1. Resource allocation framework

A centralized resource allocation scheme consists of the following steps:

Step1: Each task τ_i reports its type θ_i to the resource manager, where $\theta_i = (\phi_{i1}, \phi_{i2}, \ldots, \phi_{im})$.

Step2: Based on the types of all tasks $\theta = (\theta_1, \theta_2, \ldots, \theta_n)$, the resource manager determines the optimal resource allocation. For each task τ_i,

$$r_i(\theta) = (\phi_{i1}(u_i^*), \phi_{i2}(u_i^*), \ldots, \phi_{im}(u_i^*))$$

where $u_i^*, 1 \leq i \leq n$ is the optimal solution of the problem (P1).

The resource allocation problem is informationally decentralized, and it requires each task to report its type truthfully. However, the tasks are often thought to be self-interested in reality and they may have incentives to report their types untruthfully in an effort to obtain as much resources as possible.

The resource allocation problem with strategic tasks can be viewed as a resource allocation game. In this game, the players are all tasks, the strategies for a task are all possible types of the task, and the payoff of a task is the utility that the task achieves for any given type profile. For such a resource allocation game, we have the following proposition.

Proposition 1. When there exists at least one task that misreports its type, the resulting system utility is not more than that when each task reports its type truthfully.

Proof. Let $\hat{\theta}_i$ be the reported type of each task τ_i. Assume that there exists at least one task τ_k that reports its type untruthfully, i.e., $\hat{\theta}_k \neq \theta_k$. Then, the resulting resource allocation for each task τ_i is $r_i(\hat{\theta}) = (\hat{\phi}_{i1}(u_i^*(\hat{\theta})), \hat{\phi}_{i2}(u_i^*(\hat{\theta})), \ldots, \hat{\phi}_{im}(u_i^*(\hat{\theta})))$, where $u_i^*(\hat{\theta}), 1 \leq i \leq n$ is the optimal solution of the problem (P1) with the type profile $\hat{\theta}$. Since $r(\hat{\theta}) = (r_1(\hat{\theta}), r_2(\hat{\theta}), \ldots, r_n(\hat{\theta}))$ is a feasible solution to the problem (P) with the type profile θ, we have $\sum_{i=1}^{n} u_i(r_i(\hat{\theta}), \theta_i) \leq \sum_{i=1}^{n} u_i^*(\theta)$.

3.2   Resource Allocation Based on VCG Mechanism

Since the resource allocation problem is an informationally decentralized optimization problem and the tasks are strategic, we resort to mechanism design to obtain the optimal resource allocation.

The goal of mechanism design is to design a game which implements the desirable social choice rule in equilibrium. The basic idea of mechanism design can be depicted by Fig. 2. $\Theta = \prod_{i=1}^{n} \Theta_i$, where Θ_i is the type space of task τ_i; O is the set of outcomes; $f : \Theta \rightarrow O$ is called a social choice function, which maps a type profile $\theta \in \Theta$ to an outcome $o \in O$. A mechanism is defined by a pair $(\mathcal{M}, g)$, where $\mathcal{M} = \prod_{i=1}^{n} \mathcal{M}_i$, $\mathcal{M}_i$ is the strategy space of task τ_i, and $g : \mathcal{M} \rightarrow O$ is an outcome function. When given the preferences of each task over the outcomes, the mechanism $(\mathcal{M}, g)$ induces a game. A social choice function f is implemented by the mechanism $(\mathcal{M}, g)$ in equilibrium if there exists a profile of strategies $m = (m_1, m_2, \ldots, m_n)$ such that m is an equilibrium and $g(m(\theta)) = f(\theta)$ for all $\theta \in \Theta$.

A mechanism (Θ, f) is referred to as a direct mechanism. A direct mechanism (Θ, f) is dominant strategy incentive compatible(also known as strategy-proof) if

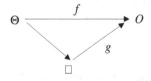

Fig. 2. Framework of mechanism design

truthful revelation is a dominant strategy for each task. According to revelation principle, if a social choice function f can be implemented by a mechanism $(\mathcal{M}, g)$ in dominant strategies, then the direct mechanism (Θ, f) is dominant strategy incentive compatible.

The mechanism $(\Theta, f = r)$ is not dominant strategy incentive compatible. In order to encourage the tasks to be truthful, the resource manager can introduce a monetary transfer function $t : \Theta \rightarrow R^n$. Then, the social choice function is the pair $f = (r, t)$. The preferences of task τ_i can be defined by a quasi-linear utility function,

$$\mathcal{U}_i(\hat{\theta}, \theta_i, r, t) = u_i(r(\hat{\theta}), \theta_i) + t_i(\hat{\theta})$$

and each task is considered to behave rationally to maximize this function.

Based on VCG mechanism, the payment of each task is defined as follows,

$$t_i^{VCG}(\hat{\theta}) = \sum_{j \neq i} u_j(r_{-i}(\hat{\theta}_{-i}), \hat{\theta}_j) - \sum_{j \neq i} u_j(r(\hat{\theta}), \hat{\theta}_j) \tag{1}$$

where $\hat{\theta}_{-i} = (\hat{\theta}_1, \ldots, \hat{\theta}_{i-1}, \hat{\theta}_{i+1}, \ldots, \hat{\theta}_n)$ and $r_{-i}(\hat{\theta}_{-i})$ is the optimal resource allocation with task τ_i taken out of the system. Then, $t_i^{VCG}(\hat{\theta})$ can be viewed as the utility loss of all other tasks due to the presence of task τ_i. The mechanism $(\Theta, (r, t^{VCG}))$ has the following properties.

Theorem 1. The mechanism $(\Theta, (r, t^{VCG}))$ is strategy-proof and allocatively efficient.

Proof. Since the transfer function is defined as (1), the net utility of task τ_i is

$$\begin{aligned}\mathcal{U}_i(\hat{\theta}, \theta_i, r, t^{VCG}) &= u_i(r(\hat{\theta}), \theta_i) - t_i^{VCG}(\hat{\theta}) \\ &= [u_i(r(\hat{\theta}), \theta_i) + \sum_{j \neq i} u_j(r(\hat{\theta}), \hat{\theta}_j)] - \sum_{j \neq i} u_j(r_{-i}(\hat{\theta}_{-i}), \hat{\theta}_j)\end{aligned} \tag{2}$$

Because the last term is independent of the reported type of task τ_i, task τ_i aims to maximize the terms in the square bracket in (2) by manipulating its type,

$$\underset{\hat{\theta}_i \in \Theta_i}{\text{maximize}} \quad u_i(r(\hat{\theta}_i, \hat{\theta}_{-i}), \theta_i) + \sum_{j \neq i} u_j(r(\hat{\theta}_i, \hat{\theta}_{-i}), \hat{\theta}_j)$$

It can be seen that truthful revelation is a dominant strategy for each task. Therefore, the mechanism $(\Theta, (r, t^{VCG}))$ is strategy- proof, from which allocative efficiency follows immediately.

Theorem 2. The mechanism $(\Theta, (r, t^{VCG}))$ is individual-rational and weakly budget-balanced.

Proof. By Theorem 1, each task reports its type truthfully. Then the net utility of task τ_i is

$$\mathcal{U}_i(\theta, \theta_i, r, t^{VCG}) = \sum_{j=1}^{n} u_j(r(\theta), \theta_j) - \sum_{j \neq i} u_j(r_{-i}(\theta_{-i}), \theta_j).$$

Since $r_{-i}(\theta_{-i})$ can be viewed as a feasible solution to the system with $r_i = 0$, we have

$$\sum_{j=1}^{n} u_j(r(\theta), \theta_j) \geq \sum_{j \neq i} u_j(r_{-i}(\theta_{-i}), \theta_j)$$

Therefore, $\mathcal{U}_i(\theta, \theta_i, r, t^{VCG}) \geq 0$, i.e., the mechanism satisfies individual rationality.

Next, we prove that the total transfer is nonnegative such that the resource manager does not require a subsidy, i.e.,

$$\sum_{i=1}^{n} t_i^{VCG}(\theta) \geq 0 \tag{3}$$

Substituting the transfer of each task by (1), we have

$$\sum_{i=1}^{n} t_i^{VCG}(\theta) = \sum_{i=1}^{n} [\sum_{j \neq i} u_j(r_{-i}(\theta_{-i}), \theta_j) - \sum_{j \neq i} u_j(r(\theta), \theta_j)]$$

Since any solution to the system with all tasks remains feasible to the system without any one task, the payment of each task is nonnegative. Therefore, (3) holds, i.e., the mechanism is weakly budget-balanced.

4   A Distributed VCG-like Resource Allocation Algorithm

The research on mechanism design mainly focuses on direct revelation mechanisms. However, direct mechanisms have some drawbacks. In the direct mechanism $(\Theta, (r, t^{VCG}))$, the tasks are asked to disclose their private information completely and the resource manager is required to compute the optimal resource allocation in a centralized manner. To overcome these drawbacks, we propose a distributed resource allocation algorithm.

In Sect. 4.1, we propose a pricing mechanism based multi-resource allocation algorithm, in which the tasks are assumed to be truthful. In Sect. 4.2, we take into account the strategic behaviors of the tasks and propose a distributed VCG-like multi-resource allocation algorithm.

4.1   A Pricing Mechanism Based Resource Allocation Algorithm

Usually, we assume that the resource consumption functions are convex. Then, the objective function $\sum_{i=1}^{n} u_i$ is concave, the inequality constraint functions $\sum_{i=1}^{n} \phi_{ij}(u_i) - R_j$ are convex, and the problem (P1) is a convex optimization problem. Thus, dual decomposition can be used to solve the problem (P1).

The Lagrangian of (P1) is defined as

$$L(u, \lambda) = \sum_{i=1}^{n} u_i - \sum_{j=1}^{m} \lambda_j \left(\sum_{i=1}^{n} \phi_{ij}(u_i) - R_j \right)$$
$$= \sum_{i=1}^{n} \left(u_i - \sum_{j=1}^{m} \lambda_j \phi_{ij}(u_i) \right) + \sum_{j=1}^{m} \lambda_j R_j$$

where $\lambda_j \geq 0$ is the Lagrange multiplier associated with the inequality constraint $\sum_{i=1}^{n} \phi_{ij}(u_i) - R_j \leq 0$ (the price of resource $\mathcal{R}_j$). The dual function is defined as the maximum value of the Lagrangian,

$$g(\lambda) = \underset{u \geq 0}{\text{maximize}} \ L(u, \lambda)$$

which is convex even if the original problem is not convex. The dual function can be decomposed into the following subproblems,

$$g_i(\lambda) = \underset{u_i \geq 0}{\text{maximize}} \ u_i - \sum_{j=1}^{m} \lambda_j \phi_{ij}(u_i) \tag{4}$$

which can be solved locally and independently. The solution to (4) is

$$u_i^*(\lambda) = \arg \underset{u_i \geq 0}{\max} \ u_i - \sum_{j=1}^{m} \lambda_j \phi_{ij}(u_i)$$

The dual problem is

$$\underset{\lambda}{\text{minimize}} \ g(\lambda) = \sum_{i=1}^{n} g_i(\lambda) + \sum_{j=1}^{m} \lambda_j R_j$$
$$\text{subject to } \lambda \geq 0$$

which is always a convex optimization problem even if the original problem is not convex.

Since the original problem is convex, under some conditions such as Slater's condition, the duality gap is zero. Hence, the original problem can be equivalently solved by solving the dual problem.

The gradient or subgradient method is often used to solve the dual problem. It is easy to show that the gradient or subgradient of the dual function is

$$R - \sum_{i=1}^{n} [\phi_{i1}(u_i^*(\lambda)), \dots, \phi_{im}(u_i^*(\lambda))]^T$$

Hence, the following gradient or subgradient method can be used,

$$\lambda_j(t+1) = [\lambda_j(t) - \alpha(R_j - \sum_{i=1}^{n} \phi_{ij}(u_i^*(\lambda(t))))]^+$$

where t is the iteration index, α is a positive step-size, and $[]^+$ denotes the projection onto the nonnegative orthant. To guarantee the gradient or subgradient method to converge to the optimal value, we can adopt a diminishing step-size rule. For convenience, however, we adopt a constant step-size. For a sufficiently small step-size, the gradient method converges to the optimal value and the subgradient method converges to within some range of the optimal value.

According to the above analysis, we propose a pricing mechanism based multi-resource allocation algorithm (PMRA),

Parameters: The resource consumption functions of each task ϕ_{ij} and the capacity of each resource R_j.

Initialization: Set the initial price for each resource $\lambda_j(0) \geq 0$.

Step 1: The resource manager informs all tasks of the price of each resource $\lambda_j(t)$.

Step 2: Each task computes the resource demand $\phi_{ij}(u_i^*(\lambda(t)))$ according to the price of each resource, and reports the result to the resource manager.

Step 3: The resource manager updates the price of each resource $\lambda_j(t+1)$ based on the resource demand of each task.

Step 4: Repeat the above steps until satisfying termination criterion.

At each iteration, we need to find a feasible solution u to the problem (P1) such that

$$\left\{ \begin{array}{l} \forall i \neq j, L_i'(u_i) = L_j'(u_j) \\ \forall j, \sum_{i=1}^n \phi_{ij}(u_i) \leq R_j \text{ and } \exists k, \sum_{i=1}^n \phi_{ik}(u_i) = R_k \end{array} \right\}$$

where $L_i(u_i)$ is the Lagrangian of task τ_i. The above problem can be solved by a bisection search algorithm.

Let u^* be the optimal solution to the problem (P1). For any feasible (u, λ), we have $\sum_{i=1}^n u_i \leq \sum_{i=1}^n u_i^* \leq g(\lambda)$. Then, it is satisfied that $\sum_{i=1}^n u_i^* - \sum_{i=1}^n u_i < \varepsilon$ provided that $g(\lambda) - \sum_{i=1}^n u_i < \varepsilon$. Thus, we can take $g(\lambda) - \sum_{i=1}^n u_i < \varepsilon$ as termination criterion.

4.2   A Distributed VCG-like Resource Allocation Algorithm

The PMRA algorithm depends on the convexity of the problem (P1). To guarantee the convexity of the resource consumption functions, we introduce convexity checking.

Convexity Checking: Let $m_i = \{u_i, (r_{i1}, r_{i2}, \ldots, r_{im})\}$ be the messages from task τ_i. For m_i^1, m_i^2, m_i^3, if $u_i^1 < u_i^2 < u_i^3$, then

$$\frac{r_{ij}^3 - r_{ij}^2}{u_i^3 - u_i^2} \geq \frac{r_{ij}^3 - r_{ij}^1}{u_i^3 - u_i^1}$$

The PMRA algorithm can be decomposed into two parts: a slave algorithm s_i for each task τ_i and a master algorithm g for the resource manager, such that $(g \circ s)(\theta) = r(\theta)$ for all θ. In the PMRA algorithm, each task is assumed to be truthful. In practice, however, the tasks are strategic and may perform the slave algorithms untruthfully.

To encourage the tasks to perform the slave algorithms truthfully, the payment of each task is defined as follows,

$$t_i = \sum_{j \neq i} u_j((g \circ s_{-i})(\hat{\theta}_{-i}), \hat{\theta}_j) - \sum_{j \neq i} u_j((g \circ s)(\hat{\theta}), \hat{\theta}_j)$$

$$= \sum_{j \neq i} u_j(r_{-i}(\hat{\theta}_{-i}), \hat{\theta}_j) - \sum_{j \neq i} u_j(r(\hat{\theta}), \hat{\theta}_j)$$

Finally, we can get a distributed mechanism $(\mathcal{M}, g)$, where $\mathcal{M} = \{s(\hat{\theta}) | \hat{\theta} \in \Theta\}$, such that $(g \circ s)(\hat{\theta}) = f(\hat{\theta})$ for all $\hat{\theta}$. The distributed mechanism $(\mathcal{M}, g)$ has the following property.

Theorem 3. The distributed mechanism $(\mathcal{M}, g)$ implements the social choice function $f = (r, t^{VCG})$ in dominant strategies $s(\theta)$ if the direct mechanism (Θ, f) is strategy-proof.

Proof. Since the direct mechanism (Θ, f) is strategy-proof, we have

$$\mathcal{U}_i(f(\theta_i, \hat{\theta}_{-i}), \theta_i) \geq \mathcal{U}_i(f(\hat{\theta}_i, \hat{\theta}_{-i}), \theta_i)$$

for all θ_i, all $\hat{\theta}_i \neq \theta_i$, and all $\hat{\theta}_{-i}$. Since $(g \circ s)(\hat{\theta}) = f(\hat{\theta})$ for all $\hat{\theta}$, we have

$$\mathcal{U}_i(g \circ (s_i(\theta_i), s_{-i}(\hat{\theta}_{-i})), \theta_i) \geq \mathcal{U}_i(g \circ (s_i(\hat{\theta}_i), s_{-i}(\hat{\theta}_{-i})), \theta_i)$$

for all θ_i, all $\hat{\theta}_i \neq \theta_i$, and all $\hat{\theta}_{-i}$, i.e., $s_i(\theta_i)$ is a dominant strategy for each task τ_i. Thus, the distributed mechanism $(\mathcal{M}, g)$ implements the social choice function $f = (r, t^{VCG})$ in dominant strategies $s(\theta)$.

Since only an approximately optimal resource allocation $\hat{r}(\theta)$ is achieved for the system with the type profile θ, Theorem 3 no longer holds [12]. Hence, we introduce a weaker notion as follows.

Theorem 4. The distributed mechanism $(\mathcal{M}, g)$ approximately implements the social choice function $f = (r, t^{VCG})$ in dominant strategies $s(\theta)$, i.e., for any $\delta_1 > 0$, $\delta_2 > 0$, there always exists $\varepsilon > 0$ such that

1. $\|g \circ s - f\| < \delta_1$,
2. $\forall i, \forall \theta_i, \forall \hat{\theta}_i, \forall \hat{\theta}_{-i}, \mathcal{U}_i(g \circ (s_i(\theta_i), s_{-i}(\hat{\theta}_{-i})), \theta_i) > \mathcal{U}_i(g \circ (s_i(\hat{\theta}_i), s_{-i}(\hat{\theta}_{-i})), \theta_i) - \delta_2$.

Proof. The PMRA algorithm is guaranteed to converge to the optimal value. Therefore, there always exists $\varepsilon > 0$ such that

$$\|g \circ s - f\| < \delta_1.$$

Since $\hat{r}(\theta_i, \hat{\theta}_{-i})$ is an approximate solution to the problem (P) with the type profile $(\theta_i, \hat{\theta}_{-i})$, we have

$$U - [u_i(\hat{r}_i(\theta_i, \hat{\theta}_{-i}), \theta_i) + \sum_{j \neq i} u_j(\hat{r}_j(\theta_i, \hat{\theta}_{-i}), \hat{\theta}_j)] < \varepsilon$$

where U is the optimal value of the problem (P). On the other hand, $\hat{r}(\hat{\theta}_i, \hat{\theta}_{-i})$ is a feasible solution to the problem (P) with $(\theta_i, \hat{\theta}_{-i})$, then we have

$$u_i(\hat{r}_i(\hat{\theta}_i, \hat{\theta}_{-i}), \theta_i) + \sum_{j \neq i} u_j(\hat{r}_j(\hat{\theta}_i, \hat{\theta}_{-i}), \hat{\theta}_j) \leq U$$

Therefore, there always exists $\varepsilon > 0$ such that

$$\mathcal{U}_i(g \circ (s_i(\theta_i), s_{-i}(\hat{\theta}_{-i})), \theta_i) > \mathcal{U}_i(g \circ (s_i(\hat{\theta}_i), s_{-i}(\hat{\theta}_{-i})), \theta_i) - \delta_2.$$

5 Experiment Results

In this section, we present the simulation results. In Sect. 5.1, we analyze the impact of the strategic behaviors on the system performance by a Bayesian game based resource allocation problem. In Sect. 5.2, we examine the convergence of the PMRA algorithm.

5.1 Impact of Strategic Behaviors on System Performance

In order to analyze the impact of the strategic behaviors on the system performance, we introduce a Bayesian game based resource allocation problem. The type space of each task is finite, i.e., $|\Theta_i| < \infty, 1 \leq i \leq n$. The joint probability distribution of the types $p(\theta), \theta \in \Theta$ is known a priori. For a task with type θ_i, its expected utility for reporting type $\hat{\theta}_i$ is

$$\sum_{\hat{\theta}_{-i} \in \Theta_{-i}} p(\hat{\theta}_{-i}|\theta_i) u_i(r_i(\hat{\theta}_i, \hat{\theta}_{-i}), \theta_i)$$

Therefore, its Bayesian Nash equilibrium strategy is

$$\theta_i^* = \arg\max_{\hat{\theta}_i \in \Theta_i} \sum_{\hat{\theta}_{-i} \in \Theta_{-i}} p(\hat{\theta}_{-i}|\theta_i) u_i(r_i(\hat{\theta}_i, \hat{\theta}_{-i}), \theta_i)$$

In Fig. 3, we compare the Bayesian Nash equilibrium solutions with the optimal solutions in different scenarios (e.g., different type sets for each task, different joint probability distributions over types). It can be seen that the system performance degrades due to strategic manipulation from the tasks.

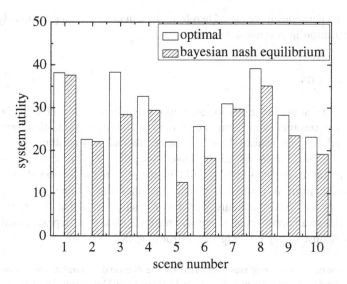

Fig. 3. Impact of strategic behaviors on system performance

5.2 Convergence of the PMRA Algorithm

Next, we examine the convergence of the PMRA algorithm. Consider a system with 10 tasks and 4 resources, and apply the PMRA algorithm with a constant step-size $\alpha = 10^{-4}$.

Figure 4 shows the iterative process of the PMRA algorithm. It can be observed that the feasible solution of the original problem converges to the optimal solution as

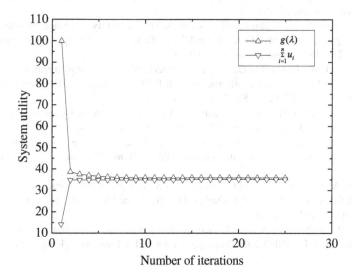

Fig. 4. Convergence of the PMRA algorithm

the number of iterations increases. Therefore, we can obtain an approximately optimal resource allocation in polynomial time.

6 Conclusions

In this paper, we study the multi-resource allocation problem for multimedia systems. We model the resource allocation problem as a convex optimization problem and propose a pricing mechanism based resource allocation algorithm. The tasks are assumed to be self-interested and behave rationally. To prevent the tasks from manipulating the resource allocation, a distributed resource allocation algorithm based on VCG mechanism is proposed, which combines the pricing mechanism based algorithm with the VCG payments. Simulation results show that the proposed algorithm can achieve an approximately optimal resource allocation in polynomial time and it is robust against strategic manipulation from the tasks.

Acknowledgments. This work was supported by the National Natural Science Foundation of China (61174065), Natural Science Fund for Colleges and Universities in Jiangsu Province, China (15KJD520002).

References

1. Rajkumar, R., Lee, C., Lehoczky, J., Siewiorek, D.: A resource allocation model for QoS management. In: 18th IEEE Real-Time Systems Symposium, pp. 298–307. IEEE Press, San Francisco (1997)
2. Lee, C., Lehoczky, J., Siewiorek, D., Rajkumar, R., Hansen, J.: A scalable solution to the multi-resource QoS problem. In: 20th IEEE Real-Time Systems Symposium, pp. 315–326. IEEE Press, Phoenix (1999)
3. Lee, C., Lehoczky, J., Rajkumar, R., Siewiorek, D.: On quality of service optimization with discrete QoS options. In: 5th IEEE Real-Time Technology and Application Symposium, pp. 276–286. IEEE Press, Vancouver (1999)
4. Stoenescu, T.M., Ledyard, J.O.: A pricing mechanism which implements a network rate allocation problem in Nash equilibria. In: 45th IEEE Conference on Decision and Control, pp. 1270–1277. IEEE Press, San Diego (2006)
5. Fu, F., Stoenescu, T.M., van der Schaar, M.: A pricing mechanism for resource allocation in wireless multimedia applications. IEEE J. Sel. Top. Sign. Proces. 1(2), 264–279 (2007)
6. Su, S., van der Schaar, M.: On the application of game-theoretic mechanism design for resource allocation in multimedia systems. IEEE Trans. Multimedia 10(6), 1197–1207 (2008)
7. Lazar, A.A., Semert, N.: Design, Analysis and Simulation of the Progressive Second Price Auction for Network Bandwidth Sharing. Department of Electrical. Engineering, Columbia University, New York (1998)
8. Maillé, P., Tuffin, B.: Multibid auctions for bandwidth allocation in communication networks. In: IEEE INFOCOM 2004, pp. 54–65. IEEE Press, Hongkong (2004)

9. Parkes, D.C., Shneidman, J.: Distributed implementations of vickrey-clarke-groves mechanisms. In: 3rd International Joint Conference on Autonomous Agents and Multiagent Systems, pp. 261–268. IEEE Press, New York (2004)
10. Shneidman, J., Parkes, D.C.: Specification faithfulness in networks with rational nodes. In: 23rd Annual ACM SIGACT-SIGOPS Symposium on Principles of Distributed Computing, pp. 88–97. ACM Press, St. John's (2004)
11. Tanaka, T., Farokhi, F., Langbort, C.: A faithful distributed implementation of dual decomposition and average consensus algorithms. In: 52nd IEEE Conference on Decision and Control, pp. 2985–2990. IEEE Press, Firenze (2013)
12. Kothari, A., Parkes, D.C., Suri, S.: Approximately-strategyproof and tractable multiunit auctions. Decis. Support Syst. **39**(1), 105–121 (2005)

An ADL Recognition System on Smart Phone

Yunfei Feng[1(✉)], Carl K. Chang[1], and Hanshu Chang[2]

[1] Computer Science Department, Iowa State University, Ames, IA, USA
{yunfei,chang}@iastate.edu
[2] Department of Computer Science and Information Engineering,
National Central University, Taoyuan, Taiwan
abc0963285350@g.ncu.edu.tw

Abstract. Multiple kinds of sensors in smart homes have been used successfully and widely on various pattern recognition tasks. In order to detect user's activities of daily living (ADLs), an array of sensors have to be installed in many places in a smart home or armed upon a user's body. Here, we present an approach for collecting and detecting activities data only via a smart phone, which largely reduces the cost of setup in a smart home and energy consumption. To the best of our knowledge, this study represents a pioneering work where a single-point smart phone is used to capture ADLs. The ADLs indoor are recognized by analyzing the data combination of sound, orientation, and Wi-Fi signals. This study engages real-life data collection, and the results from four test environments show that all of the ADL recognition rates are above 90 %.

Keywords: Auditory analysis · Audio classification · Wi-Fi RSSI fingerprinting · Orientation · SVM · Smart home

1 Introduction

Globally, older adults living independently, alone or with their spouse only, is a common trend. Researchers developed a smart assisted living (SAIL) system [1] to provide support to elderly people, patients, and the disabled. A health-driven smart home is a habitation equipped with a set of sensors, actuators, automated devices to provide ambient intelligence for daily living task support, early detection of distress situations, remote monitoring and promotion of safety and well-being [2,3].

A motivation of this work is to collect data for clinically relevant activities of daily living (ADL) (e.g. diet, personal hygiene, toilet usage, etc.) only via a single-point smart phone. Usually, staff in healthcare center collects residents' ADLs data via observation by the nurse or direct report of residents. Some commercial living-assistant products keep track of residents' ADLs, while those ADLs are recorded and typed into system manually. Some automation technologies are applied to detect ADLs in high-tech healthcare center. For instance, foot plantar pressure sensors, embedded in the foot pad of a bathroom, can detect whether the room is used. However, various sensors need to spread out to every

© Springer International Publishing Switzerland 2016
C.K. Chang et al. (Eds.): ICOST 2016, LNCS 9677, pp. 148–158, 2016.
DOI: 10.1007/978-3-319-39601-9_13

corner in a room. Our project reduces the cost of setup hardware in a smart home, so that everyone who has a smart phone with different sensor sources can eventually benefit from such a system.

2   Related Work

Multiple kinds of sensors are applied to retrieve living data for activity recognition. Based on our literature review, there are three major ways to deploy sensors to determine the elderly people's ADLs. First, most research groups built their own experimental smart home by placing a large number of traditional sensors distributed at different spots. For example, they put door contacts [2,4], infra-red sensors [4], button sensors to detect the use of utilities, such as lamp switches, faucets and microphones [2,4,5]. However, the microphones are just to detect the existence of sound, rather than to analyze the human's activities by the acoustic features. Second, nowadays, we have more advanced computer vision technology to employ. We can analyze the activity pattern on video images. Kinect, integrating audio sensors, high quality motion-tracking camera, infrared projector and many underlying algorithms make it easier to detect human's activities. However, the viewing angle of each Kinect is just a "43° vertical by 57° horizontal" field of view. Also Kinect costs much more than regular cameras. Third, many kinds of body-contact sensors help research, such as chest nodes, finger nodes, and waist nodes [6]. Some researches named the technology as the Body Sensor Network (BSN) [7].

However, the first and second methods mentioned above require high cost of equipment and installation. Once a health-driven smart home system is built, the layout of furniture is no longer flexible. In addition, the whole system should be kept working at any time. The third method makes elderly people feel burdensome by fixing many sophisticated sensors on body every morning, and feeling uncomfortable through the whole day.

A method based on extracting acoustic information from audio files is proposed. Specifically, since the acoustic characteristics of many sounds are different, typical ADLs (e.g. diet, personal hygiene, walking, etc.) can be detected and recognized by examining the sound file.

The remainder of paper is organized as follows: Sect. 3 outlines the concept of Wi-Fi RSSI fingerprinting; Sect. 4 illustrates the principle of computing orientation using Android system; Sect. 5 deals with the feature extraction from audio file; Sect. 6 describes the system architecture; Sect. 7 is the experiment design; results discussion comes in Sect. 8; and, finally, Sect. 9 concludes the paper.

3   Wi-Fi Fingerprinting

Global Positioning System (GPS) is widely used to retrieve position. Unfortunately it is difficult to use for indoor applications due to weak signal. When Wi-Fi based devices are becoming popular, and the Wi-Fi access points are widely distributed indoor, Wi-Fi Positioning System (WPS) [8,9] is a newly proposed method for localization. By combining GPS and Wi-Fi-based Received Signal Strength Indicator (RSSI) information, we can derive the location where the audible events take place. If a record has strong GPS signal and there is none or unknown Wi-Fi-based RSSI, it is more likely to be taken from outdoor. On the other hand, if a record has relatively weak GPS signal and Wi-Fi-based RSSI, it is more likely to be taken from indoor. After analyzing more on the combined strength characteristics of Wi-Fi access points (APs), it can predict indoor location more precisely. In this task, we use Wi-Fi-based RSSI from dense access points dedicated for localization.

Trilateration algorithm [10] is a traditional method to estimate the position by calculating distances from a mobile device to each access points in the signal space. However, this algorithm works better in an ideal space model, which assumes that distance is the single factor for signal loss. In a real building, the interior environment is more complicated, such as walls (non-bearing and bearing), hallways and signal reflection. Even enhanced algorithms based on this cannot deal with such complex situations. Therefore, in this work, we do not apply trilateration algorithm for localization estimation.

Fingerprint-based localization [11] is another widely used technique for location indicator. To build a Wi-Fi fingerprinting database, it is required to accumulate Wi-Fi RSSI data from several access points. In the prediction process, it uses a certain algorithm to search in a Wi-Fi fingerprinting database, find the closest records to the live targeted RSSI value, and predict potential location.

In this project, we use the existing Wi-Fi infrastructure, and accumulate the Wi-Fi RSSI data by the same smart phone with ADL recorder, which is highly recommended to guarantee the same context. The location estimation in our project is just to find the potential area (room) rather than very accurate location. Therefore, it reduces much calculation overhead. We use support vector machine (SVM) as a classifier to complete localization prediction.

The more rooms a building has, the better Wi-Fi RSSI fingerprinting each room represents. If there are more interior walls, especially load-bearing walls, and the larger distances between each segmented room, the Wi-Fi RSSI environments among other rooms differ more, so the combination of many Wi-Fi RSSIs is more distinctive. In this way, it is easier to determine locations between totally different buildings.

4   Orientation Detection

The rotation matrix in Android system computes the rotation around x, y and z axes which transforms from previous rotation matrix (prevR) to this current rotation matrix (R). System method of getRotationMatrix() computes the inclination matrix I as well as the rotation matrix R transforming a vector from the device coordinate system to the world's coordinate system which is defined as a direct orthonormal basis, where:

- x is defined as the vector product $y \cdot z$ (It is tangential to the ground at the device's current location and roughly points East).

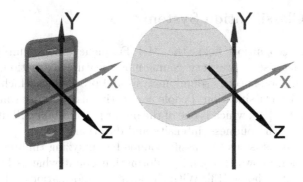

Fig. 1. The device coordinate system and the world's coordinate system

- y is tangential to the ground at the device's current location and points towards the magnetic North Pole and the device is facing the sky.
- z points towards the sky and is perpendicular to the ground.

The Android operating system is set up to calculate a rotation matrix R which is defined by $\mathbf{R} = \begin{bmatrix} E_x & E_y & E_z \\ N_x & N_y & N_z \\ G_x & G_y & G_z \end{bmatrix}$, where x, y and z are axes relative to the smartphone, see Fig. 1, and where

$$\mathbf{E} = (E_x, E_y, E_z) = \text{a unit vector which points East}$$
$$\mathbf{N} = (N_x, N_y, N_z) = \text{a unit vector which points North}$$
$$\mathbf{G} = (G_x, G_y, G_z) = \frac{\text{a unit vector which points away from}}{\text{the centre of the earth (gravity vector)}}.$$

Once R has been calculated, the Android operating system will then calculate the Euler angles ϕ, θ and ψ where

$$\begin{aligned} \text{azimuth} &= \phi = \text{rotation about } \mathbf{G} \\ \text{pitch} &= \theta = \text{rotation about } \mathbf{E} . \\ \text{roll} &= \psi = \text{rotation about } \mathbf{N} \end{aligned} \tag{1}$$

The relationship between R and (ϕ, θ, ψ) is given by

$$\begin{bmatrix} \cos\phi\cos\psi - \sin\phi\sin\psi\sin\theta & \sin\phi\cos\theta & \cos\phi\sin\psi + \sin\phi\cos\psi\sin\theta \\ -\sin\phi\cos\psi - \cos\phi\sin\psi\sin\theta & \cos\phi\cos\theta & -\sin\phi\sin\psi + \cos\phi\cos\psi\sin\theta \\ -\sin\psi\cos\theta & -\sin\theta & \cos\psi\cos\theta \end{bmatrix} . \tag{2}$$

The azimuth ϕ is a particularly important result, where $\phi = 0$ corresponds to the direction of North; $\phi = 90$ corresponds to the direction of East. The magnetic field information is available not only outdoor, but also indoor, even in a basement.

5   Sound Classification System

In the speech recognition field, the Mel Frequency Cepstrum Coefficients (MFCCs) characteristics are very common for feature extraction, while this study deals with "non-speech" sound analysis and processing, which determines the indoor activity classification. People can distinguish activity sounds by ears according to timbre [12], which is one of the major perceptual attributes of sound associated with pitch, loudness, intensity and duration.

Computers can assist us to classify sounds by analyzing timbres. Household sounds recognition allows to compile information about what is happening at any given moment at home [13]. With the location information and orientation, we can infer the individual's activity every time. For example, the sound of running water or washing dishes provides the particular acoustic information in the kitchen, etc.

Fourier analysis converts time (or space) to frequency and vice versa. A fast Fourier transform (FFT) is an algorithm to compute the discrete Fourier transform (DFT) and its inverse. For each audio file, first we convert it into mono sound. Then, it proceeds to add a sliding window to cut the frames, then to get a spectrogram for each *windowedFrame* by FFT, then to compute the climax amplitudes of the signal at each particular frequencies range. As such, we get a 3-tuple of (time, frequency, amplitude). At last, we can get fingerprints (timbre) by hashing [14] the peak frequencies and time difference between peaks.

6   System Architecture

The proposed system architecture is shown as Fig. 2. The audio files are recorded and stored in an individual's smart phone. The raw audio files will be further processed into acoustic features, and compared with audio file database to be classified into each activity category, which is a template- matching stage.

The data from multiple sensors on the smart phone are captured, including orientation of the heading of phone, light level around the phone, GPS and other features, such as StepDetector, accelerator and timestamp.

The smart phone can automatically detect the nearby Wi-Fi access points. Each position has its own Wi-Fi fingerprinting, which is the combination of Wi-Fi RSSI values from each access point. Therefore, we can determine the indoor positions by classifying the Wi-Fi fingerprinting via SVM multi-class classifier.

7   Preliminary Case Study

7.1   Experimental Living Environment

In a preliminary study, we test our ADL recognition system in four apartments. Here we only give one such apartment of size $900\,\text{ft}^2$ to illustrate, and the layout of which is shown in Fig. 3.

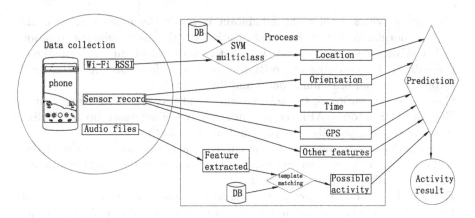

Fig. 2. System architecture, including data collection, process of sensing data, and activity prediction parts.

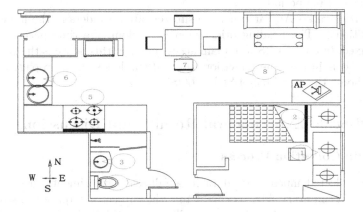

Fig. 3. Floor layout of one apartment in experiment

The circles are ADL capturing points, and the arrow around circle denotes the most frequent facing orientation in each from observation. Currently, we just use a bedroom (Position 1), a bathroom (Position 3), a living room (Position 8) with a combined kitchen (Position 5) for this work. A main Wi-Fi access point is on the top of TV set in the living room (Position 8). The smart phone used is Nexus 5 made by Google and has the latest Android 6.0.1 Marshmallow operating system.

7.2   Activities of Daily Living

In this experiment, we observe seven frequent ADLs:

– Working on desktop PC in the bedroom - The subject often works on computer and does some reading at position 1. Here, the ADL recorder can capture the sound of keyboard typing and detect heading orientation facing East.

- Hygiene activities - Once the inhabitant is inside the bathroom, he could perform normal hygiene activities at position 4 or do some washing at position 3. For privacy respect, we leave the toilet records out of our research. When the subject does washing at position 3, he has to face East, and the APP records the sound of running water and flushing toilet.
- Cooking - At position 5, the subject cooks and prepares food facing South. Here the ADL recorder APP records the sound of boiling water, boiler, jingling sound of cooking utensils, chopping and so on so forth.
- Washing dishes - At position 6, the subject washes dishes, vegetable, fruits and etc. The ADL recorder can capture the running water sound and detect that the heading orientation is West.
- Eating - If just one subject in the apartment, the seat at point 7 is most frequently used when he has meals for best convenience. So the ADL recorder can capture the sound of kitchen utensils and detect that heading orientation is North. We can distinguish the breakfast, lunch, dinner and mid-night snack in terms of time period.
- Wandering walk - Any at time, the subject often wanders in the living room at position 8. The heading orientation is random, the time period is more than fixed, but Wi-Fi RSSI of main access point in this house is the strongest, because it is just on the television set, and wireless signals propagate to the smart home through Line-of-Sight (LOS).

8   Full-Scale Experimental Results and Discussions

8.1   Data Collection Process

We then collected much more data in a full-scale experiments, from real-life situations. When every ADL is conducted, the subject is required to select the ADL label on screen, which is quite similar to the think-aloud process. A total of 3511 standard ADL records (including indoor and outdoor) are stored, and only indoor records are selected to pass on to the prediction stage.

8.2   Experiment Part 1: Location Prediction

A total of 720 valuable data records have been taken, which are from 9 APs altogether, each reading is in different combination of the parameters. Along with each ADL recorded, a real-time combination of RSSI is recorded as well, with the location of the ADL being conducted. Thus, in the prediction stage the RSSI data is further used to estimate the position.

In the study, 70 percent of the samples are used as a training set and 30 percent as a testing set. After running the SVM multi-classes algorithm, the prediction error rate on the test set is 10.22 %.

8.3   Experiment Part 2: Orientation Detection

Sometimes, external magnetic fields cause the measuring of the Earth's magnetic field inaccurate. Thus, the precision of indoor magnetic fields becomes a main issue. In real environments, different sources (metal structures, electrical apparatus, sound speaker, etc.) also generate magnetic fields, which incurs deviations to measuring. To compensate this shortcoming, we record the orientation at least twice each time, to improve the accuracy.

In the situation when the subject puts his smart phone in a direction deriving from the expected norm, or interfering magnetic fields exist, some adjustments need to be made. For example, the ideal orientation of "cooking" is South, while the results set is [Southeast, South, Southwest]. Our APP will calibrate it to the South-heading direction. One way to handle this situation is to split the experimental room into several cells according to the principle of not putting two ADLs with the same orientation in one cell. To describe it in another way, it is acceptable only when just one ADL type with the same orientation is investigated in one cell. For example, in our experimental apartment, even though kitchen and living room are two functional ranges, we still can put them into one cell. Note that cooking at position 5 is facing South, washing dishes at point 6 is facing West, eating on the dining table is facing North. Neither of them conflicts each other, so the kitchen and living room can be simplified into one cell. Another advantage of this principle is that the Wi-Fi access point is on the top of TV, and there is not a major obstacle, such as a wall, between the living room and kitchen. So in this cell, Wi-Fi signals are transmitted through line-of-sight, the received signals are in a relatively simple channel model.

8.4   Experiment Part 3: Environmental Sound Classification

The basic audio samples templates should be selected by audio experts to achieve better prediction. A total of valuable 526 indoor audio records are predicted in this process. Each audio length is no less than 15 s for better performance.

The predicted results might be either some possible activities or NONE, where NONE means this predicting module cannot classify the targeted audio file into any category.

One reason why this predicting module gives NONE result is that when someone is eating, the sound does not have any or little feature of eating sound, such as collision of dishes, moving utensils. So computer cannot predict it as an "eating" activity via audio processing. Often in such cases, even human ears cannot differentiate audio categories. In this case, in order to predict the correct activity, it is necessary to compensate the caveat by compiling information from other data, such as location, orientation, light level, etc. Another reason is that the phone is in a pocket or far from audio source, so the amplitude is not loud enough to predict accurately.

8.5   Experiment Part 4: ADL Prediction

In this section, we introduce how the ADL prediction works.

Working on PC at Home: We can find a pattern corresponding to the activity of "working on PC at home", that is the heading direction around East in the bedroom.

Wandering Walk Detection: When the subject is on the move (walking or running), the value of "stepdetector" is set into 1.0, which means steps are detected. Combined with the location and orientation information, we know where the subject is walking and his heading direction. The location information can be obtained from GPS, or from Wi-Fi fingerprinting pre-stored in database while he is indoor, no matter he is at home or in other buildings. By the increasing value of sensor STEPCOUNTER and the interval of two records, the pace can be calculated.

Other ADLs: For those activities conducted either in kitchen, living room or bathroom, we focus on the use of J48 pruned tree algorithm in the WEKA [15] tool to learn the patterns of different activities and classify them using location, orientation and sound information. The types of activities corresponds to those described in Sect. 7.2. Wandering walk belongs to "Wandering walk"; bathroom belongs to "Hygiene activities"; breakfast, lunch, dinner, midnightsnack belongs to "eating"; washinginbathroom belongs to "Hygiene activities"; and cooking, chopping, washingdishes belongs to "cooking".

A total of 980 valuable instances are fed into J48 pruned tree to train a pattern out. The number of correctly classified instances is 896, and the accuracy rate is 92.35 % by cross-validation. The confusion matrix is shown in Fig. 4.

```
 a   b   c   d   e   f   g   h   i  <---- classified as
81   0   0   0   0   0   0   0   0 | a = bathroom
 0  58   0   0   8   0   0   1   0 | b = midnightsnack
 0   0 247   0   0   1   0   8   0 | c = cooking
 0   0   0 120   2   0   0   1   0 | d = lunch
 0   9   0   0 112   0   0   4   0 | e = dinner
 0   0   0   0   0   6   0   3   0 | f = chopping
 0   0   0   0   0   0 129   0   0 | g = washinginbathroom
 0   9  20   4   5   6   0 127   1 | h = washingdishes
 0   0   0   0   0   0   0   2  16 | i = breakfast
```

Fig. 4. Confusion matrix

The sound of running water from faucet always goes with flushing toilet, so that the sound is not pure to "using bathroom". However, the two ADLs have different heading orientations, and the predictions of "using bathroom" and "washing in bathroom" gain high accuracy. "Cooking" sometimes mis-classified as "Washing dishes" can be accepted, because the sound of moving utensils, running water, collision of dishes happens together. The group of "eating" ADLs is in high accuracy, except that a small portion was mis-interpreted between "midnight snacks" and "Dinner". That is mainly because the characteristics of "midnight snacks" and "Dinner" are similar. The prediction mistakes of "washing dishes" spread to all "eating" groups and "cooking", that is because all of those categories may have the similar sound, such as moving utensils, collision of dishes, etc.

ADL recognition performances in another three apartments are 96.15 %, 99.17 % and 98.92 %, respectively.

9   Conclusions and Future Works

This paper proposes an ADL recognition system that collects data by multiple sensors on a smart phone, and extracts location, orientation information, etc. This study makes it possible to collect ADL data just by one Android-based smart phone, which can be accessible to many common users. Activity audio files are recognized by matching acoustic features with an audio feature database. The location information is retrieved by Wi-Fi RSSI values, possible activities are recognized by acoustic features, and orientations are computed by Android phones' sensing data. The activity results are determined mainly by these three sources. The preliminary results show that the average recognition rate of ADL is satisfactory. Future work will include improving the predication accuracy, and estimating the possible activities in one audio file including many micro-actions taken with interleaving sounds.

Acknowledgments. We would like to acknowledge the tremendous support provided by professor Muchun Su of National central university in order to conduct a full-scale experiment and collect a significant amount of data.

References

1. Zhu, C., Sun, W., Sheng, W.: Wearable sensors based human intention recognition in smart assisted living systems. In: International Conference on Information and Automation, ICIA 2008, pp. 954–959, June 2008
2. Sehili, M.A., Lecouteux, B., Vacher, M., Portet, F., Istrate, D., Dorizzi, B., Boudy, J.: Sound environment analysis in smart home. In: Paternò, F., de Ruyter, B., Markopoulos, P., Santoro, C., van Loenen, E., Luyten, K. (eds.) AmI 2012. LNCS, vol. 7683, pp. 208–223. Springer, Heidelberg (2012)
3. Demongeot, J., Virone, G., Duchne, F., Benchetrit, G., Herv, T., Noury, N., Rialle, V.: Multi-sensors acquisition, data fusion, knowledge mining and alarm triggering in health smart homes for elderly people. C. R. Biol. **325**(6), 673–682 (2002). longevite et vieillissement
4. Fleury, A., Noury, N., Vacher, M.: Supervised classification of activities of daily living in health smart homes using svm. In: Engineering in Medicine and Biology Society, EMBC 2009, Annual International Conference of the IEEE, pp. 6099–6102, September 2009
5. Chahuara, P., Fleury, A., Portet, F., Vacher, M.: Using markov logic network for on-line activity recognition from non-visual home automation sensors. In: Paternò, F., de Ruyter, B., Markopoulos, P., Santoro, C., van Loenen, E., Luyten, K. (eds.) AmI 2012. LNCS, vol. 7683, pp. 177–192. Springer, Heidelberg (2012)

6. Zhu, C., Sheng, W.: Multi-sensor fusion for human daily activity recognition in robot-assisted living. In: Proceedings of the 4th ACM/IEEE International Conference on Human Robot Interaction, HRI 2009, pp. 303–304. ACM, New York (2009)
7. Yang, G., Yacoub, M.: Body Sensor Networks. Springer, New York (2006)
8. Cypriani, M., Lassabe, F., Canalda, P., Spies, F.: Open wireless positioning system: a wi-fi-based indoor positioning system. In: Vehicular Technology Conference Fall (VTC 2009-Fall), 2009 IEEE 70th, pp. 1–5, September 2009
9. Lubbad, M., Alkurdi, M., AbuSamra, A.: Robust indoor wi-fi positioning system for android-based smartphone. Int. J. Res. Bus. Technol. **3**(2), 159–162 (2013)
10. Oguejiofor, O.S., Aniedu, A.N., Ejiofor, H.C., Okolibe, A.U.: Trilateration based localization algorithm for wireless sensor network (2013)
11. Lee, J.-Y., Yoon, C.-H., Park, H., So, J.: Analysis of location estimation algorithms for wifi fingerprint-based indoor localization. In: SoftTech 2013, ASTL, vol. 19, pp. 89–92 (2013)
12. Quesnel, R.: Computer-assisted training of timbre perception skills. In: ICMC, International Computer Music Conference Proceedings (1994)
13. Lozano, H., Hernáez, I., Picón, A., Camarena, J., Navas, E.: Audio classification techniques in home environments for elderly/dependant people. In: Miesenberger, K., Klaus, J., Zagler, W., Karshmer, A. (eds.) ICCHP 2010, Part 1. LNCS, vol. 6179, pp. 320–323. Springer, Heidelberg (2010)
14. Wang, A.L., F, T.F.B.: An industrial-strength audio search algorithm. In: Proceedings of the 4th International Conference on Music Information Retrieval (2003)
15. Weka data mining software. http://www.cs.waikato.ac.nz/ml/weka/

A Scalable Clinical Intelligent Decision Support System

Hua Chu, Yijing Yang, Qingshan Li[✉], Yongfei Xu, and Hongpeng Wei

Software Engineering Institute, Xidian University, Xi'an 710071, China
qshli@mail.xidian.edu.cn

Abstract. It is a known fact that Clinical Decision Support System (CDSS) can help to improve the quality of medical. But the existing CDSSs are mostly focused on a typical disease. Single knowledge base and limited decision support results have a heavy impact on the application of CDSS in clinical medicine. To improve the scalability of extending new diseases to the CDSS, this paper proposes a scalable architecture named Open Clinical Decision Support Platform (OCDSP) that can customize and develop CDSS for any kind of diseases. Using the tool sets of OCDSP, one can configure medical knowledge bases, workflows of clinical paths, and clinic rules. Finally, a concrete CDSS of a specific disease can be customized from OCDSP. The software architecture of OCDSP is discussed detailed. In order to validate the scalability of OCDSP, the case study of how to customize CDSS for fracture and coronary heart disease is put forward.

Keywords: Scalability · Clinical Decision Support System (CDSS) · Open Clinical Decision Support Platform (OCDSP)

1 Introduction

The Clinical Decision Support System (CDSS) is a computer program that uses the design principle of the expert system to realize the automation of clinical diagnosis and treatment of diseases. CDSS has commonly used in an effort to reduce medication errors [1]. It can conveniently and effectively assist doctors with complex clinical work, such as complete data collection, disease diagnosis, treatment, and prevention etc. A systematic review concluded in 2005 that CDSSs improved practitioner performance in 64 % of the studies, and patient outcomes in 13 % of the studies [2]. Because of the advantages of CDSSs, a lot of scholars and vendors are working on the development of CDSS. Velickovski et al. developed a CDSS offering a suite of services for the early detection and assessment of chronic obstructive pulmonary disease [3]. Al-Hyari et al. proposed a new CDSS for diagnosing patients with Chronic Renal Failure [4], and J S Huang et al. designed a clinical decision support model for predicting pneumonia readmission [5]. However, most of the existing CDSSs only for one type disease with a single knowledge base, limited decision support content is difficult to meet the needs of clinicians, hindering the application of the CDSS. Therefore, researching on developing a CDSS supporting diagnosis and treatment of diverse disease becomes more useful. From the above, an Open Clinical Decision Support Platform (OCDSP) is proposed in paper. A concrete CDSS for a specific disease can be customized from OCDSP through the corresponding tools provided by OCDSP.

© Springer International Publishing Switzerland 2016
C.K. Chang et al. (Eds.): ICOST 2016, LNCS 9677, pp. 159–165, 2016.
DOI: 10.1007/978-3-319-39601-9_14

2   System Architecture Design

Due to difference between diverse diseases, the medical knowledge, clinic rules and clinical paths used to treatment different patients are not same either. And with the development of medical science, medical knowledge is constantly updated. To achieve the expansion of CDSS for either existing or new disease, how to expand and updating medical knowledge base is the primary consideration. The software architecture of OCDSP is shown in Fig. 1. There are three main parts contained in OCDSP, *rules and knowledge development environment*, *knowledge management environment* and *operation support environment*.

Rules and knowledge development environment is used to develop clinical pathway rules and expert knowledge in the medical field. It guarantees the customization of medical information about different diseases. Domain experts can use the tool set in rules and knowledge development environment to generate medical knowledge, clinic rules and clinical paths for specific disease. There are three tools in this tool set. The function of the **expert knowledge modeling tool** is to design the structure and content of the knowledge base. The **clinic rules designing tool** is used to create and edit clinic rules. The **clinical paths workflow modeling tool** achieves modelling clinical pathways visibly and creating workflow files automatically.

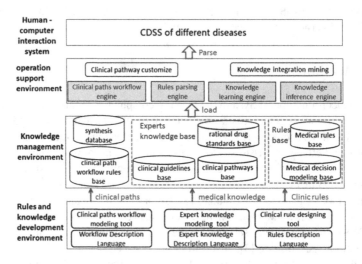

Fig. 1.   Open clinical decision support platform architecture

Knowledge management environment is responsible for the storage and management of all kinds of knowledge, rules and models, including clinical expert knowledge base, rules base, synthesis database and clinical pathway workflow rules base. Clinical expert knowledge base provides the knowledge of clinical pathways, clinical guidelines and rationale drug standards supporting the decision making and reasoning. Rules base contains clinic rules and clinical decision-making models, providing rules and expert algorithm.

Operation support environment includes platform-driven engine, open integration environment and a variety of application modules. The clinical path workflow engine controls the operational process of CDSS by analyzing workflow files. Knowledge inference engine and rules parsing engine provide diagnosis and treatment decision-making service for doctors.

Based on this architecture, the inference engine and knowledge are layered by separating the metadata and execution logic. That implements the flexible expansion of medical knowledge, clinical path rules and clinic rules for a variety of diseases.

3   Operation Mechanism of OCDSP

OCDSP uses workflow technology to modeling the care process in clinical paths, to control and manage the operational process of CDSS for different diseases. According to the characteristics of care process in clinical paths, and common workflow modeling methods jPDL4.4 and BPMN2.0, we design workflow model including activities, transfer and connections three kinds of elements. This workflow model and other details are proposed by us in the paper [6]. And, workflow modeling tool generates workflow files based on this model. Therefore, the concrete CDSS customized from OCDSP is driven by the clinical path workflow files. The operation mechanism of OCDSP is shown as Fig. 2, and the running steps are as follows.

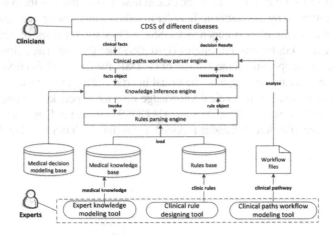

Fig. 2. Schematic overview of platform operation

Step 1: **Encapsulate Clinical Facts**. When CDSS for different diseases works, clinical path workflow engine finds and analyzes workflow model files for target disease that modeled by clinical paths workflow modeling tool, and assigns task in workflow files to appropriate execution units according to the executive order. It encapsulates clinical facts of patient that collected by clinical doctors into the facts object according to the interface defined by the system, and transfers it to the knowledge inference engine.

Step 2: **Parse Clinic Rule**. The knowledge inference engine calls rules parsing engine according to the clinical fact types. Then, the rules parsing engine loads different resources and extracts key information in clinic rules files generating rules object. The dependency between the objects is based on the concept of object-oriented model, parsing method is proposed by us in the paper [7]. Then, the rule objects are returned to knowledge inference engine.

Step 3: **Inference Decision**. The knowledge inference engine needs to make matching and reasoning according to the rules and the facts object, using a comprehensive clinical decision method based on event driven to get reasoning results. The comprehensive reasoning method includes rule-based forward reasoning, fuzzy inference decision tree and case-based reasoning method supporting for clinical decision-making. The detailed reasoning model and method are discussed in [8]. The knowledge inference engine also needs to synthesize reasoning results, and load the result evaluation system to evaluate the results' confidence level. Finally, clinical reasoning results which meet evaluation condition are returned to clinical path workflow engine, and back to CDSS client at last, so as to effectively assist clinicians in clinical work.

4   Case Study

The scalability of OCDSP shows that it can extend new disease through the corresponding custom tools provided by the platform. In order to validate this feature, the customization process and the results of two concrete CDSSs, CDSS for fractures of tibial plateau (TPFCDSS) and CDSS for unstable angina (UACDSS) are illustrated as following.

According to the operational mechanism of OCDSP, the first work of customization is configuring the clinical knowledge by the visual interface of expert knowledge modeling tool in order to generate new medical knowledge data for expert knowledge base. The Symptoms collection page of TPFCDSS and UACDSS is shown in Figs. 3 and 4, respectively. Knowledge of different diseases is added into different CDSS based on OCDSP.

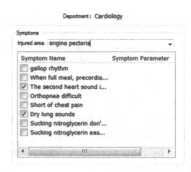

Fig. 3. Symptoms collection of TPFCDSS   **Fig. 4.** Symptoms collection of UACDSS

Then, clinical paths of fractures of tibial plateau and unstable angina must be configured. This work is implemented by drawing clinical paths using clinical paths workflow modeling tool which finally generates new workflow files to control the diagnosis and treatment process of CDSS. The running results of TPFCDSS and UACDSS are shown in Figs. 5 and 6. These system screenshots represent clinical paths of the two diseases are incorporated into the CDSS by clinical path workflow engine.

Fig. 5. Process navigation of TPFCDSS   **Fig. 6.** Process navigation of UACDSS

Finally, editing clinic rules of fractures of tibial plateau and unstable angina by clinic rules designing tool shown as Fig. 7. It can generate new clinic rules files supporting the decision-making of the CDSS automatically. The scalable clinical intelligent decision support system is shown as Fig. 8. It provides the final diagnosis decision results for fracture of tibial plateau and surgical decision making results for unstable angina, etc.

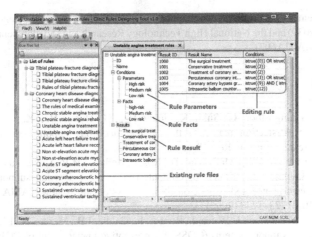

Fig. 7. Clinic rules designing tool

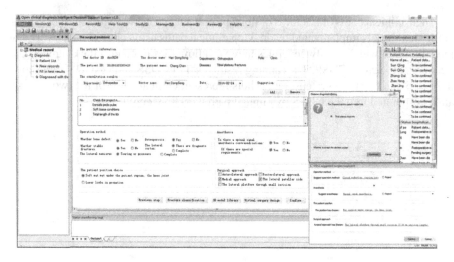

Fig. 8. CDSS and decision points

5   Conclusion and Future Work

The work describes the software architecture and operation mechanism of an Open Clinical Decision Support Platform (OCDSP). The scalability of OCDSP can help users to extend new decision-making ability of CDSS for different diseases. To validate this feature, case study of two concrete CDSS is given. Now the OCDSP is just a prototype system. In future work, we will continue to improve and complete the system. The final objective is to apply OCDSP and the customized CDSS to clinic.

Acknowledgments.   This research was supported by the National Natural Science Foundation of China (61202039) and the National High Technology Research and Development 863 Program of China (2012AA02A603).

References

1. Junghee, K., Young Moon, C., Sukil, K., Seung Hee, H., Hyong Hoi, K., Chun Bok, P.: A study on user satisfaction regarding the clinical decision support system (CDSS) for medication. Healthc. Inform. Res. **18**(1), 35–43 (2012)
2. Garg, A.X., Adhikari, N.K., McDonald, H., Rosas-Arellano, M.P., Devereaux, P.J., Beyene, J., Sam, J., Haynes, R.B.: Effects of computerized clinical decision support systems on practitioner performance and patient outcomes: a systematic review. JAMA J. Am. Med. Assoc. **293**(10), 1223–1238 (2005)
3. Velickovski, F., Ceccaroni, L., Roca, J., Burgos, F., Galdiz, J.B., Marina, N., Lluch-Ariet, M.: Clinical decision support systems (CDSS) for preventive management of COPD patients. J. Transl. Med. **12**(Suppl 2), S9 (2014)

4. Al-Hyari, A.Y., Al-Taee, A.M., Al-Taee, M.A.: Clinical decision support system for diagnosis and management of Chronic Renal Failure. In: Conference on Applied Electrical Engineering and Computing Technologies (AEECT 2013), pp. 1–6 (2013)
5. Huang, J.S., Chen, Y.F., Hsu, J.C.: Design of a clinical decision support model for predicting pneumonia readmission. In: International Symposium on Computer, Consumer and Control (IS3C), pp. 1179–1182 (2014)
6. Qingshan, L.I., Chu, H., Haidong, W.U., Yang, Z.: Workflow-based dynamic modeling for clinical path in CDSS. Int. J. Adv. Comput. Technol. $5(6)$, 596–603 (2013)
7. Gao, Y.: The Research and Implementation of Rules Engine in Open Clinical Intelligent Decision Support System. Xidian University (2013)
8. Li, Q., Feng, J., Wang, L., Chu, H., Fu, W.: Knowledge reasoning model to support clinical decision making. In: Bursa, M., Khuri, S., Renda, M. (eds.) ITBAM 2014. LNCS, vol. 8649, pp. 75–78. Springer, Heidelberg (2014)

E-Health and Chronic Disease Management

Experience Flow Mapping: Gaining Insights in Designing Tools to Support Low-Sodium Diet

Idowu Ayoola[1,2(✉)], Adriaan de Regt[2], Mart Wetzels[1], and Sander van Berlo[2]

[1] Technology University of Eindhoven, Eindhoven, The Netherlands
i.b.i.ayoola@tue.nl
[2] Onmi B.V., Eindhoven, The Netherlands

Abstract. This paper introduces a through experience flow study wherein the participants are followed throughout their groceries, cooking and eating activities to map out their experiences. The goal is to help a couple to understand their experiences in preparing a challenging meal and at the same time, keeping a low sodium diet. The ultimate goal is to develop dietary tools that can support the self-management of chronic patients. This work helps us to gain new insights to develop further three design concepts (e.g., a cooking utensil to track sodium intake, a spectrometer device to measure the nutritional content of foods and tableware to measure food whilst serving or eating). We describe the method adopted, and the results are discussed.

1 Introduction

Today, there is growing need for citizens to be central to managing their health [8]. Lifestyle factors—like healthy dieting or active lifestyle—are becoming the cornerstone in the self-management of health and wellbeing. Recent studies have shown these behavioural factors to have long-term benefits on general health performance [5]. There is a trend in using technology to empower citizens in the self-management process and to provide insights or guidance on relevant behaviours.

We are interested in chronic heart patients, managing their food content is significant for them. Many of these patients are placed on sodium restriction and should ensure to eat healthily. However, keeping a regulated nutritional composition of their meals is very challenging for many reasons. For example, the patients may not eat in isolation due to stigmatisation; the household will influence the food a chronic patient will eat; information on food composite are not easily accessible, etc. For these reasons, we are developing new sets of devices that may support the patients in regulating their diet. To obtain new insights into the development of the tools to measure sodium or other nutritional values, we at this moment perform an observational study. The study implements behavioural mapping with a focus on individual-centred mapping. Two volunteers are asked to participate in a role-playing while using tools that are represented by paper cards. The actual tools are still under development within the European

© Springer International Publishing Switzerland 2016
C.K. Chang et al. (Eds.): ICOST 2016, LNCS 9677, pp. 169–179, 2016.
DOI: 10.1007/978-3-319-39601-9_15

DoCHANGE project [4] and are not usable yet. Hence the use of paper cards to represent the tools. Relevant studies [6,9] that we found use interview methods to understand cooking behaviour but the findings were not rich on experience to help us gain early insights on how these tools should be conceived so as to develop them further from a user experience point of view. We hereby employ the use of experiential methods as a pilot study.

2   Methodology

We employed a unique combination of paper based scenario and the behaviour mapping method with a focus on individual-centered mapping. Behavioural mapping [11] is a systematic observation method to track behaviour over space and time. Individual-centred mapping requires following, or tracking, the movement of an individual by using photography or video recording; for this study the participants were visually accompanied within a specified time-frame. The study focusses on the following topics:

Context. Location and moment
Usability. Desired usage and actual usage of tools
Interaction. Shape, affordances, and interaction between participants.

The participants are asked to role-play and prepare a meal that is new to them, *Chicken Madras*. The reason for choosing a new meal is to challenge them in selecting appropriate groceries, ingredients and spices with low sodium. Alongside, they are given a set of paper cards in place of functional tools and are asked to use creatively to be aware of the sodium content in the selected and consumed foods. The interaction between participants is observed during the entire process—for grocery shopping, cooking, and dining. The parameters recorded using video, photography and taking note, during this observation are:

- Location
- Amount of time spent at location
- Tools used
- Interaction with tools
- Interaction between users

The study concluded with an interview to elaborate specific observations.

2.1   Role-Play

The two participants are asked to role-play as partners. The male partner has a heart problem and is required to watch his sodium intake while his partner usually takes charge of cooking. Compared to their normal lives, they now require drastic changes in their lifestyle, as they need to watch their activity throughout the day, fluid and sodium intake. The participants were asked to focus on lowering sodium intake for the sake of this study.

2.2   Tools

We provide the participants with four card types that include a graphic illustration of the tools they represent and a short description of their functions. The first category represented cooking utensils integrated with sensor technology that can measure salt content or the nutritional composition of food; the second represented a tableware integrated with sensor technology that can scan or identify food content and the third represents a tool that could scan food or identify food content. To facilitate the creation of new tools, the fourth type of card was added which was blank. The blank card allows the participants to specify a new tool which they thought was relevant in a situation. The tools were intentionally not described concretely to give room for the user's creativity. The participants are asked to keep the cards in their pockets until usage. They are encouraged to verbalise their thoughts and the desired functions when using the tool. The participants are free to recreate or apply the tools as they deem fit. See Fig. 1 for the tool-cards.

2.3   Activities

Participants were asked to do groceries, prepare food and dine; including a main dish and dessert. To increase the challenge of adhering to a low-sodium diet, the recipe was predefined. An unfamiliar recipe was chosen for the study to provoke consideration of the participants' interaction and behaviour during the activities. The locations of the study were defined as *the food store*, *kitchen*, and *dinner table*. To simulate reality, the study took place at the participants' home.

2.4   Participants

A couple was recruited to participate in the study. The male, 28 years of age, and his female partner, 26 years of age, agreed to participate in the study. The male participant has a professional background in technology and female participant has a background in social sciences. The participants are without children and have been living together for several months.

3   Processing

3.1   Experience Flow Mapping

The written observations, photographs, video recording, and interview results have been used to make an Experience Flow Diagram (EFD). EFD shows an overview to understand where and how the new products/services can be introduced during the performed activities. EPD is developed by Philips [10] for understanding the user experience and presenting qualitative and quantitative findings in a process diagram supported by visual and textual information. This approach enabled the communication of the concept, usability and interaction as mentioned in Sect. 2.

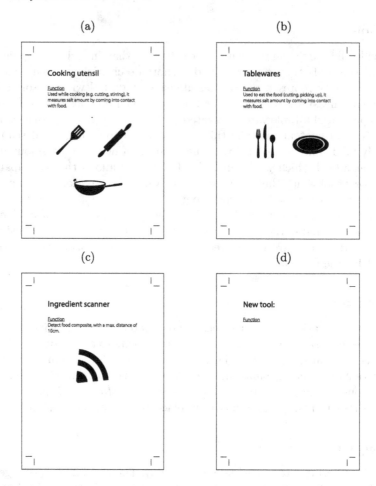

Fig. 1. (a) Cooking utensils integrated with sensor technology. (b) Tableware integrated with a sensor technology. (c) Tools used for scanning food or identifying food content. (d) Empty cards used to draw new ideas.

3.2 Affinity Diagramming

The method of Affinity Diagramming [3] was applied to abstract clusters from the collected data alongside the EFD. Similar abstractions have been clustered per *location/phase* and translated to show the inferences presented in Table 1.

4 Results

4.1 Experience Flow Mapping

The Experience Flow Diagram shown in Fig. 2 depicts the following:

– Overall scenario/experiences
– Amount of time spent at location/phase

- Used and created tools
- Quotes from participants
- Observations
- Activities in chronological order.

The duration of the role-playing scenario was 3.25 h and was positioned in four locations: living room, supermarket, kitchen, and dining table. Seven phases were identified:

1. Inventorying in the living room (5 min)
2. Selecting shopping items (30 min)
3. Purchasing in the supermarket (2 min)
4. Preparing in kitchen (25 min)
5. Cooking in kitchen (30 min)
6. Serving at the dinner table (3 min)
7. Consuming at the dinner table (20 min)

The observations are visualised in Fig. 2 and exemplified below:

Ingredient Scanner. The ingredient scanner was used 8 out of 13 tool-usages; showing recurrent usage throughout the scenario. The scanner was easily adopted in multiple scenarios and locations.

Cooking Utensils. The cooking utensil was left at home during the inventory phase because they are less applicable for grocery shopping.

New Tools. The male participant showed interest in using his own senses to measure sodium-content. For example, by determining the softness of a bread, he believed he could know how salty the bread was.

Intuition. The male participant intuitively knew what products contain high sodium levels; he was however not aware of sodium in tomatoes.

Finding Information. During the selection phase a large amount of time was spent on finding and obtaining information on the nutritional values of spices. The participants requested help from the shop-assistant and used the ingredient scanner to detect nutritional differences between fresh and grounded spices.

Old Habits. The participants were not instructed to have a specific item for desert. During the selecting phase the participants took this advantage to buy cookies which turned out to have high sodium content.

Lack of Taste. The participants jointly agreed that with less sodium, the food would lack taste and their guests would suffer from that. The male participant did not want other people to suffer due to his condition. During dinner the female participant (caretaker) added salt to her food whilst stating that "I know it's not good for me but I am addicted to the taste of salt."

Information Overload. The participants commented that the tools should not cause an information overload when cooking so they can enjoy their cooking experience.

Social Acceptance. The male participant preferred the use of the tools to be subtle to reduce stigmatisation and allow him to eventually adhere to his low sodium diet. He said: ".. the tools will most likely be used when peer pressure is high, and you would want to hide the tool, to not appear sick."

Cheating Day. The participant indicated that on occasions, they would like to be rewarded for their efforts in circumventing the challenges in keeping a healthy diet. They suggested the concept of a cheating day for which they will allow themselves to (at the least) eat some cookies.

4.2   Affinity Diagramming

The result of the Affinity diagram shown in Table 1 presents the abstracted user-needs from the Experience Flow. These are translated into clusters with descriptions shown in Table 1. The Inference column lists the interpreted requirements of the users per location and phase.

5   Discussion

It is important to examine individuals from a range of social groups and social classes as such key variables are a significant influence on attitudes about cooking and help account for variation in behaviour. The recent work in [6] interviewed 27 participants to study food-related habits in both British and French populations and was able to derive some generalisable constructs. In this paper, we included a couple which makes our findings subjective as intended as an early stage pilot study. Murcott in [9] also suggests that a limitation of mere interview-based research into food and cooking is that it has relied on what people say they do rather than observing what they actually do. We set out to circumvent this limitation by following through the experiences of the couple to gain rich insights to what they need and do.

The couple had a unifying role in preparing their meal. This role can differ in other homes depending on family culture or traditions. The female partner who was not narrated with a heart condition complied to cooking a no-sodium diet, however, maintained a different identity which allowed her to add table salt to her served meal. The article in [12] describes the construct of a home as a site for unified consumption practices wherein the household members can actively influence what they eat. For a holistic design, these separate roles should be well understood—in homes with patients with sodium restriction—and considered in the design of the tools.

Based on the inferences presented in Table 1 it is evident that products and services should be aware of purchases and consumed foods throughout the time-frame of buying and eating. The act of measuring food contents with portable tools can make it easier for users to obtain information on the content of foods at different locations. Because users become more aware of their diet contents in general, they can make informed choices. To facilitate the use of the relevant technology in multiple places, such new technology should take a discrete form to avoid stigmatisation. It was also suggested that the device should provide minimal information or interventions to allow a natural use.

A salt reduction framework [1] was initiated by the European Union in 2012 to reduce the amount of sodium that reaches one's home. This initiative supports

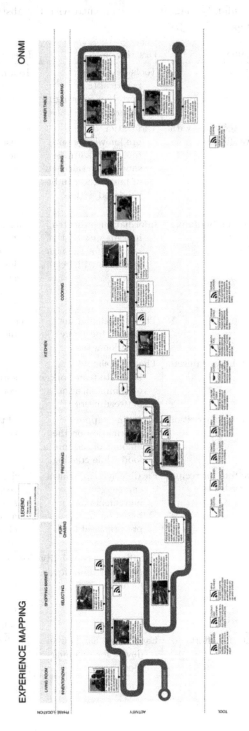

Fig. 2. Experience Flow Diagram that captures participant's shopping, cooking and dining experiences (for readability, a copy can be downloaded in [2]).

Table 1. Results from the affinity diagramming combined with the abstractions from the experience flow mapping.

Phase	Cluster name	Description	Inference
Living room (*Inventory-ing*)	Practicality	Tools have to be practical (e.g. portable) to bring to supermarket	Tool has to be relevant for the activity or food
Shopping market (*Selecting*)	Intuitive interaction with data verification	Verification of pre-knowledge with tools (e.g. softness showed the saltiness of bread and can be validated with a tool)	User can appreciate use of sense and feeling (tactile experience)
	Information on Sodium, ingredient, and additives	Information presented in a manner that is relevant for the user (e.g. filtered labels)	Information has to be relevant, accessible and instantly available (e.g. filtered, digital, or personal)
Shopping market (*Paying*)	Shopping flow	The tools should not require too many additional tasks	The tools should not disrupt shopping experience
Kitchen (*Preparing*)	Interaction between users	The tools should facilitate teamwork or communication between users	The tool should support social cooking
	Validation of composition	Providing support information on the amount of sodium in food while cooking	Need to verify food content with tool
	Suggestive tool for recipes and ingredients	Flexible system, which can suggest ingredients options based on pre-prepared foods	Desire for a recommendation system that accounts for changes in ingredients
	Avoidance	Avoiding the availability of high sodium foods at home	More engagement with food in the supermarket to persuade users from buying salty food
	Practicality for effort saving	Easy to use hands-free device for scanning food	Quick to use tool.

Continued

Table 1. *Continued*

Phase	Cluster name	Description	Inference
Kitchen (*Cooking*)	Eco-system solution	Inventory system that knows what is at home, what is bought and what is cooked	System needs to be aware of what is in house, bought and consumed (to provide accurate options)
	Worry-free cooking	Only buy healthy foods. This takes away the risk of cooking or eating unhealthy	System should provide guidance in the inventorying or selecting phases
	Verify by taste	Taste and measure the food to verify sodium content	The cook should be encouraged to monitor food content by taste
	Enjoy cooking	When preparing food, they go into intimate details with the food items as compared to the purchasing phase	The products or services should provide only subtle guidance or clues at this stage of preparing meals
	Challenging tool	When tools are used for a longer time, the participants desired new surprises in using the tools (This is similar to the notion of challenge vs. skill [7])	The tools or services should have a game element to it
	Tool for multiple locations	Ability to use the tool outside of home	The tool should be portable
	Sensual coach	The tools can teach the user to use their own senses to know the sodium content of food (e.g. to measure saltiness by taste)	Coaching can train the person cooking to rely on taste
Dinner table (*Serving*)	Less information regarding sodium content	At this stage, the need for information decreases. They simply want to enjoy the meals that has been prepared	Less coaching is desired when approaching the consumption phase
Dinner table (*Consuming*)	Validation and reward	Validating that the food has been properly prepared. At this point, little or nothing can change	They should be encouraged to monitor nutritional content at the various phases of preparing their meal. They can be rewarded for keeping a healthy diet
	Common understanding	There may be a common understanding with the partner or companion to be aware of the nutritional targets and be involved in the process of changing	The tools or services should enable collaborators to facilitate the involvement and understanding of others

a strategy wherein, series of chained behaviour are altered to avoid eventually eating high sodium foods. Using the tools as a means to provide early stage intervention at the planning and purchasing phases becomes plausible to limit acquiring unhealthy foods that can ultimately lead to consumption.

The following are the main requirements abstracted from the study:

- The products and services should aid the user in defining appropriate ingredients (required for a healthy and low sodium diet) during the planning phase.
- Aid the user in purchasing the ingredients that are defined as appropriate.
- Create awareness for the user during the cooking phase on how individual ingredients, either purchased or already in-house, contribute to the total nutritional value of the dish.
- Validate the low sodium content of the dish during the consuming phase.

6   Summary

A user observational study was conducted with a couple to understand their experiences in preparing a challenging meal and at the same time, keeping a low sodium diet. The methodology explored enabled participants to use a "new" and as yet non-envisaged technology solution. Additional evaluation is required to further substantiate the outcome measures.

It was evident that the products or services that will benefit from this study should be aware of the phases between inventorying items for groceries and dining. The couple took relatively little time to shop for the ingredients, as they had already decided ingredients in the inventory phase. Without intervening in the inventorying phase and guidance throughout the selection phase, we think they are more likely to fall back on their usual shopping behaviour. The inventorying and selection phases are essential to prevent buying unhealthy foods. When preparing food, they go into intimate details with the food items. Hence, little or subtle guidance is needed not to ruin their cooking experience. The dining phase should be about confirming the healthy nutritional value of the food, and allow participants to be rewarded and feel at ease. Overall care should be taken to avoid disrupting their regular shopping, cooking and eating rituals.

7   Conclusion

This paper presents an early stage pilot (user observational study) in preparation for a larger study which aims to examine the use of technology for promoting self-management of diet. At the time of writing, the technology toolset required to facilitate the application area remains undeveloped, and so we simulate their usage via a paper-based scenario, and we reveal some of the discovered user-requirements that the anticipated system should consider.

Acknowledgments. We like to thank the two participants for spending their time and for providing so much feedback during and after the study.

References

1. Eu salt reduction framework (2012)
2. Ayoola, I.: Experience flow diagram for understanding cooking experience (2016). https://goo.gl/fCnfVl
3. Beyer, H., Holtzblatt, K.: Contextual Design: Defining Customer-Centered Systems. Elsevier, Amsterdam (1997)
4. Do CHANGE: Do cardiac health advance new generation ecosystem. http://www.do-change.eu. Accessed 15 Feb 2016
5. Forouzanfar, M.H., Alexander, L., Anderson, H.R., Bachman, V.F., Biryukov, S., Brauer, M., Burnett, R., Casey, D., Coates, M.M., Cohen, A., et al.: Global, regional, and national comparative risk assessment of 79 behavioural, environmental and occupational, and metabolic risks or clusters of risks in 188 countries, 1990–2013: a systematic analysis for the global burden of disease study 2013. Lancet **386**(10010), 2287–2323 (2015)
6. Gatley, A., Caraher, M., Lang, T.: A qualitative, cross cultural examination of attitudes and behaviour in relation to cooking habits in france and britain. Appetite **75**, 71–81 (2014)
7. Koufaris, M.: Applying the technology acceptance model and flow theory to online consumer behavior. Inf. Syst. Res. **13**(2), 205–223 (2002)
8. Lorig, K.R., Sobel, D.S., Ritter, P.L., Laurent, D., Hobbs, M.: Effect of a self-management program on patients with chronic disease. Effective Clin. Pract. ECP **4**(6), 256–262 (2000)
9. Marshall, D.W.: Food Choice and the Consumer. Springer Science & Business Media, New York (1995)
10. Philips: Experience flows, 4 May 2015
11. Sommer, B., Sommer, R.: A Practical Guide to Behavioral Research: Tools and Techniques. Oxford University Press, New York (1991)
12. Valentine, G.: Eating in: home, consumption and identity. Sociol. Rev. **47**(3), 491–524 (1999)

Design and Implementation of Fall Detection System Using MPU6050 Arduino

Ziad Tarik Al-Dahan[2], Nasseer K. Bachache[1(✉)], and Lina Nasseer Bachache[2]

[1] University College of Humanity Studies, Najaf, Iraq
Tech_n2008@yahoo.com
[2] Al-Nahrain University, Baghdad, Iraq

Abstract. Fall is the most significant causes of injury for Elderly or Epilepsy. This has led to develop a many types of automatic fall-detection systems. However, prevalent methods only use accelerometers to isolate falls from activities of daily living (ADL). This paper proposes combination of a simple threshold method and acceleration measurement to detect falls and fall-detection. To demonstrate the activity of proposed scheme a device has been designed. We used an Arduino-UNO, also we used MPU6050 as a sensor and we can measure the velocity and acceleration by calculate the derivative for the phase this program was C-language. Several fall-feature parameters and possible falls are calibrated through an algorithm. The implementation of program built to read an analogue variable from its port as an additional adjustment to fixed the upper and the lower. The total sum acceleration vector ACC to distinguish between falling and ADL. The results using the simple threshold, PMU, and combination of the simple method and MPU were compared and analyzed. The proposed MPU reduced the complexity of the hardware also the algorithm exhibited high accuracy.

Keywords: Fall Detection Systems (FDS) · Activities of Daily Living (ADL) · MPU6050-Arduino

1 Introduction

Fall is the most significant causes of injury for elderly. These falls are because many disabling fractures that could eventually go in front to death due to complications. Most elderly (over 75 years old) have fallen at least once a year, and 24 % of them have severe injuries [1]. Among people affected by Alzheimer's disease, the probability of a fall increases by three times. Elderly care can be improved by using sensors that monitor the vital signs and activities of patients, and remotely communicate this information to their doctors and caregivers. For example, sensors installed in homes can alert caregivers when a patient falls. Some fall detection algorithms also assume falls happen when the body lies prone on the floor. But they are less effective when a person's fall posture is not horizontal as shown in Fig. 1.

The consequences of a fall can vary from scrapes to fractures and in some cases lead to death. Even if there are no immediate consequences, the long-wait on the floor for help increases the probability of death from the accident. For this reason, fall detection is an active area of research. Most of the research on falls in which accelerometers is

© Springer International Publishing Switzerland 2016
C.K. Chang et al. (Eds.): ICOST 2016, LNCS 9677, pp. 180–187, 2016.
DOI: 10.1007/978-3-319-39601-9_16

Fig. 1. Falls of patient's body on the floor

used focus on determining the change in magnitude of acceleration. When the acceleration value exceeds a critical threshold, the fall is detected [2, 3]. A contribution is made towards such standardization by collecting the most relevant parameters, data filtering techniques and testing approaches from the studies done so far. State-of-the-art fall detection techniques were surveyed, highlighting the differences in their effectiveness at fall detection. A standard database structure was created for fall study that emphasizes the most important elements of a fall detection system that must be considered for designing a robust system [4], as well as addressing the constraints and challenges. In addition, fall activity patterns are particularly difficult to obtain for training systems. These systems successfully detect falls with sensitivities. However, focusing only on large acceleration can result in many false positives from fall-like activities such as sitting down quickly and running. Furthermore, previous studies used complex algorithms like support vector machine (SVM) [5] and Markov model [6] to detect the fall. However, accuracy of these systems has not been proven to be highly effective. They also use excessive amounts of computational resources and cannot respond in real time. In this paper we propose a new device based on microcontroller (Arduino-UNO) and the sensor is MPU6050 Accelerometer and Gyro Chip.

2   Fall Risk Factors

A person can be more or less prone to fall, depending on a number of risk factors and hence a classification based on only age as a parameter is not enough. In fact, medical studies have determined a set of so called risk factors:

- Intrinsic:
  1. Age (over 75)
  2. Chronic disease
  3. Previous falls
  4. Poor balance
  5. Low mobility and bone fragility

6. Sight problems
7. Cognitive and dementia problems
8. Parkinson disease
9. Use of drugs that affect the mind
10. Incorrect lifestyle (inactivity, use of alcohol, obesity)

- Internal Environment:
  1. Need to reach high objects
  2. Slipping floors
  3. Stairs
  4. Incorrect use of shoes and clothes
- External Environment:
  1. Damaged roads
  2. Dangerous steps
  3. Poor lighting
  4. Crowded places.

3   Mpu-6050

ITG MPU-6050 is a sensor that contains MEMS accelerometer and a MEMS gyroscope in one chip. Both accelerometer and gyroscope contains 3 axis that can captures x, y and z with 16-bits analog to digital conversion hardware for each channel. Mpu-6050 uses I2C for communication which is a multi-master, multislave, single-ended, serial computer bus with low speed but very useful because uses only two wires: SCL (clock) and SDA (data) lines. Although the breadboard and the wires are optional items, the two pull-up resistor are essential. The diagram in Fig. 2 shows how to connect the sensor to a Arduino Uno. It is also important connect all the sensor pins with the correct arduino pins. The pull-up resistor will always keep a small amount of current flowing between VCC and the pin, in other words, it will keep a valid logic level if it is not flowing current in the pin 5. Sensor VDD - Arduino 3.3 v or 5 v. Sensor GND - Arduino GND. Sensor INT - Arduino digital pin 2.

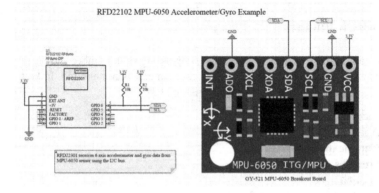

Fig. 2.   Source: RFduino, image by unknown

Sensor SCL - Arduino SCL dedicated pin = A5. Sensor SDA - Arduino SDA dedicated pin = A4.

4   Fall Detection Algorithm

The total sum acceleration vector Acc, contain both dynamic and static acceleration components [3, 7], is calculated from sampled data as indicated in Eq. (1)

$$Acc = \sqrt{(A_x)^2 + (A_y)^2 + (A_z)^2} \tag{1}$$

Where A_x, A_y, A_z are the acceleration in the x, y, z axes, respectively.

Similarly to the acceleration, the angular velocity is calculated from sampled data as indicated in Eq. (2)

$$w = \sqrt{(w_x)^2 + (w_y)^2 + (w_z)^2} \tag{2}$$

Where w_x, w_y, w_z the acceleration in the x, y, z axes, respectively.

When stationary, the acceleration magnitude, Acc, from tri-axial accelerometer is a constant, and angular velocity is 0°/s. When the subject falls, the acceleration is rapidly changing and the angular velocity produces a variety of signals along fall direction.

Since the Fall Index (Acc) requires high sampling frequency and fast acceleration changes, it will miss falls that happen slowly. Hence, Acc is not used unless we want to compare the performances of our systems with previous studies that have used the same positions but with deferent speed and accelerations.

The lower and upper fall thresholds for the acceleration and angular velocity used to identify the fall are derived as follows [8]:

1- Lower fall threshold (LFT): the negative peaks for the resultant of each recorded activity are referred to as the signal lower peak values (LPVs). The LFT for the acceleration signals are set at the level of the smallest magnitude lower fall peak (LFP) recorded.
2- Upper fall threshold (UFT): the positive peaks for the recorded signals for each recorded activity are referred to as the signal upper peak values (UPVs). The UFT for each of the acceleration and the angular velocity signals were set at the level of the smallest magnitude UPV recorded. The UFT is related to the peak impact force experienced by the body segment during the impact phase of the fall.

Fall detection algorithms using thresholds are normally divided into two groups, one is based on the LFT comparison and the other is based on UFT comparison of acceleration data. Although past research has achieved some significant results, the accuracy is still below desired levels. In this study adjust the UFT and LFT and found the performance to be 83.33 % and 67.08 %, respectively [9]. Figure 3 shows the flowchart of our algorithm which implemented in the program of Arduino_UNO in C-language this program built to read an analogue variable from its port as an additional adjustment to fixed the upper and the lower ACC.

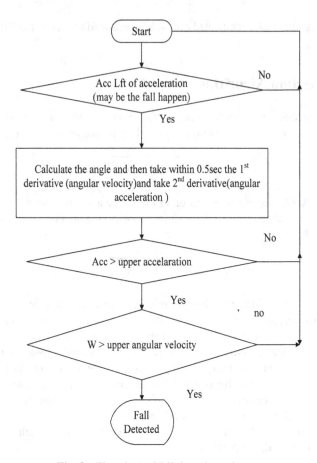

Fig. 3. Flowchart of fall detection schema.

5   Results and Discussion

Some existing acceleration-based fall detection systems are only used to distinguish falls from ADL. However, some activities like sitting down fast also feature large vertical acceleration. Figure 4 shows the acceleration and rotational rate of the trunk where the cases as follows: (a) run on a damaged road, (b) walking fast (c) step up a Stair. In Fig. 4 along three cases there is no fall then there is no alarm. Figure 5 shows the acceleration and rotational rate of the trunk and thigh for sitting fast. Where the cases as follows: (a) is a dangers fall detected, (b) is a fall posture. In Fig. 5.a the fall detected very fast and give alarm in the first moment and continued along 30 s while in Fig. 5.b give alarm after 10 s because there is no fall.

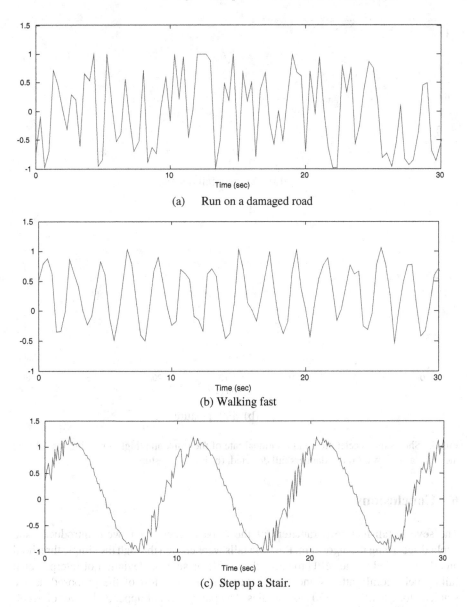

(a)   Run on a damaged road

(b) Walking fast

(c) Step up a Stair.

Fig. 4. Shows the acceleration and rotational rate of the trunk where the cases as follows: (a) run on a damaged road, (b) walking fast (c) step up a Stair.

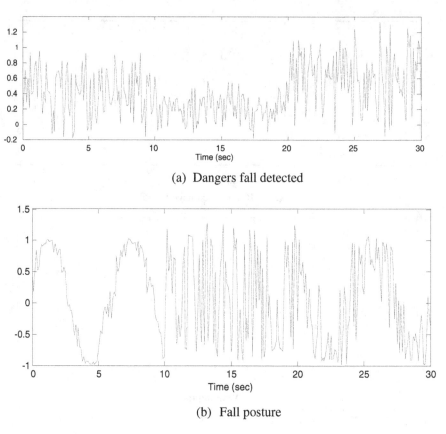

(a) Dangers fall detected

(b) Fall posture

Fig. 5. Shows the acceleration and rotational rate of the trunk and thigh for sitting fast. Where the cases as follows: (a) is a dangers fall detected, (b) is a fall posture.

6   Conclusions

The several fall-feature parameters of the 6-axes acceleration were introduced and applied according the algorithm. Possible falls were chosen through the simple threshold and then applied to the MPU to solve the problems such as deviation of interpersonal falling behavioral patterns and similar fall actions. The test of the proposed device studied along a different 350 case studies. The parameters of upper and lower of acceleration and velocity have adjusted to give best fall detection with sensitivity, specificity, and accuracy which were over than 95 %. These results demonstrate the reduction of the computing effort and resources, compared to those of using all the events applied. Then the proposed algorithms were very simple because it depend on a simple sensors (measure the angle) and the program calculate the angular velocity and acceleration. They can be implemented into an embedded system such as an 8051-based microcontroller with 128 Kbyte ROM. In the future, if the proposed algorithms are implemented to the embedded system, its performance will be tested in a real time.

References

1. Hwang, J.Y., Kang, J.M., Jang, Y.W., Kim, H.C.: Development of novel algorithm and real-time monitoring ambulatory system using Bluetooth module for fall detection in the elderly. In: Engineering in Medicine and Biology Society, IEMBS 2004, 26th Annual International Conference of the IEEE, vol. 1, pp. 2204–2207, September 2004

2. Lindemann, U., Hock, A., Stuber, M., Keck, W., Becker, C.: Evaluation of a fall detector based on accelerometers: a pilot study. Med. Biol. Eng. Comput. **43**(5), 548–551 (2005)

3. Kangas, M., Konttila, A., Lindgren, P., Winblad, I., Jämsä, T.: Comparison of low-complexity fall detection algorithms for body attached accelerometers. Gait Posture **28**(2), 285–291 (2008)

4. Abbate, S., Avvenuti, M., Corsini, P., Light, J., Vecchio, A.: Monitoring of human movements for fall detection and activities recognition in elderly care using wireless sensor network: a survey, pp. 1–20. InTech (2010)

5. Zhang, T., Wang, J., Xu, L., Liu, P.: Fall detection by wearable sensor and one-class SVM algorithm. In: Huang, D.-S., Li, K., Irwin, G.W. (eds.) ICIC 2006. LNCIS, vol. 345, pp. 858–863. Springer, Heidelberg (2006)

6. Ganti, R.K., Jayachandran, P., Abdelzaher, T.F., Stankovic, J.A.: Satire: a software architecture for smart attire. In: Proceedings of the 4th International Conference on Mobile Systems, Applications and Services, pp. 110–123. ACM, June 2006

7. Klenk, J., Becker, C., Lieken, F., Nicolai, S., Maetzler, W., Alt, W., Zijlstra, W., Hausdorff, J.M., van Lummel, R.C., Chiari, L., Lindemann, U.: Comparison of acceleration signals of simulated and real-world backward falls. Med. Eng. Phys. **33**(3), 368–373 (2011)

8. Bourke, A.K., O'donovan, K.J., Olaighin, G.: The identification of vertical velocity profiles using an inertial sensor to investigate pre-impact detection of falls. Med. Eng. Phys. **30**(7), 937–946 (2008)

9. Bourke, A.K., Van de Ven, P., Gamble, M., O'Connor, R., Murphy, K., Bogan, E., Nelson, J.: Evaluation of waist-mounted tri-axial accelerometer based fall-detection algorithms during scripted and continuous unscripted activities. J. Biomech. **43**(15), 3051–3057 (2010)

Modeling the In-home Lifestyle of Chronic Anorectal Patients via a Sensing Home

Xiaohu Fan[1,2(✉)], Li Wang[2], Changsheng Xie[3], Jing Cao[4], Jing Zeng[1], and Hao Huang[5(✉)]

[1] School of Computer Science and Technology, HUST, 1037 Luoyu Road, Wuhan, China
{fanxiaohu,zengjing}@hust.edu.cn
[2] Information Center of Mayinglong Pharmaceutical Group Co., Ltd.,
8 Nanyuansi Road, Wuhan, China
web_wli@163.com
[3] Wuhan National Laboratory for Optoelectronics, 1037 Luoyu Road, Wuhan, China
CS_xie@hust.edu.cn
[4] School of Economics, HUST, 1037 Luoyu Road, Wuhan, China
U201316553@hust.edu.cn
[5] School of Software Engineering, HUST, 1037 Luoyu Road, Wuhan, China
thao@hust.edu.cn

Abstract. The prevalence rate of anorectal disease is relatively high in China. Life style is one of the most important correlation factors with chronic anorectal disease. However, clinical diagnosis is insufficient to collect the data from patients' homes because the whole set of previous facilities is too expensive for patients to afford. In this paper, we propose a feasible wireless-based solution to deploy a cost-effective data collection scheme. We compare and analyze the living data sampled from volunteers during 28 days. Furthermore, an understandable behavior routine model presented as heat-map can be provided to clinicians. With this auxiliary data, professional guidance on living habits might be greatly beneficial for augmenting the life quality of patients suffering from chronic diseases.

Keywords: Anorectal E-Health · Chronic management · Smart home · Living routine · Cost-effective

1 Introduction

Due to improvements in public health, nutrition, medicine and personal hygiene, there has been a continual increase in life expectancy all over the world. Information technology and computer science, combined with electronic instruments, have served as important auxiliary tools and are widely used by clinicians. Technological advancements in electronic health can be a driving force for new management models, especially in chronic care.

Anorectal diseases are a series of common diseases of human beings [1], although they are not fatal. These kinds of diseases seriously affect the patient's work and life and give patients a great deal of pain. Numerous advanced therapeutic approaches, and monitoring equipment and supporting facilities are provided in the hospital.

© Springer International Publishing Switzerland 2016
C.K. Chang et al. (Eds.): ICOST 2016, LNCS 9677, pp. 188–199, 2016.
DOI: 10.1007/978-3-319-39601-9_17

According to the results of a Chinese adult common anorectal disease epidemiology survey [2], the factors closely related with anorectal diseases can be listed in the order of their most common appearance as follow: the highest is work environment and life-style, followed by eating habits. The third is psychological status. The fourth is bowel habits. Based on the characteristics of this kind of chronic disease, there is only a little time required for patients to be hospitalized for surgery or treatment, leaving a long period at home for rehabilitation. However, the symptoms and signs of patients at home are unavailable. Besides, clinical diagnostic practice might fail to identify health problems for evaluating the patients' living habits in the early stages because individual self-reported data is confused or limited, not suitable or insufficient for clinical assessments [3].

Fortunately, with the continuous development of technology and the popularity of the network, home-level electronic equipment has become plentiful in function with wallet-friendly prices. Blood pressure, blood sugar, BMI and the quality of sleep can be sampled at home, all by the patients themselves [4]. Innovations around Ambient Assisted Living (AAL) and Telemedicine systems are continuously advancing. One of the fields in this development and innovation of modern technologies is the Smart Home [5], which enables independent living for citizens in the household environment with the option of assisted care. However, these advanced technologies are temporary and still too expensive for residents.

Sensing Home [6] is our previous work, and it is a cost-effective solution of smart home, which is able to sample the environment and motion of the resident for activity recognition via ZigBee in a home setting. The motivation of this paper is to provide a solution for living behavior collection in a home setting, with lower cost and higher dimensional data to help patients with chronic illness get professional living guidance for recovery.

The main contributions of this paper are summarized as follows: (1) We simplify the sensing home to be more cost-effective, to sample behavior in a functional location-based method to model the lifestyle of patients; (2) collaborate with the Anorectal Health Cloud, so more healthcare providers and patients are able to fight against anorectal diseases together; (3) recruit four families as volunteers with diversity distributions for age, occupation, household environment and resident area, sampled for 28 days of data for research, and (4) attempt to provide heat-map records. In this way, data gathered from sensors will be easily understood by the clinical physician; thus, professional guidance can help patients recover better.

The remainder of the paper is organized as follows. In Sect. 2, we introduce the related work about applications in home level healthcare. In Sect. 3, we describe the preliminary results of this solution. Subsequently, in Sect. 4, the implementation and architecture of each service provider is described in detail. Section 5 gives the results to verify the applications and the lifestyle model. Finally, we summarize the discussions and give some conclusions in Sect. 6.

2 Related Work

With the continuous development of the economy, the demand for better and more efficient healthcare is not only promising but also a primary concern in the budgets of public and private health service providers. The high cost of the existing approaches of clinical health services is due to professional human resources and advanced equipment. According to a US national survey [7], fewer than 10 % could afford formal paid healthcare services, and the majority of individuals relied on informal health aid from family, friends and volunteers. In terms of a suitable solution for the healthcare system [8], there are three major factors of concerns: human labor, cost and quality of service. Instances of emergencies and fatal diseases require professional instruments and services provided in the hospital while, for chronic conditions, wearable devices or Ambient Assisted Living systems with regular clinical diagnoses might be feasible. Everyday home life presents unique challenges for chronic patients at home, and ongoing efforts by technologists and healthcare providers are required to collaborate to develop effective and innovative solutions.

Telemedicine [9] is a health service especially fit for chronic patients living at home [10]. These programs [11] are generally divided into two categories: connected health [12] and integrated care [13]. There are research projects like Smart Medical Home [10], U-Health [14, 15] ubiquitous health care [16]. At the same time, there are numerous devices, like Electrocardiography (ECG) devices [17] and a smart walking analyzer [18] with proprietary usage. Although there are no standard criteria to evaluate those products, cost and complexity are the major concerns of the users.

Computer vision based solutions [19, 20] serve as a traditional monitoring system with image processing functions. Computed Tomography [21], fall detection [22, 23] and a security system are currently the most common applications. Except for the consideration of total own cost (TOC), individuals do not want to be monitored for privacy protection.

Therefore, binary sensor based solutions that are cost-competitive and pervasive information and communication systems can be used in the creation of new products to make the home smart, thereby providing ubiquitous healthcare. An important component in the connected health ecosystem is data analytics, giving value and meaning to the collected data and enabling personalized healthcare decisions in the full circle of care around an individual, specifically, the data collected via sensors. With respect to other related projects like House_n [24], CASAS [25], Smart House [26], GETALP [27], Adaptive House [28], Aware Home [29] and Intelligent Workspace [30], a variety of different deployment scenarios and network architectures of the system are presented. Besides, RFID technology could join these systems for identification or location tracking [31, 32].

These approaches gathered ADLs [33] and IADLs [34], which enabled in-home healthcare [35] with activities recognition (AR) [36]. Kasteren implemented a temporal probabilistic hidden Markov model (HMM) and conditional random fields (CRF) algorithms [37], Riboni et al. [38] attempted a fine-grained hybrid reasoning model, Asma solved multi-occupant problems [39], Ordónez used hybrid algorithms to deploy a long term AR for evaluation [40] and Zeng [41] put forward a better design-flow to enhance the quality of experiences. Most of ambient assisted living systems are context aware, scenarios based or statistically based recognition approaches, and it is difficult to deal with unknown historical conditions.

Smart wearable devices accelerated the development of the mobile healthcare system [42]. In addition to professional home medical equipment, a large number of consumer electronics are emerging, such as Apple watch, Microsoft band and so on. Although these devices have neither a uniform data format nor transmission protocol standards, they are still emerging and facilitate our life and work.

Unlike seniors or the disabled, most chronic anorectal patients are functionally stable and capable of performing essential daily activities on their own. We use wireless sensors installed in the patients' homes to track their daily living routines. The sensing home provides the statistical results detected, which are reported to the clinicians and patients. With these auxiliary data of living routines, combined with interrogation to get mental state and diet information, professional guidance can be provided to the chronic patients.

3   Preliminary

The Chinese adult common anorectal disease epidemiology survey was jointly organized by the MaYingLong Pharmaceutical Group Co., Ltd. and the Chinese Association of Chinese medicine of the Anorectal Branch. This survey was launched in Nov. 2012, and 68906 valid samples were included from 31 provinces and 195 counties/districts all over China.

We used the test of goodness for fit [43] to check the statistical quality of our data. Adapting the sixth national population census of China [44] as the Population, the detailed result is shown in Table 1. The degree of freedom is 3 (K-1-2, K is the number of age groups), and the Chi square value is 2.98 while the P value is > 0.05. Thus, there was no significant difference between our sample age structure and population distribution, which means the sample data is representative.

Table 1. Sample test of goodness for fit with the national population.

Age group	National proportion (P_i)	Sample proportion (S_i)	$(S_i-P_i)^2/P_i$
18 ~ 24	16.1	12.1	0.9938
24 ~ 34	18.8	24.46	1.704
35 ~ 44	23.04	21.86	0.0604
45 ~ 54	17.49	18.12	0.0227
55 ~ 64	13.28	13.64	0.0098
>= 65	11.29	9.82	0.1914
Total	100	100	
Chi square value			*2.9792*

According to the results of our survey, there are 34522 individuals suffering from anorectal diseases, and the prevalence rate of anorectal disease in China is 50.1 %. We collected additional information through the questionnaire and used the statistical covariance and the Maximal Information Coefficient (MIC) [45] index to find out that the factors highly correlation with anorectal diseases are: (1) work environment and life style, (2) customary diet, (3) mental state, (4) bowel evacuation habit and (5) bedtime routine.

Diet habit, occupation and the mental state of the patients can be collected in traditional clinical diagnosis. However, the living style and bowel and bedtime routine of patients at home cannot be sampled in detail. Obtaining better treatment and consolidating the curative effect for the patients require the data mentioned above. Although the smart home with video surveillance is capable of accomplishing this, this kind of solution costs human resources for recording and hurts the privacy of the patients. Besides, the patients' home environments might be heterogeneous. So, we discarded the camera and behavior recognition and abstracted each room in the household into its basic function, as shown in Fig. 1.

Fig. 1. Location based activity abstract of a volunteer's home. Each room requires a frontend sampling device with PIR sensors to collect human motions.

Fig. 2. Xizhilang R2274 smart electronic toilet seat cover.

We used passive infrared (PIR) sensors to sample the motions of the daily routines and living habits of the patients. To further simplify the model, we used a Boolean variable to mark the status as active or not, leaving the temperature and humidity as an integer value for reference. For the bowel evacuation data, we used the customized R2274 electronic toilet seat cover shown in Fig. 2.

4   Architecture and Implementation

In order to provide long term remote medical rehabilitation for chronic anorectal patients, a combination of three aspects of service was required: a traditional healthcare provider, a professional anorectal cloud service and the customized sensing home. The general architecture is shown in Fig. 3.

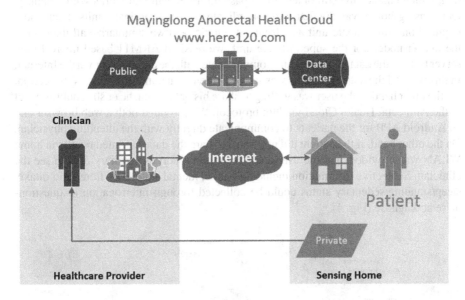

Fig. 3.   Architecture of the 3 roles of the service provider.

Mayinglong Co, Ltd. as a traditional medicinal materials production plant, acquisitioned several specialist anorectal hospitals and was ready to provide professional services. The Anorectal Health Cloud, available at www.here120.com, is a specialized cloud communication platform open for correlative patients and clinicians all over China. Our customized sensing home is required to reduce the video camera for privacy protection and uses the PIR sensors to sample the living routines at minimal power consumption with much easier deployment. To verify the effectiveness of the method to collect household behavior, we recruited four volunteers among the patients who were willing to share their data for research. We selected diversity distribution volunteers for age, occupation, household environment and housing dimension area, as shown in Table 2.

Table 2. Characteristics of volunteers.

Age group	Number	Work status	Residential area
20 ~ 30	Single	Work	56 m^2
30 ~ 40	Couple	Work	76 m^2
55 ~ 65	Single	Retired	92 m^2
65 ~ 75	Couple	Retired	118 m^2

The deployment process should be simple and easy; besides, the whole set of equipment should be cost-effective and not disturb the patients' normal lives. We adapted the HC-SR501 PIR sensors to detect human motions. This was combined with DHT11 to collect the temperature and humidity for the living environment of the households. For data transmission, we used the low power consumption TI-cc2530 based ZigBee solution, which enables the equipment to be pasted on the wall and works with a battery. Our sensing home was divided into subordinate and superordinate units. Each room required one subordinate unit as a frontend sample, and we summarize all the data to the master node. For the superordinate unit, we used an ARM11 based micro Linux server to store the data of patients and communicate with the cloud server via the Internet. In this way, all the data of patients was stored in their own homes for privacy protection. On the other hand, if the user was willing to share his or her data, he or she could connect to the Anorectal Health Cloud via http protocol. We provided both a web browser and an Android APP for the patients to communicate directly with the attending physician. On the other hand, if the patient did not want to share the data, a printed result via home WLAN was provided, and the user could bring the report as auxiliary data to see the clinician. Subjective information including habits, mental state, diet, fibre/fluid intake, sleep/standing/sedentary status could be collected through interrogation or questionnaire at diagnose (Fig. 4).

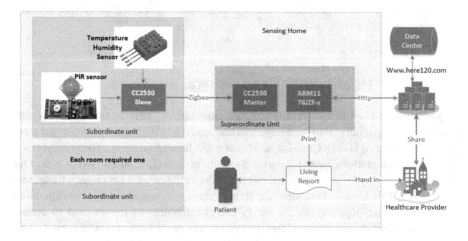

Fig. 4. Implementation of the sensing home to collect the living habits of patients.

The main factors affecting anorectal disease were thus divided into four parts to be summarized and submitted to the physician: (1) traditional clinical data provided by the hospital, (2) a living style report provided by the sensing home, (3) bowel evacuation reports by the R2274 electronic toilet seat cover and (4) occupation, eating habits and mental state obtained at the time of diagnosis. Clinicians were presented with the higher dimensions of the data provided by our work to help patients recover. Currently, this approach is an initial attempt, leaving clinical trials with larger sample size should be completed by the physicians to further explore the relationship between data and the anorectal diseases.

5   Experiment Result

The average power consumption of the sensing home is about 1.8 watts per hour; we collected from four weeks of the four sampled volunteers. In order to provide an intuitive presentation to both the clinician and the patient, we used a heatmap diagram to express the behavior routine. We scaled and normalized the average data during the 28 days of the sample. The detailed results are shown in Fig. 5, and living routines are readable for common users. Consistent with our previous assumptions, the results show that the home environments of patients are diverse and their living habits are various. For privacy protection, frequency and time length of excretory data preserved.

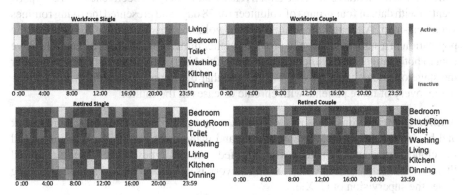

Fig. 5. Average living routine of volunteers.

As can be seen in Fig. 5, the household routine of the retired individuals seems more regular than that of those in the work force. Considering the effect of the difference between working days and holidays, we extracted the data from 6:00 PM of Friday to 11:59 PM of Sunday as the weekend data to verify whether the workday lifestyle is different from that of the weekend. As Fig. 6 shows, the working individuals perform more activities at weekends and sleep and get up later than on workdays.

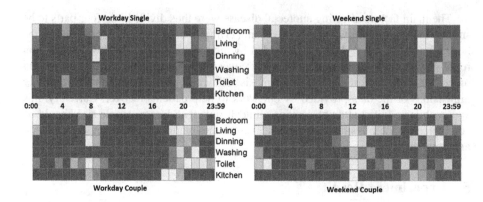

Fig. 6. Different lifestyles between the workday and weekend.

6   Conclusion

In this paper, we have compared home environment healthcare projects and examined the major factors according to the results of the Chinese adult common anorectal disease epidemiology survey. This paper introduces a simple solution to implement behavior collection with features of cost-effectiveness and energy-effectiveness. We experimented with data of four groups of volunteer for 28 days and presented the living routines via a heat-map. Although the sample data of volunteers is insufficient to represent the population in a statistical sense, it provides higher dimensions and more comprehensive data to both patients and clinicians. Currently, this kind of auxiliary data model is under the stage of research and testing. We believe that the improved solution will facilitate the recovery of more patients with chronic diseases in the future.

Author Contributions. This research work is part of X. Fan's Ph.D dissertation work and he defined the theme, data processing and manuscript writing. L. Wang designed the cloud server and website. J. Cao proofed text and typesetting. J. Zeng analyzed literature and refined the architecture. This work is conducted by X. Fan and H. Huang under the supervision of C. Xie.

Conflicts of Interest. The authors declare no conflict of interest.

Acknowledgments. This work is supported in part by East Lake National Innovation Foundation under grants number 2013-dhfwy-012, by 2015 R&D support foundation of Shenzhen Virtual University Park: Shenzhen branch of DSSL, project of research and platform construction, and in part by Independent innovation research foundation of HUST.

References

1. Bharucha, A.E., Wald, A., Enck, P., Rao, S.: Functional anorectal disorders. Gastroenterology **130**(5), 1510–1518 (2006)
2. Tian, Z.G., Chen, P., et al.: China Adult Common Anorectal Disease Epidemiology Survey. Wuhan University Press, Wuhan (2015)
3. Gordon, N.P., Hiatt, R.A., Lampert, D.I.: Concordance of self-reported data and medical record audit for six cancer screening procedures. J. Nat. Cancer Inst. **85**(7), 566–570 (1993)
4. Chobanian, A.V., et al.: Seventh report of the joint national committee on prevention, detection, evaluation, and treatment of high blood pressure. Hypertension **42**(6), 1206–1252 (2003)
5. Dhawan, A.P., Heetderks, W.J., Pavel, M., Acharya, S., Akay, M., Mairal, A., Wheeler, B., Dacso, C.C., Sunder, T., Lovell, N., et al.: Current and future challenges in point-of-care technologies: a paradigm-shift in affordable global health-care with personalized and preventive medicine. IEEE J. Trans. Eng. Health Med. **3**, 1–10 (2015)
6. Fan, X., Huang, H., Qi, S., Luo, X., Zeng, J., Xie, Q., Xie, C.: Sensing home: a cost-effective design for smart home via heterogeneous wireless networks. Sensors **15**(12), 30270–30292 (2015)
7. Anderson, G., Knickman, J.R.: Changing the chronic care system to meet peoples needs. Health Aff. **20**(6), 146–160 (2001)
8. Deen, M.J.: Information and communications technologies for elderly ubiquitous healthcare in a smart home. Pers. Ubiquitous Comput. **19**(3–4), 573–599 (2015)
9. Association, A.T., et al.: What is telemedicine (2013). http://www.americantelemed.org/about-telemedicine/what-is-telemedicine. Accessed 31 March 2014
10. Wootton, R.: Twenty years of telemedicine in chronic disease management–an evidence synthesis. J. Telemedicine Telecare **18**(4), 211–220 (2012)
11. Fitzpatrick, G., Ellingsen, G.: A review of 25 years of CSCW research in healthcare: contributions, challenges and future agendas. Comput. Support. Coop. Work (CSCW) **22**(4–6), 609–665 (2013)
12. Kvedar, J., Coye, M.J., Everett, W.: Connected health: a review of technologies and strategies to improve patient care with telemedicine and telehealth. Health Aff. **33**(2), 194–199 (2014)
13. Valentijn, P.P., Schepman, S.M., Opheij, W., Bruijnzeels, M.A.: Understanding integrated care: a comprehensive conceptual framework based on the integrative functions of primary care. Int. J. Integr. Care **13**(1) (2013)
14. Kim, J., Park, S.O.: U-health smart system architecture and ontology model. J. Supercomputing **71**(6), 2121–2137 (2015)
15. Jung, E.Y., Kim, J.H., Chung, K.Y., Park, D.K.: Home health gateway based healthcare services through U-Health platform. Wirel. Pers. Commun. **73**(2), 207–218 (2013)
16. Deen, M.J.: Information and communications technologies for ubiquitous healthcare. In: 2012 5th International Conference on Computers and Devices for Communication (CODEC), pp. 1–3. IEEE (2012)
17. Goldberger, A.L.: Clinical electrocardiography: a simplified approach. Elsevier Health Sciences (2012)
18. Jin, B., Thu, T.H., Baek, E., Sakong, S., Xiao, J., Mondal, T., Deen, M.J.: Walking-age analyzer for healthcare applications. IEEE J. Biomed. Health Inf. **18**(3), 1034–1042 (2014)
19. Seo, J., Han, S., Lee, S., Kim, H.: Computer vision techniques for construction safety and health monitoring. Adv. Eng. Inf. **29**(2), 239–251 (2015)
20. Han, J., Shao, L., Xu, D., Shotton, J.: Enhanced computer vision with microsoft kinect sensor: a review. IEEE Trans. Cybern. **43**(5), 1318–1334 (2013)

21. Schulze, D., Heiland, M., Thurmann, H., Adam, G.: Radiation exposure during midfacial imaging using 4-and 16-slice computed tomography, cone beam computed tomography systems and conventional radiography. Dentomaxillofacial Radiol. **33**(2), 83–86 (2014)
22. Mubashir, M., Shao, L., Seed, L.: A survey on fall detection: principles and approaches. Neurocomputing **100**, 144–152 (2013)
23. Igual, R., Medrano, C., Plaza, I.: Challenges, issues and trends in fall detection systems. Biomed. Eng. Online **12**(66), 1–66 (2013)
24. MIT House_n. http://web.mit.edu/cron/group/house_n/
25. CASAS. http://ailab.wsu.edu/casas/datasets.html
26. Duke University Smart House. http://smarthome.duke.edu/
27. GETALP. http://getalp.imag.fr/xwiki/bin/view/HISData/
28. Adaptive house, University of Colorado. http://www.cs.colorado.edu/~mozer/nnh/
29. Georgia tech aware home. http://awarehome.imtc.gatech.edu
30. Carnegie Mellon's intelligent workspace. http://www.arc.cmu.edu/cbpd/iw/
31. Li, N., Becerik-Gerber, B.: Performance-based evaluation of RFID-based indoor location sensing solutions for the built environment. Adv. Eng. Inf. **25**(3), 535–546 (2011)
32. Kim, S.C., Jeong, Y.S., Park, S.O.: Rfid-based indoor location tracking to ensure the safety of the elderly in smart home environments. Pers. Ubiquitous Comput. **17**(8), 1699–1707 (2013)
33. Kim, E., Helal, S., Lee, J., Hossain, S.: The making of a dataset for smart spaces. In: Yu, Z., Liscano, R., Chen, G., Zhang, D., Zhou, X. (eds.) UIC 2010. LNCS, vol. 6406, pp. 110–124. Springer, Heidelberg (2010)
34. Ciol, M.A., Rasch, E.K., Hoffman, J.M., Huynh, M., Chan, L.: Transitions in mobility, ADLs, and IADLs among working-age medicare beneficiaries. Disabil. Health J. **7**(2), 206–215 (2014)
35. Roldán-Merino, J., García, I.C., Ramos-Pichardo, J.D., Foix-Sanjuan, A., Quilez-Jover, J., Montserrat-Martinez, M.: Impact of personalized in-home nursing care plans on dependence in ADLs/IADLs and on family burden among adults diagnosed with schizophrenia: a randomized controlled study. Perspect. Psychiatr. Care **49**(3), 171–178 (2013)
36. Fan, X., Chen, S., Qi, S., et al.: An ARM-Based hadoop performance evaluation platform: design and implementation. In: Collaborative Computing: Networking, Applications, and Worksharing, pp. 82–94. Springer International Publishing (2015)
37. Van Kasteren, T., Noulas, A., Englebienne, G., Kröse, B.: Accurate activity recognition in a home setting. In: Proceedings of the 10th International Conference on Ubiquitous Computing, pp. 1–9. ACM (2008)
38. Riboni, D., Bettini, C., Civitarese, G., Janjua, Z.H., Bulgari, V.: From lab to life: fine-grained behavior monitoring in the elderly's home. In: 2015 IEEE International Conference on Pervasive Computing and Communication Workshops (PerCom Workshops), pp. 342–347. IEEE (2015)
39. Benmansour, A., Bouchachia, A., Feham, M.: Multioccupant activity recognition in pervasive smart home environments. ACM Comput. Surv. (CSUR) **48**(3), 34 (2015)
40. Ordóñez, F.J., de Toledo, P., Sanchis, A.: Activity recognition using hybrid generative/discriminative models on home environments using binary sensors. Sensors **13**(5), 5460–5477 (2013)
41. Zeng, J., Yang, L.T., Ning, H., Ma, J.: A systematic methodology for augmenting quality of experience in smart space design. IEEE Wirel. Commun. **22**(4), 81–87 (2015)

42. Luo, N., Ding, J., Zhao, N., Leung, B.H., Poon, C.C.: Mobile health: design of flexible and stretchable electrophysiological sensors for wearable healthcare systems. In: 2014 11th International Conference on Wearable and Implantable Body Sensor Networks (BSN), pp. 87–91. IEEE (2014)
43. Anderson, T.W., Darling, D.A.: A test of goodness of fit. J. Am. Stat. Assoc. **49**(268), 765–769 (1954)
44. National statistical offices of China. http://www.stats.gov.cn
45. Reshef, D.N., Reshef, Y.A., Finucane, H.K., Grossman, S.R., McVean, G., Turn-baugh, P.J., Lander, E.S., Mitzenmacher, M., Sabeti, P.C.: Detecting novel associations in large data sets. Science **334**(6062), 1518–1524 (2011)

E-Health Technology Assessment and Impact Analysis

Evaluation Framework for Smart Technology Mental Health Interventions

Cheryl Forchuk[1,6(✉)], Abraham Rudnick[2], Josephine MacIntosh[3], Fatima Bukair[4], and Jeffrey Hoch[5]

[1] Faculty of Health Sciences, Arthur Labatt Family School of Nursing, Western University, London, ON, Canada
cforchuk@uwo.ca
[2] Department of Psychiatry and Behavioural Neurosciences, McMaster University, Hamilton, ON, Canada
[3] Vancouver Island Health Authority, Mental Health and Substance Use Services, Victoria, BC, Canada
[4] Health and Rehabilitation Science, Western University, London, ON, Canada
[5] Institute of Health Policy, Management and Evaluation, University of Toronto, Toronto, ON, Canada
[6] Lawson Health Research Institute, 750 Baseline Road East, London, ON, Canada

Abstract. Evaluations of technological mental health interventions are often too narrow to support the uptake of such technologies. This report describes the evaluation framework used for a mobile technology study, the Mental Health Engagement Network (MHEN). The framework presented here includes four types of analyses: effectiveness, economic, policy, and ethics analysis. When technological mental health interventions are evaluated in each of these four areas, research can be more comprehensive and set the stage for spreading the innovation. Particularly, inclusion of economic analysis may speak to potential funders, ethical analysis may encourage adoption in clinical settings, and policy analysis may encourage uptake from decision-makers. This report provides a framework that can be adapted to a variety of technological mental health interventions to assess and compare not only effectiveness, but also economic, policy and ethical challenges and opportunities. Findings from the MHEN study are presented as a case study of the applied framework.

Keywords: Mobile technology · Mental health care · e-Mental health · Evaluation framework · Effectiveness · Economic analysis · Policy analysis · Ethical analysis · Mental Health Engagement Network (MHEN)

1 Introduction

In a 2014 briefing paper, the Mental Health Commission of Canada [1] concluded that technological innovations in e-Mental health presented an enormous opportunity to transform an overburdened, underfunded mental heath care delivery system, and that scaling-up e-Mental health, sooner rather than later, would benefit the mental health and well-being of all Canadians. Technological mental health interventions seek to provide

© Springer International Publishing Switzerland 2016
C.K. Chang et al. (Eds.): ICOST 2016, LNCS 9677, pp. 203–210, 2016.
DOI: 10.1007/978-3-319-39601-9_18

psychiatric support services to individuals with mental disorders in such a way that supplement, rather than replace, face-to-face interaction with health care professionals. Mobile and web-based technologies in particular, allow clients to connect with their health care providers electronically, and provide mechanisms by which clients can manage and track their own mental health. Although such interventions show promise, their evaluations are often limited as they primarily – if not solely – focus on demonstrating effectiveness, rather than assessing a range of potential outcomes and impacts.

Issues plaguing technological evaluations are multi-faceted, but largely stem from their limited scope [2]. Particularly, evaluations often fail to include a range of stakeholders throughout the evaluation process. This approach may limit the uptake of such technologies, since front-line providers and other decision-makers were not involved in the evaluation process. Additionally, effectiveness analyses assessing usability, acceptability and client readiness, typically exclude other factors affecting technology adoption, such as ethical and related privacy considerations [1]. Finally, economic evaluation is often lacking in the area of mental health interventions in general, and in technological evaluations more specifically; this lack of economic consideration may preclude technology adoption from decision-makers [3, 4]. Each of these aspects represents a gap in the current evaluation of technological mental health interventions. In order to address these gaps, the current report advocates for the adoption of a new framework by which technological mental health interventions can be evaluated. The Mental Health Engagement Network (MHEN) intervention will be used as an example of how this evaluation framework can be applied in practice.

2   Evaluation Framework

The evaluation framework presented here consists of four parts. First, effectiveness analysis seeks to assess aspects of technology use and how this relates to mental health outcomes. Second, economic analysis evaluates 'value for money', as it relates to health and social service use. Third, policy analysis aims to incorporate considerations of decision-makers identified throughout the research process. Finally, ethical analysis explores issues such as privacy and data storage, which may address some practical considerations of decision-makers and clients alike. Each of these aspects will help ensure that evaluations of technological mental health interventions are more comprehensive, and speak to as many clients, health care professionals, policy- and decision-makers as possible. This framework is summarized in Fig. 1.

2.1   Effectiveness Analyses

Effectiveness analyses comprise the majority of current evaluations of mental health technologies. Although these analyses are crucial, we submit, based on our own research experiences and reviews of the literature, that the components included in effectiveness analyses ought to be more comprehensive. Traditional effectiveness analyses measure the use of technology in relation to health outcomes (such as reduced symptoms). While this is clearly important, other measures of effectiveness would enhance evaluations.

Specifically, such evaluations should include measurements of actual use of technology over time, which will allow researchers to determine effectiveness for different types of users (e.g., youth vs. seniors) and the rate at which clients adopt new technologies. Additionally, consumer usability and the extent of adoption of technology in life patterns should be assessed. This will allow researchers to determine areas for future enhancement to improve ease of use and uptake. Finally, identifying priority populations may help to tailor technologies to best suit the needs of clients and health care professionals.

While these effectiveness guidelines apply to many intervention studies, they can be tailored to technological mental health interventions as these interventions may have distinct considerations. Particularly, Doherty et al. [2] advocate that effectiveness analyses should include quantitative *and* qualitative measures; application logging (so that researchers can determine how often different applications are accessed in the aggregate); and tracking of declined and withdrawn participants. By addressing these factors, evaluations may be able to address barriers to uptake of technological interventions. Also, many evaluations of technological mental health interventions stop at effectiveness analyses; while such analysis is crucial, a comprehensive analysis of technological interventions for mental health requires more.

2.2 Economic Analyses

In the financially constrained world of health care, economic analyses are becoming increasing important as a way to examine actual and likely cost savings of interventions [1]. Basically, economic analyses consist of 'value for money' considerations that incorporate the intervention's costs and its economic benefits. This involves the collection of person level cost and outcome data for each study participant, as well as an analysis of costs and benefits on a societal level that identify specific subcategories such as caregiver, health care costs, and other government costs, such as disability support payments and policing costs.

Economic aspects are under-examined in the literature, and are too often missing from mental health intervention evaluations in general [3, 4]. However, economic analysis is of critical importance, especially for involving other stakeholders aside from care providers, i.e., employers. Although there are many types of economic analyses, cost-effectiveness analysis is the most common in mental health intervention evaluations, with comparatively little use of cost-utility analysis or cost-benefit analysis [3]. Cost benefit analysis is useful to address these shortcomings, but such analyses can be difficult to undertake. Although technological mental health interventions may be demonstrated to be effective, there is a gap between research and knowledge translation to practice – economic analysis can help with this, as it may be more understandable to policy decision-makers.

2.3 Policy Analyses

Policy analyses are another overlooked aspect of technological mental health intervention evaluations. We conceptualize policy analyses as those that identify specific policy implications in data exchange, secure storage, and use of technologies, and address policy implications arising from the issues identified throughout the research process. Including key stakeholders in identifying both problems and solutions is useful throughout any evaluation, but is particularly useful in policy analyses. For technological mental health interventions to have optimal effects, they must have the support of a variety of clinical and non-clinical stakeholders beyond service users. Clinical stakeholders include nurses, physicians, and other allied health professionals, while non-clinical stakeholders include administrators, government representatives, and researchers. This approach is supported by Doherty et al. [2], whose guidelines for evaluation of mental health technologies specifically suggests incorporating both clinical practitioners and non-clinical peers into a comprehensive evaluation. This may help to increase technology adoption, which historically has been slow in the field of mental health.

2.4 Ethical Analyses

Ethical analyses may be the most commonly overlooked pillar of the proposed evaluation framework. We define ethical analyses as including the identification of specific ethical implications in data exchange, secure storage, and use of technologies, and the comparison of ethical standards to the project's findings in relation to views of fairness, autonomy, privacy, social justice and other moral matters. Such ethical considerations seem to be assumed on the basis of research ethics board approval for the study. However, while this approval protects the research participants, it often fails to consider long-term ethical considerations that may affect the adoption of technological interventions. In fact, privacy and ethical considerations are often a major challenge to the successful adoption of such technology [1, 5]. Therefore, a more comprehensive ethical evaluation is necessary to ensure users that their privacy and other moral needs are being protected to the best degree possible. Further, through the use of an action research methodology, users may be able to identify ethical considerations as they arise, so that they can be evaluated and addressed in a timely manner.

3   MHEN Case Study

3.1   Background

The MHEN is a mobile, web-based intervention funded by Canada Health Infoway. Briefly, MHEN employed a mixed methods, delayed implementation research design. A sample of mental health services clients (N = 394) were recruited from the caseloads of 54 mental health professionals from 4 community mental health agencies in an large urban centre in Ontario, Canada. Participants were then randomized into two groups, where Group 1 (n = 192) received early intervention, and Group 2 (n = 202) received delayed intervention (beginning 6 months later). Thus, Group 2 initially acted as the control group. A baseline comparison found no significant demographic differences between the two groups.

During the course of the study, each participant completed four interviews (at baseline, 6, 12, 18 months), each of which included eight standardized questionnaires (a demographic

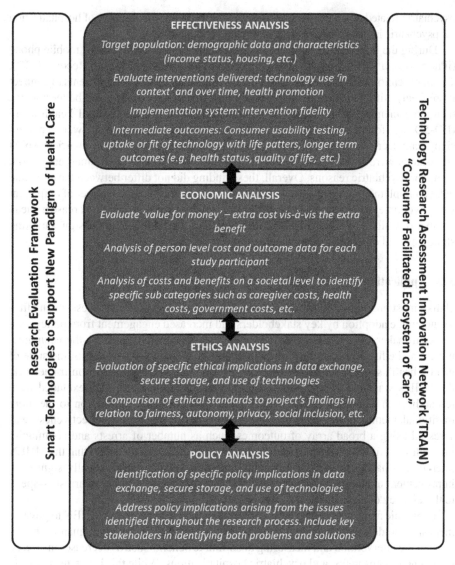

Fig. 1. A framework developed to study the latest technological advances on the market deploying them at core gaps as identified by the researchers, care providers and consumers.

form, the Quality of Life –Brief Version (QoL-BV), Health, Social, and Justice Service Use form, Medical Outcomes Study 36-item Short-Form Health Survey (SF-36), the European Quality of Life -5 Dimensions (EQ-5D), the Community Integration Questionnaire, the Adult Consumer Empowerment Scale, and the Perception of Smart Technology Form). Statistical analyses for repeated measures (analysis of variance (ANOVA) and general estimating equations (GEE)) were conducted to assess changes over time in relation to quality of life, overall health score, number of arrests, number of out-patient visits, number of psychiatric-related emergency room visits, and the presence (or absence) of hospitalization for psychiatric issues in the previous six month period.

During the intervention stage, each client was equipped with a smart mobile phone (iPhone 4S), a TELUS health space™ account and a Personal Health Record (PHR). The intervention was intended to supplement usual care by allowing patients to connect more freely with their healthcare professionals, particularly nurses, and better manage their own mental health. While no significant change in mean overall health score (EQ-5D) was found, small but significant improvements in quality of life were reported, significant decreases in the number of arrests, outpatient visits, and psychiatric hospital admissions were found, along with a downward trend in number of emergency room visits for psychiatric reasons. Overall, these finding did not differ between the early and delayed implementation groups, with the exception of the average number of outpatient visits over time, where the early treatment group demonstrated a larger decrease in mean number of visits. For a more detailed description of the MHEN study design, sampling strategies, and outcome measures, please see Forchuk et al. [6, 7].

3.2 Application

Unlike most previous studies, which have focused mainly on effectiveness, in an effort to encourage adoption by key stakeholders and increased engagement from policy- and decision-makers, the MHEN research team also endeavored to assess the economic, policy, and ethical implications of including mobile technology as part of the suite of mental health supports currently on offer. By utilizing such an evaluation framework, the MHEN was able to engage a range of stakeholders that are often excluded from research, such as nurses, social workers, and policy-makers. In addition to the more traditional mental health metrics (e.g., quality of life measures), effectiveness was assessed using a broad array of outcomes, such as number of arrests and community integration. This allowed for a more thorough examination of the effect that the MHEN intervention had on clients. The findings here—a small, yet statistically significant improvement in quality of life, and a significant reduction in number of arrests—speak to the efficacy of e-mental health supports.

Economic analyses are also being undertaken to help propose the MHEN to government stakeholders and other decision-makers. Specifically, this involves quantifying the costs of the intervention and measuring quantifiable benefits such as decreases in arrests, emergency rooms visits, and psychiatric hospitalizations. While this is not an easy task, we have found that economic analyses speak to decision-makers in a way that traditional effectiveness analyses alone cannot. We expect that when translated to dollars saved, the statistically significant decreases in the number of arrests, outpatient visits, and psychiatric hospital admissions, coupled with the downward trend in number of emergency room visits for psychiatric reasons, will speak loudly.

Policy and ethical analyses were also undertaken using qualitative data. Focus groups with both clients and care providers allowed us to identify issues related to privacy, data collection, storage and more. However, these focus groups also identified other concerns that researchers had not anticipated. For example, clients cited timeliness of the response by care providers as an ethical consideration. While it is understandable that care providers are not always available to address the immediate concerns of their clients, alternative methods for allowing clients to seek care (which may require policy changes) are especially important when the intervention allows for real-time interaction.

The MHEN evaluation was far-reaching in its scope and there are important lessons to be learned from it. For example, choosing measures that are important to clients, but also well characterized and quantifiable, can be difficult. For example, quality of life may be of vital importance, and few would argue that technological mental health interventions that improve quality of life are not beneficial. However, it is challenging to attach a monetary value to quality of life, so incorporating an economic analysis may miss some important outcomes from a client perspective.

Additionally, it can be difficult to address the needs of all relevant stakeholders. This can lead to an insufficiently deep approach to evaluation, where different aspects are included that speak to different stakeholders, but time may not permit each aspect to be analyzed in depth. Nonetheless, it remains important to include a variety of stakeholders in the evaluation process, as this increases the breadth of the research, and may translate into increased knowledge transfer, and hopefully increased funding for, and adoption of, technology to support mental health services clients and professionals. Our team is also currently using this same approach to evaluate web-based and text messaging-based mental health interventions, which will allow for direct comparisons of different modes of technological support.

4   Conclusion

Historically, technological mental health interventions have seen slow uptake by community stakeholders. It is our opinion that more comprehensive evaluations will help not only to improve interventions, but may also improve knowledge translation and uptake. Evaluations should include the above four pillars (effectiveness, economics, policy and ethics), but must also incorporate the feedback of multiple stakeholders, including the central role of service users. Additionally, evaluations should be done in a staged and iterative manner, so that issues can be identified and addressed early and further evaluated. By incorporating as many of these aspects as possible, it is our hope that evaluations of technological mental health interventions will move beyond effectiveness analysis toward evaluations that are more comprehensive, and speak to more stakeholders.

Acknowledgments. This research program has been funded by Canada Health Infoway with support from TELUS Health.

References

1. Mental Health Commission of Canada. E-Mental Health in Canada: Transforming the Mental Health System Using Technology (2014). http://www.mentalhealthcommission.ca
2. Doherty, G., Coyle, D., Matthews, M.: Design and evaluation guidelines for mental health technologies. Interact. Comput. **22**, 243–252 (2010)

3. Trepel, D., Ali, S.: Health-related quality of life measures in economic evaluations of child and adolescence mental health interventions: a systematic review. J. Ment. Health Policy Econ. **15**, S22 (2012)

4. Hamberg-van Reenen, H.H., Proper, K.I., van den Berg, M.: Worksite mental health interventions: a systematic review of economic evaluations. J. Occup. Environ. Med. **69**, 837–845 (2012)

5. Richards, H., King, G., Reid, M., Selvaraj, S., McNicol, I., Brebner, E., Godden, D.: Remote working: survey of attitudes to eHealth of doctors and nurses in rural general practices in the United Kingdom. Fam. Pract. **22**, 2–7 (2005)

6. Forchuk, C., Rudnick, A., Reiss, J., Hoch, J., Donelle, L., Corring, D., Godin, M., Osaka, W., Campbell, R., Capretz, M., Reed, J., McKillop, M.: Mental health engagement network: an analysis of outcomes following a mobile and web- based intervention. J. Technol. Soc. **10**, 1–13 (2015)

7. Forchuk, C., Rudnick, A., Hoch, J., Godin, M., Donelle, L., Rasmussen, D., Campbell, R., Osaka, W., Edwards, B., Osuch, E., Norman, R., Vingilis, E., Mitchell, B., Reiss, J., Petrenko, M., Corring, D., McKillop, M.: Mental health engagement network (MHEN). Int. J. Adv. Life Sci. **5**, 1–10 (2013)

Pervasive Mobile Services for Active Aging: An Exploratory Investigation into the Relationship Between Willingness-to-Adopt Mobile Devices and Shopping Experience

Susan E. Reid[1(✉)], Bessam Abdulrazak[2], Monica Alas[1], and Jillian Bibeau[1]

[1] Bishop's University, Lennoxville, QC, Canada
sreid@ubishops.ca
[2] Université de Sherbrooke, Sherbrooke, QC, Canada
bessam.abdulrazak@usherbrooke.ca

Abstract. The main purpose of research presented in this paper is to create a simplified senior shopping typology utilizing a values-based segmentation approach. This typology is then used to see whether and how certain segment's characteristics may influence the usage of and willingness-to-adopt mobile devices related to shopping tasks. Understanding the way senior consumers shop and how pervasive mobile services can meet their needs is important to help build applications and devices which can enhance seniors' quality of life. The research presented in this paper examines the relationship between the willingness-to-adopt mobile devices on the part of senior consumers (i.e. +65) and the relative ease they experience during shopping.

Keywords: Mobile devices · Willingness-to-adopt · Shopping experience · Seniors

1 Introduction

Understanding the fast growing market of senior consumers and how pervasive mobile services can meet their needs is essential in order to better develop and propose applications that enhance senior's quality of life, including during shopping activities. One pertinent trend relating to senior consumers is that this segment is at an all-time peak and continuing to grow. According to the World Health Organization (WHO) [33], by 2025, the number of people 65+ globally will jump from 390 to 800 million, an almost 50 % increase. An aging population, combined with lengthening life expectancies around the globe, fueled by rapid urbanization, increasingly sedentary lifestyles, changing diets and rising obesity is expected to increase the demands for life science products [7] and technological products that will assist this market with aging well (e.g., pervasive mobile services and applications). As per the Institute for Healthcare Informatics (IMS), in 2013, the smartphone penetration rate among the 65+ age category in the United States was 18 % and their downloading application rate was

© Springer International Publishing Switzerland 2016
C.K. Chang et al. (Eds.): ICOST 2016, LNCS 9677, pp. 211–221, 2016.
DOI: 10.1007/978-3-319-39601-9_19

8 % [2]. While research shows increased technology use by and interest from seniors [9, 18], senior health-related applications still represent a very small target category and very few applications specific to seniors have been developed [2, 21]. In fact, most applications have been designed for their caregivers, who are typically part of a younger population. As such, we are interested in developing a better under-standing of the mobile device needs of such consumers when they are shopping outside the home and how best to support them in those activities if desirable and feasible. The growth of the 65+ demographic, along with its wealth and disposable income, makes it worthwhile to study shopping services and experiences specifically desired by seniors [20, 28, 31]. That said, seniors experience challenges during the shopping process and, as such, it is important to view the process from a social and services provision perspective as well. One avenue for providing better shopping experiences, both in terms of overcoming challenges and in terms of enhancing experiences, may be through the use of mobile devices. As such, the purpose of this research is to compare senior citizens' willingness-to-adopt mobile devices based on their shopping activities and behaviors and to see whether in fact the use of such devices is linked to a better facilitated shopping experience.

Lian and Yen [16] note that most online shopping applications have been devel-oped ignoring the potential of the senior market. As such, we propose a typology of seniors related to their health and psychographic characteristics based around shopping patterns and we propose relationships of these to their mobile device use. This paper considers data from both the literature and our own research, integrating our findings and outlining shopper typologies by considering whether mobile phones have the potential to become a component of their shopping experience.

2 Literature Review

One of the most important underlying theories of marketing, segmentation theory, relates to how markets 'hang together' as a result of various consumer characteristics such as demographics, personality, values, lifestyle and psychographics. In 1983, Mitchell proposed the 'VALS' typology as a way of understanding the values and lifestyles of consumers [22]. While there are several versions of the typology and it has been expanded substantially over the years, the three main original factors were as follows: the first, was a 'need-driven' type (related to what we call 'functional'); the second, is an 'outer-directed' type (related to what we refer to as 'social') and the third, is an 'inner-directed' type (what we refer to here as 'experiential'). The use of such a 3-factor typology (i.e., functional, social, experiential) is well supported by studies specifically investigating motivations linked to the grocery shopping function in the literature such as that conducted by Geuens et al. [10].

Aging encompasses (A) health/biological, (B) psychological/social and (C) envi-ronmental changes and these impact the activities and roles, which seniors play in society. One critical activity for seniors, impacted by these three aspects of aging, is their shopping activities [19, 25]. Due to the growth and interest in this segment, seniors and their shopping behaviors exhibit a fast-growing area of research interest, where there has been little previous focus. As such, the following literature review is organized around this three-factor framework.

A. **Health/Biological.** The procurement of food is a fundamental task that must be carried out by most people and can be considered a cumbersome task that must be performed frequently [30]. Senior shoppers are exposed to the shopping task for longer periods of time than younger shoppers due to declining fitness and agility, and/or simply due to having more disposable time [29]. Consumers who have ambulation and dexterity problems, as do many of the shoppers in the senior demographic, find this chore especially challenging [32]. Personal mobility plays a large role in grocery shopping [13] and the accessibility of stores becomes more important for senior consumer cohorts [23]. For example, struggling to reach products on a top or bottom shelf may prove a struggle for seniors. Goodwin & McElwee [11] researched how the product-selecting process is also more challenging for older consumers. Reading product labels and getting an overview of categories of products on a shelf may present difficulties due to deteriorating eyesight [14]. Mobile devices and smartphones can play a significant role in maintaining Quality of Life for seniors [1]. These devices have been used increasingly in the field of telehealth. Notwithstanding, in this study we are interested in seeing whether there are tasks, which can be facilitated by pervasive computing applications.

B. **Psychological/Social.** Moschis et al. [23] state that the behavior of seniors differs significantly from that of other age groups, especially in the grocery retail environment. For example, given the fact that seniors are usually retired, they generally take their time and enjoy browsing [4]. That said, senior shoppers should not be considered as a homogeneous segment. Rather than seeing seniors as a homogeneous market, and instead looking at it as heterogeneous [12, 24], in terms of the 'psychographics' underlying what makes seniors tick, could help retailers better manage and market to this sector and also provide better tools or applications on mobile devices tailored to various psychographic groups within this demographic. It is therefore important to understand how they differ and to examine how their shopper motivation goes beyond mere 'provisioning' activity [21]. Ultimately, we need to understand and learn how to better serve psychographic sub-groups within the senior's category.

C. **Environmental.** According to Angell et al. [4] and Bellenger et al. [5], store choices are determined by key store attributes including: accessibility, type and availability of merchandise, the store environment (everything from the physical to the social environment), price/promotions and store/customer services. Based on these considerations, Angell et al. have developed a typology of six groupings of shoppers based on a combination of income, product orientation, accessibility and store environments. Similarly, Teller, Gittenberger & Schneditz [29] outline attributes as determinants of satisfaction of the store: accessibility of the store, products within the store, pricing and product-related attributes, and atmosphere [13]. Depending on the person's age, the role of such attributes varies so they have different effects on satisfaction with their patronized store [11, 17, 23].

Shopping styles and needs of the aging population are therefore expected to vary with health condition (A), the individual shopping style (B) and retail environment (C).

If these factors are not taken into account, they may result in low adoption [1, 15]. We therefore combine all three aging-related factors in the shopping context: to come up with a simplified typology of three types of shopper based largely on psychographic distinctions: functionalist, social and experiential. The basis for understanding shoppers using this breakdown comes from extensive research in the field of marketing [3, 8]. This typology does not utilize income as a determinant, however, we do have data that demonstrate that income level is significantly related to adoption of mobile devices. Once we remove income from the equation, we can then look more closely at how the other factors are playing out in terms of adoption of mobile devices and their potential relationship to shopping tasks.

3 Propositions

The aim of this study is to build on previous research and undergo the creation of a simplified senior shopping typology utilizing a psychographics approach and the potential usage of mobile phones within their shopping experience. Consequently, we propose a typology that is based on the factors presented in the literature review and on the behavioral shopping traits that resulted from our pre-test results. More precisely, we developed three propositions to capture senior's willingness to adopt pervasive mobile services devices specific to each psychographic trait. Our typology of senior shoppers can be summarized as follows:

(i)   the *'functionalist'* who wants to get in and out of the store as quickly as possible (and this may be motivated by and/or related to various health issues),
(ii) the *"social shopper"* who is primarily motivated by the social aspects of shopping (those who are highly social, those who have high need of helping behavior with the various tasks affiliated with shopping) and
(iii) the *"experiential shopper"* who is primarily motivated by the experience with products, promotions and the store environment.

More specifically, the *functionalist shopper* is a practical shopper who does not like to shop and values the merchandise selection, service policies and accessibility of their grocery store. These shoppers tend to view shopping as a chore that is to be done as quickly as possible and are oriented to getting the products which they desire in the most efficient and best fashion. They also tend to be more selective. On the other spectrum, the *social shopper*, the main focus is on the customer service aspect of a grocery store and fellow shoppers. This is the segment that is most likely to shop with friends. This consumer is likely to expend a large amount of time grocery shopping, as long as they are socializing. Similarly, the *experiential shopper* enjoys shopping but for the store experience aspect. Preferring to spend a leisurely amount of time doing their groceries, this shopper has the potential to buy a mobile phone and its applications to heighten their overall experience.

Proposition 1. The behavior of each of these three types of senior shopper is likely to be mitigated by health issues. In particular, however, the functionalist shopper, who does not like shopping may either not like the task, or this could be related to health issues; in particular, more significant mobility and cognition issues. These shoppers are likely to depend on others to help with their shopping and are also less likely to utilize and be willing to adopt mobile devices.

(P1):   Functionalists due to mobility and cognition issues are less likely to be willing to adopt mobile devices.

Proposition 2. Social shoppers, are those who have high social requirements in terms of liking to spend time including shopping with friends and also are more likely to socialize with employees and not be shy to ask for in-store help. Such shoppers are considered likely to not be as dependent on mobile devices for facilitating their shopping experience as they rely on live networking to enable their information needs.

(P2):   Social shoppers are less likely to be willing to adopt mobile devices.

Proposition 3. Mobile use is likely to be most affiliated with the experiential types of shoppers, because mobile devices facilitate the activities which they enjoy doing (i.e., comparing pricing information, promotions, finding things in store).

(P3):   Experiential shoppers are more likely to be willing to adopt mobile devices.

4   Method

A survey methodology was used to test our propositions among participants aged between 65 and 95. The survey was conducted during 2013. This section covers the main subsets of our survey, the types of analysis employed and presents the demographic profiles.

A. The Pre-test and Questionnaire. The survey was first performed with a group of 9 pre-test participants. Based on analysis of the initial results from the pre-test, questions were added and then distributed to a larger number of seniors invited by two research assistants (who are also seniors) to attend hosted gatherings in Ontario and Quebec (Canada). In total, the survey was administered to 103 participants, aged 65–95, and respondents were classified into 4 clusters based on their 'willingness-to-adopt' mobile phones: (Cluster 1) Does not use a mobile device and is not willing/or able to; (Cluster 2) Would like to use a mobile device but does not know how; (Cluster 3) Would like to use a mobile device, knows how/where to obtain one, but has not done so yet; (Cluster 4) Already uses a mobile device. Utilizing SPSS (Version 20) to analyze the data, it was discovered that the greatest level of significant difference along the 'willingness-to-adopt' spectrum occurred between Cluster 1 and 4 participants: i.e., the "non-adopters" (participants that rejected the idea of using a mobile phone) and the "adopters" (those who already owned a mobile device) and therefore the results have been tabulated based on the comparisons of these two clusters. As such, while the overall survey results included 103 participants, our first data analysis focused primarily on the results of the 73 participants comprising these two clusters. The other analyses including demographic profiles, frequency tabulations and the rest of our data analysis do include all 103 survey results.

The data on health demographics were divided into groups based on a self-reported 5- and 6- point scale, known as the 'Health Utilities Index (the 'HUI'), used by health professionals across Canada to assess general health (vision, speech, ambulation, dexterity, cognition, social activities and general health). Comparisons were made, using these indices, to better understand the difficulties any such restrictions may present while grocery shopping.

The shopping-related questions, examining how seniors shop and potential challenges experienced, were presented in the survey based on Likert self-report scales: 1 being the 'strongly disagree'/'never' category and 7 being the 'strongly agree'/'always' category. The frequency tables demonstrate the percentage of participants who experienced certain difficulties related to issues that might be addressed by the supermarket to facilitate and accommodate these difficulties.

B. **Participants.** Participants were a mix between male (35) and female (68). Of those interviewed, 4.95 % were in the income bracket of less than $10,000 (5 participants); 7.92 % between $10,001 and $15,000 (8 participants); 7.92 % between $15,001 and $20,000 (8 participants); 12.87 % between $20,001 and $25,000 (13 participants); 19.80 % between $25,001 and $40,000 (20 participants) and 46.53 % over $40,000 (47 participants) and two did not state their income bracket. The age of respondents varied between 65–95 years of age with distributions as follows:

65- < 70	70- < 75	75- < 80	80- < 85	85- < 90	90- < 95	95+
35 (33.98 %)	29 (28.16 %)	21 (20.39 %)	13 (12.62 %)	4 (3.9 %)	1 (0.9 %)	0 (0 %)

5 Results

We used an ANOVA statistical comparison [26] in order to examine the results based on each proposition and note which, if any, demographic and health indicators had an impact on mobile device adoption (Table 1).

Proposition 1 Result: The Demographic and health factors, indicated in Table 2, show that income, dexterity capabilities and general health show a distinction between non-adoption and adoption of mobile devices. Specifically, willingness-to adopt mobile devices (in this case, represented by those seniors who had actually adopted either mobile phones or tablets) was strongly related to income, regardless of age. On the other hand, non-adoption of mobile devices was significantly related to problems with dexterity and also, poor general health as proposed in Proposition 1 but no support was found in terms of cognition issues.

Proposition 2 Result: The psychological/social factor related to shopping was assessed, as indicated in Table 2, by asking a simple question: "How do you usually do your shopping at the grocery store?" The responses were aimed at seeing whether they preferred to go on their own or with others. The results show clearly that non-adopters of mobile devices differ significantly from adopters in terms of shopping more with friends. Non-adopters also showed significance at the 10 % level in terms of desiring to have

Table 1. Relationships between demographics/Health indicators and mobile device adoption

Factor	F value	P value
Age	1.002	0.320
Income	4.785	**0.032**[a]
Vision	0.328	0.569
Speech	0.146	0.704
Ambulation	2.490	0.119
Dexterity	2.950	**0.090**[b]
Cognition	0.511	0.477
Social activities	0.572	0.452
General health	2.880	**0.094**[b]

[a] significant impact in terms of mobile device adoption at the 5 % level
[b] significant impact in terms of mobile device non-adoption at the 10 % level

Table 2. Social

Q: how do you usually do your shopping at the grocery store?	F value	P value
On your own	.000	.998
With friend(s)	3.928	.051[a]
With family member(s)	1.825	.181
With non-family caregiver(s)	1.344	.250
Having someone pick things up for me	3.172	.079
Having things delivered	.683	.411

[a] significant impact in terms of mobile device non-adoption at the 5 % level

someone pick things up for them at the store. This is an interesting finding as "having things delivered" was not found to be significant; in other words, those who for whatever reason were not able to get to the store, preferred the social contact of having a known individual picking up items for them in the grocery store to having things delivered by an unknown person, thereby exhibiting a desire for social contact. The most important and clear finding here that is in line with Proposition 2, however, was that the social shopper prefers shopping with friends and is a non-adopter of mobile devices.

Proposition 3: While most of the tasks we asked about were considered to be difficult by the majority of respondents (i.e., finding products in the store, figuring out the price, reading price tags, figuring out the labeling of ingredients, comparing products based on quality or price, figuring out how promotions work), they did not all show a difference between adopters and non-adopters of mobile devices. Moreover, the situations where non-adoption was correlated to the environment of the store seemed to occur around figuring out complex, or out-of-the ordinary tasks such as figuring out how much a person required given multiple size options, figuring out price given price/weight rather than a unit price or figuring out the origin of products. Additionally, finding assistance and bathrooms proved to be challenging for non-adopters. As such, having access to a mobile device may provide opportunities given the challenges seniors currently face in the shopping environment. The following Table 3 outlines the tasks in grocery stores found to show a larger and significant difference for non-adopters of mobile devices over adopters.

Table 3. Experiential significant results when comparing adopters to non-adopters of mobile devices

Figuring how much I need given the size of the package or weight	4.282	.042[a]
Figuring out the cost given the price/weight	3.995	.049[a]
Figuring out where a product comes from	4.150	.045[a]
Selecting appropriate products for my diet	4.308	.042[a]
Finding assistance	9.515	.003[a]
Finding bathroom facilities	7.204	.009[a]

[a] significant impact in terms of mobile device non-adoption at the 5 % level

6 Discussion and Managerial Implications

The main purpose of the research presented in this paper was to build on previous research and undergo the creation of a simplified senior shopping typology utilizing a psychographics approach and the potential usage of mobile phones within their shopping experience to create three senior segments: the functionalist shopper, the social shopper and the experiential shopper.

(i) **The Functionalist Shopper.** Shopping is not perceived as a pleasant outing but rather as a chore that must be done, for functionalist shoppers. This type of shopper focuses on getting their products in the most efficient manner as quickly as possible. It was expected that they would be less inclined to adopt mobile devices. As health issues may potentially be related to this psychographic segment, these seniors could benefit from a mobile device while they shop that would include applications that make ingredients and products easier to read, notify them of promotions and make sure they do not get lost in the grocery store by planning out their trip in advance (e.g., app that details the layout of aisles, what is on sale, the easiest route, through the store given their product needs etc.). Our results demonstrated that non-adoption of mobile devices is significantly related to dexterity issues and overall poor general health. In fact, those with general health issues are less likely to adopt mobile devices and if combined with the functionalist personality, this might preclude the functionalist from seeking such services through mobile devices. For those functionalists who would prefer not to shop, and/or for those with specific health issues and/or dexterity issues there is likely a solid market for grocery delivery at the right cost and potentially for mobile apps supporting delivery services

(ii) **The Social Shopper.** The social shopper sees shopping as a way to socialize with fellow shoppers or customer service staff. They are the most likely to spend time shopping and be accompanied by friends. From the results of our data, this shopper has the least potential to adopt a mobile phone. That said, given the social nature of this shopper, apps that encourage communication (e.g., Instagram, texting) might encourage adoption of mobile devices, but not necessarily for use during the shopping process [27]

(iii) **The Experiential Shopper.** According to our findings, the experiential shopper enjoys the store experience. This consumer may value an app that lets them take a survey at the end of each grocery outing to inform the store how their experience was. They may enjoy having a GPS which informs them of select stores in their area based on set criteria they select. These customers appreciate a personalized coupon application, as they enjoy getting deals on the products they already buy. The data support the existence of this type of shopper, but unfortunately those with the most 'experiential challenges' in their shopping behaviors are non-adopters and are those who would probably benefit the most in terms of overcoming these challenges through adoption.

As such, while functionalists and social shoppers, in general are not adopters of mobile devices, this is not to say that these segments of senior shoppers would not benefit from mobile device use. Instead, they may prefer applications that are not used **during** the shopping process, but **beforehand**, e.g., a type of 'chatroom' that keeps track of when their friends are free to shop, a page that allows them to set up rideshares, a receipt tracker or a coupon app attached to a loyalty card, such as the successful app created by Nielson [6]. The mobile app/coupon customers tended to be more loyal shoppers of the participating retailer. They spent 66 % more per month than people not using the app and they made 44 % more trips to the store. This is an application that could be well-used by the experiential and functional shoppers within the senior sector.

Another option for consideration would be to enable information access utilizing in-store kiosks, particularly for functionalists and experiential shoppers. This approach could allow syncing with at-home devices or data cards, calling help when needed and/or looking up required and more complex information at the store.

In sum, there are a multitude of opportunities that exist to enrich the shopping experience for each of the three types of senior shoppers discussed in this paper: the functionalist, the social shopper and the experiential shopper. These opportunities for experiential improvement can be largely enriched through the encouragement of use of mobile devices, although clearly to-date, functionalists and socials show lower adoption rates. Adoption can be encouraged through simplification of services, lowering of price and education on how to use services of interest to each segment. As mentioned, the timing of access may be better facilitated through links to on-site kiosks or information provision prior to shopping.

7   Conclusion

Seniors have very specific capabilities, limitations and needs that affect their day-to-day activities such as shopping. This ever-fast growing market, that is expected to reach 800 million people by 2025 [33] could benefit widely from pervasive technologies such as applications, pending that their needs are well understood. We presented in this paper how a typology that harmonizes the aging-related factors with psychographic distinctions was developed to meet the ubiquitous needs of this segment and develop appropriate applications. Functionalist, social and experiential shoppers have different shopping experiences and challenges that can be improved and enhanced by pervasive computing. Given the influence of peer review on the adoption of technology, future research should test for how social influence plays a role in this market's willingness to adopt mobile devices. Moreover, this typology should also be tested across different cultures and identify the motivating factors for adopting such devices.

Acknowledgments. The authors would like to acknowledge the generous financial support of the Fonds de recherche du Quebec nature et technologie, awarded through the INTER research team, the University of Sherbrooke and Bishop's University, as well as the volunteer assistance of Lizzy Fontana and Mary Jean Reid.

References

1. Abdulrazak, B., Malik, Y., Arab, F., Reid, S.: PhonAge: adapted smartphone for aging population. In: Biswas, J., Kobayashi, H., Wong, L., Abdulrazak, B., Mokhtari, M. (eds.) ICOST 2013. LNCS, vol. 7910, pp. 27–35. Springer, Heidelberg (2013)
2. Aitken, M.: Patient Apps for Improved Healthcare From Novelty to Mainstream. IMS Inst. Healthc. Inf., October, 61 (2013)
3. Amatulli, C., Guido, G.: Determinants of purchasing intention for fashion luxury goods in the Italian market: a laddering approach. J. Fash. Mark. Manag. 15(1), 123–136 (2011)
4. Angell, R., et al.: Understanding the older shopper: a behavioural typology. J. Retail. Consum. Serv. 19(2), 259–269 (2012)
5. Bellenger, D.N., et al.: Shopping center patronage motives. J. Retail. 53(2), 29–38 (1977)
6. Cameron, D., et al.: Nielsen personalizes the mobile shopping app. J. Advert. Res. 52(3), 333–338 (2012)
7. Deloitte Touche Tohmatsu Limited.: 2015 Global life sciences outlook. Adapting in an era of transformation. www.deloitte.com/lifesciences
8. Flint, D.J., et al.: Shopper Marketing: Profiting from the Place where Suppliers, Brand Manufacturers, and Retailers Connect. Pearson Education, USA (2014)
9. Gabriel, M., Benoit, U.: The web accessible for all: guidelines for seniors. Univers. Access HCI. 4, 872–876 (2003)
10. Geuens, M., et al.: An exploratory study on grocery shopping motivations. In: Groeppel-Klien, A., Esch, F.-R. (eds.) E - European Advances in Consumer Research, pp. 135–140. Association for Consumer Research, Belgium (2002)
11. Goodwin, D.R., Mcelwee, R.E.: Grocery shopping and an ageing population: research note. Int. Rev. Retail. Distrib. Consum. Res. 9(4), 403–409 (1999)
12. Gunter, B.: Understanding the Older Consumer: The Grey Market. Psychology Press, Routledge (1998)
13. Hare, C., et al.: Identifying the expectations of older food consumers: more than a "shopping list" of wants. J. Mark. Pract. Appl. Mark. Sci. 5(6), 213–232 (1999)
14. Hare, C.: The food-shopping experience: a satisfaction survey of older Scottish consumers. Int. J. Retail Distrib. Manag. 31(5), 244–255 (2003)
15. LeRouge, C., et al.: User profiles and personas in the design and development of consumer health technologies. Int. J. Med. Inform. 82, 11 (2013)

16. Lian, J.-W., Yen, D.C.: Online shopping drivers and barriers for older adults: Age and gender differences. Comput. Hum. Behav. **37**, 133–143 (2014)
17. Lumpkin, J.R., et al.: Marketplace needs of the elderly - determinant attributes and store choice. J. Retail. **61**(2), 75–105 (1985)
18. Melenhorst, A.-S., et al.: The use of communication technologies by older adults: exploring the benefits from the user's perspective. Proc. Hum. Factors Ergon. Soc. Annu. Meet. **45**, 221–225 (2001)
19. Meneely, L., et al.: Elderly consumers and their food store experiences. J. Retail. Consum. Serv. **16**(6), 458–465 (2009)
20. Metz, D., Underwood, M.: Older, Richer, Fitter: Identifying the Consumer Needs of Britain's Ageing Population. Age Concern England, England (2005)
21. Miller, D.: A Theory of Shopping. Wiley, Hoboken (2013)
22. Mitchell, A.: The Nine American Lifestyles. Macmillan, New York (1983)
23. Moschis, G., et al.: Patronage motives of mature consumers in the selection of food in grocery stores. J. Consum. Mark. **21**(2), 123–133 (2004)
24. Moschis, G.P.: Marketing to Older Consumers. CT Quorum. Books, Wesport (1992)
25. Mumel, D., Prodnik, J.: Grey consumers are all the same, they even dress the same – myth or reality? J. Fash. Mark. Manag. **9**(4), 434–449 (2005)
26. O'Brien, R.G.: A general ANOVA method for robust tests of additive models for variances. J. Am. Stat. Assoc. **74**, 877–880 (1979)
27. San-Martín, S., et al.: The impact of age in the generation of satisfaction and WOM in mobile shopping. J. Retail. Consum. Serv. **23**, 1–8 (2015)
28. Stroud, D.: The 50-plus Market. Kogan Page Ltd., United Kingdom United States (2005)
29. Teller, C., et al.: Cognitive age and grocery-store patronage by elderly shoppers. J. Mark. Manag. **29**(3–4), 317–337 (2013)
30. Teller, C., et al.: The relevance of shopper logistics for consumers of store-based retail formats. J. Retail. Consum. Serv. **19**(1), 59–66 (2012)
31. Tréguer, J.-P.: 50 + Marketing: Marketing, Communicating and Selling to the Over 50 s Generations. Palgrave Macmillan, New York (2002)
32. Whelan, A., et al.: Life in a " Food Desert". Urban Stud. **39**(11), 2083–2100 (2002)
33. World Health Organization: World Health Report 2013: Research for Universal Health Coverage. Switzerland, Geneva (2013)

SmartSwim: An Infrastructure-Free Swimmer Localization System Based on Smartphone Sensors

Dong Xiao[1], Zhiwen Yu[1(✉)], Fei Yi[1], Liang Wang[1,2],
Chiu C. Tan[3], and Bin Guo[1]

[1] Northwestern Polytechnical University, Xi'an, China
{charyxiao, yifei93219}@mail.nwpu.edu.cn,
{zhiwenyu, guob}@nwpu.edu.cn,
[2] Xi'an University of Science and Technology, Xi'an, China
wangliang@xust.edu.cn
[3] Temple University, Philadelphia, China
cctan@temple.edu

Abstract. Many works have focused their attention on the sports activity monitoring and recognition using inherit sensors on the smartphone. However, distinct from many on-the-ground activities, swimming is not only hard to monitor but also dangerous in the water. Knowing the position of a swimmer is crucial which can help a lot in rescuing people. In this paper, we propose a system called SmartSwim employing smartphone as a sensor for swimming tracking and localization. In detail, we first present a sensor based swimming status classification and moving length estimation. A swimmer locating algorithm is then proposed drawing on the experience of pedestrian dead reckoning (PDR) concept. We implemented the system on commercial smartphones and designed two prototype applications named WeSwim and SafeSwim. Experimental results showed the accuracy of swimming status classification reaches more than 99 % and the Error Rate value for length estimation is lower than 7 % overall.

Keywords: Swimmer tracking · Localization · Drown detection · Social network

1 Introduction

Swimming pools are one of the major venues where accidental drowning occur, with young children especially vulnerable [2]. Such tragic accidents can potentially be minimized, as swimming pools usually have trained lifeguards on duty to rescue victims, provided they can get to them in time. This has prompted academic researchers [19, 20], as well as commercial companies [21], to propose systems to help identify potential drowning incidents in time.

Another equally important problem, apart from determining *who* are potential drowning victims, is to determine *where* the victims are exactly located. Lifeguards have a short period of time to reach a potential drowning victim, and an accurate method to pinpoint exactly where a swimmer is located in a pool is invaluable. This is,

© Springer International Publishing Switzerland 2016
C.K. Chang et al. (Eds.): ICOST 2016, LNCS 9677, pp. 222–234, 2016.
DOI: 10.1007/978-3-319-39601-9_20

in essence, an entity localization problem which is actively studied in the research community [5–9]. Most existing localization techniques can be classified as either infrastructure-based techniques, or device-based techniques.

Infrastructure-based localization relies on deploying infrastructure such as Wi-Fi access points to use the propagation of radio signals to estimate distance. Such techniques are accurate, but require the installation of additional infrastructure in swimming pools. However, existing device-based localization techniques cannot be applied directly to locate swimmers. The main reason is that, unlike walking or running, the swimmer may use different styles (e.g., breaststroke, freestyle, etc.) during swimming, which will cause different distance and different location of the swimmer.

In this paper, we propose *SmartSwim*, a smartphone-based system to accurately locate a swimmer in swimming pool. The smartphone running *SmartSwim* is encased in a waterproof carrier strapped onto the person while swimming. *SmartSwim* first learn the patterns for different styles of swimming (e.g., breaststroke, freestyle) by collecting the accelerometer and gyroscope values while people are swimming. It then automatically classifies the swim activity into different styles by using a sliding window technique and lightweight supervised learning algorithm. After identifying the specific style, *SmartSwim* then estimates the distance by calculating the location of a swimmer using the swimmer's original position, thus providing an accurate position of each swimmer in real-time. In addition, we can use *SmartSwim* to collect swimming data and share the activities on health social networks.

The remaining of this paper is organized as follows. In Sect. 2, we review the related work. The system framework is presented in Sect. 3. In Sect. 4, we describe the approach of swimming behavior recognition, followed by swimmer locating methods in Sect. 5. Then, two prototype applications based on the proposed system are demonstrated in Sect. 6. In Sect. 7, experimental results are presented. We conclude the paper in Sect. 8.

2   Related Work

Entity Localization: Infrastructure-based techniques use the Wi-Fi signal to determine the location of an entity [5, 6]. Closer to our work are smartphone-based techniques. Hsu et al. [7] designed an indoor localization system using the accelerometer and gyroscope sensors in a smartphone. Qian et al. [8] proposed an improved method using the inertial sensors with pedestrian dead reckoning (PDR) to determine the relative location change of a pedestrian.

Smartphone as a Sensor: Sports related applications based on smartphone sensing include running [1], golf [3], and snowboarding [4]. Similar to our work, Marshall et al. [13] proposed a system to use the smartphone to track swim coaching, allowing swimmers to access timely feedback and improve their swimming skills. However, the system cannot give the locations of potential drowning victims.

Swim Tracking and Analyzing: There have been several studies that used non-smartphone hardware to perform swim monitoring. Bächlin et al. [11] proposed a wearable assistant for swimmers, which consists of acceleration sensors with micro-controllers and feedback interface modules that a swimmer wears during swimming. The study of Siitola et al. [12] showed that tracking can be done with high accuracy using simple method that are fast to calculate with a really low sampling frequency.

In general, the system we proposed aims at swim tracking and swimmer locating by leveraging on the inherit sensors on smartphones. Compared to prior research, our work mainly focuses on swimming status classification, swimming length estimation, and swimmer localization.

3   System Architecture

In this section, we introduce the proposed framework for supporting swimming assistant applications as illustrated in Fig. 1. The system consists of three components: data capture, swimming behavior recognition, and swimming localization. We first collect data from the built in sensors on smartphone wore by a swimmer. Then, the data is pre-processed and features are extracted for swimming behavior recognition. Finally, the swimming localization is performed based on the recognized swimming behavior, stroke counts, and estimated depth.

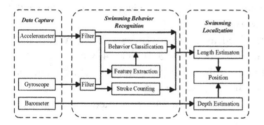

Fig. 1. *SmartSwim* system architecture.

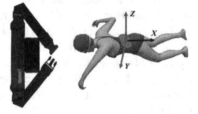

Fig. 2. The smartphone with a waterproof and the mounting position.

Data capture: We used the accelerometer, gyroscope and barometer sensors in a smartphone to capture the necessary data. Since a typical smartphone is not water resistant, we encased the phone in a waterproof pouch which is strapped onto the swimmer's lower back. Figure 2 shows the pouch and how it is worn by a swimmer.

Swimming Behavior Recognition: This module uses the collected sensor data to determine the swimming style. It first pre-processes the raw data using a combination of moving average filter to identify outliers and a sliding window technique to sample the data. After processing, the component extracts several features and applies supervised learning models for classification. The swimming behavior recognition component is able to recognize three main swimming styles, i.e., breaststroke, freestyle, and backstroke, in addition to walking and turning.

Swimming Localization: This module determines the actual real-time location of a swimmer. It consists of three parts: stroke counting, length estimation, and depth estimation. For stroke counting, we used the gyroscope data to detect each stroke. Then, a moving length estimation algorithm inspired by [10] is used to estimate distance. Unlike

[10] however, our proposed system can estimate five types (breaststroke, freestyle, backstroke, walking, and turning) of moving length. Finally, depth estimation is accomplished using barometer as an indicator. The swimmer's position is calculated by combining these factors with the swimmer's starting location.

4   Swimming Behavior Recognition

We first filter the raw sensor, and then extract features from the cleaned data, and finally recognize the swimming style using the extracted features.

Data Filtering: We collect the sensor data from the smartphone's 3-axis accelerometer and 3-axis gyroscope. Another extra m-axis sensing data for each sensor is then calculated from the root-mean-square value of 3-axis data individually using the Eq. (1).

$$m_s = \left(x_s^2 + y_s^2 + z_s^2\right)^{\frac{1}{2}} \tag{1}$$

$$G_{xyzfilterd}[i] = \frac{1}{M} \times \sum_{j=-(M-1)/2}^{(M-1)/2} G_{xyz}[i+j] \tag{2}$$

where s represents accelerometer or gyroscope sensor, and x, y and z represent the 3-axis data respectively. Thus, we have totally 8 dimensions, which are x, y, z and m axis data for accelerometer and gyroscope respectively.

However, each dimension of the sensing data consists of outliers which distort the patterns in the data. We compared three different filtering algorithms: moving average filter, mean filter, and Prewitt horizontal edge-emphasizing filter. Figure 3 illustrates the results of applying these three techniques on the original data. From the results, we can see that the moving average filter performs the best, as it removed the noise in the data effectively, and the filtered results are close to the real value. The equation that the moving average method used is as Eq. (2). where G_{xyz} is the original data obtained from the sensors, M is the window width and $G_{xyzfilterd}$ is the filtered data.

As indicated in the Eq. 2, the different width of the window M is directly related to the sampling rate of the data. We then use a slide window technique with 50 window width (frequency 100 Hz) to acquire the most ideal data. In practice, we chose about 2 s long window with a slide of 0.5 s between two sequential windows (see Fig. 4). Therefore, every two consecutive windows will have an overlap of 1.5 s and we classify the ongoing activity in each half second. The method has been widely used in existing studies and proved effective [12, 14, 15].

Feature Extraction: We classify swimming behavior into five types: breaststroke, freestyle, backstroke, walking, and turning. We found that different swimming behavior results in different body movement or posture. For example, when a swimmer is performing the breaststroke, his waist arches upward with every stroke to lift his head above the water for air. This folding motion of the waist is less pronounced when he is utilizing freestyle. When swimming with the freestyle, the swimmer's body will rotate more with each stroke as he rotates his body sideways for air. Based on these

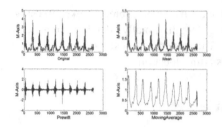

Fig. 3. Comparison of different filtering methods.

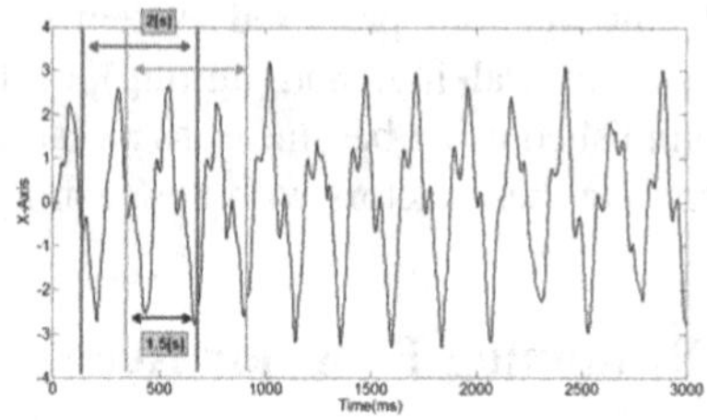

Fig. 4. Schematic view of sliding window.

observations, we extract three types of features which describe the posture of body activities as follows:

Body Folding Feature (BFF): A swimming style like breaststroke requires the swimmer's waist to be folded upwards every time he takes a breath, thus, the BFF describes the level how a swimmer folds his waist upwards. This is obtained from the m-axis accelerometer records, which is defined as Eq. (3).

$$BFF = \underset{0 \le i \le WS}{Max} \left(Acceler_i^m \right) \tag{3}$$

$$BRF = \underset{0 \le i \le WS}{Mean} \left(Gyr_i^m \right) \tag{4}$$

$$BDF_{Ver} = \underset{0 \le i \le WS}{Max} \left(Acceler_i^x \right) \tag{5}$$

$$BDF_{Par} = \underset{0 \le i \le WS}{Mean} \left(Acceler_i^z \right) \tag{6}$$

where *WS* represents the window's size for data sampling and $Acceler_i^m$ is the value in the corresponding window.

Body Rotation Feature (BRF): This feature describes the body rotation level while swimming. For example, when a swimmer performs an arm pull, his body is consequently rotated to keep balance. We use the BRF as a factor to indicate the rotation of body and it is extracted from m-axis gyroscope records, which is defined as Eq. (4), where Gyr_i^m represents the m-axis data from gyroscope in each sampling window.

Breast Direction Feature (BDF): A swimmer's breast direction could be classified into two types in a swimming pool: vertical against the horizontal plane when he is standing and parallel with the horizontal plane while he is swimming. Thus, we use BDF to distinguish these two body postures which is extracted from different axis data of accelerometer as Eqs. (5) and (6), where BDF_{Ver} and BDF_{Par} represents the vertical and parallel posture respectively, $Acceler_i^x$ represents x-axis data from accelerometer, and $Acceler_i^z$ is z-axis data in each sampling window.

Behavior Recognition: We explored various supervised learning methods in our behavior recognition. One constraint is that the method should be efficiently implemented with the limited computational resources of the smartphone. We found that tree-based classifiers such as J48, LADTree, and RandomTree were suitable for our purpose. As concluded by Woohyeok et al. [15], the specific user model which uses one user's data for training and testing at the same time can achieve high accuracy. Thus, we build different models for different swimmers.

5 Swimmer Locating

In order to locate a swimmer's position in real-time, we need to address three issues: swimming stroke counting, moving length estimation, and depth estimation. In this section, we will introduce the methods solving these problems respectively.

Swimming Stroke Counting: Based on our analysis of accelerometer, gyroscope and barometer data, we found that m-axis gyroscope data can be used as an indicator for recognizing breaststroke cycle while x-axis gyroscope data can be used for backstroke and walking cycle. Figure 5 shows the triaxial gyroscope signal collected from a smartphone during breaststroke. We can observe that m-axis gyroscope data shows better periodicity than the other axis of data, thus we adopt m-axis gyroscope data for cycle discovery on breaststroke.

Peak detection is a common method to discover cycles in time series data, in which sliding window [16] and criteria algorithm [8] are widely used. Prior work usually adjusts the size of window to realize peak detection manually. But this results in poor peak recognition accuracy, as the algorithm is largely dependent on the size of the window. As shown in Fig. 6, one cycle of a stroke is detected by discovering the peaks during the swimming period. There are several features in each cycle of data (see Fig. 6, one cycle of a stroke ranges from A to B). On the one hand, it is obvious that during the period from A to B, the curve has to cross the threshold value δ_k from negative to positive twice, and the corresponding time slot is Δt_k. On the other hand, there must be two peaks within this time period and the corresponding amplitude is defined as ΔG_k.

However, as the cycle detection process is a real-time procedure, it is impossible to obtain the current Δt_k at time t_k, and the threshold for period Δt_k is undefined as well. In order to estimate a relative accurate value of the threshold δ_k for period Δt_k, we use an empirical formulation based on the information from last cycle which is already detected, and the equation is defined as follows:

$$
\delta_k = \begin{cases} \dfrac{1}{4 \times WS} \displaystyle\int_0^{4 \times WS} G_m(t)dt, k = 0 \\[2ex] \dfrac{1}{2 \times \Delta t_{(k-1)}} \displaystyle\int_{t_{(k-1)}}^{t_{(k-1)} + 2 \times \Delta t_{(k-1)}} G_m(t)dt, k > 0 \end{cases} \tag{7}
$$

where WS represents the window's size, thus, for the first time to estimate δ_k, we use the first 4 window data of G_m. The following δ_k for time period Δt_k is then estimated employing the time slot at $t_{(k-1)}$, which is $\Delta t_{(k-1)}$ in particular. Therefore, after δ_k is estimated, it is possible to detect point A and B respectively for cycle detection as well as stroke counting.

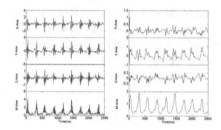 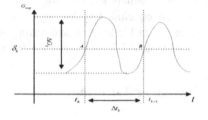

Fig. 5. Triaxial gyroscope data for breast-stroke: raw data and filtered data.

Fig. 6. One cycle of a stroke.

Although the above algorithm with an appropriate threshold δ_k is able to estimate the cycle time, a cycle verification mechanism must be introduced. The reason is that there still exists small disturbances which would influence the accuracy for cycle detection.

Intuitively, there is little difference between two consecutive swim strokes as people swim regularly, which means Δt_k fluctuates around $\Delta t_{(k-1)}$ and ΔG_k also fluctuates around $\Delta G_{(k-1)}$. Thus, it is unacceptable when Δt_k or ΔG_k is much shorter than $\Delta t_{(k-1)}$ or $\Delta G_{(k-1)}$ respectively. Therefore, Range Feature (RF) mechanism is then applied to distinguish the reasonable Δt_k and ΔG_k using history information.

Here, we define $\Delta t_k^{\min}$, $\Delta t_k^{\max}$, $\Delta G_k^{\min}$ and $\Delta G_k^{\max}$ as follows:

$$\Delta t_k^{\min} = \alpha \times \frac{\left(\Delta t_{(k-1)}^{\min} + \Delta t_{(k-1)}\right)}{2} \tag{8}$$

$$\Delta t_k^{\max} = \beta \times \frac{\left(\Delta t_{(k-1)}^{\max} + \Delta t_{(k-1)}\right)}{2} \tag{9}$$

$$\Delta G_k^{\min} = \alpha \times \frac{\left(\Delta G_{(k-1)}^{\min} + \Delta G_{(k-1)}\right)}{2} \tag{10}$$

$$\Delta G_k^{\max} = \beta \times \frac{\left(\Delta G_{(k-1)}^{\max} + \Delta G_{(k-1)}\right)}{2} \tag{11}$$

where $\Delta t_k^{\min}$ and $\Delta t_k^{\max}$ represent the upper and lower bound for a candidate Δt_k, $\Delta G_k^{\min}$ and $\Delta G_k^{\max}$ is the upper and lower bound for a candidate ΔG_k. Two adjustment factor α and β are considered in practice which are empirically set to be 2/3 and 4/3 respectively. As for different swim style, we initiate $\Delta t_k^{\min}$ and $\Delta t_k^{\max}$ with different fixed values manually and the ΔG_0 is calculated within the first 4 windows. Then, if any Δt_k is larger than the corresponding $\Delta t_k^{\min}$ and smaller than $\Delta t_k^{\max}$, as well as the value of ΔG_k is between $\Delta G_k^{\min}$ and $\Delta G_k^{\max}$ respectively, we can say that a swim stroke is discovered.

Figure 7 illustrates the results of stroke detection for breaststroke with the above algorithm, in which 9 strokes were detected. Once the stroke is discovered, it is easy to count the number of strokes, thus, each stroke length becomes the significant factor in moving length estimation.

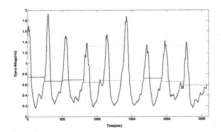

$$M_k = \sigma \times \frac{\sqrt[3.5]{\frac{\sum_{i=1}^{N} |a_i|}{N}} \times \sqrt[6]{a_{peak,diff}} \times \sqrt[7]{H}}{\sqrt[8]{\Delta t_k}}$$

(12)

Fig. 7. Results of stroke detection for breaststroke.

Moving Length Estimation: Our moving length estimation method is inspired by prior work on localization of walking subjects [10]. We present a moving distance empirical formulation, which is learned from the observations of the relationship between step length and other factors during walking.

First, we calculate M_k, which is the moving distance, defined as Eq. (12), where σ is an empirical coefficient with different fixed values in different strokes, a_i is the vertical acceleration, $a_{peak,diff}$ represents the difference between the maximum and minimum of vertical acceleration during one stroke, H is the height of swimmer, and Δt_k is the time for a cycle calculated by swimming stroke counting method.

The empirical coefficient can be customized through adjusting the value of σ. Assuming M_{real} is the ground truth of swimmer's moving distance, $M_{estimate}$ is the estimated value, the next moving distance σ_{new} is calculated as follows:

$$\sigma_{new} = \sigma_{old}^{\frac{M_{real}}{M_{estimate}}}$$

(13)

$$\begin{cases} X_{k+1} = X_k + C_k \times M_k \\ H_{k+1} = H_k + \Delta H \end{cases}$$

(14)

Depth Estimation: The barometer sensor is commonly integrated in modern smartphones, and the data from this sensor can be translated to height [17]. We found that the barometer is capable to measure height change under water with low sensing error. For instance, the change in the ambient pressure of 1 hPa requires the change in depth of only 0.01 m under water; this change can be achieved by altering the height of 7.9 m in the air [18].

Using the above three methods, we can locate the user with the Eq. (14). where X_k is the location on time k and X_0 is obtained from the user's original position, C_k is the stroke count, M_k is the average moving distance during the C_k strokes, H_k is the depth in the swimming pool of time k, and ΔH is calculated by using the barometer data.

6   Prototype Applications

We developed two prototypes to showcase the potential applications of *SmartSwim*. The first is a social network application, *WeSwim*, and the second is a safety monitoring application called *SafeSwim*.

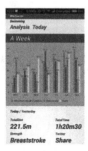

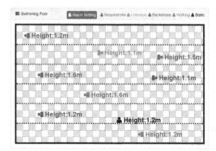

Fig. 8. WeSwim application.

Fig. 9. SafeSwim application. (Color figure online)

WeSwim: There have been considerable interests in developing social network applications that allow users to share their fitness records with their friends. For example, mobile applications such as Nike + Running allow users to share data, e.g., the number of steps, and the distance of walks, which improves the enthusiasm of each user. *WeSwim* is a similar application designed for swimming fans to share their swimming data (e.g., swimming distance, time, and style) with others through social networks. The user can check his/her personal records or share his/her records on social networks with smartphone after swimming, as shown in Fig. 8.

SafeSwim: To ensure the safety of swimming in a pool, lifeguards need to know the position of each swimmer. This is currently done by visually scanning the pool periodically. However, this type of visual scanning is prone to human errors. We developed the *SafeSwim* prototype to help lifeguards determine the location and status of each swimmer in a pool by visualizing their swimming data captured with the *SmartSwim* system. Figure 9 illustrates the interface of the application. As shown in Fig. 9, each swimmer is a point in the monitor, different color indicates different status: red for breaststroke, orange for freestyle, blue for backstroke, green for walking and black for static (standstill). And the depth of every swimmer is attached on the right side of each point. Using this monitoring application, lifeguards are able to get the overview of the locations of all swimmers in real time, making it easier to identify and reach potential downing victims in time.

7 Experimental Results

In this section, we evaluate the proposed system and methods based on a real-life swimming data set.

Data Collection: We recruited five college students (male, 23–24 years old) to collect data for experiments. The smartphone we used is XiaoMi 2 which integrates accelerometer, gyroscope and barometer. Each swimmer swam a distance of more than 100 m using different swimming styles. During their swimming, different kinds of strokes are recorded, including breaststroke, freestyle, backstroke and walking. The dataset is shown in Table 1.

Table 1. Swimming Data

Swimmer ID	Swimming status				Total(m)
	Breaststroke	Freestyle	Backstroke	Walking	
1	40	65	70	50	225
2	30	35	55	50	170
3	50	70	60	50	230
4	28	45	60	50	183
5	32	55	70	50	207

Results of Swimming Behavior Classification: As for distinguishing different swimming behaviors, we evaluate our extracted features by employing the effective feature quantities and the feature space of collected data shown as Figs. 10 and 11.

Figure 10 shows two features, BDF_{Ver} and BFF with different swimming behavior. Different color and shape indicates different records of swimming behavior, thus, we could find out that different magnitude of value on BDF_{Ver} or BFF leads to different swimming behaviors, specifically, when the value is lower than −5, a walking behavior can be inferred (in red dots) and a backstroke is detected (in pink stars) when the value of BFF is larger than 10 respectively. Figure 11 is similar with Fig. 10 but using the other two features which are BDF_{Par} and BRF. Therefore, combining these four features, it is possible for us to classify different swimming behaviors.

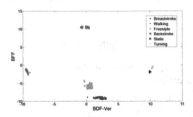
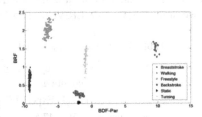

Fig. 10. Feature space for BDF_{Ver}-BFF. (Color figure online)

Fig. 11. Feature space for BDF_{Par}-BRF. (Color figure online)

We conclude the ability of different features to distinguish different swimming behaviors in Table 2. We can observe that the four extracted features have different ability for classifying different swimming behaviors. BDF_{Ver} is effective for indicating walking, BDF_{Par} has the ability to distinguish backstroke, BFF can be used to differentiate breaststroke from backstroke, while BRF performs well in recognizing freestyle.

Table 2. Effective feature quantity to differentiate swimming behaviors

Feature quantity	Possible classification
BDF_{Ver}	walking-(breaststroke-freestyle-backstroke)-(static-turning)
BDF_{Par}	(breaststroke-freestyle)-(static-walking-turning)-backstroke
BFF	breaststroke-freestyle-(static-walking-turning)-backstroke
BRF	freestyle-(backstroke-turning)-(breaststroke-walking)-static

$$ER = \frac{|\exp er - real|}{real} \times 100\% \quad (15)$$

Employing these features, we trained three tree-based supervised learning models: J48, LADTree, and RandomTree. The average accuracy for swimming behavior classification is 99.5 %. RandomTree outperforms the other two models with an accuracy of 99.75 %.

Results of Stroke Counting: Here we adopt metric Error Rate (ER) to evaluate the performance of stroke counting, which is calculated as Eq. (15). where $\exp er$ is the average number of estimated stroke counts, *real* stands for real stroke counts. We calculate the average stroke counts of breaststroke, freestyle, backstroke and walking for all swimmers respectively, and test the performance of our stroke counting algorithm, the results are demonstrated in Table 3.

As we can see, the ER is lesser than 5 % overall. Different status has different ER values, the lower value of ER means better accuracy for stroke counting. The accuracy of breaststroke and walking are the best and its ER value is 4 %, while backstroke has the worst accuracy as its ER value is 5 %.

Table 3. The accuracy of stoke counting and moving length estimation

Status	Accuracy of stoke counting			Accuracy of moving length estimation		
	Real	Exper	ER (%)	Real(m)	Exper(m)	ER (%)
Breaststroke	50	47.5	5.00	36	34.2	5.00
Freestyle	60	57.5	4.17	54	57.8	7.03
Backstroke	50	48	4.00	63	67.5	7.14
Walking	100	96	4.00	50	47.3	5.40

Results of Moving Length Estimation: In this experiment, we estimate the moving length of different strokes and compute the ER with the real moving length. The results are shown in Table 3. The ER value is around 7 % or less. Moving length estimation with breaststroke got the best accuracy with an ER of 5 %.

8 Conclusion and Future Work

In this paper, we propose a swimming localization system based on smartphone sensors, such as accelerometer, gyroscope, and barometer. The system estimates the distance with different strokes using the stroke classification and stroke counting. The depth is estimated with barometer. The experimental results show the effectiveness of the proposed approach. Two prototype applications were built based on the system.

Although our results show that the proposed system performs well, there are still several aspects can be improved. First, we plan to take more swimming status into consideration, which would be important to some emergencies such as convulsions and drawn. Second, in the current system, we only conduct experiments on a single straight line in swimming pool, however, it is more useful to achieve tracking arbitrary curves. Finally, developing more applications for different purpose based on this system can be of great value in everyday life.

Acknowledgment. This work was supported in part by the National Basic Research Program of China (No. 2015CB352400), the National Natural Science Foundation of China (No. 61222209, 61373119, 61332005), and the Specialized Research Fund for the Doctoral Program of Higher Education (No. 20126102110043).

References

1. Auvinet, B., Gloria, E., Renault, G., et al.: Runner's stride analysis: comparison of kinematic and kinetic analyses under field conditions. Sci. Sports 17(2), 92–94 (2002)
2. World Health Organization. Drowning fact sheet number 347 (2010)
3. Fitzpatrick, K., Anderson, R.: Validation of accelerometers and gyroscopes to provide real-time kinematic data for golf analysis. In: Moritz, E.F., Haake, S. (eds.) The Engineering of Sport 6, pp. 155–160. Springer, New York (2006)
4. Spelmezan, D,, Borchers, J.: Real-time snowboard training system. In: CHI 2008 Extended Abstracts on Human Factors in Computing Systems, pp. 3327–3332. ACM (2008)
5. Martin, E., Vinyals, O.: Friedland, G., et al.: Precise indoor localization using smart phones. In: Proceedings of the International Conference on Multimedia, pp. 787–790. ACM (2010)
6. Xiong, J., Jamieson, K.: ArrayTrack: a fine-grained indoor location system. In: NSDI, pp. 71–84 (2013)
7. Hsu, H.H., Peng, W.J., Shih, T.K., et al.: Smartphone indoor localization with accelerometer and gyroscope. In: 2014 17th International Conference on Network-Based Information Systems (NBiS), pp. 465–469. IEEE (2014)
8. Qian, J., Ma, J., Ying, R., et al.: An improved indoor localization method using smartphone inertial sensors. In: 2013 International Conference on Indoor Positioning and Indoor Navigation (IPIN), pp. 1–7. IEEE (2013)

9. Haverinen, J., Kemppainen, A.: Global indoor self-localization based on the ambient magnetic field. Robot. Auton. Syst. **57**(10), 1028–1035 (2009)

10. Deng, Z.A., Hu, Y., Yu, J., et al.: Extended kalman filter for real time indoor localization by fusing WiFi and smartphone inertial sensors. Micromachines **6**(4), 523–543 (2015)

11. Bächlin, M., Förster, K., Tröster, G.: SwimMaster: a wearable assistant for swimmer. In: Proceedings of the 11th International Conference on Ubiquitous Computing, pp. 215–224. ACM (2009)

12. Siirtola, P., Laurinen, P., Röning, J., et al.: Efficient accelerometer-based swimming exercise tracking. In: 2011 IEEE Symposium on Computational Intelligence and Data Mining (CIDM), pp. 156–161. IEEE (2011)

13. Marshall, J.: Smartphone sensing for distributed swim stroke coaching and research. In: Proceedings of the 2013 ACM Conference on Pervasive and Ubiquitous Computing Adjunct Publication, pp. 1413–1416. ACM (2013)

14. Kon, Y., Omae, Y., Sakai, K., et al.: Toward classification of swimming style by using underwater wireless accelerometer data. In: Ubicomp/ISWC 2015 Adjunct, Osaka, Japan

15. Woohyeok, C., Jeungmin, O., Taiwoo, P., et al.: MobyDick: an interactive multi-swimmer exergame. In: Proceedings of the 12th ACM Conference on Embedded Network Sensor Systems, SenSys 2014, Memphis, Tennessee, USA, 3–6 November 2014

16. Anhua, L., Jianzhong, Z., Kai, L., et al.: An efficient outdoor localization method for smartphones. In: 23rd International Conference on Computer Communication and Networks, ICCCN 2014, Shanghai, China, 4–7 August 2014

17. Kartik, S., Minhui, Z., Guo, X.F., et al.: Using mobile phone barometer for low-power transportation context detection. In: Proceedings of the 12th ACM Conference on Embedded Network Sensor Systems, SenSys 2014, Memphis, Tennessee, USA, 3–6 November 2014

18. Muralidharan, K., Khan, A. J., Misra, A., et al.: Barometric phone sensors: more hype than hope! In: Proceedings of the 15th Workshop on Mobile Computing Systems and Applications, p. 12. ACM (2014)

19. Eng, H.-L., et al.: DEWS: a live visual surveillance system for early drowning detection at pool. In: IEEE Transactions on Circuits and Systems for Video Technology, vol. 18, no. 2, pp. 196–210 (2008)

20. Kharrat, M., et al.: Near drowning pattern recognition using neural network and wearable pressure and inertial sensors attached at swimmer's chest level. In: 2012 19th International Conference on Mechatronics and Machine Vision in Practice (M2VIP). IEEE (2012)

21. iSwimband wearable drowning detection device. https://www.iswimband.com/

Tele-Assistance and Tele-Rehabilitation

Design of a Tele-Ophthalmology System
for Comprehensive Eye Examination and DR Screening
and Its Preliminary Implementation

Di Xiao[1(✉)], Janardhan Vignarajan[1], Tingting Chen[2], Tiantian Ye[2],
Baixiang Xiao[2], Nathan Congdon[2], and Yogessan Kanagasingam[1]

[1] The Australian e-Health Research Centre, Health and Biosecurity Flagship,
CSIRO, 147 Underwood Ave., Floreat, WA 6014, Australia
{Di.Xiao,Janardhan.Vignarajan,Yogi.Kanagasingam}@csiro.au
[2] Zhongshan Ophthalmic Centre, Sun Yat-sen University,
54 South Xianlie Road, Guangzhou, China
cttlxy@163.com, yolanda46514@gmail.com,
xiaobaixiang2006@126.com, ncongdon1@gmail.com

Abstract. We have developed a prototype version of telemedicine system, which combines web-based application, tablet app and digital retinal imaging, for comprehensive eye examination and diabetic retinopathy screening. Patient treatment and follow-up examination are implemented in the system. In the paper, we introduced the design of system architecture and main workflows and their preliminary implementations. The system provided a new service model through one grading center linking with multiple remote hospitals for eye care in Guangdong province, China. The early stage of the project practice and study also undertook the responsibility of educations for remote-area doctors and image graders for DR diagnosis and image grading. The project has successfully demonstrated the telemedicine system and associated workflows can be used for providing DR screening and eye disease diagnostic services in remote and rural hospitals in China.

Keywords: Tele-ophthalmology · Diabetic retinopathy screening · Telemedicine · Comprehensive eye examination · Diabetic retinopathy grading

1 Introduction

In 2015, 415 million adults had diabetes in the world. If without effective actions, the number will rise to 642 million by 2040 [1]. It was estimated every 6 s a person died from diabetes and five million people had died from diabetes [1]. According to the World Health Organization (WHO), in 2030, diabetes will be the 7th leading cause of death [2].

Diabetic retinopathy (DR) is one of the major and long-term microvascular complications of diabetes. DR is the most common cause of vision loss and blindness in the working-age adults. With the increased prevalence of Type 1, and especially Type 2 diabetes, it is anticipated that the impact of vision impairment and blindness associated with DR will invariably increase in the coming decades.

© Springer International Publishing Switzerland 2016
C.K. Chang et al. (Eds.): ICOST 2016, LNCS 9677, pp. 237–249, 2016.
DOI: 10.1007/978-3-319-39601-9_21

With the high prevalence of diabetes in the USA, the American Diabetes Association and American Academy of Ophthalmology recommended annual eye examination for Type I and Type II diabetes patients. Some early DR screening programmes were developed and practiced in countries, especially in USA and Europe [3–5], such as the French DR screening program in 1990 s, Diabetes 2000 program in USA from 1990 to 2000, and UK DR screening program before 2003.

In the past decade, the combination of telemedicine and digital retinal imaging technology was gradually applied in DR screening programs. In USA, there have been several long-term and large-scale DR screening programs, which screened millions of people and achieved success, such as the US Veterans Administration VistA program, EyePACS (University of California Berkley), Joslin Vision Network Diabetes Eye Care Program (JVN), and UPMC DR screening project (University of Pittsburgh Medical Centre). In France, "Ophdiat" diabetes telemedicine network created in the Île-de-France area [6] was a successful one, which included 7 hospitals, 11 primary healthcare centres and 2 prisons. UK National Health Service Program, which screened nearly 2 million people with diabetes per year, has been an example in the well-established DR screening programs [7]. The practices of these programs have shown that a telemedicine approach for DR screening can effectively increase the rates of eye examinations, thereby potentially reducing the rates of vision loss and blindness in the diabetes patients.

It is estimated that by year 2030 the increase of diabetes is disproportionately more in developing countries (69 % in developing countries vs. 20 % in developed countries with 2010 as baseline). This will result in a heavy burden on the health care system because of several DM related complications. In the past decades, China became one of regions with highly increased DR populations. It was estimated in 2030, the number of diabetes patients would be 42 million or even much higher [8]. Early DR screening for the populations is increasingly required [9].

This project has been supporting by World Diabetes Foundation and ORBIS. The goal of the project was to provide a telemedicine-based service model for remote and rural patients' eye care and DR screening based on local hospitals. Leaded by Zhongshan Ophthalmic Centre (ZOC), Guangzhou, China and Australian e-Health Research Centre, CSIRO, the project aimed at building a diabetic retinopathy grading (DR grading) centre in ZOC and linking with 10 remote hospitals in Guangdong province by a tele-ophthalmology system for patients' DR screening and other eye disease diagnosis and further providing efficient treatment and follow-up management for serving rural populations. The project also aimed at training ophthalmic doctors in remote hospitals for the improvement of diabetic retinopathy diagnosis and training image graders for DR grading.

This paper presents the preliminary design and implementation of the telemedicine system for meeting the above goals. In this paper, we stress system architecture, functional components and workflows, and present initial prototype of the system as well as its early practice in Guangdong, China for rural and remote patients' eye examination and DR screening.

2 Method

2.1 System Architecture

According to the project requirement, 10 remote and rural hospitals would conduct patient's comprehensive eye examination, retinal imaging and eye disease diagnosis according to their clinical settings. Image grading centre at ZOC (Guangzhou, capital city of Guangdong province) would conduct DR image grading and DR recommendation. Patient's treatment would be managed and operated by ZOC cooperating with each remote hospital for arranging eye surgery or laser photocoagulation. Most of the rural eye doctors had the skills to diagnose and give treatment suggestions to DR patients. ZOC trainers had been supporting them for better practice.

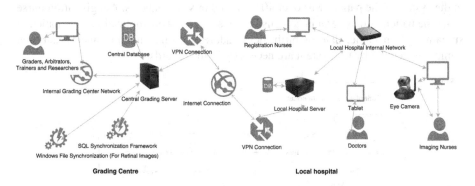

Fig. 1. System architecture.

Figure 1 shows the system architecture. In each local hospital, an independent work station with local web server and database server were built for storing all medical records and providing internet service, web-page service and Web Service for tablet application. Microsoft ASP.Net and MS SQL server technology were utilized for the server construction. Visual Basic.Net and MS Silverlight were employed for the web application and Web Service development. The server was protected by physical security at all times in the local hospital. Patient registration nurses and imaging nurses used the web-based application by web browsers in desktop computers for patient retinal image uploading, patient medical information recording and clinical workflow management. An android app using Java language was developed for the doctors to recording patient's comprehensive examination result, disease diagnosis and treatment plan by a step-by-step guide in the app. Standard wireless encryption protocols were used within a Wi-Fi router for data exchanges between the tablet app and the server.

In ZOC grading centre, the similar database server and web server were developed by the same Microsoft technology. Same web-based application was built but could be accessed only by image graders, image grading arbitrators, treatment trainers, researchers and system administrators based on their roles in the system assigned. The ZOC server system also consisted of SQL Synchronization framework and Windows File Synchronization framework for synchronizing all medical records and retinal images from the 10 servers in 10 hospitals to the central server in ZOC, by wrapping some proprietary software. The local hospital servers were connected with the central server by VPN connection.

Under the system architecture, there were several workflows designed for patient registration, retinal imaging, eye examination, image grading, disease diagnosis and treatment plan. In the following, we only discuss several core workflows.

2.2 Modeling and Main Workflow

Figure 2 illustrates a main workflow in the 10 local hospitals for conducting patient registration and disease diagnosis for DR and other eye diseases. When a patient first time visited a Department of ophthalmology in a hospital, he/she would be registered in the system if the patient was over 40 years old or with diabetes. A registration nurse input the patient's demographics by using the system's web application. The patient's surname, given name, date of birth, home address, mobile number and registration number generated by the system are necessary in the records.

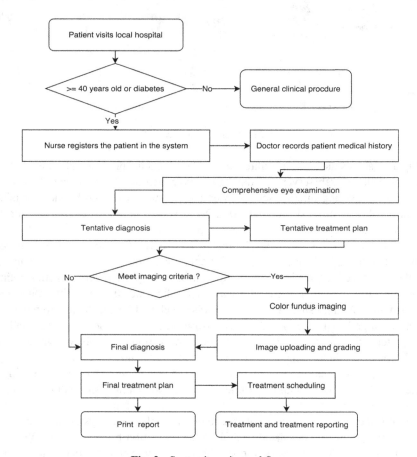

Fig. 2. System's main workflow.

The registered patient's name would be displayed in the doctors' patient pending examination list in their tablet apps. Once a doctor selected the patient, he/she first recorded the patient's medical history. Then he/she instructed the patient to complete all necessary comprehensive eye examinations. The doctor recorded the patient's eye examination results in the tablet app's eye examination page. Then the doctor could make the patient's tentative diagnosis and tentative treatment plan. If the patient met the project's imaging selection criteria, the patient would be sent for retinal imaging. An imaging nurse could conduct the imaging process and upload the captured retinal images to the system by the system's web application. The system then transmitted the patient's images to ZOC grading centre for image grading. After the grading result being sent back to the hospital, the doctor could open and view the image grading result as a reference and make his/her final diagnosis and treatment plan. If the patient didn't meet the imaging selection criteria, the doctor could directly make the final diagnosis and treatment plan and print the patient's clinical report.

2.3 Image Grading and Workflow

After the patient's retinal images were transferred to the ZOC grading center. The graders in ZOC could start DR image grading. A basic DR grading workflow is illustrated in Fig. 3. The workflow was designed by referring to the DR grading standard

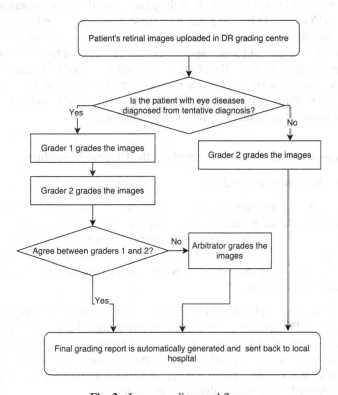

Fig. 3. Image grading workflow.

from UK National Screening Committee (UK NSC). The images collected from the 10 % normal patients based on the tentative diagnosis in each hospital (randomly selected by the system and uploaded) were directly assigned to the grader 2 for image grading. For the images with DR signs, the system assigned the grading task to the grader 1 first. After the grader 1 completed the grading, the system then assigned the task to the grader 2. The system arranged a back-to-back grading rule between the grader 1 and grader 2. After the grader 2 completed the grading task, the system automatically compared the grading results from the two graders and judged the consistency between them. If the two grading results were consistent, the result would be used as the final grading report. If inconsistent, the system would assign the task to an arbitrator. The arbitrator's grading result would be used as the final grading report. The report was sent back to the corresponding hospital automatically by the system. In the grading procedure, the grader 1, grader 2, and the arbitrator used the same web-based application for the image grading but with different access roles.

2.4   Treatment Scheduling and Treatment

If a patient was diagnosed with eye diseases and needed further treatment, the doctor needed to complete the treatment plan for the patient in the tablet app. If the patient needed revisit, a revisit date must be assigned. If the patient needed laser photocoagulation or eye surgery, the system would put the patient in the group of waiting for treatment scheduling. A trainer from ZOC could view the group from the web application and make a treatment appointment by calling and consulting with the registration nurse in the local hospital. The patient might be arranged for photocoagulation or surgery in local hospital supervised by ZOC trainers or surgery in ZOC. The treatment schedule presented in the calendar component in the system could be accessed by nurses, doctors and trainers by using the web application. After finishing the treatment, the trainer or doctor who conducted the treatment needed to complete an online treatment report and sign it.

2.5   Selection Criteria and Key Contents in the Clinical Procedure

Two key selection criteria were designed in the system:

1. Selection criteria for recruiting patients in the project: patients need to meet either: (1) with age equal and greater than 40 years old; or (2) with diabetes.
2. Selection criteria for recruiting patients in the fundus imaging: patients need to meet: (1) diagnosed with eye diseases and doctors decide the patients need retinal imaging; or (2) If diagnosed without eye diseases but selected randomly by the system (10 % opportunity) for imaging.

Some key contents implemented in the system in each phase of the eye examination, disease diagnosis, DR screening and treatment were designed and implemented.

In the patient medial history page, the tablet app enabled a doctor record a patient's following information, categorized as: symptoms, associated symptoms, incentives, intraocular laser history, eye surgery history, surgical approaches, type of surgery (time, location), systemic history and family medical history.

In the patient comprehensive examination page, the tablet app enabled a doctor record a patient's comprehensive examination results, including: vision and intraocular pressure, pupil examination, eye movement examination, slit lamp examination, gonioscopy, fundus examination, and the item of other comments. Each examination included some sub-examination items, such as fundus examination including the examination items of mydriasis, vitreous body, optic disc and cup; macula and retinal vascular, and the item of other comments.

The tentative and final diagnosis pages enabled the diagnostic result records for cataract, glaucoma possibility, glaucoma type, diabetic retinopathy, history of photocoagulation, ametropia, eye injury and eye inflammation, as well as the item of other comments.

The ZOC grading report page from the web application enabled the grading result records for diabetic retinopathy, diabetic macular edema, history of photocoagulation, image gradable or not and possibility of glaucoma. For DR grading, the system enabled the levels of DR input, as R0: No DR; R1: DR (background); R2: Non-proliferative DR (NPDR); R3a: Active PDR; R3s: Stable PDR. The levels of diabetic macular edema (DME) included: M0: No DME; M1: DME.

The tentative and final treatment plan pages in the table app had the similar contents for information record. They contained medication (text input), optometry, laser photocoagulation, eye surgery and revisit observation. The differences were that in the final treatment plan, photocoagulation type and surgery type were listed that needed a doctor to make selection.

The patient treatment record enabled a trainer/doctor record the following information after completing a treatment, including: patient basis information, DR diagnosis, location of treatment, treatment approaches of laser photocoagulation, laser photocoagulation parameter settings, revisit date, and type of eye surgery.

3   Results

3.1   Web Application

Figure 4 illustrates the homepage of the tele-ophthalmology system, which was named CREST electronic medical record (EMR) system. All functional components of the system are arranged in the homepage. At the top-right, there are 6 functional buttons for reporting, refreshing web page, displaying calendar, creating new patient, and exiting system. Once a registration nurse clicks the "Creating new patient" button, a pop-up window comes out and let the nurse input the patient's personal information, as shown in Fig. 5. After the new patient episode is created, the patient's name will be listed and displayed in the first tab T1-"Waiting for examination", which represents the current state of the patient. Tabs T1 to T7 (top-left portion of the homepage) in sequence represent the different states of the patients in the EMR system (refer to Fig. 4 for the tab names). A patient may or may not go through all the states, as we mentioned in the main workflow in Sect. 2. The nurse can access each tab and view patient list (lower portion of the homepage). The nurse can also view a patient's full information including personal contact, examination result, diagnosis result and treatment plan etc. in a pup-up window once the nurse clicks the patient name in a patient list (Fig. 6). In some tabs, the nurse has editing access authorized.

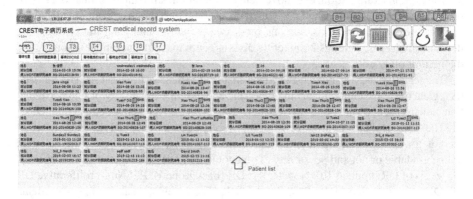

Fig. 4. Homepage of CREST EMR system (web app – demo version). Comments with red text: all tabs: T1-Waiting for examination; T2-Waiting for imaging; T3-Waiting for grading; T4-Waiting for final diagnosis; T5-Waiting for treatment scheduling; T6-Waiting for treatment; T7-Archived. All functional buttons: B1-Reporting; B2-Refreshing; B3-Calendar; B4-Searching; B5-Creating new patient; B6-Exit (Note: the patient names are test data rather real). (Color figure online)

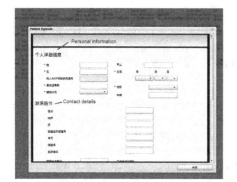

Fig. 5. Window for creating new patient episode.

Fig. 6. Window for reviewing a patient's full information in one episode.

Figure 7 illustrates the pop-up reporting window when a ZOC trainer or researcher clicks the "Reporting" button in the homepage. The trainer can use the first two items "trainer's schedule" and "treatment schedule" to arrange and view the appointments for the patients listed in the "waiting for treatment scheduling" state and "waiting for treatment" state, respectively. The researchers from ZOC can use the third item "statistical report" to define a specific period to generating a statistical report for a selected hospital, which will be implemented in future.

Nurses, doctors, trainers and researchers can also use the calendar button to open a calendar window to view specific events. In the calendar window, users can view patient list in the schedules under the categories of "patient revisit", "laser photocoagulation", "surgery in local hospital" and "surgery in ZOC" in a selected week. Figure 8 shows the "revisit" patient list in the first week of October 2015.

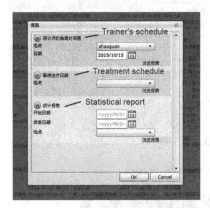

Fig. 7. Window for reports.

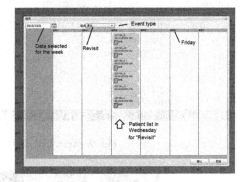

Fig. 8. Window of event calendar.

3.2 Tablet App

Doctors in local hospitals use the tablet app to complete the records about patient's medical history, examination result, disease diagnosis and treatment plan. After logging in, a doctor can select "My Current Patient" page and view three categories in order: patients pending for examination and tentative diagnosis, patients pending for ZOC grading and patients pending for final diagnosis. Each category lists all the patients in that state. The doctor can access any category at any time, however he/she usually needs follow the order of the categories for completing a diagnostic process. For examining and diagnosing a new patient, the doctor needs to access the first one and can view all patients listed there. After the doctor selects a patient, a new page with all categories of completing a patient's tentative diagnosis is displayed (as shown in Fig. 9, English version is shown in the right pane). The doctor can follow the categories in sequence in the left panel of the page to complete the patient's medical history enquiry, comprehensive eye examination, tentative diagnosis and tentative treatment plan as introduced in the workflow in Sect. 2.

Back to the upper-level three main categories, the "Patients Pending for ZOC Grading" category can let the doctor check the patients waiting for the grading feedbacks from the ZOC grading center. The doctor can access and view all the information about the patients from his/her tentative diagnosis phase but cannot make any edition.

After selecting the "Patients Pending for Final Diagnosis" category, the doctor can view patient list and select one patient, then can access a final diagnosis page as shown in Fig. 10. In the page, besides the similar categories in the previous tentative diagnosis page, underneath them, the "ZOC Grading Result", "Final Diagnosis" and "Final Treatment Plan" categories are added. The doctor can view his/her previous tentative diagnosis, further refer to the ZOC's DR grading result (including the patient's color fundus images) and make his/her final diagnosis and finalize the final treatment plan (Fig. 11).

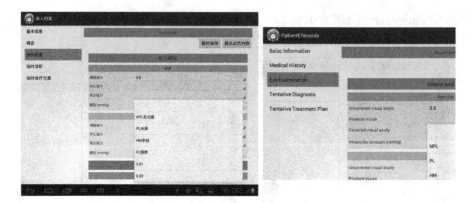

Fig. 9. Tentative diagnosis procedure page.

Fig. 10. Final diagnosis page – ZOC grading result category.

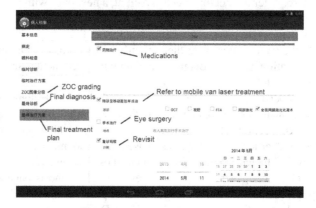

Fig. 11. Final diagnosis page - final treatment plan category and contents. (Color figure online)

3.3 Preliminary Clinical Trials and Discussions

Imaging camera adopted in the system was 3nethra classic non-mydriatic fundus camera with 45 degrees angle of field view (Forus Health Pvt. Ltd, Bengaluru, India). After completing retinal imaging by the system, an imaging nurse can use the web application to upload the images. The images associated with patient's basic information will be transferred to the ZOC grading center.

The first prototype version of the system with basic functions was completed in June 2013 and installed in one hospital at Shaoguan, Guangdong province for initial system test and evaluation by our working group. ORBIS team visited ZOC in June 2013 and discussed with ZOC team to understanding the progress of the project. In the following half year, more functional components were added step-by-step and system improvement was made, according to the feedbacks from our working group and clinical staff. At the end the year, the system was installed in 10 remote hospitals (one hospital from one city) in Guangdong province for clinical trials. Table 1 lists the name of 10 cities and the number of doctors from each hospital using the system. At ZOC, there were 2 image graders and 1 arbitrator for image grading. 2 researchers used the system for monitoring the workflows and analyzing the data.

After completing system evaluation in 3 months in 10 hospitals, in March 2014, a new version (version 3) was updated and installed. Figure 12(a) shows a clinical environment in a Hospital in Shaoguan, while a nurse is conducting a retinal imaging. Figure 12(b) shows one color fundus image with DR signs.

A preliminary statistical data collected in April 2015 presented that 9100 patients were recorded in the system and 2275 patients were with different levels of diabetic retinopathy. However, some functional components were still under improvement based on the feedbacks from our clinical working group.

Table 1. Number of doctors using the system in each hospital (in each city).

City	JieYang	Chenghai	Yangjiang	Huidong	Wuchuan
No. of doctors	2	4	1	8	2
City	Sihui	Yunan	Luoding	Yingde	Shaoguan
No. of doctors	2	2	4	1	3

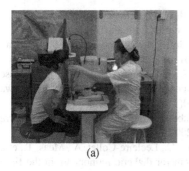 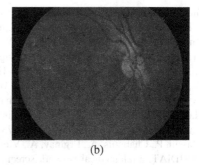

(a)   (b)

Fig. 12. A clinical environment for retinal imaging. (Color figure online)

A general telemedicine-based DR screening system, simply for referral/no referral decision, cannot replace a comprehensive eye examination in terms of overall ocular evaluation. In this project, we have combined the two in one telemedicine system for increasing the rates of patient access, eye disease assessment and DR screening in remote areas in the level of hospitals in small- or medium-sized cities in China.

Because of involving eye comprehensive examination, the whole clinical process would be longer than usual. On the tablet app, how to select and utilize the examining items effectively would be depending on doctor's experience and decision. At the early stage, imaging procedure might take longer time. With the improvement of operating skill, the nurses could control the process within 5 min. For education and research purpose, tentative and final diagnoses and treatment plans are two separate steps, how to make it more efficient is an issue that we need to think about in future. We are targeting to improve the efficiency of system in our next stage after collecting enough feedbacks from the doctors and nurses.

4   Conclusion

We have developed a telemedicine system for comprehensive eye examination and DR screening, eye disease diagnosis, DR treatment through our cloud-based web application and tablet application. The tele-ophthalmology system provided a new service model to support DR screening and eye care by linking multiple remote hospitals and one grading centre in Guangdong province, China.

In our preliminary clinical trials of the system, we have shown that the telemedicine system can be used for diabetic retinopathy screening and eye disease diagnosis with its usability and scalability. The system is currently continuing its usage and some new functional components are being added, such as statistical report. In future, some research and training components can be simplified or switched off once these components have been verified for their functionalities and completed their missions. Then the entire system will be more efficient.

References

1. International Diabetes Federation. Diabetes atlas. 7th edn. http://www.idf.org/diabetesatlas
2. WHO Media Centre Diabetes. www.who.int/mediacentre/factsheets/fs312/en/index.html
3. Rubino, A., Rousculp, M.D., Davis, K., Wang, J., Girach, A.: Diagnosed diabetic retinopathy in France, Italy, Spain, and the United Kingdom. Prim. Care Diab. 1(2), 75–80 (2007)
4. Kilstad, H.N., Sjølie, A.K., Gøransson, L., Hapnes, R., Henschien, H.J., Alsbirk, K.E., Fossen, K., Bertelsen, G., Holstad, G., Bergrem, H.: Prevalence of diabetic retinopathy in Norway: report from a screening study. Acta Ophthalmol. 90(7), 609–612 (2012)
5. Hansen, A.B., Andersen, M.V.N.: Screening for diabetic retinopathy in Denmark: the current status. Acta Ophthalmol. Scand. 82(6), 673–678 (2004)
6. Massin, P., Chabouis, A., Erginay, A., Viens-Bitker, C., Lecleire-Collet, A., Meas, T., et al.: OPHDIAT: a telemedical network screening system for diabetic retinopathy in the Île-de-France. Diab. Metab. 34(3), 227–234 (2008)

7. Peto, T., Tadros, C.: Screening for diabetic retinopathy and diabetic macular oedema in the United Kingdom. Curr. Diab. Rep. **12**(4), 338–345 (2012)
8. Ding, J., Zou, Y., Liu, N., Jiang, L., Ren, X., Jia, W., Snellingen, T., Chongsuvivatwong, V., Liu, X.: Strategies of digital fundus photography for screening diabetic retinopathy in a diabetic population in urban China. Ophthalmic Epidemiol. **19**(6), 414–419 (2012)
9. Peng, J., Zou, H., Wang, W., Fu, J., Shen, B., Bai, X., Xu, X., Zhang, X.: Implementation and first-year screening results of an ocular telehealth system for diabetic retinopathy in China. BMC Health Serv. Res. **11**, 250 (2011)

Handling Gait Impairments of Persons with Parkinson's Disease by Means of Real-Time Biofeedback in a Daily Life Environment

Alberto Ferrari[1(✉)], Pieter Ginis[2], Alice Nieuwboer[2],
Reynold Greenlaw[3], Andrew Muddiman[3], and Lorenzo Chiari[1]

[1] Department of Electrical, Electronic and Information Engineering, "Guglielmo Marconi",
University of Bologna, Bologna, Italy
{alberto.ferrari,lorenzo.chiari}@unibo.it
[2] Neuromotor Rehabilitation Research Group, Department of Rehabiliation Sciences,
KU Leuven, Leuven, Belgium
{pieter.ginis,alice.nieuwboer}@kuleuven.be
[3] Oxford Computer Consultants Limited, OCC, Oxford, UK
{reynold,andrew.muddiman}@oxfordcc.co.uk

Abstract. A smartphone app with telemedicine capability integrating data from foot-mounted inertial measurement units (CuPiD-system) was developed to realize a portable gait analysis system and, on top of it, to provide people with Parkinson's disease (PD) remote supervision and real-time feedback on gait performance. Eleven persons with PD were recommended to perform gait training for 30 min, three times per week for six weeks. The app offered praising/corrective verbal feedback, encouraging participants to keep the spatio-temporal gait parameters within a clinically determined 'therapeutic window'. On average, persons performed 20 training sessions of 1.8 km in 24 min and received 28 corrective and 68 praising messages. The mean walking rhythm was 58 strides/min with a stride length of 1.28 m. System's usability was determined as positive by the users. In conclusion, CuPiD resulted to be effective in promoting gait training in semi-supervised conditions, stimulating corrective actions and promoting self-efficacy to achieve optimal performance.

Keywords: Parkinson's disease · Wearable sensors · Android APP · Tele-rehabilitation · Biofeedback · Gait

1   Introduction

Wearable sensors combined with smartphone apps for health monitoring and coaching are an emerging research field. It is expected that it will enable proactive personal health management and continuous treatment of several medical conditions [1–3]. These systems, comprising various types of small motion sensors and telemedicine back-end services, promise to change the future of personal healthcare by exploiting low-cost unobtrusive solutions for all-day and ubiquitous supervision of health and life style [4, 5].

Overall, innovations in wearable monitoring systems are shifting the medical sector from the traditional approach reactive to healthcare–treating problems at the crisis level,

© Springer International Publishing Switzerland 2016
C.K. Chang et al. (Eds.): ICOST 2016, LNCS 9677, pp. 250–261, 2016.
DOI: 10.1007/978-3-319-39601-9_22

to a proactive health management approach which allows health issues to be postponed, discovered and promptly addressed at an early stage [6]. The design and development of such devices in the context of major orthopedical and neurological conditions focuses on the treatment of the motor symptoms and aims to promote a healthier lifestyle and support clinical decisions making [7]. Consumer-grade smartphones in association or not with additional sensors are more and more successfully employed to support patients in the management of their pathologies [8]. In addition, smartphones easily enable the transfer of preprocessed information, acquired via wearable sensors, to specialized clinical facilities by means of highly automated telemedicine services. This feature allows the implementation of remote clinical supervision overcoming logistical limitations such as travel distances and lack of local expertise. By this, expenses are strongly reduced for both patients and healthcare systems [8].

In this technology-enhanced healthcare context, some of the most promising applications exploiting the use of sensors and smartphones that goes beyond simply monitoring the progression of symptoms, have been developed for persons with Parkinson disease (PD). Such applications aim to achieve a therapeutic function, treating motor impairments through practice enhanced with cues or biofeedback [9–12]. Biofeedback refers to the provision of external stimuli during or immediately after a motor act such as a step, which supplements sensory (proprioceptive) pathways to guide motor performance. In such a framework, subjects' cognitive engagement is stimulated and effects of motor exercise are enhanced [12–15].

Gait in PD is particularly impaired when automaticity is required, precluding patients to walk safely while performing a secondary task. Due to this automatization deficit, people with PD require more attentional resources to perform gait optimally, such as maintaining walking speed, large steps, cadence, upright trunk posture, etc. [16]. As the disease progresses, most of the balance and gait impairments become resistant to the pharmacological and surgical treatments [17]. Yet, to circumvent the dopamine deficits, physical therapy and rehabilitation can be effective to counteract motor impairments [18]. Taking into account the chronic and neurodegenerative nature of PD, rehabilitation and exercise therapy should be incorporated on the long-term into the everyday routine in order to reach maximal effectiveness [19, 20].

Innovatively, but building on both patients' needs [21, 22] and recent evolutions of mobile health technology, Casamassima et al. [23] developed a unique wearable sensors and smartphone-based system that provides real-time, personalized feedback in order to improve the dynamic balance and gait performance of people with PD [10, 24, 25]. Unlike commercially available systems, this tailor-made tool is based on state-of-the-art principles of rehabilitation and motor learning. The system was referred to as CuPiD: Closed-loop system for personalized and at-home rehabilitation of people with Parkinson's disease, and can be used as a walking aid, providing online verbal corrections, intelligent cueing and performance feedback. CuPiD has been designed by a multidisciplinary team of experts in the fields of PD care and biomedical engineering together with PD patients, who took direct part in careful addressing effectiveness and user-friendliness of the tool.

The technological solution consists of a fully portable and wearable architecture based on Inertial Measurement Units (IMUs) connected via Bluetooth to an Android smartphone which functions as a portable processing platform. CuPiD performs an accurate step-by-step real-time gait analysis by processing the inertial data and, on top of it, provides persons with PD biofeedback on gait performance in a closed-loop architecture. Feedback provision is regulated by a logic flow of states and conditions automatically adapting to the reality and aimed at challenging the person to maintain their gait performance close to a personalized target. This target is subject-specific and periodically customizable during a calibration trial in which the patient is asked to walk at her/his best. From the selected calibration trial, the stride length, cadence and gait speed are computed and saved as reference values, subsequently used during routinely training sessions. Conversely, two gait training parameters do not require any reference values. Gait asymmetry continuously compares the right and left performance and provides feedback when the difference exceeds the clinically preset threshold. Similarly, upper body posture takes into account the gravity component to provide feedback upon the recognition of the stooped posture seen in people with PD [23].

During the training sessions, verbal corrective feedbacks are provided to the user each time the difference, expressed as a percentage, between the real-time value and the reference value is above an upper or below a lower tolerance (i.e. therapeutic window). On the contrary, if the person is able to maintain within this therapeutic window, a verbal reinforcement is played. The therapeutic window (intended as the area between the upper and lower tolerances) is a measure of the adherence to the clinical target and determines the level of difficulty and challenge of the training.

Before the start of the training, the initial frequency of feedback provision and size of the therapeutic window are manually adjustable by the user or the clinical operator. During training these settings are automatically controlled and handled by the CuPiD app itself, which dynamically looks for an operating point corresponding to a training level neither too demanding and verbose, with an excessive number of vocal instruction or messages per time unit, neither useless and silent, with too few messages. Furthermore, in the attempt to increase adherence, following approaches were implemented. Firstly, verbal messages were prerecorded with the voice of the patient's physiotherapist. Secondly, each verbal message provided to the patient was randomly selected from three different mp3 files, each containing a different expression of the same content. Thirdly, as long as the patient is able to provide a correct performance remaining within the therapeutic window the frequency of praising feedbacks is progressively reduced. Fourthly, CuPiD automatically identifies resting periods or moments without walking and enters in a standby mode, disabling the biofeedback. Finally, verbal messages have been accurately formulated by clinicians to stimulate the motor adjustments usually prompted during rehabilitation sessions in the clinical settings [25].

CuPiD is intended to foster daily walking in a semi-supervised condition lasting, according to patient capabilities, around half an hour. Noteworthy, the system has been designed not just to improve physical fitness but especially to train and rehabilitate the motor control aspect of gait attempting to regain the automaticity of gait execution, normally coordinated by the central pattern generators. For example, by setting both gait speed and stride length as monitored parameters patients are forced to maintain a certain walking speed without incrementing the cadence but using just the stride length as the regulating strategy [10].

Ginis et al. have recently reported the results of a pilot randomized controlled trial about the CuPiD app's feasibility and clinical effectiveness [10].

Aims of the present study were: (i) to test users' acceptance in an extended use of the CuPiD system; (ii) to assess the adherence of patients in using the system to practice safe walking independently, during outdoor walking in various settings; and (iii) to propose an intelligent telemedicine infrastructure for remote monitoring and supervision of the rehabilitation program by a clinician.

2   Materials and Methods

Eleven persons with PD undertook gait training during a period of six weeks (10 Males, age: 65 ± 9 years, height 174 ± 7 cm, weight 83 ± 18 Kg, disease duration 12 ± 5 years, Hoehn & Yahr 2.3 ± 0.4, UPDRS III [0–132] 36 ± 16.2, ON L-Dopa). The study was approved by the local ethic committee of the University Hospitals of Leuven. All participants gave written consent according to the declaration of Helsinki. Nine participants completed the training. The reason for one dropout was due to difficulties operating the CuPiD system without any supervision present and for the second dropout was unrelated to CuPiD.

Participants received weekly home visits from the researcher during the six weeks intervention and were instructed to walk at least 3 times per week for 30 min, according to ACSM's exercise guidelines for health benefits. In the first session, patients were explained how to use the system by an expert. Participants were also taught on how to apply the IMUs to their shoes by means custom made holders, and to carry the smartphone in a pocket. A booklet with pictures and personalized instructions was left in the home and consultation by telephone was offered in case of difficulties using the system. The optimal performance walk was recorded during the initial visit and repeated on average twice over the 6-week study period. At the end of the study patients were asked to fill in an ad-hoc questionnaire similar to QUEST [26]. Results on system usability and feasibility are reported.

During their walks participants were instructed on how to run the CuPiD app and follow the feedbacks via earphones on a set of gait parameters preselected on a daily basis according to a personalized rehabilitation program determined by the patient's clinician. The app offered praising/corrective verbal feedback, encouraging to keep the pre-set gait spatio-temporal parameters to remain within the therapeutic window.

Data showing the average amount of training sessions performed as well as the average time and distance walked, steps taken, cadence, gait speed and both praising and corrective messages delivered per session are reported. Exemplary data from one PD patient of CuPiD's functioning during a single trial as well as over the entire 6 weeks course are also reported.

The Tele-rehabilitation infrastructure was developed addressing the concerns of recent telemedicine reviews: interoperability, accessibility and reliability [8]. The aim of this service is the delivery of the training data to a server resulting in a secured and accessible way for rehabilitation specialists, allowing them to monitor and upgrade the training protocols remotely. As soon as the user's domestic Wi-Fi connection is detected, app data is automatically uploaded from the local smartphone gateway to a central server via an encrypted store-and-forward network. Software running on the central server checks the integrity of the received data, handles errors and decrypts to the original file. The access to the data storage is being regulated through a web application, implementing an authentication via a single sign on mechanism and differentiating between users and clinicians. From the web application clinicians have access to raw data, aggregated data and automated training reports displayed in charts summarizing information related to both single and multiple training sessions.

3 Results

The average scores of the 10 PD persons involved in the study for system usability and feasibility were obtained on a Likert scale which goes from 1 "totally disagree" to 5 "fully agree" and are reported in Table 1.

In general, participants were very positive about the CuPiD system, as scores on user-friendliness were on average above 4. However, attaching and removing the IMUs and using the CuPiD system without technical support resulted in more variable answers, as

Table 1. CuPiD usability and feasibility.

Likert scale for CuPiD usability and feasibility	1: totally disagree - 5: fully agree
I can turn on the foot sensors easily	4.5 (0.7)
I can wear the foot sensors easily	4.4 (1.0)
I can wear the trunk sensor easily	4.6 (0.5)
I can turn on the mobile phone easily	4.7 (0.5)
I can turn on the CuPiD APP easily	4.7 (0.5)
It is easy to connect the app with the sensors	4.5 (0.7)
The system reacts to the changes in my walking	4.6 (0.5)
The feedback that is provided is easy to understand	4.6 (0.5)
The feedback that is provided is consistent with the training I received	4.6 (0.7)
I think I can use the system independently	4.4 (0.8)
In my opinion, the training is suitable for patients with Parkinson's disease	4.6 (0.7)
The auditory feedback is heard well	4.9 (0.3)
I can remove the foot sensors easily	4.6 (0.5)
I can remove the trunk sensor easily	4.6 (0.5)
I can operate the CuPiD APP easily	4.5 (0.7)
I think the CuPiD APP is simple to use	4.2 (0.8)
The manual is clear and simple to understand	4.4 (0.7)
I find 3 times a week training feasible to my condition	4.3 (0.9)
I enjoyed the home training and find it interesting	4.1 (1.1)
I find the home training challengeable	3.9 (0.9)

indicated by the standard deviations (Table 1). It was observed that participants with previous smartphone experience had the least problems using the system. Some participants were so enthusiastic about CuPiD that expressed disappointment after its withdrawal.

The dosage of the intervention carried out by CuPiD is summarized in Table 2.

Table 2. CuPiD dosage.

CuPiD Dosage – mean values over the 6 weeks	
Number of trials	20
Distance travelled	1.8 km
Total number of left plus right strides	2844
Training duration	24 min
Cadence	116 steps/min
Stride length	1.3 m
Stride duration	1.05 s
Gait speed	1.24 m/s
Number of praising messages	68
Number of correcting messages	28

An example of CuPiD's functioning during a single trial is reported in Fig. 1. In particular, the figure shows that 1736 strides were performed and also displays the therapeutic window, when praising and corrective feedbacks were provided as well as the percentage difference of the (a) strides length and (b) gait speed with respect to the corresponding reference values.

Figure 1 is an example of how the app requires attention and trains motor control of gait aspects. Initially the patient had difficulties to maintain the optimal gait speed (up till around step 700). This while, between steps 800 until 1200, the patient attempted to adjust the gait speed by reducing the stride length, which was clinically unwanted and therefor elicited corrective feedbacks. Finally, from step 1200 the patient was able to maintain at the personalized and pre-recorded optimal stride length and gait speed.

Figure 2 shows the effect of CuPiD training over the 6 weeks period. The figure allows the assessment of both intra-and inter-session results. First of all, on this figure it is possible to determine within one session (intra-session): (i) the amount of corrective feedbacks; (ii) the onset of fatigue at the end of training (not visible in Fig. 2 nor in Fig. 1); (iii) how close the patient could perform with regard to the reference value and; (iv) the trend of the upper and lower limits of the therapeutic window. Furthermore, over the subsequent sessions (inter-sessions) following information can be distilled: (i) the trend of changes in reference values (shown in Fig. 2 from session 3 to session 4); (ii) the effect of having (or not) a parameter set as the primary or secondary training parameter and; (iii) the overall effect CuPiD has over the different weeks.

Figure 3 reports four screenshots of the web application of the telemedicine service. In particular, this web application comprises an authentication page (Fig. 3a) in which the clinician or the user can login. The sole purpose of this login is to allow clinicians to access only their patients' information and to guarantee privacy for the patients' training data. Following login, the clinician directly comes to a home page containing

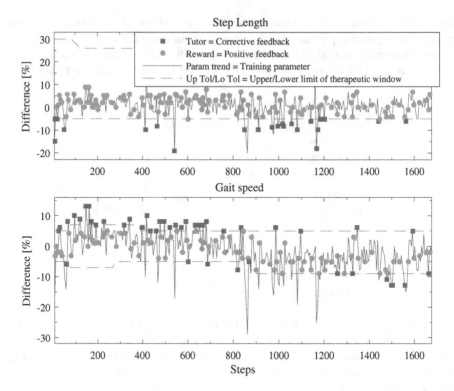

Fig. 1. The x-axis reports the number of steps acquired. The solid (blue) line shows the % difference of the (a) stride length and (b) gait speed with respect to the corresponding reference values. The dashed (red) lines mark the upper and lower values of the therapeutic window, the dots (green) mark a praising message and the squares (red) mark a corrective message. (Color figure online)

a table, listing his patients alphabetically with some basic details (Fig. 3b). It is clearly indicated whether patients have new logs, or if they have entered new contact requests. This way the clinician has an immediate and proper overview of the required actions. All data collected is de-identified and subjects are provided with study numbers to maintain confidentiality.

The CuPiD telemedicine server assures that all incoming and outgoing transmissions are encrypted using the SSL protocol (https). Unencrypted connections are rejected. The server is divided into a Repository and a CuPiD Clinical UI each lying behind a firewall. The server employs Microsoft identity credentials to map from the CuPiD Repository to the CuPiD Clinical UI as to ensure the integrity of the information. Clinicians and devices are given a username and password to allow each of them to access the allocated services and data of patients to which they are assigned. A username may or may not be the same as an identifier. Identifiers are intended to be anonymous, whereas usernames are not necessarily anonymous. A user may choose to waive its anonymity by having their username and identifier identical. All passwords are hashed and salted.

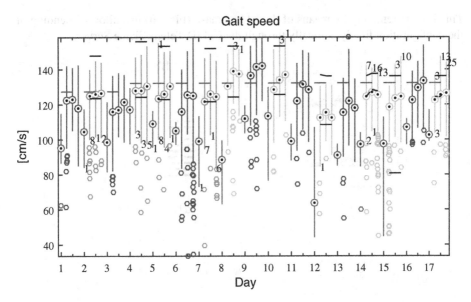

Fig. 2. The figure shows on the x-axis the 16 different trainings organized in such a way that the data of a single session is divided over 4 box plots, the first one in red contains values of the gait speed before the first feedback was provided to the patient and the following three box plots show, equally divided, the remaining steps of the training session. The numbers above and below each box plot indicate the amount of corrective feedbacks provided in the three different phases of the training. The black horizontal lines mark the upper and lower levels of the therapeutic window with in between as green line the pre-recorded reference (target) value. Green box plots indicate that the gait parameter, in this example gait speed, was selected as the primary training parameter. Cyan box plots indicate that the gait parameter was selected as the secondary training parameter. Blue box plots indicate that the particular training parameter was not monitored in real-time by the app. (Color figure online)

All mobile devices only connect via individual patient credentials with the CuPiD Repository which is an implementation of the Apache WebDAV. This is an established protocol, which runs on HTTPS and has been chosen for reliability, familiarity for IT staff and because HTTPS is relatively easy to allow through firewalls. This way, the app will not interact directly with the CuPiD Clinical interface. A service running in the background on the smartphone and upon active Wi-Fi detection initiates the synchronization of all data and reports generated by the app (raw data, processed data and high-level reports) with the server through a secure connection. Next, it is possible to remotely edit or change the entire rehabilitation protocol and by simply uploading a configuration text file to the data folder of the CuPiD app running on the smartphone.

The flexibility of the telemedicine design allows the clinician to review the raw training data and outcomes of both single and multiple trials by means of centralized charting and data visualization tools (Fig. 3c). When the results of the trial have been reviewed, the clinician can take the decision to change the rehabilitation protocol, e.g. the amount and type of gait parameters, initial limits of the therapeutic window, etc.

This is done remotely by means of the ad hoc mask (Fig. 3d) that allows amending of the configuration file dynamically through the CuPiD Telemedicine Server.

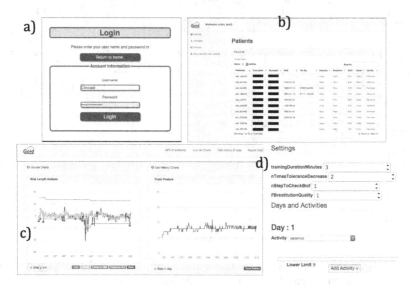

Fig. 3. Telemedicine web application: (a) authentication page for the login of clinician or user; (b) home page with patients basic details; (c) centralized charting and data visualization tools for revision of raw training data and outcomes of both single and multiple trials; (d) mask enabling the modification of the rehabilitation protocol.

4 Discussion

Positive effects of endurance exercise training on both motor and non-motor features of PD have been recently demonstrated [20]. An innovative system (CuPiD) based on wearable inertial sensors and a smartphone has been developed to promote physical activity and improve quality of walking in PD patients. Beyond current endurance training, whose benefits in tackling PD symptoms are still limited due to the lack of supervision and guidance, CuPiD was developed in order to target and rehabilitate specific aspects of motor control such as dynamic balance, coordination and proprioception. The system design was intended to improve gait in terms of safety, fluency and energetic consumption by augmenting via biofeedback the self-awareness on the ongoing performance and on undesired gait changes. As well, CuPiD aimed at postponing the onset of festination or freezing during the training session. In fact, it is described in literature that freezing often initiates with a parallel decrease in stride length (amplitude) and an increase in cadence (frequency). As the system checks these two parameters continuously, the origination of freezing or festination is promptly detected and counteracted soliciting the person to recover and maintain a proper gait pattern.

The system proved to be easy to use and face validity seemed high for PD patients. Patients perceived the system almost as if a physical therapist walked with the subject and provided appropriate feedback (e.g., keep it up - you are doing great, or increase your step length).

CuPiD was independently and successfully used during six weeks by 9 PD patients. The system allowed the patients to train their gait performance and collected copious numbers of consecutive gait cycles. Given the stand-alone provision of motor exercises, the continuous supervision and the user-friendliness, CuPiD appears to be well suited for unsupervised gait training in people with PD and this in a real-life setting.

Furthermore the system makes it possible to evaluate a wide range of intra- and inter-session aspects related with the adherence of treatment and the improvement of physical fitness and motor control.

CuPiD supplements the Rehabilitation System with a Telemedicine infrastructure, which allows remote supervision (telesupervision) of the rehabilitation program once it is carried out by the patient in the home setting. The telemedicine architecture has been implanted to ensure complete transparency from the patient's perspective, provide secure data transfer and be easy to use by the clinical staff with a vast amount of charts showing relevant preprocessed information. This opens opportunities for further in depth clinical research as well as providing personalized therapy in a home setting boosting motor-learning effects with daily exercises and increasing adherence by lowering the logistical burden of regular clinical visits. Telesupervision also allows scalability, by having multiple CuPiD systems operating by a single clinician. This makes it possible to start PD specific rehabilitation already in the early stages of the disease as well as increasing the supervised training time of PD patients.

CuPiD proved to be well-accepted and effective, but further optimization of the system and larger power-based studies spanning longer training periods are warranted to corroborate these findings.

The current study is part of the EU-funded CuPiD-project (FP7 grant agreement No. 288516, www.cupid-project.eu).

Acknowledgments. The research leading to these results has received funding from the European Union Seventh Framework Programme (FP7/2007-2013) under grant agreement No. 288516 (CuPiD project).

References

1. Appelboom, G., Yang, A.H., Christophe, B.R., Bruce, E.M., Slomian, J., Bruyère, O., Bruce, S.S., Zacharia, B.E., Reginster, J.-Y., Connolly, E.S.: The promise of wearable activity sensors to define patient recovery. J. Clin. Neurosci. **21**, 1089–1093 (2014)
2. Shull, P.B., Jirattigalachote, W., Hunt, M.A., Cutkosky, M.R., Delp, S.L.: Quantified self and human movement: a review on the clinical impact of wearable sensing and feedback for gait analysis and intervention. Gait Posture **40**, 11–19 (2014)
3. Pasluosta, C.F., Gassner, H., Winkler, J., Klucken, J., Eskofier, B.M.: An emerging era in the management of Parkinson's disease: wearable technologies and the internet of things. IEEE J. Biomed. Health Inform. **19**, 1873–1881 (2015)
4. Lowe, S.A., Ólaighin, G.: Monitoring human health behaviour in one's living environment: a technological review. Med. Eng. Phys. **36**, 147–168 (2014)

5. Lee, Y.-S., Ho, C.-S., Shih, Y., Chang, S.-Y., Róbert, F.J., Shiang, T.-Y.: Assessment of walking, running, and jumping movement features by using the inertial measurement unit. Gait Posture **41**, 877–881 (2015)
6. Li, Y., Guo, Y.: Wiki-health: from quantified self to self-understanding. Future Gener. Comput. Syst. **56**, 333–359 (2015)
7. Lieber, B., Taylor, B.E.S., Appelboom, G., McKhann, G., Connolly, E.S.: Motion sensors to assess and monitor medical and surgical management of Parkinson disease. World Neurosurg. **84**, 561–566 (2015)
8. Qiang, J.K., Marras, C.: Telemedicine in Parkinson's disease: a patient perspective at a tertiary care centre. Parkinsonism Relat. Disord. **21**, 525–528 (2015)
9. Nonnekes, J., Snijders, A.H., Nutt, J.G., Deuschl, G., Giladi, N., Bloem, B.R.: Freezing of gait: a practical approach to management. Lancet Neurol. **14**, 768–778 (2015)
10. Ginis, P., Nieuwboer, A., Dorfman, M., Ferrari, A., Gazit, E., Canning, C.G., Rocchi, L., Chiari, L., Hausdorff, J.M., Mirelman, A.: Feasibility and effects of home-based smartphone-delivered automated feedback training for gait in people with Parkinson's disease: a pilot randomized controlled trial. Parkinsonism Relat. Disord. **22**, 28–34 (2015)
11. Lopez, W.O.C., Higuera, C.A.E., Fonoff, E.T., de Oliveira Souza, C.: O., Albicker, U., Martinez, J.A.E.: Listenmee and Listenmee smartphone application: synchronizing walking to rhythmic auditory cues to improve gait in Parkinson's disease. Hum. Mov. Sci. **37**, 147–156 (2014)
12. Rochester, L., Baker, K., Hetherington, V., Jones, D., Willems, A.-M., Kwakkel, G., Van Wegen, E., Lim, I., Nieuwboer, A.: Evidence for motor learning in Parkinson's disease: acquisition, automaticity and retention of cued gait performance after training with external rhythmical cues. Brain Res. **1319**, 103–111 (2010)
13. Nieuwboer, A., Kwakkel, G., Rochester, L., Jones, D., van Wegen, E., Willems, A.M., Chavret, F., Hetherington, V., Baker, K., Lim, I.: Cueing training in the home improves gait-related mobility in Parkinson's disease: the RESCUE trial. J. Neurol. Neurosurg. Psychiatry **78**, 134–140 (2007)
14. Rocha, P.A., Porfírio, G.M., Ferraz, H.B., Trevisani, V.F.M.: Effects of external cues on gait parameters of Parkinson's disease patients: a systematic review. Clin. Neurol. Neurosurg. **124**, 127–134 (2014)
15. Spaulding, S.J., Barber, B., Colby, M., Cormack, B., Mick, T., Jenkins, M.E.: Cueing and gait improvement among people with Parkinson's disease: a meta-analysis. Arch. Phys. Med. Rehabil. **94**, 562–570 (2013)
16. Jones, D., Rochester, L., Birleson, A., Hetherington, V., Nieuwboer, A., Willems, A.-M., Van Wegen, E., Kwakkel, G.: Everyday walking with Parkinson's disease: understanding personal challenges and strategies. Disabil. Rehabil. **30**, 1213–1221 (2008)
17. Rubinstein, T.C., Giladi, N., Hausdorff, J.M.: The power of cueing to circumvent dopamine deficits: a review of physical therapy treatment of gait disturbances in Parkinson's disease. Mov. Disord. **17**, 1148–1160 (2002)
18. Goodwin, V.A., Richards, S.H., Taylor, R.S., Taylor, A.H., Campbell, J.L.: The effectiveness of exercise interventions for people with Parkinson's disease: a systematic review and meta-analysis. Mov. Disord. **23**, 631–640 (2008)
19. Tomlinson, C.L., Patel, S., Meek, C., Herd, C.P., Clarke, C.E., Stowe, R., Shah, L., Sackley, C.M., Deane, K.H.O., Wheatley, K., Ives, N.: Physiotherapy versus placebo or no intervention in Parkinson's disease. Cochrane Database Syst. Rev. **9**, CD002817 (2013)
20. Lamotte, G., Rafferty, M.R., Prodoehl, J., Kohrt, W.M., Comella, C.L., Simuni, T., Corcos, D.M.: Effects of endurance exercise training on the motor and non-motor features of Parkinson's disease: a review. J. Parkinsons Dis. **5**, 21–41 (2015)

21. Schipper, K., Dauwerse, L., Hendrikx, A., Leedekerken, J.W., Abma, T.A.: Living with Parkinson's disease: priorities for research suggested by patients. Parkinsonism Relat. Disord. **20**, 862–866 (2014)
22. Fok, P., Farrell, M., McMeeken, J., Kuo, Y.: The effects of verbal instructions on gait in people with Parkinson's disease: a systematic review of randomized and non-randomized trials. Clin. Rehabil. **25**, 396–407 (2011)
23. Casamassima, F., Ferrari, A., Milosevic, B., Ginis, P., Farella, E., Rocchi, L.: A wearable system for gait training in subjects with Parkinson's disease. Sens. (Basel) **14**, 6229–6246 (2014)
24. Ferrari, A., Ginis, P., Hardegger, M., Casamassima, F., Rocchi, L., Chiari, L.: A mobile kalman-filter based solution for the real-time estimation of spatio-temporal gait parameters. IEEE Trans. Neural Syst. Rehabil. Eng. (2015). doi:10.1109/TNSRE.2015.2457511
25. CuPiD.: Closed-loop system for personalized and at-home rehabilitation of people with Parkinson's disease.: FP7-ICT-288516, 2011–2014
26. Demers, L., Weiss-Lambrou, R., Ska, B.: Development of the Quebec user evaluation of satisfaction with assistive technology (QUEST). Assist. Technol. **8**, 3–13 (1996)

Supporting Referential Gestures in Mobile Remote Presence: A Preliminary Exploration

Victor Kaptelinin[(✉)]

Department of Informatics, Umeå University, 90531 Umeå, Sweden
victor.kaptelinin@umu.se

Abstract. The paper discusses recent developments in mobile remote presence (MRP) and argues that providing support for referential gesturing is critically important for exploiting the full potential of MRP systems in creating inclusive smart environments. By bringing in insights from research in interaction design and related fields the paper proposes a set of tentative requirements to referential gesturing support for MRP systems. Some of the key challenges for designing referential gesturing in the context of mobile remote presence are identified.

Keywords: Mobile remote presence · Embodied telepresence · Referential gestures · Interaction design · Human-computer interaction · Computer supported cooperative work

1 Introduction

Mobile Remote Presence (MRP) systems are remotely controlled devices that serve as physical avatars of their "pilots" and support pilots' embodied social presence in a local setting. MRP systems are increasingly common in various contexts, including healthcare and elderly care environments. The use of MRP systems opens up a possibility to extend the range of physical and social activities available to the elderly and people with special needs, as well as their family, friends, and caretakers, and thus provides more favorable conditions for societal inclusion and empowerment. However, interaction capabilities of existing MRP systems (at least, affordable ones) are limited, which undermines the prospects for using this technology for creating inclusive smart environments.

This paper argues that one of the most significant limitations of many existing MRP systems, which need to be addressed in further research, is a lack of support for referential gesturing. A preliminary exploration, from an interaction design perspective, of challenges and potential solutions associated with addressing this limitation is presented. The paper reports on a work in progress: the analysis in the paper introduces the rationale and general conceptual point of departure for a recently started research project, supported by the Swedish Research Council, which aims to investigate interaction design issues related to mobile remote presence in smart environments.

C.K. Chang et al. (Eds.): ICOST 2016, LNCS 9677, pp. 262–267, 2016.
DOI: 10.1007/978-3-319-39601-9_23

2 Mobile Remote Presence, Interactional Empowerment, and Social Inclusion

STAND

SEAT

Fig. 1. Telepresence robot Double by Double Robotics (www. doublerobotics.com); SEAT: a sitting height, STAND: a standing height

Mobile Remote Presence (MRP) systems, or telepresence robots, typically comprise the following parts (see Fig. 1): (a) a "head", that is, a video-conferencing unit, including a camera, microphone, speakers, and a display; in some models, such as Double by Double Robotics, the unit can simply be a standard tablet computer, (b) a wheeled base, which can be used to move the device in a setting, and (c) an elongated vertical part, such as a pole, which connects the video-conferencing unit and the wheeled base; this part is often designed so that the height of the "head" can be adjusted depending on the context, for instance, on whether the communication partner is standing or sitting. A diversity of MRP systems, which differ in the size of their displays, quality and quantity of cameras, inclusion of additional equipment (such as a laser pointer), and so forth, is currently available on the market (see, e.g., [3, 9, 10]). MRP systems can be controlled by their "pilots" from remote locations via computing devices connected to the Internet.

A key advantage of MRP systems compared to conventional video-conference technologies is that they serve as embodied social proxies of their pilots in a local setting. The pilots can move around in the setting, view people and the environment from various angles, start conversations where and when it is appropriate, join discussions taking place in different locations, and so forth. A number of studies have been conducted into the effect of robotic telepresence on the quality of interaction (e.g., [2–5, 7, 11]). The effect was found to be generally positive: the perceived social presence of remote workers using the technology was almost at the same level as that of people who were physically present in a setting.

One area, in which the use of MRP systems demonstrated a positive impact on the quality of interaction, is elderly care [2–4]. Implementation of MRP systems, such as Giraff by Giraff Technologies, in assisted living settings provided advantages to the elderly, as well as their relatives and caregivers [3]. Since the visits did not require physical travel, the elderly could enjoy more visits and spend more time interacting with other people.

Arguably, current uses of telepresence robots are just the first steps, and exploiting the full potential of MRP systems in healthcare and assisted living requires further research and development. First, the interaction between local people, e.g., elderly persons, and their visitors, embodied as MRP systems is not always optimal and needs to be improved (e.g., [4]). Second, and more importantly, there are promising novel ways of using the technology, which need to be explored. For instance, one can envision inclusive smart cities of the future that support the elderly, as well as people with special needs, in using MRP technology for visiting, with social presence, remote places that cannot be visited physically.

As argued below, a condition for successfully accomplishing these goals is the development of more advanced solutions for grounding MRP system-mediated social interactions in the specific physical and social contexts of a local setting, and, in particular, providing support for referential gestures.

3   Enabling MRP Systems with Referential Gesturing Capabilities: Why Is It Essential?

While a wide range of telepresence robots is currently commercially available [3, 9], most of them are, essentially, just video conferencing systems on wheels. It is true that remote pilots can move around in a local setting, view it from different angles, approach people they want to communicate with, and take an active part in deciding on the place and time of a conversation. However, when a conversation commences, it is usually similar to a conventional videoconference session in the sense that references to the local physical context are not particularly extensive.

Referencing instruments, which are most commonly used in MRP systems, such as QB and MantaroBot [3, 9], are laser pointers. Such pointers can be used for instance, for highlighting certain areas of a large screen display, jointly viewed by the pilot and local participants. A disadvantage of laser pointers is that the signals they produce can be easily overlooked if a person is not expecting them, and therefore using such pointers does not necessarily support efficient attention management. In addition, the use of laser pointers can be unsafe. Another solution, implemented in PEBBLES, an MRP system primarily designed for educational settings (e.g., classrooms), is providing robots with a "hand" that can be controlled by the pilot. Empirical evaluation of PEBBLES suggests that the hand may not be an optimal solution: the use of the hand is limited to very simple gestures, such as waving it to draw teacher's attention. In addition, the hand raises some safety concerns [3].

Probably, the most advanced functionality for pointing and referential gesturing by a telepresence robot is implemented in a series of experimental systems named Ges-tureMan, created at the University of Tsukuba [5, 10]. The design of GestureMan robots provides a number of potentially useful insights. It should be noted, however, that the robots are not intended as general-purpose embodied social proxies. Instead, they are designed for specific purposes, such as remote instruction on physical tasks. It is not clear whether the solutions implemented in these technologies are practical or affordable if they are used in other contexts.

Therefore, typical MRP systems support interactions *in* the physical context of a local setting, but not so much *about* the context. Arguably, in many cases this limi-tation is not critical. For instance, when workers have an impromptu work-related discussion in a hallway, they usually do not discuss the physical context (that is, the hallway) itself. In such cases existing telepresence robots may be generally sufficient to meet workers' communication needs. In a similar vein, when a relative, embodied as an MRP system, visits an elderly person, they do not necessarily talk about objects in the local setting, so supporting referential gestures may not be important.

However, both logical arguments and empirical evidence indicate that users of MRP systems may need something more than just "video conferencing systems on wheels", and extended gestural capabilities is likely to be one of the most needed features. First, supporting referential gesturing is important for a successful collaborative work on a shared object, as opposed to mere communication about the object, so a deeper appropriation of MRP systems for collaboration is likely to require supporting referential gesturing. Second, in some cases communication about the local context appears to be important for successful interaction in existing healthcare and assisted living environments (e.g., in the case of questions like "Did you take *these* pills?"). Third, supporting referential gesturing by telepresence robots is crucial for making it possible for the elderly and people with special needs to employ MRP systems for virtual trips, e.g., in inclusive smart cities. If such scenarios are realized then, apparently, communication with a direct reference to objects in the local context is going to be a key type of communication between the pilot and people in a local setting. Fourth, empirical studies of communication involving MRP systems deployed in real-life settings reveal a number of problems with making appropriate spatial arrangements during such communication (e.g., [4]). Supporting referential gestures, which may help coordinate participants' mental models of their shared spatial context, appears to be a promising way to alleviate these problems.

4 Interaction Design of Referential Gesturing in Mobile Remote Presence: Identifying Tentative Requirements

Enhancing MRP systems with referential gesturing capabilities can be approached from different perspectives, including software and hardware development, management, and so forth. The analysis in this paper adopts an interaction design perspective. In interaction design and related fields, such as HCI and CSCW, the focus of research is on how people interact with technology and employ it in their everyday activities, rather than on technology per se. Pointing and referential gesturing have been studied from an interaction design perspective for over two decades [8], and some of these studies offer a number of useful insights for exploring possible strategies for supporting referential gesturing in mobile remote presence. The discussion below capitalizes on these studies (e.g., [1], which presents an evaluation methodology for shared workspace groupware) to identify a set of tentative requirements to referential gesturing in mobile remote presence.

Supporting a diversity of communicative purposes. In face-to-face communication gestures serve a diversity of roles. A gesture performed by an actor can refer, for instance, to (a) actor's actual or intended *communication partner*, (b) an *object* in the local setting the actor wants to bring to communication, (c) the communicative *intention* of the actor, or (d) actor's *request for action*, directed to people in the setting. When designing robots' gestural capabilities one should aim for supporting a range of such purposes. It should be noted that it is not uncommon for the same gesture to have several purposes at the same time.

Making the Difference Between Inactive Communication Mode and Active Communication Mode Clearly Visible. To avoid possible confusion and address privacy concerns a telepresence robot should provide clear cues signifying its current mode, that is, whether the robot is in an inactive mode (no gesture or other communicative action is performed or planned to be performed) or active mode (a gesture or other communicative action is being performed or can be expected soon).

Coordinating Gestures with Other Communication Modalities. The meaning of a referential gesture often depends on how the gesture in question is related to other communication modalities, such as voice, gaze, and posture. For instance, pointing to an object while maintaining eye contact with person A can have a different meaning than pointing to the same object while maintaining eye contact with person B.

Employing Unambiguous, Widely Known, and Easily Recognizable Gestures. Gestural communication with robots is a rather unusual type of activity for many people, and if the gestures performed by telepresence robots are complicated and unclear, people in the local setting may be disoriented.

Providing Simple and Intuitive Gesture Control. Typical users serving as pilots of MRP systems and employing widely available technologies, such as conventional computers, may find it challenging to even navigate a system. To avoid potential cognitive overload caused by the need to carry out additional tasks, gesture control features of the pilot's user interface should be as simple and intuitive as possible.

Ensuring Safety. Physical gestures performed by telepresence robots in a local setting are associated with an increased risk of causing harm to people and material damage to objects in the environment (including the MRP system itself). A key requirement, therefore, should be taking all necessary steps to minimize the risk. It can be done, for instance, by imposing constraints on robot's movements, introducing emergency controls to be available to local people, and using soft-impact components (e.g., [6]).

Enabling Low Effort Interruption Management. MRP systems' pilots are present in two settings simultaneously, which makes them especially prone to interruptions. To avoid sudden disruptions in a local setting (e.g., when an MRP system freezes in the middle of a gesture because the pilot is distracted by what happened in his or her physical setting), pilots should be able to easily deal with such cases, for instance, starting a standard interruption management procedure by simply pressing a button.

This tentative list is intended as a starting point in identifying a more comprehensive set of requirements. It should be noted that meeting the above requirements are associated with a number of challenges. For instance, coordinating gestures with other communication modalities is complicated by problems with using gaze in telerpesence in general, and employing widely known and easily recognizable gestures is complicated by cross-cultural differences in gestural communication.

5   Conclusion

This paper argues that referential gesturing, a centrally important aspect of human communication, should be supported in the design of MRP systems to fully exploit the potential of such systems in the search for novel solutions for assisted living and inclusive smart cities. This paper reports on a work in progress; the analysis presented in the paper has been conducted to inform further design-based exploration of mobile remote presence in smart environments within an ongoing research project.

Acknowledgments. The study was funded by The Swedish Research Council. The author is grateful to Patrik Björnfot and two anonymous reviewers for their helpful comments.

References

1. Baker, K., Greenberg, S., Gutwin, C.: Empirical development of a heuristic evaluation methodology for shared workspace groupware. In: Proceedings of the 2002 ACM Conference on Computer Supported Cooperative Work, pp. 96–105. ACM Press, NY (2002)
2. Beer, J.M., Takayama, L.: Mobile remote presence systems for older adults: acceptance, benefits, and concerns. In: Proceedings of the 6th International Conference on Human-Robot Interaction (HRI 2011), pp. 19–26. ACM Press, NY (2011)
3. Kristoffersson, A., Coradeschi, S., Loutfi, A.: A review of mobile robotic telepresence. Adv. Hum.-Comput. Interact. **2013**, 17 (2013). article ID 902316
4. Kristoffersson, A., Coradeschi, S., Severinson Eklundh, K., Loutfi, A.: Assessment of interaction quality in mobile robotic telepresence: an elderly perspective. Interact. Stud. **15** (2), 343–357 (2014)
5. Kuzuoka, H., Suzuki, Y., Yamashita, J., Yamazaki, K.: Reconfiguring spatial formation arrangement by robot body orientation. In: Proceedings of the 5th International Conference on Human-Robot Interaction (HRI 2010), pp. 285–292. ACM Press, NY (2010)
6. Mihaj, D.: Pneuduino: A Modular Platform for Controlling Airflow and Pressure. Smashing Robotics, 2 February 2016 (2016). http://smashingrobotics.com/pneuduino-modular-platform-for-controlling-airflow-and-pressure/
7. Rae, I., Mitlu, B., Takayama, L. Bodies in motion: mobility, presence, and task awareness in telepresence. In: Proceedings of CHI 2014, pp. 2153–2162. ACM Press, NY (2014)
8. Schmauks, D., Wille, M.: Integration of communicative hand movements into human-computer-interaction. Comput. Humanit. **25**(2), 129–140 (1991)
9. TelepresenceRobots.com. http://telepresencerobots.com/comparison
10. Veloso, M., Aisen, M., Howard, A., Jenkins, C., Mutlu, B., Scassellati, B.: WTEC Panel Report on Human-Robot Interaction: Japan, South Korea, and China. WTEC (2012)
11. Tsui, K.M., Desai, M., Yanco, H.A., Uhlik, C.: Exploring use cases for telepresence robots. In: Proceedings of the 6th International Conference on Human-Robot Interaction (HRI 2011), pp. 11–18. ACM Press, NY (2011)

Modeling of Physical and Conceptual Information in Intelligent Environments

Wellness Concepts Model Use and Effectiveness in Intelligent Knowledge Authoring Environment

Taqdir Ali and Sungyoung Lee[(⊠)]

Department of Computer Science and Engineering,
Kyung Hee University, Seocheon-Dong, Giheung-Gu, Yongin-Si
Gyeonggi-Do 446-701, Republic of Korea
{taqdir.ali,sylee}@oslab.khu.ac.kr

Abstract. Intelligent recommendation systems have high impact on users to adopt healthy routines towards the optimal health and wellbeing. The wellbeing recommendation and decision support systems need up-to-date wellness knowledge for effective recommendations to the users. Lack of evolutionary knowledge base is the most prominent barrier in the effectiveness of wellness recommendation system and its applications for assisting in healthier life choices. Domain experts can transform their knowledge into the evolutionary knowledge base of intelligent recommendation system, when they have access to an intelligent and supportive knowledge authoring environment. We have proposed a system that provides an intelligent and supportive knowledge authoring environment with the help of scalable wellness concepts model (WCM). WCM helps in contextual selection of concepts and their values set using Intelli-sense approach during the rule creation. The use of WCM, in knowledge authoring environment, enhances experts' performance and decreases the chance of errors in wellness knowledge creation. It maximizes the concepts recall ratio of domain experts and provides guidance to some extent during rule creation process. We evaluated our system using user-centric evaluation by 6 domain experts. Each domain expert created 5 rules, containing 2 simple and 3 complex using the proposed system. The results suggested that the proposed system has user-satisfaction level up to 80.42 %.

Keywords: Wellness · Wellness concepts model · Intelligent environment · Knowledge authoring · Recommendation system

1 Introduction

Wellness has broader scope than health-care, health-care considered as part of the wellness domain. In illness-health-wellness continuum [1], individuals mainly focus on positive aspects of health and wellness sides to protect from illness. In the past few decades, the number of counseling approaches, in health and wellness domains, has grown exponentially [2, 3]. In current technological era, intelligent recommendation systems play very important role in recommending and counseling the users about healthier life. These systems depend on evolutionary knowledge base and which is

© Springer International Publishing Switzerland 2016
C.K. Chang et al. (Eds.): ICOST 2016, LNCS 9677, pp. 271–282, 2016.
DOI: 10.1007/978-3-319-39601-9_24

considered as core component of the system [4, 5]. Knowledge acquisition is a challenging task and also a key barrier to adopt evolutionary knowledge base expert systems [6]. This is because of the cumbersome and unsystematic interaction between knowledge engineers and the domain experts.

Knowledge engineering "bottleneck" in expert systems adoption has encouraged the knowledge acquisition researchers to provide a controlled and assistive knowledge authoring environment to domain experts without doing extensive tasks [7]. In addition to interactive and easy to use features of authoring environment, the knowledge should be shareable, interoperable, and easily integratable to heterogeneous databases of the legacy systems [6]. All the three aspects of knowledge acquisition; easiness, shareability and interoperability, can be achieved by utilizing standard data models and standard terminologies [6, 8]. Domain experts feel comfort with standard terminologies in creating knowledge rules. Standard terminologies such as SNOMED CT [5, 10] and data model standards like Virtual Medical Record (vMR) [9] are designed for use in decision support systems. The list of standards in clinical domain is not limited to only these standards. Unlike clinical domain, wellness domain is lacking in standards and there exist neither the data models nor the terminological standards.

Without controlled vocabulary in authoring environment, domain experts utilize their own concepts that may differ from one expert to another. Therefore, inconsistency prevails in the knowledge rules created by different experts with their own terminologies. This lack of conceptual consistency leads to the interoperability issue of knowledge base with the legacy systems [6]. Additionally, the controlled vocabulary also helps the experts to maximize the recall of concepts during the rule creation. Experts feel comfort with controlled vocabulary and it enhances the performance of the experts. In similar way, the controlled vocabulary in the form of contextual selection of concepts [11] reduces the chance of errors during the rules creation. In current study, we take initiative to propose wellness concepts model (WCM), based on physical activities and nutrition domain, verified by the domain experts. This WCM is incorporated in Intelligent Knowledge Authoring Environment and used by the experts for rules creation. This WCM is a way towards standardization and controlled terminology in the wellness domain. In our proposed system, WCM facilitates domain experts to create knowledge rules using contextual selection of concepts.

Last two decades of 20th century, the wellness has been defined as a new paradigm in the health-care [12]. Many researchers have proposed different wellness models for different purposes; one of the popular wellness models is *The Indivisible Self* [3], which we have selected as a baseline for our proposed WCM. We have derived our WCM from the five second-order factors of *The Indivisible Self*. We extended the model in three basic areas *Essential, Physical,* and *Nutrition.* The main reason behind selecting these three components is the focus of evolutionary knowledge base for an innovative personalized health and wellness recommendation system called Mining Minds [13, 14]. Mining Minds is a novel framework that focuses on digital health and wellness paradigms to enable the provision of personalized health and wellness support [13–15]. Therefore, our proposed knowledge authoring environment primarily focuses on the knowledge of users' physical activities, health status, and nutrition components in the wellness domain. Other components of wellness domain like mental health, spiritual and social life can easily be integrated with WCM for intelligent recommendations in corresponding domains.

The proposed knowledge authoring environment allows the domain experts to utilize the WCM concepts for keys as well as values in all facts of rules. The experts can easily select their desired concepts from the WCM tree in the rule editor, while the corresponding possible values set is shown in the immediate window as Intelli-sense. Therefore, the authoring environment provides the controlled vocabulary of wellness in two different ways like WCM tree and Intelli-sense window.

2 Related Work

2.1 Wellness Concepts Model (WCM)

Ardell, D.B. [16] have proposed definition of wellness and model for high level of wellness in nutrition knowledge, physical fitness, stress management and environmental awareness. In same way, Hettler B. [17] also categorized the wellness model in high level of concepts like physical, nutrition and social categories. Both of these high level model are considered as pioneer models in wellness domain.

A theoretical model based on counseling theory called *Wheel of Wellness*, was first introduced in early 1990 s by Sweeney and Witmer [18, 19]. The authors have identified a number of characteristics that are related to the healthy living, quality of life and longevity. They organized these characteristics according to life tasks, friendship and love. The original *Wheel of Wellness* model has seven sub-tasks in the life tasks. According to this model, the life forces that effect an individual's life are family, religion, education/industry, media, government, and community.

After an extensive survey, Myers and Sweeney [3] have proposed an evidence-based model of wellness *The Indivisible Self*. The authors have realized that the structure of *Wheel of Wellness* should be re-examine due to hypothesized relationships among its components and the complex structure of it. *The Indivisible Self* has proposed a higher-order wellness factor, which is based on the Adler's [20] theory of holism, the indivisibility of self. Five main concepts are considered as second-order factors; *Essential Self, Social Self, Creative Self, Physical Self*, and *Coping Self*. These second-order factors are further categorized into 17 sub components. This model provides strong support for basic Adlerian concepts related to holism and the indivisibility of human existence is supported by this research findings. In our proposed WCM, we have considered this model as fundamental concepts in second-order of hierarchy. We enhanced wellness model by adding more concepts based on extensive literature with the help of a team of experts.

2.2 Knowledge Authoring Environment

There are knowledge authoring tools available in clinical domain, while specifically wellness domain lacks these tools. A multiple-method knowledge acquisition shell is proposed in [21] that generates knowledge acquisition tools without a specific model of problem solving. The system provides very generic environment to create knowledge for multiple domain, but domain expert needs help in technical aspects to formalize domain knowledge. In this case, the domain experts have dependency on knowledge engineers to build a domain knowledge base.

A collaborative ontology editor and knowledge acquisition tool WebProtege is proposed by Tudorache, T et al. in [22]. The system was built using the existing protégé infrastructure that supports collaboration on the backend side. The authors have developed a useful ontology editor for knowledge acquisition, but this editor is difficult to use for domain experts without semantic web knowledge to create domain knowledge. Dustin Dunsmuir et al. have proposed a system in [23], which enables clinicians to create knowledge rules without the help of knowledge engineers and programmers. The system is based on the "pattern and outcome" approach and works in the domain of anesthesia. However, its scope is limited and difficult to extend to other domains. This system creates rules directly in XML files; therefore, physicians are involved with XML files, which require the tedious extra task of XML training.

3   Methodology

3.1   Wellness Concepts Model (WCM) Paradigm

The focus of healthcare domain is transforming from disease to wellness, and wellness domain is shifting towards user centric model with innovative platforms [13]. The Mining Minds [13, 15] is an innovative platform that exploits digital health and wellness paradigms to the end users by providing wellbeing services and recommendations. Mining Minds mainly focuses on the health and wellness recommendations and guidelines. The structure of Mining Minds is divided into different layers and each layer is responsible to perform its related activities. Knowledge Curation Layer (KCL) [15] is one of these layers is designed to maintain the evolutionary knowledge base for the essential requirement for intelligent recommendation services. In KCL, our proposed Knowledge Acquisition Tool (KAT) facilitates expert to transform their knowledge and experience in to computer interpretable knowledge base. The KAT currently emphasizes on physical activities and nutrition knowledge for recommendations. Using KAT, the physical instructors and nutritionist transforms their knowledge utilizing the concepts of physical, nutrition, and user's essential information. These concepts are part of WCM and are related to each other through different relationships. Figure 1 illustrates the development and integration paradigm of WCM with KAT to evolve the wellness knowledge for Mining Minds.

A team of domain experts including 2 nutritionists and 3 physical instructors designed the conceptual model and provided the higher level blueprint of WCM. A collaborative study between the teams of domain experts and knowledge engineers took place to initialize design and implementation of WCM. The knowledge engineers' team provided the identified relationships among the concepts represented the model in ontological format for computer interpretation. The domain experts' team validated the design and verified the WCM implementation. Eventually model is persisted in the repository. This WCM repository is integrated to KAT, which facilitates experts to evolve the knowledge base in user-friendly manner.

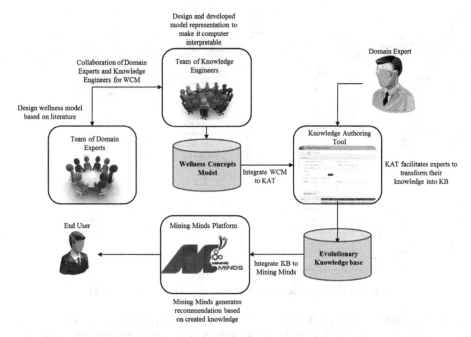

Fig. 1. Integration of wellness concepts model and knowledge acquisition tool paradigm

3.2 Wellness Concepts Model (WCM) Design

The *Indivisible Self* [3] provides very comprehensive evidence-based wellness model, which we selected as a core model for this study. We modified the model according to the health and wellness requirements of a recommendation system, specifically for physical activities and nutrition domains. The Indivisible Self model is composed of the second-order factors including Essential, Creative, Coping, Social, and Physical Self. The proposed WCM model extends the second-order hierarchy with multiple level of depth in Creative, Essential, and Physical components based on the nature of components. The Creative category contains Thinking, Emotions, Control, Positive Humor, and Work. Usually the wellness recommendation systems use emotion and work related information of the users. Therefore, we extended the Emotion and Work categories under the Creative hierarchy. In same way, we have added many other concepts under the Essential category as shown in Fig. 2. For instance, under the Profile Information, we put the demographic information, anthropometrics parameters, and bio-medical parameters. Under Self-care, which is subcategory of Essential, we have related all the behaviors and habits of users that play important role in self-care, like risky habits, healthy habits, preferences in food, activities, hobbies, and transportation.

In Physical self, we added Health Status as subcategory and related it to diseases, symptoms, and other health related concepts. We put concepts that belong to physical activities under the exercise hierarchy while diet concepts under the nutrition hierarchy. Health status, physical activities, and nutrition are the main focus of wellness

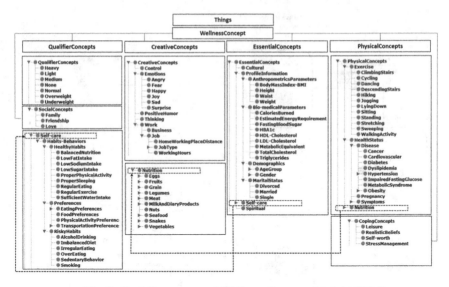

Fig. 2. Partially represented Wellness Concepts Model (WCM)

recommendation systems. We have introduced a new category qualifier concepts in second-order factors, which contains all the concepts that illustrate possible values set of other concepts. For instance, normal, heavy, light are some possible values set for dinner, lunch, and breakfast. We have provided maximum semantics in all these concepts that are usually use in wellness recommendations. For instance, each user has some preferences in food, physical activities, transportation, and eating time. New concepts can be plugged-in easily in a related hierarchy because of the flexible hierarchical structure of the model. Figure 2 shows wellness concepts model hierarchies partially, while Fig. 3 demonstrates the attribute relationships among some concepts. For instance, the three attribute relationships (a) *containsFoodOf* (b) *containsActivitiesOf* and (c) *foodIntake* are used to connect different concepts. The (a) relates food Preference with Nutrition, (b) relates Physical Activities Preferences with Exercises, and (c) *relates* Eating Preferences (Breakfast, Lunch, and Dinner) with Qualifier Concepts (Light, Medium, Heavy).

3.3   Implementation of WCM Integrated KAT

In Fig. 4, we present the implementation architecture of our proposed WCM integrated Knowledge Acquisition Tool (KAT). It consists of six sub-components Domain Model Manager, Rule Editor, Situation Event Manager, Knowledge Transformation Bridge, Knowledge Base and Knowledge Sharing Interfaces.

Domain Model Manager: This component is responsible to manage the wellness model. It loads the WCM into the Rule Editor to use in rule editing activity.

Rule Editor: As a core component of KAT, rule editor provides a user-friendly environment to domain expert to create knowledge rules. The knowledge rules

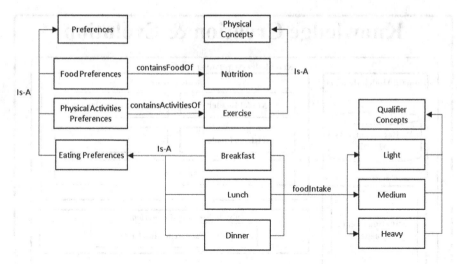

Fig. 3. Attribute relationships in WCM

represented in form of unordered production rules. The rule base reasoning (RBR) used to generate final recommendations to end users. It comprises of five further sub-components to perform distinct functionalities. **Model Loader** is in charge of loading WCM concepts into the rules editor in tree structure for easy selection of desired concepts. This sub-component shows all the concepts in a single tree or sub-tree based on the top categories like Profile Information, Diseases, and Physical Activities. The **Intelli-sense Manager** provides a list of related concepts which are used to facilitate the experts to choose the desired value from the list. For instance, when expert wants to write Physical Activity = Sitting, the possible values set for Physical Activity are reflected to appear such as; Standing, Sitting, Walking, Jogging, and others. A separate inner Intelli-sense window is shown to reflect all possible values. **Artifacts Controller** fetches the operators into the Rule Editor and facilitate experts to select required operators from the list. The **Rule Creator** module creates the rule from all facts and conclusion created by experts in conditions and conclusion parts. It creates the hierarchy of conditions and conclusion in the created rules. The **Rule Validator** validates the rule and finds the duplications and conflicts of the new rule with the existing rules in the knowledge base.

Situation Event Manager: Some rules may consist of some salient features that should monitor by the system as events, those features are called situation events. Whenever an abnormal situation occurs, the system generates recommendation and passes as an alert to the user. It facilitates expert to identify and select the desired facts as situation event.

Knowledge Transformation Bridge: This module transforms plane rule into a computer executable format. We use relational schema representation for persisting rules in the knowledge base.

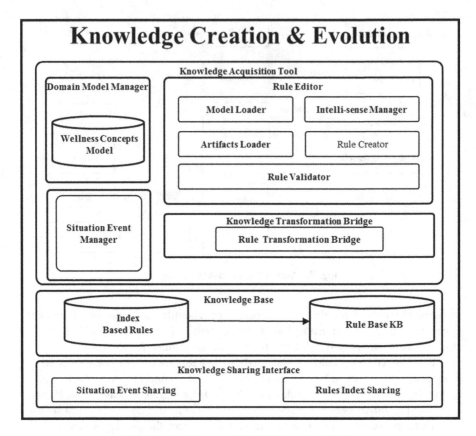

Fig. 4. Architecture of WCM integrated KAT

Knowledge Base: In knowledge base, we have two repositories one for persisting the whole rules as *Rule Base KB* while the second repository as *Index Based Rules* for persisting the situations events in rules. These repositories are closely coupled to each other based on identifiers of situations and rules.

Knowledge Sharing Interfaces: This component consists of two types of sharing interfaces. *Situation Event Sharing* interface shares the situation events with monitoring systems to observe the abnormal situations of the users. While *Rule Index Sharing* interface is responsible to share the knowledge rules with reasoning engine of the recommendation system.

4   Results and Evaluations

The main objective of WCM integration with knowledge acquisition tool is facilitating domain experts to transform and represent their knowledge to computer interpretable knowledge base. When domain experts are satisfied and comfortable in knowledge acquisition then adoption of wellness recommendation systems will be increase.

.**Fig. 5.** Rule Editor

Therefore, we evaluated the proposed WCM integrated KAT from domain experts to assess their satisfaction over the claimed facilitation of WCM augmented knowledge authoring environment.

Experimental Setup: (a) We provided the developed knowledge acquisition tool to the domain experts. Figure 5 shows the main Rule Editor of the system that we deployed on the web server. (b) In order to easily understand the usage of authoring environment, we also provided the system manual. (c) A visual representation of WCM is provided in a graphical format to understand the hierarchies of concepts. (d) A set of questions is provided in a questionnaire form. Eight of the questions in the questionnaire are related to the; (i) organization of the information, (ii) concepts of WCM, (iii) performance and help of WCM in Rule Editor, (iv) coverage of desired concepts in WCM, and (v) user-friendliness of the system. (e) Overall six domain experts are assigned including two physical instructors, two nutritionists, and two nurses to evaluate the system on the basis of questions.

Table 1. Possible answers' weightage

Question evaluation criteria	Weightage (%)
Highly Satisfied	100
Satisfied	80
Less Satisfied	60
Not satisfied	40

During experiment session, each domain expert created five rules in corresponding fields using their experience and knowledge. After knowledge creation, each domain expert provided answers to the relevant questions in our provided questionnaire. Each question has 4 possible answers and we have assigned a weightage to each answer as shown in Table 1 based on the methods and protocols suggested in [24].

We evaluated the user satisfaction level based on the domain experts' feedback. And users' satisfaction level at average 80.42 % has recorded. In Table 2, the domain experts' feedback (in percentage) is illustrated to each question. We first found out the average values for each question and then we calculated the system performance by determining the overall average value (80.42 %) from the averages of individual questions.

Table 2. Domain Experts' feedback

User satisfaction (%)								
Evaluators	Q1	Q2	Q3	Q4	Q5	Q6	Q7	Q8
Physical instructor - 1	80	60	100	80	80	80	80	60
Physical instructor - 2	100	80	80	60	80	80	60	100
Nutritionist - 1	80	100	80	80	100	80	80	80
Nutritionist - 2	100	60	100	80	80	100	60	60
Nurse - 1	80	80	80	100	80	80	60	80
Nurse - 2	60	60	80	80	100	80	100	80
Average	**83.33**	**73.33**	**86.67**	**80.00**	**86.67**	**83.33**	**73.33**	**76.67**
Total average	**80.42 %**							

5   Conclusion and Future Work

Every individual intend healthier life, which is possible with healthier physical activities and balanced diet. Wellness model is run by these categories. Without evolutionary knowledge base, a recommendation system is difficult to adopt. Our proposed intelligent knowledge authoring environment is beneficial to create evolutionary knowledge base with the use of a comprehensive wellness concepts model. It provides user-friendly environment to author wellness knowledge by domain experts without knowledge engineers intervention.

Currently, we have validated knowledge rules with respect to duplication and conflict of rules, but in future we will also focus on the semantic validation of rules that will enhance satisfaction level of domain experts.

Acknowledgments. This work was supported by the Industrial Core Technology Development Program (10049079, Develop of mining core technology exploiting personal big data) funded by the Ministry of Trade, Industry and Energy (MOTIE, Korea) and This research was supported by the MSIP, Korea, under the G-ITRC support program (IITP-2015-R6812-15-0001) supervised by the IITP, and by the MSIP(Ministry of Science, ICT and Future Planning), Korea, under the ITRC(Information Technology Research Center) support program (IITP-2015-H8501-15-1015) supervised by the IITP(Institute for Information & communications Technology Promotion).

References

1. Els, D.A., De La Rey, R.P.: Developing a holistic wellness model. SA J. Hum. Resour. Manage. **2**, 46–56 (2006)
2. Lenz, A.S., Smith, R.L.: Integrating wellness concepts within a clinical supervision model. The Clinical Supervisor **29**(2), 228–245 (2010)
3. Myers, J.E., Sweeney, T.J.: The indivisible self: An evidence-based model of wellness. J. Individ. Psychol. **60**, 234–244 (2004)
4. Fehre, K., Adlassnig, K.P.: Service-oriented Arden-syntax-based clinical decision support. In: Proceedings of eHealth 2011, pp. 123–128. Austrian Computer Society, Vienna (2011)
5. Ali, T., Hussain, M., Khan, W.A., Afzal, M., Kang, B.H., Lee, S.: Arden syntax studio: creating medical logic module as shareable knowledge. In: 2014 IEEE International Symposium on Innovations in Intelligent Systems and Applications (INISTA) Proceedings, pp. 266–272. IEEE, June 2014
6. Ali, T., Hussain, M., Ali Khan, W., Afzal, M., Lee, S.: Authoring tool: acquiring sharable knowledge for Smart CDSS. In: 2013 35th Annual International Conference of the IEEE Engineering in Medicine and Biology Society (EMBC), pp. 1278–1281. IEEE, July 2013
7. Shortliffe, E.H.: Medical expert systems—knowledge tools for physicians. West. J. Med. **145**(6), 830 (1986)
8. Osheroff, J.A., Teich, M.J., Middleton, B., Steen, E.B., Wright, A., Detmer, D.E.: A roadmap for national action on clinical decision support. J. Am. Med. Inform. Assoc. **14**(2), 141–145 (2007)
9. Kawamoto, K., Del Fiol, G., Starsberg, H.R., Hulse, N., Curtis, C., Cimino, J.J., Beatriz, H.R. et al.: Multi-national, multi-institutional analysis of clinical decision support data needs to inform development of the HL7 virtual medical record standard. In: AMIA Annual Symposium Proceedings, vol. 2010. American Medical Informatics Association (2010)
10. Summary of SNOMED CT Benefits. http://www.ihtsdo.org/snomedct/whysnomedct/benefits/. Accessed Feb. 2016
11. Ali, T., Hussain, M., Khan, W.A., Afzal, M., Lee, S.: Customized clinical domain ontology extraction for knowledge authoring tool. In: Proceedings of the 8th International Conference on Ubiquitous Information Management and Communication, p. 23. ACM, January 2014
12. Larson, J.S.: The conceptualization of health. Med. Care Res. Rev. **56**(2), 123–136 (1999)
13. Banos, O., Amin, M.B., Ali Khan, W., Ali, T., Afzal, M., Kang, B.H., Lee, S.: Mining minds: an innovative framework for personalized health and wellness support. In: 2015 9th International Conference on Pervasive Computing Technologies for Healthcare (PervasiveHealth), pp. 1–8. IEEE, May 2015

14. Mining Minds Overview, http://www.miningminds.re.kr/english/. Accessed Feb. 2016
15. Banos, O., Amin, M.B., Khan, W.A., Afzal, M., Hussain, M., Kang, B.H., Lee, S.: The Mining Minds Digital Health and Wellness Framework
16. Ardell, D.B.: High Level Wellness, an Alternative to Doctors, Drugs, and Disease. Bantam Books, New York (1979)
17. Hettler, B.: Wellness: encouraging a lifetime pursuit of excellence. Health Values 8(4), 13 (1984)
18. Sweeney, T.J., Witmer, J.M.: Beyond social interest: Striving toward optimum health and wellness. Individ. Psychol. 47, 527–540 (1991)
19. Witmer, J.M., Sweeney, T.J.: A holistic model for wellness and prevention over the lifespan. J. Couns. Dev. 71, 140–148 (1992)
20. Adler, A.: Understanding Human Nature. Fawcett, New York (1954). Original work published 1927
21. Puerta, A.R., Egar, J.W., Tu, S.W., Musen, M.A.: A multiple-method knowledge-acquisition shell for the automatic generation of knowledge-acquisition tools. Knowl. Acquisition 4(2), 171–196 (1992)
22. Tudorache, T., Nyulas, C., Noy, N.F., Musen, M.A.: WebProtégé: A collaborative ontology editor and knowledge acquisition tool for the web. Semant. Web 4(1), 89–99 (2013)
23. Dunsmuir, D., Daniels, J., Brouse, C., Ford, S., Ansermino, J.M.: A knowledge authoring tool for clinical decision support. J. Clin. Monit. Comput. 22(3), 189–198 (2008)
24. Barua, A.: Methods for decision-making in survey questionnaires based on Likert scale. J. Asian Sci. Res. 3(1), 35 (2013)

Sedentary Behavior-Based User Life-Log Monitoring for Wellness Services

Hafiz Syed Muhammad Bilal[1], Asad Masood Khattak[2], and Sungyoung Lee[1(✉)]

[1] Department of Computer Engineering, Kyung Hee University,
Seocheon-dong, Giheung-gu, Yongin-si, Gyeonggi-do 446-701, Korea
{bilalrizvi,sylee}@oslab.khu.ac.kr
[2] College of Technological Innovations, Zayed University, Dubai, United Arab Emirates
asad.khattak@zu.ac.ae

Abstract. Ubiquitous computing and smart gadgets have revolutionized the self-quantification in tracking and logging activities for improving daily life and inducing healthy behavior. Life-log monitoring is the process of monitoring the daily life routines of user in an efficient manner in terms of time and amount of activities. The effective utilization of life-log monitoring is to correctly identify and intimate user unhealthy activities in a timely manner. For monitoring life-log, the knowledge of sedentary behavior first need to be formulated by the domain expert in the form of unhealthy situations, these situations are used as the monitoring unit. In this study we proposed a method for automatically monitoring users' unhealthy situations in the domain of sedentary behavior with prolonged activities. The proposed method simultaneously filters out multiple sedentary activities of users simultaneously while ignoring the activities having no situations. The results depict that the monitoring method intimates the stakeholder with delay less than the monitoring interval cycle.

Keywords: Life-log · Automatic monitoring · Sedentary behavior · Unhealthy situation · Wellness

1 Introduction

Health is a reflection of lifestyle and active lifestyle has great impact on wellness. The choice of energetic lifestyle may lead to a fuller, healthy and long lifetime. The element of human well-being may be specified as: safety; availability of livelihood (e.g. food, shelter, energy); freedom; social interaction and physical health [1]. Active routine is an important ingredient in addition to diet, hydration, leisure and finance. A lifestyle with a small or no regular physical activity is a sedentary. A sedentary person is the one who has irregular or insufficient amount of physical activity in daily life routine [2].

1.1 Consequences of Sedentary Behavior

A sedentary person is more vulnerable to health issues like muscular weakness, bone health, blood pressure, obesity and risk of diabetes [3]. Involvement in moderate-vigorous level physical activity is an economical measure to improve health and reduce

© Springer International Publishing Switzerland 2016
C.K. Chang et al. (Eds.): ICOST 2016, LNCS 9677, pp. 283–292, 2016.
DOI: 10.1007/978-3-319-39601-9_25

disability [4]. Disability increases the risk of hospitalization and institutionalization and is a major concern of economy [5].

Those, who follow physical activity guideline's recommendations, proposed by ACSM [6] and AHA [3], still have high potentials of health risk due to prolonged sedentary living time. Consider a person who sits more than 4 h per day has 40 percent higher health risk than those who sit less than that [7]. Those having regular interrupts in sedentary activities have a better metabolic profile than those who remain inactive for long periods [8]. Living an active life requires intimation and basic knowledge with connections to healthcare experts.

1.2 Life-Log Monitoring and Wellness Applications

Over the past few years, the focus of software applications is trending towards health and wellness applications. The trend is considered as a prompt and useful resource for analyzing users' data to recommend healthy lifestyle [11]. Thousands of desktop as well as mobile applications are available for logging user activities and enabling users in visualizing the cumulative impact of activities on daily or weekly basis. Routine life activities are quantified through different sensors to manage personalized healthcare and wellness [9]. *Microsoft Health, Apple Healthkit, Samsung S Health*, and *Google Fit* are a few among the numerous applications which collect and analyze users' data to generate healthy lifestyle recommendations [11].

Life-log monitoring is a challenging task; it determines a person's health and wellness state which is more than simply collecting and storing the person's activity data. Therefore, automatic mechanisms are required to process personal data and transform it into information. The monitoring technique can be leveraged by healthcare and wellness systems to extend, adapt and evolve the knowledge provided by domain experts [9]. Generally, life-log monitoring services are used to generate alerts or recommendations to stakeholders in a human-understandable format. These services can provide support for customization of recommendation on the basis of user preferences and demands.

2 Mining Minds: At a Glance

Technology revolution and the modern age of information facilitate the community in terms of on-spot context based health informatics [14]. The information technology is reshaping the world by using cloud computing infrastructure for managing big data from internet of things to support personalize recommendations. Our ongoing project, Mining Minds MM [9, 11, 12] is an innovative platform that constitutes of state-of-art information technologies to motivate users for healthy lifestyle after monitoring their life-log. The innovative platform is necessary to cope with the challenges in healthcare and wellness domains that is more converging towards a user centric model [13].

Mining minds platform's services collectively collect and analyze human's daily life data, generated from multiple sensors and give context based personalized wellness recommendations [12]. Considering the requirements, MM platform consists of five layers, respectively, Data Curation Layer (DCL), Information Curation Layer (ICL),

Service Curation Layer (SCL), Knowledge Curation Layer (KCL) and Supporting Layer (SL). The SCL is responsible for generating personalized recommendation. The hybrid-CBR technique is used to generate personalized recommendations according to the user context and preferences by manipulating recognized activities, user context and user profile information [14].

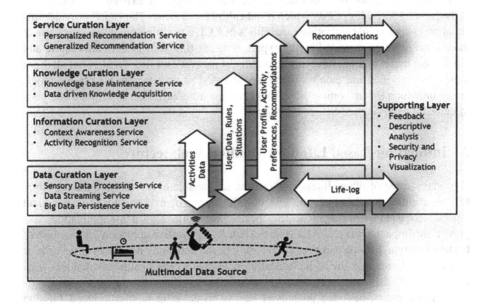

Fig. 1. Mining minds platform

The goal of KCL is to manage and create knowledge for wellness and healthcare. It provides a rule editor environment to expert for expressing his wellness knowledge and healthcare experience in the form of executable guidelines. These guidelines provide the situation for identifying the unhealthy patterns with respect to context and remedies for clutched unhealthy patterns in term of actions [15].

The SL is in charge of the user interface, visualization, and descriptive analytics. The supporting layer creates a unique interface which has the adaptive and personalized approach towards building and managing the user interfaces. The analytics gives users and experts different insights into the habits, activities and different classification of the application [14, 15].

ICL is responsible to infer and recognized the activity of a user by manipulating the data generated by multiple sensors. The data is converted into concepts or categories like physical activities and location. It is the core of MM services which identify the context and activity, e.g. sitting in office, with the help of sensory data. These recognized contexts and activities are essential for identification of user lifestyle pattern [15].

DCL provides the foundation of the MM platform architecture. Data from multimodal data sources is gathered, persisted and processed at DCL. It consists of different modules for data streaming and communication, data representation and mapping and big data. The big data addresses the 3Vs (volume, velocity and variety) aspects of raw sensory data acquired using multiple sensors [14]. DCL is curating the user data in a temporal manner to build the life-log. Life-log records all those activities which are recognized by the ICL along their temporal credentials. It supports to analyze and identify the lifestyle pattern to highlight the unhealthy activities and abnormal behavior of the user.

Life-log evaluation is an essential concept to highlight the existence of a situation in the running activities of user which is unhealthy for the user. The expert provides this situation using the rule authoring capabilities of KCL e.g. sitting more than one hour. If there is no situation provided by the expert, it means that activity does not require any monitoring and it will not have any unhealthy impact on user life. To filter out all those unhealthy activities and monitor them, we proposed an architecture for life-log monitoring on which the activation of wellness service from SCL and descriptive analytics of unhealthy activities of SL are dependent.

3   Intimation-Based Life-Log Monitor Architecture

Nowadays, most of the wellness applications are capable of recognizing the user time to time activities, log them into one's life-log and present them in an interactive graphical representation [11]. Besides, presenting the user's activities logs, a few applications also present the impact of co-related activities [10]. As a proactive approach for adaption of healthy lifestyle, life-log can be used to highlight the unhealthy behaviors at the time of occurrence. Intimating the to-be unhealthy activities to the health stakeholders adds more comprehension and perfection towards the user wellness.

Health consciousness and proactivity lead us to drive an intimation-based Life-log Monitor (LLM). The derived architecture, shown in Fig. 1, is designed for the LLM constitutes of three major components. These components manage the unhealthy situation information provided by experts and monitor the life-log on the basis of these situations which are the driving force for the monitoring. The provided instructions are guidelines used to monitor the life-log at run time to filter out all those conditions which are needed to be

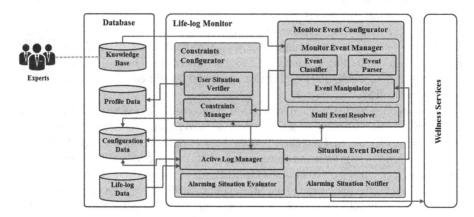

Fig. 2. Architecture of intimation-based life-log monitor

identified and triggers the wellness services. The three main components are Monitor Event Configurator, Constraints Configurator and Situation Event Detector as shown in Fig. 2.

3.1 Monitor Event Configurator

This component is responsible for managing the monitoring situations shared by experts in a common configuration format. The monitoring situation is a guideline to examine the activity of a user at the occurrence time. It constitutes of activity, duration of activity and additional constraints. Monitor Event Configurator (MEC) identifies the situation components and keeps it as configuration data. Beside, storing the information related to situation, MEC has to find out the suitable monitoring situation for situation event detection. MEC has a sub component, Multi Event Resolver (MER), which acts as a conflict resolver in case there are more than one situations related to a single activity.

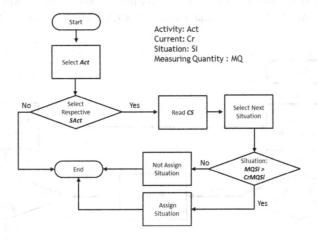

Fig. 3. Flow chart of Conflict resolver in multiple Situations

An activity may have multiple sedentary situations. The choice of appropriate situation for an activity is quite significant. Think there are two situations related to sitting activity. Ace is one hour and the other is three hours. In both cases the wellness actions are different, which are proposed by the expert and notified by wellness services. In this example, if a user starts sitting activity, the appropriate target for intimation is first one hour and then three hours. Figure 3 shows the operation of MER that is getting out the suitable situation on the basis of current activity status of the user.

3.2 Constraint Configurator

This component is responsible for managing the constraints related to a particular monitor-able situation and verifying before monitoring that the user's profile data is matching the constraints. The constraints related to situations are managed by a constraint manager in the form of key - value pairs. The key-value pair provides dynamicity in handling multiple constraints related to a situation.

To monitor a situation against an activity User Constraint Verifier (UCV) search the user profile. As there are multiple constraints may associate with a single situation, therefore UCV has to cater for all the constraints to verify that the user fulfills the situation constraints. If it is not able to find the information with the given constraints, the monitoring of that activity of the user does not start.

3.3   Situation Event Detector

Situation Event Detector (SED) is the key component of the LLM and is responsible for identifying the situation when activity is transformed into sedentary one according to the monitor-able situation. These situations are identified from the rules generated by the expert. This module consists of three sub components, as shown in Fig. 2, which are Active Log Manager (ALM), Alarming Situation Evaluator (ASE) and Alarming Situation Notifier (ASN).

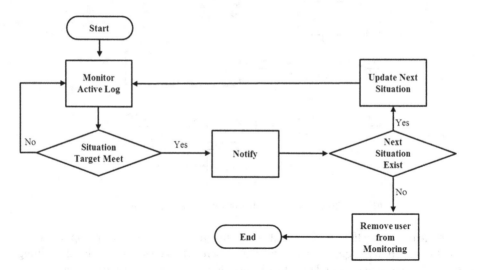

Fig. 4.   Flow chart of life-log monitoring

There are lots of activities going on in a life span of the user, all of these activities are not considered as sedentary ones. ALM is the component that filters out the monitorable sedentary activities and manage them separately. Therefore, the Active Log consists of only those activities which are considered as monitor-able with respect to the situation and verifies against all constraints associated to the constraints matching with the user profile. Consider, if age and gender of user is not according to the constraints of situation then that activity of respective user is not selected for the monitoring. Similarly, if there is no sedentary situation related to an activity then that activity is also not considered for monitoring. In active log, every activity is registered with its starting time and the situation targeted time.

The ASE is responsible for monitoring the Active Log at regular intervals. It carries out the comparison of monitor-able target duration with the difference of starting time and current time as shown in Fig. 4. The benefit of the ASE is that we can filter out different activities of users at the same time. We don't need to consider every activity individually.

4   Evaluation Methodology

To evaluate the working of proposed LLM in a real environment, we integrated it with Mining Minds platform V2.0. It is a platform for person centric health and wellness [9, 12]. It provides the facility to recognize these activities of the user through sensor-based technology. It supports the real time data acquisition of user activity, analysis and recognition of activity and wellness services to intimate the user at run time. The intimation is done in the form of appropriate action message alert on user mobile phone. Before integrating the proposed LLM, the user has to interact with the wellness services to know about activity status.

4.1   Experimental Setup

We have considered all those activities which are evaluated on the basis of time consumption. So that we can validate LLM against time base monitoring activities to highlight the prolonged duration of activity to avoid sedentary behavior. We selected users of different ages and gender, divided them into three age groups, as shown in Table 1, and they performed different activities concurrently.

Table 1.   User age groups and ranges

Sr.#	Age group	Age range
1	Kid	Age <=17
2	Adult	Age > 17 && Age <=45
3	Old	Age > 45

We have selected five different activities: sitting, standing, walking, stretching and lying. The Mining minds platform expressed very high accuracy to identify the above mentioned activities [15]. Our expert (Physiotherapist) provides different prolonged unhealthy situations related to sitting and standing activities. Specific gender and age-group are provided to setup the constraints for the monitoring situations. For example a situation that is related to sitting activity i.e., sitting more than one-hour for healthy

Table 2.   Situations for monitoring the activities

Sr.#	Activity	Duration	Age group	Gender
1	Sitting	1 h	Adult	Male & Female
2	Lying	3 h	Adult	Male & Female
3	Standing	2 h	Adult	Male & Female

adults. For evaluation, the situations are provided by the expert through the knowledge authoring tool of Mining Minds as shown in the Table 2. The table represents the continuous duration of activities when that become unhealthy for an adult male/female and need to be intimated so that the activity or posture should be changed. Consider an adult person continuously sit for one hour or more, it is not good for his/her health and it is consider as a sedentary activity. In this situation it is good to intimate him/her, so that he/she may take small walk or little exercise.

We have selected 10 volunteers who are fully informed for the usage of the system and provided guidelines to perform different actions regarding the alert messages. About 20 % of the volunteers do not fulfill the constraints of the situations. Rest of the volunteers are directed to perform different activities and follow the instructions on and off. In this way we are able to judge the working of LLM against multiple situations of an activity.

4.2 Evaluation Criteria

The performance of the LLM is monitored on efficiency basis that how correctly and timely it has generated the intimation for the wellness services on the occurrence of prolonged sedentary event. The delay between crossing the threshold value set against a particular activity and intimation is evaluated. We crossed check it with the help of intimation log and number of notifications generated for the expert in expert panel. The panel supports the expert while generating rules and defining situations against different activities.

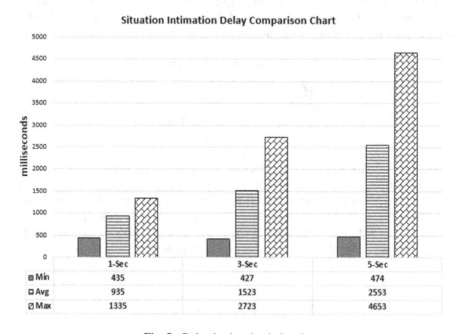

	1-Sec	3-Sec	5-Sec
Min	435	427	474
Avg	935	1523	2553
Max	1335	2723	4653

Fig. 5. Delay in situation intimation

4.3 Experimental Result Analysis

LLM starts monitoring of the activities which have a registered situation of sedentary from experts and the constraints of the situation match with the user profile. LLM intimates the stakeholders when the activity becomes sedentary with the maximum delay less than the interval of monitoring cycle as shown in Fig. 5. Results show that when we keep the interval duration greater than 1 s, all the situations are intimated in less than monitoring interval cycle for situation.

The delay in intimation is due to the wait for executing the next cycle. If duration of the activity reached the limits of the situation and there is no monitoring cycle at that time, then it has to wait for next cycle to be intimated. The platform is deployed on Microsoft Azure cloud that is the reason that execution of services required nearly 400 to 500 ms. The overall delay in intimation is quite affordable for our volunteers. The intimation log status is verified with the expert panel as shown in Fig. 6.

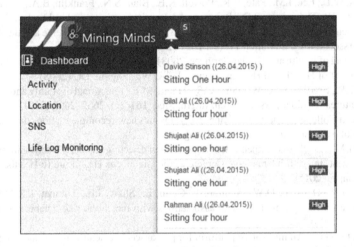

Fig. 6. Expert dashboard for Activity Log Analysis

5   Conclusion and Future Work

The designed LLM monitors the activities which become sedentary due to prolonged duration. It informs the wellness services as soon as the activity becomes sedentary. It is a novel way to monitor activities and push information instead of waiting for the user or expert to examine the daily or weekly routine. This novel technique can support the wellness applications in becoming proactive to avoid the sedentary behavior. The precautionary approach is adopted for more effective intimation against sedentary activities. Currently, the LLM monitors all those activities which have a situation designed by experts and are related to time domain i.e. sitting more than one hour. In wellness domain the diet has a big influence, in the future we will extend the LLM for monitoring the diet in term of calories.

Acknowledgments. This research was supported by Basic Science Research Program through the National Research Foundation of Korea(NRF) funded by the Ministry of Science, ICT & Future Planning(2011-0030079), this work was supported by the Industrial Core Technology Development Program (10049079, Develop of mining core technology exploiting personal big data) funded by the Ministry of Trade, Industry and Energy (MOTIE, Korea) and this research work was also supported by Zayed University Research Initiative Fund# R15098.

References

1. Millennium Ecosystem Assessment, Ecosystems and Human Wellbeing: A Framework for Assessment. Island Press, Washington, DC (2003)
2. Thorp, A.A., Owen, N., Neuhaus, M., Dunstan, D.W.: Sedentary behaviors and subsequent health outcomes in adults: a systematic review of longitudinal studies, 1996–2011. Am. J. Prev. Med. **41**(2), 207–215 (2011)
3. Haskell, W.L., Lee, I.M., Pate, R.R., Powell, K.E., Blair, S.N., Franklin, B.A., Macera, C.A., Heath, G.W., Thompson, P.D., Bauman, A.: Physical activity and public health: updated recommendation for adults from the American College of Sports Medicine and the American Heart Association. Circulation **116**(9), 1081 (2007)
4. Department of Health and Human Services: 2008 Physical Activity Guidelines for Americans. Department of Health and Human Services USA, Washington, DC (2008)
5. Fried, T.R., Bradley, E.H., Williams, C.S., Tinetti, M.E.: Functional disability and health care expenditures for older persons. Arch. Intern. Med. **161**(21), 2602–2607 (2001)
6. American College of Sports Medicine. ACSM issues new recommendations on quantity and quality of exercise (2011). Accessed 3 Aug. 2011
7. Hussain, M., Lee, S.: Recommendation framework for detecting sedentary behavior in smart home environment. In: 12th International Conference on Ubiquitous Healthcare (u-Healthcare 2015), Osaka, Japan (2015)
8. Healy, G.N., Dunstan, D.W., Salmon, J., Cerin, E., Shaw, J.E., Zimmet, P.Z., Owen, N.: Breaks in sedentary time beneficial associations with metabolic risk. Diabetes Care **31**(4), 661–666 (2008)
9. Banos, O., et al.: An innovative platform for person-centric health and wellness support. In: Ortuño, F., Rojas, I. (eds.) IWBBIO 2015, Part II. LNCS, vol. 9044, pp. 131–140. Springer, Heidelberg (2015)
10. Azumio: Argus quantify your day-to-day (2015). http://www.azumio.com/s/argus/index.html
11. Ahmad, M., Amin, M.B., Hussain, S., Kang, B.H., Cheong, T., Lee, S.: Health fog: a novel framework for health and wellness applications. J. Supercomputing, 1–19 (2016)
12. Banos, O., Amin, M.B., Ali Khan, W., Ali, T., Afzal, M., Kang, B.H., Lee, S.: Mining minds: an innovative framework for personalized health and wellness support. In: 2015 9th International Conference on Pervasive Computing Technologies for Healthcare (PervasiveHealth), pp. 1–8. IEEE, May 2015
13. Khan, W.A., Amin, M.B., Banos, O., Ali, T., Hussain, M., Afzal, M., Hussain, S., Hussain, J., Ali, R., Ali, M., Kang, D.: Mining Minds: Journey of Evolutionary Platform for Ubiquitous Wellness
14. Ali, R., Afzal, M., Hussain, M., Ali, M., Siddiqi, M.H., Lee, S., Kang, B.H.: Multimodal hybrid reasoning methodology for personalized wellbeing services. Comput. Biol. Med. **69**, 10–28 (2016)
15. Banos, O., Amin, M.B., Khan, W.A., Afzal, M., Hussain, M., Kang, B.H., Lee, S.: The Mining Minds Digital Health and Wellness Framework

Cloth Wrinkle Enhancement Based on the Coarse Mesh Simulation

Mi Jing[✉], Bing He, and Yue Lv

State Key Lab of Virtual Reality Technology and Systems, Beihang University,
Xueyuan Road No. 37, Haidian District, Beijing, China
{jingmi2014,hebing,lvyue2014}@buaa.edu.cn

Abstract. Wrinkle simulation can reflect the texture and simulation effect of clothes. In this paper, we realize a new cloth wrinkle enhancement method based on the coarse mesh simulation. Firstly, we extend the deformation tensor to generate the mesh vertex stretch tensor, so as to obtain one measuring factor for the three-dimensional cloth mesh vertex deformation. Then, we introduce a new method to extract the wrinkle baseline in the 2D mesh which is stretching from 3D coarse mesh and mapping it to 3D coarse mesh. Finally, we use the convolution surface as framework to simulate the wrinkle shape. We also propose and realize the wrinkle surface adjustment method. Experiment result proves the effectiveness of this method, namely this method can significantly improve the cloth wrinkle effect based on the coarse mesh simulation.

Keywords: Cloth simulation · Wrinkle enhancement · Wrinkle baseline · Mesh deformation

1 Introduction

For purpose of simulating the wrinkle effect with visual authenticity, finer meshes are usually required to capture the detailed changes of wrinkle. However, the cloth simulation directly using fine meshes needs to consume a huge amount of calculation resources and the simulation speed is low. In accordance with the scholars' analysis [1], formation of wrinkles and overall movement of cloth can be divided into two independent processes. The cloth simulation based on coarse mesh can capture the most obvious feature of clothes, while the authentic wrinkle can subdivide the deformation through coarse mesh. Therefore, cloth simulation can implement physical simulation on the coarse mesh and further add the wrinkle method on this basis, so as to obtain the cloth simulation effect with more visual authenticity.

In our research work, we design a cloth wrinkle enhancement demonstration system that is developed under the Microsoft Windows 7 platform by using MFC, and the development language is C++. In the system, the wrinkle enhancement experiment is implemented by following the steps as shown in the Fig. 1.

The research work is mainly based on the existing cloth simulation adopting the coarse meshes. In the work of this paper, Blender software is used to implement the physical simulation deformation of initial coarse mesh so as to generate the deformation

© Springer International Publishing Switzerland 2016
C.K. Chang et al. (Eds.): ICOST 2016, LNCS 9677, pp. 293–301, 2016.
DOI: 10.1007/978-3-319-39601-9_26

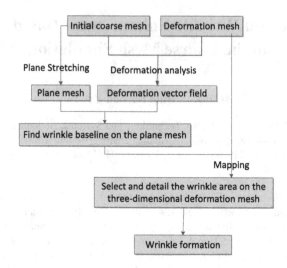

Fig. 1. Schematic diagram for the research contents

coarse mesh. The following figure shows the schematic diagram for the main research contents of this paper.

The input for the solution system researched in this paper is the initial coarse mesh and its formation mesh, while its output is the cloth mesh after enhancement of the deformation mesh wrinkle. With deformation analysis on the initial coarse mesh and deformation mesh, we extract the winkle baseline on the stretched plane of initial mesh, and then map the wrinkle baseline onto the three-dimensional deformation mesh. Select and detail the wrinkle area on the deformation mesh and finally add wrinkle to the three-dimensional deformation mesh, so as to achieve the purpose of enhancing the wrinkle effect of clothes.

Figure 2 shows an example verifying the wrinkle enhancement method which display the wrinkle enhancement effect picture of this cloth model. This three-dimensional cloth model has 1249 vertexes and 2386 triangle patches. In the Fig. 2, (a) and (c) is the effect diagram of skirt before adding the wrinkle, and (b) and (d) is respectively the wrinkle enhancement effect diagram.

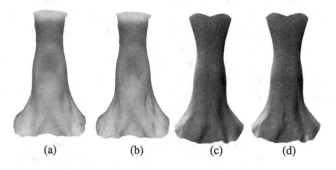

Fig. 2. Wrinkle enhancement effect diagram of skirt

2   Research Status

There are many cloth wrinkle simulation methods. In which, the commonly used methods include the method based on bitmap and method based on geometry, etc.

In 1978, Blinn [3] introduced the Bump Mapping in his chapter, namely: modify the surface normal vector prior to lighting computing so as to generate the visual effect of wrinkle provided that the surface geometry properties are not changed. Volino [5] simulated the wrinkle of deformation model through adjusting the given amplitude of wrinkle mode, added the wrinkle pattern template on the initial deformation mesh surface to integrate the complicated wrinkle deformation, and realizes the subdivision of mesh in some pattern areas to be detailed. Reference [6] applied the above methods to the simulation of cloth wrinkle and obtained a good visual effect. However, just as described in Kono [7], users in the Bump Mapping method shall draw the complicated wrinkle mode and adjust the mode parameters.

Clothes will have bend when covered over the body part of cylinder. Decaudin [8], etc. used this kind of priori knowledge of clothes to form the pre-defined wrinkle. This method is only applicable to the circumstance when the surface of cylindrical clothes has some pre-defined small deformation and will not be applicable to the deformation of any clothes. Larboulette [4], etc. and Wang Yu [9], etc. adopts the principle of keeping the side length unchanged and added wrinkle on the wrinkle baseline defined by users. In this paper, we adopt the deformation tensor defined by Talpaert, etc. [13] in the continuum mechanics to evaluate the wrinkle.

Li [10], etc. extracted human facial wrinkle baseline from pictures, mapped the 2D curve to 3D facial pattern, obtained the three-dimensional wrinkle shape through adjustment of curve function of wrinkle profile shape and further subdivided the wrinkle model through detailing of the curve surface. In this paper, we also use the wrinkle baseline to argument the wrinkle, but we introduce a new method to generate the wrinkle baseline from plane mesh which is obtained by unfold 3D coarse mesh.

Cutler [11], etc. marked the wrinkle baseline at the corresponding location of cloth surface, and finally generated the three-dimensional wrinkle in accordance with these wrinkle baseline as well as the defined wrinkle shape and adjustable parameter – wrinkle shape radius. Rohmer [2], etc. adopted the same concept and simulated the wrinkle on the basis of wrinkle baseline. The different point is that the location of wrinkle baseline in the method of Rohmer, etc. is obtained by the program in accordance with the analysis on the coarse simulation effect, which is to replace the human interference with the automatic post-processing method. We are inspired by this work and do some further study.

The wrinkle simulation method based on multi-resolution mesh divides the wrinkle formation and overall movement of cloth into two independent processes. Many scholars add the high-resolution mesh (fine mesh) along the normal direction of the low-resolution ground mesh (coarse mesh) to form the wrinkle.

3   Realization of Wrinkle Enhancement Method

3.1   Deformation Analysis and Plane Stretching of Coarse Mesh

When clothes suffer compression force at both sides, the clothes will have bending wrinkle due to the incompressibility and good bending property in its surface, so as to make the clothes reach the final force equilibrium. This kind of characteristic is reflected in the three-dimensional cloth model made of triangle meshes, which is the deformation of triangle meshes. Theoretically speaking, larger deformation of one triangle mesh patch means that this triangle patch suffers large compression.

For deformation analysis, we first need to use Blender to simulate physical simulation on initial coarse mesh and generate the deformation mesh. Then adopts the deformation tensor defined by Talpaert, etc. [13] to evaluate the deformation of cloth surface.

Angle value of triangles in the triangle mesh has a large impact on the process of finding the wrinkle baseline. Therefore, we optimize the angle-preserving plane stretching method on the basis of the ABF++ method proposed by Sheffer, etc. [14], and implements the calculation of plane triangle angle through the given plane triangle angle constraint condition and suitable constraint of the triangle angle along the vertical direction. Finally, fix one side of the triangle mesh on the two-dimensional plan in accordance with the solved triangle angle value, and convert the solution problem of triangular two-dimension coordinate to the matrix solution problem, so as to obtain the two-dimensional plane coordinate of mesh and realize the plane stretching of three-dimensional mesh.

3.2   Extraction of Wrinkle Baseline Based on Coarse Mesh

Prior to tracing the wrinkle baseline, sort all vertexes on the plane from small to large in accordance with the characteristic value μ_{i1} of stretch tensor of each vertex, and place all vertexes into one priority queue in accordance with the size of characteristic value μ_{i1}. Then trace the wrinkle baseline according to the following steps:

Step 1: select the vertex with the minimum characteristic μ_{i1} value from the queen as the seeded starting vertex, namely it will be selected as the first vertex on the wrinkle baseline; the adjacent vertex in the seeded starting vertex will the smallest characteristic value μ_{i1} will be regarded as the second vertex on the wrinkle baseline. Then calculate the direction of connection line between these two vertexes. Then proceed in accordance with the direction on this connection line. As there are two directions on the connection line between the first two selected vertexes, we trace the remaining wrinkle baseline along these two directions respectively. Finally, the tracing results on these two directions will be integrated together.

Step 2: select one tracing direction according to the step 1;

Step 3: define the current vertex as the tail vertex of wrinkle baseline along this direction, as shown in the Fig. 3.

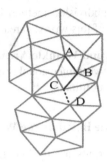

Fig. 3. Schematic diagram for tracing of wrinkle baseline

The extracted wrinkle fold line shall be smoothened after extracting the wrinkle fold line, so as to form the smooth wrinkle baseline. We adopt the simplest Laplacian smoothing method.

The iterative process of smoothing operation of the wrinkle fold line L is as follows:

(1) Save and make one copy of vertex information on L.
(2) For the internal vertex p_i (p_i is the vertex not on the boundary) on the fold line L, perform the calculation $L(p_i) = \frac{1}{2}(p_{i+1} - p_i) + \frac{1}{2}(p_{i-1} - p_i)$ and then calculate $p'_i = p_i + \lambda L(p_i)$. In which, p'_i is the coordinate of p_i at the new location.
(3) Terminate the iteration if reaching the cycle number; otherwise, start a new cycle of iteration starting from the step (1).

For convenience of expression, we redefine the concept of shortest path between two points, geodesic distance, etc., and will continue to use these re-defined concepts in subsequent part. The definition is as follows:

(1) The shortest path between two points is defined as the path with the least path segments in all paths connecting two points.
(2) Geodesic distance between two points is defined as the number of segments on the shortest path between two points.
(3) Geodesic distance between any point and one line (can be straight line, curve or annulus) on the mesh is defined as the smallest geodesic distance among the geodesic distances between this point and point on this line.

In accordance with above definitions, the selection process of wrinkle area can be briefly described by taking the following specific steps:

(1) Firstly add the vertex on the wrinkle baseline into the wrinkle area, and mark the wrinkle baseline.
(2) Select the vertexes having a geodesic distance of 1 from the wrinkle baseline in accordance with the selected wrinkle baseline, and add to the corresponding wrinkle area of this wrinkle baseline.
(3) Select the vertex having a geodesic distance of 1 from the area boundary in accordance with the current scope of wrinkle area, and add to this wrinkle area.

Then, adopt the Loop mesh subdivision method in the extracted wrinkle area to realize the local mesh subdivision of this wrinkle area.

Integration of Wrinkle Baseline and Wrinkle Area. We adopt the concept of barycentric coordinates [12] to map the two-dimensional coordinate on the smoothed wrinkle baseline to the three-dimensional coordinate.

3.3   Generation of Cloth Wrinkle Based on the Wrinkle Baseline

Ordering $p_1, p_2, \ldots, p_m$ as the end points arranged in order on the fold line, The wrinkle baseline can be expressed as:

$$s(t) = \begin{cases} p_1 + ta_1, 0 \leq t \leq l_1 \\ p_2 + (t - l_1)a_2, l_1 < t \leq l_1 + l_2 \\ \cdots \\ p_{m-1} + \left(t - \sum_{i=1}^{m-2} l_i\right)a_{m-1}, \sum_{i=1}^{m-2} l_i < t \leq \sum_{i=1}^{m-1} l_i. \end{cases} \tag{1}$$

For the point p in the space, the value is 1 when p is the point on the wrinkle baseline, and conversely the value is 0.

The field function of convolution surface adopted in this paper is defined as the convolution of kernel function $k(p)$ and geometric function $g(p)$:

$$f(p) = \int_{V_u} \omega(u)k(p - u)du. \tag{2}$$

In which, V_u is the domain of definition of skeleton, and $\omega(u)$ is the weighting function controlling the wrinkle deformation radius. We uses the weight function $\omega(u)$ proposed by Rohmer [2], etc. in calculating the convolution surface. In this paper, $v(u)$ is the tension amount of the point u, and ξ is manual setting value taking 0.0004.

Kernel function in this paper adopts the Cauchy kernel function. In order to calculate field function $f(p)$ of point p in the space, it is necessary to solve the integral of the formula (2). When $\omega(u)$ is constant ω_0, $f(p)$ equals the product of ω_0 multiplying the kernel function:

$$f(p) = \omega_0 \int_u k(p - u)du. \tag{3}$$

Assuming that the wrinkle fold line has M fold line segments, we divide each segment of fold line skeleton into N small segments. It is believed that the weight function of each small segment is a constant and equals to the value of weight function in the middle position of small segment, then:

$$f(p) = \int_u \omega(u)k(p - u)du = \sum_{k=1}^{M} \sum_{i=1}^{N} \omega_{ki} \int_{u_{ki}} k(p - u_{ki})du_{ki}. \tag{4}$$

In which, ω_{ki} is the corresponding weight of the i th small segment of fold line on the k th wrinkle fold line segment. u_{ki} is the point on the i th small segment of fold line of the k th wrinkle fold line segment.

To map the patch on the original mesh surface to the implicit wrinkle surface. For one vertex p_1 in the original triangle mesh, if it is included in the scope of implicit wrinkle surface (namely, the field function used for calculating its convolution surface $f(p_1) > 1$, then it is necessary to implement mapping of it; otherwise if $f(p_1) <= 1$, this means that the point p_1 will not be affected by the wrinkle surface and does not need mapping. If p_1 needs to be mapped to the wrinkle surface, it is firstly necessary to calculate its mapping direction and then calculate the coordinate of points mapped by p_1 to the convolution surface along the mapping direction. The mapping direction vector v_{map} of the point p_1 can be obtained through calculating the normal vector of this point. We define the corresponding normal vector $v_{normal}(p)$ of the vertex p on the triangle mesh as the average normal vector of adjacent triangle surface of the point p and also the normalized result:

$$v_{normal}(p) = \frac{\sum_i u_{pi}}{\left\|\sum_i u_{pi}\right\|}. \tag{5}$$

In which, u_{pi} is the corresponding normal vector p of the i th adjacent triangular facet, and $\|v\|$ modulus taking of vector v. Starting from the point p_1, the radial along the direction $v_{normal}(p_1)$ can be expressed as:

$$g(t)_{p_1} = p_1 + tv_{normal}(p_1), 0 \le t < +\infty \tag{6}$$

Thus, the problem of solving the p_1 mapping point equals to the solution of equation $f(g(t)_{p_1}) = 1$. Therefore, we use the method of searching for approximate solution to obtain the mapping point of p_1 on the wrinkle surface.

The cross section of wrinkle simulated by using the above methods is the arc shape, while it is found through observation of wrinkles in the real world that the cross-sectional shape of wrinkles is more close to the shape of the following function:

$$g(x) = A\cos^2(x). \tag{7}$$

Thus, the location of vertex in the wrinkle area is further adjusted on the basis of the mapping result of implicit surface. In accordance with the above methods, function of any shapes can be used to adjust the sectional shape of three-dimensional cloth wrinkle, so as to further simulate the diversified wrinkle state.

4   Conclusion and Prospect

We research and realizes a set of cloth wrinkle enhancement simulation method based on the coarse mesh simulation, which is aimed at obtaining more fine wrinkle details and enhancing the wrinkle simulation effect on the basis of physical simulation result of cloth by adopting the coarse mesh and in accordance with the deformation analysis on the initial mesh and deformation mesh. Through the plane stretching of mesh, the wrinkle baseline extraction method realized in this paper not only avoids high complexity of searching for wrinkle baseline directly on the three-dimensional mesh, but also improves the higher integration and operability of the final wrinkle baseline on the final three-dimensional mesh. We realize the method for selection of wrinkle area and formation of wrinkle. After obtaining the wrinkle baseline, simulation wrinkle can be made more effectively through the local mesh subdivision of the original coarse mesh. It can be seen from the experiment effect that this method can obtain a better wrinkle enhancement effect.

In future work, we would consider not subdivides the front and rear part of the three-dimensional mesh of cloth to extracts the wrinkle baseline, which will affect the continuity of wrinkle baseline surrounding the subdivision line. The stretched planes of two cloth meshes can be spliced together. In addition, the wrinkle baseline is subdivided into many small line segments in formation of convolution surface in this study, and the tension amount of line segment between two points is regarded as equivalent. In the further study, we will consider that the tension amount on this curve section shall have some changes.

Acknowledgements. This work was supported by grant No.61272346 from NSFC (National Natural Science Foundation of China).

References

1. Zurdo, J., Brito, J., Otaduy, M.: Animating wrinkles by example on non-skinned cloth. IEEE Trans. Vis. Comput. Graph. **19**(1), 148–158 (2013)
2. Rohmer, D., Popa, T., Cani, M.P., et al.: Animation wrinkling: augmenting coarse cloth simulations with realistic-looking wrinkles. ACM Trans. Graph. (TOG) **29**(6), 157 (2010)
3. Blinn, J.F.: Simulation of wrinkled surfaces. In: SIGGRAPH, pp. 286–292 (1978)
4. Larboulette, C., Cani, M.P.: Real-time dynamic wrinkles. In: The Computer Graphics International, pp. 522–525. IEEE Computer Society (2004)
5. Volino, P., Magnenat-Thalmann, N.: Fast geometrical wrinkles on animated surfaces. In: Seventh International Conference in Central Europe on Computer Graphics and Visualization (WSCG) (1999)
6. Hadap, S., Bangerter, E., Volino, P., et al.: Animating wrinkles on clothes. In: IEEE Visualization, pp. 175–182 (1999)
7. Kono, H., Genda, E.: Wrinkle generation model for 3d facial expression. In: ACM SIGGRAPH Sketches & Applications, p.1. ACM (2003)
8. Decaudin, P., Julius, D., Wither, J., et al.: Virtual garments: a fully geometric approach for clothing design. Comput. Graph. Forum **25**(3), 625–634 (2006)
9. Wang, Y., Wang, C.C., Yuen, M.M.: Fast energy-based surface wrinkle modeling. Comput. Graph. **30**(1), 111–125 (2006)
10. Li, L., Liu, F., Li, C., et al.: Realistic wrinkle generation for 3D face modeling based on automatically extracted curves and improved shape control functions. Comput. Graph. **35**(1), 175–184 (2011)

11. Cutler, L.D., Gershbein, R., Wang, X.C., et al.: An art-directed wrinkle system for CG character clothing. In: Proceedings of the ACM SIGGRAPH/Eurographics Symposium on Computer Animation, pp. 117–125. ACM (2005)
12. Liu, T., Bargteil, A.W., O'Brien, J.F.: Fast simulation of mass-spring systems. ACM Trans. Graph. (TOG) **32**(6), 214 (2013)
13. Talpaert, Y.: Tensor Analysis and Continuum Mechanics. Kluwer Academic Publishers, Dordrecht (2002)
14. Sheffer, A., Lévy, B., Mogilnitsky, M., et al.: ABF++: fast and robust angle based flattening. ACM Trans. Graph. (TOG) **24**(2), 311–330 (2007)

Medical Big Data Collection, Processing, and Analysis

Challenges in Managing Real-Time Data in Health Information System (HIS)

Usman Akhtar[1], Asad Masood Khattak[2], and Sungyoung Lee[1]([✉])

[1] Department of Computer Science and Engineering, Kyung Hee University,
Seocheon-dong, Giheung-gu, Yongin-si, Gyeonggi-do, South Korea
{usman,sylee}@oslab.khu.ac.kr
[2] College of Techological Innovation, Zayed University, Dubai, UAE
asad.khattak@zu.ac.ae

Abstract. In this paper, we have discussed the challenges in handling real-time medical big data collection and storage in health information system (HIS). Based on challenges, we have proposed a model for real-time analysis of medical big data. We exemplify the approach through Spark Streaming and Apache Kafka using the processing of health big data Stream. Apache Kafka works very well in transporting data among different systems such as relational databases, Apache Hadoop and non-relational databases. However, Apache Kafka lacks analyzing the stream, Spark Streaming framework has the capability to perform some operations on the stream. We have identified the challenges in current real-time systems and proposed our solution to cope with the medical big data streams.

Keywords: Stream processing framework · Health-care Information System (HIS) · Kafka messaging

1 Introduction

Over the past two decades, the technology advancements have led to increase data from many domains like health care and other scientific sensors. Big data in health is concerned with the datasets that are too big and complex to process and interpret with the existing tools and these datasets present a problem with the storage, analysis and visualization. Big data is unstructured and normally require real-time analysis. Big data refers to those datasets that are very large and complex to manage with traditional software or common data management tools. Big data in health-care is growing enormous not only because of its volume but also with the diversity of the datatypes. In health-care sector, there are three main types of digital data: clinical records, health research records and organization operations records. Clinical records consist of a variety of data like electronic medical records, images and wireless medical devices and these devices are the major contributors to the flood of big data. Health research records also generate large amount of data that are unstructured. Genetic differences

© Springer International Publishing Switzerland 2016
C.K. Chang et al. (Eds.): ICOST 2016, LNCS 9677, pp. 305–313, 2016.
DOI: 10.1007/978-3-319-39601-9_27

study, which include more than 100,000 the participants, generate approximately 1.5 GB of data per person. Organization operations records such as billing and scheduling have been digitized resulting in large amount of data generation.

Designing a scalable big data system faces a series of challenges. First, due to the heterogeneous and huge volume of data, it is difficult to collect data from the distributed locations. Second, storage is the main problem for heterogeneous datasets. Big data system need to store while providing performance guarantee. Third challenge is related to mining massive datasets at real-time that include visualization. These challenges demand a new processing paradigm as the current data management systems is not efficient in dealing with the real-time or heterogeneous nature of data. However, traditional database management system is based on storing the structured data in relational database management system (RDBMS). These traditional systems do not provide any support for unstructured or semi-structured data. From the view of scalability, there are many flaws in traditional RDBMS in scaling for managing with the hardware in parallel, which is not suitable to manage growing data. To address these challenges, many solutions have been proposed by the research community such as NoSQL [1], which is more suitable for dealing with the massive heterogeneous data. MapReduce [2] programming model is more suitable for processing large datasets as it consists of map and reduce function. Apache Hadoop is a batch processing system that allows distributed processing of large datasets. It also integrates storage, data processing and other management modules to provide a powerful solution. One of the major limitation of Hadoop is dealing with the real-time stream processing or in memory processing.

Real-time management of data stream and providing data analytics is the key requirement in health care [3]. Data stream refer to those data that continuously arrive without persistent in the storage. Fast inference in real-time is still a major research problem. The streaming processing paradigm will normally analyze data as soon as it arrives and data is in the form of stream. Only a small portion of the stream is stored in limited memory. Some of the distributed stream computing framework include Storm, S4, Kafka and Storm Streaming [4].

Research on health-care management is constantly growing. Research community is interested in storing data captured from medical devices. Managing stream is an ongoing research issue and much of the research work is related to the querying stream data and management. Data storage is one of the crucial part of the health-care information system as the data are coming from the different sources, PolyglotHIS [5] combines relational, graph and other document models to conciliate variety of information. In the recent past, there has been a growing attempt to utilize medical signal analytics to improve patient care management [6].

1.1   Motivation

Research on real-time health-care data acquisition and management is constantly growing. The main motivation is to figure out the challenges in health information system (HIS), while dealing with the real-time data stream. Moreover, we

Table 1. Real-time systems spectrum

Current focus	Batch processing	Relational database management system
Technologies	HDFS, MapReduce	MySQL, PostgreSQL
Limitations	Suitable for batch processing not for the real-time streams	Not suitable for unstructured data
Challenges	Continuous processing of stream, load balancing	Not suitable for generating real-time analytics
Possible solution	Use KafKa for distributed stream processing and Apache Spark streaming to perform operations on the streams	Use of NoSQL, Apache Hive and ApacheHbase for both the structured and unstructured data

have worked out to find the limitations of existing technologies. Our main goal is to develop a model that is capable of handling medical big data streams and provide analytics.

Table 1, showing the current real-time system spectrum as shown, the current focus is mainly on the batch processing and using the relational database management system. For managing real-time medical streams batch processing is not the appropriate solution. Possible solution is the uses of distributed messaging system like Apache KafKa and store the data in NoSQL databases for analytics.

We have discussed the challenges for the health information system while dealing with the big data in Sect. 2. Based on the challenges discuss in this paper we have proposed our model in Sect. 3.

2   Big Data: Challenges in Health Information System

Health-care industry is generating the massive amount of data. To analyze and store real-time management of medical stream is a challenging task. We have identity the challenges in health information system and briefly describe the current technology available to cope with these challenges. We also consider the limitation of the current technology.

2.1   Challenges in Health-Care Informatics

The speedy growth of health-care organization and also the continuously increasing number of patients has led to the greater use of the clinical support system. Modern medical imaging techniques are capable of producing high resolution images but they require High Performance Computing. Many monitoring devices continuously generate data and the data is normally stored for a small period of time. However, many attempt have been made to utilize the data from telemetry and other physiological monitoring devices. Many areas in health-care can be improved by the use of computational intelligence. In variety of medical applications different image acquisition techniques have been utilized.

For health-care informatics challenge current technology like HBase and MongoDB are becoming more common in research communities. Apache Hadoop is highly scalable and open source framework which render variety of computing modules such as Spark Streaming and Apache Storm [7]. For performing variety of operations while dealing with the medical streaming data spark and storm is promising platform. These platforms are capable of ingesting and computing streaming data. In intensive care unit (ICU), vast amount of data is produced and there is a need to develop clinical decision support system (CDSS) [8].

For the streaming data in health-care, there is a need to develop a platform as the current technologies are limited to handle medical devices data. Moreover, data acquisition and ingestion is required for clinical health-care setting, while dealing with the streaming data. The main challenges while dealing with the data acquisition are network bandwidth, scalability and cost issues.

2.2   Increased Cost with Low Health-Care Services

There are plenty of challenges that health-care are facing specially hospital administrator and researchers. However, consumers are experiencing increased cost without any gain in health services.

Currently, health-care application uses very expensive system to manage data. The health-care system should use Hadoop, as it is an open source software from Apache and it include MapReduce framework for running applications. Hadoop is very scalable and supports many other modules for distributed storage and computations. Hadoop also provides many high language support like Pig Latin [9] and Hive [10] and many vendors are offering commercial distributions including Cloudera, MapR, and Hortonworks.

2.3   Stream Computing for Smarter Health-Care

To improve the patient outcome and to detect the warning signs of the complications, there is a need for stream computing platform. In modern health-care patients are routinely connected to the medical equipment that continuously monitor blood pressure and heartbeat.

Consequently, data processing engines are gaining popularity in health-care such as Spark Streaming, Apache Storm and Apache Kafka. Apache Kafka is mainly used for stream processing and it supports wide range of the scenarios and claims high throughput and reliability. Apache Storm processes data in real-time and it is extremely useful in processing high velocity of data. While Apache Spark is in-memory data processing and includes rich APIs support to efficiently execute streaming and allow SQL for iterative access of data. While dealing with the fast moving big data analytics, Apache Storm and Apache Kafka complement each other. Most stream distributed processing systems, like Apache Storm, work on a record at a time model, where each node is responsible for receiving the data and update internal state.

These models raise many challenges in cloud environment in term of fault tolerance, consistency and fusion with the batch processing. A new programming model was proposed which consists of discretized streams (D-Streams). Apache Spark model uses small intervals and treats the stream a series of deterministic batch processing computations. Apache Spark is efficient in building a modern health care application that fuses well with the batch processing. While dealing with the streaming data, Apache Spark is fault tolerant as it employs a new approach called parallel recovery.

2.4   Transforming Health-Care Data into Information

In the recent advancements there are lot of Real-Time technologies like Kafka, Storm, and Spark Streaming, but the main problem is the lack of knowhow in using these technologies.

The Stream Data Platform: The stream data processing is different than the query processing in traditional relational database management system. Our main goal is to the design a system that stores the patients physiologic features and displays the analytics in real-time. These analytics help the medical staff to initiate medical intervention earlier to save lives.

But there are some challenges while dealing with the stream data platform. The first problem in building the health-care application is the transportation of the data between systems. A lot of data systems are involved in building some health-care applications, such as, relational databases, Hadoop, search system and other analytics system. As in the distributed system all of these need reliable feeds of data and this raises the problem of data integration when you have to cope with the unstructured data.

Second problem is related to the analytical data processing e.g. processing in data warehouse. The inefficient data integration between the system makes it hard to perform richer analytical data processing.

Stream Data Collection: In a typical hospital, nurses are responsible for monitoring patients vital signs manually. They visit each patient to record the critical signs but the condition of the patient may decline after the visit. Currently, new wireless sensors are available that can transmit the patient conditions at much higher frequencies and these measurements can be streamed to Hadoop for storage. In ICU, patient monitoring system monitor the vital signs such as heart rate, respiration rate, body temperature and blood pressure. Data stream of these vital signs can be sent via a communication port supported by the interface software and sequentially stored in Hadoop for distributed data storage.

3 Discussion

Based on the challenges discuss in the health-care application we have proposed a solution based on the KaKfa data streaming and Spark Streaming. We believe that this model can work indecently and with the existing application. Efficient processing of data in health-care increases the quality of patient monitoring. Consider, the Patient with a Cardiac problem, and often wear Cardiac Event Recorders (CERS), which constantly record the Hearts Electrical Activity (ECG). In CERS data is manually transferred to other device. So, this stream can be utilized to perform real-time analysis. Medical devices are the ultimate source of sending the data. But these data cannot be sent directly to the HDFS for storage and analysis. Kafka is used to buffer the data before writing into the HDFS. Frameworks are used to perform some operations on the stream, these frameworks are Spark Streaming and Apache Storm. To query the historical data in HDFS, Apache Hive and Apache Impala are widely used Fig. 1. Shows data sources coming from the medical devices to Kafka as it provides the functionality of the messaging system. To perform operations on the stream, Spark Streaming is applied. This will process the stream and finally write it on the HDFS. Hive runs on top of the Hadoop to query the data inside the HDFS for visualization and analytics.

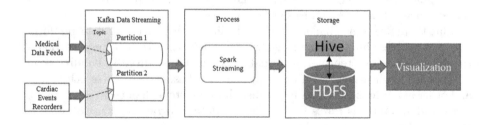

Fig. 1. Transforming health-care data into information

Kafka data streaming module is responsible for managing the events streams. A stream that is coming in the Kafka is modeled by a topic which gives name to the data. As Kafka is a publish-subscriber messaging system each message has its own key, which is useful way to partition the data on cloud. In medical big data application ETL (extract, transform and load) pipelines are needed as data platform is being able to stream data between systems to provide analytics.

4 Related Work

Big Data application are widely used in health-care, medical and government services. Recently, national health authority of Australia encloses Personally Controlled Electronics Health Record (PCEHR) to manage the individual health records as an electronics health records (eHR) [11]. The volume of these health-care systems are very large and it is very useful for the doctors and other health-care providers to provide the best possible care. Ehealth system are gaining lot of importance in research community and researchers put emphasis on the privacy, data integrity and storage. Some commercial companies are trying to propose there own solution to deals with the stream processing like IBM InfoSphere Streams which has the capability to analyze data in motion and can easily integrate with the development framework like Eclipse and enable you to analyze, visualize and test with the help of Streams Processing Language (SPL) [12].

In Table 2, we have shown the comparison of different eHealth frameworks proposed in the literature. Now researchers are trying to propose a model that include Big Data ecosystem technologies in more effective way. Health-care need real-time data analysis, we have taken a step to propose a model that uses Big Data processing and analytics for Health-care scenarios.

Table 2. Comparison of different eHealth frameworks

eHealth proposed models	Big data system	Real-time analysis	Privacy and security	Limitation
A privacy-preserving framework for personally controlled electronic health record (PCEHR) system [13]	No	No	Yes	Major focus is on the privacy, storage of large health record is still the main challenge
An open platform for personal health record apps with platform-level privacy protection [14]	No	No	Yes	Proposed a cloud based solution but uses relational database for storage. Not suitable for real-time
Privacy preservation and information security protection for patients portable electronic health records [15]	No	No	Yes	Useful for safeguarding the EHR, but storage and visualization is not covered
The Taiwanese method for providing patients data from multiple hospital EHR systems [16]	Yes	No	Yes	Useful for safeguarding the EHR, but storage and visualization is not covered

5 Conclusion and Future Work

To improve the patient outcome and to detect the warning signs of the complications, there is a need of a streaming computing platform. The traditional relational system does not provide any support for unstructured nature of medical data stream. From the view of scalability, there are many flaws in traditional RDBMS in scaling with the hardware in parallel, which is not suitable to manage growing data. After analyzing the challenges we have proposed a cheap commodity health-care information system which can successfully process real-time streaming and store data on Hive warehouse on the top of the HDFS. The main limitation of the work is not able to perform end-to-end evaluation of the work along with the response time. In future, we will continue to work on how we can efficiently capture data from the medical devices regardless of the data format.

Acknowledgments. This work was supported by the Industrial Core Technology Development Program (10049079, Develop of mining core technology exploiting personal big data) funded by the Ministry of Trade, Industry and Energy (MOTIE, Korea) and This research was supported by Basic Science Research Program through the National Research Foundation of Korea (NRF) funded by the Ministry of Science, ICT and Future Planning (2011-0030079). This research work was also supported by Zayed University Research Initiative Fund R15098.

References

1. Cattell, R.: Scalable SQL, NoSQL data stores. SIGMOD Rec. **39**(4), 12–27 (2010). http://doi.acm.org/10.1145/1978915.1978919
2. Dean, J., Ghemawat, S.: Mapreduce: simplified data processing on large clusters. Commun. ACM **51**(1), 107–113 (2008). http://doi.acm.org/10.1145/1327452.1327492
3. Peek, N., Holmes, J., Sun, J.: Technical challenges for big data in biomedicine and health: data sources, infrastructure, and analytics. Yearb Med Inform **9**(1), 42–7 (2014)
4. Zaharia, M., Das, T., Li, H., Shenker, S., Stoica, I.: Discretized streams: an efficient and fault-tolerant model for stream processing on large clusters. In: Proceedings of the 4th USENIX Conference on Hot Topics in Cloud Computing, HotCloud 2012, Berkeley, CA, USA, p. 10. USENIX Association (2012). http://dl.acm.org/citation.cfm?id=2342763.2342773
5. Kaur, K., Rani, R.: Managing data in healthcare information systems: many models, one solution. Computer **3**, 52–59 (2015)
6. Apiletti, D., Baralis, E., Bruno, G., Cerquitelli, T.: Real-time analysis of physiological data to support medical applications. Trans. Info. Tech. Biomed. **13**(3), 313–321 (2009). http://dx.doi.org/10.1109/TITB.2008.2010702
7. Raghupathi, W., Raghupathi, V.: Big data analytics in healthcare: promise and potential. Health Inf. Sci. Syst. **2**(1), 1–10 (2014). http://dx.doi.org/10.1186/2047-2501-2-3

8. Hussain, M., Khattak, A., Khan, W., Fatima, I., Amin, M., Pervez, Z., Batool, R., Saleem, M., Afzal, M., Faheem, M., et al.: Cloud-based smart cdss for chronic diseases. Health Technol. **3**(2), 153–175 (2013)

9. Olston, C., Reed, B., Srivastava, U., Kumar, R., Tomkins, A.: Pig latin: a not-so-foreign language for data processing. In: Proceedings of the 2008 ACM SIGMOD International Conference on Management of Data, SIGMOD 2008, pp. 1099–1110. ACM, New York (2008). http://doi.acm.org/10.1145/1376616.1376726

10. Thusoo, A., Sarma, J.S., Jain, N., Shao, Z., Chakka, P., Anthony, S., Liu, H., Wyckoff, P., Murthy, R.: Hive: a warehousing solution over a map-reduce framework. Proc. VLDB Endow. **2**(2), 1626–1629 (2009). http://dx.doi.org/10.14778/1687553.1687609

11. Rabbi, K., Kaosar, M., Islam, M.R., Mamun, Q.: A secure real time data processing framework for personally controlled electronic health record (PCEHR) system. In: Tian, J., Jing, J., Srivatsa, M. (eds.) SecureComm 2014, pp. 141–156. Springer, Heidelberg (2014)

12. Nabi, Z., Wagle, R., Bouillet, E.: The best of two worlds: integrating IBM infosphere streams with apache YARN. In: 2014 IEEE International Conference on in Big Data (Big Data), pp. 47–51. IEEE, (2014)

13. Begum, M., Mamun, Q., Kaosar, M.: A privacy-preserving framework for personally controlled electronic health record (PCEHR) system (2013)

14. Van Gorp, P., Comuzzi, M., Jahnen, A., Kaymak, U., Middleton, B.: An open platform for personal health record apps with platform-level privacy protection. Comput. Biol. Med. **51**, 14–23 (2014)

15. Huang, L.-C., Chu, H.-C., Lien, C.-Y., Hsiao, C.-H., Kao, T.: Privacy preservation and information security protection for patients portable electronic health records. Comput. Biol. Med. **39**(9), 743–750 (2009)

16. Jian, W.-S., Wen, H.-C., Scholl, J., Shabbir, S.A., Lee, P., Hsu, C.-Y., Li, Y.-C.: The taiwanese method for providing patients data from multiple hospital EHR systems. J. Biomed. Inform. **44**(2), 326–332 (2011)

Placement Scheduling for Replication in HDFS Based on Probabilistic Approach

Dinh-Mao Bui and Sungyoung Lee[✉]

Department of Computer Engineering, Kyung Hee University, Suwon, Korea
{mao,sylee}@oslab.khu.ac.kr

Abstract. Along with the rapid evolution in Big Data analysis, Apache Hadoop keeps the important role to deliver the high availability on top of computing clusters. Also, to maintain the high throughput access for computation, the Apache Hadoop is equipped with the Hadoop File System (HDFS) for managing the file operations. Besides, HDFS is ensured the reliability and high availability by using a specific replication mechanism. However, because the workload on each computing node is various, keeping the same replication strategy might result in imbalance. Targeting to solve this drawbacks of HDFS architecture, we proposes an approach to adaptively choose the placement for replicas. To do that, the network status and system utilization can be used to create the individual replication placement strategy for each file. Eventually, the proposed approach can provide the suitable destination for replicas to improve the performance. Subsequently, the availability of the system is enhanced while still keeping the reliability of data storage.

Keywords: Placement scheduling · HDFS · Execution time · Throughput · Probabilistic approach

1 Introduction

Big Data is the terminology to describe the large and complex dataset that the common processing techniques are inadequate to conduct the mining. The obstacles include but not limited to the analysis, capture, curation, search, storage and visualization. To solve these problem, the Apache Hadoop is known to be one of the most efficient framework. Not only used to achieve the high availability, Apache Hadoop is designed with an assumption that the hardware failures of computing nodes are commonplace and should be handle to maintain the data reliability.

The fundamental components of Apache Hadoop include the storage part (Hadoop Distributed File System (HDFS)) and the processing part (MapReduce). The HDFS has been expected to provide the reliable, high-throughput access to parallel computing. As time goes by, this component grows up as a suitable storage framework for parallel and distributed processing, especially for MapReduce solution.

© Springer International Publishing Switzerland 2016
C.K. Chang et al. (Eds.): ICOST 2016, LNCS 9677, pp. 314–320, 2016.
DOI: 10.1007/978-3-319-39601-9_28

In essence, HDFS splits files into large blocks and distributes to commodity nodes. When tasks is generated in the system, the MapReduce categorizes and transfers these task to nodes in parallel according to the data requirement. This mechanism is to take advantage of data locality characteristic to improve the performance. To ensure the reliability, HDFS is initially configured to replicate three copies of every data file regardless the status of the computing nodes. As time goes by, this replication strategy may lead the system into imbalanced status by creating the hot-spot (the special node that attracts many jobs) [1,2]. Thus, this configuration slows down performance and wastes the resources [3,4].

In this research, we would like to introduce an approach choosing the placement for replicas more effectively. In this approach, not only the nature of system capability is taken into account, but also the task characteristic is considered. As a result, the replicas is dynamically scheduled based according to the utilization of the system. By implementing this framework, the task execution time and the throughput can be improved and benefit the Hadoop system.

The remainder of this paper is organized as follows. In Sect. 2, the system architecture of the proposed approach is presented. Section 3 includes the performance evaluation. Finally, the conclusion is summarized in Sect. 4.

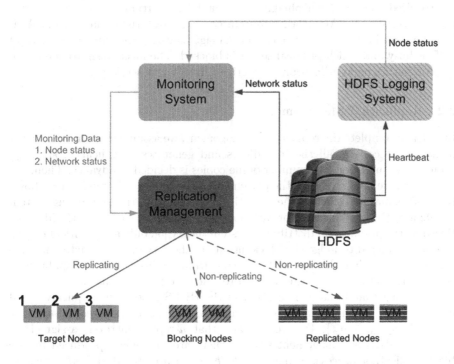

Fig. 1. Architecture of Replication Placement Management (RPM) system.

2   Proposed Architecture

2.1   System Architecture

The purpose of the proposed idea is to design an Replication Placement Management system (hereinafter, RPM) for HDFS. In other words, the main function of this system is to dynamically schedule the placement for replicas based on the system utilization. Constructing on top of the Hadoop File System and Open Nebula Orchestrator, the proposed system takes responsibility to manage the replication over the virtualized HDFS instances. An overview of the proposed RPM is described in Fig. 1. In this architecture, instead of using the physical servers for the computing nodes, the virtual machines are preferred because of the flexibility, elasticity, multi-tenancy and on-demand deployment features.

As described in Fig. 1, the system starts by periodically collecting the heartbeat from the HDFS Logging System. After that, this data goes to the Monitoring System as the first input source. The second input source is the network utilization which is polled directly from the computing nodes. It is essential to introduce the Monitoring System. Mainly based on the Ganglia framework, the Monitoring System is simple, robust and easy to configure for monitoring most of the required metrics. After plugging into the HDFS virtual nodes as well as the physical servers, the Monitoring System can collect statistic via Ganglia API. This information helps the replication management to determine which virtual node is busy and which physical server is blocked. The mechanism to determine the computing node utilization is described in the next section.

2.2   Replication Management

In order to complete the replication management, we assume that the replication management collects all the ingredients and generates a replication strategy. From this assumption, the number of file copies is decided in advance. Then, the only issue is related to choose the placement of the replicas. As mentioned above, this task is mainly based on the statistics retrieved from the monitoring system to calculate the blocking rate for each node and assign the replicas to the idle one. Based on the parallel and distributed system theory [5], only a few critical factors can be considered to judge the blocking rate of the server. These factors include the network bandwidth, the number of concurrent accesses and the capability of the server. Following is the mechanism to calculate the blocking rate.

Assuming that a file X is utilized in the HDFS system, it is quickly sliced into m blocks by the Namenode. These m blocks can be denoted as an array $X = \{b_1, b_2, b_3, \cdots b_m\}$. Due to the fact that n-replica factor is assigned for this file by HDFS management system, there are nm blocks produced by the block replicating process. Suppose $b_1, b_2, b_3, \cdots b_j$ are stored at VM_i. Because the limited number of concurrent accesses of VM_i is c_i, there must be at least one client that is denied the access if the concurrent access increases to $c_i + 1$. The probability of VM_i refusing a client access defines the blocking rate of VM_i, which is represented by $\mathcal{BR}(VM_i)$. Furthermore, this formula needs to be generalized. Suppose that the visiting rate from clients to VM_i again follows the Poisson Process with an arrival rate λ_i. Naturally the service process of VM_i is considered to be of the $M/M/c/c$ queuing model. Because the capacity of VM_i is c_i, the client leaves VM_i immediately if all the communication lines of VM_i are busy. As a result, the blocking rate of VM_i follows the Poisson Arrival See Time Averages (PASTA) theory [6] and is defined below

$$\mathcal{BR}(VM_i) = \frac{(\lambda_i \tau_i)^{c_i}}{c_i!} \left[\sum_{k=0}^{c_i} \frac{(\lambda_i \tau_i)^k}{k!} \right]^{-1} \tag{1}$$

in which, c_i is the limited number of concurrent accesses provided by VM_i, λ_i is the arrival rate of the visiting client, τ_i is the average processing time of each block in VM_i. In HDFS, the access mode is exclusive writing and concurrent reading, then τ_i might be considered as the average time of VM_i reading a block. Thereafter, by evaluating the blocking rate, it is easy for the Replication Management to select a location for assigning the replicas. As described in Fig. 1, only the virtual machine satisfying two conditions is chosen as the destination for replication. The first condition is low-blocking rate and the second one is not to not store the replicas in advance. While the latter condition is obvious, the former condition of low-blocking rate is chosen to balance the system. By placing the replication on the low utilization worker nodes, the approach helps to increase the access to these specific nodes rather than putting more stress on the busy one. As time progresses, this philosophy can improve the overall system performance, which would be shown on the performance evaluation in the next section.

3 Performance Evaluation

3.1 Experiments

We use the experiment of testDFSIO to evaluate the effectiveness of our proposed method. The testDFSIO is a benchmark tool to discover the HDFS capability. In essence, this tool is developed to evaluate the I/O performance for HDFS. The computing system used for these experiments is described in Table 1.

3.2 Results

On the execution time benchmark of testDFSIO experiment (Fig. 2), it can be seen obviously that RPM outperforms DARE [2] and ERMS [3] when file size increases. In the last experiment case of 4 GB of file size, RPM finishes the tasks in 17.38 % and 62.36 % faster than ERMS and DARE, respectively. The same situation happens when investigating the read throughput factor in Fig. 3. RPM continues surpassing ERMS and DARE in every experiment cases of file size. The result is obvious because of acceptable utilization of network traffic as well as of disk-writing operation when applying RPM in comparison with others.

Table 1. System configuration

	Configuration
Computing Nodes	01 Name Node, 8 Data Nodes
Node Types	XEN's Virtual Machine
Platform	64bit
CPU Cores	Intel®Core™ i7-3770, 3.40 GHz 4 cores for Name Node 1 cores for each Data Node
Storage	500 GB for Name Node 100 GB for each Data Node
Memory	16 GB for Name Node 8 GB for each Data Node
Network	Gigabit NIC
OS	CentOS 6.5 (final) Kernel: 2.6.32-431.el6.x86_64
Software	Apache Hadoop 2.0.0-cdh4.7.0

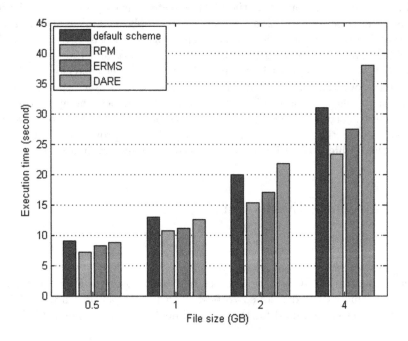

Fig. 2. Execution time benchmark of testDFSIO (lower is better).

In fact, when engaging ERMS and DARE, the HDFS system has to reserve too much network bandwidth and CPU cycles for transferring and writing the replicas because of the hot-spot issue. In this issue, the hot-spot becomes the most crowded node and make the system imbalance. Subsequently, the HDFS system keeps scheduling the tasks to this special node because of high density of local data. It can lead the whole system into the 'traffic jam' and disk-operation overhead.

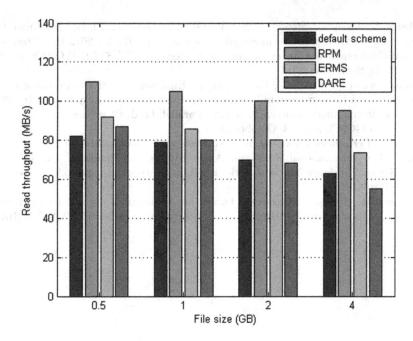

Fig. 3. Read throughput benchmark of testDFSIO (higher is better).

4   Conclusion

The main purpose of this research is to improve the balance and the performance of HDFS system by proposing the comprehensively replication placement management component. With rigorous analysis of the characteristics of file operation in HDFS, the uniqueness of our idea is to create an adaptive and effective solution to extend the capability of Big Data systems. For further development, some parts of the source code developed for testing our idea would be made available under the terms of the GNU general public license (GPL).

Acknowledgment. This work was supported by the Industrial Core Technology Development Program (10049079, Develop of mining core technology exploiting personal big data) funded by the Ministry of Trade, Industry and Energy (MOTIE, Korea); and supported by the National Research Foundation of Korea (NRF) grant funded by the Korea government (MSIP) NRF-2014R1A2A2A01003914.

References

1. Wei, Q., Veeravalli, B., Gong, B., Zeng, L., Feng, D.: Cdrm: a cost-effective dynamic replication management scheme for cloud storage cluster. In: 2010 IEEE International Conference on Cluster Computing (CLUSTER), pp. 188–196, September 2010
2. Abad, C.L., Lu, Y., Campbell, R.H.: Dare: adaptive data replication for efficient cluster scheduling. In: CLUSTER, pp. 159–168. IEEE (2011)

3. Cheng, Z., Luan, Z., Meng, Y., Xu, Y., Qian, D., Roy, A., Zhang, N., Guan, G.: Erms: an elastic replication management system for hdfs. In: 2012 IEEE International Conference on Cluster Computing Workshops (CLUSTER WORKSHOPS), pp. 32–40, September 2012
4. Kousiouris, G., Vafiadis, G., Varvarigou, T.: Enabling proactive data management in virtualized hadoop clusters based on predicted data activity patterns. In: 2013 Eighth International Conference on P2P, Parallel, Grid, Cloud and Internet Computing (3PGCIC), pp. 1–8, October 2013
5. Wu, X.: Performance Evaluation Prediction and Visualization of Parallel Systems. The International Series on Asian Studies in Computer and Information Science. Springer US, New York (1999). http://books.google.co.kr/books?id=IJZt5H6R8OIC
6. Gallager, R.: Stochastic Processes: Theory for Applications. Cambridge University Press, Cambridge (2013). http://books.google.co.kr/books?id=CGFbAgAAQBAJ

Context Aware Computing for Ambient Assisted Living

Peter Wlodarczak$^{(\boxtimes)}$, Jeffrey Soar, and Mustafa Ally

University of Southern Queensland, Toowoomba, Australia
wlodarczak@gmail.com

Abstract. With the prevalence of wireless technologies, cloud computing and the rapid growth of deployed smart sensors in the past few years, we live in an increasingly interconnected world. These technologies have fostered the dissemination of the Internet of Things (IoT). They form the foundation for smart homes and smart cities. Context aware devices and ambient computing techniques have expanded the application of the IoT into new areas such as assisted living, eHealth, and elderly care. However, there are challenges to analyze the large volumes of sensor and context data generated by these devices. Also, there are serious security and privacy concerns especially in the area of health care that need to be addressed. This paper gives an overview of the state-of-the-art technologies for ambient assisted living (AAL) and proposes an architecture based on SOA.

Keywords: Internet of Things · Context aware computing · Ambient computing · Assistive technologies · eHealth · Smart home · SOA

1 Introduction

This paper discusses the emergence of context aware computing in the healthcare domain. It explores the enabling technologies such as the Internet of Things (IoT) and ambient computing and proposes an architecture for an IoT-based eHealth solution. The Internet of Things (IoT) intelligently connects devices, humans and systems through the Internet. IoT is defined as a service-oriented network and a mandatory subset of future Internet where every virtual or physical object can communicate with every other object giving seamless service to all stakeholders [1]. Whereas Social Media can be considered the Internet of People (IoP) where real world persons interconnect and communicate with each other, with the IoT devices such as sensors, actuators, GPS enabled systems or cameras communicate with each other, Machine to Machine (M2M), via the Internet. The devices can be considered virtual identities that communicate in smart spaces. The IoT forms the 'glue', connecting devices, things, to other things and databases. The devices include among other sensors, Smart watches, fitness monitors, Smartphones, tablets, vehicles, machine components, consumer products and even clothe. Enabling technologies of the IoT are miniaturization of sensors, wireless sensor networks (WSN), integration and RFID chips. Medical supervision and healthcare services provisioning is about to change in the near future as a result of these new technologies [2].

Connecting devices through a network such as the Internet is nothing new per se. It was initially used in control applications to implement different automation functionalities:

© Springer International Publishing Switzerland 2016
C.K. Chang et al. (Eds.): ICOST 2016, LNCS 9677, pp. 321–331, 2016.
DOI: 10.1007/978-3-319-39601-9_29

monitoring, supervision and direct control [3]. But usually these sensors or actuators have proprietary interfaces and communication protocols that are not designed to work together, and orchestration of different devices cannot be easily achieved. They are connected through proprietary industrial networks or fieldbuses and were usually designed for a specific purpose and for small, periodic data. For instance, a thermostat is connected to a heating system to regulate the room temperature, but it might not be easily integrated into an Internet home control app, where an owner can switch on the heating a day before going to his holiday house. Devices that are part of the IoT, sometimes called smart dust or smart motes, are supposed to act with autonomous behavior. For instance, an intelligent temperature sensor should be able to be a part of a home automation system, a security system and an eHealth solution concurrently.

Interconnected sensors, actuators, cameras and other devices in a building that can be steered remotely, form what's called a smart home. The concept of smart homes can be extended citywide to form smart cities, where traffic is regulated automatically, vehicle-mounted terminals find the nearest parking space, power and water supply and garbage collection is optimized, and travel routes are calculated automatically. Ultimately, this will lead to the sensing planet that can capture natural processes and phenomenon.

The term context aware computing has its origin in ubiquitous computing. It originally refers to location awareness, but more generally means awareness of changes in the environment that are otherwise static, such as the identity, or activity and time. Context is any information that can be used to characterize the situation of an entity such as the current location, users accessing the entity, state of the entity (on or off), etc. An entity is a person, place, or object that is considered relevant to the interaction between a user and an application, including the user and applications themselves [4]. In computer science, context awareness, also called sentient, refers to devices that can sense and react to their environment. If the awareness is towards persons, it is called Ambient Intelligence (AmI). AmI refers to computers that are aware of and responsive to the presence of people. It builds on context awareness and is a form of human-centric computer interaction. For instance, cars with ambient intelligence can stop or evade if they sense a pedestrian crossing the street. AmI is a new paradigm in information technology aimed at empowering people's capabilities using digital environments that are sensitive, adaptive, and responsive to human needs, habits, gestures, and emotions [14].

Modern societies face the challenges of caring for their aging population and exploding health care costs [5]. These difficulties will exacerbate even more due to an increasingly aging population, which translates into a multitude of chronic diseases and tremendous demand for various healthcare services [14]. Context aware computing combined with the IoT opens new possibilities for noninvasive monitoring of patients, surveillance of the elderly, pervasive healthcare systems, on-line medical consultations, or even robotic arm control for surgical interventions [6]. It has the potential to reduce waiting queues in hospitals, lower health care cost, and remotely monitor patients with chronic diseases. Smart cities improve health care services and safety by detecting emergencies, finding the best route for an ambulance, turning all traffic lights on green if an ambulance approaches, and detecting the type of emergency, so the emergency team is already prepared if the patient arrives.

The purpose of this paper is to give an overview on the current state-of-the-art technologies of AmI and the IoT for eHealth and elaborates an architecture based on Service Oriented Architecture (SOA).

2 Overview of Technologies

2.1 The Internet of Things

Technically, the IoT can be divided into four layers, a sensing layer, a communication layer, a management layer and an application layer.

The sensing layer collects data from the physical devices such as sensors, smartphones, tablets, RFID enabled devices, cameras or actuators and transmits it to interconnected devices using field networks.

The communication layer consists of various IP WAN protocols such as ATM, xDSL, fiber, or mobile networks such as GPRS, 3G, and LTE. With the pervasiveness of wireless technologies, the signals are increasingly transmitted using protocols such as Wi-Fi or Bluetooth. They support multi-hop routing and self-organization. Wireless technologies allow M2M devices to be deployed more flexibly and promoted 3G and 3G + networks to be the preferred medium for M2M communication. They are the preferred technology for mobile devices such as smart bands, smart watches or smart clothe.

The management layer comprises management, control and operations of terminals. Usually, a middleware abstracts the basic function set of the management layer such as device management, authentication, and authorization, logging and auditing.

At the application layer, the data is analyzed, visualized and depending on the application an alert is triggered, for instance when a sensor threshold has trespassed, or a device is malfunctioning. The application layer can be on a local server or in the cloud (Fig. 1).

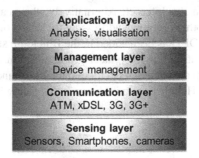

Fig. 1. Internet of Things layer model

One characteristic of the IoT is that virtually an unlimited number of devices can be connected to the Internet and processing all data is not feasible. Context-awareness will play a critical role in deciding what data needs to be processed [3]. What data needs to be processed is usually decided on in the application layer, but can also happen at lower layers.

Another characteristic of the IoT is that it is not developed for a specific application such as home automation or security. It is a general purpose sensor network that supports scalability, extensibility, mobility support, and has no single point of control.

2.2   Components of an IoT-Driven Healthcare System

eHealth systems are part of an ecosystem for medical prevention, supervision, and treatment [2]. There are three main components in an IoT-driven eHealth system: Sensors that collect patient data, microcontrollers to process, analyze and transmit the data to backend systems or into the cloud, and computers to graphically visualize the data.

Their characteristics are:

1. Embeddedness, often integrated into the environment
2. Context awareness
3. Personalized
4. Adaptive
5. Anticipatory.

Embeddedness means the software is embedded in everyday objects such as smartphones, watches or cloth, to support different types of users and applications [7]. These objects receive stimuli from the environment and the users, and are thus context aware. The applications are personalized in that they provide an ecosystem of medical sensors for user-specific monitoring of vital signs or movement tracking of elderly, disabled or recovering people. They need to adapt to different situations such as different movement patterns during weekdays or on the weekend. They need to anticipate problematic situations through the analysis of heterogeneous sensor data and react or alert and are thus also called anticipatory systems.

Wireless sensors can communicate through Wi-Fi or the mobile network through 3G or LTE directly with the Internet. Alternatively, they can communicate with a gateway through Bluetooth. A protocol addressing the needs of medical devices called Health Device Profile (HDP) has been added to the Bluetooth stack. HDP uses connection-oriented channels that quickly reconnect if a connection is broken. It acts as the sender to transmit medical data and as receiver of data for instance from a mobile phone.

A typical IoT-based eHealth system is shown in the following figure (Fig. 2):

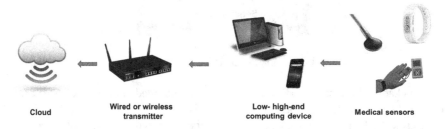

| Cloud | Wired or wireless transmitter | Low- high-end computing device | Medical sensors |

Fig. 2. IoT-based eHealth system

A sensor such as a smart band can connect e.g. through Bluetooth to a low or high-end device that then transmits the data to the cloud through a wireless transmitter. However, a device such as a smartphone can directly transmit e.g. location data to the Internet without using an intermediate device or wireless transmitter. The data can aslo be stored in a database instead of the cloud.

2.3 Data Collection

The information lifecycle management of an eHealth system can be divided into following steps:

collection -> relevance filtering -> classification -> transmission and transportation -> handling and storage -> manipulate, conversion and alteration -> release -> backup -> retention -> destruction.

The sensors deliver raw sensor data, e.g. the coordinates produced by a GPS system, and context information, e.g. the geographic location the coordinates point to. The data can be requested from the sensor periodically, through a pull mechanism, or the sensor delivers the data through a push mechanism to the data acquisition software.

Relevance filtering is usually done during analysis, but it can already happen on the sensor level. For instance, a blood pressure sensor might only deliver data if the pressure change is above a certain threshold, whereas a temperature sensor is polled periodically. Relevance filtering can happen at the analysis level. For instance, GPS-enabled devices such as wearables, smartphones, smartwatches, smart bands or activity tracker can record movement patterns of a patient. However, it is only analyzed if the movement patterns show deviant behavior.

2.4 Data Analysis

The collected data has to be analyzed for patterns that can, for instance, point to certain diseases or indicate that a patient has become symptomatic. This is a classification problem where data is classified into two or more categories. When data from more than one sensor is collected, it is a Distributed data mining (DDM) problem.

This is where knowledge discovery in databases (KDD) and data mining technologies come into play, since these technologies provide possible solutions to find the information hidden in the data of IoT, which can be used to enhance the performance of the system or to improve the quality of services this new environment can provide [9]. Typical data mining techniques include clustering, classification, and frequent pattern mining.

2.4.1 Clustering

Clustering groups data into centroids using some distance measure such as the Euclidian, Manhattan or Jaccard distance. It is used to depict the characteristics of the groups. Some clustering algorithms allow one instance to belong to more than one cluster [10]. The classic clustering technique is called k-means clustering [10], but there are others such as hierarchical clustering, and distribution-based or density-based clustering methods.

In k-means clustering, k denotes the number of clusters, the points around which the centroids, or means, are grouped.

Clustering is used to understand the underlying structure of data and in an eHealth setting usually not really useful since data mining is supposed to find deviant user behavior or predict if a patient is becoming symptomatic. However, clustering techniques can be used for data pre-processing tasks such as data deduplication or entity resolution.

2.4.2   Classification

Classification is used to predict if a patient is becoming symptomatic or if he starts to show deviant behavioral patterns. Unlike clustering, a form of unsupervised learning, where no prior knowledge is assumed to guide the partitioning process, classification assumes some prior knowledge to construct classifiers to represent the possible distribution of patterns. It is called a supervised learning process since the class label is known. In an eHealth system, the class label corresponds to a medical condition such as hypertension or depression. An eHealth system classifies sensor data into normal and abnormal values and can alert the hospital if it has diagnosed a medical condition. For instance, certain blood sugar and cholesterol levels are normal. If a threshold is exceeded, a patient might have to adjust his medication dosage or arrange a doctor's appointment for further diagnosis. The thresholds might have to be individually adjusted based on age, gender, previous medical history or the like. A classifier can be trained on previous patient data and adjust to personal conditions of a specific patient. While recognizing predefined activities often relies on supervised learning techniques, unsupervised learning is valuable for its ability to discover recurring sequences of unlabeled sensor activities that may comprise activities of interest [14]. It should be mentioned that classifiers usually calculate the probability that a certain pattern belongs to a certain class, i.e. a disease, and should not be considered a conclusive diagnose.

Typical classifiers include naïve Bayes, k-Nearest Neighbor (k-NN), Support Vector Machines (SVM) and Artificial Neural Networks (ANN). They are well documented in literature [5, 10–12, 18] and are not explained in more detail here.

3   A SOA-Based IoT eHealth System

SOA is an acronym for Service Oriented Architecture. There is no agreed on definition in literature for SOA. SOA is not a concrete architecture: it is something that leads to a concrete architecture [13]. However, there are several principles of SOA that makes it an interesting paradigm for an IoT-based eHealth system and for the IoT in general.

SOA aims to be flexible and interconnect heterogeneous resources in a network. It is based on three technical core principles:

1. Services
2. Loose coupling
3. Interoperability.

The resources expose their interfaces as services. In an eHealth setting, the resources are the sensors such as a sphygmomanometer or a thermometer. An interface would then expose its service through a function:

getTemperature( )

An eHealth system based on SOA principles can call this function to get the body temperature of a patient. A SOA system supports service orchestration, defining what service should be called in what order. For instance, if one blood value is too high, it can call another blood value if needed for a better diagnosis.

Another principle of SOA is loose coupling. This means that the sensors don't have to be constantly connected to the eHealth system. They only connect when some data is needed.

A typical SOA system uses an Enterprise Service Bus (ESB). An ESB is a piece of software that can interconnect different devices. Using an ESB has several advantages. The devices can support different data formats, for instance, XML, JSON, plain text or other. The ESB supports different data formats and can convert them into other formats if needed, a process called transformation. Also, an ESB supports different communication protocols. It can, for instance, connect to a sensor through the Internet using the TCP/IP protocol, or using a messaging system such as the Java Messaging Service (JMS) and to a database to permanently store the sensor data. ESBs usually support encryption so sensitive medical data can be transmitted encrypted. An ESB also provides the flexibility to integrate new devices if needed.

For an eHealth application, the ESB provides an abstraction layer in that the developer doesn't have to deal with different data formats and communication protocols but can focus on the data analysis part. Also, a SOA-based eHealth system can have several applications in parallel, for instance, one to diagnose heart conditions, and another application to analyze blood levels.

The eHealth system can store the data in a database or in the cloud. Alternatively, the whole eHealth system can be hosted in the cloud.

Following figure shows an entire SOA-based eHealth system (Fig. 3):

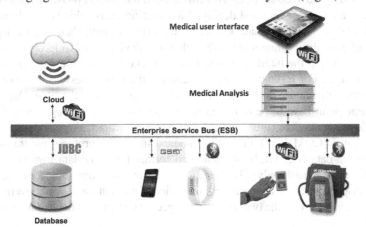

Fig. 3. SOA-based eHealth system

3.1 Service Interface

The interfaces of the devices can have simple REpresentational State Transfer (REST) interfaces. REST is the architectural style of the World Wide Web (WWW). It has the advantage that it is widely supported by most programming languages, and the services can be called through URL calls, for instance:

http://www.patient1.com/getTemperature

Instead of using a REST interface, Web Services (WS) can be used. Services designed as WS using SOAP (Simple Object Access Protocol) messages as defined by the W3C consortium add complexity, since the sensor data is transmitted as SOAP messages in XML format. The OASIS (Open Standards for the Information Society) non-profit consortium has defined Devices Profile for Web Services (DPWS) guidelines based on WS-* specifications to provide interoperability between different devices [8]. Despite the higher complexity, there are several advantages. Web Services are based on web-related standards. Also, there is a set of security standards such as WS-Security and WS-Trust, defined by the OASIS consortium.

WS-Security focuses on signing XML messages so they cannot be tampered with and encrypt them so they cannot be intercepted. WS-Trust is focused on establishing trust between participants that exchange XML messages to avoid unknown systems to make service calls. This adds security and privacy to sensitive medical data. Security and privacy measures are mandatory in some regulations enacted in certain countries.

The disadvantage is that XML-based Web Services generate an overhead for devices such as medical sensors that typically have limited processing power.

4   Challenges

The success of the IoT is due to standards that have been established on the Internet such as HTTP, XML, and Web services. Nevertheless, in the current phase of the IoT, most applications are independent and deployed for specific users. This is mainly due to a lack of standards on the terminals. Currently, most devices have their proprietary interfaces. To effectively communicate with each other, devices need to have standardized abstraction layers at the interface level. This is crucial for effective data fusion at the application layer. For instance, a sensor measures the blood pressure; another sensor measures the temperature at the same time. The context here is the time. Data from a specific time point have to be retrieved in an easy, standardized way. Some attempts were made to standardize some medical transmission formats. For instance, there is a standard (e.g. DICOM) for transmitting medical images, a protocol for transmitting patient related data (e.g. HL7) or a standard format for ECG data transmission [2]. However, these standards only solve some aspects of the data communication and fusion problem. Aspects such as secure access or device identification are not covered. Only by fusing the values from the two sensors in a specific context, a reliable diagnose might be possible.

Medical sensors are typically resource-constraint devices with limited computing power, limited storing and energy capabilities. If the devices are mobile and are battery powered, the battery needs to be recharged regularly. This limits the amount of logic that can be built into the devices and also limits a patients' mobility, for instance, if he wants to go traveling.

For eHealth systems, protocols and technologies must meet the high real-time, safety and security requirements. Communication protocols of the Internet or mobile services are not optimized for those requirements. For instance, if a patient falls or blood levels have reached a certain threshold, an alert has to be triggered immediately since it is a potential life threatening situation. If a patient is in a location with low network coverage, he might be in danger. The IoT is vulnerable to attacks since communications are mostly wireless, unattended things are usually vulnerable to physical attacks, and most IoT components are constrained by energy, communications, and computation capabilities necessary for the implementation of complex security-supporting schemes [15].

There are many devices on the market, for instance, ECG monitors, sphygmomanometers, thermometers, etc., but their communication protocols are not open, and a given device cannot be integrated into other (or multiple) applications.

Different devices have different capabilities. A patient might need several sensors, and this might be unpractical since he has to carry several devices with him and learn how to use properly and maintain them.

IoT-based eHealth solutions have to be able to maintain dynamic topologies where sensors can be added and removed dynamically. Even in a SOA system, new devices cannot easily be added or removed. It is expected that things can be identified automatically, can communicate with each other, and can even make decisions by themselves [9].

Supervised methods have to learn user behavior bevor they can make predictions. Annotating behavioral data is a very laborious task. Due to physical, mental, cultural, and lifestyle differences, not all individuals perform the same set of tasks [16]. Depending on individual behavior, supervised techniques might not perform equally well for each individual. When real-world environments are used, more complexities appear, such as situation interruption, multi-tasking, multiple users, and unexpected user behaviour [18]. Including situations where more than one person is involved should be a focus of future research.

eHealth systems need to be privacy enabled, and access control (AC) to these devices is critical. Privacy preserving data mining techniques have to be adopted to ensure doctor-patient confidentiality. Healthcare related data is subject to regulations in many countries, such as HIPPA (Health Insurance Portability and Accountability Act) in the US. eHealth systems have to be compliant with these regulations.

Symbolic access has to be secured, e.g. through a private Domain Name System (DNS) to translate symbolic requests into physical, IPv6 addresses. For instance, using DNSSEC, a security extension of DNS, and using a Hardware Security Module (HSM) for securely storing the encryption keys. Otherwise, they might be visible to non-authorized persons with malicious intents.

5 Conclusions

IoT using AmI will change our health care system by improving the life quality of patients, and help professionals react more quickly and automatically in emergency situations.

This new Internet has led the evolution of the Ubiquitous Web 2.0, in integrating physical world entities into virtual world things [7]. It will enable an ecosystem of applications and devices that will simplify citizens' lives, and make it more safe and efficient. Although ambient intelligence was not part of the original IoT paradigm, integration of both concepts paves the way to future computing with embedded intelligence (EI). EI brings artificial intelligence to the IoT. It has the capability to learn individual behaviors, special context, social patterns and urban dynamics. However, due to the heterogeneity of devices and data formats, data fusion and analysis of EI enabled IoT is still a challenging task and standards, such as Web Services or SOAP based device interfaces need to be developed.

Designing AAL systems for the elderly requires special attention, because of their cognitive, perceptual, or physical limitations [16]. The users might not be technology savvy, and an AAL system should not depend on user effort. Learning systems have the advantage that they don't require predefined rules, and the training doesn't require any user interaction. A new type of learners called deep learners have been appearing, and big progress has been made in areas such as speech recognition, multimedia mining and natural language processing [17]. It is to be expected that deep learning algorithms will be increasingly used in eHealth systems too.

The SOA paradigm can be used to ensure reusability and interoperability of heterogeneous, distributed things. SOA enables the orchestration of services running on devices. Cloud computing promotes the seamless integration of physical devices in humans lives by providing location autonomy. It fosters a new, proactive computing approach and gives way to new types of applications that can deliver eHealth services quicker and more efficiently. Future service-oriented Internet devices will offer their functionality via service-enabled interfaces adopting the vision of the Web of Things (WoT) (inspired by the IoT), e.g. via Simple Object Access Protocol (SOAP) based Web Services or RESTful APIs [7]. It will pave the way for Sensing-as-a-Service eHealth systems, where the applications are hosted in the cloud and can be accessed by many, for instance by doctors and hospitals and not just by one single health care provider.

Future eHealth systems will provide natural-feeling human interfaces that can sense feelings such as anxiety, distress or depression and expand the capabilities of medical applications dramatically. Advances in robotics will also have an impact assistive eHealth. Assistive robots allow the older adults to overcome their physical limitations by helping them in their daily activities [16].

Ultimately, more devices such as cars, electronics such as fridges and home entertainment will be interconnected and improve security and life quality citywide or even worldwide.

References

1. Tsirmpas, C., Anastasiou, A., Bountris, P., Koutsouris, D.: A new method for profile generation in an Internet of Things environment: an application in ambient assisted living. IEEE Internet Things J., vol. PP, no. 99, pp. 1–8 (2015)
2. Sebestyen, G., Hangan, A., Oniga, S., Gal, Z.: eHealth solutions in the context of Internet of Things. In: Proceedings of the 2014 IEEE International Conference on Automation, Quality and Testing, Robotics, pp. 1–6 (2014)
3. Perera, C., Zaslavsky, A., Christen, P., Georgakopoulos, D.: Context aware computing for the Internet of Things: a survey. IEEE Commun. Surv. Tutorials **16**(1), 414–454 (2014)
4. Abowd, G.D., Dey, A.K., Brown, P.J., Davies, N., Smith, M., Steggles, P.: Towards a better understanding of context and context-awareness. In: Gellersen, H.-W. (ed.) HUC 1999. LNCS, vol. 1707, pp. 304–307. Springer, Heidelberg (1999)
5. Wlodarczak, P., Soar, J., Ally, M.: Reality mining in eHealth. In: Yin, X., Ho, K., Zeng, D., Aickelin, U., Zhou, R., Wang, H. (eds.) HIS 2015. LNCS, vol. 9085, pp. 1–6. Springer, Heidelberg (2015)
6. Sim, H., Yip, S., Cheng, C.: Equipment and technology in surgical robotics. World J. Urol. **24**(2), 128–135 (2006)
7. Cubo, J., Nieto, A., Pimente, E.: A cloud-based internet of things platform for ambient assisted living. Sensors (14248220) **14**(8), 14070–14105 (2014)
8. OASIS.: Devices Profile for Web Services (DPWS) (2009). http://docs.oasis-open.org/ws-dd/ns/dpws/2009/01
9. Chun-Wei, T., Chin-Feng, L., Ming-Chao, C., Yang, L.T.: Data mining for Internet of Things: a survey. IEEE Commun. Surv. Tutorials **16**(1), 77–97 (2014)
10. Witten, I.H., Frank, E., Hall, M.A.: Data Mining, 3rd edn. Elsevier, Burlington (2011)
11. Wlodarczak, P., Ally, M., Soar, J.: Data Process and Analysis Technologies of Big Data. Chapman and Hall/CRC, Boca Raton (2015)
12. Wlodarczak, P., Soar, J., Ally, M.: Genome mining using machine learning techniques. In: Geissbühler, A., Demongeot, J., Mokhtari, M., Abdulrazak, B., Aloulou, H. (eds.) ICOST 2015. LNCS, vol. 9102, pp. 379–384. Springer, Heidelberg (2015). Chap. 39
13. Josuttis, N.: Soa in Practice: The Art of Distributed System Design. O'Reilly Media Inc., Sebastopol (2007)
14. Acampora, G., Cook, D.J., Rashidi, P., Vasilakos, A.V.: Survey on ambient intelligence in healthcare. Proc. IEEE **101**(12), 2470–2494 (2013)
15. Abie, H., Balasingham, I.: Risk-based adaptive security for smart IoT in eHealth. In: Proceedings of the 7th International Conference on Body Area Networks, Oslo, Norway, pp. 269–275 (2012)
16. Rashidi, P., Mihailidis, A.: A survey on ambient-assisted living tools for older adults. IEEE J. Biomed. Health Inf. **17**(3), 11 (2013)
17. Wlodarczak, P., Soar, J., Ally, M.: Multimedia data mining using deep learning. In: IEEE Xplore, pp. 190–196 (2015)
18. Ye, J., Dobson, S., McKeever, S.: Situation identification techniques in pervasive computing: a review. Elsevier Pervasive Mob. Comput. **8**(1), 36–66 (2012)

Human Machine Interfaces

Hierarchical Self-organizing Maps of NIRS and EEG Signals for Recognition of Brain States

Katsunori Oyama[1(✉)], Kaoru Sakatani[2], Hua Ming[3],
and Carl K. Chang[4]

[1] Department of Computer Science, Nihon University, Koriyama, Japan
oyama@cs.ce.nihon-u.ac.jp
[2] Department of Electrical and Electronics Engineering,
Nihon University, Koriyama, Japan
sakatani.kaoru@nihon-u.ac.jp
[3] Department of Computer Science and Engineering,
Oakland University, Rochester, USA
ming@oakland.edu
[4] Department of Computer Science, Iowa State University, Ames, USA
chang@iastate.edu

Abstract. Recent advances in temporal data mining of brain activity with NIRS and EEG signals allow us to recognize *brain states* in higher resolution. However, brain states are not always distinct from each other and often differ in temporal granularity. This paper revisits Dennett's three levels of stance, the DIKW model for the design of two self-organizing maps (SOMs), which contributes to recognition of a hierarchy of brain states with finer granularities. The experimental results show that two brain states at different levels can be accurately identified by applying different training data for each level of SOM.

Keywords: Brain state · NIRS · EEG · Self-organizing map · DIKW model

1 Introduction

Temporal data mining of brain activity using near-infrared spectroscopy (NIRS) and electroencephalography (EEG) signals is an emerging area of research with the objective of using an e-health system to detect disease during an early stage, before its physical symptoms become apparent. However, brain states are not always distinct; for example, two brain states, such as fatigue and sleeping, can occur simultaneously.

This study takes both unsupervised and supervised learning approaches to recognizing brain states by simultaneous monitoring of NIRS and EEG recordings. In this paper, we begin by reviewing Dennett's three levels of stance (physical stance, design stance, and intentional stance) [1] and the data-information-knowledge-wisdom (DIKW) model [2] in order to illustrate the challenges in temporal data mining. To identify the brain states, we cascade a system of two self-organizing maps (SOMs) in which the feature vectors have different segment lengths; that is, the segment length of a sample in the lower SOM is 1 s and that in the upper is 30 s. In an experiment, we

© Springer International Publishing Switzerland 2016
C.K. Chang et al. (Eds.): ICOST 2016, LNCS 9677, pp. 335–344, 2016.
DOI: 10.1007/978-3-319-39601-9_30

applied SOM analysis to NIRS and EEG signals obtained during a mental arithmetic task, and the brain states of *resting* and *listening* were identified in parallel by applying different training data for each level of the SOMs. We discuss the inductive relation between classification accuracy and the types of brain state.

2   Brain States and Their Granularities

During the past decade, simultaneous monitoring of brain activity with wearable NIRS and EEG sensors has been intensively investigated in order to evaluate cognitive and emotional processing [3]. These sensor modalities have enabled the recognition of various types of brain states, including not only motor images but also affective states [4]. Our approach examines the use of simultaneous NIRS and EEG recordings to capture feature vectors x_n related to the prefrontal cortex (PFC), as discussed in the following sections.

2.1   Feature Vectors from NIRS Recordings

Recent studies have identified the PFC as a key region for the experience and regulation of emotional responses, and NIRS is a technique that is well suited for investigating PFC activity. The degree of right-lateralized asymmetry in PFC activation patterns is known to be positively correlated with changes in heart rate during a mental task [5], and the results of this analysis contributes to the recognition of affective states related to negative valence.

First, we define a feature of the concentration changes in oxy-hemoglobin (HbO_2) in the left and right PFCs at time t as $o_i(t)$, where the subscript i denotes the position of the NIRS sensor, and $o_1(t)$ and $o_2(t)$ are assigned to left and right PFC, respectively. A feature of the concentration changes in deoxy-hemoglobin (Hb) is defined as $h_i(t)$, with the subscripts having the same meaning as for $o_i(t)$. These features are discretized into $O_i(n)$ and $H_i(n)$ with segments of length $t_n - t_{n-1}$ as follows:

$$O_i(\mathrm{n}) = \frac{\int_{t_{n-1}}^{t_n} o_i(t)dt}{t_n - t_{n-1}}, \tag{1}$$

$$H_i(n) = \frac{\int_{t_{n-1}}^{t_n} h_i(t)dt}{t_n - t_{n-1}}. \tag{2}$$

These four features, $O_1(n)$, $O_2(n)$, $H_1(n)$, and $H_2(n)$, are periodically captured from NIRS recordings as elements of the feature vectors that are then used as input for the SOMs.

2.2   Feature Vectors from EEG Recordings

EEG changes are obtained directly from neurons firing within the brain, and this can be monitored noninvasively by placing electrodes on the scalp. For EEG analyses, both event-related desynchronization (ERD) and event-related potential (ERP) have been chosen to measure mental work or memory load, and both have been found to have statistical significance [6]. In particular, the ERD-based approach decomposes EEG signals into a power spectra; for example, division into theta (4–6 Hz), low-alpha (6–8 Hz), middle-alpha (8–10 Hz), high-alpha (10–12 Hz), and beta (12–30 Hz) bands can be used to determine the ERD, i.e., the reduction in power at a particular frequency in response to an event, such as the initiation of a mental task.

The EEG index $w_i(t)$ is defined as the ratio of $d_i(t)$ to $s_i(t)$ for an electrode at position i. The spectral power between 8 Hz and 12 Hz is assigned to $d_i(t)$, and the spectral power between 13 Hz and 30 Hz is assigned to $s_i(t)$, which is sensitive to the brain states related to working memory:

$$w_i(t) = \frac{d_i(t)}{s_i(t)}. \tag{3}$$

The corresponding feature is then discretized into n time segments, and the values of $W_i(n)$ are obtained from EEG recordings of length $t_n - t_{n-1}$, as follows:

$$W_i(n) = \frac{\int_{t_{n-1}}^{t_n} w_i(t)dt}{t_n - t_{n-1}}. \tag{4}$$

In this study, eight electrodes were used to collect the EEG data; these were placed at the following positions: left PFC: AF3, F3, F7, T3; and right PFC: AF4, F4, F8, T4. Thus, eight values, $W_1(n)$ through $W_8(n)$, were periodically captured as elements of the feature vector used as input for the SOMs.

2.3 Hierarchical SOM Model of Brain States

Identification of brain states has been an active area of research for many years by many researchers, and consequently, classification accuracy has improved to the point where it is of practical use in healthcare monitoring. However, in reality, the granularity of various brain states are not completely distinct, and they have hierarchical relations. For healthcare monitoring, the identification of a single state is preferable, and the data, which imply the co-occurrence of brain states, cannot easily be used for understanding, explaining, or predicting an individual's health status.

Brain states are one aspect of human intention, and can be abstracted using Dennett's three levels: physical stance, design stance, and intentional stance [1]. The key idea here is that we can choose to view intention at varying levels of abstraction when attempting to understand, explain, or predict an object's behavior (in this paper, the brain state). The more concrete the level is, the more accurate are our predictions, while the irrelevant details can be ignored by the analysis. On the other hand, the level of abstraction can also be evaluated using the DIKW model [7, 8], in which the definitions of the super and sub relations between the objects is dependent on the choice of layer: data, information, knowledge, or wisdom. For example, in the wisdom layer, the brain states of *working* for an experiment and *writing* can be hierarchically classified according to their relative priority relative to achieving a given task.

The growing hierarchical SOM [9] has a hierarchical architecture composed of independent SOMs, and this allows an exploratory analysis within a holistic view. The SOMs in the lower level each use a subset of the feature vectors from the upper level, and the temporal granularity of each feature vector is the same in each level. In practice, the segment length of a brain state often varies depending on the type of brain activity and the purpose of the analysis. For example, 2 min segments of the brain states of *resting* and *working* can be recognized from the simultaneous NIRS and EEG recordings shown in Fig. 1; lower-level brain states with shorter segment lengths, such as *listening* and *writing,* are ignored.

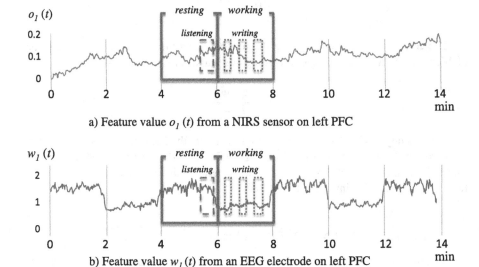

a) Feature value $o_1(t)$ from a NIRS sensor on left PFC

b) Feature value $w_1(t)$ from an EEG electrode on left PFC

Fig. 1. Example of differences in temporal granularity of NIRS and EEG recordings.

3   SOMs for Classification of Brain States

The features discussed in the previous sections can be used to form feature vectors when generating a SOM; this allows the visualization and exploration of a high-dimensional data space by nonlinearly projecting it onto a 2-D plane [10]. NIRS and EEG signals may involve outliers and unknown patterns of waveforms. A SOM results in robust learning compared to other types of cluster analyses, such as k-means clustering [11].

Each feature vector x_n for a SOM includes twelve feature values: $O_1(n)$, $O_2(n)$, $H_1(n)$, $H_2(n)$, $W_1(n)$, $W_2(n)$, $W_3(n)$, $W_4(n)$, $W_5(n)$, $W_6(n)$, $W_7(n)$, and $W_8(n)$. In this study, two SOMs are cascaded as shown in Fig. 2, and each SOM has different feature vectors of the stated segment length: the samples in the lower SOM have a length of 1 s, and those in the upper SOM have a length of 30 s.

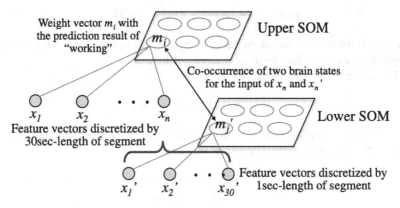

Fig. 2. Hierarchical SOMs of NIRS and EEG signals.

This study takes both unsupervised and supervised learning approaches to the recognition of brain states: the unsupervised SOM is used for exploratory analysis to find the optimal segment length so that the brain states can be classified, and the supervised SOM is examined for validation of the classification accuracy; this is discussed in detail in the following sections.

3.1   SOM (Unsupervised SOM)

Given a self-organizing map $\mathbf{M}$ with K units (i.e., nodes), each unit is associated with a weight vector m_i ($i = 1, 2,..., K$), and these are connected by the feature vectors $x_1, x_2, ..., x_n$. In the SOM learning algorithm, each m_i is updated by competitive learning with x_n. In this process, the Euclidean distances to all weight vectors are computed for each input feature vector x_n, and the best-matching unit (BMU) is selected as the one for which the weight vector is the most similar to the input vector. After some number of iterations of the competitive learning algorithm, similar feature vectors are mapped to the same unit.

The SOM competitive learning algorithm is as follows:

Step 1. Randomize the weight vectors on each of the units.

Step 2. Draw the feature vectors x_n from the input data set in order of n.

Step 3. Find the weight vector m_i that is most similar to x_n and the corresponding unit c that is the BMU, defined as follows:

$$c = \arg \min_i \|x_n - m_i\|. \tag{5}$$

Step 4. Select the units within the neighboring area N_c of the BMU (this includes the BMU), and the radius $n_c(\tau)$ of N_c is calculated as follows:

$$n_c(\tau) = 1 + (n_c(0) - 1) \cdot (1 - \tau/T), \tag{6}$$

where $n_c(0)$ is the initial value of the radius $n_c(\tau)$, τ is the current number of iterations in the algorithm, and T is the maximum number of iterations.

Step 5. Update m_i on the selected units, as follows:

$$m_i \leftarrow m_i + h_{ci}(\tau)[x_n - m_i], \tag{7}$$

where $h_{ci}(\tau)$ is a neighborhood function as defined below, and $\alpha(\tau)$ is a learning parameter that depends on the number of iterations:

$$h_{ci}(\tau) = \begin{cases} \alpha(\tau) & \text{if } i \in N_c(\tau) \\ 0 & \text{otherwise} \end{cases},$$

$$\alpha(\tau) = \alpha_0 \cdot (1 - \tau/T).$$

Step 6. Repeat Step 2 through Step 5 until $\tau = T$ (iterate T times).

3.2   Supervised SOM

The supervised version of SOM uses the algorithm for unsupervised SOM, except the components of the feature vector x_n are separated into an input set s_n and a training set t_n. A weight vector m_i on the unit i of the supervised SOM is then composed of the input set s_i and training set t_i. After the competitive learning of the supervised SOM with the components of s_n and t_n, the prediction result for each new input of s_n can be acquired from an element of the training set on the BMU, as follows.

Step 1.   Find the BMU on the trained SOM by using the Euclidean distance, Eq. (5), for the new input s_{n+1}.

Step 2.   Obtain t_i for the BMU, and output one of the components of t_i as the prediction result.

One version of supervised SOM, the X-Y fused Kohonen network (XYF) [12] is known to have improved classification accuracy, and thus we use it for the analysis in this study. One feature vector of the object in XYF is created by concatenating the X and Y spaces as a SOM, and it is then trained in the same way as above. The only difference between this and the supervised SOM discussed above is that the distance of the object to a unit is defined as the sum of the separate distances in the X and Y spaces. Prediction is done using only the X space.

4 Results

We conducted an experiment in which a mental arithmetic task was performed by ten participants (young males); the goal was to observe the transition between the brain states of *resting* and *working*. Each participant performed a mental arithmetic task by writing down answers to various problems (e.g., 131–57 = ?) and then rested for three cycles, over a period of 12 min. The brain states of *resting* and *working* thus changed every 2 min, as shown in Fig. 1. NIRS sensors (2 optodes) and EEG sensors (8 electrodes) were placed to monitor brain activity in the PFC area. Body movements, except those required for reading the arithmetic problems, were prohibited during the experiment. Low-pass and high-pass filters were applied to the NIRS and EEG signals, and thus body-movement-related artifacts in this experiment were reduced to less than 5 %.

Each feature vector in this experiment is composed of the input set $s_n = (O_1(n),$ $O_2(n),$ $H_1(n),$ $H_2(n),$ $W_1(n),$ $W_2(n),$ $W_3(n),$ $W_4(n),$ $W_5(n),$ $W_6(n),$ $W_7(n),$ $W_8(n))$ and its corresponding training set $t_n = (n, b)$, where the integer n is the number of time periods, and b represents the brain state to be validated. The brain state can be chosen as either *resting* or *working* for the upper SOM and as either *eye-closing, listening, writing,* or *writing_and_listening* for the lower SOM.

In the SOM competitive learning, components in s_n are normalized by their standard deviation so that they are comparable. Table 1 shows the feature vectors used for the upper SOM, while Table 2 shows those used for the lower SOM. The upper SOM (training length T: 300, map size K: 4 × 4) was created with the feature vector shown in Table 1, whereas the lower SOM (training length T: 300, map size K: 8 × 8) was created with the feature vector shown in Table 2.

(1) **Results of Unsupervised Learning.** From the result shown in Fig. 3(a), the feature vectors of the 30 s segments were classified as *resting* and *working*; seven units were assigned to *resting,* and all of the *resting* feature vectors were mapped into these seven units. One of these units had feature values labeled "4 resting" and "12 resting;" these are highlighted in the rounded rectangle (dashed line) as examples of upper-SOM feature vectors that correspond to the lower-SOM feature vectors shown in the rounded rectangle in Fig. 3(b). Note that Fig. 3(b) shows the feature vectors of the 5 s segment with the lower-SOM mapping result.

From these results, we observe a situation in which upper- and lower-level brain states co-occur: the feature vectors with the segment numbers 18, 21, 22, and 23 in the lower SOM are part of the feature vector labeled "4 resting" in the upper SOM. Similarly, the rest of the segment numbers, 68, 69, 70, and 71, belong to the feature vector labeled "12 resting" in the upper SOM.

(2) **Results of Supervised Learning.** Classification accuracy for the feature vectors of one of the ten subjects was calculated by leave-one-out cross-validation. In the upper SOM, both of the brain states were successfully classified 92 % of the time (all but two), as shown in Table 3, and the two prediction errors both occurred at the transition between *resting* and *working*. There were fewer observations of *listening* and *writing_and_listening* in the lower SOM due to the limited number of samples, i.e., there were thirteen feature vectors used to recognize the brain state of *listening*. The brain states of *eye-closing* and *writing* were recognized with

Table 1. Feature vectors for the upper SOM with segment length of 30 s. This is an example from one of the subjects. A total of 24 feature vectors were acquired from each subject.

t_n		s_n						
n	b	$O_1(n)$	$O_2(n)$	$H_1(n)$	$H_2(n)$	$W_1(n)$	...	$W_8(n)$
1	resting	−0.04	−1.25	1.51	1.27	0.89		0.13
2	resting	−0.63	−2.22	2.29	2.10	0.52		0.35
3	working	−0.38	−1.80	2.29	2.10	0.92		0.71
4	working	0.01	−0.70	2.00	1.89	0.27		0.18
5	resting	1.24	0.83	1.22	0.66	−2.01		−1.98
6	resting	1.58	−0.01	0.54	−0.99	−0.92		−1.37
...	...	...	...	...	...	...	...	...
24	working	0.06	1.10	−0.81	−0.17	−0.50		−0.07

Table 2. Feature vectors for the lower SOM with segment length of 5 s. This is an example from one of the subjects. A total of 144 feature vectors were acquired from each subject.

t_n		s_n						
n	b	$O_1(n)$	$O_2(n)$	$H_1(n)$	$H_2(n)$	$W_1(n)$	...	$W_8(n)$
1	eye-closing	0.92	0.12	1.89	1.87	0.59		0.35
2	eye-closing	0.35	−0.65	1.34	0.88	1.38		0.57
3	eye-closing	−0.19	−1.0	1.20	0.82	0.85		0.08
4	eye-closing	−0.27	−1.54	1.29	1.12	0.17		−0.01
5	eye-closing	−0.32	−1.86	1.55	1.34	0.73		0.29
6	eye-closing	−0.69	−1.96	1.65	1.58	1.09		−0.51
...	...	...	...	...	...	...	...	...
144	listening	0.03	0.84	−0.67	−0.18	0.50		0.31

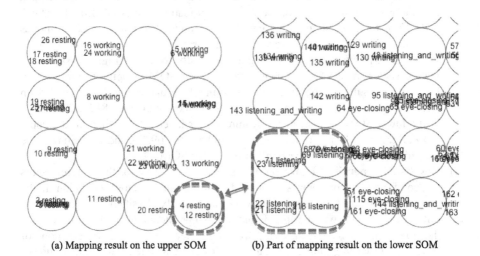

(a) Mapping result on the upper SOM   (b) Part of mapping result on the lower SOM

Fig. 3. Mapping results of the two SOMs with feature vectors in the 30 s and 5 s segments. Each feature vector is labeled with segment number n and brain state b.

Table 3. Classification accuracy for the brain states from the example shown in Fig. 3.

Brain state		Accuracy (# correct/total)	Accuracy (%)
Upper SOM	*resting*	11/12	92 %
	working	11/12	92 %
Lower SOM	*eye-closing*	81/81	100 %
	listening	10/13	77 %
	writing	66/66	100 %
	writing_and_listening	4/6	67 %

100 % accuracy, because there were sufficient samples. From the results shown in Table 3, the brain state of *resting* can be found with either *eye-closing* or *listening*. These combinations mean that the subject has closed eyes while listening for a voice command to signal the start of the mental arithmetic task. On the other hand, the brain state of *working* was found with either *writing* or *writing_and_listening*.

5   Conclusions

From the experimental results of a SOM analysis, the detection of brain states gave information about two different levels. Specifically, the lower SOM is useful for identifying brain activity related to actions with a shorter period, whereas the upper SOM can suggest human intentions about the activities in this experiment. The two SOMs therefore imply that it is possible to use health-monitoring devices to determine details about brain states.

For the experiment in this paper, two SOMs were cascaded; however, it is important to consider more than two levels of SOMs in order to determine whether more information can be gained from a SOM analysis. Also, in this paper, we analyzed the feature vectors of only one subject; for a full SOM analysis, it will be necessary to examine the feature vectors of all ten subjects, that is, ten pairs of upper and lower SOMs. Achieving interchangeability of the weight vectors between the trained SOMs at the same level will be critical for building a common SOM for all ten subjects.

This paper presented and evaluated a hierarchical approach using two SOMs to recognize brain states from data obtained by simultaneous NIRS and EEG monitoring. The SOMs were used to recognize brain states with finer granularities. We conducted an experiment with simultaneous NIRS and EEG monitoring during a mental arithmetic task; the states of *resting* in the upper SOM and that of *listening* in the lower SOM were identified to occur simultaneously. Future investigations will involve application of the SOM to a case study of healthcare monitoring. Development of an algorithm for real-time monitoring of mental states may eventually make possible the early detection of disease.

Acknowledgments. This work was supported by JSPS Grant-in-Aid for Young Scientists (B) Grant Number 26730079.

References

1. Dennett, D.: The Intentional Stance. MIT Press, Cambridge (1989)
2. Ackoff, R.L.: From data to wisdom. J. Appl. Syst. Anal. **16**(1), 3–9 (1989)
3. Sawan, M., Salam, M.T., Gelinas, S., Lan, J.L., Lesage F., Nguyen, D.K.: Combined NIRS-EEG remote recordings for epilepsy and stroke real-time monitoring. In: IEEE International Symposium on Circuits and Systems (ISCAS), pp. 13–16 (2012)
4. Balconi, M., Grippa, E., Vanutelli, M.E.: What hemodynamic (fNIRS), electrophysiological (EEG) and autonomic integrated measures can tell us about emotional processing. Brain Cogn. **95**, 67–76 (2015)
5. Tanida, M., Katsuyama, M., Sakatani, K.: Relation between mental stress-induced prefrontal cortex activity and skin conditions: a near-infrared spectroscopy study. Brain Res. **1184**, 210–216 (2007)
6. Dong, S., Reder, L.M., Yao, Y., Liu, Y., Chen, F.: Individual differences in working memory capacity are reflected in different ERP and EEG patterns to task difficulty. Brain Res. **1616**, 146–156 (2015)
7. Oyama, K., Chang, C.K., Mitra, S.: Inference of human intentions in smart home environments. Int. J. Robot. Appl. Technol. **1**(2), 26–42 (2013)
8. Ming, H., Chang, C.K., Yang, J.: Dimensional situation analytics: from data to wisdom. In: IEEE Computer Society International Computer Software and Applications Conference (COMPSAC), pp. 50–59 (2015)
9. Dittenbach, M., Merkl, D., Rauber, A.: The growing hierarchical self organizing map. In: Proceedings of the International Joint Conference on Neural Networks (IJCNN), pp. 24–27 (2000)
10. Kohonen, T.: Essentials of the self-organizing map. Neural Networks **37**, 52–65 (2013)
11. Bação, F., Lobo, V., Painho, M.: Self-organizing maps as substitutes for k-means clustering. In: Sunderam, V.S., van Albada, G.D., Sloot, P.M., Dongarra, J. (eds.) ICCS 2005. LNCS, vol. 3516, pp. 476–483. Springer, Heidelberg (2005)
12. Melssen, W., Wehrens, R., Buydens, L.: Supervised Kohonen networks for classification problems. Chemom. Intell. Lab. Syst. **83**, 99–113 (2006)

A Multi-modal BCI System for Active and Assisted Living

Niccolò Mora[✉], Ilaria De Munari, and Paolo Ciampolini

Università degli Studi di Parma, Parco Area delle Scienze 181/A, 43124 Parma, Italy
{niccolo.mora,ilaria.demunari,paolo.ciampolini}@unipr.it

Abstract. Brain Computer Interface (BCI) technology is an alternative/augmentative communication channel, based on the interpretation of the user's brain activity, who can then interact with the environment without relying on neuromuscular pathways. BCI can thus be placed in the context of human-machine interfaces and, considering a possible application scenario to smart homes, they can serve as a technological bridge to make Active and Assisted Living (AAL) systems' functionalities accessible to subjects who would not otherwise be able to actively use. In this paper, BCI is specifically conceived for AAL system control experience, developed ad-hoc, considering cost and compactness constraints, besides classification performance. The implemented solution is quite general, as it can handle multiple bio-potentials: this feature allows to exploit different information channels, namely, ElectroEncephaloGraphy (EEG) and ElectroMyoGraphy (EMG). Each subsystem (EEG, EMG) is presented and its performance discussed; both can operate in real-time and in self-paced mode (i.e. they automatically recognize if a command is being issued and, in this case, which one). In particular, the EEG part, based on Steady State Visual-Evoked Potentials (SSVEP), can achieve very good results in terms of false positive rejection, improving over the state of the art (False Positive Rate: 0.16 min^{-1}). Moreover, such results are achieved without any initial system calibration phase. Meanwhile, the EMG subsystem can be used as a smart switch for SSVEP stimuli control (on/off), improving user's comfort when no control periods are desired.

Keywords: Brain Computer Interface (BCI) · hybrid BCI (hBCI) · Steady State Visual Evoked Potential (SSVEP) · ElectroEncephaloGraphy (EEG) · ElectroMyoGraphy (EMG)

1   Introduction

A Brain Computer Interface (BCI) is an alternative, augmentative communication channel [1] which aims at providing the user with an interaction path based on the sole interpretation of her/his brain activity. BCI can have multiple fields of application, such as control of mobile robots [2], artificial limbs [3] or electrical wheelchair [4]. Also, in the context of intelligent environments and homes, BCI could serve as a technological bridge to enable Active and Assisted Living (AAL) systems control [5, 7].

As with any other conventional AAL system interfaces (tablet, smartphone, remote controller etc.), in order to promote the BCI acceptance and effectiveness, the user needs to perceive BCI-enabled control as easy and natural as possible; in other terms, BCI

© Springer International Publishing Switzerland 2016
C.K. Chang et al. (Eds.): ICOST 2016, LNCS 9677, pp. 345–355, 2016.
DOI: 10.1007/978-3-319-39601-9_31

operation should be continuous and self-paced [8–10], i.e. the device must be able to discern user's intentional control periods from nonintentional ones, providing reliable command decoding in the former case. Moreover, in such a scenario, user interactions with the system are quite rare and sparse in time. In light of this, practical and effective BCI-enabled home control should follow a "Plug&Play" approach as much as possible. This means that the user should be allowed to interact with the system without needing neither complex and time-consuming "ad personam" calibration procedures, nor demanding training sessions. In addition, such behavior should be uniform across different users, i.e. they should be able to consistently use the device with the same settings (realizing a so-called subject-independent BCI), and fine performance tuning should be just limited to a few high-level parameters. Finally, another aspect worth remarking is that, in this context, accuracy in the command selection and false positives minimization are of primary concern, with respect to interaction speed.

Considering all the aspects above, the SSVEP (Steady State Visual Evoked Potentials) paradigm [9–11] was chosen for core BCI operation; SSVEP has recently received much attention, especially in communication or control applications where fast, reliable interaction is needed and multiple simultaneous choices are presented to the user. SSVEP is a periodic brain response elicited by a visual stimulus, flickering at a constant frequency: a peak in the brain power spectrum, synchronous with such frequency, can be produced just by looking at the visual stimulus. SSVEP are regarded as robust features for BCI [9], given their inherently higher SNR (Signal to Noise Ratio) with respect to other paradigms (e.g., motor imagery [13], as discussed in [10]). Moreover, since it exploits involuntary response, SSVEP do not require, in principle, any specific user skill and thus involve no user training. In addition, the steady-state, repetitive nature of such potentials makes it possible to design calibration-free classification methods.

Other input channels can be added to a BCI system in order to improve its reliability. In particular, some BCI users could still have some residual motor ability: information on muscular activation could be picked up and monitored by means of ElectrMyoGraphy (EMG). In this case EMG signals from (possibly weak) muscular activations could be integrated into a hybrid BCI (hBCI) framework and be used to switch on and off the SSVEP visual stimulation unit when not needed. This can improve user's comfort (less eye fatigue on the long run), as well as further reduce the BCI false positives (long inactive periods with SSVEP stimuli are excluded).

Finally, another major aspect worth considering in promoting accessibility to this kind of technology is its cost. Lowering costs does not merely means saving money, but rather broadening the spectrum of users and uses for BCI-enabled devices, generating new concepts and ideas, just as in the commercial electronic realm happens. Closely related to this aspect is the adoption of scalable, compact technological solutions; future BCI-embedded implementations could potentially allow to discover new methods and applications, just as wearable devices are re-inventing the way we intend sensors.

The above discussion introduces the context for which our BCI device was realized: this paper presents the complete implementation, focused on enabling effective AAL system control.

2   Bio-Potential Acquisition Module

A dedicated hardware module was designed and realized for acquiring bio-potentials, shown in Fig. 1. The module features 16 input channels in a small, 100×130 mm form factor, and can be powered by means of 4 AA alkaline batteries. Production costs are also contained, with respect to current, commercial EEG devices: in medium scale, device manufacturing amounts to, approximately, 300 € (i.e. a fraction of most commercial EEG modules). The module communicates via a full-speed USB 2.0 link (12 Mbps), and can be controlled and set-up directly by a host computer.

Fig. 1. A photo of the realized bio-potentials acquisition module (dimensions: 130×100 mm)

The module is built around two high-resolution (24-bit) δ-Σ Analog to Digital Converters (ADCs), featuring DC-handling capability. Data rate can be adjusted in the range of 250-16 kSPS (Samples Per Second). In our experimental setups, it is common practice to set 250 SPS for EEG studies (in order to achieve the best noise performance) and up to 2000 SPS for EMG acquisition. An input gain is also applied, our default being 24, yielding a maximum $\pm$ 188 mV input dynamic range.

The module was validated and compared against a reference, commercial EEG module [6, 12], namely a *g.tec USBamp*. Referred-To-Input (RTI) noise was found to be within 1.4 μV_{pp}, more than sufficient to reliably acquire EEG signals (which, compared to EMG ones, exhibit lower signal levels, as low as a few μV). The module was also validated against the reference one in a dynamic setup, performing a p300 session. The EEG was acquired, holding the cap and electrode set fixed, and simply switching the input connectors for recording waveforms in an interleaved scheme (i.e. run1 REF, run2 DUT, run3 REF etc.). The collected waveforms were compared, showing consistent behavior [6, 12]. All these hints allow us to conclude that the realized module does not introduce significant noise or bias, when compared with a high-end, reference device, and can, therefore, be equivalently used in BCI experiments.

3   EEG-Based BCI: Signal Processing

As mentioned in the introduction, SSVEP was chosen as the operating paradigm for the EEG-based BCI. Many algorithms exist in literature for SSVEP classification; among the most popular ones are: MEC [14] (Minimum Energy Combination), AMCC [15] (Average Maximum Contrast Combination) and CCA [16] (Canonical Correlation Analysis). A review of such methods goes beyond the scope of this article; the interested reader could refer, for example, to [11, 17]. Our implementation choice stems from a CCA-based approach, and proposes an extension in order to improve the system immunity against false positives.

CCA is a statistical method, generally used for finding the correlations between two sets of multi-dimensional variables. It seeks a pair of linear combinations (canonical variables, characterized by weight vectors $\mathbf{w_x}$, $\mathbf{w_y}$) for the two sets, such that the correlation between the two linear combinations $\mathbf{x_L} = \mathbf{w_x}^T X$ and $\mathbf{y_L} = \mathbf{w_y}^T Y$ is maximized:

$$\max_{w_x, w_y} \rho = \frac{E\left[x_L y_L^T\right]}{\sqrt{E\left[x_L x_L^T\right] E\left[y_L y_L^T\right]}} = \frac{w_x^T XY^T w_y}{\sqrt{w_x^T XX^T w_x \, w_y^T YY^T w_y}} \tag{1}$$

Here X, Y are the input and the SSVEP reference matrix, respectively. Y is composed by N_h (*sin, cos*) couples representing a steady state sinusoidal response, with N_h representing the number of considered harmonics:

$$X = \begin{bmatrix} \sin 2\pi ft_1 \cos 2\pi ft_1 & \cdots & \sin 2\pi N_h ft_1 \cos 2\pi N_h ft_1 \\ \vdots & \vdots & \vdots \\ \sin 2\pi ft_{Nt} \cos 2\pi ft_{Nt} & \cdots & \sin 2\pi N_h ft_{Nt} \cos 2\pi N_h ft_{Nt} \end{bmatrix} \tag{2}$$

In case multiple SSVEP frequencies are being considered, the aforementioned procedure is performed for every target.

Eventually, a simple classifier can pick the largest correlation coefficient among the stimuli set. Doing so, however, could potentially lead to a high false positives rate, especially if the BCI runs in self-paced mode: in that case, a method for discerning intentional control periods from rest ones is mandatory. A common solution to this problem is to smooth the classifier output, validating the classifier output only if n previous samples agree with the current one. In the following we adopt a different methodology, identifying a feature which could be used to assess the level of confidence in the prediction and that can be exploited to discern between user control and rest periods.

3.1   Confidence Indicator: Improving Basic CCA Accuracy

In the following, we consider an offline 4-class SSVEP problem (namely, {16, 18, 20, 22} Hz) and introduce the notion of a confidence indicator for improving baseline CCA accuracy, the main performance index we consider for our application. Should such indicator result in a low confidence, classification is not validated: we call this new "no-reliable-decision" state a neutral state. The neutralization mechanism can positively impact on the overall prediction accuracy, at the expense of discarding a fraction of epochs (considered non-informative).

We define such confidence indicator as the absolute difference between the largest correlation coefficient and the second largest one as such indicator, from here on referred to as parameter d.

$$d = \max_{f \in Fstim} |\rho_f| - \max_{f \in Fstim \setminus \{fmax\}} |\rho_f| \qquad (3)$$

where ρ_f is the correlation coefficient yielded by CCA as described in Eq. (1), $Fstim$ is the set of possible stimuli frequencies and $fmax$ the frequency associated to the largest ρ_f. The expected advantage in choosing such an indicator is that uncertainty is inferred by the relative comparison of the ρ_f's, rather than referring to a subject-dependent and, possibly, frequency-dependent threshold on the maximum value of ρ_f.

In Fig. 2, distribution of correctly and wrongly classified epochs (each one containing a SSVEP) with respect to d parameter is shown by a histogram approximation. Ideal behavior should associate all errors (black bars) to low values of d, with correct classification (light grey bars) associated to largest values instead. An optimal threshold, d^*, could then be easily determined and a rejection criterion set up to discard all epochs associated with low d values ($d \leq d^*$). However, since actual data show overlaps between the correct and wrong classification distributions, a tradeoff between prediction accuracy and data yield (i.e. the fraction of non-neutral epochs) is needed. In order to assess such tradeoff, the following procedure was adopted: for a given value of d^*, a subset of epochs is selected, fulfilling the condition $d \geq d^*$; then, wrong and correct classification are counted within the subset, keeping track of the fraction of rejected epochs, and accuracy is computed accordingly. Such procedure is repeated, sweeping the parameter d^*, in order to assess its effect on error count (or accuracy) and neutralization rate. We characterized the method on the whole population of the test, instead of relying on a per-user basis analysis: this is in line with our view of subject-independent approach.

Figure 3 graphically report such results. In order to appreciate the improvement carried by neutralization strategy, the performance achieved with no neutralization is also reported (grey solid line). Consistent improvement is achieved over the reference case, even at lower neutralization rates, i.e., without implying too relevant data loss.

The quality metric introduced above can also be exploited to introduce some adaptive features in the SSVEP classification stage. In particular, we can check the quality of the current prediction at runtime by looking at the indicator d: we may start with a short time window length, to be increased whenever d does not exceed a given threshold. This could potentially improve the user's experience and comfort: each time, the required SSVEP persistence time for classification is dynamically chosen, so as to be as short as possible (i.e. the user needs to focus for less time on the stimulus, provided sufficient quality of the SSVEP response is reflected in the d value); at the same time, avoiding to choose a fixed, short window, may help in improving immunity to false positives.

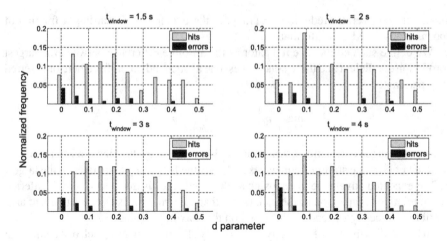

Fig. 2. Distribution of classifiers' hits and errors (light grey and black, respectively; each is normalized to the sample size) as a function of the parameter d. The distributions are also plotted for different EEG window lengths.

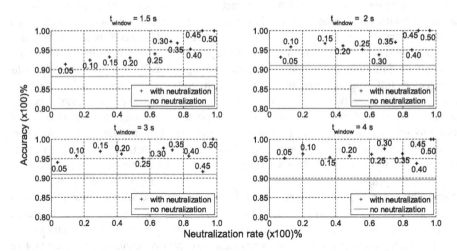

Fig. 3. Accuracy as a function of neutralization rate, at different values of threshold d*. The solid grey line represents the original, "raw" accuracy level, without neutralization (i.e., d* = 0). The graphs are plotted for different EEG window lengths.

3.2 Confidence Indicator: Improving Basic CCA Accuracy

Based on the algorithms described so far, a self-paced, online BCI, exploiting a 4-class SSVEP paradigm was implemented and tested.

Experimental setup is as follows: 4 visual stimuli (LED, organized in a rectangular pattern over a box) are shown simultaneously, with blinking frequencies equal to {16, 18, 20, 22} Hz; the subject is seated approximately 1 m away from the visual stimuli. Only 6 passive Ag/AgCl electrodes are used to acquire signals form scalp locations Pz,

P3, P4, POz, O1, O2. The protocol associates a particular home automation task (namely on/off switching of a light and opening of a motorized shutter) to each stimulus, and the user is asked to perform several control actions, at his own pace and will. Moreover, in order to assess the immunity to false positive events, long idle periods are introduced on purpose, during which the subject does not make any intentional choice and is allowed to talk and, partially, move. A total of 10 healthy volunteers (age 24–61, 4 females) participated in this study, none of them with any prior BCI-control experience, nor was involved in any calibration/training phase.

As far as the online signal processing is concerned, a classification is attempted every 200 ms, using the neutralization technique we introduced before, to ensure classification reliability. The adaptive window-length choice mechanism is also used: at first, classification is attempted using the shortest available window (2 s). In case no prediction can be made reliably (at least according to the confidence indicator d), the window is allowed to grow in pre-determined steps, attempting classification at each time step until either a reliable choice is obtained or an upper time limit is reached (4 s).

In addition, in order to further improve immunity to false positives, a post-smoother is optionally added, which averages the last 5 classification outputs for each class (the 4 targets plus the neutral state): if the average for a class exceeds a given threshold, the choice is validated, otherwise a null output is assumed.

3.3 Results

As previously stated, in order to provide smoother operation in BCI-enabled control applications, we are primarily concerned with maximizing the accuracy (i.e. correctly classifying the command when the user is trying to issue one) and, at the same time, minimizing the false positives. That also requires being able to discern when the user is actively controlling the device, or is just resting or performing other tasks.

Table 1 reports the online experiment results (mean and standard deviation), in terms of true positive, false negative and false positive rates. A very good performance is achieved, both in terms of true positive and false positive rates.

In particular, the advantage of adopting the aforementioned confidence indicator is that false positives are kept to a very small amount (≈ 0.16 min^{-1} on average, i.e. approximately a false positive event every 6'15''), when compared to state of the art performance, such as in [18, 19]. Of course, such performance, as is, may still be not suitable for some applications, but provides a solid base for further improvements, e.g. by exploiting EMG signals, as explained in the next section.

All the results are achieved without any subject-specific parameter tuning: in other words, all user share the exact same setup, in line with our subject-independent BCI approach.

Another test was performed in less controlled conditions with respect to a lab environment. In particular, the entire system was deployed during the *Handimatica 2014* exhibition, where greater interfering sources were present, such as high background luminosity, noise and electromagnetic interference. Moreover, during this test, the BCI user was relatively free to move and speech, in order to interact with people. Overall, 6

Table 1. Online performance on the self-paced, 4-class experiment: mean (std. dev.)

Subject	False Positive Rate [min^{-1}]	True Positives [%]
1	0.094	89.1
2	0.202	96.9
3	0.037	96.9
4	0.094	89.1
5	0.261	100
6	0.077	92.2
7	0.071	92.2
8	0.100	90.6
9	0.489	100
10	0.142	96.9
Mean	0.156	95.0
Std	0.134	4.2

live demos were performed, for the approximate duration of 30 min each. Although non-conclusive from a statistical point of view, promising results were achieved: the subject was able to successfully operate the BCI, and the false positive rate was as low as 0.14 min^{-1}, in line with the results achieved in lab conditions.

This encourages the transition of such technology also outside of lab environments.

4   EMG as Auxiliary Input Channel in H-BCI

In this section we present some preliminary results on the use of EMG as an alternative input channel for our BCI system.

We can think of several possible scenarios for EMG-EEG integration: for example, the EMG channel could be used as a binary switch for enabling the EEG signal analysis. In this case, the user could help the BCI in discerning intentional control periods from non-intentional ones. However, it is still important for the EEG-based BCI section to be able to make such a distinction on its own, since false activations could be triggered by the EMG part.

In order to test the suitability of EMG as a binary switch for the BCI part we define the following protocol: the user will signal his intention to activate/turn off the BCI by slightly clenching the jaw. In the future hybrid BCI architecture, this action will also imply turning on/off the visual stimulation unit, to minimize user's discomfort (coming from being unnecessarily exposed to flashing lights for long time). Moreover, turning LED stimuli off when not needed could mean improving BCI robustness against false positives, since peaks at the specific target frequencies are less likely to occur.

EMG is acquired from the masseter muscle via a single, differential channel. Sampling rate is set to 1000 SPS to pick-up relevant signal features. After collection, the signal undergoes basic pre-processing, including band-pass filtering ([100–350] Hz bandwidth, optimized to extract the more significant signal features) and squaring. Before extracting the necessary features, the observed signal window is inspected for potentially interesting peaks based on a percentile criterion. Based on this, two features are extracted from the isolated signals: the integral and the mean. Those features are then passed to a linear kernel SVM, which takes care of the classification between epoch with or without muscular activation.

The training phase consisted of a series of 100 activations performed by a single subject. Online, real-time performance was then assessed on two subjects, and no further subject-specific training was performed. A real-time test session consisted of 50 attempts to achieve control by a slight jaw clench, performed in a self-paced fashion, with at least 6 s between consecutive activations. In this scenario, a false positive event represents a detected activation while the subject was not trying to achieve control, whereas a false negative is a missed activation attempt. The first subject (the one which performed the training phase) was able to achieve perfect control over the whole real-time test session; the other subject did achieve a very good performance too, with just one false positive (≈ 0.07 min^{-1}) and two false negatives (4 %).

A preliminary experiment was then carried out, for testing the feasibility of a hybrid-BCI (h-BCI) architecture. As previously explained, the EMG signal can be used as an auxiliary channel to improve system's robustness against false positives. In particular, the EMG signal is used as a binary switch to enable/disable processing of the EEG signals; in other words, the h-BCI acts as a conventional EEG-based BCI when the EMG channel signals the user's intention to interact with it.

The following experiment protocol was adopted: the user is asked to achieve control of the h-BCI via a light jaw clench. At this point, the user must issue a command via the SSVEP paradigm (introduced in the previous sections). If the user does not issue any command (i.e. no SSVEP response is detected) within a given amount of time (10 s in this experiment), the h-BCI reverts to the initial status, waiting for an event on the EMG channel.

A run is composed of 50 self-paced trials, and long inactive periods are introduced within trials to assess immunity to false positives. For performance estimation purposes, the event in which the user is not able to activate the h-BCI (either via EMG or EEG) is considered a False Negative, whereas a misclassification or a spurious activation are considered False Positives.

One subject performed two runs of the aforementioned experiment, reporting an average false positives rate of 0.072 min^{-1} and an average 10 % false negative rate. It is worth highlighting that the EMG part was responsible for just one false positive, whereas the EEG part accounts for a total of 4, concentrated in the last trials of each run and probably related to increased eye fatigue. These findings, although very preliminary and bearing scarce statistical significance, are indeed quite promising and encourage in moving towards a hybrid BCI architecture, capable of fusing EMG and EEG information to achieve a more robust interaction paradigm.

5 Conclusions

In this paper, we discussed a complete implementation of a SSVEP-based BCI and discussed a possible extension using EMG as an auxiliary input signal.

The whole signal processing chain for a self-paced, SSVEP-based BCI was presented. Given the application scope of home automation control, in which user interactions are quite rare and sparse in time, the accuracy and robustness constraints prevail over high data throughput requirements. From this perspective, undergoing long or periodical system calibration phases could be perceived as an excessive burden by the user (this spoiling acceptance and usability chances), so that a calibration and training-free approach was pursued. Subject-independent operation was demonstrated, at the same time achieving remarkably good performance.

To this purpose, a CCA-based algorithm was exploited: after assessing its reference performance, improvement in accuracy and robustness were obtained by accounting for neutralization of unreliable choices, based on the estimation of a classification confidence index. Such an index was also exploited to implement adaptive, dynamic selection of optimal duration of EEG epoch, thus increasing efficiency of the classification process and consequently allowing to improve the BCI responsiveness towards the user.

Finally, devised methods were implemented and tested in an online, self-paced BCI experiment. Obtained results are very promising: high true positive rates ($\approx$ 94 %) and low false positive rates (≈ 0.16 min^{-1}) were achieved, outperforming literature data. Moreover, the entire setup was also replicated outside lab-controlled conditions, in the scope of the *Handimatica 2014* exhibition, with very promising results. This may encourage the adoption of such technology in more realistic contexts.

Also, a possible hybrid BCI architecture was discussed, exploiting EMG as an auxiliary input channel, acting as a binary activation switch for the EEG-based part. This behavior could improve both user's comfort, turning off visual stimulation when not needed, as well as resilience towards false positives. Preliminary results for the detection of a slight jaw clench via EMG show that this auxiliary channel could be suitable for controlling and aiding the EEG-based section of the BCI. Furthermore, a proof-of-concept test of the complete h-BCI was presented, showing promising results.

References

1. Wolpaw, J.R., Birbaumer, N., McFarland, D.J., Pfurtscheller, G., Vaughan, T.M.: Brain-computer interfaces for communication and control. Clin. Neurophysiol. **113**(6), 767–791 (2002)
2. Bi, L., Fan, X., Liu, Y.: EEG-based brain-controlled mobile robots: a survey. IEEE Trans. Hum. Mach. Syst. **43**(2), 161–176 (2013)
3. Horki, P., Solis-Escalante, T., Neuper, C., Müller-Putz, G.: Combined motor imagery and SSVEP based BCI control of a 2 DoF artificial upper limb. Med. Biol. Eng. Comput. **49**(5), 567–577 (2011)
4. Carlson, T., Millán, J.D.R.: Brain-controlled wheelchairs: a robotic architecture. IEEE Robot. Autom. Mag. **20**(1), 65–73 (2013)
5. Mora, N., Bianchi, V., De Munari, I., Ciampolini, P.: A BCI platform supporting AAL applications. In: Stephanidis, C., Antona, M. (eds.) UAHCI 2014, Part I. LNCS, vol. 8513, pp. 515–526. Springer, Heidelberg (2014)
6. Mora, N., Bianchi, V., De Munari, I., Ciampolini, P.: Improving BCI usability as HCI in ambient assisted living system control. In: Foundations of Augmented Cognition, pp. 293–303 (2015)

7. Carabalona, R., Grossi, F., Tessadri, A., Castiglioni, P., Caracciolo, A., De Munari, I.: Light on! Real world evaluation of a P300-based brain-computer interface (BCI) for environment control in a smart home. Ergonomics **55**(5), 552–563 (2012)
8. Millan, J.D.R., Mourino, J.: Asynchronous BCI and local neural classifiers: an overview of the adaptive brain interface project. Trans. Neural Syst. Rehabil. Eng. **11**(2), 159–161 (2003)
9. Cecotti, H.: A self-paced and calibration-less SSVEP-based brain-computer interface speller. IEEE Trans. Neural Syst. Rehabil. Eng. **18**(2), 127–133 (2010)
10. Mora, N., De Munari, I., Ciampolini, P.: A plug&play brain computer interface solution for AAL systems. Stud. Health Technol. Inf. **217**, 152–158 (2015)
11. Mora, N., Bianchi, V., De Munari, I., Ciampolini, P.: Simple and efficient methods for steady state visual evoked potential detection in BCI embedded system. In: 2014 IEEE International Conference on Acoustics, Speech and Signal Processing (ICASSP), pp. 2044–2048 (2014)
12. Mora, N., De Munari, I., Ciampolini, P.: Exploitation of a compact, cost-effective EEG module for plug-and-play, SSVEP-based BCI. In: 2015 7th International IEEE/EMBS Conference on Neural Engineering (NER), pp. 142–145 (2015)
13. Pfurtscheller, G., Brunner, C., Schlögl, A., Lopes da Silva, F.H.: Mu rhythm (de) synchronization and EEG single-trial classification of different motor imagery tasks. NeuroImage **31**(1), 153–159 (2006)
14. Volosyak, I.: SSVEP-based Bremen-BCI interface - boosting information transfer rates. J. Neural Eng. **8**(3), 036020 (2011)
15. Garcia-Molina, G., Zhu, D.: Optimal spatial filtering for the steady state visual evoked potential: BCI application. In: 5th International IEEE/EMBS Conference on Neural Engineering, pp. 156–160 (2011)
16. Lin, Z., Zhang, C., Wu, W., Gao, X.: Frequency recognition based on canonical correlation analysis for SSVEP-based BCIs. IEEE Trans. Biomed. Eng. **54**, 1172–1176 (2007)
17. Mora, N., De Munari, I., Ciampolini, P.: Subject-independent, SSVEP-based BCI: trading off among accuracy, responsiveness and complexity. In: 2015 7th International IEEE/EMBS Conference on Neural Engineering (NER) (2015)
18. Pfurtscheller, G., Solis-Escalante, T., Ortner, R., Linortner, P., Muller-Putz, G.R.: Self-paced operation of an SSVEP-based orthosis with and without an imagery-based "brain switch:" a feasibility study towards a hybrid BCI. IEEE Trans. Neural Syst. Rehabil. Eng. **18**(4), 409–414 (2010)
19. Pan, J., Li, Y., Zhang, R., Zhenghui, G., Li, F.: Discrimination between control and idle states in asynchronous SSVEP-based brain switches: a pseudo-key-based approach. IEEE Trans. Neural Syst. Rehabil. Eng. **21**(3), 435–443 (2013)

Post-test Perceptions of Digital Tools by the Elderly in an Ambient Environment

Elizabeth Bougeois[4], Jenny Duchier[3], Frédéric Vella[1],
Mathilde Blanc Machado[1], Adrien Van den Bossche[1], Thierry Val[1],
Damien Brulin[2], Nadine Vigouroux[1(✉)], and Eric Campo[2]

[1] IRIT, Université de Toulouse,
CNRS, INPT, UPS, UT1, UT2 J, Toulouse, France
{Vella,Mathilde.Blanc-Machado,vigourou}@irit.fr,
{vandenbo,thierry.val}@univ-tlse2.fr
[2] LAAS-CNRS, Université de Toulouse, UT2 J, Toulouse, France
eric.campo@univ-tlse2.fr
[3] INSERM, UMR 1027 INSERM-UPS, Toulouse, France
jenny.duchier@inserm.fr
[4] LERASS, UT2 J, Toulouse, France
elizabeth.bougeois@univ-tlse2.fr

Abstract. This article presents the first results about the perception of 33 elderly people about interaction tools in a digital ambient environment. The evaluation of this study is based on the filling of a short questionnaire, and interviews after a presentation of the different possible technologies and the use of a digital automated living lab, centred on a life scenario, by volunteers. The first results show a significant interest of the elderly in the voice interaction mode, in comparison with tactile interaction or switches, as well as a good opinion of the technological tools presented, in the context of a potential future use, for their health, better autonomy and well-being.

Keywords: Ambient digital environment · Usability · Perception · Interaction mode · Elderly · Living lab

1 Introduction

Longer life increases the number of people with loss of autonomy and may lead to dependence [1]. Needs in terms of securing a dependent elderly person, or a disabled person and needs for a response to isolation and social ties deficit have been identified as well as key ingredients [2] and challenges [3] for Ambient Assisted Living (AAL) systems [4]. The issue of home support is justified by a social necessity and by individual aspirations or for savings in health spending and social protection [5].

The use of ICT (Information Technology and Communication) can enable frail people or people with disabilities to live better by giving them the means to be more independent at home [6]. Many efforts have been made to increase accessibility to ICT –communication devices, assistive and health technologies ...– for old people but the solutions are not yet at the appointment. This is mainly due to the lack of study of the

© Springer International Publishing Switzerland 2016
C.K. Chang et al. (Eds.): ICOST 2016, LNCS 9677, pp. 356–367, 2016.
DOI: 10.1007/978-3-319-39601-9_32

real needs and a clear definition of the elderly profiles (dependent, frail, socially iso-lated, digital exclusion, etc.). Some specific characteristics prevent or put a brake on the access to these new technologies. The behaviour and interaction modes of these people in their use and access to these technologies as well as their perception of technology are not fully understood because of the many influencing factors.

[7, 8] explored the potential for voice user interface to interact with home-based services. [9] reported studies comparing touch screen and traditional mouse input and [10] described the design and the use of handheld computers for older adults. These modalities of interaction adapted to the home are still a challenge in connection with home automation and ambient technologies. Another significant challenge when studying technologies within the True Life Lab concept [11] is the living context where the research is carried out to inform about the acceptability of future innovative technologies or services.

Methods and tools from social sciences and ICT need to be merged to explore and analyse the behaviour of users with these innovative technologies to design, adapt them, on the basis of related ICT experiences. It is also important to consider how a new numeric ambient technology including intuitive interaction based on gesture, tactile and speech enables to fit the profile of the user.

Therefore, a methodology [12] mixing ethnographic observation [13] of actions and interviews [14] needs to be investigated. This innovating methodology must take into account several restraints, for instance the fact that the elderly people cannot endure a long experimentation time and may be stressed by the numeric ambient environment with observers.

We propose an interdisciplinary methodology to anticipate the use and the acceptance of these technologies by an elderly population, to build real models of habitat and solutions tailored to their expectations. In this way, it is necessary to study the relationship of these people with digital technologies in a smart home environment. This is the reason why the paper presents the preliminary results of an experiment conducted in living lab on a sample of 33 volunteers (aged > 60 years). A test protocol was implemented, so that the volunteers could test the technological tools available in a smart home and perform, alone, independently a real-life test scenario. The last step of the study was the filling of a questionnaire on the utility and relevance of the tools used. The change in perception about the technologies used between the before and after testing was particularly studied.

The paper is organized as follows: Sect. 2 describes the experimental protocol. Section 3 presents the test environment. Section 4 gives the method and the observation tools. Section 5 gives preliminary results. Section 6 offers a discussion. Section 7 ends the paper with a conclusion and comments about future work.

2 Experimental Protocol

The only criteria retained for the inclusion of participants in this project are the age –at least 60 years of age– and being retired. There is no exclusion criterion about diseases, disabilities or loss of independence.

Up to three participants are called on a half day during which researchers accompany them. The experiment session is divided into seven phases:

- The signature of a consent letter with the presentation of the scientists' team, the objectives of the study and the different phases of the experiment.
- The response to a questionnaire on a tactile tablet. A researcher accompanies each participant to help him to use the tablet or to understand the questions. The goal of this questionnaire is to know socio-cultural profiles of elderly, their current uses of ICT, the intentions of using new technologies, the anticipation of the place of settlement and their adaptation.
- The visit of a smart home (cf. Sect. 3) and the presentation of the different technologies and services available. Participants discover the smart home where they will carry out a scenario and they can ask any questions concerning the functioning of the equipment.
- The appropriation period of the three different interaction techniques. This phase allows participants to try classic switches and the touch screen user interface to control the home equipment. They are also informed that they can speak with the smart home but without spoken example. This choice was retained to avoid influencing the participant and to let them discover this interaction mode during the test.
- The individual experimentation into the smart home, according to a scenario simulating the awakening of the participants. They are asked to carry out their usual activities after getting up in the morning. They can use classic switches and/or tactile interface on tablets and/or voice control of the smart home.
- The post-experimentation semi-structured interview with researchers in human and social sciences. The researchers have observed the participants during the scenario. By mixing the information collected both during the observation phase and during the interviews, the researchers aim to understand the participant's behavior, to discuss about their feelings and their projection in the use of the ambient technologies.
- The response to a post-experimentation questionnaire. This step enables to quantify the qualitative data from the previous interview.

3 Smart Home Test Environment

The experimentation was set up in the smart home of the university institute of technology of Blagnac in France (MIB), [15]. This smart home is a technological, scientific and human platform. In the standard configuration, this flat of 80 m^2 is equipped with a networking infrastructure adaptable to a valid, a frail or a disabled person (Fig. 1). It enables interconnectivity between commercial equipments and devices for intelligent management of the living environment, the implementation of technological solutions for monitoring and study of uses in the home setting. This home is equipped with various kinds of sensors (comfort, domestic security, access management, remote assistance...) and technical aids. The person can use classic switches, a touch screen interface (Fig. 2), or his/her voice. Interoperability is an important issue because of the heterogeneity of technological devices [16]; Interoperability is ensured through a middleware accepting standard protocols such as KNX or HTTP and also proprietary wireless protocols.

4 functions are proposed:

- E-health functions to follow the health-status of the person,
- Comfort and assistive functions to support person with automatism equipment,
- Access functions for safety and security,
- Communication functions to control home equipment and to keep social ties with the outside (family, caregivers...).

In this study, only comfort and assistive functions are considered (Fig. 2).

Fig. 1. The experimental smart home [15]

Fig. 2. A volunteer using the tablet in the kitchen

The control switches are completed with pictograms (kind of help) to explain the role of each button (Fig. 3-a). The tablet has an intuitive user interface with buttons affected to each room. Ergonomic criteria –size of buttons, space between buttons [17], and background colour to maximize the contrast– have been applied to facilitate the accessibility by older persons. Pressing the affected button provides access to the list of possible equipment commands. Same pictograms are used for the buttons on tablet and wall switches (Fig. 3-b). Voice input is recorded through an ambient sensitive microphone set up in the flat. The spoken message is displayed in the smart home by means of a text-to-speech synthesis.

A platform (called MIOZ) was designed to simulate the process chain of a spoken dialogue –speech recognition, understanding system, management of dialogue and generation of message– between the participant and the smart home without the knowledge of the participant. MIOZ sends and receives orders and feedbacks to sensors, actuators… regardless of the communication technology available in the MIB. Thus, the experimenter can track the participant's actions through the sensors' feedback and interact with him through. To achieve this goal, a specific lightweight middleware "MiCom" has been developed. MiCom enables connections with various technologies and insure interoperability thanks to a HTTP-based command set to interact with sensors and actuators, regardless of the communication technology. Each device of the environment can be managed by calling HTTP URLs.

The participant is also observed thanks to four cameras deployed in the smart home.

 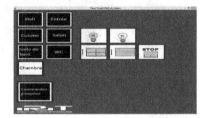

Fig. 3. a- Pictograms associated to wall switches **b-** Touch screen user-interface

4 Method and Observation Tools

4.1 Ethnography and Communication Tool

The social science process of the study is inductive, based on grounded theories. The analysis of the qualitative data is focused both on the actions performed by the elderly people and their behaviour during the observation stage, and on their discourse about their experiment, during the interviews.

The interview lasts between 15 and 20 min and is focussed on five items:

- How the participant felt during the experiment?
- Which ICT the participant likes best and which are convincing?
- What could be the participant's motivation to use the ICT at home?
- When? –that is to say: anticipation of the adaptation of the home and intentions in terms of investment,
- In case of social contribution: which ICT would come first and how is the participant ready to carry out administrative procedures?

Following the interview, the short questionnaire is presented on tablet. This questionnaire is presented as a resume of the total experiment. It focusses on the opinion of the participant about ICT's.

4.2 Questionnaire

According to the experiment protocol (cf. Sect. 2) participants were invited to answer to a questionnaire focussed on four items:

- The view about technologies,
- The wish to settle domotic equipment and ICT at home. If positive answer: which items? (Voice input system, talking machine, touch screen user interface, control switches, light path, carephone and adjustability of furniture to abilities and needs, several items could be selected). If negative answer: justification (no perception of usefulness, too expensive, lack of confidence in technologies, intrusive technology, fears about the use of collected data),
- Interaction mode preferences,
- Easiness of the different interaction modes (prioritisation).

The analysis of the whole data gives comprehensive elements of the way the elderly consider the use of ambient technologies dedicated to palliate the loss of autonomy.

4.3 Justification of Our Approach

Carrying out semi structured interviews enables the researchers to collect information that were not possible to anticipate: the participants engage, during the interviews, their authentic living experience as elderly people, their representations and projections about aging, loss of autonomy or dependence, their eventual fears about the future, their level of information and their representations about ICT's in an ambient environment.

Their discourse is therefore incarnated, grounded on their life experience and freely contextualized.

In such a protocol, this way of investigating enables to qualify quantitative data and gives a vision or orientation from which it is possible to define new tracks for the analysis of the results. This come and go between qualitative and quantitative information leads to precise, sharp and authentic consideration of human beings as far as their health is concerned and benefits into better understanding of their real needs. The qualitative investigation enriches the quantitative data, and vice versa.

5 Results

We have proceeded to an experimentation period of 33 volunteers and have carried out an analysis of both post experiment interviews and questionnaires.

5.1 Population

33 volunteers (21 female and 12 male) were recruited (Table 1). Among them, there is a person with motor impairment (lower limbs) and another with cognitive impairment.

Table 1. Population profile

	60–64 years	65–74 years	75–90 years and older	Total
Female	4	10	7	21
Male	2	8	2	12
Total	6	18	9	33

All the others have no deficiency except visually impairment corrected by wearing glasses. All of them have signed the consent letter and agree with the goal of the experiment protocol.

5.2 Quantitative Results

Figure 4 shows that 90.91 % of older people surveyed have changed their opinion on new technologies (about 87.88 % in a positive way towards 3 in a negative way). 9.09 % have not changed their opinion after the experiment.

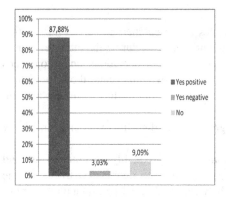
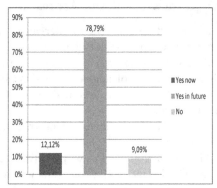

Fig. 4. The change of opinion about technologies

Fig. 5. The intentions about being equipped with such devices

We notice that only 12 % of elderly are ready to use currently the home automation and ICT technologies. However, when they are projected in the future, about 79 % are interested in these technologies (Fig. 5). 81.82 % of the participants say they are ready to carry out administrative procedures to adapt their home.

Figure 6 shows the different wishes about ICT in smart home, several answers could be given by the participants for a same question. We can see a strong preference for speech technologies (75.76 % respectively for voice recognition and 57.58 % for voice synthesis). The light path when the person gets up is also highly chosen (51.52 %). A lower interest (42.42 %) is reported for the touch screen user interface even if this interaction mode is available everywhere on tablet and smartphone. The lowest interests are respectively for control switches and carephone. These intention

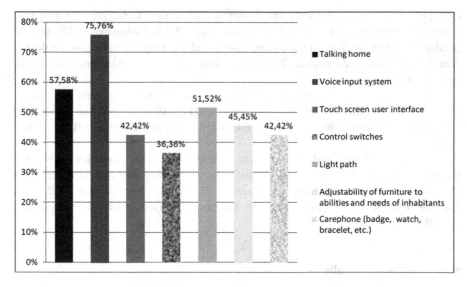

Fig. 6. Which devices at home?

rates are surprising because of the usual use of control switches in a standard home and the importance of teleassistance for frail or dependent people. Negative reasons reported concerns mainly the cost (6.6 %) and rate equality (3.3 %), the lack of perception of usefulness and the potentially intrusive dimension.

Figure 7 shows the high preference for voice input as interaction mode to control the smart home (about 70 % as first choice). The tactile interaction appears as a second choice (about 55 %, Fig. 8) while the switch control is chosen as a third choice (about 58 %). A Pearson's chi-squared test

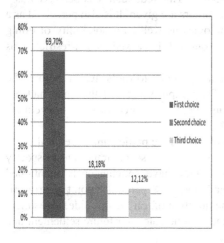

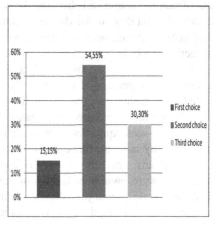

Fig. 7. Voice input system ranging (preference criteria)

Fig. 8. Touch screen user interface ranging (preference criteria)

($\chi 2$) [18] was applied between the variables (interaction technique and range of selection). Pearson's chi-squared test data are: Table 10-squared = 42, df = 4, p-value = 1.668e-08. The interaction technique and the range of selection are dependant for the preference criteria. This means that there is a significant statistic link between these two variables.

The same tendency is observed from the ease criteria (first choice for voice input (Fig. 9), second choice for touch screen interface (Fig. 10). However the rate for the second choice is respectively (51.52 % for touch screen and around 40 % for switch control).

A Pearson's chi-squared test ($\chi 2$) was applied between the variables (interaction technique and range of selection) for the ease criteria (Figs. 9 and 10). Pearson's chi-squared test data are: Table 10-squared = 37.091, df = 4, p-value = 1.725 e-07. The two variables (interaction technique and range of selection) are also dependant from the ease criteria.

5.3   Qualitative Results

First, the possible voice interaction with the MIB smart home through the MIOZ platform appears as the favorite equipment, from a qualitative point of view. It is perceived as a personalization of the smart home, a reassuring presence and a strong element of comfort: "the voice tranquilizes me, it reassures me"; "I am most impressed, amazed by the voice"; "one feels less lonely with the voice". Even when a negative perception occurs, it is nuanced: "the voice is stressful…but I suppose one gets used to it". This element matches with the quantitative results (cf. Fig. 6).

However, the most important result of the study is clearly the need to offer several modes of interaction to the inhabitant. The experimented protocol allows redundancy of the equipment, which gives, according to the discourse of the participants, the possibility of an extended comfort and well-being. This redundancy is perceived as a means of keeping acting and choosing the way orders are given. It is also perceived as a warranty of reliability of the different technologies as well as a possibility of doing several tasks or giving several orders simultaneously. It is viewed as non-restrictive as far as acting freely is concerned.

The participants sometimes had a defiant attitude towards ICT's before the experiment. This perception changed after. They express the fact that they had not expected such easiness in the use of the equipments: "I feared to be overwhelmed; these technologies now seem more feasible".

The cost of such equipments remains a problem, as the participants, even if they do not mention any amount; think that it is too expensive. It seems important to specify that, without any question about this aspect, they have spontaneously mentioned whether they were owners or tenants of their home. This particular point clearly orientated their thoughts and projections into the question of, on the one side, investment and, on the other side, equipment. Tenants tend to anticipate their future settlement in a nursing home.

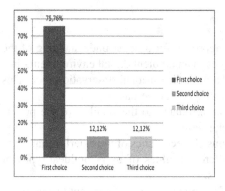

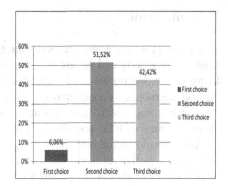

Fig. 9. Voice input system ranging (ease criteria)

Fig. 10. Touch screen user interface ranging (ease criteria)

6   Discussion

The technologies tested during the experiment appear to elderly people as a means of independence and a way to avoid going to a nursing home and stay healthy at home. However, some participants found that these innovative devices were too "medicalized", others wonder about the system reliability or costs at home. The novel interaction techniques (voice and tactile) are preferred: the voice input is natural and touch screen is fun and easy to use.

Even though the participants declare themselves as "concerned" and "convinced" by the technologies in the MIB, they also say that they don't need it immediately but in the future. Some of them clearly express their difficulty to project themselves into the loss of autonomy. This may be analyzed as ambivalence, or reluctance about palliative technologies as far as free and independent aging is concerned.

During the interviews, some participants have a contradictory discourse, compared to their behaviour during the experiment, such as, for instance, being very keen about the voice interaction with the MIB and not using it at all. It seems that the experience has changed their views positively as far as technologies are concerned. This remark has to be understood in the restraint context of the study: the experiment is new, enjoyable, both experiment and interviews were carried out in a short duration.

The corpus of participants up till now studied is very heterogeneous: age, social and cultural background, previous uses of technologies, representations and experience of aging…

The age of the participants (60 up to 90 years) does not seem to have any influence on the results: there is –in the ongoing results– no specificity in the use of the ICT's according to the age. These criteria are to be taken into account because the ongoing results do not always reflect this heterogeneity: the further experiments will allow a more accurate analysis.

7　Conclusion

This paper proposes a new methodological approach for a better understanding of the needs of the elderly and the use of technologies in an ambient digital environment –in a living lab– based on the implementation of a multidimensional observation tool. This method interconnects a qualitative regard with quantitative data.

The ongoing results lead to a new question, related to the stability of the preferences, in terms of ICT modalities, in the long term.

This remark, linked with the heterogeneous characteristics of the elderly, enables to anticipate a further difficulty to qualify different profiles of users or ideal-types of inhabitants or modes of connected settlements.

The study aims a better understanding of the potential uses of ambient technologies by the elderly. The next step is to carry on the experiments with about one hundred more people, in order to sharpen the previous observations and to interpret these results according to the social, cultural and health profiles of the elderly.

The multimodal way of using ICT's appears as essential for a complete consideration of the different representations, needs, uses of the elderly, as well as for an optimized acceptability and accessibility of these technologies. Also, other interaction modes could be tested, such as gesture or partial body movement, which are more natural interactions.

Acknowledgments. This work is partially funded by the MSH-T of Toulouse and AG2R La Mondiale Insurance group.

References

1. Chappell, N.L., Cooke, H.A.: Age related disabilities - aging and quality of life. In: Stone, JH, Blouin, M (eds.) International Encyclopedia of Rehabilitation (2010). http://cirrie.buffalo.edu/encyclopedia/en/article/189/
2. Sun, H., De Florio, V., Gui, N., Blondia, C.: The missing ones: key ingredients towards effective ambient assisted living sytems. J. Ambient Intell. Smart Environ. Arch. **2**(2), 109–120 (2010)
3. Coughlan, T., Mackley, K.L., Brown, M., Martindale, S., Schlögl, S., Mallaband, B., et al.: Current issues and future directions in methods for studying technology in the home. PsychNology J. **11**(2), 159–184 (2013)
4. Bierhoff, I., van Berlo, A., Abascal, J. et al.: Chapter 3. Smart home environment. Towards an inclusive future: impact and wider potential of information and communication technologies. In: Roe, P.R.W. (ed.), pp.110–156 (2007)
5. Coughlin, J., D'Ambrosio, L., Reimer, B., Pratt, M.: Older adult perceptions of smart home technologies: implications for research, policy & market innovations in healthcare. Engineering in Medicine and Biology Society. In: 29th Annual International Conference of the IEEE, EMBS 2007, pp. 1810–1815 (2007)
6. Curry, R., Trejo-Tinoco, M., Wardle, D.: The Use of Information and Communication Technology to Support Independent Living for Older and Disabled People. Department of Health, London (2003)

7. Schlögl, S., Chollet, G., Garschall, Tscheligi, M.M., Legouverneur, G.: Exploring voice user interfaces for seniors. In: 6th Conference on Pervasive Technologies Related To Assistive Environments, Rhodes Greece (2013)

8. Vacher, M., Portet, F., Rossato, S., Aman, F., Golanski, F., Dugheanu, R.: Speech-based interaction in an AAL-context. Gerontechnology 11(2), 310–316 (2012)

9. Findlater, L., Froehlich, J.; Fattal, K., Wobbrock, J. O.; Dastyar, T.: Age - related differences in performance with touchscreens compared to traditional mouse input. In: CHI 2013, pp. 1–4 (2013) ISBN 9781450318990, S

10. Zhou, J., Rau, P.-L.P., Salvendy, G.: Use and Design of Handheld Computers for Older Adults: A Review and Appraisal. Int. J. Hum.-Comput. Interact. 28(12), 799–826 (2012)

11. Vigouroux, N., Rumeau, P., Boudet, B., Vella, F., Salvodelli, M.: Wellfar-e-link®: true life lab testing of a homecare communication tool. Non-pharmacological therapies in dementia, Nova science publishers 3(2), 133–142 (2015)

12. Olivier de Sardan, J.-P.: Epistemology, Fieldwork, and Anthropology. Palgrave MacMillan, New York (2015)

13. Goffman, E.: The interaction order. Am. Sociol. Rev. 48, 1–17 (1983)

14. Corbin, J., Strauss, A.L.: Basics of Qualitative Research: Techniques and Procedures for developing Grounded Theory, 4th edn. San Jose State University, Sage (2015)

15. Campo, E., Daran, X., Redon, L.: Une maison intelligente au carrefour des sciences technologiques et des sciences humaines. In: 2nd International Conference sur l'accessibilité et les systèmes de suppléance aux personnes en situation de handicap; Paris, France, pp. 33–42 (2011)

16. Le Guilly, T., Olsen, P., Ravn, A.P., Rosenkilde, J.B., Skou, A.: HomePort: middleware for heterogeneous home automation networks. In: 2013 IEEE International Conference on Pervasive Computing and Communications Workshops (PERCOM Workshops), pp. 627–633 (2013)

17. Jin, Z.X., Plocher, T., Kiff, L.: Touch screen user interfaces for older adults: button size and spacing. In: Stephanidis, C. (ed.) HCI 2007. LNCS, vol. 4554, pp. 933–941. Springer, Heidelberg (2007)

18. Pearson, K.: On the criterion that a given system of deviations from the probable in the case of a correlated system of variables is such that it can be reasonably supposed to have arisen from random sampling. Philos. Mag. Series 5 50(302), 157–175 (1990)

Wearable Sensors and Continuous Health Monitoring

Research on Continuous Vital Signs Monitoring Based on WBAN

Lina Yu, Liqun Guo, Huanfang Deng, Kequan Lin, Limin Yu,
Wanlin Gao$^{(\boxtimes)}$, and Iftikhar Ahmed Saeed

Key Laboratory of Modern Precision Agriculture System Integration Research,
Ministry of Education, China Agricultural University, No. 17 Qinghua East
Road, Haidian District, Beijing 100083, People's Republic of China
{linda-3740,dengfang0831,Linkequan,yulimin1978,
cau_szmtyjs}@163.com, guoliqun@cau.edu.cn,
2690684625@qq.com

Abstract. Vital signs are the indicators which evaluate the existence of health status and life quality. Hospitals may provide medical services for acute and chronic diseases and injuries. However, continuous monitoring and long-term treatment becomes difficult in such type diseases. In this paper, continuous vital signs monitoring system (CVSMS) based on wireless body area network (WBAN) is designed. And the gathered data is transmitted to a mobile phone via Bluetooth and then transferred to a remote server and stored in the database. In this way, a variety of vital signs such as body temperature, pulse rate, blood pressure, and ECG information would be acquired. Through the analysis and assessment of CVSMS, the results showed that the measurements are accurate and it provides an effective method for continuous health monitoring.

Keywords: Wireless body area network · Vital signs · Continuous monitoring · Bluetooth

1 Introduction

China's aging society is drawing near, the elderly population of China is expected to reach 300 million by 2025 [1]. Patients with chronic diseases are also increasing day by day. According to statistics, the number of patients diagnosed at a younger age with chronic diseases had been more than 260 million by 2012 [2]. However, the diagnosis and treatment of hospital-centered model cannot accommodate the increasing health care needs, and community health care centered model will be the future direction of health care, including home and personal care [3]. Vital signs (temperature, blood pressure, pulse, ECG, etc.) are the assessment of existence and the index of quality life [4]. The Changes in said vital signs are often precursors of physical disease. Therefore, it is vitally important to obtain real-time information about the vital signs for the elderly and chronically ill [5]. WBAN (Wireless Body Area Network) combines medical sensor technology and wireless sensor network technology [6, 7]. The application of WBAN for real-time monitoring of human characteristic information could greatly improve the level of medical care [8–10].

© Springer International Publishing Switzerland 2016
C.K. Chang et al. (Eds.): ICOST 2016, LNCS 9677, pp. 371–382, 2016.
DOI: 10.1007/978-3-319-39601-9_33

In recent years, physiological monitoring systems have been widely studied and applied. Inchoate signs monitoring instruments are essentially bedside monitors. However, they have many limitations such as simple functions, non-continuous and low accuracy [11]. With the development of remote technology, modern monitoring system can collect and deal with the multiple physiological parameters of each part of human body using a wide variety of sensors [12, 13]. Monitoring system operation has become simpler and the results are also more accurate. Multi-parameter signs monitoring system mainly monitors ECG signal, which has been used by hospitals and the welfare institutions. And its main approach is based on regular checkups of individual. But this typical medical monitoring instrument has the characteristic of medical professional and operational difficulties, which don't allow the users do a full signs monitoring by themselves. On the contrary, family-oriented signs monitors can meet the above needs. But the prices of existing signs monitoring instruments are usually above $1000. Therefore, a continuous physiological parameters monitor with low cost and simple operation is significant for elderly guardianship and chronic care.

This paper aims to design a continuous vital signs monitoring system (CVSMS). Signs sensors are used for collecting the information of human body, such as temperature, blood pressure, pulse rate, blood oxygen saturation and heart rate.

2   Methods

CVSMS illustrated in Fig. 1 comprises of monitoring sensors, wireless transmission network and data servers. Human physiological parameter's data collected by WBAN is displayed on monitoring software screen in real time and transmitted to mobile phone via Bluetooth [14, 15], then uploaded to the remote database server (vital signs database) for further analysis [16].

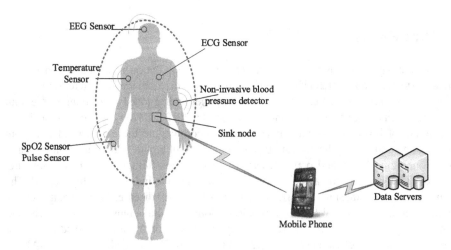

Fig. 1. The structure of CVSMS.

In order to meet the multi-parameter measurement requirements, a dedicated processor is required for data collection and processing. In this paper, we designed a treatment stratagem using symmetric multi-processing. The ATOM Z520 processor is capable of providing the human interaction. The master control chip uses C8051F005 for the data acquisition and processing of wide variety of body signs parameters. For the consistent and stable data transmission between the control module and the display module, the serial transmission approach was adopted. Resistive touch screen is selected which control the screen through the touch pen. Compared with conventional monitoring system, CVSMS is more advantageous and convenient for elderly people.

2.1 Overall Design

C8051F005 is used as the master chip of collecting part and Bluetooth module is adopted for data transmission process. The ATOM Z520 processor provides the human-machine interaction. The overall design of CVSMS is shown in Fig. 2.

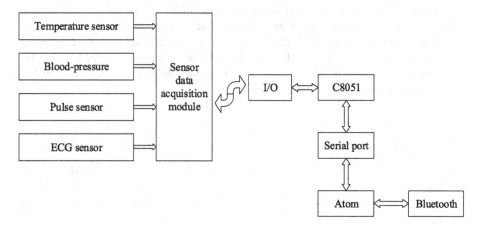

Fig. 2. The overall design of CVSMS.

Some parts of CVSMS have been integrated well on the development board, which need not to carry too much development, such as part of ATOM human-computer interaction and Bluetooth module. The master module used for data acquisition need circuit board design, plate making and commissioning.

2.2 CVSMS Hardware Design

(1) **Temperature Measurement Module.** The common sensor used for measuring the body temperature mainly consists of the following four types: thermistor, thermocouple, RTD (Resistance Temperature Detector) and IC temperature sensor. Considering the sensor cost, size, accuracy, stability, measurement range and the ease of use, the YSI-400 series thermistor sensor used for medical purposes is selected.

The AD of micro controller unit collects TEMP signal VT. According to the formula:

$$\frac{V_{cc}}{R_{10} + R_T} = \frac{V_T}{R_T} \tag{1}$$

$$R_T = \frac{V_T \times R_{10}}{V_{cc} - V_T} \tag{2}$$

R_T is the thermistor resistance. According to the thermistor's temperature-resistance curve, the current measured temperature can be received.

(2) **Blood Pressure Measurement Module.** In this study, we selected the FGN-605PGSR blood pressure sensor to collect the blood pressure signal. The principle of the sensor is based on double-ended differential voltage signal output due to resistance located in Wien bridge whose power supplied by a constant current source and changes with pressure. It measures the pressure in the range of −34.47 ∼ +34.47 kPa and accords with the requirement of blood pressure measurement. The schematic and block diagram of blood pressure measurement module are shown in Figs. 3 and 4 respectively. This module is composed of pressure sensor (FGN-605PGSR), constant flow source (LM324 × 1), differential amplifier (LM324 × 3), 0.8 Hz second-order high-pass filter (LM324 × 1), 200 times magnification (LM324 × 2), 38 Hz second order low-pass filter (LM324 1), blood pressure pulse trigger (LM311 × 1).

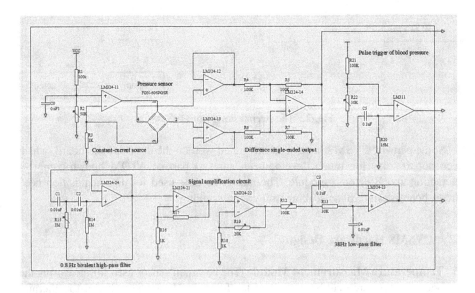

Fig. 3. The schematic of blood pressure measurement module.

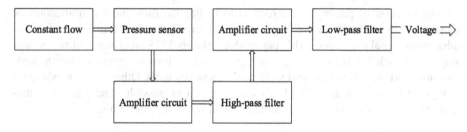

Fig. 4. The block diagram of blood pressure measurement module.

(3) **Blood Oxygen Measurement Module.** The block diagram of blood oxygen measurement module is shown in Fig. 5. A fingertip blood oxygen sensor is adopted. Two juxtaposed light emitting diodes are fixed on fingertip and emit red light whose wavelength is 660 nm and infrared light whose wavelength is 905 nm respectively. Lower wall is a photodiode. The measurements are carried out by turning red and infrared light that transmitted through the fingers into electrical signal. When blood oxygen module operates, two light-emitting diodes (LED) driven by time-sharing and circuit gives light respectively under more stringent duty cycles at regular intervals. Using the ratio of LEDs luminous intensity and the intensity of light received by photodiode, we can calculate whole blood absorption rate of 660 nm red light and 905 nm infrared light. Then the displayed oxygen values could be realized by calculating the ratio of the two wavelength light and referencing R curve.

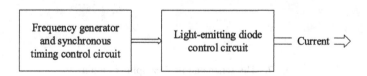

Fig. 5. The block diagram of blood oxygen measurement module.

(4) **ECG Measurement Module.** The block diagram of ECG measurement module is shown in Fig. 6. ECG acquisition module mainly encompasses electrode module, preamplifier circuit, band-pass filter circuit, main amplifier circuit and electrical level rising circuit. Electrode extracts the ECG signal, and after amplification, filtering, two amplifier, and electrical level rising, the treatment of A/D conversion and software filtering can be in progress. Then the correct data can be received.

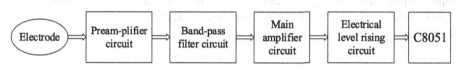

Fig. 6. The block diagram of ECG measurement module.

The function of preamplifier circuit is to realize the differential amplification of signals, which is crucial in the whole sampling circuit, because this is the basis for subsequent signal processing. This paper adopts the INA118 precision instrumentation amplifier, which has the advantages of high accuracy, low power consumption, high common-mode rejection ratio and wide work frequency band. Other circuit needs to be configured properly to play INA118's role as much as possible. The method of differential amplification ensures the high common mode rejection ratio.

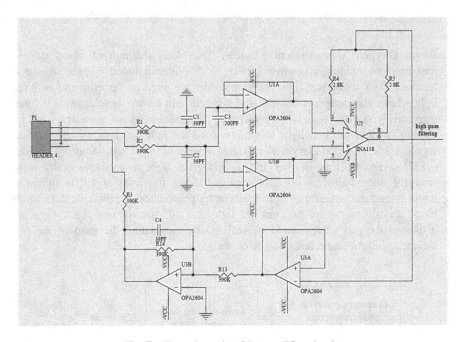

Fig. 7. The schematic of Preamplifier circuit.

The schematic of Preamplifier circuit is shown in Fig. 7. In the design of circuits, U1A and U1B make up emitter follower, which can stabilize input signal and improve the input impedance and common mode rejection ratio. U3, R13, R14 and C10 make up floating drive circuit, which can amplify the common mode signal, so as to inhibit the interference of 50 Hz frequency strongly.

The input level of A/D converter is 0 ∼ 3.3 V, so the ECG signal must be amplified 800 ∼ 1000 times. The preamplifier circuit magnifies about 10 times, so that the main amplifier circuit magnifies about 100 times so can meet the demand. This paper adopts/foster two stage amplification. The first stage magnifies 10 times and the second stage adjusts the best magnification, so as to receive the gain output that meet the needs.

2.3   CVSMS Software Design

CVSMS is designed to collect physiological parameters data including temperature, blood pressure, blood oxygen and its waveform, and ECG through the serial port, and display the received data in real time. It acquires two critical features i.e. setting module and Monitoring module. Setting module addresses configuration of the serial port, ECG filter mode, inflatable blood pressure values, and the associated calibration values. Monitoring module initializes the serial port, sends the appropriate testing instructions (temperature, blood pressure, blood oxygen and ECG detection instruction), receives, interprets data and displays in real time. The system's overall frame diagram is shown in Fig. 8.

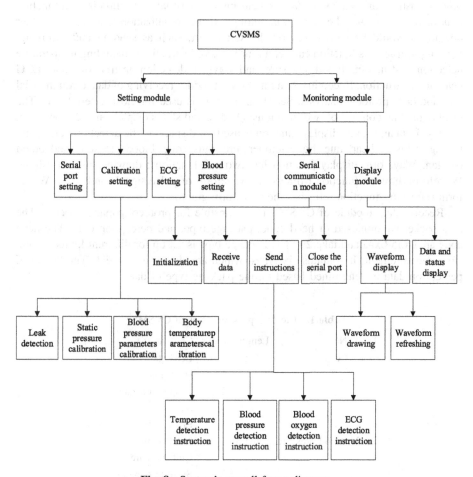

Fig. 8. System's overall frame diagram.

The setting module has four main functions: serial port setting, ECG setting, blood pressure setting and calibration setting. Serial port settings function is used for setting the serial port number, baud rate, parity data bits and stop bits. ECG setting function depicts the ECG filtering mode and ECG gain. Blood pressure setting function configures the blood pressure measurement mode (including adult mode, child mode, neonatal mode), and pre-inflation pressure value. Calibration settings include leak detection, static pressure calibration, blood pressure and body temperature calibration. The leak detection function is used for setting the pre-charge pressure value. Static pressure calibration function is used for setting the cuff pressure. Blood pressure parameters calibration function is used for setting the pressure deviation according to the measured pressure. Temperature parameters calibration function is used for setting the temperature deviation according to the measured temperature.

The monitoring module consists of two sub-modules including serial communication module and display module. Serial communication modules includes initializing, sending instructions, receiving data and closing of the serial port. Initialization function is used for initializing the serial port settings. If the initialization is successful, other operations would be carried out on the serial port, such as sending and receiving. Sending instructions function can send four types of instructions, including temperature detection instruction, blood pressure and oxygen detection instruction, and ECG detection instruction. Receiving data function is used for receiving of data through serial port and does protocol analysis. Serial off function is used for closing serial port. The display module consists of two functions: (1) data and status display and (2) waveform display. Data and status display function is used for displaying the detection values and testing status of heart rate, body temperature, pulse rate, blood pressure, and blood oxygen. Waveform display function has two sub-functions: drawing and refreshing. Waveform drawing function r draws the waveform of pulse signals and ECG. Waveform refreshing function refreshes the waveform graph.

Receive data module of CVSMS is responsible for protocol parsing process. The data packet is composed of head code, package type, and perception data. The head code are 0x55 0xaa and take 2 bytes. Package type is set up for different kinds of vital signs measurement. It contains six types, which are shown in Table 1. The length of perception data is determined based on the package type of data.

Table 1. The data package types of CVSMS

Type	Name	Length	Index	Content
0x01	ECG	5 bytes	0	ECG status
			1	Heart rate
			2	Respiration rate
			3	ST
			4	Error code
0x02	Blood pressure	5 bytes	0	NIBP status
			1	Cuff pressure
			2	Systolic pressure
			3	Mean pressure
			4	Diastolic pressure

(*Continued*)

Table 1. (*Continued*)

Type	Name	Length	Index	Content
0x03	SpO$_2$	3 bytes	0	SPO$_2$ status
			1	SPO$_2$
			2	Pulse rate
0x04	Temperature	3 bytes	0	Temperature status
			1	Temp1
			2	Temp2
0x05	ECG wave	8 bytes	0	ECG Wave1
			1	ECG Wave2
			2	ECG Wave3
			3	ECG Wave4
			4	ECG Wave5
			5	ECG Wave6
			6	ECG Wave7
			7	ECG Wave8
0x06	SpO$_2$ wave	1 bytes	0	SPO$_2$ Wave

3   Result

According to observations, compared with traditional instruments, we made a long time signs monitoring for a various samples. One of the samples observation result from 8:00 to 22:00 is shown in Tables 2 and 3. The records indicated that the CVSMS and traditional instruments groups showed no statistical significance (p > 0.05) in vital signs data measurement.

Table 2. The results of vital signs data measurement by CVSMS and traditional instruments. Temp: Temperature; SBP: Systolic blood pressure; DBP: Diastolic blood pressure; PR: Pulse rate; SpO$_2$: Blood oxygen saturation; A: CVSMS measurement; B: Traditional instruments measurement

No.	Time	Temp(°C)		SBP (mmHg)		DBP (mmHg)		PR(bpm)		SpO$_2$(%)	
		A	B	A	B	A	B	A	B	A	B
1	8:00	36.5	36.5	136	135	90	90	76	75	98	98
2	9:00	36.5	36.5	135	130	90	90	75	74	97	98
3	10:00	36.5	36.5	130	130	85	85	74	75	97	98
4	11:00	36.5	36.5	128	125	84	85	75	75	98	97
5	12:00	36.5	36.6	125	125	83	85	78	77	99	98
6	13:00	36.7	36.6	122	120	84	85	78	78	99	98
7	14:00	36.7	36.7	120	120	85	85	77	77	98	98
8	15:00	36.7	36.7	120	120	85	85	78	77	98	97

(*Continued*)

Table 2. (*Continued*)

No.	Time	Temp(°C)		SBP (mmHg)		DBP (mmHg)		PR(bpm)		SpO$_2$(%)	
		A	B	A	B	A	B	A	B	A	B
9	16:00	36.8	36.8	123	125	85	85	77	75	97	97
10	17:00	36.8	36.8	134	135	89	90	77	75	98	98
11	18:00	36.7	36.6	122	120	84	85	75	75	99	98
12	19:00	36.5	36.6	118	115	85	85	74	75	99	98
13	20:00	36.5	36.5	115	115	85	85	76	75	98	98
14	21:00	36.5	36.5	112	110	82	80	75	76	98	98
15	22:00	36.5	36.5	110	110	79	80	75	75	98	98

Table 3. Group statistics of data measured by the CVSMS and traditional instruments. Temp: Temperature; SBP: Systolic blood pressure; DBP: Diastolic blood pressure; PR: Pulse rate; SpO$_2$: Blood oxygen saturation; A: CVSMS measurement; B: Traditional instruments measurement

	Group	N	Mean	Std. Deviation	Std. Error Mean
Temp	A	15	36.5933	0.12228	0.03157
	B	15	36.5933	0.10998	0.02840
SBP	A	15	123.3333	8.05930	2.08090
	B	15	122.3333	7.98809	2.06252
DBP	A	15	85.0000	2.90320	0.74960
	B	15	85.3333	2.96808	0.76636
PR	A	15	76.0000	1.41421	0.36515
	B	15	75.6000	1.12122	0.28950
SpO$_2$	A	15	98.0667	0.70373	0.18170
	B	15	97.8000	0.41404	0.10690

4 Discussion

WBAN technology for vital signs monitoring is promising to alter the traditional chronic monitoring routine, especially for family care. However, the designing of non-invasive body-worn sensors system is a challenging work, often requiring a broad insight into the nature of the disease and its effect on physiological parameters. Although there are sensors available for vital signs monitoring, there is still a need for improvement to achieve continuous monitoring of these parameters. The main constraints for systems such as our CVSMS design are low power requirements, security and reliability.

In order to achieve continuous and unobtrusive monitoring, implementation of wireless modules is vital. This paper, using Bluetooth technology, designs communication circuit module to achieve short distance wireless. Integration of wireless modules to CVSMS not only provides support for patients' mobility, but also has the potential to change the conventional healthcare service to real-time feedback communication. The benefits of employing multi-parameter monitoring systems for the prevention, prediction and management of diseases are myriad. CVSMS with multiple sensors are capable of providing an extensive database of the patient's medical history. It will be more reliable and useful, compared to single-parameter monitoring devices.

5 Conclusion

From a practical standpoint, this paper analyzed the current demands and developed a CVSMS solution for the continuous monitoring of vital signs, and described the design of each function module. After the implementation of hardware platform, the data frame format of command and transport were developed. On the above basis, according to the need of continuous monitoring, the overall function design of CVSMS was accomplished. Finally, after assessment, the results showed that CVSMS and traditional instruments groups showed no statistical significance ($P > 0.05$) in vital signs data measurement.

Acknowledgments. This work was supported by Chinese Universities Scientific Fund (Grant #: 2016XD002) and National Key Technology R&D Program of China (Grant #: 2012BAJ18B07).

References

1. Li, J.: The report of national people's congress standing committee law enforcement inspection team on inspecting the implementation of "the people's republic of China guarantee law of the senior citizens' rights and interests". Gaz. Standing Committee Nat. People's Congr. People's Repub. China **6**, 612–618 (2011)
2. The number of chronic diseases in China has over 260 million, incidence increases and shows younger trend. People's Daily. http://www.chinanews.com/jk/2012/01-05/3582573.shtml
3. Zhu, M., Jia, Q.: The analysis of demand for long term care and its insurance system constructing in China. Chin. J. Health Policy **2**, 32–38 (2009)
4. Evans, D., Hodgkinson, B., Berry, J.: Vital signs in hospital patients a systematic review. Int. J. Nurs. Stud. **38**, 643–650 (2001)
5. Xuan, Y., Zhao, Z., Fang, Z., et al.: A wireless body sensor network for the elderly health monitoring. J. Comput. Res. Dev. **2**, 355–359 (2011)
6. Alghamdi, B., Fouchal, H.: A mobile wireless body area network platform. J. Comput. Sci. **5**, 664–674 (2014)
7. Ullah, S., Khan, P., Ullah, N., Saleem, S., Higgins, H., Kwak, K.S.: A review of wireless body area networks for medical applications. Int. J. Commun. Netw. Syst. Sci. **2**, 797–803 (2009)
8. Yilmaz, T., Foster, R., Hao, Y.: Detecting vital signs with wearable wireless sensors. Sensors **10**, 10837–10862 (2010)
9. Latre, B., Braem, B., Moerman, I., et al.: A survey on wireless body area networks. Wireless Netw. **17**, 1–18 (2011)

10. Lou, D.D., Chen, X.X., Zhao, Z., Xuan, Y.D., Xu, Z.H., Jin, H., Guo, X.Z., Fang, Z.: A wireless health monitoring system based on android operating system. In: 2013 International Conference on Electronic Engineering and Computer Science (EECS 2013), vol. 4, pp. 208–215 (2013)
11. Xia, L., Xia, L., Zhang, Y., et al.: Basic feature and application of multi- parameter monitor. Inf. Med. Equip. **22**, 56–58 (2007)
12. Tang, W., Huang, X., Yang, C.: The development and future of multi- parameter monitor. Beijing Biomed. Eng. **1**, 72–74 (2003)
13. Mok, W.Q., Wang, W.R., Liaw, S.Y.: Vital signs monitoring to detect patient deterioration: An integrative literature review. Int. J. Nurs. Pract. **21**, 91–98 (2015)
14. Challoo, R., Oladeinde, A., Yilmazer, N., Ozcelik, S., Challoo, L.: An overview and assessment of wireless technologies and co-existence of zigbee, bluetooth and wi-fi devices. Procedia Comput. Sci. **12**, 386–391 (2012)
15. Laine, T.H., Lee C., Suk H.: Mobile gateway for ubiquitous health care system using zigbee and bluetooth. In: Proceedings of the 2014 Eighth International Conference on Innovative Mobile and Internet Services in Ubiquitous Computing (IMIS), pp. 139–145 (2014)
16. Su, Y., Gao, W., Yu, L., Hu, H., Luo, X.: Wireless Body Area Network data storage method based on HBase. Appl. Mech. Mater. **427–429**, 2273–2277 (2013)

A Wearable Sensor for AAL-Based Continuous Monitoring

Valentina Bianchi, Claudio Guerra, Ilaria De Munari, and Paolo Ciampolini[✉]

Dipartimento di Ingegneria dell'Informazione, Università degli Studi di Parma,
Viale delle Scienze 181/a, 43124 Parma, Italy
{valentina.bianchi,ilaria.demunari,paolo.ciampolini}@unipr.it,
claudio.guerra@studenti.unipr.it

Abstract. Continuous monitoring of safety and health conditions are among the primary goals of Ambient Assisted Living technologies. Effective solutions, aimed at fostering independent life of elderly persons, need for carefully balancing system intrusiveness, perspicacity, reliability and cost features. Heterogeneous networks, including different combination of environmental and personal (wearable) sensors can be used, with relevant value coming from data fusion: analysis techniques, aiming at inferring safety and health-related information in an indirect fashion from behavioral features are being deeply investigated with this aim. Device cooperation and interoperability are thus key factors: in this paper, the development of a wearable sensor suitable for broad range AAL application is introduced, addressing features specifically oriented to behavioral analysis. First, the device itself is capable of analyzing different features of the user motion patterns, synthesizing high-level information (simple task identification, energy expenditure) on board. This result in better battery management (less data transferred over the radio link) and interoperability (thanks to data abstraction). Second, by means of a suitable operating protocol, it cooperates with environmental sensors (e.g., a toilet sensor) providing the latters with user identification information, and thus allowing to exploit related data even in a multi-user context. This avoid the need of more expensive and complex indoor localization techniques or of more intrusive identification technologies (e.g., NFC/RFID tags).

Keywords: Ambient Assisted Living · Wearable sensors · Sensor networking · Behavioral analysis

1 Introduction

The Ambient Assisted Living (AAL) paradigm exploits innovative ICT technologies to foster independent life of elderly people in their preferred living environment, by providing more safety, by compensating motor or sensing impairments, by promoting social inclusion and participation [1]. AAL encompasses a wide range of enabling technologies, among which smart sensors play a key role. As AAL technology progressed, in fact, its focus shifted from mere safety and automation functionalities to smarter services, involving a wider range of heterogeneous devices and relying on intelligent interpretation of sensor data [2].

© Springer International Publishing Switzerland 2016
C.K. Chang et al. (Eds.): ICOST 2016, LNCS 9677, pp. 383–394, 2016.
DOI: 10.1007/978-3-319-39601-9_34

Accessibility and acceptability of such technology is of paramount importance, besides actual technical performance: minimizing intrusiveness and impact on daily living habits is needed to make the approach effective and sustainable. More specifically, a sensible balance between the additional user burden involved by the adoption of a new technology and the subjective perception of benefits needs to be taken into account.

A meaningful example of such statement comes from telemedicine domain. Remote monitoring of health condition is indeed a key to "ageing in place" policies [3]. This may rely on clinical sensors, suitable for self-checking of relevant health parameters and enabled for network connectivity. Such techniques have shown promising effectiveness: in [4], for instance, a study involving cohorts of patients suffering from congestive heart failure disease (CHF) shown a much better six-months survival probability (80 % vs 60 %) for patients exploiting telemedicine facilities, with respect to the control group receiving conventional cure.

However, such techniques suffer from some inherent limitations: clinical devices can be expensive, and necessarily require some skill and awareness to the end-user. This, together with boredom and carelessness, may result in poor compliance with required check routines, thus jeopardizing the effectiveness of the approach. Moreover, dimensionality of the telemedicine approach is necessarily limited, due to limited availability of inexpensive devices suitable for self-managed measures. Thus, while telemedicine is appropriate indeed for the management of a specific medical condition, it is less suitable for a broader prevention and early diagnosis scenario. Within the AAL scenario, a more comprehensive insight of user health condition can be gained in an indirect way, exploiting information coming from a wider set of sources, including simple environmental sensors, as well as wearable devices. Behavioral profiles can be built upon such data and searched for health-relevant events, anomalies and trends [5].

Within the "HELICOPTER" project (funded by the EU in the framework of the AAL-JP programme [6]), such an approach is exploited in a hierarchical fashion, accounting for both the direct (i.e., based on clinical sensors) and indirect (i.e., based on non-clinical ones) schemes in a coordinated approach. In this paper, Sect. 2 below introduces the overall HELICOPTER approach, while some specific features of the sensing infrastructure are described in deeper details in Sect. 3. We focus, in particular, on the central role the wearable sensor MuSA plays in the data fusion and interpretation strategy. Some preliminary results coming from living-lab tests are also shown. Conclusions are eventually drawn in Sect. 4.

2   The HELICOPTER Concept

The HELICOPTER (*HEalthyLIfe support through COmPrehensive Tracking of individual and Environmental Behaviors*) project aims at implementing behavioral monitoring features, suitable for supporting the early diagnosis of several common age-related diseases. It is based on a holistic vision, merging clinical, wearable and environmental sensors within the same interoperable network. The actual sensor list is given in Table 1:

Table 1. Sensor list in the HELICOPTER framework.

Environmental	Wearable	Clinical
Room presence	Alarm button	Body Weight
Door/drawer	*Fall*[a]	Blood Pressure
Fridge sensor	Identification	Pulse oxymeter
Hob sensor[a]	Energy expenditure	Glucometer
Bed occupancy		*Portable ECG*[a]
Chair occupancy		
Toilet usage		
Electric Power[a]		

[a] Sensors available, but not exploited in current pilots

Interaction of the user with sensors occurs in different modes: environmental sensors do not need to be intentionally operated by the user. Wearable sensors require more awareness (remembering to wear, battery check,...) but still no direct operation. Clinical sensors provide most accurate measurements, at the expense of some further operating burden. On the other hand, environmental sensors are suitable for continuous monitoring, wearable ones provide data only when worn, and clinical sensors provide figures when operated (usually at given intervals, depending on the prescription and on the adherence to it).

Therefore, as illustrated by Fig. 1, environmental, wearable and clinical devices exhibit different tradeoffs among data accuracy and continuity, intrusiveness and ease of use (of course, further options exist, with clinical sensors suitable for continuous monitoring; such devices, however, are usually meant for dealing with medical conditions and are scarcely suitable in a low-cost, low-intrusiveness prevention scenario). Given such complementary features, a suitable data fusion strategy may help in attaining better overall performance.

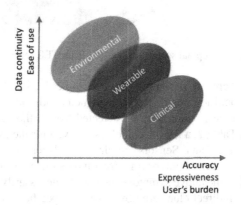

Fig. 1. Sensors hierarchy in the HELICOPTER framework

The monitoring strategy is based on the layered view given in Fig. 2. The user interacts, throughout his day, with environmental sensors scattered into the home and with a tiny device worn on his belt (described below). Data coming from such sensors are fed to a behavioral model, which hunts for patterns, anomalies and trends which may be consistent with the onset of a given diseases. If some sign emerges from such indirect inference, the user is addressed to more accurate monitoring, based on clinical measurements. Outcome of suggested (or periodic) clinical checks enter the model as well, providing a more comprehensive and coherent view: should the overall vision confirm the "diagnostic suspicion", the system issue proper feedbacks to the user and alerts the care system. The caregiver or the GP is then allowed to review the sensor "symptoms" and to assess the situation, providing for appropriate actions. I.e., the HELICOPTER system is not meant for "automatic" diagnosis of diseases, but instead for providing continuous attention to possible indicators requiring medical attention. In this sense, it can be regarded as a tool for an elementary "automatic triage", which possibly yield a "double-win" result: the user peace of mind can be fostered by the awareness of a system watching over the user himself in a non-intrusive way, whereas the care system may take advantage of the preliminary screening, which could reduce unnecessary demand for clinical intervention.

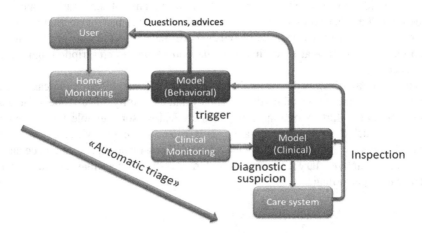

Fig. 2. Conceptual scheme of the HELICOPTER service view

To clarify the concept, we may refer to an example: let's consider the congestive heart failure (CHF) condition mentioned above. Such condition, indeed, may result in several "behavioral" clues, which may be detected trough the sensing infrastructure introduced above. In Table 2, a list of such clues is given for the example at hand, and correlated to sensing elements. Sensors are classified depending on whether a direct clinical measurement is carried out, or if indirect indicators are provided.

Of course, not all of the above symptoms need to be necessarily present to diagnose a CHF episode; also, indirect clues are obviously nonspecific, and may be caused by many other conditions. So, there is no deterministic correlation between a given set of symptoms and the CHF diagnose; a probabilistic approach is to be pursued instead, assessing the likeliness of such condition, based on available clues. To estimate such

Table 2. Sensor clues (Heart failure example)

Clue	Sensors	
Feeling tired, lack of energy	Wearable, measuring cumulative quantity and intensity of motion Bed and chair occupancy TV usage	Indirect
Sleep difficulties, due to bad breathing	Bed and chair occupancy Room presence TV usage	
Lack of appetite	Fridge sensor Cupboard sensor Room presence (kitchen)	
Increased urination frequency, especially at night	Toilet sensor Bed sensor	
Confusion, memory issues	Wearable Room presence Bed and chair occupancy Appliance usage	
Irregular heartbeat	Blood pressure monitor Pulsoxymeter	Direct
Bodyweight increase	Bodyweight scale	
Blood oxygen concentration decrease	Pulsoxymeter	

probability, we exploit a Bayesian Belief Network (BBN) approach, modeled upon clinical knowledge, and trained on the specific user activity profile.

The model first evaluates the probability based on the indirect sensor set only; should the estimated probability become significant, the clinical (direct) sensors are taken into account: the user is addressed to a clinical self-check. Clinical sensor measures re-enter the model, and a more precise assessment of the probability is carried out. If the probability exceeds a given threshold, the "diagnostic suspicion" is issues, and professional caregivers are involved.

Similar to the CHF example, a set of 8 models is being defined, including: hyper- and hypoglycemia, reduced physical activity, cystitis, depression, prostatic hypertrophy, bladder prolapse. Extensive discussion of such models goes beyond the scope of this paper, and will be presented elsewhere. Here we shall focus on some specific features

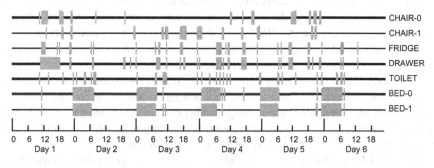

Fig. 3. Sample of environmental sensor data, coming from a pilot home. Gray ticks indicate "active" status of sensors

we have implemented into a wearable sensor to make its cooperation with the HELI-COPTER environment more effective.

The HELICOPTER system has been deployed at homes of about 50 users, and is been tested in such a living-lab environment. Pilots started at the beginning of 2016, and results are expected within a few months. In Fig. 3, a sample of environmental sensor data coming from an actual pilot site is shown.

3 Wearable Sensor and AAL

The overall HELICOPTER networking infrastructure is based on heterogeneous wireless communication standards: environmental and wearable sensors exploits the IEEE 802.15.4/ZigBee standard, while clinical devices are compliant with IEEE 802.15.1/ Bluetooth protocol. A common gateway aggregates data coming from both domains and takes care of network supervision, data logging, and forwarding information through the Internet to relevant stakeholders. The end-user interacts with the system (getting feedbacks, advices, requests) by means of an app running on an Android tablet.

User data are collected over the cloud at a service center, which runs the BBN software models and infers "diagnostic suspicions".

Although the service concept is almost straightforward, a number of implementation issues need to be taken into account to make it viable and effective.

3.1 Sensor Data Tagging

For instance, the concept relies on the exploitation of data coming from sensors deployed in the living environment to track meaningful habits and build behavioral profiles. If more than a single person lives in the house, we therefore need to "tag" sensor informations, distinguishing the actual user interacting with the sensor. Since sensors are placed at known locations, this can be done by tracking the user position within the environment. A number of different techniques [7] can be applied to the indoor localization task: most of them, however, does not comply with the cost and intrusiveness constraints which need to be matched here. Artificial vision methods [8] imply the use of cameras, which are not well received in the home familiar environment; radiolocation methods [9, 10] (based on multilateration and exploiting time-of-flight or signal strength information) usually rely on the accurate calibration of the radio network ("finger-printing") which makes the installation in a dynamic living environment not practical. Methods based on NFC/RFID devices [11] require dedicated technologies and imply the user cooperation in "check-in" operations.

On the other hand, the purpose here is just to "tag" sensor data, i.e., to associate a sensor-detected activity to a specific user, so that a geographically accurate positioning is not needed. Moreover, since the envisaged data processing is based on a probabilistic approach, some "noise" (i.e., misinterpreted tags) is likely to be tolerable, and we may hence content ourselves with less expensive/intrusive approaches.

In the HELICOPTER approach, we start from the assumption that the monitored users wear a wearable device, which records their physical activity and inherently carries identification information. In this project we use a wearable device called "MuSA" (Multi Sensor Assistant, [12]) exploits the same ZigBee radio communication protocol adopted by environmental sensors and may therefore exchange messages with each of them over the radio link. While communicating in a single-hop mode, the Received Signal Strength Index (RSSI) can be extracted and correlated [13] to the spatial distance d between transceivers (i.e., the wearable device and the environmental sensor):

$$d = k * 10^{-RSSI}$$

where k is a constant involving signal propagation features, related to the actual signal path. If we assume that k does is uniform enough in the region of interest (i.e., the space close to the environmental sensor), RSSI can be considered as an inverse distance indicator. In practice, whenever an environmental sensor (a chair occupancy sensor, for instance) is activated, a simple polling protocol is implemented: the sensor itself exchanges a message with all known wearable devices (i.e., pertaining to different monitored people) and assign the action tag to the closest one (i.e., the one featuring the higher RSSI). A threshold is introduced: if the RSSI does not exceeds a given value, the wearer of the mobile node is assumed to be too far from the actual sensor for being responsible of the sensor activation. This allows for discriminating actions taken by "third" persons (family members, guests) not wearing a wearable device.

The accuracy of such an approach, of course, is limited by uncertainties and irregularities along electromagnetic waves propagation path; nevertheless, it is more than adequate to the aimed purpose: tests carried out in a simulated environment exhibited satisfactory discrimination features in all cases of practical interest [14].

It is worth to be emphasized that the procedure inherently exploits components already in place, so that the tagging procedure comes at no additional cost. Moreover, such a simple method is based on areal-time comparison, so that is virtually free of calibration procedures depending on the actual sensor placement and on the environment features. Consistently, installation and subsequent interventions for maintenance and upgrades does need to be concerned with this.

3.2 On-Board Activity Monitoring

Physical activity is a relevant component in many of the "Diagnostic Suspicion" models mentioned above. More generally speaking, monitoring quantity and quality of daily physical activity is meaningful to the overall behavioral picture and contributes to the assessment of health and wellbeing. In principle, some information about the user movement can be obtained in an indirect fashion too, by correlating environmental sensor outcomes. In many cases, passive infrared (PIR) presence sensors are exploited to this purpose [5]. Such approach, however, suffers from some inherent limitations: (*i*), PIR devices operating range is not compatible with activity tagging techniques based on proximity or localization, so, in the general case, detected activity cannot easily be ascribed to a specific user and, (*ii*), they return a binary information about the presence of someone moving in the observed field, but cannot provide any hint about the movement speed or intensity, which is instead quite relevant to health assessment purposes.

Hence such approaches, besides being minimally invasive, can provide only large-grain, average indicators. Much more detailed information can be obtained by exploiting wearable sensors: the MuSA device embeds an Inertial Measurement Unit (IMU), originally aimed at fall detection and consisting of integrated 3-axis accelerometer, 3-axis gyroscope and 3-axis magnetometer. The embedded IMU can provide a quite detailed picture of the user movement: from the nine degrees of freedom information, accurate assessment of motion features can be obtained by means of suitable processing algorithms. However, wearable devices need to cope with stringent power consumption constraint, to preserve battery lifetime. This limits the available resources, both in terms of computing power and memory, and of radio link usage. To extract accurate motion information, suitable for activity recognition, speed estimation, etc., relatively high IMU sampling rates are needed to fulfill the Nyquist-Shannon criterion. This rules out the possibility of streaming IMU data in real-time to an external processing units, since it would imply continuous transmission and thus jeopardize battery lifetime. Hence, basic processing need to be carried out on board, limiting activity of the radio link to the transfer of a much lower number of synthesized data. Such real-time processing needs to coexist with other tasks the MuSA device is in charge of (fall detection, management of the tagging procedure described in previous section, emergency button calls, etc.) and, therefore, its computational demand need to be minimized.

Although many physiology models [15] assume the walking speed as a meaningful health indicator, inferring such a speed from IMU data is not a trivial task. In fact, velocity can be extracted by integrating acceleration data, projected along the walking average direction. The drift error inherently associated to numerical integration, together with the noise coming from motion components not directly related to the walk, require to introduce complex compensation mechanisms [16].

In the case at hand, however, we are not interested neither in absolute velocity estimation, nor in navigation path reconstruction, so integration over long time bases are not needed and we may refer to simpler approaches. In particular, in the formulation of BBN models, we adopt a differential scheme, according to which we just look for relative changes in the variables, instead of comparing them with fixed thresholds. On the one hand, this allows for minimizing the need of user-specific model calibration; on the other one, common-mode errors are inherently rejected, this in turn relaxing constraints on offset and drift errors. In a more general sense, since the model does not rely on the physical value of the variables, but only on its changes, we may safely select alternative variables, provided they follow a similar change pattern.

Hence we selected, as a meaningful indicator, the Energy Expenditure (EE, [17]), which is a popular choice for assessing the intensity of physical activity.

Among many methods to evaluate EE, the use of accelerometers has been often adopted, and many algorithms have been proposed [18]. In this work, we adopt the simple formulation suggested by Bouten in [19], which requires to integrate the acceleration vector components over a short time base.

The acceleration components (a_x, a_y, a_z) are sampled at a 60 Hz rate. Then a high-pass filter (Butterworth, 4th order) is applied, to eliminate frequency components at baseband. Acceleration components are then integrated over a time window of T_W length, and summed:

$$I_{A,tot} = \int_{T_W} a_x dt + \int_{T_W} a_y dt \int_{T_W} a_z dt$$

eventually yielding the following expression for the energy expenditure:

$$EE = k_1 + k_2 I_{A,tot}$$

where k_1 and k_2 are suitable constants.

The algorithm was encoded in the MUSA firmware, coexisting with fall detection and identification tasks, and was first tested in a lab environment. The test involved several subjects of different ages, who were invited to walk on a motorized treadmill. At 1 min intervals, the treadmill pace was increased by 1 km/h steps.

Test results are summarized in Fig. 4: tests were carried out with different subjects of different age classes. Replicable patterns were found, with differences among homogeneous class ages: for instance, at the 5–6 km/h transition, younger subject tended to start running, while middle-agers keep walking. Older subjects, instead, were unable to stand the transition 1–2 km/h, due to fatigue. In general, such indications were found to be suitable for entering the HELICOPTER BBN models, and the EE estimation algorithm was included in the pilot studies.

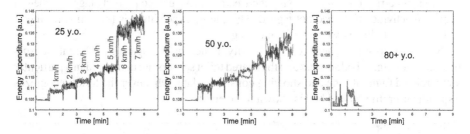

Fig. 4. MuSA on-board energy expenditure calculation.

3.3 Preliminary Pilot Results

By deploying the MUSA device at the pilot dwellings, we were able to test the two features introduced in previous subsections within a real living environment.

Results are summarized in Fig. 5: for the sake of readability, only a two days timeframe is shown. The test case refers to a house in which a couple of elderly persons live. Each person was given his own wearable sensor, while environmental sensors (except for the bed sensors) were common to both. The left diagram refers to the picture coming from the environmental sensors only, while the diagram on the right shows improvements obtained by introducing MUSA features. In particular, personal energy expenditures appear on the two lowermost rows, and environmental sensors outputs were tagged.

The color code is the following: green ticks refer to activity attributed to "user 0", while blue ticks stand for "user 1" actions. Red ticks instead, stand for actions not tagged (either because performed by a third person, or because the users didn't wear the MUSA device while acting). The overall picture is quite clear and sound: in the experiment, users wore the device during the night and the morning, while not wearing it in the afternoon. Consistently,

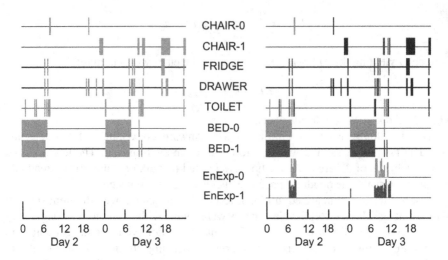

Fig. 5. MUSA introduced features. Left: environmental sensors only, Right: EE calculation, sensor data tagging.

all activities carried out while carrying the wearable device were properly tagged, whereas afternoon activities remained not tagged. The energy expenditure is low while resting in bed, and raises to higher values in the morning.

Some consistency check can be easily done, by comparing different sensors outcomes. In Fig. 6, bed sensors and the shared toilet sensors are compared in a particular view, related to night time and showing consistent data: whenever the toilet recognizes a specific user, the related bed is shown to be empty.

Fig. 6. Tag consistency checks among different sensors.

4   Conclusions

In this paper, we present the HELICOPTER system infrastructure, aimed at supporting an "automatic triage" service. The system relies on a heterogeneous set of devices, including environmental, wearable and clinical sensors, seamlessly connected in an open and interoperable framework.

Environmental sensors provide low-density, continuous information in a non-intrusive fashion, whereas clinical sensors are suitable for more deep and punctual health information, at the expense of more demanding user cooperation and awareness.

Sensor information is thus hierarchically organized, in order to optimize user experience and system perspicacity. All data converge in a data fusion and analytics scheme, aimed at early detection of common diseases. A probabilistic approach is exploited, which may provide a "diagnostic suspicion", to be eventually corroborated or rejected by health professionals.

In this paper, the specific role of the wearable sensor MUSA is discussed in supporting such a vision. First, it cooperates with environmental sensors for tagging detected actions with specific user labels, making the approach suitable for a multi-user context as well. Then, it processes dynamic data to estimate (on board) energy expenditure, to be fed to probabilistic models for the diagnostic suspicion inference.

The overall system infrastructure has been designed and implemented, and is currently being tested in a pilot study involving about 50 users. Preliminary results and lab tests are given, showing that a quite rich and consistent picture of the user behavior can be obtained in a minimally invasive fashion.

In the immediate future, as soon as user data needed for the probabilistic model training will be available, the whole system chain will be activated, involving end-users, their caregivers and health professionals in the service picture.

Acknowledgments. This work has been supported by the Ambient Assisted Living Joint Program (HELICOPTER project, AAL-2012-5-150). The authors acknowledge contribution of the project partners to the system conception and design.

References

1. Bianchi, V., Grossi, F., Matrella, G., De Munari, I., Ciampolini, P.: A wireless sensor platform for assistive technology applications. In: 11th EUROMICRO Conference on Digital System Design Architectures, Methods and Tools, pp. 809–816. IEEE Press (2008)
2. Losardo, A., Grossi, F., Matrella, G., De Munari, I., Ciampolini, P.: Getting out of the lab: a real-world AAL experience. Gerontechnology **13**(2), 256 (2014)
3. Losardo, A., Bianchi, V., Grossi, F., Matrella, G., De Munari, I., Ciampolini, P.: Web-enabled home assistive tools. Assistive Technol. Res. Ser. **29**, 448–455 (2011)
4. Pedone, C., Rossi, F.F., Cecere, A., Costanzo, L., AntonelliIncalzi, R.: Efficacy of a physician-led multiparametric telemonitoring system in very old adults with heart failure. J. Am. Geriatr. Soc. **63**(6), 1175–1180 (2015)
5. Losardo, A., Grossi, F., Matrella, G., DeMunari, I., Ciampolini, P.: Exploiting AAL environment for behavioral analysis. Assistive Technol. Res. Ser. **33**, 1121–1125 (2013)
6. Guerra, C., Bianchi, V., Grossi, F., Mora, N., Losardo, A., Matrella, G., De Munari, I., Ciampolini, P.: The HELICOPTER project: a heterogeneous sensor network suitable for behavioral monitoring. In: Cleland, I., et al. (eds.) IWAAL 2015. LNCS, vol. 9455, pp. 152–163. Springer, Heidelberg (2015). doi:10.1007/978-3-319-26410-3_15
7. Kundra, I., Ekler, P.: The summary of indoor navigation possibilities considering mobile environment. In: 3rd Eastern European Regional Conference on the Engineering of Computer Based Systems, pp. 165–166. IEEE Press (2013)

8. Yu, S., Mellon, C., Yang, Y., Hauptmann, A.: Harry Potter's marauder's map: localizing and tracking multiple persons-of-interest by nonnegative discretization. In: Computer Vision and Pattern Recognition, pp. 3714–3720. IEEE Press (2013)

9. Santinelli, G., Giglietti, R., Moschitta, A.: Self-calibrating indoor positioning system based on zigbee devices. In: IEEE Instrumentation and Measurement Technology Conference, pp. 1205–1210. IEEE Press (2009)

10. Guerra, C., Bianchi, V., De Munari, I., Ciampolini, P.: CARDEAGate: Low-cost, ZigBee-based localization and identification for AAL purposes. In: International Instrumentation and Measurement Technology Conference, vol. July 2015, pp. 245–249. IEEE Press (2015)

11. Shang, M., Shi, Y.: A scalable passive RFID-based multi-user indoor location system. In: Wireless Communications, Networking and Mobile Computing, pp. 1–4. IEEE Press (2011)

12. Bianchi, V., Grossi, F., De Munari, I., Ciampolini, P.: Multi sensor assistant: a multisensor wearable device for ambient assisted living. J. Med. Imaging Health Inform. 2(1), 70–75 (2012)

13. Parker, S.J., Hal, J., Kim, W.: Adaptive filtering for indoor localization using ZIGBEE RSSI and LQI measurement. Adapt. Filtering Appl. 14, 305–324 (2007)

14. Guerra, C., Bianchi, V., De Munari, I., Ciampolini, P.: Action tagging in a multi-user indoor environment for behavioural analysis purposes. In: Annual International Conference of the IEEE Engineering in Medicine and Biology Society, vol. November 2015, pp. 5036–5039. IEEE Press (2015)

15. Studenski, S., Perera, S., Patel, K., Rosano, C., Faulkner, K., Inzitari, M., Brach, J., Chandler, J., Cawthon, P., Connor, E.B., Nevitt, M., Visser, M., Kritchevsky, S., Badinelli, S., Harris, T., Newman, A.B., Cauley, J., Ferrucci, L., Guralnik, J.: Gait speed and survival in older adults. JAMA 305(1), 50–58 (2011). 2011 Jan 5

16. Yang, S., Li, Q.: Inertial sensor-based methods in walking speed estimation: a systematic review. Sensors 2012 12, 6102–6116 (2012)

17. Manini, T.M.: Energy expenditure and aging. Ageing Res. Rev. 9(1), 1–11 (2010)

18. Altini, M., Penders, J., Vullers, R., Amft, O.: Estimating energy expenditure using body-worn accelerometers: a comparison of methods, sensors number and positioning. IEEE J. Biomed. Health Inform. 19(1), 219–226 (2015)

19. Bouten, C.: Assessment of energy expenditure for physical activity using a triaxial accelerometer. Med. Sci. Sports Exerc. 26(12), 1516–1523 (1994)

The Study to Track Human Arm Kinematics Applying Solutions of Wahba's Problem upon Inertial/Magnetic Sensors

M. Sajeewani Karunarathne[✉], Nhan Dang Nguyen,
Medhani P. Menikidiwela, and Pubudu N. Pathirana

Deakin University, 75 Pigdons Road, Waurn Ponds, Geelong, VIC, Australia
skmaddum@deakin.edu.au

Abstract. Long-term, off-site human monitoring systems are emerging with respect to the skyrocketing expenditures engaged with rehabilitation therapies for neurological diseases. Inertial/magnetic sensor modules are well known as a worthy solution for this problem. Much attention and effort are being paid for minimizing drift problem of angular rates, yet the rest of kinematic measurements (earth's magnetic field and gravitational orientation) are only themselves capable enough to track movements applying the theory for solving historical Wahbas Problem. Further, these solutions give a closed form solution which makes it mostly suitable for real time Mo-Cap systems. This paper examines the feasibility of some typical solutions of Wahba's Problem named TRIAD method, Davenport's q method, Singular Value Decomposition method and QUEST algorithm upon current inertial/magnetic sensor measurements for tracking human arm movements. Further, the theoretical assertions are compared through controlled experiments with both simulated and actual accelerometer and magnetometer measurements.

Keywords: Wearable sensors · Arm activity monitoring · MEMS sensors · Wahba's problem and solutions

1 Introduction

The orientation estimation of a dynamic self-framed object, based on its observation vectors and corresponding global frame's observations, was initiated with minimising loss function proposed by Grace Wahba in 1965 [1,2]. Later, this problem was generally known as *Wahba's Problem* in applied mathematics [3]. Thereupon, the solutions for this problem have been improved and these solutions have been applied various applications including aerospace and ship navigation, bio-medical advancements and multi camera calibration in computer vision [4].

When we consider the theoretical insights of the Wahba's problem, importantly following three main factors should be satisfied to apply the solutions of Wahba's problem,

© Springer International Publishing Switzerland 2016
C.K. Chang et al. (Eds.): ICOST 2016, LNCS 9677, pp. 395–406, 2016.
DOI: 10.1007/978-3-319-39601-9_35

1. There should be a dynamic object with its own coordinate system, but moved in a global coordinate system
2. The orientation of the object respect to the global coordinate system is required to determine using the observation vectors
3. There should be static observation vectors which are common to both local and global coordinate system.

Under the Wahba's problem, the special orthogonal matrix for the corresponding rotation is found between two coordinate system from a set of weighted observation vectors [2,5]. The unit vectors measured in local body are noted as b_i and the corresponding vectors in reference body are noted as r_i. Here A and a_i are respectively the rotation matrix between two coordinate systems and the non negative weight.

$$L(A) \equiv \frac{1}{2} \sum_i a_i |b_i - Ar_i|^2 \tag{1}$$

When we consider the applicability of Wahba's problem for tracking human arm movements, we can state some similarities which satisfying the above three conditions. In other words, the inertial/magnetic sensor worn on human arm has different coordinate system respect to the earth frame. The inertial sensors self-contained with magnetometers are able to measure static vectors: earth gravity vector and magnetic field which are common in the earth frame too. Hence the Wahba's solutions can be applied in the scenario of tracking human arm movements [6].

The major benefit of applying these techniques is that usage of gyroscope readings can be avoided. The gyroscope readings are very accurate measurement in local frame, though the integration of gyroscope measurements to determine the movement angle in earth frame is caused deficiencies in inaccuracy due to drift [7]. Further the solutions of Wahba problem have closed form estimation which are efficient to compute [6,8].

The purpose of this paper is to give an overview of the most popular and most promising algorithms in solving Wahba's problem. Further, the feasibility of determining the human arm movements using historical solutions of Wahba's problem will be investigated. Under this study, four algorithms such as TRIAD Method, Daveport's q method, Singular Value Decomposition method and QUaternion ESTimator method, will be compared with simulated arm movements and real time data. This paper is structured as the next Sect. 2 discusses the historical approaches for Wahba's problem. The third section will be examined efficinecy and accuracy for the simulated arm movement behaviour with the four methods in our consideration. Then, the succeeding section will explore the applicability of discussed Wahba's solutions for real time human arm movement capturing experiments. The paper will be concluded with the discussion and future work in last section.

2   Historical Approaches of Wahba's Problem

First of all, we abbreviated reference frame coordinate system as RCS and local body coordinate system as LCS to enhance the clearness of explanations. As the Eq. 1, the Wahba's problem is basically a minimizing problem to determine least variance of orientation estimation between RCS ($r_i, i = 1, 2..n$) and LCS ($b_i, i = 1, 2..n$). Here, i from 1 to n is the number of different observation vectors. This theory is originally used for spacecraft's attitudes estimation where the observation vectors are unit vectors of a star or sun [9–11]. However, each potential solutions of Wahba's problem are attempted to minimise the loss function in the Eq. 1 [2]. Later, this equation is simplified as Eq. 2.

$$L(A) \equiv \lambda_0 - tr(AB^T) \tag{2}$$

where B is $\sum_{i=1}^{n} a_i b_i r_i^T$. It is obvious that the matrix B is maximised when the least error of estimation $L(A)$ is minimized. Each following approaches were attempted to find optimal solution based rotation matrix or quaternion presentation from the cost function in Eq. 2. In the following sections, these methods will be discussed in detail.

2.1   TRIAD Method

Among the number of solutions, the TRIAD method which is a preliminary approach, firstly applied to solve this problem [12]. The TRIAD method was introduced by Harold Back. He attempted to find optimal solution through cosine matrix of two common observation vectors from LCS and RCS. In this approach, the observation vectors in LCS (b_1 and b_2) and the corresponding observation vectors in RCS (r_1 and r_2) are normalized and the normalized cross product of each vectors were used to calculate optimal rotation matrix (A) as follows.

$$A = \left[\frac{R_1}{\|R_1\|}, \frac{R_1 \times R_2}{\|R_1 \times R_2\|}, \frac{R_1}{\|R_1\|} \times \frac{R_1 \times R_2}{\|R_1 \times R_2\|} \right] \left[\frac{r_1}{\|r_1\|}, \frac{r_1 \times r_2}{\|r_1 \times r_2\|}, \frac{r_1}{\|r_1\|} \times \frac{r_1 \times r_2}{\|r_1 \times r_2\|} \right]^T. \tag{3}$$

2.2   Singular Value Decomposition (SVD) Method

Later, SVD method was introduced to solve this problem [13,14]. The speciality of this method is that its outstanding performance with even noisy observation vectors [2,14]. Under this method, the U and V orthogonal value is determined using B matrix in Eq. 2. Then, the determinant of U and V are found which are $detU$ and $detV$. Later, the optimal rotation matrix is estimated using following equation.

$$L(A) = U \begin{bmatrix} 1 & 0 & 0 \\ 0 & 1 & 0 \\ 0 & 0 & detU * detV \end{bmatrix} V^T \tag{4}$$

However, this method will ultimately find the optimal rotation matrix in Euler angles which leads to singularity issues. The quaternion is usually used to avoid those singularity issues and gimbal lock situations [6,15]. In addition to that, the use of quaternions eliminates the need for computing trigonometric functions [6]. Hence the next two methods in our consideration are produced the optimal estimation as a quaternion.

2.3   Davenport's q Method

Davenport introduced this method as relevant to determine the attitude of spacecraft [8,16]. Under this method, trace of AB^T in the Eq. 2 is written as a homogeneous quadratic function of quaternion q [2,8] as follows.

$$tr(AB^T) = q^T K q \tag{5}$$

where K is the symmetric traceless matrix

$$K \equiv \begin{bmatrix} S - Itr(B) & z \\ z^T & tr(B) \end{bmatrix} \tag{6}$$

Here, S is equal to the summation of B and its transpose $(B + B^T)$. z is a 3 by 3 matrix which is equal to the summation of cross product of r_i and b_i of all observation vectors. In other words, $z = \sum_{i=1}^{n} a_i b_i \times r_i$.

Then, the optimal quaternion for the movement is given by the normalized eigenvector (V) of K with the largest eigenvalue (D).

$$K q_{opt} = \lambda_{max} q_{opt} \tag{7}$$

$$q_{opt} = V < -max(D)) \tag{8}$$

However, this method will fail, if the all eigenvalues are equal or more than one of eigenvalues are equal. Since K is traceless, the sum of eigenvalues become to zero and there is not unique solution if the two largest eigenvalues are zero. It means the data is not sufficient to determine the attitudes [2]. This is the main disadvantage of this method.

2.4   QUEST Method

The QUaternion ESTimator (QUEST) method was initially introduced in 1979 [2,17,18]. Thereupon, this method is considered as the most applied algorithm for attitude estimation of spacecraft. Under this method, the fourth order quadratic method is found λ_{max} in Eq. 7. The fourth quadratic equation can be formulated as follows.

$$0 = \gamma \left[\lambda_{max} - tr(B) \right] - z^T \left[\alpha I + \lambda_{max} - tr(B)S + S^2 \right] \tag{9}$$

where

$$\alpha = \lambda_{max}^2 - [tr(B)]^2 + tr(adj[S])$$

and

$$\gamma = \alpha[\lambda_{max} + tr(B)] + det(S)$$

Then, we can find λ_{max} for the optimal quaternion using Newton -Raphson iteration [3]. When the loss function is very small, the λ_0 will be close to λ_{max}. In such times, we required to conduct several cycles or iterations of this method to get optimal(maximum) λ in order to get the optimal result.

Through out this study, this four approaches will be investigated with inertial sensor measurements: accelerometer readings and magnetometer readings as in the flow chart in Fig. 1.

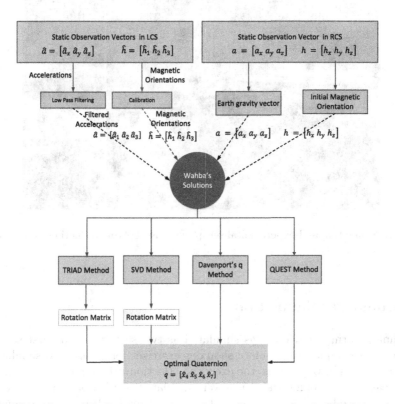

Fig. 1. Flow chart of finding orientation using each approaches in Wahba's solutions upon inertial/magnetic sensor measurements

The inertial sensor contains orthogonally mounted 3 DOF (Degree of Freedom) accelerometer, 3 DOF gyroscope and 3 DOF magnetometer. In general, the accelerometer and gyroscope are used to measure linear acceleration and angular rates of a rotation [7,19]. The magnetometer readings are used to identify the magnetic orientation. Since the magnetic north and geographical north are different and it highly depends on external magnetic fields in the environment, the proper calibration is required before obtaining measurements [7]. However, inertial/magnetic sensor based instruments are outperforming in rehabilitation, because it is a convenient, low-cost and affordable option compared to a traditional motion analysis laboratory [7]. Further, the inertial/magnetic sensor can be used in non-clinical settings providing continuous monitoring for an extended period of time. Hence that is considered more cost-effective approach to deliver post-stroke rehabilitation services in home [20]. Therefore, the findings of this paper is more important to such inertial/magnetic sensor based motion capturing systems.

Fig. 2. Simulation and experimental setup: Exercise 1-Arm Abduction/Adduction

3   Computer Simulation

The human arm behaviour was simulated as two scenarios. The first scenario (exercise 1) is aimed to simulate shoulder exercises for whole arm shoulder to wrist as one limb. Under this, the exercise abduction/adduction was considered. The measurements of inertial sensor were simulated as it is worn on wrist but not bending from elbow. Then, the second scenario (exercise 2) is aimed to simulate the arm bending exercise from elbow, apparently a day-to-day activity: lifting a water bottle. At this exercise, the elbow was lifted 45 degrees in Y-Z plane and the wrist was moved by 153 degrees in same plane. The Figs. 2 and 3 show the simulated scenarios for exercise 1 and exercise 2 respectively.

Initially, these scenarios were simulated without accounting noise of accelerometer and magnetometer measurements. Then, the noise was introduced to each measurements as decreasing Signal-to-Noise Ratio (SNR) from 60 dB to 5 dB. The accelerometer measurements were simulated with $\bar{a}_t, a, C_t, M_t$ and WA_t

Fig. 3. Simulation and experimental setup: Exercise 2-Lifting a bottle of water

which are the measured accelerometer readings, true arm rotation, a constant offset or bias, a moving bias and noise at time t respectively [21].

$$\bar{a}_t = a + C_t + M_t + WA_t, \tag{10}$$

Similarly, the magnetometer readings were modelled as Eq. 11

$$\bar{h}_t = h + C_t + M_t + Wh_t \tag{11}$$

where $\bar{h}_t, h, C_t, M_t$ and Wh_t are the measured magnetometer readings, actual arm rotation, a constant offset, a moving bias and a wide band sensor noise at time t respectively [21]. Here, WA_t and Wh_t are normally distributed. Later, the optimal estimation of movement angle from each algorithm with noise was compared with the ideal movement without noise. The noise levels under our consideration for this analysis was designed as starting from 60 dB and decreasing by 5 dB at each time until 5 dB.

The angles derived from each approaches such as TRIAD method, Davenport's q method, SVD method and QUEST method, were identical at the absence of noise. However, when the noise was introduced to accelerometer readings and magnetometer readings, the estimated angles of each axis were changed. According to the Fig. 4, initially the root mean square error (RMSE) was very small in both exercises. However when the Signal-to-Noise-Ratio (SNR) was decreased from 50 dB to 20 dB, the RMSE was increased approximately three times than the rate of RMSE change from 60 dB to 50 dB. The RMSE was tremendously changed when the ample noise (lesser than 20 dB) was introduced. The same phenomenon could be seen in sub figures (d), (e) and (f) for the exercise for day-to-day activity. However, considering sub figures (a) and (b) for exercise 1 and (d) and (f) for exercise 2, the QUEST algorithm was outperforming compared to other approaches. The QUEST algorithm has the least RMSE in all

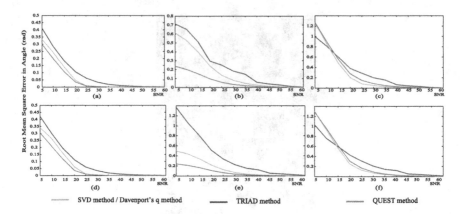

Fig. 4. Simulation Result: (a), (b) and (c) - The root mean squared error of movement angle in X, Y and Z axis for shoulder exercise, (d),(e) and (f) - The root mean squared error of movement angle in respectively X, Y and Z axis for lifting a bottle exercise

noise levels from 5 dB to 60 dB in those figures. The second least RMSE could be seen in SVD approach and Davenports q method. Further, both SVD method and Davenport's q method were equally performing hence the trajectories from each approaches were overlapping in every figure. The least performing algorithm was the TRIAD method, Although, when we consider the subfigures (e) and (f), the QUEST algorithm, SVD method and Davenport's q method are equally performing until the SNR level is less than 15 dB. Then, the TRIAD method is outperforming than the other methods which is a valuable insight of TRIAD method (see Fig. 4(f)).

4   Real Data Experiment, Result and Discussion

The exercises as in Sect. 3 were performed under the real time experiments, in order to validate and compare the most suitable approach for arm exercises using inertial sensors. The experiments to validate the algorithm were conducted with ten healthy subjects (eight males and two females) without any history of orthopaedic or intramuscular impairments. However, under the Sect. 3, the each exercises were simulated under constant speed. So the actual exercises were conducted having relatively low speed compared to gravity or constant velocity in order to closely relate with the simulated environment.

The exercise for abduction/adduction and flexion/extension were conducted wearing the inertial sensors (Biokin WMS [22]) on the left wrist and elbow. The second exercise was designed as lifting a water bottle from the front of the body to the mouth. The experiment was conducted wearing two inertial sensors (Biokin WMS [22]) closer to elbow and wrist of the left arm. The motion was simultaneously recorded using the VICON optical motion capture system (VICON T40S System) equipped with eight cameras sampling at 250 Hz. The angles were derived from output of the VICON system which is considered as the

The Study to Track Human Arm Kinematics Applying Solutions   403

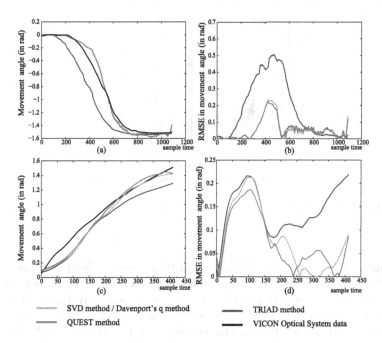

Fig. 5. Experiment Result: (a) - The movement angle for Abduction exercise, (b) - Root Mean Square Error in movement angle for Abduction exercise, (c) - The movement angle for lifting water bottle exercise and (d) - Root Mean Square Error in movement angle for lifting a bottle exercise

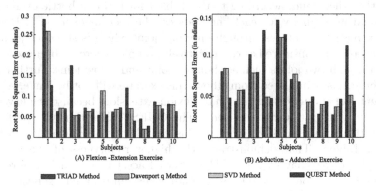

Fig. 6. Experiment Result: (a), (b) - The root mean squared error of movement angle for *extension/flexion* exercise and *abduction/adduction* exercise respectively

gold standard. During the analysis, VICON data were re-sampled at 140 Hz for comparison purposes. Under this exercise, the movement of wrist was analysed.

The root mean square errors of movement angles for the abduction/adduction, flexion/extension exercises and lifting a bottle exercise were analysed. According to the Fig. 6 for abduction/adduction exercise and Fig. 7

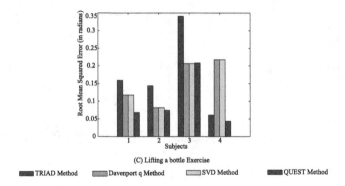

Fig. 7. Experiment Result: (c) - The root mean squared error of movement angle for lifting a bottle exercise

for lifting water bottle, the QUEST algorithm have the least error compared to other methods. The average RMSE values for all subjects for exercise 1:*abduction/adduction* and *flexion/extension* were respectively 0.0651 radians and 0.0608 radians. Further, the average RMSE for drinking exercise is 0.0987 radians for QUEST algorithm. The Davenport's q method and SVD method were equally performing in each exercises and they have the second least error. The highest error could be observed in TRIAD method for three exercises. This result is shown in Fig. 6. Importantly, the same phenomenon could be observed in simulation for the same exercise in Sect. 3.

On the other hand, according to the Table 1 for lifting a bottle exercise, the same trend in accuracy for each methods can be seen as exercise 1. However, under exercise 1, it rotates through only one joint which is shoulder joint. The second exercise is considered as comparatively complex exercise, because the arm rotates through two joints such as shoulder joint and elbow joint. Further, when the lower arm is being lifted from elbow, this exercise will not be longer a planar movement like abduction-adduction or flexion-extension, because the lower limb is slightly twisting towards the body. The QUEST algorithm was performing superior than other methods even in this complexity of kinematics as in the result in Table 1. That demonstrates the higher robustness of the algorithm for complex day-to-day exercises. The external acceleration such as force from arm muscles, will be observed when conducting complicated exercise such as exercise 2. The second least RMSE was observed in Davenport's q method and SVD which is 0.1559 radians. Likewise, the highest error was shown in TRIAD method. However we can see the accuracy is slightly reduced in this exercise than the first exercise. Importantly, the impact of external accelerations may also be affected to the estimation.

However, the QUEST method was well-performing in real-time environment which is very similar to our previous observation in simulation.

Table 1. Root mean square error for lifting a water bottle

	TRIAD method	Davenport's q method	SVD method	QUEST method
Subject 1	0.1593	0.1178	0.1178	0.0681
Subject 2	0.1441	0.0817	0.0817	0.0745
Subject 3	0.3408	0.2067	0.2067	0.2085
Subject 4	0.0611	0.2174	0.2174	0.0438
Overall	0.1763	0.1559	0.1559	0.0987

5   Conclusion

In this paper, we have investigated the applicability of four solutions for Wahba's problem such as TRIAD Method, Davenport's q method, Singular Value Decomposition method and QUaternion ESTimator method for tracking human arm kinematics. These algorithms were simulated for two scenarios and discussed the most robust algorithm for two scenarios with introduced signal noise. Further they are tested with the "Gold Standard" VICON optical motion capture system and verified the feasibility for determining movement angle in human arm kinematics. The QUEST algorithm is outperforming for both simple exercises such as arm abduction-adduction, flexion-extension and complicated exercises such as internal/external rotation of arm for day-to-day activities. However, the QUEST method should be improved for complicated exercises to enhance accuracy by accommodating powerful filtering mechanism such as Kalman filter, which will be a future work of this study.

References

1. Wahba, G.: A least squares estimate of satellite attitude. SIAM Rev. **7**(3), 409 (1965)
2. Markley, F.L., Mortari, D.: Quaternion attitude estimation using vector observations. J. Astronaut. Sci. **48**(2), 359–380 (2000)
3. Markley, F.L., Mortari, D.: How to estimate attitude from vector observations (1999)
4. Lima, S.M.R.C.P.: Comparison of small satellite attitude determination methods (2000)
5. Markley, F.L., Crassidis, J.L.: Fundamentals of Spacecraft Attitude Determination and Control. Springer, New York (2014)
6. Yun, X., Bachmann, E.: Design, implementation, and experimental results of a quaternion-based kalman filter for human body motion tracking. IEEE Trans. Rob. **22**(6), 1216–1227 (2006)
7. Karunarathne, M.S., Ekanayake, S.W., Pathirana, P.N.: An adaptive complementary filter for inertial sensor based data fusion to track upper body motion. In: 2014 7th International Conference on Information and Automation for Sustainability (ICIAfS), pp. 1–5. IEEE (2014)

8. Shuster, M.D.: A survey of attitude representations. Navigation **8**(9), 439–517 (1993)
9. Shuster, M.D., Dellinger, W.F.: Spacecraft attitude determination and control. In: Fundamentals of Space Systems, pp. 236–325 (1994)
10. Wertz, J.R.: Spacecraft Attitude Determination and Control. Springer Science & Business Media, Heidelberg (2012)
11. Sidi, M.J.: Spacecraft dynamics, control: a practical engineering approach. Cambridge University Press, Cambridge (1997)
12. Black, H.D.: Early development of transit, the navy navigation satellite system. J. Guidance, Control Dyn. **13**(4), 577–585 (1990)
13. Hajiyev, C., Cilden, D., Somov, Y.: Gyroless attitude and rate estimation of small satellites using singular value decomposition and extended kalman filter. In: 2015 16th International Carpathian Control Conference (ICCC), pp. 159–164, May 2015
14. Markley, F.L.: Attitude determination using vector observations and the singular value decomposition. J. Astronaut. Sci. **36**(3), 245–258 (1988)
15. Moon, F.C.: The Machines of Leonardo Da Vinci and Franz Reuleaux: kinematics of machines from the Renaissance to the 20th Century. Springer, Netherlands (2007)
16. Davenport, P.B.: A vector approach to the algebra of rotations with applications. National Aeronautics and Space Administration, vol. 4696 (1968)
17. Shuster, M.D.: Approximate algorithms for fast optimal attitude computation. In: Guidance and Control Conference, vol. 1, pp. 88–95 (1978)
18. Markley, F.L.: Equivalence of two solutions of wahbas problem. J. Astronaut. Sci. **60**(3–4), 303–312 (2013)
19. Tseng, S.P., Li, W.-L., Sheng, C.-Y., Hsu, J.-W., Chen, C.-S.: Motion and attitude estimation using inertial measurements with complementary filter. In: Control Conference (ASCC): 8th Asian, pp. 863–868. IEEE (2011)
20. van Exel, N.J.A., Koopmanschap, M.A.: Cost-effectiveness of integrated stroke services. J. Med. **98**(6), 415–425 (2005)
21. Flenniken, W., Wall, J., Bevly, D.: Characterization of various IMU error sources and the effect on navigation performance. In: ION GNSS, pp. 967–978 (2005)
22. Biokin. http://biokin.com.au/

A Model for Automated Affect Recognition on Smartphone-Cloud Architecture

Ying Su[1], Rajib Rana[2], Frank Whittaker[2], and Jeffrey Soar[2(✉)]

[1] Institute of Science and Technology for China, Beijing, China
[2] University of Southern Queensland, Springfield, Australia
soar@usq.edu.au

Abstract. This paper proposes a model for automated affect recognition on a smartphone-cloud architecture. Whilst facial-mood recognition is becoming more advanced, our contribution is in analysis and classification of voice to supplement mood recognition. In the model we build upon previous work of others and supplement these with new algorithms.

Keywords: Smart phone · Affect recognition

1 Introduction

Affect, which is the observable display of feelings, carries rich latent information about the state of the caller. Affective behaviour is usually displayed through facial expressions, the tone of voice, gestures, and other emotional signs such as laughter or tears, which are referred to as affect displays. Out of these, voice and facial expressions are most powerful affective displays [22]. Previously researchers have attempted to extract affective information from them in a controlled laboratory setting [1, 15]. A controlled environment can significantly bias affective response [16], which poses the need for evaluating affective behaviour in a natural setting. Due to the current advancement in the smartphone technology and that many people have their smartphones with them 24×7, smartphones make a promising platform for assessing spontaneous affective behaviour. On a smartphone platform voice offers flexibility for affect recognition, as the microphone is less sensitive to the location and orientation of the phone as compared with cameras. We propose a model to capture affect from the spontaneous speech during phone calls. In order to sense affect from spontaneous speech on the smartphone, it is imperative to fulfil three key criteria: (1) robustness, (2) energy efficiency and (3) privacy. Speech is likely to be compounded with background noise, therefore the proposed affect recognition method needs to be robust to noise. Despite the advancement in the smartphone technology, smartphones are still constrained by limited battery power; the proposed method therefore needs to be energy- efficient. Rapid battery depletion could cause user dissatisfaction, which could eventually hinder adoption. There are some attempts for processing audio on the smartphone [3, 14] where the conventional Mel Frequency Cepstral Coefficient (MFCC) with Gaussian Mixture Models (GMM) has been used as the classifier for audio classification. The use of MFCC features poses security risks as it can be used to reconstruct the original audio [14]. GMM is not

C.K. Chang et al. (Eds.): ICOST 2016, LNCS 9677, pp. 407–414, 2016.
DOI: 10.1007/978-3-319-39601-9_36

robust to noise [10]. Very recently, speech recognition researchers have put an orthogonal viewpoint forward from Microsoft [6], who found that Deep Neural Networks (DNN) can significantly outperform the accuracy of the GMM for speech recognition, especially in noisy condition. We identify a number of gaps that need to be addressed to use DNN for affect recognition subject to robustness, energy efficiency and privacy.

1.1 Background

In "speech recognition" a DNN approach called "Deep Speech" has significantly outperformed several commercial speech systems, such as Google Speech API and Apple Dictation. It achieves a word error rate of 19.1 % where the best commercial systems achieve 30.5 % error [10]. Despite this significant outcome, to the best of our knowledge no studies have yet considered DNN for emotion recognition from "noisy" speech.

One of many solutions to accommodate heavy-duty processing on the smartphone is to offload processing to a cloud server. But cloud offloading sometimes poses security risks when the information stored in the cloud can be used to reconstruct the data content. For example, MFCC audio features of a speech segment can be used to reconstruct the original speech; MFCC features are not ideal for privacy preservation. To get around this problem one can choose the spectral features, such as, high-frequency energy ratio and frequency centroid, which do not allow reconstruction of the data content and discriminative for noisy scenarios as well; but directly using the spectral features in DNN has not generated satisfactory performance [9]. An optimal feature set is yet to be defined that will maximise the robustness and privacy trade-off while using DNN for affect recognition from noisy speech.

Due to the advent of the low-power co-processors on the current smartphones, it is possible to conduct continuous processing incurring very low-power consumption. Co-processors can perform some specific continuous tasks without intervening the power-consuming main processor. Co-processors, however, have severe memory constraints and limited processing capacity, and therefore may not able to accommodate all kind of tasks. In some other cases although it can accommodate a task but can cause a massive processing delay. It is, therefore, necessary to execute tasks in a joint phone-cloud architecture, where data can be made non-identifiable or non-reconstructible on the phone and the rest of the processing can be done at the cloud. Until today only one study [12] has shown the feasibility of aphone-cloud shared approach for DNN based emotion classification, but this study uses aone-layer DNN, which does not fully utilise the benefits of the deep neural network. A multilayer DNN offers significantly higher accuracy but at the expense of large processing load and power consumption on the phone. In order to utilise DNN in its full potential, development of a power-efficient load sharing strategy between the phone and the cloud is therefore warranted.

1.2 Aims

The aims of this paper are to present a conceptual model complete with design. In our current pilot data is captured and managed through cloud services. An evaluation and validation strategy has been designed for both the pilot and full study and will be reported on once findings from the pilot are available.

This paper proposes to combine the ubiquity of smartphone, the computation power of cloud and sophisticated algorithms to automatically recognise emotion changes. Using sound for emotion detection has already been well studied by many other researchers including for emotion detection and has proven to be an effective approach. The contribution of this work is to build upon previous research through enhancing algorithms to improve quality to a level to be clinically useful.

The issue of how the phone will need to be placed is not material as the target group (young mental health patients) use their phone frequently as do any other young people. Data capture occurs at time of interaction and due to the frequency of interactions there is still adequate capture even if some are missed or not usable.

2 Conceptual Model

This paper proposes a model for continuously monitoring patients' affective behaviours, which can be used to prevent relapse by early detecting a negative change in the patient's mental health. It will advance knowledge by demonstrating how two emerging techniques: DNN and SRC can be used in a combination for accurate emotion recognition from noisy speech. The model aims to share the load between phone and cloud server to maximise accuracy, power-efficiency and privacy. Currently data collection is mostly patient initiated, which is at risk due to the low uptake and motivation in mental illness. Without patients' data, their platform is of limited or no use. The proposed system will enable passive assessment of mental illness through voice as one of the key affective displays. It will passively assess the voice and will look for markers related to mental illness. A complex mood rating will be made based on the presence of various markers in the voice. Clinicians can receive rich information about patient's mood status over any desired period. This would help them to tailor the treatment strategy to individual patient's need. Mood information can be provided to patients so that they can better self-manage their illness through developing coping strategies based on a mood diary. Many symptoms of physical and mental illness are common; it is not trivial for a chronic disease expert (such as an oncologist) to isolate the symptoms of mental illness from that of physical illness. The proposed system can be beneficial in realising this integrated platform since it will mine information about patient's mental health from their daily life and will make it available to a specialist who can initiate mental health diagnosis/treatment when a persistent declination is observed. The best-reported performance of affect sensing using smartphone audiocomes from the use of Gaussian Mixture Model (GMM) [14]. In the case of discriminativetraining, features corrupted by noise are ignored by the GMMs whereas the DNN can potentially extract some useful information from them through the layers of nonlinear processing [19]. GMM produces a much poorer performance for speech recognition in the presence of noise [10]. The spontaneous speech is highly likely to be compounded with ambient noise. The use of DNN for emotion recognition from noisy speech has not yet been explored. Our model aims to translate the current success of DNN in "noisy speech recognition" to "emotion recognition from spontaneous speech". We propose a non- conventional adaptation of the Sparse

Random Classifier (SRC) to exploit its high accuracy in classifying audio signals. In our previous research, we have shown that SRC outperforms many powerful classifiers, especially Support Vector Classifier while classifying acoustic signals [20]. We choose audio features that cannot be used to reconstruct the speech segments to protect patient privacy. Unlike previous designs of running DNN fully on the smartphone to maintain privacy at the expense of compromising accuracy [8], we propose DNN in shared phone-cloud architecture. On the phone we execute a small amount of tasks sufficient to make data non-identifiable and non-reconstructable at the server and conduct rest of the processing at the server.

The model uses publicly available Database of Emotional Speech to develop the affect-sensing algorithm. We mix noise of various natural sources with these clean speech (this is a standard approach used in the literature [18]) to generate noisy speech signals. Using these noisy speech data the algorithm can assist in recognising various emotions such as disgust, fear, joy and sadness. We divide the speech signal into segments and then extract the segment-level features to train a DNN. The trained DNN computes the emotion state distribution for each segment. From these segment-level emotion state distributions, utterance-level features are constructed and fed into a Sparse Random Classifier (SRC) to determine the emotional state of the whole utterance. In order to develop a robust classifier, unlike the recently proposed methods, which usually substitute DNNs for other classifiers such as SVMs, our approach exploits DNN to learn the non-linear relationship between the noise and clean signal through the multiple layers of nonlinear processing in DNN. Tasks in order to develop the proposed affect sensing method on a shared phone- cloud architecture, we perform the following three major tasks.

3   Design and Discussion

The first stage of the algorithm is to extract features for each segment in the whole utterance. The input signal is converted into frames with overlapping windows. The feature vector $z(m)$ extracted for each frame m consists of features. Some possible candidates are pitch-based features and their delta feature across time frames. We choose features to maximise the privacy and accuracy trade-off. Because the emotional information is often encoded in a relatively long window, one method to form the segment level feature vector is by stacking features in the neighbouring frames as, $x(m) = [z(m - w), ..., z(m), ..., z(m + w)]$, where w is the window size on each side. We empirically determine the window size. With the segment-level features, we train a DNN to predict the probabilities of each emotion state. We assume that many segments are corrupted with noise and assume that therelationship between clean features and noisy features are non-linear. Encouragingly, as the DNN is composed of multiple layers of nonlinear processing; the network, therefore, has the capacity to learn this relationship directly from the data. To enable this, we augment each observation input to the network with an estimate of the noise present in the signal. In this case the networks input vector is appended with a noise estimate: $x(m) = [z(m - w), ..., z(m), ..., z(m + w), \hat{n}]$, where $\hat{n}$ is the noise estimate. Selection of $\hat{n}$ is critical for our scenario as we aim to develop a robust classifier to characterise emotion from spontaneous speech. Modelling various background noise using Maximum Likelihood Estimate, we will seek to estimate the best value for ^n. The number of input units of the DNN is consistent with the segment-level feature vector size. It uses a softmax output layer whose size is set to the number of possible emotions K. The number of hidden layers and the hidden units will be chosen from cross-validation. Using the trained DNN we will aim to produce a probability distribution t over all the emotion states for each segment: $t = [P(E\,1), ..., P(EK)]\,T$. Emotion states in all segments might not be identical to that of the whole utterance, however, we anticipate that there would be certain patterns in the segment-level emotion states, which can be used to predict utterance-level emotions by a higher-level classifier.

Given the sequence of the probability distribution over the emotion states generated from the segment-level DNN, we can form the emotion recognition problem as a sequence classification problem, that is, based on the segment information, we need to make a decision for the whole utterance. The features in the utterance-level classification can be computed from the statistics of the segment-level probabilities. If $Ps(Ek)$ denotes the probability of the k-th emotion for the segment s, some feasible features for the utterance i for all $k = 1, ..., K$ are $f\,k1 = \max_{s \in U} Ps(Ek)$, $f\,k2 = \min_{s \in U} Ps(Ek)$, $f\,k3 = \frac{1}{|U|}\sum_{s \in U} Ps(Ek)$, $f\,k4 = Ps(Ek) > \theta\,|U|$ (1) where, U denotes the set of all segments used in the segment-level classification and θ is a threshold. The features $f\,k1$, $f\,k2$, $f\,k3$ correspond to the maximal, minimal and mean of segment-level probability of the k-th emotion over the utterance, respectively. The feature $f\,k4$ is the percentage of segments, which have a high probability of emotion k. Since the segment-level outputs already provide considerable emotional information and the utterance-level classification does not involve too much training, it is unnecessary to use DNNs for the utterance-level classification. We will use Sparse Random Classifier for the utterance level classification.

The Sparse Random Classifier (SRC) has been developed extending the emerging theory of Compressive Sensing [21]. In our previous research, we have extended SRC and showed that it can outperform the powerful Support Vector classifiers [4, 17]. Consider that we have $n\,i$ training samples from emotion class i, $i \in [1, 2, k]$. Consider that each training sample is represented by m dimensional feature vector. Then the $n\,i$ training samples from the i-th activity class can be represented by a matrix $A\,i = [v\,i, 1, v\,i, 2, ..., v\,i, n\,i] \in R\,m \times n\,i$. The building block of SRC is that any test object $y \in R\,m$ from the same activity class will approximately lie in the linear span of the training samples associated with object i. The mathematical representation of this assumption with $\alpha i, j \in R, j = 1, 2, ..., n\,i$ as the coefficients can be given by: $y = [\alpha\,i, 1\,v\,i, 1 + \alpha\,i, 2\,v\,i, 2 + ... + \alpha\,i, n\,i\,v\,i, n\,i]$. The membership of the test sample is unknown primarily. We define a new matrix A for the entire training set as the concentration of the all n training samples of k object classes: $A = [A\,1, A\,2, ..., A\,k] = [v\,1, 1, ..., v\,1, n\,1, v\,2, 1, ..., v\,2, n\,2, v\,k, 1, ..., v\,k, n\,k,]$. Then the linear representation of the training object y can be rewritten in terms of training samples: $y = Ax\,0 \in R\,m$, where $x\,0 = [0, ..., 0, \alpha\,i, 1, ..., \alpha\,i, n\,i, 0, ..., 0]\,T \in R\,n]$ is a coefficient vector whose entries are zero except those associated with i-th class. Given the success of the emerging SRC, we aim to use it for emotion classification using utterance level features. We can stack the features $(f1..., f4)$ in columns for each segment in an utterance and then do the same for all other utterances and construct a "training" matrix. For a test utterance, we represent it as a linear combination of the training matrix and identify the test label. This will be a non-conventional use of SRC as the features are probabilistic. Such as, $f\,k1$ is the maximal of the segment-level probability of the k-th emotion over the utterance. Extending the foundation of SRC to use in this problem setting, we would make a unique contribution.

Admission control strategies assist in power savings by reducing unnecessary processing. The low-power DSP co-processor is utilised to execute the related tasks with a minimum CPU involvement. A large proportion of the time users are situated in quiet environments. In such cases performing audio processing is a waste of phone resources. This stage of the processing can be delegated to the low-power co-processor [13] and thus eliminate the need for adopting duty cycling schemes which may miss sound events. If any specific emotion is dominant, methods can be developed to quickly determine if the utterance belongs to that group or not, to achieve significant savings in processing. If a coarse-grained model can be developed to isolate speech from non-speech, this could save power by not processing non-speech segments. Human affective states last much longer than a few seconds. Much computation can be saved if a consecutive utterance segment is not further processed when it only has a fractional difference from the previous utterance. To protect privacy the model allows us to (a) capture audio data during phone call and break them into audio segments as discussed in T1.1 and (b) implement the DNN and SRC classification framework in the server and a two-way communication link between the mobile and the server.

A feature management module on the phone allows for generating the various combinations of segment level features and can calculate the corresponding classification accuracy, resource usage and latency. Datasets to be considered include the Danish Emotional Speech Corpus (DES) [7], Berlin Emotional Speech Database (EMO-DB) [2], Polish emotional speech [5], and Simulated and Actual Stress (SUSAS) [11] will be where the first three datasets contain clean speech phrases with various emotions (e.g., disgust, fear, joy, sadness and surprise). The fourth dataset contains noisy voice samples encompassing stress and various emotions collected during real stressful situations, such as a roller coaster and helicopter ride. In order to simulate noise-corrupted speech signals (to combine with the clean speech phrases), the DEMAND noise database (http://parole.loria.fr/DEMAND/) can be used to sample noise segments. This database involves 18 types of noises including white noise and noises at the cafeteria, car, restaurant, train station, bus and park. b. Admission control strategies and segment level feature extraction tasks (T3) can be optimised for the phone to obtain the best resource usage (CPU, Battery) and accuracy trade-off.

4   Conclusion

This paper presents a conceptual model for automated affect recognition on smartphone-cloud architecture. This is a relatively new field that is experiencing significant attention and we aim to make a contribution to the field in analysis and classification of voice to supplement mood recognition.

References

1. Alghowinem, S., Goecke, R., Wagner, M., Epps, J., Parker, G., Breakspear, M.: Characterising depressed speech for classification. In: Interspeech, pp. 2534–2538 (2013)
2. Burkhardt, F., Paeschke, A., Rolfes, M., Sendlmeier, W.F., Weiss, B.: A database of German emotional speech. In: Interspeech, vol. 5, pp. 1517–1520 (2005)
3. Chang, K.-H., Fisher, D., Canny, J., Hartmann, B.: How's my mood and stress? an efficient speech analysis library for unobtrusive monitoring on mobile phones. In: Proceedings of the 6th International Conference on Body Area Networks, BodyNets 2011, ICST, Brussels, Belgium, ICST (Institute for Computer Sciences, Social-Informatics and Telecommunications Engineering), pp. 71–77 (2011)
4. Chew, S.W., Rana, R., Lucey, P., Lucey, S., Sridharan, S.: Sparse temporal representations for facial expression recognition. In: Ho, Y.-S. (ed.) PSIVT 2011, Part II. LNCS, vol. 7088, pp. 311–322. Springer, Heidelberg (2011)
5. Cichosz, J., Slot, K.: Application of selected speech-signal characteristics to emotion recognition in polish language. In: International Conference on Signals and Electronic Systems, pp. 409–412 (2005)
6. Deng, L., Yu, D.: Deep Learning. Now Publishers Incorporated, Hanover (2014)
7. Engberg, I.S., Hansen, A.V.: Documentation of the Danish emotional speech database. DES. Internal AAU report, Center for Person Kommunikation, Denmark, p. 22 (1996)
8. Georgiev, P., Lane, N.D., Rachuri, K.K., Mascolo, C.: DSP. Ear: leveraging co- processor support for continuous audio sensing on smartphones. In: Proceedings of the 12th ACM Conference on Embedded Network Sensor Systems, pp. 295–309. ACM (2014)
9. Han, K., Yu, D., Tashev, I.: Speech emotion recognition using deep neural network and extreme learning machine. In: Proceedings of INTERSPEECH, ISCA, Singapore, pp. 223–227 (2014)
10. Hannun, A.Y., Case, C., Casper, J., Catanzaro, B.C., Diamos, G., Elsen, E., Prenger, R., Satheesh, S., Sengupta, S., Coates, A., Ng, A.Y.: Deep speech: scaling up end-to-end speech recognition. CoRR, abs/1412.5567 (2014)
11. Hansen, J.H., Bou-Ghazale, S.E., Sarikaya, R., Pellom, B.: Getting started with susas: a speech under simulated and actual stress database. In: Eurospeech, vol. 97, pp. 1743–1746 (1997)
12. Lane, N.D., Georgiev, P.: Can deep learning revolutionize mobile sensing? (2015)
13. Lu, H., Bernheim Brush, A.J., Priyantha, B., Karlson, A.K., Liu, J.: SpeakerSense: energy efficient unobtrusive speaker identification on mobile phones. In: Lyons, K., Hightower, J., Huang, E.M. (eds.) Pervasive 2011. LNCS, vol. 6696, pp. 188–205. Springer, Heidelberg (2011)
14. Lu, H., Frauendorfer, D., Rabbi, M., Mast, M.S., Chittaranjan, G.T., Campbell, A.T., Gatica-Perez, D., Choudhury, T.: StressSense: detecting stress in unconstrained acoustic environments using smartphones. In: Proceedings ofthe 2012 ACM Conference on Ubiquitous Computing, pp. 351–360. ACM (2012)
15. McIntyre, G., Göcke, R., Hyett, M., Green, M., Breakspear, M.: An approach for automatically measuring facialactivity in depressed subjects. In: 3rd International Conference on Affective Computing and Intelligent Interaction and Workshops, 2009, ACII 2009, pp. 1–8. IEEE (2009)
16. Picard, R.W.: Affective computing for HCI. In: HCI, vol. 1, pp. 829–833 (1999)
17. Rana, R., Kusy, B., Wall, J., Hu, W.: Novel activity classification and occupancy estimation methods for intelligent HVAC (heating, ventilation and air conditioning) systems. Energy **93**, 245–255 (2015)

18. Schuller, B., Arsic, D., Wallhoff, F., Rigoll, G.: Emotion recognition in the noise applying large acoustic feature sets. In: Speech Prosody, Dresden, pp. 276–289 (2006)

19. Seltzer, M.L., Yu, D., Wang, Y.: An investigation of deep neural networks for noise robust speech recognition. In: 2013 IEEE International Conference on Acoustics, Speech and Signal Processing (ICASSP), pp. 7398–7402. IEEE (2013)

20. Wei, B., Yang, M., Shen, Y., Rana, R., Chou, C.T., Hu, W.: Real-time classification via sparse representation in acoustic sensor networks. In: Proceedings of the 11th ACM Conference on Embedded Networked Sensor Systems, p. 21. ACM (2013)

21. Wright, J., Yang, A.Y., Ganesh, A., Sastry, S.S., Ma, Y.: Robust face recognition via sparse representation. IEEE Trans. Pattern Anal. Mach. Intell. **31**(2), 210–227 (2009)

22. Zeng, Z., Pantic, M., Roisman, G., Huang, T.: A survey of affect recognition methods: audio, visual, and spontaneous expressions. IEEE Trans. Pattern Anal. Mach. Intell. **31**(1), 39–58 (2009)

Social, Privacy, and Security Issues

A Heuristic Method of Identifying Key Microbloggers

Lidong Huang[1,2,3(✉)], Wenxian Wang[2], Xiaozhou Chen[1],
and Junhua Chen[3]

[1] School of Mathematics and Computer Science, Yunnan Minzu University,
Kunming 650000, People's Republic of China
lidonghuang@yahoo.com
[2] Network and Trusted Computing Institute, College of Computer Science,
Sichuan University, Chengdu 610000, People's Republic of China
[3] Key Laboratory of IOT Application Technology of Universities in Yunnan
Province, Yunnan Minzu University, Kunming 650000, China

Abstract. In microblogosphere, some microbloggers are not only active but also influential, called them key microbloggers, who enable information diffuse faster, wider and deeper. The knowledge of key microbloggers is crucial for developing efficient methods to either hinder the rumor spread or promote useful information dissemination. In this paper, we discuss how to evaluate a microblogger's influence, investigate microblogging-specific features that constitute a microblogger's active index, and present a model attempting to quantify key microbloggers. We conduct experiments with data, which was crawled from Sina Weibo, and evaluate ranking accuracy of the proposed model. Experimental results attest that the proposed method is able to identify key microbloggers effectively in the microblogging behavior.

Keywords: Social media · Key microblogger · Influence · Active index

1 Introduction

Microblogging has recently become one of the most popular social media services for people to communicate with each other. Compared to common blogging, microblogging meets the need for an even faster mode of communication. In a microblogosphere, there exists some users who are not only active but also influential, called key microbloggers. Aral s et al. [1] suggest that influential individuals, who have influential friends, may be helpful in the spread of information in the social network. It is a significative and difficult issue to how to identify them from millions users.

Many microblogging services, including Twitter and Sina Weibo, rank influence or authority of microblogger according to the number of followers who he has or the total number of posts which he published. But it is not enough to identify key microbloggers only using these factors. In this paper, we present the definition of key microbloggers for the first time, discuss influence and activity separately, and combine influence with active index for identifying key microbloggers, and present a model which quantifies key microbloggers with regard to a specific domain.

© Springer International Publishing Switzerland 2016
C.K. Chang et al. (Eds.): ICOST 2016, LNCS 9677, pp. 417–426, 2016.
DOI: 10.1007/978-3-319-39601-9_37

The rest of this paper is organized as follows. Section 2 investigates the related work of measuring user's influence or authority in the social media network. The proposed model of identifying key microbloggers is presented in Sect. 3. In Sect. 4, we report our experimental study. Finally, we conclude our paper and discuss our future work in Sect. 5.

2 Related Works

Currently, the study about influential propagate in a social network has been an area of much interest. The problem of influence maximization is to find a small set of users in a social network in order to maximize the spread of influence. Unfortunately, Kempe et al. prove that this problem is NP-hard [2]. [3–5] employ the greedy algorithm to obtain good approximation solution for influence maximization. However, the greedy algorithm is apt to suffer from a combination explosion.

M Kitsak et al. [6] found that influential spreaders are those located within the core of the network as identified by the K-shell decomposition analysis. K Subbian et al. [7] proposed a predictive perspective of influence, and present a new approach to supervised rank aggregation.

[8, 9] presented ranking approaches for microblog search taking into account the social network properties of users and the properties of microblogging itself. Duan et al. [10] proposed a new tweet ranking strategy which used the content relevance of tweet, author authority and tweet-specific features. Cha M et al. presented a comparison of three measures of influence (i.e., indegree, retweets and mentions) [11].

The aforementioned works give us some enlightenment. However, their researches are orthogonal to the problem discussed here.

The only work directly relevant to our problem is that reported in [12], which propose TwitterRank, an extension of PageRank algorithm, measures influence of users in twitter taking both the topical similarity between users and the link structure into account. However, TwitterRank ignores the twitter-specific features, such as the number of followers which a user in the twitter has, and the number of posts which he published.

In order to quantify user influence in a social network, [13] propose an adaptive and parameter-free algorithm, the LeaderRank, another extension of PageRank algorithm with adding the ground node which connects to every node. However, LeaderRank is not content-based but linkage-based analysis. The proposed model in this paper will smooth over their faults.

3   The Model of Identifying Key Microbloggers (MIKM)

3.1   The Framework of Identifying Key Microbloggers

Wing S. Chow et al. [14] analyze the role of social network in organizational knowledge sharing and find that social network significantly contributed to a person's volition to share knowledge. It is noticed that diverse users are interested in different domains. Therefore, it is more meaningful to identify key microbloggers with regard to different domains respectively. Then the search for key microbloggers can be narrowed down to the question of how to identify key microbloggers in different domains. Based on this finding, we present the framework of identifying key microbloggers which is shown in Fig. 1.

As shown in Fig. 1, users' posts and profiles are crawled from microblogging site firstly. Then domains that microbloggers are interested in are classified automatically by analyzing the content of posts which they published. Based on classified domains, domain-specific relationship networks among microbloggers are constructed, and microbloggers' influence and active index are calculated. Finally, we leverage MIKM to calculate the score of microbloggers and rank them according to their scores. The users of top K are key microbloggers.

3.2   Domain Classification

Every microblogger concentrates on his areas of interest. Therefore, it is higher meaningfulness to identify key microbloggers with regard to specific domains respectively. The goal of domain classification is to automatically determine the appropriate domain which a microblogger is interested in through an analysis of the text in his posts. In this paper, we focus on Naïve Bayes classification [15], which has been shown to efficiently model in text classification.

In addition, a microblogger's interest maybe changes in a different period. In order to alleviate the effects of interest drift and improve the effectiveness of classification, we propose a sliding-window classifying approach for adaptive domain classification. During a fixed period of days, we collect all messages posted by a microblogger, classify these messages, and then find out which domain the microblogger has an interest in.

There is an open question: What is the best size of sliding window. According to [16], most of the active periods of topics are a week or shorter. This indicates that the period of a microblogger's interest drift is about one week. Therefore we choose 7 days as the size of sliding window.

3.3   The Definition of Key Microblogger

In general, posts published by influential microbloggers may receive many comments or be forwarded many times; during a given period, the more quantity of posts a microblogger publishes, the more active he is. These phenomena give us much enlightenment on this research.

Definition 1 (Influential): If a microblogger attract many followers and his posts are forwarded or commented many times, we can say he is influential.

Definition 2 (Active Index): A microblogger, who often publishes a lot of posts, follows many other users, may be thought to be active. Microblogger's activity is indicated with active index.

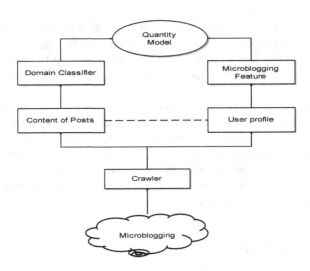

Fig. 1. The framework of identifying key microbloggers

An active microblogger may not be a good information disseminator without powerful influence; and in the same way, an influence microblogger may not be a good information disseminator if he was not active. Therefore, we put forward key microblogger which is defined as follows:

Definition 3 (Key Microblogger): Key Microblogger is a type of user who is not only influential but also active in microblogosphere, and plays a key role in information diffusion.

3.4   The Measurement of Influence

In order to quantify the influence, we compute three scores for each microblogger representing her/his influence independently.

Definition 4 (Followers Score): The Followers Score of a microblogger i is defined as

$$f_{FS}(i) = \log(N_F(i))\tag{1}$$

with $N_F(i)$ denotes the number of followers which a microblogger i has.

Definition 5 (Forward Score): The Forward Score of a microblogger i is defined as

$$f_{FWS}(i) = \frac{1}{N} \sum_{n=1}^{N} F_n^T(i)\tag{2}$$

with N is the number of posts published by microblogger i, and $F_n^T(i)$ denotes the number of n-th post is forwarded during a given T days.

Definition 6 (Commented Score): The Commented Score of a microblogger i is defined as

$$f_{CDS}(i) = \frac{1}{M} \sum_{m=1}^{M} C_m^T(i) \tag{3}$$

with M is the number of posts commented by microblogger i, and $C_m^T(i)$ denotes the number of m-th post is commented during a given T days.

According to the definition 1, the influence of microblogger i can be measured by:

$$Influence(i) = \omega_F f_{FS}(i) + \omega_{FW} f_{FWS}(i) + \omega_{CD} f_{CDS}(i) \tag{4}$$

where ω_F, ω_{FW}, and ω_{CD} denote the weight of $f_{FS}(i), f_{FWS}(i)$, and $f_{CDS}(i)$ respectively, and $\omega_F + \omega_{FW} + \omega_{CD} = 1$.

3.5 The Measurement of Active Index

If an influential microblogger is not active, his influence will be limited. Therefore, activity is very essential to identify key microbloggers. Active index, which is used to measure microblogger's activity, is defined as follows:

In order to quantify the active index, we compute three scores for each microblogger representing her/his active index.

Definition 7 (Friend-Score): the Friend-Score of a microblogger i is defined as

$$f_{FDS}(i) = \log(Q_{FD}(i)) \tag{5}$$

with $Q_F(i)$ denotes the number of friends a microblogger i has. The number of friends each user has is limited to 2000 in Sina Weibo.

Definition 8 (Post-Score): the Post-Score of a microblogger i is defined as

$$f_{PS}(i) = \frac{Q_P^T(i)}{T} \tag{6}$$

with $Q_P^T(i)$ denotes the number of the post published by microblogger i during a given T days.

Definition 9 (Comment-Score): the Comment- Score of a microblogger i is defined as

$$f_{CS}(i) = \frac{Q_C^T(i)}{T} \tag{7}$$

with $Q_c^T(i)$ denotes the number of comments a microblogger i gives during a given T days.

According to the definition 2, the active index of microblogger i can be measured by:

$$AIndex(i) = \omega_P f_{PS}(i) + \omega_{FD} f_{FDS}(i) + \omega_C f_{CS}(i) \tag{8}$$

where ω_P, ω_{FD} and ω_C denote the weight of $f_{PS}(i)$, $f_{FS}(i)$ and $f_{CS}(i)$ respectively, and $\omega_P + \omega_{FD} + \omega_C = 1$.

3.6 The Measurement of Key Microbloggers

Every factor score is normalized to lie between 0 and 1. According to the definition 3, the final score of each microblogger is calculated as:

$$K(i) = H(i) \times (\mu \times Inflence(i) + (1 - \mu) \times AIndex(i)) \tag{9}$$

where μ is weighting coefficient, which can be dynamic adjusted according to the requirement of different application.

4 Experimental Results

4.1 Data Set

The data is crawled from Sina Weibo, which is one of the most popular microblogging sites in China. Every user in Sina Weibo keeps a simple profile about oneself, which include ID, screen name, the number of followers and the number of post, etc. Users' profile data can be easy to crawl by calling APIs which are open officially by Sina Weibo. We gather the content of users' all posts by crawling on web page. The crawler adopt a breadth-first search (BFS) crawling strategy. The crawlers are launched on November 28th, 2014. Until May 30th, 2015, the dataset consists of 40,598,896 posts and 63,607,362 users along with their profiles.

4.2 Discussion of Weighted Coefficients

In this paper, we employ the analytic hierarchy process(AHP) [17] to determine weight coefficient of each factor. AHP is a combination of qualitative and quantitative, flexible and hierarchical analysis method.

Firstly, we model the problem of identifying key microbloggers as a hierarchy. Then a series of pair-wise factors are compared against our research goal for importance. Based on pair-wise comparisons of the factors, we can establish priorities among the factors of the hierarchy. Finally, according to the priority of each factor, we endow it with a weight coefficient.

Table 1 shows all the weight coefficients. Here, we think the importance of influence is the same as the one of activity, so the μ is set to 0.5.

Table 1. Weight coefficients

Type	Weight	Value	Normalization
Influence	w_F	0.50	**0.213**
	w_{FW}	0.84	**0.380**
	w_{CD}	0.95	**0.407**
Active	w_P	0.55	**0.367**
	w_{FD}	0.23	**0.153**
	w_C	**0.72**	**0.480**

4.3 Evaluation Standard and Result

4.3.1 Comparison with Related Ranking Algorithms

Many existing studies have proposed different algorithms of ranking users [11–13]. In this paper, we compare our model with other related algorithms. The related algorithms include:

- **Followers** (FS) measures microbloggers by the number of followers. This is the measurement currently employed by Sina Weibo and many other microblogging services.
- **PageRank** (PR) measures microbloggers with only link structure of the network.
- **TwitterRank** (TR) that measure microbloggers with the structure of network and the content of microblogging taken into account.

4.3.2 Correlation

We first investigate the correlation of our algorithm with other three algorithms. We employ Kendall's Tau rank correlation coefficient (τ) to measure the correlation between the rank lists generated by the different algorithms [18]. Kendall's Tau is computed as below:

$$\tau = \frac{2(n_c - n_d)}{n^2 - n} \tag{10}$$

where n_c is the number of concordant pairs, n_d is the number of discordant pairs and n is the total number of items in a rank list. τ *takes* a value within the range of $[-1,1]$. $\tau = 1$ if the two lists are completely the same; if one list is the reverse of the other, $\tau = -1$. For other values in the range, a larger value of τ implies higher agreement between the two lists.

Table 2 shows the τ values between the rank lists generated by various algorithms in the different domains, include politics, sport, entertainment and technology. We also examine the average τ values between the four algorithms. It is observed that our algorithm has higher agreement with TR than with FS and PR. This is because both MIKM and TwitterRank take the structure of network and the content of microblogging into account, while FS and PR do not.

Table 2. Kendall's rank correlation coefficients

Domain	MIKM vs. FS	MIKM vs. PR	MIKM vs. TR
#Politics	0.440	0.462	**0.683**
#Sport	0.404	0.425	**0.661**
#Technology	0.467	0.512	**0.695**
#Entertainment	0.421	0.446	**0.676**
AVG	**0.433**	**0.461**	**0.679**

4.3.3 Accuracy

Normalized discounted cumulative gain (NDCG) is a measure of accuracy of a rank algorithm, often used in information retrieval. In this experiment, we employ NDCG to compare the ranking accuracy of each algorithm. The NDCG accumulated at a particular rank position p is defined as:

$$NDCG@p = \begin{cases} \frac{1}{N_p}\sum_{j=1}^{p} 2^{r_j} - 1 & j = 1 \\ \frac{1}{N_p}\sum_{j=1}^{p} \frac{2^{r_j}-1}{\log_2 j} & j > 1 \end{cases} \tag{11}$$

where r_j is the relevant label of the item with position j in the ranked list, and N_p is a constant which denotes the maximum value of $NDCG@p$ given the query.

In the experiment, we employ 50 volunteers to evaluate Popularity Index score (PIs) of microbloggers by scoring 4 to 0 by scanning their lasted 100 posts. We show top 25 users generated by each algorithm. There are total 39 different users to be evaluated. Figure 2 illustrates the NDCG@p of Top k users of four algorithms.

Figure 2 shows that MIMK successfully suggests relatively high ranking accuracy for the entire range. Both MIMK and TR outperform the other two algorithms. The result suggests the content of microblogging is high relevance to key microbloggers. The fact that MIMK performs better than TR indicates that key microbloggers in the microblogging social network can be better determined by both the content of microblogging and microblogging-specific features than only by the content of microblogging.

5   Conclusions

Identifying key microbloggers in microblogosphere is a significant issue. We address a novel problem of identifying key microbloggers by presenting a framework and a quantification model. We propose a classifying approach with sliding-window to determine which domain microbloggers are interested in. In order to quantify key microbloggers, we take both the influence and active index into account. The experimental results show that the proposed algorithm outperforms other related algorithms. Nevertheless, as an early attempt to identify key microbloggers, our approach still has space for improvement. We are going to refine and extend our work.

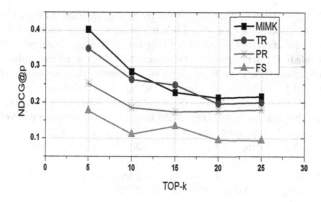

Fig. 2. The value of NDCG@p of Top k users of four algorithms

Acknowledgements. This work was sponsored by the National Key Technology R&D Program (Grant No. 2012BAH18B05). The authors also gratefully acknowledge the helpful comments and suggestions of the reviewers, which have improved the presentation.

References

1. Aral, S., Walker, D.: Identifying influential and susceptible members of social networks. Science **337**, 337–341 (2012)
2. Kempe, D., Kleinberg, J., Tardos, É.: Maximizing the spread of influence through a social network. In: Proceedings of the Ninth ACM SIGKDD International Conference on Knowledge Discovery and Data Mining, pp. 137–146. ACM (2003)
3. Saito, K., Kimura, M., Ohara, K., Motoda, H.: Efficient discovery of influential nodes for SIS models in social networks. Knowl. Inf. Syst. **30**, 613–635 (2012)
4. Chen, W., Wang, Y., Yang, S.: Efficient influence maximization in social networks. In: Proceedings of the 15th ACM SIGKDD International Conference on Knowledge Discovery and Data Mining, pp. 199–208. ACM (2009)
5. Wang, Y., Cong, G., Song, G., Xie, K.: Community-based greedy algorithm for mining top-k influential nodes in mobile social networks. In: Proceedings of the 16th ACM SIGKDD International Conference on Knowledge Discovery and Data Mining, pp. 1039–1048. ACM (2010)
6. Kitsak, M., Gallos, L.K., Havlin, S., Liljeros, F., Muchnik, L., Stanley, H.E., Makse, H.A.: Identification of influential spreaders in complex networks. Nat. Phys. **6**, 888–893 (2010)
7. Subbian, K., Melville, P.: Supervised rank aggregation for predicting influencers in twitter. In: 2011 IEEE Third International Conference on Privacy, Security, Risk and Trust, and 2011 IEEE Third International Conference on Social Computing, pp. 661–665. IEEE (2011)
8. Zhao, L., Zeng, Y., Zhong, N.: A weighted multi-factor algorithm for microblog search. In: Zhong, N., Callaghan, V., Ghorbani, A.A., Hu, B. (eds.) AMT 2011. LNCS, vol. 6890, pp. 153–161. Springer, Heidelberg (2011)
9. Nagmoti, R., Teredesai, A., De Cock, M.: Ranking approaches for microblog search. In: Proceedings 2010 IEEE/ACM International Conference on Web Intelligence-Intelligent Agent Technology (WI-IAT), pp. 153–157, (2010)

10. Duan, Y., Jiang, L., Qin, T., Zhou, M., Shum, H.-Y.: An empirical study on learning to rank of tweets. In: Proceedings of the 23rd International Conference on Computational Linguistics, Association for Computational Linguistics, Beijing, China, pp. 295–303 (2010)

11. Cha, M., Haddadi, H., Benevenuto, F., Gummadi, K.P.: Measuring user influence in twitter: the million follower fallacy. In: Proceedings of the Fourth International AAAI Conference on Weblogs and Social Media, Washington, DC, pp. 10–17 (2010)

12. Weng, J., Lim, E.-P., Jiang, J., He, Q.: TwitterRank: finding topic-sensitive influential twitterers. In: Proceedings of the Third ACM International Conference on Web Search and Data Mining, ACM, New York, New York, USA, pp. 261–270 (2010)

13. Lü, L., Zhang, Y.C., Yeung, C.H., Zhou, T.: Leaders in social networks, the delicious case. PLoS ONE 6, e21202 (2011)

14. Chow, W.S., Chan, L.S.: Social network, social trust and shared goals in organizational knowledge sharing. Inf. Manage. 45, 458–465 (2008)

15. McCallum, A., Nigam, K.: A comparison of event models for naive bayes text classification. In: AAAI-98 Workshop on Learning for Text Categorization, Citeseer, pp. 41–48 (1998)

16. Kwak, H., Lee, C., Park, H., Moon, S.: What is twitter, a social network or a news media? In: Proceedings of the 19th International Conference on World Wide Web, pp. 591–600. ACM 2010

17. Saaty, T.L.: Decision making with the analytic hierarchy process. Int. J. Serv. Sci. 1, 83–98 (2008)

18. Kendall, M.G.: A new measure of rank correlation. Biometrika 30, 81–93 (1938)

Signed Network Label Propagation Algorithm with Structural Balance Degree for Community Detection

Lei Fang[✉], Qun Yang, Jiawen Wang, and Weihua Lei

College of Computer Science and Technology,
Nanjing University of Aeronautics and Astronautics, Nanjing, China
fanglei_nuaa@139.com, Qun.Yang@nuaa.edu.cn,
{287568706,623659607}@qq.com

Abstract. Social networks are usually modeled as signed networks. The community detection is an important problem for the research of signed networks. The time complexity of signed label propagation algorithm is lower than most existing algorithms for community detection in the signed networks. However, bad performance on robustness and accuracy in the algorithm should not be ignored. Thus, we propose a structural balance degree to measure the balance of an edge in the local network and the local network density. Then a novel signed network label propagation algorithm with structural balance degree is proposed for community detection in signed networks. Besides, the algorithm is tested on several real-world social networks. Experimental results prove that the optimized algorithm can enhance both the robustness and the effectiveness. Its convergence rate is also faster than current algorithms.

Keywords: Community detection · Signed networks · Structural balance degree · Label propagation algorithm

1 Introduction

There are various interpersonal relationships in real world, such as friends, relatives and even enemies. The network with binary relationship cannot simply be modeled as an unsigned network, which can cause the core information loss of the edge. For this reason, the network is usually modeled as a signed network with both positive and negative edges. The community detection problem [1, 2] is a key research point in social network analysis. Nodes located in the same community are usually closely connected, but they may be sparsely connected to other nodes in different communities. Many approaches, such as user interaction based algorithm [3], clustering algorithm [4, 5], information cascade-based model [6], and semantic network-based algorithm [7] have been proposed to tackle the community detection problem. Raghavan et al. proposed the label propagation algorithm (LPA) for community detection in unsigned networks [8]. It is easy to implement and it has linear time complexity [9]. Šubelj et al. [10] found that random node update orders within the algorithm severely hamper its robustness, and consequently also the stability of the identified community structure.

© Springer International Publishing Switzerland 2016
C.K. Chang et al. (Eds.): ICOST 2016, LNCS 9677, pp. 427–435, 2016.
DOI: 10.1007/978-3-319-39601-9_38

So they proposed a balanced propagation that counteracts for the introduced randomness by utilizing node balancers. It is for the unsigned network which is not our research point in this paper.

Triangle structural balance theory [11], which is considered as the basis of the social psychology analysis of the signed network theory, has a great impact on the research of the signed network. Nakanishi et al. [12] research whether software agents can influence human relations by using balance theory in agent-mediated communities. It shows that the balance theory can be used in social network analysis. But the problem which they research on is not a community detection problem.

Compared to unsigned networks, it is necessary to consider about the sign information of edge when detecting communities in the signed network. As for the problem, we presented the signed network label propagation algorithm based on LPA first. Then, we presented the structural balance degree which is used to measure the balance of each edge in the signed network. Last, we presented the signed network label propagation algorithm with structural balance degree. The algorithm can detect communities in signed networks effectively and its results are stable.

2 Related Works

Researchers tend to adopt two kinds of methods to solve the community detection problem in signed network now.

2.1 Whole-Network-Based Algorithm

It sets an objective function of the signed network as the measurement of the network partitioning result and it is based on the whole network information. It finds optimal partition ways by optimizing the objection function solution of the case. The modularity is put forward and used to measure different network partitioning results in unsigned complex networks. Gomez et al. [13] developed the modularity function to discover communities in signed networks. It splits network into a positive part and a negative part and then the corresponding subgraph modularity is calculated respectively. The weighted sum of plus and minus modularity is the overall modularity of the signed network. Modularity is a measurement function originated from the concept of network connection density. Thus, this classification method is rather closer to the definition of the community.

Traag et al. [14] extend an existing Potts model to incorporate negative links as well, resulting in a method similar to the clustering of signed graphs. They opted for simulated annealing to minimize an objective function. Its time complexity is much higher than the time complexity of LPA and the improved algorithms.

Li et al. [15] proposed a two-stage signed network community discovery algorithm. In the first phase, the GN algorithm is used to get a preliminary division in subnet composed of positive edges. In the second phase, a hierarchical clustering method is used to combine the negative edges between different positive subnets.

Bansal et al. [16] introduced the correlation clustering algorithm into the document network and proposed two clustering goals. One is to maximize the sum of the number of internal plus edges in clusters and the number of negative edges between different clusters. The other is to minimize the sum of the number of internal negative edges in cluster and the number of positive edges between different clusters. They also proved that the two kinds of clustering goals in the signed network are NP- hard problems.

2.2   Local-Information-Based Algorithm

It is a local community discovery algorithm. Yang et al. [17] presented finding extracting community (FEC) algorithm of local random walks on the signed network to find communities. The time complexity of FEC algorithm is linear and it performs well in terms of time efficiency. But the weakness is that the experimental results are not stable because of the random selection of initial node in the process of random walks and the uncertainty of random walks steps.

Shama et al. [18] proposed a two-step cluster CRA (clustering re-clustering algorithm) algorithm. Compared to FEC, CRA is more stable because the two step clustering could be affirmatory without the artificial set of parameters.

3   Signed Network Label Propagation Algorithm

In some particular cases, if there are two strong communities in the signed network, which are only connected by negative edges, labels cannot spread across them. The problem is also related to label propagation in two unsigned subnets and it suggests that the label propagation algorithm is feasible on the signed network. For this reason, we develop a sign network label propagation algorithm (SLPA). It does not require the division of the positive and negative subsets in the clustering process. Combining label propagation algorithm with edges' sign, SLPA detects communities directly instead of dividing network into positive and negative subnets.

$G(V, E_+, E_-)$ is an unweighted and undirected graph which can represent the signed social network. V stands for all the nodes in graph G, and E_+ is the set of all positive edges; E_- is the set of all negative edges. e_{ij} is the edge that connects the node v_i with the node v_j.

l_i is the label of the node $v_i(v_i \in V)$ and the set of the node v_i's neighbors is represented by N_i. N_i^+ is the set of nodes connected with the node v_i by positive edges, and N_i^- is the set of nodes connected with the node v_i by negative edges. $N(v) = N_i^+ \cup N_i^-$, and $N_i^+ \cap N_i^- = \emptyset$.

Each node is only affected by its neighbors. If there is a positive edge between the node and its neighbor, it would get the label from the neighbor node. But if there is a negative edge between the node and its neighbor, it would reject the label from the neighbor node. After several iterations, the nodes, which are closely-connected to positive edges, receive the same label. Finally, the nodes with the same label are clustered into the same community. The formula of l_i is shown below:

$$l_i = \underset{l}{\arg max} \left(\left| N_i^+ (l) \right| - \left| N_i^- (l) \right| \right) \tag{1}$$

$N_i^+ (l)$ is the set of nodes with the label l in N_i^+. $N_i^- (l)$ is the set of nodes with the label l in N_i^-. The formula shows that if there are nodes with the label l in neighbor nodes of v_i and the difference value of nodes with the label l in N_i^+ and N_i^- is the maximum, the node v_i selects the label l as its new label.

SLPA can detect communities in signed networks, but it does not perform well in terms of robustness due to its strong randomness. Besides, neither network density relations nor the structural balance of the signed network are taken into consideration. Thus, the label propagation algorithm remains to be improved to solve the problems.

4 The Structural Balance Degree of Signed Network

In an unsigned network, if two adjacent nodes have a common adjacent node, the two nodes and their common adjacent node would constitute a triangle. When calculating the similarity of the two nodes, the number of their common adjacent nodes is an essential part of the operator. According to the definition of the community, the joint situation between adjacent nodes of the two nodes reflects the connection density of the local network which the two nodes belong to. Since each edge in the signed network can be positive or negative, there exist two kinds of relationships between two connected nodes: attraction and mutex. And their common adjacent node can have various relations with the two nodes.

There may be a positive edge or a negative edge between two nodes in the signed network. If the edge e_{12} is a positive edge, there are four types of triangles, which the edge maybe belong to, as shown in Fig. 1:

According to the triangle structural balance theory of the signed network, Fig. 1(a) and (d) are balanced, but Fig. 1(b) and (c) are unbalanced. In these unbalanced triangles, the relation among the three nodes still changes dynamically and their final status remains unknown. For example, in Fig. 1(b), if the positive relationship of edge e_{13} and e_{12} is very strong, but the negative relationship of node 2 and node 3 is not strong, the negative relationship of edge e_{23} is likely to be converted to the positive relationship. Thus, in unbalanced triangle, the positive or negative nature of the edges may gain more possibility to change. The unbalanced triangle in the signed network does not take part in the calculation of the structural balance degree of edges.

The structural balance degree is used to measure the balance degree of each edge in the signed network. Its value can use the number of balanced triangles which are constituted of the edge and its adjacent edges. For the edge e_{ij}, its structural balance degree is K_{ij}.

If the structural balance degree of the edge e_{ij} is higher, its sign nature would be more stable, and its local network density would be bigger. For a positive edge, if the structural balance degree is higher, the two nodes connected by the edge would be closer and they gain more probability to be in the same community. For a negative

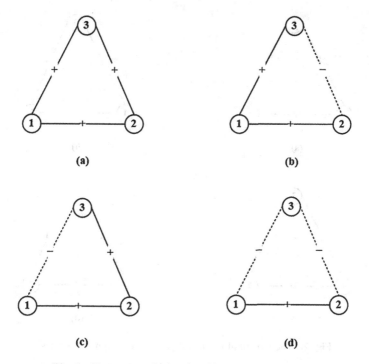

Fig. 1. Four types of triangle with a positive edge e_{12}.

edge, if the structural balance degree is higher, the two nodes connected by the edge would be more distant and they gain less probability to be in the same community.

As edges have the nature of plus or minus sign, the structural balance degree of the positive edge should be positive and that of negative edge should be negative. The product decision method helps to determine whether a triangle is balanced. For a triangle, if the product of the three edges' signs is $+1$, the triangle would be balanced else the triangle would be unbalanced. Figure 2 shows the calculation examples of the structural balance degree of the four basic triangles.

Concrete steps of the structural balance degree are as follows:

1. In a signed network, $e_{ij} \in E$ and its structural balance degree is set by its sign. If it's a positive edge, its default structural balance degree K_{ij} would be $+1$. If it's a negative edge, its default structural balance degree K_{ij} would be -1.
2. For the edge $e_{ij} \in E$, the nodes connected to v_i and v_j make up a set N_{ij}.
3. For each $v_k \in N_{ij}$, v_i, v_j and v_k constitute a signed triangle. If the product of e_{ij}, e_{ik} and e_{jk} is $+1$, the structure of the triangle would be balanced. If the product of e_{ij}, e_{ik} and e_{jk} is -1, the structure of the triangle would be unbalanced. When the triangle is balanced, if e_{ij} is positive, K_{ij} add 1; if e_{ij} is negative, K_{ij} minus 1.
4. The resulting K_{ij} is the structural balance degree of e_{ij}.

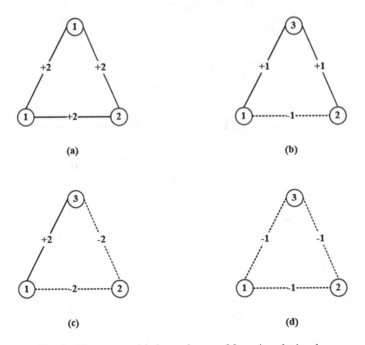

Fig. 2. The structural balance degree of four signed triangles

5 Signed Network Label Propagation Algorithm with Structural Balance Degree

Neither the network density nor the structural balance of the signed network is taken into consideration in SLPA. Thus, the structural balance degree is proposed to measure the balance of each edge in the signed network. It not only reflects the stability of the sign, but also measures local network density. This is primarily because the structural balance degree also has sign. It can cause the label to spread easily in dense positive subnets but difficultly in dense negative subnets. For this reason, we propose the sign network label propagation algorithm with structural balance degree (SBDSLPA). The label updating strategy is shown as the following formula.

$$l_i = \frac{\arg max}{l} \sum_{l_j=l, v_j \in N_i} K_{ij} \tag{2}$$

l_i is the label of the node $v_i (v_i \in V)$. If v_i is connected with v_j, $e_{ij} \in E$, and its structural balance degree is K_{ij}.

The steps of SBDSLPA are as follows:

1. Each node in the signed network is labeled by a unique integer value. This label represents the community that the node belongs to.
2. Compute the structural balance degree of each edge in the signed network.

3. All nodes in V are arranged in a random order, and node's labels are updated in turn. The new label of the node v_i is calculated according to the formula (2).
4. Repeat step 3 until labels of all nodes no longer change and the algorithm convergence. At last nodes with the same label belongs to the same community.

If there are both positive and negative edges between v_i and the nodes which belong to the Community C, it would be easy to judge whether the positive relationship or the negative relationship is stronger between Community C and v_i, according to the sign of the sum value of the edges' structural balance degree. This determines whether the node v_i belongs to the community C. Label propagation algorithm is an intelligent clustering algorithm based on the label preference of nodes. The structural balance degree can give the spontaneous clustering a control guide.

6 Experiments and Discussion

In order to compare SLPA with SBDSLPA, some experiments are conducted on three different benchmark signed network data sets. The algorithms are implemented by the standard C language.

The experimental environment is shown in Table 1:

Table 1. The experimental environment

Operating system	Ubuntu 12.10
Compiler	gcc 4.8
Memory	4 GB
CPU	3.20 GHz

The experiment network data sets are three true signed networks. Their specific data attributes are as shown in Table 2.

Table 2. The signed social network datasets

Network	Nodes	Edges	Edges(+)	Edges(-)
Gahuku-Gama Subtribes Network (GGSN)	16	116	58	58
Sampson Monastery Network (SMN)	18	158	80	78
Slovene Parliamentary Network (SPN)	10	45	18	27

We run SLPA and SBDSLPA for 50 times on the three datasets. For the generating communities, the average signed network modularity (SQ) and average normalized mutual information degree are computed and the statistical results are shown in Tables 3 and 4 respectively. The average running time is displayed in Table 5.

The average signed network modularity of SLPA and SBDLPA on the three different network data sets is recorded in the Table 3. The average signed network

Table 3. The average signed network modularity

Network	SLPA	SBDSLPA
GGSN	0.35	0.43
SMN	0.44	0.57
SPN	0.41	0.45

Table 4. The average normalized mutual information

Network	SLPA	SBDSLPA
GGSN	0.83	0.97
SMN	0.85	0.92
SPN	0.93	1.00

Table 5. The average execution time (ms)

Network	SLPA	SBDSLPA
GGSN	45	37
SMN	41	29
SPN	43	35

modularity of SBDSLPA is larger than SLPA by 20.7 percent. It shows that the result of SBDSLPA is closer to the real community classification.

Table 4 provides the average normalized mutual information of the experimental results on the three signed network data sets. The larger the value of NMI is, the more stable the results from the community detection algorithms are. From the table, the average value of NMI of the SBDSLPA is larger than SLPA on all the three test network datasets. On average, SBDSLPA's NMI is larger than SLPA's NMI by 10.9 percent. So SBDSLPA is more stable than SLPA.

The average execution time of SLPA and SBDSLPA on the three datasets is given in Table 5. From the table we can see that the average execution time of SBDSLPA is shorter than the SLPA. SBDSLPA's average execution time is shorter than SLPA by 21.9 percent. This shows that the convergence rate of SBDSLPA is much faster than SLPA on the same datasets.

7   Conclusions

Label propagation algorithm is a linear time algorithm for community detection without using any prior parameters. It is widely used for solving community detection problems in unsigned networks. In this paper, we analyze the triangle structural balance theory of signed networks and propose a community detection algorithm in the signed network called Signed Network Label Propagation Algorithm with Structural Balance Degree (SBDSLPA). First, we present a novel measurement to the structural balance degree of each edge in the signed network. Then, this measure is used to control the label propagation process. It makes labels propagate easily in the subset where the positive edges are intensive, but difficultly in the subnet where the negative edges are intensive. The experimental results show that SBDSLPA is more effective and stable than SLPA in the signed network.

References

1. Girvan, M., Newman, M.E.: Community structure in social and biological networks. Proc. Natl. Acad. Sci. **99**, 7821–7826 (2002)
2. Newman, M.E.: The structure and function of complex networks. SIAM Rev. **45**, 167–256 (2003)
3. Dev, H.: A user interaction based community detection algorithm for online social networks. In: Proceedings of the 2014 ACM SIGMOD International Conference on Management of Data, pp. 1607–1608 (2014)
4. Lin, W.Q., Kong, X.N., Yu, P.S., Wu, Q.Y., Jia, Y., Li, C.: Community detection in incomplete information networks. In: Proceedings of the 21st International Conference on World Wide Web, pp. 341–350 (2012)
5. Jin, H., Wang, S.L., Li, C.Y.: Community detection in complex networks by density-based clustering. Phys. A Stat. Mech. Appl. **392**, 4606–4618 (2013)
6. Barbieri, N., Bonchi, F., Manco, G.: Cascade-based community detection. In: Proceedings of the Sixth ACM International Conference on Web Search and Data Mining, pp. 33–42 (2013)
7. Xia, Z.Y., Bu, Z.: Community detection based on a semantic network. Knowl. Inf. Syst. **26**, 30–39 (2012)
8. Raghavan, U.N., Albert, R., Kumara, S.: Near linear time algorithm to detect community structures in large-scale networks. Phys. Rev. E **76**, 036106 (2007)
9. Šubelj, L., Bajec, M.: Unfolding communities in large complex networks: combining defensive and offensive label propagation for core extraction. Phys. Rev. E **83**, 885–896 (2011)
10. Šubelj, L., Bajec, M.: Robust network community detection using balanced propagation. Phys. Condens. Matter **81**, 353–362 (2011)
11. Heider, F.: Attitudes and cognitive organization. J. Psychol. **21**, 107–112 (1946)
12. Nakanishi, H., Nakazawa, S., Ishida, T., et al.: Can software agents influence human relations?: balance theory in agent-mediated communities. In: International Joint Conference on Autonomous Agents & Multiagent Systems, AAMAS 2003, 14–18 July 2003, Melbourne, Victoria, Australia, Proceedings, pp. 717–724 (2003)
13. Sergio, G., Pablo, J., Alex, A.: Analysis of community structure in networks of correlated data. Phys. Rev. E Stat. Nonlinear Soft Matter Phys. **80**, 016114 (2009)
14. Traag, V.A., Bruggeman, J.: Community detection in networks with positive and negative links. Phys. Rev. E **80**, 036115 (2009)
15. Li, X., Chen, H., Li, S.: Exploiting emotions in social interactions to detect online social communities. In: PACIS (2010)
16. Bansal, N., Blum, A., Chawla, S.: Correlation clustering. Mach. Learn. **56**, 89–113 (2004)
17. Yang, B., Cheung, W.K., Liu, J.: Community mining from signed social networks. IEEE Trans. Knowl. Data Eng. **19**, 1333–1348 (2007)
18. Sharma, T., Charls, A., Singh, P.K.: Community mining in signed social networks—an automated approach. In: Proceedings of the International Conference on Computer Engineering and Applications, pp. 152–157. IACSIT Press, Singapore (2009)

Towards Modeling Confidentiality in Persuasive Robot Dialogue

Ivor D. Addo[1(✉)], Sheikh Iqbal Ahamed[1], and William C. Chu[2]

[1] Marquette University, Milwaukee, WI, USA
{ivor.addo,sheikh.ahamed}@marquette.edu
[2] Tunghai University, Taichung City, Taiwan
cchu@thu.edu.tw

Abstract. In many persuasive health interventions, humanoid robots and other intelligent systems are capable of carrying out meaningful conversations with human subjects in an effort to influence humans towards behavior or attitudinal change. In human-to-human conversations, the listening party often has the ability to discern whether or not certain aspects of the conversation should be kept confidential. Consequently, in conversational service robot scenarios (including elderly care use cases), humans often have the expectation that humanoid robots are capable of preserving the privacy and confidentiality of a given human-robot dialogue. In this literature, we explore the inherent challenges and approaches to modeling confidentiality in human-robot interaction (HRI) dialogue scenarios involving a cloud-enabled networked robot. As a result, we share a novel reference model for designing persuasive dialogue systems.

Keywords: HRI dialogue · Persuasive robots · Confidentiality · Privacy · Reference model · Privacy framework

1 Introduction

Doctor-patient confidentiality and counselor-patient confidentiality are well documented as essential aspects of the code of ethics that allows human subjects to freely discuss private and revealing information concerning their lives [1]. Yet, very little has been done to advance these tenets in persuasive dialogue systems which often play the role of a health coach or counselor to humans. Persuasive systems often employ dialogue systems to support intervention towards attitude and behavior change. The dialogue system in a persuasive system may be implemented as an intelligent software agent or, in some cases, as an intelligent companion robot.

In most human-to-human communications, there is often a need to evaluate both verbal and non-verbal communication signals to truly understand the situation at hand. Verbal communication often involves the use of spoken words while non-verbal communication involves visual cues including facial expressions, body movement, proximity, body language, and more [5, 6]. Generally, when a human stands further away from another human (i.e. proximity) it indicates their level of comfort with the other party. In other scenarios, a human might say something positive through spoken

© Springer International Publishing Switzerland 2016
C.K. Chang et al. (Eds.): ICOST 2016, LNCS 9677, pp. 436–442, 2016.
DOI: 10.1007/978-3-319-39601-9_39

word, while simultaneously exhibiting contradicting signals through non-verbal cues. A combination of verbal and non-verbal signals can be used by intelligent systems to discern confidentiality in dialogue systems.

Imagine a simple dialogue exchange between a teenage girl (*Amy*) and her friend (*Chloe*) at a college party, *Amy* whispers to *Chloe* the spoken word "I'm pregnant" (as illustrated in Fig. 1 – left image). Even though, *Amy* did not explicitly indicate to *Chloe* that her pregnancy should be kept confidential, the combination of the "*whisper*" (i.e. low pitch sound and close proximity to *Chloe* during the exchange), content of the verbal communication (i.e. "*pregnant*"), and the context of the scenario (i.e. at a crowded party scene) can be enough grounds for suggesting confidentiality. Arguably, if Chloe's next utterance in response to the news is a loud pitched celebratory response (e.g. "Wow, congratulations!") it might damage *Amy*'s trust and comfort with sharing future confidential dialogue with *Chloe*. This is the type of implicit confidentiality that this literature seeks to enable companion robots with. The ability to detect and preserve confidentiality through their day-to-day interactions with humans is critical.

Fig. 1. On the left, we illustrate an exhibition of non-verbal cues in a human-to-human conversation regarding a confidential subject (involving whispering). On the right, we illustrate a sample conversation gesture between a futuristic Android robot and a human in an HRI dialogue as the robot shares spoken word regarding a confidential subject.

A common design practice in dialogue systems involves implementing a dialogue manager (DM) [2, 3] to generate, consume, and coordinate both verbal and non-verbal dialogue interactions between the human subjects and the intelligent systems involved. In the traditional dialogue system, there is often an Automatic Speech Recognition (ASR) module and a Text-to-Speech (TTS) module involved with consuming verbal content and exuding speech capabilities in the intelligent system, respectively [4]. That notwithstanding, non-verbal cues including gestures and facial expression can be identified using the camera inputs on the dialogue system. In investigating an approach to modeling confidentiality in HRI dialogue, we implemented our solution using the NAO T14 humanoid robot platform.

In the ensuing literature, we discuss our motivation for this study, the challenges and requirements associated with implementing confidentiality in dialogue systems, and a resulting reference architecture model. Previous studies have examined best practices for designing dialogue systems [2–4]. However, at the time of publication, we were unable to find any published model for implementing confidentiality in HRI dialogue systems.

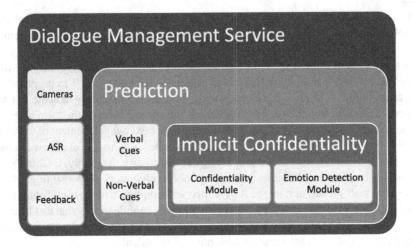

Fig. 2. Reference model for the DMS

Accordingly, we view the proposed reference model as our novel contribution. We conclude with a review of opportunities for using and extending the model in the future.

2   Motivation and Application Scenarios

Intelligent conversational systems can be used to motivate behavior change among people who are interested in behavior change towards curbing obesity [5], risky behavior change among Post-Traumatic Stress Disorder (PTSD) patients, smoking cessation, and more. There are other applications of conversational robots in elderly care monitoring scenarios [8]. Our primary motivation is to enable autonomous systems with an ability to implicitly detect confidentiality and preserve privacy in HRI dialogue systems.

2.1   Relevant Use Cases

Two use cases that we considered in an effort to validate the implementation of the reference model include the following:

- Simulation of a humanoid robot as an interaction partner in an elderly care scenario.
- Simulation of a humanoid robot as a health coach in a childhood obesity scenario.

In both scenarios, the human parties would expect to use the robot as a socially assistive partner with human-like social capabilities in lieu of treating it as a meager tool. In such interaction scenarios, the robot is expected to be able to exhibit communication skills by using natural language, emotion, and maintain social relationships over a period of time [5, 8].

2.2 Common Challenges and Requirements

Among the scenarios that we examined, the dialogue system would be expected to be able to cater to the following challenges and requirements:

- **Explicit:** Detect explicit confidential conversations when the human subject explicitly states (either before or after a dialogue interaction) that the conversation should be kept confidential
- **Implicit:** Detect implicit confidential conversations when the human subject attempts to confide in the robot without explicitly stating that the ensuing conversation should be treated as confidential content
- **Response:** Determine an appropriate way to respond to confidential content uttered by the human subject so that the human is encouraged to freely share additional private information
- **Consent:** Determine how to store confidential content in a centralized intelligent storage system such that it is not shared with other intelligent systems that share a common knowledge base
- **Compliance:** In a US-based smart environment, the Health Insurance Portability and Accountability Act's (HIPAA) compliance rules [1] will apply when personal health information is collected and stored by the dialogue system.

3 Reference Architecture Model

The proposed reference architecture model seeks to address the common concerns described in Sect. 2, by implementing a Confidentiality Module (CM) in the Dialogue Management Service (DMS). Using multimodal sources including the ASR module and the cameras on the intelligent system, the robot system will feed input signals (including both verbal and non-verbal cues) to the DMS to help discern implicit confidentiality. Using supervised machine learning techniques, the CM component will evaluate communication patterns while establishing several input signals as features, in an effort to classify a specific dialogue pattern as implicitly confidential. Collaborative filtering feedback from the end user will be used as additional input to refine the DMS while making use of machine learning techniques.

The challenges identified earlier, are addressed in the reference model by having the robot confirm confidentiality verbally when it is unsure of its confidential classification. Where necessary, the robot can state to the human subject that the conversation in question will be kept confidential unless the conversation involves harm to the subject or others. Once a dialogue is determined to be confidential, it will be tagged with metadata indicating that it is confidential prior to persisting it to a HIPAA-compliant central storage system so other intelligent knowledge systems cannot access it without informed consent. When the DMS detects personal health information (PHI) it will remind the end user of its privacy preservation feature.

3.1 Machine Learning Techniques

Machine Learning (ML) is often considered a domain of computational intelligence which is concerned with building software solutions that automatically improve with experience [12]. Notably, a time series is often viewed as a sequence of observations, $St \in R$ that is ordered in time [12]. Invariably, detection of confidential information in natural language is expected to take the shape of time series data. This approach lends itself to the prediction of future outcomes based on the past and perhaps offers an opportunity to be able to control the process that creates the series data and also understand the mechanism for creating the series data. In this work, we consider multivariate time series data where several measurements about a given class of dialogue pattern can be collected repeatedly. The proposed framework is depicted in Fig. 3, below.

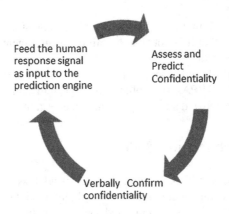

Fig. 3. Proposed strategy for the confidentiality detection engine

Machine learning techniques for *Feature Selection* can be used to determine evidence-based features that tend to be more relevant to predicting confidentiality in dialogue. Each raw feature will have an associated score indicating its level of intensity. Some of the raw features that we explored include *low tone of voice, whispering gesture pattern, oration of specific spoken words* associated with confidentiality. A weight can be applied to some of the features based on ratings by experts.

3.2 Exuding Trust and Eliciting Confidentiality

To encourage the human subject to share additional private information and promote trust between the human and the robot, the conversational robot will seek to select and respond to the human using a conversation pattern that acknowledges the detection of confidentiality. Empathetic conversation patterns will be, in turn, selected by the DMS and spoken by the robot through the Text-to-Speech (TTS) feature.

4   Evaluation

To test the efficacy of the proposed strategy, we plan on using a number of approaches including:

- *An end-user survey* to determine the perceived accuracy of the system in identifying implicit confidentiality. A representative sample size with a diverse demographic background will be employed to take the survey.
- *Performance analysis* of various classification algorithms. Multiple classification algorithms including the following can be evaluated to dynamically select the best algorithm or model for a given set of input features: *Support Vector Machines (SVM), Boosted Decision Tree, Regression Trees, Random Forests, Neural Networks*, and *Nearest Neighbors*.

  It is important to quantify the performance of the selected classifiers in a bid to measure and improve their accuracy. Our available data set will be split between the *Training Set* and the *Test Set* using an 80:20 split ratio. The classifier will be trained using the 80 % set and evaluated with the remaining 20 % of the data set. The classifier accuracy will be measure as a percentage score of test data points that are correctly classified by the classifier. We propose the use of *ROC* curves for comparing the various models. We expect a greater area under the curve (*AUC*) to indicate a more accurate model. The *Gini-statistic* can also be computed from the ROC curves.

We also propose the use of the *K-fold cross-validation* technique to minimize potential prediction errors. With this approach, we will divide the training set into k (=10) folds and use the kth fold for testing each of the planned k experiments. This will help minimize issues pertaining to an unfortunate data split. In addition, the inclusion of a real-life feedback loop, as illustrated in Fig. 2 will be useful for minimizing uncertainty in the predictions. We find the need for *ongoing validation* critical to minimizing model decay over time. In the same token, we expect the model to be fine-tuned or rebuilt when deterioration in the model accuracy measures are discovered.

5   Conclusion

With the advent of persuasive robots and intelligent systems, we are confident that the proposed reference model will be very useful for implementing confidentiality in future persuasive systems.

References

1. American Psychology Association: Protecting your privacy: understanding confidentiality. http://www.apa.org/helpcenter/confidentiality.aspx
2. Lee, C., Cha, Y., Kuc, T.: Implementation of dialogue system for intelligent service robots. In: 2008 International Conference on Control, Automation and Systems, ICCAS 2008, Seoul, pp. 2038–2042 (2008)

3. Oinas-Kukkonen, H., Harjumaa, M.: Persuasive systems design: key issues, process model, and system features. Commun. Inf. Syst. **24**(1), 485–500 (2009). Article no. 28
4. Nakano, M., et al.: A two-layer model for behavior and dialogue planning in conversational service robots. In: 2005 IEEE/RSJ International Conference on Intelligent Robots and Systems (IROS 2005), pp. 3329–3335 (2005)
5. Addo, I.D., Ahamed, S.I., Chu, W.C.: Toward collective intelligence for fighting obesity. In: COMPSAC, pp. 690–695 (2013)
6. Breazeal, C.: Designing Sociable Robots. MIT Press, Cambridge (2004)
7. Kanda, T., Shiomi, M., Hagita, N.: Communication robots: application challenges of human-robot interaction. In: Advances in Interaction Studies – New Frontiers in Human-Robot Interaction, pp. 235–256 (2011)
8. Meerbeck, B., Saerbeck, M.: Communication robots: application challenges of human-robot interaction. In: Advances in Interaction Studies – New Frontiers in Human-Robot Interaction, pp. 257–277 (2011)
9. Ogawa, T., Morita, K., Kitagawa, H., Fuketa, M., AOE, J.-I.: A study of dialogue robots with haptic interactions. In: 2011 7th International Conference on Natural Language Processing and Knowledge Engineering (NLP-KE), Tokushima, pp. 285–288 (2011)
10. Marsland, S.: Machine Learning an Algorithmic Perspective. CRC Press, Boca Raton (2009)
11. Sutton, R.S., Barto, A.G.: Reinforcement Learning: An Introduction. MIT Press, Cambridge (1998)
12. Gianluca, B.: Machine learning strategies for time series prediction. In: Machine Learning Summer School (2013). http://www.ulb.ac.be/di/map/gbonte/ftp/time_ser.pdf

What Make You Sure that Health Informatics Is Secure

Bian Yang[✉]

Norwegian Information Security Laboratory (NISlab) and Center of Cyber
and Information Security (CCIS), Norwegian University of Science and Technology (NTNU),
Teknologivegen 22, 2815 Gjøvik, Norway
bian.yang@ntnu.no

Abstract. We show in this poster the various types of threats to information security in health informatics and try identifying the promising technical solutions to addressing these threats. In addition, we contend that information security in health informatics does not rely merely on technical solutions but on a holistic solution incorporating more socio-technical understandings. Though the challenges to adoption of information security controls in health informatics are usually reflected on the technologies' usability aspect, they are deeply rooted on the socio-technical level involving various human factors such as the gap in the working culture, in the professional language and its implications, and in the understanding of the workflow and the operational mechanisms in the two fields - healthcare and security. We will preliminarily investigate in this poster a promising approach to modelling and measuring the influences from the socio-technical aspect.

Keywords: Information security · Health informatics · Socio-technical understanding · Usability · Human behavior and response modelling · Human factors · Biometric sensing · Data analysis

1   Introduction

Along with the penetration of information and communications technologies in the healthcare domain, security and privacy concerns are growing in recent years triggered by the increasing real-life security accidents such as medical database breaches [1, 2], data and system ransom [3, 4], medical device hacking [5, 6], online privacy leakage [7, 8], *etc.* In many cases, health informatics can unexpectedly open another way to the attackers besides serving its original purpose. The changes brought by health informatics in the past decade include, but not limited to, (1) digitization of health and medical records; (2) proliferation of Bring-Your-Own-Devices (BYOD) in the healthcare context, for both medical staffs and patients; (3) telemedicine and electronic records sharing; (4) connection of medical devices to the cyber space; (5) delivery of Internet and cloud based healthcare services across the borders. Most of these trends, while improving the accuracy, efficiency, and availability of healthcare services, increase the attack surface from the adversary's perspective. For example, taking the advantage of electronic health records and cloud-based data management applications, *e.g.*, Microsoft HealthVault, Google Health, and Dossia, an attacker could collect full profiles of the target patients. In addition, BYOD and electronic health records sharing

© Springer International Publishing Switzerland 2016
C.K. Chang et al. (Eds.): ICOST 2016, LNCS 9677, pp. 443–448, 2016.
DOI: 10.1007/978-3-319-39601-9_40

increase the chances of identity theft and data breach, due to the loss of devices or negligent/malicious security and privacy policy violation [9]. Wired or wireless connection enabled medical devices, e.g., a Bluetooth-enabled pacemaker [6], can open a channel to cyberattacks. Under the increasing privacy concerns, the scope of legal entities has been expanding to include business associates [10], which in turn requires more stakeholders to adopt technology safeguards for data protection and technology integrity. On the other hand, statistics showed that most security breaches can be attributed to socio-technical and human factors [9, 11, 12], such as insiders' negligence or social engineering based attacks, which go beyond the scope of technology.

We will summarize in Sect. 2 some trends happening or being envisioned in the future healthcare sector, and the typical security and privacy vulnerabilities. Section 3 preliminarily analyzes the socio-technical essence of the security problem with health informatics, and presents a concept design of human behavior analysis based approach to modelling the human factors and to enhancing the health informatics' security from the socio-technical perspective. Section 4 concludes this poster paper.

2   Trends, Vulnerabilities, and Enabling Technologies

Healthcare is a complex ecosystem in which multiple players, *e.g.*, patients, healthcare practitioners, healthcare research and education institutes, healthcare infrastructure maintainers, funders such as governments and insurers, ICT service providers, and information and cyber security experts, get involved with different interests, mindsets, and working cultures. We need to understand the trends in the healthcare domain taking place in the next decades. Some examples are:

Shifts of healthcare patterns including (1) from hospital to home and cyber space to reduce the cost, and to maximize the availability of healthcare resources; (2) from in-hospital treatment to prevention, to reduce the cost and improve the healthcare quality from a long-term perspective; (3) from the doctor-centered model to the patient-centered model, to maximize the healthcare quality based on understanding and respecting patients' expectation and making personalized healthcare plans; (4) from pay-for-service to pay-for-quality in cost model [13, 14], to improve the whole eco-system's benefit-cost efficiency; (5) from healthcare organizations to more stakeholders in liability to security breaches [10].

Adoption of new technologies including mobile health, off-the-shelf setups for heath monitoring, virtual reality and augmented reality for rehabilitation and virtual clinical trials, cloud based health analytics, crowd data sourcing, social media and online health forum for case studies and second opinions generation, *etc.*

Personalized health including the adoption of personal health records (PHR), personalized health data analytics, personalized medicine, data-driven inference and information fusion as done by the IBM Dr. Watson platform [15].

In terms of information security, the vulnerabilities of the existing health informatics system can be categorized into two types – the technique vulnerabilities and the socio-technological ones. The former include, for example, lack of security-by-design and privacy-by-design guideline in the technology concept design phase (*e.g.*, the pacemaker's cyber-threat case [5, 6]), lack of lightweight and low-energy-consumption cybersecurity mechanisms for Internet-of-Things [16], BYOD in the working environment, lack of efficient and secure identity management in the healthcare workflow, lack of convenient access controls for the cloud and social media based data storage and sharing, and those obsolete ICT sub-systems which are un-patchable or not yet patched but still at service [17, 18]. With such technique vulnerabilities existing in other sectors as well, we found there are some socio-technical ones being more typical for the healthcare sector including the usability challenges [19] which have been widely aware of, the difference in working culture, the hindrance from the law and regulation aspect [20] especially for those Internet-based health services delivered across borders, etc.

   In recent years, more efforts have been invested in the search of new enabling technologies for security and privacy enhancement, which can be promising for the use in health informatics especially for applications devoted to the cloud environment and data analysis uses, such as statistical privacy for outsourced data analysis [21], full homomorphic encryption [22], privacy-preserving biometrics [23], anonymity communications and data sharing [24], attribute-based authentication [25], etc.

3   The Human Factors

The socio-technical aspect, a.k.a. technological challenges attributed to human and social factors, characterizes the security problem in the healthcare sector in a unique way because of many features of the healthcare sector: the beneficence-first principle, trust-based practice, interruptive and sometimes stressful working environment, etc. In security relevant cases, such human factors can be reflected on different aspects. It is noted that there is a gap in working culture between the security and the healthcare fields. One example is the beneficence-first principle respected by the healthcare practitioners, which may precede the need of the patients' privacy during emergencies. In other scenarios a healthcare practitioner may choose to deliver the healthcare services to patients without strong requirement of identity verification, which may unexpectedly encourage the actions of identity theft and faking in order to milk the healthcare or social benefit resources. Another challenges is, for instance, the difference in working language, such as the term "health security", which can be interpret as healthcare service assurance on the strategy and policy level by professionals working in the public health domain, or as patient safety understood by a medical staff, or as information security of the healthcare services from the view of an information security expert. The trust issue is another typical challenge to the healthcare practitioners, such as blind trust showed in the survey results disclosed in [19] on the adoption of PKI (choosing to believe they do not need to care about other security requirements once PKI is adopted), or such as sharing accounts, leaving the screen open, speaking out passwords, believing that identity frauds do not exist by their own experience, not expecting an ID verification from their colleagues [19], etc. All these challenges in trust management can be exploited easily by attackers via social engineering based tricks. However, from the healthcare practitioner's perspective, some good practices in the eye of an information security expert such as ID checks, system login and sign-off, screensaver, diversified passwords for different systems, *etc.*, can seriously degrade the efficiency and availability of the services to be delivered to the patients. One security concern is that such inconvenient information security controls actually end up to an encouragement to circumvent such controls by other insecure but more efficient ways. Other socio-technical challenges include the lack of security training and awareness, negligence [9] towards security policy under emergencies or other stressful situations, lack of individualized guideline for security incident response, *etc.*

Aware of such socio-technical challenges, we are so far short of a quantitative way to modelling human factors from the information security perspective. We might need to resort to an interdisciplinary and socio-technical approach to this end. The future security and privacy designs for health informatics should incorporate knowledge created from the behavioral analysis of human responses to account for the socio-technical and human factors for incident prevention, detection, response, and disaster recovery. We propose a concept design towards the future human factors modelling for health informatics security, as illustrated in Fig. 1. The concept design assumes that the human factors can be modelled by mapping the measured human responses (*e.g.*, the subjects' behaviors captured by the audio/video system and the inner states captured by wearable sensors) to the security incidents logged by the information systems (*e.g.*, the ICT infrastructure in the work place, the medial equipment, and the BYOD devices) and humans (colleagues, patients, *etc.*) interacted with the subject under the study, *i.e.*, healthcare practitioners in his/her working place. The mapping could be established by

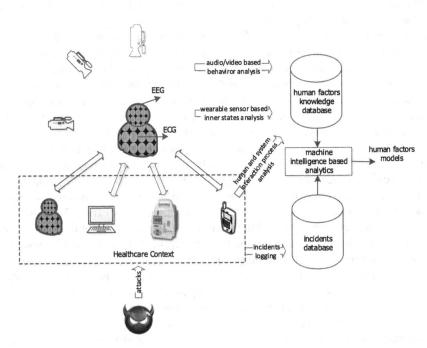

Fig. 1. Human factors modeling based on human response measurement and analysis during security incidents

the advanced machine intelligence such as the deep learning technologies popularly adopted nowadays.

4 Conclusions

We presented in this poster a status of the security and privacy threats to the healthcare sector and health informatics, and especially noted the unique socio-technical essence of the security challenges. In addition, we proposed a concept design to use biometric sensing to measure human responses to security incidents and use machine intelligence for modelling these human factors, as a potential approach to identifying the socio-technical patterns in order to better understanding the security and privacy problems in the healthcare sector.

Acknowledgments. This work is partially funded by the strategical funding from the Center for Cyber and Information Security (ccis.no) to support the research initiative on health and welfare security.

References

1. Wikipedia: Medical Data Breach. https://en.wikipedia.org/wiki/Medical_data_breach. Accessed 07 Apr 2016
2. Ahmed, M., Ahamad, M.: Combating abuse of health data in the age of eHealth Exchange. In: 2014 IEEE International Conference on Healthcare Informatics, pp. 109–118. IEEE Press (2014)
3. Boatman, K.: Beware the Rise of Ransomware. http://us.norton.com/yoursecurityresource/detail.jsp?aid=rise_in_ransomware. Accessed 07 Apr 2016
4. Los Angeles Hospital Paid Hackers $17,000 Ransom in Bitcoins. http://www.reuters.com/article/us-california-hospital-cyberattack-idUSKCN0VR085. Accessed 07 Apr 2016
5. Sametinger, J., Rozenblit, J., Lysecky, R., Ott, P.: Security challenges for medical devices. Commun. ACM **58**(4), 74–82 (2015)
6. Vallance, C.: Could Hackers Break My Heart via My Pacemaker? http://www.bbc.com/news/technology-34899713. Accessed 07 Apr 2016
7. Subedar, H., El-Khatib, K.: Privacy and security concerns for health data collected using off-the-shelf health monitoring devices. In: IEEE 11th International Conference on Wireless and Mobile Computing, Networking and Communications, pp. 341–348 (2015)
8. Libert, T.: Privacy implications of health information seeking on the web. Commun. ACM **58**(3), 68–77 (2015)
9. SANS Institute Survey: New Threats Drive Improved Practices: State of Cybersecurity in Health Care Organizations (2014). https://www.sans.org/reading-room/whitepapers/analyst/threats-drive-improved-practices-state-cybersecurity-health-care-organizations-35652. Accessed 07 Apr 2016
10. The HITECH Act. https://en.wikipedia.org/wiki/Health_Information_Technology_for_Economic_and_Clinical_Health_Act#cite_note-20. Accessed 07 Apr 2016
11. Annual report to congress: FISMA, 18 March 2016. https://www.whitehouse.gov/sites/default/files/omb/assets/egov_docs/final_fy_2015_fisma_report_to_congress_03_18_2016.pdf. Accessed 07 Apr 2016

12. 2015 HIMSS Cybersecurity Survey - Full Report. http://www.himss.org/2015-cybersecurity-survey/full-report. Accessed 07 Apr 2016

13. Leonard, K.: Hospital of Yesterday: The Biggest Changes in Health Care. http://health.usnews.com/health-news/hospital-of-tomorrow/articles/2014/07/15/hospital-of-yesterday-the-biggest-changes-in-health-care. Accessed 07 Apr 2016

14. Ritchie, A., Marbury, D., Verdon, D., Mazzolini, C., Boyles, S.: Shifting reimbursement models: the risks and rewards for primary care. http://medicaleconomics.modernmedicine.com/medical-economics/content/tags/aca/shifting-reimbursement-models-risks-and-rewards-primary-care?page=full. Accessed 07 Apr 2016

15. Keim, B.: IBM's Dr. Watson will see you…someday. IEEE Spectr. **52**(6), 76–77 (2015)

16. Maksimovi, M., Vujovi, V., Perii, B.: A custom internet of things healthcare system. In: 10th Iberian Conference on Information Systems and Technologies (2015)

17. Dimick, C.: Healthcare Still Unprepared for Cybersecurity Attacks. http://journal.ahima.org/2015/10/20/report-healthcare-still-unprepared-for-cybersecurity-attacks/. Accessed 07 Apr 2016

18. Kovacs, E.: 1,400 Flaws Found in Outdated CareFusion Medical Systems. http://www.securityweek.com/1400-flaws-found-outdated-carefusion-medical-systems. Accessed 07 Apr 2016

19. Fernando, J.: The elephant in the room: health information system security and the user-level environment. In: International Conference for Internet Technology and Secured Transactions (2009)

20. Mirkovic, J., Skipenes, E., Christiansen, E.K., Bryhni, H.: Security and privacy legislation guidelines for developing personal health records. In: Second International Conference on eDemocracy & eGovernment (2015)

21. Machanavajjhala, A., Kifer, D.: Designing statistical privacy for your data. Commun. ACM **58**(3), 58–67 (2015)

22. Popa, R.A., Zeldovich, N.: How to compute with data you can't see. IEEE Spectr. **52**(8), 42–47 (2015)

23. Breebaart, J., Yang, B., Dulman, I., Busch, C.: Biometric template protection. Datenschutz und Datensicherheit-DuD **33**(5), 29–304 (2009)

24. Feigenbaum, J., Ford, B.: Seeking anonymity in an internet panopticon. Commun. ACM **58**(10), 58–69 (2015)

25. Guo, L., Zhang, C., Sun, J., Fang, Y.: A privacy-preserving attribute-based authentication system for mobile health networks. IEEE Trans. Mob. Comput. **13**(9), 1927–1941 (2013)

Workshop 1: Mobile Health Services

Towards Crowd-Sourced Air Quality and Physical Activity Monitoring by a Low-Cost Mobile Platform

Bian Yang[1]([✉]), Núria Castell[2], Junjie Pei[1], Yang Du[1],
Alemayehu Gebremedhin[1], and Øyvind Kirkevold[1]

[1] Norwegian University of Science and Technology (NTNU),
Teknologivegen 22, 2815 Gjøvik, Norway
{bian.yang, alemayehu.gebremedhin,
oyvind.kirkevold}@ntnu.no
[2] Norwegian Institute for Air Research (NILU),
Instituttveien 18, 2007 Kjeller, Norway
nuria.castell@nilu.no

Abstract. Crowd-sourced air quality monitoring has been becoming popular in recent years for environmental surveillance and public health study. Most of such air quality monitoring programs merely invites volunteers to collect air quality data by portable or mobile air quality sensors. However, we assume it could be more interesting to measure a person's physical activity intensity and his/her exposure to the air quality in a synchronized way in order to measure the air quality's personalized impact on health, because different persons' physical activities can differ in location, time, *etc.*, and can be very individualized as well. To this end, during the 2014–2015 winter-spring season, we designed and implemented a low-cost mobile platform for recording air quality (both sensor data and subjective feeling data) and participants' physical activity intensity. The developed platform is supposed to assist in future crowd-sourced environmental health studies. Data collection activities were arranged to prove the feasibility of the developed mobile platform. Over the data collected, preliminary analysis have been done identifying the correlations among air quality indicators, participants' subjective feelings of air quality, physical activity status measured by wearable sensors, and reported health symptoms. The data collection operation and the data analysis results demonstrate the feasibility of the adopted methodology and the developed platform towards future user-centered, personalized, and crowd-sourced environmental health and health care studies.

Keywords: Crowd-sourcing · Air quality · Physical activity · Environmental monitoring · Health care · Mobile platform

1 Introduction

Air pollution is considered harmful to health and has been linked with respiratory diseases and cancer [1]. The WHO reported that in year 2012 around 7 million people's death were linked to air pollution [2]. A recent report [3] based on the survey data

© Springer International Publishing Switzerland 2016
C.K. Chang et al. (Eds.): ICOST 2016, LNCS 9677, pp. 451–463, 2016.
DOI: 10.1007/978-3-319-39601-9_41

collected during year 1990–2013 by the research [4] confirmed the air pollution's impact on premature death and health in general. Quantifying air quality's impact on human health needs reliable data collected from both environmental monitoring and public health sectors. However, existing environmental health studies face several challenges: first, data collection activities from the two sectors are not always synergized and therefore in most cases only cross-sectional studies instead of control or cohort studies can be done; second, due to the cost and size factors, professional air quality measurement equipment are usually sparsely installed on the town/district level and not portable, which impacts the trustworthiness of data precision on the community and street levels; third, public health studies are based on large-scale data collection which is usually both costly and time consuming; the last but not the least, existing environmental health studies aim at generating trustworthy global statistics from a large-scale data survey instead of analyzing personal profiles or giving personalized health advice from a longitudinal study perspective. While technologies advancement in recent years in personal smart devices, wireless sensors, and compact electronics makes air quality data recording devices portable and low in cost [5, 6], and crowd data sourcing makes data collection easier such as what happened in the EU project CITI-SENSE [7], there is so far few research and innovation on exploiting such new technologies and the crowd data sourcing methodology for longitudinal studies of air quality on human health. In this work we aimed to test the feasibility of using low-cost portable sensors to measure the air quality and the physical activity and using crowd data sourcing for data collection. Thanks to the fact that the two types of data are collected from the same subjects, the developed data collection platform can therefore enable both cohort studies generating public health statistics and longitudinal studies generating personalized health advice.

The remaining part of the paper is organized into the following sections: Sect. 2 describes the methodologies we used, Sect. 3 describes the data collection platform we developed, Sect. 4 describes the data collection settings, Sect. 5 presents the preliminary data analysis results, and Sect. 6 concludes this paper.

2 Background and Methodologies

City residents, especially those sensitive to air quality, such as asthma, Chronic Obstructive Pulmonary Disease (COPD), and cardiovascular diseases patients, may suffer from very localized air pollution, such as at a specific location at a specific time point, which cannot be accurately extrapolated from the stationary air quality monitors due to distance and other geographic and human factors in the city. Therefore, a system that can be used to obtain higher resolution (e.g., on the street and residential block level) air quality monitoring results, preferably in real time, could be very helpful to those local residents who care about air quality around their specific living environment or a location they perform most of the activities at. In addition, long-term data collection and analysis may disclose the air quality dynamics of a specific location inside a city so both the local residents and the city facility planning agencies have sufficient evidence to reason and make an informed and evidence-based decision in personal activity planning and city transportation and facility planning.

In Norway, the major air pollution sources include particulate matter (PM) and nitrogen dioxide (NO_2). The particulate matter is mainly contributed by traffic emission, the use of studded winter tires, and wood burning in winter. NO_2 is mainly from the traffic emission. The Mjøsa lake valley area where the authors' research institute is located, is especially of interest for a study in this project because of its valley geometric conditions (thus harder for polluted air to disperse) and cold weather (thus more wood burning) in winter seasons.

To prove the concept of using low-cost mobile data collection platform and crowd data sourcing for future environmental health study, we adopted the following methodologies when devising the data collection plan.

Synchronized Data Collection. In order to collect data for case control or cohorts based public health study, the air quality data and the persons' activity and health data should be synchronized, *i.e.*, the person whose health data are examined should be the same person who was actually exposed to the air quality environment. To this end, we invited the participants to collect the air quality data and their activity and health data in the same time.

Multiple Data Collection Sessions. Multiple data collection sessions should be arranged to obtain enough data along the time axis for longitudinal study on personal health history analysis and trend prediction. Such cumulated personal data can be used to find known health patterns or be contributed as a case to large-scale public health databases.

Activity Based Exposure Measurement. In a city, the air quality can be varied in geographic locations. To increase the sampling density, mobile sensors can be adopted to measure the air quality in different locations and time as a low-cost means compared to the case distributed stationary sensors are installed. However, health impacts are directly caused by human exposures, and therefore persons travelling in the same route in a city could have different health impacts due to the variance in their exposure intensity. For instance, travelling in vehicles and by walking usually have different exposure degrees [8]. We assumed, in our data collection activities, participants may have different walking routes, and when passing the same geographic location they may have different exposure degrees which can be reasonably estimated by their physical activity intensity, for instance, indicated by the heart beat rate [8]. This assumption inspired us to adopt human activity sensors to estimate the actual exposure of a specific participant in a specific location.

Combined Objective and Subjective Data Collection. To ensure the accuracy of a crowd-sourced data collection platform, we'd better to have the measured results calibrated with those stationary professional sensors (for both air quality and physical activity) to ensure the quality of the collected data. Combined objective and subjective data collection, *i.e.*, recording both the sensors' output and the participant's subjective feeling in the form of a real-time questionnaire in a smartphone, can be another way to roughly cross-check the quality of the collected data by examining the correlation between the objective data and the subjective data.

Low-Cost Mobile Devices. To encourage citizens' participation, the platform components, namely the air quality sensor, the physical activity sensor, and the smartphone used to collect the subjective feeling and sensors' output, should be both compact, light in weight, and low in cost in terms of the affordability to normal families in the authors' country.

Usability Enhanced by Efficient Data Logging and Data Sharing. The two types of data – objective data from sensors' output and subjective data from participant's input – should require as less effort from the participant as possible. Data logging and transmission to the smartphone from the sensors should be automated. The smartphone interface for taking participant's input should be easy to operate, *e.g.*, by limiting the times of screen-touch interaction and setting all questionnaire contents in a linear way. The collected data should be saved in the smartphone after measurement at each location and backed up in a remote server. One specific participant can also browse all the non-sensitive shared data contributed by other participants in a real time.

Privacy and Data Security. Though air quality collected in public outdoor areas inside a city has little privacy concerns, physical activity and some subjective feeling data concerning personal health status should be well protected from being shared to other participants. In addition, the data stored in both smartphones and the remote server should rigidly comply with the data separation principle to avoid the linkage of any personally identifiable information of the participant with the data she/he collected and contributed. All collected data are indexed by the participant pseudonymous code which was assigned to a participant before the first session started. On the other hand, to guarantee the participant's privacy right to access or revoke her/his own data in a later phase, the participants identifiable IDs (*e.g.*, name, contact, address, *etc.*) and the pseudonymous code should also form a one-to-one mapping to avoid the confusion caused by the complete anonymity. This one-to-one mapping table should be carefully kept in a physically separate place. Other general security measures, such as SSL/TLS based secure data transmission, data encryption in the remote servers' hard disk, and network firewall configured to limit the accesses to the server to authorized users, should be adopted as well.

3   The Developed Low-Cost Mobile Data Collection Platform

During the 2014–2015 winter-spring season, we developed a data collection platform consisting of a smartphone and low-cost air and physical activity sensors. Volunteered citizens were invited to walk inside the city Gjøvik where the research team lies to collect at specified geographic locations the air quality data Particular Matters (PM) in six particle size channels and the participants' physical activity data including heart beat and cadence of walking. In addition, the participants are required to answer the questionnaire on her/his smartphone App after air quality measurement at each predefined geographic location in the city. The data collection platform consists of the following components: PM sensor CEM DT-9881 (Fig. 1), WAHOO fitness sensor TICKR RUN [9], a general-purpose smartphone installed with a questionnaire App

Fig. 1. The CEM DT-9881 PM sensor compared in size to a mouse

named CrowdAir and the corresponding software serving the WAHOO sensor, and a remote server for data backup and sharing.

The CEM PM sensor is relatively compact in size and designed to be hand-held. The PM sensor can record data types including air temperature, relative humidity, dew point, wet-bulb temperature and PM (with 6 particle size channels: 0.3 μm, 0.5 μm, 1.0 μm, 2.5 μm, 5.0 μm, 10 μm) cumulative counts within maximum 60 s. In our data collections, the PM measurement time window was set as 20 s. The output is the number of particles in each size channel. The air flow rate of this sensor is 0.1ft3 (2.83 L/min). These air quality data can be read out right after each measurement session (20 s) on the screen. They are also recorded in an SD card in the device and can be output manually. The CEM sensor cost around $340 while most portable PM sensors in the market have a price range $3,000 to $11,000. With increasing interest in PM pollution detection from general public and decreasing prices of electronics, we envision a consumer-electronics level PM sensor with no more than $400 would be interesting for general public to purchase for home use in the authors' country.

We make use of the Wahoo Fitness sensor (TICKR RUN) to capture the heart rate and the cadence (walking or cycling speed) of participants who wear this sensor at the chest. The Wahoo sensor are worn with participants all the way during a session. The sensor works together with smart phone by Bluetooth. The heart rate is normally correlated with the ventilation rate, and can thus be used as an indicator of the air inhalation. If the ventilation rate is high we consider it a high-dose exposure to the ambient air environment. The price of the Wahoo sensor is around 90 EUR which is deemed affordable for most people for fitness data tracking use.

In addition to the sensor based objective data, subjective data about the feelings of air quality and the symptoms (*e.g.*, cough, sore throat, eye itchiness, *etc.*) reported via the smartphone App CrowdAir from the participants are recorded as well.

The types of data and the means for collection are summarized in Table 1.

The Resource Oriented Architecture (ROA) was adopted as the overall architecture for implementing the platform. ROA is widely used in distributed systems thanks to its re-usability feature. As an energy-saving solution compared to the Simple Object Access Protocol (SOAP) based architecture, ROA suits mobile applications. The App CrowedAir, developed in Java using Eclipse, is intended for different O/S platforms. To this end, PhoneGap, as a web-based tool towards building cross-platform apps with HTML, was used in the App development. Windows 2012 R2 was deployed as the server. We adopted MySQL to implement the database thanks to its open-source and

Table 1. Data types and collection means

Category	Data types	Collection means
Objective data from the sensors	Basic air status[a] and PM 0.3, 0.5, 1, 2.5, 5, and 10 μm	PM sensor
	Heart beat rate	Wahoo
	Cadence	Tickr-Run
Subjective data from the participant's input	Feeling of air quality in 4 levels: "excellent, good, poor, bad", and	Questionnaire App CrowdAir
	Feeling of symptoms in 4 levels: "none, mild, moderate, severe"	

[a]The basic air status includes air temperature (AT), dew point (DP), relative humidity (RH), and wet bulb (WB).

cross-platform features. In addition, a web service was established to synchronize the collected data between the smartphone and the remote server.

As is shown in the Fig. 2, the overall system architecture consisted of two components: the client side and the server side. On the client side, each participant has two tasks in the workflow. First, a participant operates the PM sensor to collect the air quality data while Wahoo sensor automatically records the physical activity data. Second, a participant completes a questionnaire about their subjective feelings via the smartphone App CrowdAir. After measurement at each location, the collected data and questionnaire answers are transmitted via the 3G/4G telecommunications network to the backend database on server side hosted as a web service. The server side delivers two services to the participants: (1) pooling all participants' recorded data, including the sensor-generated data and the questionnaire answers, to the backend database; (2) answering queries from participants about publishable data (*e.g.*, the PM data contributed from all participants and the subjective feeling data about air quality) at a specified location. The collected data and questionnaire answers will be temporarily saved on a smartphone as an XML files when the 3G/4G network is not available.

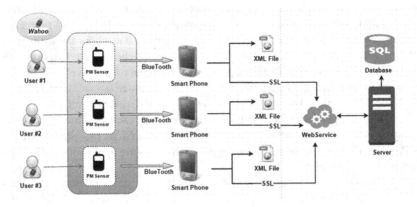

Fig. 2. The overall system structure of the developed data collection platform

The system will synchronize the data with the server in real time as long as 3G/4G telecommunications network is re-gained. To ensure the privacy of the participants, all personally identifiable information were physically separated from the collected data, and no symptoms data reported by the participants are shared to other participants via the platform. To ensure the user experience, all questions listed in the smartphone App CrowdAir based questionnaire were arranged in a linear way so as to reduce the users' interaction times to the minimum while keeping the answer options as simple and understandable as possible.

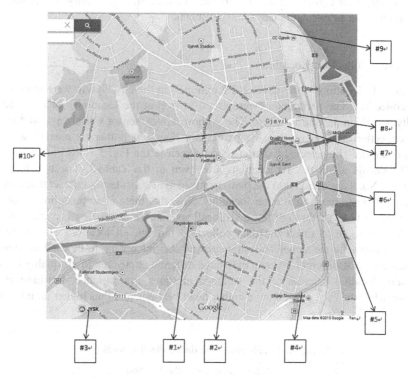

Fig. 3. Locations for data collection in the city (red-colored: required; black-colored: optional) (Color figure online)

4 Data Collection Settings

4.1 Participant Group

In total 12 citizens from the city Gjøvik were recruited as participants in the data collection. The participants are assigned with time slots according to both their preference and the balance of sessions across a week. In average 2 or 3 sessions were planned in each day per week including the weekends. Finally, data cumulated in 8 weeks were recorded.

Constrained by budget and time resources, the number of participants became a challenge to data collection. Due to the limited number of participants and the crowd data sourcing essence, the data collected were not always aligned in quality and completeness. But this is within our expectation because in real operation of such crowd data sourcing activities, data quality and completeness shall be varied across different participants as well. Data quality assessment and control is thus of great importance when processing crowd-sourced data. A typical challenge is that in such crowd data sourcing scenarios the collected data are hard to evaluate in quality without reference. Some indirect evaluation method could be used to estimate the data quality such as using user experience as a rough estimation of the data quality which has been proven effective in our data analysis experiments.

4.2 Data Collection Locations

A total of 10 locations (8 required and 2 optional) in the city Gjøvik were selected for data collection. The participants were asked to stop at the locations, measure the air quality and fill in the questionnaire. The Wahoo activity sensor was always on during a data collection session so that the participant does not bother to interact with the Wahoo sensor. The selected locations can be seen in the Fig. 3.

The details about the 10 locations are given in the Table 2. The two locations No. 3 and No. 9 are optional to the participants to visit considering the fact that they are relatively farer to reach than other locations. Note that there is no predefined route for the participants to go through these 10 locations and we assume each participant has her/his own route to finish the data collection through all locations which are not necessarily exactly the same. This strategy was also interesting to be used to simulate the real case that different citizens may have different exposures to air quality even at the same location because of the variance in route. For instance, finishing at the location #1 in the Fig. 3 could have higher heart beat rate and thus higher air inhalation

Table 2. Details about the data collection locations

No.	Information about the location
1 (required)	Main entrance of the university building
2 (required)	Residential area
3 (optional)	Area close to a biomass heat plant
4 (required)	Bus stop
5 (required)	Lake shore
6 (required)	Gas station
7 (required)	City hall vicinity
8 (required)	Park close to the central bus station
9 (optional)	Outside a shopping mall
10 (required)	Pedestrian area in the city center

volume and rate than the case starting from the location #1, as in most cases a participant has performed a lot of physical activities approaching the end of a session.

All collected data have timestamp and GPS tags in order to get associated with locations without confusion caused by different routes adopted by different participants. To better ensure the accuracy in data collection locations, a picture was required to take per location by the participant after each measurement.

5 Preliminary Data Analysis

Some preliminary data analysis had been done over the collected data by the developed data collection platform. Note that the data analysis results given in this section should not be over interpreted in addition to proving the feasibility in functionality of the developed platform and the crowd data sourcing methodology.

5.1 Subjective Air Quality Feeling and PM Measurement in Different Locations

The participants' subjective feelings of the air quality, which were voted in 4 levels representing "1(excellent)", "2(good)", "3(poor)", and "4(bad)", respectively, are presented in the Table 3 for 7 different locations namely #2, #4, #5, #6, #7, #8, #10. The two optional locations #3 and #9 are distinctly less in record amount compared to other locations and thus were not counted in the table to avoid biased comparisons. The #1 location has a low record amount as well possibly because quite a lot participants forgot to collect the data at the starting point. The corresponding PM measurements in the 7 locations were given in Table 4.

It is observed that the subjective feeling votes in Table 3 show obvious correlation with those PM measurements in Table 4, as expected. The two locations #4 (bus stop) and #6 (gas station) with bad air quality measured can be attributed to the traffics. The locations such as #2 (residential area), #5 lake shore, and #10 pedestrian area are relatively faraway from traffics. The traffic is a main source of PM10 and that has been reflected in lower PM count measured at those locations. Also, it is possible to see a correlation between presence of traffic and the perception that the air quality is worse.

Table 3. Votes on air quality by subjective feelings

Location	Level 1 (best)	Level 2	Level 3	Level 4 (worst)
#2	67	11	0	0
#4	40	28	10	0
#5	66	11	1	0
#6	44	26	8	0
#7	57	20	1	0
#8	54	23	1	0
#10	64	13	1	0

Table 4. Average particle counts measured in 20 s with the air flow rate 0.1ft3 (2.83 L/min)

Location	PM 2.5	PM 10
#2	581.5	67.6
#4	1128.6	144.4
#5	1036.3	95.0
#6	1328.1	151.4
#7	771.1	89.4
#8	701.9	87.1
#10	668.5	70.5

5.2   Regression Analysis Over Sensor Data and Subjective Feelings

Table 5 presents the regression analysis results across the collected data types. In order to explore the relationship between the air quality and the physical activity, a regression was performed using the air quality as explanatory variables and the human biometric data, including heart rate and cadence, as dependent variables. The same method was applied to estimate the relation between the sensor-generated air quality and human subjective feeling of the air quality and their health status from questionnaire.

Note that the data collected during this campaign were not enough to draw conclusions on the air quality, physical activity, and health status. The results obtained in the small pilot study should not be generalized without regarding the specific data collection environment in the studied city. The aim of the analysis is to show the potential of crowd-sourced environmental monitoring of air quality and human health. The adopted statistic regression method was random effect regression, because the data pair (air quality/physical activity and air quality/subjective feelings) was obtained by random sampling and each pair is independent of every other pair. Random effect model will allow the individual characteristics to be modelled. The software used to achieve the estimation results is STATA.

Table 5. Regression analysis results

	Heart rate	Cadence	Air quality feeling	Health symptom
PM2.5	−0.000368	0.000283	−0.0000126	−0.00000823
	(−1.13)	(−0.85)	(−0.99)	(−1.25)
PM10	0.00228	−0.00379	0.000849***	0.000395***
	(0.50)	(−0.80)	(4.78)	(4.31)
AT	−1.373***	−0.574**	−0.0193**	−0.0108**
	(−6.72)	(−2.85)	(−2.79)	(−3.12)
_cons	120.8***	111.4***	1.551***	1.162***
	(41.23)	(40.24)	(17.21)	(26.09)
N	721	728	728	728

t statistics in parentheses
* p < 0.05, ** p < 0.01, *** p < 0.001

The values outside parenthesis in Table 5 are the coefficients of the regressions, and the numbers inside parenthesis are the t-value from statistics. The further of the t-value deviates from zero, the stronger is the correlation.

Note that the correlation results between {PM2.5 and PM10} and {heart rate and cadence} should not be over-interpret for a causal relationship between the air quality and the heart rate/cadence. Though long-term exposure to air pollution may impact on health status indicated by heart rates, the data collected in this proof-of-concept project is far too less to draw such a conclusion. Instead, we intended to examine, in the 10 locations, whether the geometric condition or the route selection or other unknown factors can cause high physical activity intensity (reasonably indicating high air inhalation rate) under highly polluted air environment, which poses a threat to the participant's health and should therefore trigger an alert to the participant.

We can see from the regression results that the measurement of the air quality PM10 does have a significant correlation with the participants' subjective feelings of both air quality and health symptom, which may be interpret in a way that either PM10 intensity is detectable to some degree in the sense of human feeling or PM10 emission usually accompanies other pollutants that are detectable in the sense of human feeling. It is also observed that the air temperature has a significant correlation with both physical activity and the subjective feelings. Considering the temperature dynamic range which is roughly [0, 23] degree centigrade in the data collection city, we tentatively assume that colder weather condition may cause the participants to walk faster and feel worse in terms of health symptom. The air temperature and the subjective feeling of the air quality shows also noticeable correlation, which is consistent with the general understanding that there is more particular matters emission during colder weather dates caused by wood burning and winter-tyre use in the studied city.

5.3 Physical Activity Intensity's Variance Within Participants in Locations

As the regression analysis between the air quality and the physical activity did not show distinct correlations from the average values, we further studied whether we can find some participants who has distinctly different physical activity intensities from others at the same locations, or has distinctly varied physical activity intensities at different locations. We randomly picked up 2 participants' physical activity values (averaged from all sessions) on the 7 locations mentioned above and this time indeed observed diversity in the physical activity intensity across different locations and among different participants. The exemplar values are given in Table 6. These examples verified our assumption in Sect. 2 that participants when passing the same geographic location (*e.g.*, #4 and #6 which are locations with relatively heavier air pollution) may have different exposure degrees which can be estimated by their physical activity intensity. This methodology could be important to capture a person's daily routine physical activity patterns that can, when combined with air pollution exposure, greatly impact one's health. Such personalized data collection and analysis could greatly facilitate the patient-centric environmental health study and personalized healthcare in the future.

Table 6. Examples of diverse physical activity intensity (averaged number per minute from all sessions) across the same set of locations by two different participants A and B

	Heart rate		Cadence	
	Partic. A	Partic. B	Partic. A	Partic. B
# 2	112.8	106.8	126.2	80.4
# 4	114.1	97.6	108.6	128.6
# 5	109.2	162.8	101.6	184.5
# 6	102.0	101.1	118.7	123.9
# 7	81.4	132.1	112.9	110.4
# 8	151.7	95.1	126.7	109.9
# 10	111.5	96.6	138.0	81.8

6 Conclusions

In this work we described the concept of crowd-sourced environmental health study and the methodologies we adopted in developing such an air quality, human activity, and health status data collection and sharing platform based on low-cost, portable, and mobile sensors, a smartphone, and a remote server with a database. Though the preliminary data analysis results generated from this work should not be over interpreted due to the scale and geographic constraints of the collected data, the data collection process itself and the main analysis results proved the feasibility of such a low-cost crowd-sourced data collection platform serving future environmental health study. Future work efforts will be invested on improving data quality control methods, testing such crowd-sourced data collection methodology in large-scale public health and personalized health care studies, adopt real-time big data analytics as a service to the platform, and improve the usability and social cost models while availing crowd data sourcing's high efficiency in benefit-cost.

Acknowledgement. This work was funded by Norwegian Regionale Forskningsfond Innlandet's pilot research project Air Quality Crowd Awareness (CrowdAir) (project number 236584). We also thank the following colleagues: Kari Eikerol and Magnar Eikerol for their cooperation in site identification and measurements, Jingjing Yang for drafting the data collection plan, and Guoqiang Li for technical discussions.

References

1. Ambient (outdoor) Air Quality and Health. http://www.who.int/mediacentre/factsheets/fs313/en/. Accessed 15 Feb 2016
2. Seven Million Premature Deaths Annually Linked to Air Pollution. http://www.who.int/mediacentre/news/releases/2014/air-pollution/en/. Accessed 15 Feb 2016
3. Polluted Air Causes 5.5 million Deaths a Year New Research Says. http://www.bbc.com/news/science-environment-35568249. Accessed 15 Feb 2016

4. Brauer, M., Freedman, G., Frostad, J., Donkelaar, A., Martin, R., Dentener, F., Dingenen, R., Estep, K., Amini, H., Apte, J., Balakrishnan, K., Barregardh, L., Broday, D., Feigin, V., Ghosh, S., Hopke, P., Knibbs, L., Kokubo, Y., Liu, Y., Ma, S., Morawska, L., Sangrador, J., Shaddickr, G., Anderson, H., Vos, T., Forouzanfar, M., Burnett, R., Cohen, A.: Ambient air pollution exposure estimation for the global burden of disease 2013. Environ. Sci. Technol. **50**(1), 79–88 (2015)
5. Yang, Y., Li, L.: A smart sensor system for air quality monitoring and massive data collection. In: Proceedings of International Conference on Information and Communication Technology Convergence (ICTC), pp. 147–152 (2015)
6. Jafari, H., Li, X., Qian, L., Chen, Y.: Community based sensing: a test bed for environment air quality monitoring using smartphone paired sensors. In: Proceedings of 36th IEEE Sarnoff Symposium, pp. 12–17 (2015)
7. EU FP7 Research Project CITI-SENSE. http://www.citi-sense.eu/. Accessed 15 Feb 2016
8. Zuurbier, M., Hoek, G., Hazel, P., Brunekreef, B.: Minute ventilation of cyclists, car and bus passengers: an experimental study. Environ. Health **8**(48), 1–10 (2009)
9. Wahoo Tickr Run sensor. http://eu.wahoofitness.com/devices/hr.html. Accessed 15 Feb 2016

A Gesture-Based Smart Home-Oriented Health Monitoring Service for People with Physical Impairments

Md. Abdur Rahman[1(✉)] and M. Shamim Hossain[2]

[1] Computer Science Department, College of Computer and Information Systems, Umm Al-Qura University, Makkah, Saudi Arabia
marahman@uqu.edu.sa
[2] Software Engineering Department, College of Computer and Information Sciences, King Saud University, Riyadh, Saudi Arabia
mshossain@ksu.edu.sa

Abstract. Smart home shows great potential in providing ubiquitous services within one's home environment. With the advent of gesture recognition hardware and frameworks, it is now envisioned that most of the household activities that are used on a daily basis, can now be operated using gestures. This will allow people with special to use their natural gestures to interact with different interfaces, whether it be appliances or accessing Internet-based healthcare services. In this article, we present a gesture based natural user interface framework, which supports a set of smart home services through gestures. In order to get feedback from the user interaction, a reverse feedback mechanism is implemented, which keeps track of how many gestures are working correctly. We have developed a mathematical model to represent proposed framework. From the user feedback and analysis of the gathered system testing data, we are optimistic about the deployment of the proposed framework in real life scenarios.

Keywords: Smart home · Gesture based interaction · Natural user interfaces · Remote health monitoring

1 Introduction

Research on smart home aims to make our life comfortable, especially for those who are at old age or have physical impairments and hence needs caregiver support for their daily life activities. The evolution of user interfaces has changed the shapes of smart home research. Among the emerging next-generation user interfaces, use of the biological features of a human body is gaining popularity [1]. Gesture-based interface is suitable for the control of the networked home appliances due to its intuitive and natural characteristics [2]. As a result, gesture based systems tend to show potential in diversified spectrum of real-life applications such as smart home, in-home health monitoring, natural user interfaces for medical applications, serious games for kids with special needs, controlling media within a car entertainment system, gesture based communication via sign languages, etc. [3]. It offers a simple yet powerful control

© Springer International Publishing Switzerland 2016
C.K. Chang et al. (Eds.): ICOST 2016, LNCS 9677, pp. 464–476, 2016.
DOI: 10.1007/978-3-319-39601-9_42

mechanism that is appropriate to all users including those with special needs like children, elderly people and people with physical impairments.

Due to the movement problem of old age people and lack of all-time caregiver support, gesture based smart home control services play a significant role in assisting people of physical impairments [4]. In addition to controlling various appliances and other services such as sending SMS, browsing Internet, writing emails, and chatting, the gestures can be a source of physical or occupational therapy monitoring [4], which requires a subject to perform a number of exercises. Hence, a smart home can be a means of rehabilitation space for a subject [5, 6]. Moreover, with the advancements of gesture tracking technologies, it is now possible to use off the shelf sensors for daily life gesture tracking in a smart home environment [7]. Examples of economically priced sensor devices are Microsoft KinectV2, the LeapMotion and the EMG-based Myo [8].

This paper presents a natural user interface framework for next-generation smart homes in which people with physical impairments can use gestures to control appliances and also consume Internet-based services. In the passive form, the framework supports occupational therapy by mapping each smart home control motion to a specific therapy outcome [4]. Through gestures, a subject can interact with both appliances at home as well as control software. The framework mashes up 3 state of the art gesture tracking sensors, namely Myo, Leap Motion and Kinect2, to support a wide range of smart home related gestures. The Myo armband reads the hand muscle tone and uses Bluetooth low energy (BLE) to transmit the gesture data to a PC or a smart phone. Since the operating range of BLE 4.0 is around a home area network, it can cover appliance control over a typical home. In order to support the complete and very rich gestures, the framework combines all the three sensors to recognize complex smart home control actions. In addition to gestures targeting a specific appliance or software control (e.g., using gestures to turn a light bulb off or type an email), the sensors also collect occupational therapy data. The gesture data corresponding to occupational therapy, often called kinematic data, is collected in the background when a subject interacts with different smart home services through gesture. We have developed analytics that help us in kinematic data analysis, which assists a therapist in observing the phenomena "how many different types of daily life activities can be performed by a subject him/herself through gestures". We have developed natural user interfaces, which allows a subject to control home appliances such as lights or to access Internet-based services through gestures.

The remainder of the paper is organized as following. Section 2 describes the architecture and modeling of the proposed system. Section 3 illustrates the technologies behind the implementation. Section 4 presents the test results followed by conclusive remarks.

2 Proposed Framework and Modeling

We assume a smart home where a family is living. There are m number of family members within the smart home that is equipped with n number of gesture tracking sensors. All the l number of appliances and the gesture-enabled Internet-based services in the home are interconnected through our proposed framework. In every room, the gesture tracking sensors are available along with the visualization interface. Gestures performed within any room by any individual is recognized in a personalized way [7]. The framework uses a state machine modeling approach where each gesture is assigned a state, and when a user makes certain gestures at any room, at any time within the smart environment, specific gesture data is collected by the gesture tracking sensor. We present the gesture modeling by leveraging a gesture vocabulary, which expresses possible states of gestures and represent those using mathematical expressions. A high-level gesture is represented as a collection of primitive joint motions [8], which can be combined to form a high-level smart home gesture. Next, we elaborate the gesture vocabulary.

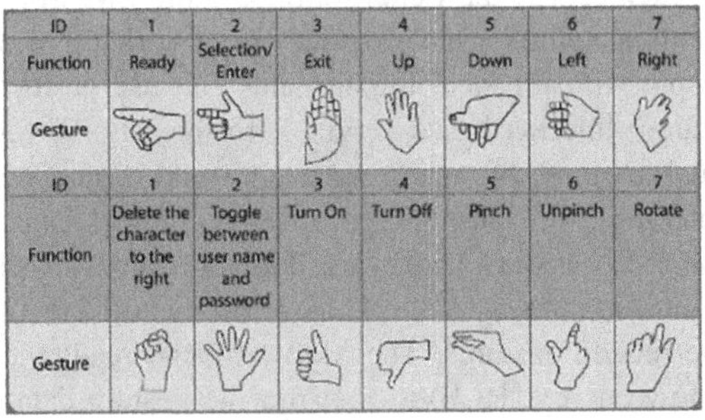
ID
1
2
3
4
5
6
7
Function
Ready
Selection/ Enter
Exit
Up
Down
Left
Right
Gesture
ID
1
2
3
4
5
6
7
Function
Delete the character to the right
Toggle between user name and password
Turn On
Turn Off
Pinch
Unpinch
Rotate
Gesture

Fig. 1. Gestures related to various control actions.

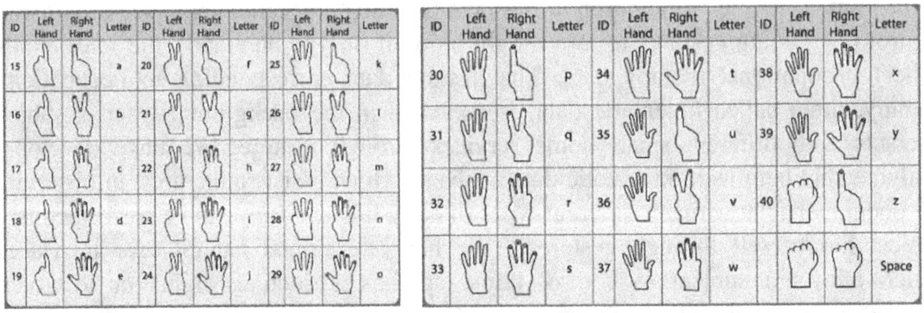
ID
Left Hand
Right Hand
Letter
15 a
16 b
17 c
18 d
19 e
20 f
21 g
22 h
23 i
24 j
25 k
26 l
27 m
28 n
29 o
30 p
31 q
32 r
33 s
34 t
35 u
36 v
37 w
38 x
39 y
40 z
Space

Fig. 2. Gestures related with letters (both hands at pronation).

2.1 Gesture Vocabulary Design

Figure 1 shows a set of gestures that are related to various control actions for navigating within the control menu items. This set of gestures are also used for sending control signals to the smart home appliances. In order to support control for software based services such as typing SMS, browsing web pages, writing emails, etc., we use the gesture vocabulary shown in Figs. 2, 3 and 4. Figures 1, 2, 3 and 4 listed below show the various gesture vocabularies used in this literature.

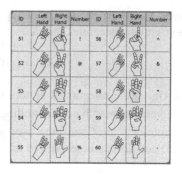

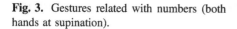

Fig. 3. Gestures related with numbers (both hands at supination).

Fig. 4. Gestures related with special characters (both hands at supination).

2.2 Modeling Primitive Gesture-Based Services

We first define necessary gesture control variables related to context-based services modeling. To express the user defined smart home control gestures, we use the primitive gestures defined in [8] to express a complete smart home gesture context. We express the set of gesture primitives as following [8]:

$$GC = \{gc_1, gc_2, gc_3, \ldots, gc_l\} \qquad (1)$$

where GC is the atomic smart home gesture context primitive. An example of gesture context primitive can be as follows: "*a subject has to perform an elbow bend and turn motion to control a light bulb*". Using the modeling described in [8], we can deduce the high-level context into primitive contexts.

gc_1 = USER Palm SUPINATED
gc_2 = USER Elbow FLEXED
gc_3 = USER Wrist FLEXED
gc_4 = USER Index Fingertip FULLY EXTENDED
gc_5 = USER Index Fingertip TOUCHES SHOULDER

If (gc_1) and (gc_2) and (gc_3) and (gc_4) and (gc_5).

Then Context = USER *performing elbow bend and turn exercise to control a light bulb*.

Similarly, other high-level smart home control gestures can be expressed using primitive actions, which can be recognized by gesture tracking sensors. However, a user can personalize all such user gestures based on her preference. In our framework modeling, we assume two types of sensors: *gesture-tracking* sensors and *non-gesture-tracking* sensors. *Gesture-tracking* sensors are Kinect, Leap and MYO. *Non-gesture-tracking* sensors are those that a user might use for sensing geo-location, sweat level, SpO2, etc.

Each element of the set GC is called specific smart home gesture context as it defines one single and unique aspect of the gesture definition. The gesture primitives are physically limited to the human body anatomy and therefore limited to a fixed set of gestures. However, parameters of Eq. (1) do not mention categories of gestures. To support gesture categories, we define:

$$GC' = \{GC'_1, GC'_2, GC'_3, GC'_4\} \tag{2}$$

where GC' is the categorized gesture set; C'_1 represents geo-location related contexts, GC'_2 represents smart home controlling context, GC'_3 represents temporal contexts and GC'_4 represents inter and intra user personalization contexts. The relation between Eqs. (1) and (2) can be expressed as follows:

$$GC'_i \subseteq GC \tag{3}$$

$$\bigcup\nolimits_{i=1}^{4} GC'_i = GC \tag{4}$$

Once the atomic or primitive gesture context primitives have been defined, a high-level gesture expression can be expressed as follows:

$$GC^* = \{gc^*_1, gc^*_2, .., gc^*_n\} \tag{5}$$

where gc^*_i represents a high-level gesture context available from the sub-sets GC'_1, GC'_2, GC'_3 and GC'_4 (see Eq. 4). In order to make a complex categorized expression, zero or more gesture primitive contexts can be taken from each category as shown in Eq. (5). A particular context of GC^* i.e. gc^*_i represents a complete and unique smart home gesture context such as "*user makes a gesture to close his window AC of dining room in the afternoon*". Because gestures are tracked by *gesture-tracking* sensor sets, a particular gesture context can be expressed in terms of type of sensor as follows:

$$GC'' = \{GC_s, \ GC_{sc}, \ GC_{sd}\} \tag{6}$$

where GC'' represents contexts based on which sensor provides the gesture data. For example, GC_s represents the gesture set that are tracked by *gesture-tracking* sensor Kinect2, GC_{sc} represents gesture primitives available from *gesture-tracking* sensor LEAP, and GC_{sd} represents smart home gestures recognized by the *Gesture-tracking* sensor MYO. The relationship among GC_s, GC_{sc}, GC_{sd} and GC can be expressed as $GC_s \cup GC_{sc} \cup GC_{sd} = GC$. Each sub-set element in Eq. (6) can be rewritten as follows:

$$GC_s = \{gc_{s1}, gc_{s2}, gc_{s3}, \ldots gc_{sk}\} \tag{7}$$

where $gc_{si} \in GC$ and $GC_s \subset GC$.

$$GC_{sc} = \{gc_{sc1}, gc_{sc2}, gc_{sc3}, \ldots gc_{scj}\} \tag{8}$$

where $gc_{scj} \in GC$ and $GC_{sc} \subset GC$

$$GC_{sd} = \{gc_{sd1}, gc_{sd2}, gc_{sd3}, \ldots gc_{sdl}\} \tag{9}$$

where $gc_{sdl} \in GC$ and $GC_{sd} \subset GC$ and $GC'' = GC_s \bigcup GC_{sc} \bigcup GC_{sd}$.

2.3 Modeling High-Level Gestures

We assume that a subject within a smart home can perform m numbers of diversified types of gesture-based services S, from both hardware controlling gestures and software controlling gestures, as follows:

$$S = \{s_1, s_2, s_3, \ldots s_m\} \tag{10}$$

where $s_i|\{1 \leq i \leq m\}$ represents a high level gesture-based service. We also assume that a user uses d number of *non-gesture-tracking* sensors, which can be expressed as the follows:

$$NGC = \{ngc_1, ngc_2, ngc_3, \ldots ngc_d\} \tag{11}$$

Combining both *non-gesture-tracking* sensors NGC with that of *gesture-tracking* set GC_s as follow:

For any particular gesture-based context $gc \in GC_s$ and non-gesture based context $ngc \in NGC$ (derived from Eqs. (7) and (11) respectively), we claim that a one-to-one function f exists on ngc into gc, $f : ngc \rightarrow gc$ so the following relation holds

$$GC_s(gc_{si}) = \{(gc_{si}) | \exists ngc_i \in NGC, f(ngc_i) = gc_{si}\} \tag{12}$$

For a single gesture service $s \in S$ and any instance of gesture tracking context $gc \in GC_{sc}$ (derived from Eq. (8) and (9) respectively), we claim that a one-to-one function f' on s into gc, $f' : s \rightarrow gc$ so the following relation holds

$$GC_{sc}(gc_{scj}) = \left\{(gc_{scj}) | \exists s_i \in S, f'(s_i) = gc_{scj}\right\} \tag{13}$$

We now map a set of gesture-based services with a particular context expression. For any gesture service $s \in S$ and any instance of context $gc \in GC^*$, a one-to-one function g on s into gc, $gc : s \rightarrow gc$. For a particular context $gc_i^* \in GC^*$, a context-aware smart home gesture service can be mapped as follows:

$$CGS(gc_i^*) = \{(s_i) | s_i \in S, \forall s_i : g(s_i) = gc_i^*\} \tag{14}$$

Equation (14) shows a complete smart home user context from GC^* in terms of gesture services from S. Therefore, context-aware gesture services (CGS) can be define in terms of user context as follows:

$$CGS = \{CGS(gc_i^*)|gc_i^* \in GC^*\} \tag{15}$$

The context-aware gesture services can be expressed based on *gesture-tracking* Kinect2 sensor GC_s as follows:

$$CGS(gc_{si}^*) = \{(s_i)|s_i \in S, \forall s_i : g(s_i) = gc_{si}^*\} \tag{16}$$

The context-aware gesture services based on *gesture-tracking* LEAP sensor GC_{sc} can be expressed as follows:

$$CGS(gc_{scj}^*) = \{(s_i)|s_i \in S', \forall s_i : g(s_i) = gc_{scj}^*\} \tag{17}$$

The context-aware gesture services based on *gesture-tracking* MYO-based EMG signal sensing set GC_{sd} can be express as follows:

$$CGS(c_{sdk}^*) = \{(s_i)|s_i \in S', \forall s_i : g(s_i) = gc_{sdk}^*\} \tag{18}$$

Context-aware gesture services (*CGS*) can be defined in terms of user context as well as sensory media as follows:

$$CGS = \{(CGS(gc_{sdk}^*)|gc_{sdk}^* \in GC^*)U(CGS\left(gc_{scj}^*\right)| \\ gc_{scj}^* \in GC^*)U(CGS(gc_{si}^*)|gc_{si}^* \in GC^*)\}. \tag{19}$$

2.4 High-Level Architecture

Salient components of the proposed gesture tracking system within a smart home is shown in Fig. 5.

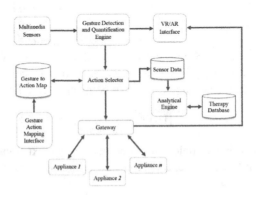

Fig. 5. Salient components of the proposed smart home.

Gesture data from gesture tracking sensors, called *Multimedia Sensors,* is processed by *Gesture Detection and Quantification Engine*. It processes the raw media as well as skeletal data and supplies to the *Gesture to Action Map* component, which is a repository that contains all the smart home supported gestures available within the system. It also stores a mapping table for each user's personalized gesture commands. The framework provides a *Gesture Action Mapping Interface* which can be used to customize gesture and corresponding gesture tracking sensors. The *Action Selector* receives the real-time gestures performed by a user through *Gesture Detection and Quantification Engine*, reads the relevant gesture from the *Gesture to Action Map* repository and shares the gesture with the *Gateway*. The *Gateway* incorporates a set of gesture interfaces related to different hardware and software based controls of different smart home services. To see the live gesture animations that are being performed, the framework provides *Virtual Reality/Augmented Reality (VR/AR)* Interface. Since the framework also supports occupational therapies, an *Analytical Engine* reads the sensory data corresponding to the gestures and queries the *Therapy Database* to produce gesture activity reports from historical or live sessions, and deduce various quality of improvement graphs.

3 Implementation

The framework has been implemented using a PC having 8 GB RAM running Windows 10. A KinectV2 gesture tracking sensor was used that can recognize most significant 20 joints of a human body. A Leap motion controller was used to recognize hand gestures. Figure 6 shows smart home environment where KinectV2, Leap, and MYO are integrated within same environment. The web based interface was developed using Laravel running within Apache, HTML5, Angular JS and three.js JavaScript framework. Three.js helps us rendering LEAP, MYO, and KinectV2 frames in 3D WebGL environment.

We have developed customized web sockets to intercept frames from the multiple sensors that needs to run on the client computer, which provides the raw skeletal stream to the HTML4 objects. Gesture-based skeletal data is stored in either JSON or industry standard BVH format. The relational data containing user, health, gesture to appliance control mapping data etc. is stored in a PostGreSQL database. Analytical output is plotted using the Laravel and Angular JS plotting libraries. The live animated skeletal data are rendered using the three.js library. We have developed both web and smartphone based user interfaces that allows a user to visualize live gestures as well as consume different smart home services using gestures. A user can personalize gestures for each type of service from the web based interface. The framework automatically engages the right sensor from the gesture tracking sensor array. The gesture data from MYO can be captured by both smartphone or a PC. The mapping action corresponding to a gesture is intercepted by right sensor and a control signal is sent to the appropriate appliance. We have also developed PC and smartphone-based visualization interfaces to reflect the status of the smart appliances.

Fig. 6. Smart home environment with three gesture recognition sensors

4   Test Results

We have established collaboration with 4 disability centers that support in-home physio and occupational services for patients having physical impairments. We have learnt different gestures, their normal range of motion, types of difficulty in motion of old age people or people with movement problem, collected therapy details and observed quality of improvement metrics corresponding to different in-home gesture-based activities.

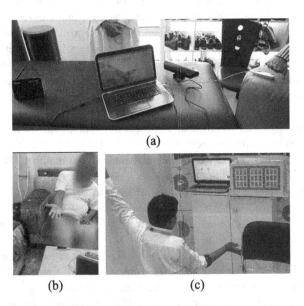

Fig. 7. Different test scenarios with different gesture tracking sensors (a) a disabled child in a disabled children hospital using both Kinect and LEAP together (b) a right hemiplegic disabled user uses LEAP attached with a laptop for performing a therapy and (c) a child wearing a MYO armband controlling smart home appliances.

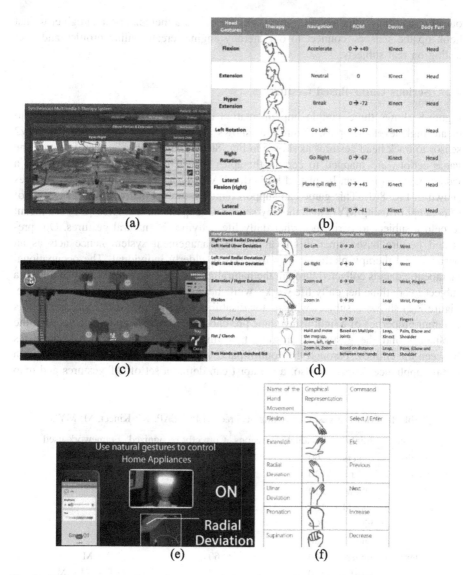

Fig. 8. Serious games used as a therapy consisting of a set of gestures for different game actions (a–b) a user plays a Kinect-based flight game (c–d) a user plays a LEAP and Kinect based ladder game and corresponding therapeutic gestures and (e–f) a set of therapeutic gestures based on LEAP and MYO.

4.1   Experience with Human Subjects

Thanks to the support of the therapists from the 4 centers, we have been able deploy our proposed system both in patient homes and therapy centers. The test conditions in each of the 4 hospitals are different in nature. For example, Fig. 7 shows setup in three different scenarios where LEAP, MYO armband and Kinect have been used. Thanks to our plug and play middleware framework, it requires a therapist or a caregiver to just hook up the sensors, connect to our therapy engine, create online profiles and start testing on real subjects.

4.2 Serious Game-Based Gestures

Figure 8 shows three sample implementation cases where the gestures are used to create high level therapies. Figure 8(a) shows a flying game, which uses Kinect v2 sensor to track head gestures as shown in Fig. 8(b) to control the flight movement. The game actions are mapped to certain therapies related to head. Figure 8(c) shows a ladder game which can be played by both LEAP and Kinect v2, the tracked gestures shown in Fig. 8(d). This game can support hand gestures. Finally, Fig. 8(e) is a proof of concept of using MYO as a therapy sensor. Occupational therapies (OT) are meant to help a subject to perform his/her daily life activities by natural gestures. Our presented gesture based smart home appliance management system hence acts as an occupational therapy platform for a disabled or elderly individual. The occupational therapeutic data is collected through the natural gesture of each subject, which allows a subject to continue her daily life works, while her health is examined at the same time. Figure 8(e) shows a subject with motor disability wearing the MYO sensor controls different properties of a light using some pre-chosen gestures. To interface between the appliances and the gesture of a subject, a smartphone is used which coordinates between the entities. Through the control panel a subject can map each gesture with a certain appliance property. Also, a therapist can define a set of OT gestures and map

Table 1. Primitive gesture tracking accuracy (LP: LEAP, KI: Kinect, M: MYO)

Motion	Joint	Conducted sessions	Correctly recognized	Framework used
Flexion	fingers	60	60	LP + M
	wrist	120	118	LP + KI + M
	elbow	210	207	KI
	shoulder	185	178	KI
	hip	200	189	KI
	knee	180	173	KI
Extension	fingers	60	60	LP + M
	wrist	120	117	LP + KI + M
	elbow	210	208	KI
	shoulder	185	179	KI
	hip	200	192	KI
	knee	180	170	KI
Supination	forearm	350	350	LP + M
Pronation	forearm	350	350	LP + M
Adduction	shoulder	150	148	KI
	hip	155	151	KI
Abduction	shoulder	150	143	KI
	hip	155	152	KI

Table 2. Analysis of primitive ROM values for the joints of the SPINE

Therapy name	Joint	Movement	Range of motion
SPINE_CERVICAL_FLEXION _EXTENSION	Spine Cervical (Kinect: Spine)	Flexion	0 → 45
		Extension	
		Hyperextension	
SPINE_CERVICAL_ABDUCTION _ADDUCTION	Spine Cervical (Kinect: Spine)	Lateral flexion (abduction)	0 → 45
		Reduction (adduction)	
		Rotation	
SPINE_CERVICAL_ROTATION	Spine Cervical (Kinect: Spine)	Rotation	60
SPINE_THORACIC_FLEXION _EXTENSION	Spine Thoracic, Lumbar (Kinect: Hip_center)	Flexion	0 → 90
		Extension hyperextension	
SPINE_THORACIC_ABDUCTION _ADDUCTION	Spine Thoracic, Lumbar (Kinect: Hip_center)	Lateral flexion (abduction)	0 → 40
		Reduction (adduction)	
		Rotation	
SPINE_THORACIC_ROTATION	Spine Thoracic, Lumbar (Kinect: Hip_center)	Rotation	20 → 45

with a set of appliance control signals to test how many of such actions can be performed by a patient per day.

4.3   Gesture Tracking Accuracy

Table 1 shows the gesture tracking accuracy and the tracking sensor (s) i.e. Kinect, LEAP or MYO. For example, let us assume a scenario where a patient names Alice has weakness in completely extending her hand via elbow joints. Hence, she has difficulty in opening doors or doing other house hold activities. The framework captures the range of motion of elbow joint of Alice from the appliance control gesture data as follows: starting elbow flexion 15°, instead of 0° and highest elbow flexion is 140°, which is 145° for a normal person. Hence, Alice has 15° gesture weakness in elbow flexion at the lower bound and 5° near the upper bound. Alice can configure gestures for controlling appliances or other software services that can accommodate this weakness and at the same time show the instantaneous as well as statistical data about elbow joint improvement. Using our proposed gesture model, we can deduce the accuracy of gestures shown in Tables 1 and 2. Although the framework can detect the gestures with more than 98 % accuracy, we are still working on further increasing the accuracy.

5   Conclusion and Future Work

Using off the shelf gesture tracking sensors such as LEAP 3D motion sensor, Kinect2 and MYO, we have developed a smart home gesture monitoring system for people with special needs. A gesture vocabulary has been developed, which can be emulated through a set of primitive mapping gestures. The primitive gestures can be combined to express high level gestures, which can be used by subjects to control home appliances or performing software interactions such as sending SMS, sending emails, controlling browser actions, browsing maps, etc. The mapped high level activities can then be saved to a user profile and recognized by the multimedia gesture tracking sensors. Since old age people or people with special needs require occupational therapies, the proposed framework can also be used to support occupational therapies by tracking how many daily life activities can be performed by gestures. The kinematic therapy data is then made available to the caregiver medical institution. Our proposed gesture-based framework has been tested by practicing therapists from 4 hospitals and their feedback is positive. The accuracy of gesture tracking lies within acceptable range of motion limit.

Acknowledgement. This project was supported by the NSTIP strategic technologies program (11-INF1703-10) in the Kingdom of Saudi Arabia.

References

1. Ding, I.-J., Chang, C.-W.: An eigenspace-based method with a user adaptation scheme for human gesture recognition by using Kinect 3D data. Appl. Math. Model. **39**(19), 5769–5777 (2015)
2. Suryanarayan, P., Subramanian, A., Mandalapu, D.: Dynamic hand pose recognition using depth data. In: Proceedings of ICPR, pp. 3105–3108 (2010)
3. Wachs, J.P., Kölsch, M., Stern, H., Edan, Y.: Vision-based hand-gesture applications. Commun. ACM **54**(2), 60–71 (2011)
4. Qamar, A.M., et al.: A multi-sensory gesture-based occupational therapy environment for controlling home appliances. In: Proceedings of the ACM ICMR 2015, Shanghai, China (2015)
5. Rahman, M.A.: i-Therapy: a non-invasive multimedia authoring framework for context-aware therapy design. Multimed. Tools Appl. **75**(4), 1843–1867 (2016)
6. Alankus, G., Kelleher, C.: Reducing compensatory motions in motion-based video games for stroke rehabilitation. Hum.-Comput. Interact. **30**(3–4), 232–262 (2015)
7. Gips, J., Betke, M., DiMattia, P.A.: Early experiences using visual tracking for computer access by people with profound physical disabilities. In: Stephanidis, C. (ed.) Proceedings of the 1st International Conference on Universal Access in HCI (UA-HCI): Towards an Information Society for All, pp. 914–918. Lawrence Erlbaum Associates, Mahwah (2001)
8. Rahman, M.A., Hossain, M.S., El Saddik, A.: Context-aware multimedia services modeling: an e-Health perspective. Multimed. Tools Appl. **73**(3), 1147–1176 (2014)

Health Assistant Based on Cloud Platform

Guoyan Huang[✉], Liangyuan Chen, and Zhangchi Feng

School of Data and Computer Science, Sun Yat-sen University, Guangzhou, China
{huanggy7,chenly23,fengzhch}@mail2.sysu.edu.cn

Abstract. With the rapid growth of machine learning algorithms, the artificial intelligence classification technology serves as a useful and an important reference for physicians or non-specialists to make a diagnosis. In this paper, we designed a health assistant that aims at enhancing the quality and the performance of healthcare services. We intend to develop communication technologies between cloud platform and mobile applications to resolve the data-storage shortage of portable devices. Contribution of our work includes the use of effective and efficient machine learning algorithms (i.e. Bayesian Network, C5.0, Neural Network and Neural-C5.0) which have been compared and applied to diagnosis a heart disease. Our study conducted four experiments and constructed a model on the cloud. And this article summaries the implementation details and presents the results of our study.

Keywords: Machine learning algorithms · Cloud based · Auxiliary diagnosis system · Bayesian Net · C5.0 · Neural network

1 Introduction

As of the internet era, the utilization ratio of medical applications [1,2] by clinicians, patients, and others has increased rapidly. These applications aim at reducing turnaround time in hospitals, and unnecessary expenses [3]. They provide us with useful and timely functionalities including clinical guidance, hospital registration, location-based services and access to health knowledge [2,4,5] They improve our health outcome, healthcare service and help to solve the shortage of medicinal human resources via mobile devices and the Internet.

Heart disease, which is known as coronary artery disease (CAD), occurs when plaque, a sticky substance, narrows or partially obstructs coronary arteries and can result in decreased blood flow. This decreased blood flow may cause chest pain (angina), a warning sign of potential heart problems such as a heart attack. There are many risk factors associated with CAD. Some risk factors, such as high cholesterol, obesity, high blood pressure and diabetes [6], related to patients lifestyle and cannot be ignored. So diagnosing a heart disease involves experience and highly skilled [7]. One possible improvement is the introduction of machine learning algorithms in medical diagnosis.

The authors contributed equally to this work.

© Springer International Publishing Switzerland 2016
C.K. Chang et al. (Eds.): ICOST 2016, LNCS 9677, pp. 477–488, 2016.
DOI: 10.1007/978-3-319-39601-9_43

Advances in the field of artificial intelligence gave rise to the emergence of the auxiliary medical diagnosis system. Machine learning [8–10] is an important branch of artificial intelligence and indeed, it is also one of the most rapidly developing sub fields. In recent years, machine learning algorithms are designed to analyze medical data sets. Data with correct diagnosis for patients is available in the form of medical records. Records of the patients are required to be entered with the known correct diagnoses into a computer program to run a machine learning algorithm. The program will derive a trained classifier and some medical diagnostic knowledge automatically. The classifier will either assist a physician to diagnose a new patient and improve the speed and accuracy, or to help inexperienced physicians and non-specialists to diagnose patients regarding special problems [11].

Motivated by the need to improve the medical services, we designed an auxiliary diagnosis system for heart disease, combining the cloud platform and mobile terminal. Initially, the medical records were prepared and mined to make the training process more efficient. The medical data was afterwards classified using SPSS, a tool for data analysis. Then we compared the performance of several supervised machine learning algorithms (i.e. Bayesian Network, C5.0, Neural Network and Neural-C5.0). Later on, our system was evaluated on a cloud-based mobile application.

2   Related Work

In these recent decades, several machine learning algorithms have been proposed by researchers for developing effective medical diagnosis system. For breast cancer, the majority of surgeons recommended the breast biopsy. However, it was point out [12] that the rate of positive findings is very low. Hence, the author described a new computer-aided diagnosis (CADx) system by decision tree. After analyzing the training data consisting of digital ultrasonographic (US) images of breasts containing pathologically proven tumors, the author adapted the covariance as their features and the texture parameters were used as the inputs to construct the decision tree model. The results suggested that the CADx system performs better than an experienced physician in various indexes, such as accuracy and sensitivity.

Das et al. [7] constructed a neural network ensemble based methodology, focusing on heart disease diagnosis. Three neural networks were used to build the fully automatic model. In [13], three examples about myocardial infarction, back pain and survival probability after severe injury were given so as to prove his conclusion. These examples indicated that the network has the same performance as that of an experienced expert. Medical analysis and diagnosis by Neural Networks will not only release the burden of doctors but also increase the accuracy and efficiency of diagnosis.

Kukar [14] improved the characteristic performance (sensitivity and specificity) of non-invasive symptomatic methods (i.e. clinical examinations of the patients, exercise ECG testing) by evaluating all available diagnostic information with machine learning techniques.

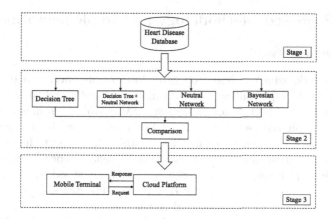

Fig. 1. Framework of the Health Assistant.

However, some issues should be concerned in these work. When we deal with a medical diagnosis problem, it is important to give users the transparency of learned knowledge and the explanation for reasoning process. Thus a comprehensive and efficient machine learning algorithms should be used to solve this problem.

3 An Overview for the Health Assistant

Our design aims at building a cloud-based medical application, taking the advantages of both in Android and cloud platform with a visual human interface. Android platform enables users to use full functionality conveniently with their mobile devices. The cloud platform supplies users with a variety of resources, available computing power and integrated data management. The combination of these techniques is bound to offer better healthcare service to all the users and developers. By merging mobile medical applications and cloud computing, online data management and off-line medicinal healthcare can offer some useful functionality. The framework of the system is shown in Fig. 1.

The increased availability of health data and the urgent need to learn from our previous observations to improve the effectiveness of diagnostic has been led to the formulation of predictive models in clinical studies, public health and individual health. We get the medical records from the UCI machine learning repository. Then we input the medical records of known correct diagnosis to some machine learning techniques (i.e. Bayesian Net, C5.0, and Neural Network) and the program derives predictive classifiers. The performance of different algorithms will be compared and evaluated. Finally, the application will be built on the cloud platform and tested on mobile terminals. Users can diagnose a heart disease by sending a request to the cloud and getting the response from the cloud database through any portable devices anytime and anywhere.

4   The Proposed Methodology and Implementation

4.1   Bayesian Network

Bayesian network, which is based on probabilistic inference, is a probabilistic graphical networks representing a set of random variables and their conditional dependencies via a directed acyclic graph (DAG) [15]. This means that each node of the graph represents a random variable, and each arc represents a direct dependence between two variables. Graphs that reflect the structure of the domain make great difference - they normally reflect expert's understanding of the domain, which can be easily extended and understood by others.

A Bayesian network for U is a pair $B = \langle G, \Theta \rangle$. The first component, namely G, is a DAG whose vertices correspond to the random variables $X_1,...,X_n$, and whose edges represent direct dependencies between the variables. The second component of the pair, called Θ, represents the set of parameters which quantifies the network. It contains a parameter $\theta_{x_i | \Pi_{x_i}} = P_B \left(x_i \mid \Pi_{x_i} \right)$ for each possible value x_i of X_i, and Π_{x_i} of Π_{X_i}, where Π_{X_i} denotes the set of parents of X_i in G. A Bayesian network B defines a unique joint probability distribution over U given by

$$P_B \left(X_1, ..., X_n \right) = \prod_{i=1}^{n} P_B \left(X_i \mid \prod_{X_i} \right) = \prod_{i=1}^{n} \theta_{X_i | \Pi_{X_i}}. \tag{1}$$

4.2   Neural Network

Artificial neural network is a type of computing which is based on the way that a brain performs computations. Neural networks are good at fitting non-linear functions and recognizing patterns by combining many simple computing elements into a highly interconnected system. Knowledge is represented by the strength of connections between nodes and is required by adjusting the connections through a process of learning.

A simple neural model (see in Fig. 2) consists of three (or four) basic elements: a set of synapses, a linear combination, an activation function and bias term B_k (Optional). In our project, the number of units in the input layer equals the amounts of attributes. We use the following formula to determine the number of units in the hidden layer [16], and we set m as zero.

$$N_{hidden} = \sqrt{N_{input} + N_{output}} + m \quad (-5 \le m \le 5). \tag{2}$$

4.3   C5.0

Different from a general statistical classification model, decision tree model, is also known as a rule inference model, is based on logical rules. The decision tree model induces the rules from training samples, and classifies the new samples with these rules. Decision tree model is also known as supervised learning. To build the model, we need only two kinds of variables, target variables and

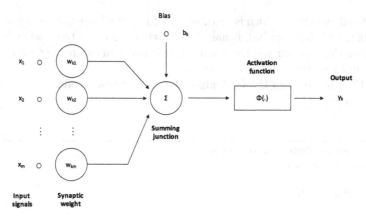

Fig. 2. Structure of a simple neural model.

attribute variables. Thus, a decision tree model can deal with non-numerical data, and it reduces the work of data preprocessing compared to neural network.

The basic requirement to establish a decision tree is to maximize the "difference" between nodes. There are many algorithms to calculate the "difference," and the method of measurement is the major difference between the models. ID3 (Interactive Dichotomiser 3) chooses the attribute which has the optimal information gain to become the child node of decision trees. The formulas of the information theory include entropy and conditional entropy.

$$H(X) = - \sum_{x \in X} p(x) \log_2 p(x) \tag{3}$$

$$H(Y|X) = \sum_{x \in X} p(x)H(Y|X = x) = - \sum_{x \in X} \sum_{y \in Y} p(x)p(y|x) \log_2 p(y|x) \tag{4}$$

So the definition of the mutual information between class label D and attribute A is described below.

$$Gain(D, A) = H(D) - H(D|A) \tag{5}$$

Obviously, the weakness of ID3 is that the model prefers to the attribute which has more values. To tackle this problem, C4.5 algorithm applies the information gain ratio to quantify the "difference". The information gain ratio of attribute A is indicated below.

$$SplitInfo_A(D) = - \sum_{i=1}^{n} \frac{|D_j|}{|D|} \times \log_2 \frac{|D_j|}{|D|} \tag{6}$$

$$GainRatio_A(D) = \frac{Gain(D, A)}{SplitInfo_A(D)} \tag{7}$$

The C5.0 algorithm which is suitable for processing large data sets is a revised version of the C4.5 algorithm. It has also known as boosting trees, since it adapts boosting method to increase the accuracy. It is faster in computing, and occupies less memory resources than C4.5 algorithm.

The C5.0 is based on the C4.5 algorithm. The pseudo code of C5.0 is shown in Algorithm 1.

Input: an attribute-valued data set D
Output: Optimal $Tree$
1 $Tree = \Phi$;
2 **if** D *is "pure"* **then**
3 $\quad$ STOP;

4 **end**
5 **for** *all attribute a belong to D* **do**
6 $\quad$ Compare information-theoretic criteria if we split on a;

7 **end**
8 a_{best} = best attribute according to the above computed criteria;
9 $Tree$ = create a decision node that tests a_{best} in the root;
$\quad$ D_v = induced sub-data sets from D based on a_{best};
$\quad$ **for** *all D_v* **do**
10 $\quad$ $Tree_v$ = C5.0(D_v);
11 $\quad$ Attach $Tree_v$ to the corresponding branch of Tree;
12 **end**
13 return $Tree$;

Algorithm 1. Framework of C5.0

4.4   Neural-C5.0

As it is known to us, the decision tree can learn fast and is robust against noise data. It has excellent comprehensibility but may cause the problem of over-fitting without pruning. While the neural network has strong self-organizing ability and fault-tolerant ability, it is also easily extended to approximate the exact results. However, this algorithm has the shortcoming of low explanation and complex operation. When we deal with a medical diagnosis problem, it is important to give users the transparency of learned knowledge and the explanation for reasoning process. Generally speaking, the decision tree and the neural network can be highly complementary to each other. In our work, we combine the C5.0 algorithm with the neural network algorithms, aiming at improving the performance of medical diagnosis. Neural-C5.0 is a novel algorithm which trains a neural network algorithm ensemble at first and then uses the new result training set as the input of C5.0 to generate the result. We use the SPSS to implement this model, and the visual interface is shown in Fig. 3.

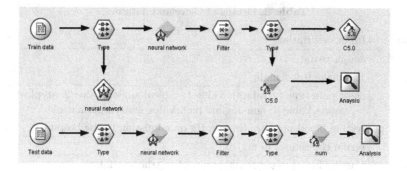

Fig. 3. Neural-C5.0 in SPSS.

Table 1. Division of the Cleveland dataset

Dataset	# of instances	percentage	#presence	#absence
Train set	209	70 %	94	115
Test set	94	30 %	45	49

5 Experiment

Our project conducted four machine learning algorithms on a heart disease database with the help of SPSS. SPSS is a data mining software built by IBM. It was used to build predictive models and conduct other tasks. We compared and analyzed the performance of the algorithms. For a case study, we built the classifier on the cloud platform and evaluated the feasibility of our system on the mobile devices.

5.1 Dataset Description

The heart disease data set was taken from the UCI machine learning repository [17]. We choose the Cleveland database which was created by Cleveland Clinic Foundation. There are 303 instances in the data set of which 297 are complete samples, and six are samples with missing values. We apply 70 % of the heart disease data set to the proposed model, and use the rest of the data set for validation of the system. The detailed information of the data set is shown in Table 1.

The database contains 76 attributes, but all published experiments refer to use a subset of 13 of them. The Cleveland database has concentrated on simply attempting to distinguish presence (values 1) from absence (value 0) of heart disease. The attributes are listed in Table 2.

5.2 Results and Analysis

Four experiments used the identical training and testing sets in order to provide the alike experimental conditions. We use SPSS to conduct four machine

Table 2. Details of Cleveland dataset

Input	Input description
age	age in years
sex	1 = male; 0 = female
cp	chest pain type (4 values): Value 1: typical angina, Value 2: atypical angina, Value 3: non-anginal pain, Value 4: asymptomatic
threstbps	resting blood pressure (in mm Hg on admission to the hospital)
chol	serum cholestoral in mg/dl
fbs	(fasting blood sugar > 120 mg/dl);1 = true,0 = false
restecg	resting electrocardiographic results, Value 0: normal, Value 1: having ST-T wave abnormality (T wave inversions and/or ST elevation or depression of > 0.05 mV), Value 2: showing probable or definite left ventricular hypertrophy by Estes' criteria
thalach	maximum heart rate achieved
exang	exercise induced angina (1 = yes; 0 = no)
oldpeak	ST depression induced by exercise relative to rest
slope	the slope of the peak exercise ST segment, Value 1: upsloping, Value 2: flat, Value 3: downsloping
ca	number of major vessels (0-3) colored by flourosopy
thal	3 = normal; 6 = fixed defect; 7 = reversable defect
Output	Output description
num	diagnosis of heart disease (angiographic disease status), Value 0: < 50 % diameter narrowing Value 1: > 50 % diameter narrowing

learning algorithms and derive predicted classifiers. The classifier learns from the training set and evaluates the performance on the testing set, it finally classifies the data set into two diagnosis classes: a healthy patient, or a patient who possibly has heart disease. Classification results of the system are displayed by using a confusion matrix, which allows visualization of the performance of an algorithm. And we compare the performance of each algorithm by calculating the classification accuracy, sensitivity and specificity. These three indexes are defined in the following formulas.

$$accuracy = \frac{\#true\ postitives + \#true\ negatives}{\#all\ patients} \quad (8)$$

$$sensitivity = \frac{\#true\ postitives}{\#all\ patients\ with\ the\ disease} \quad (9)$$

$$specificity = \frac{\#true\ negatives}{\#all\ patients\ without\ the\ disease} \quad (10)$$

The comparison results in terms of four machine learning techniques are reported in the confusion matrix and Fig. 4. It is obvious that Neural-C5.0 and

Table 3. Confusion matrix of four machine learning algorithms

Cleveland dataset		Train		Test	
		Present	Absent	Present	Absent
Bayesian Net	Positive	79	104	28	42
	Negative	15	11	17	7
C5.0	Positive	83	110	30	42
	Negative	11	5	15	7
Neural network	Positive	80	91	34	40
	Negative	14	24	11	9
Neural-C5.0	Positive	84	113	33	41
	Negative	10	2	12	8

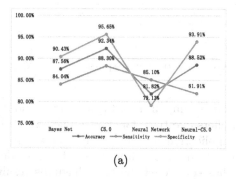
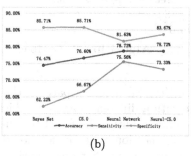

(a)   (b)

Fig. 4. Performance comparison of four machine learning algorithms: (a) Evaluations on training set, (b) Evaluations on testing set.

Neural Network are more accurate than Bayesian Network and C5.0 though C5.0 performs well on the training set. It is easy for a single decision tree to have over fitting problems if the pruning severity is not optimal enough. However, for Neural-C5.0, the neural network process can select the representative features and reduce the scale of the decision tree in the next step. In this way, we dont need to adjust a high pruning severity and can be able to produce a decision tree with better performance than that of a single C5.0 tree (Table 3).

5.3 Case Study

For further use, we built an application as a carrier to evaluate the performance of the system. Focusing on diagnosing patients by themselves privately, our application consists of two parts: mobile terminal and cloud platform. In the android system, the application includes a visual 3D human mannequin. With the mannequin, users can precisely locate the uncomfortable part of their body. Moreover, a 3D mannequin is much more interactive and responsive by rotating or zooming-in/out the model and clicking the screen. The application can have a medical diagnosis on heart disease. Users can send a request to the cloud platform and start answering questions stored on the node of a decision tree. The cloud platform stores the structure of the neural-C5.0 model and sends a response to the mobile devices. Soon it will send the result and feedback to mobile devices.

Algorithm 2 shows the schema of a feedback mechanism to user requests.

Input: *parameters* in a url request
Output: response
1   **if** *parameters reach the nodes* **then**
2   return *Question* on the node;
3   continue to receive the data from Android platform.
4   **end**
5   **if** *parameters reach the leaves* **then**
6   return *diagnosis result*;
7   STOP.
8   **end**

Algorithm 2. Feedback Mechanism to User Request

In Fig. 4(a), clicking parts of the mannequin will lead to the corresponding page with a different database, which offers questions for users. When we click the confirm button in Fig. 4(b), the application would send the answer in a URL to the cloud and request for the next question after choices being made. Figure 4(c) shows that our algorithm has conducted the final diagnosis result and it can be displayed on the screen of the mobile terminal (Fig. 5).

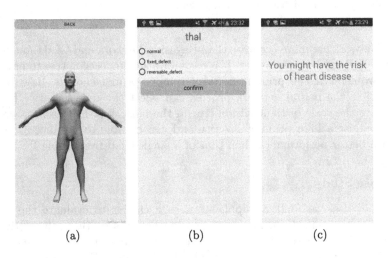

(a)   (b)   (c)

Fig. 5. Workflow of the Health Assistant: (a) Mannequin, (b) Question, (c) Diagnosis result.

6   Conclusion

The paper has presented a medical diagnosis system which combines with a cloud based mobile application. Users are able to diagnose heart diseases via a mobile device freely. A 3D mannequin which supports zooming and panning to locate the involvement area precisely is provided. By evaluating the performance of four machine learning algorithms, we constructed a decision tree model on the cloud platform, succeeded in establishing the connection between cloud server and mobile devices by implementing some simple and useful API interfaces. Also, a highly-reliable, timely-available and scalable services is offered which not only improve user experience, but also benefiting doctors, patients and others. As for future work, it may include improving the security of user authentication techniques on the connection between mobile devices and cloud platform, making the full use of the cloud platform and etc.

References

1. Lewis, T.L., Wyatt, J.C.: mHealth, mobile medical apps: a framework to assess risk and promote safer use. J. Med. Internet Res. **16**(9), e210 (2014)
2. Varshney, U.: Pervasive healthcare and wireless health monitoring. Mob. Netw. Appl. **12**(2–3), 113–127 (2007)
3. Armbrust, M., Fox, A., Griffith, R., Joseph, A.D., Katz, R., Konwinski, A., Lee, G., Patterson, D., Rabkin, A., Stoica, I., et al.: A view of cloud computing. Commun. ACM **53**(4), 50–58 (2010)
4. Varshney, U.: Pervasive healthcare computing: EMR/EHR, wireless and health monitoring. Springer Science & Business Media, New York (2009)
5. Maglogiannis, I., Doukas, C., Kormentzas, G., Pliakas, T.: Wavelet-based compression with ROI coding support for mobile access to dicom images over heterogeneous radio networks. IEEE Trans. Inf. Technol. Biomed. **13**(4), 458–466 (2009)
6. Rajkumar, A., Sophia Reena, G.: Diagnosis of heart disease using datamining algorithm. Glob. J. Comput. Sci. Technol. **10**(10), 38–43 (2010)
7. Das, R., Turkoglu, I., Sengur, A.: Effective diagnosis of heart disease through neural networks ensembles. Expert Syst. Appl. **36**(4), 7675–7680 (2009)
8. Adeli, H., Hung, S.-L.: Machine Learning: Neural Networks, Genetic Algorithms, and Fuzzy Systems. Wiley, New York (1994)
9. Dietterich, T.G.: Ensemble methods in machine learning. In: Kittler, J., Roli, F. (eds.) MCS 2000. LNCS, vol. 1857, pp. 1–15. Springer, Heidelberg (2000)
10. Shavlik, J.W., Dietterich, T.G.: Readings in Machine Learning. Morgan Kaufmann, San Francisco (1990)
11. Kononenko, I.: Machine learning for medical diagnosis: history, state of the art and perspective. Artif. Intell. Med. **23**(1), 89–109 (2001)
12. Kuo, W.-J., Chang, R.-F., Chen, D.-R., Lee, C.C.: Data mining with decision trees for diagnosis of breast tumor in medical ultrasonic images. Breast Cancer Res. Treat. **66**(1), 51–57 (2001)
13. Brause, R.: Medical analysis and diagnosis by neural networks. In: Crespo, J.L., Maojo, V., Martin, F. (eds.) ISMDA 2001. LNCS, vol. 2199, pp. 1–13. Springer, Heidelberg (2001)

14. Kukar, M., Kononenko, I., Grošelj, C., Kralj, K., Fettich, J.: Analysing and improving the diagnosis of ischaemic heart disease with machine learning. Artif. Intell. Med. **16**(1), 25–50 (1999)
15. Friedman, N., Geiger, D., Goldszmidt, M.: Bayesian network classifiers. Mach. Learn. **29**(2–3), 131–163 (1997)
16. Kurkova, V., Kainen, P.C., Kreinovich, V.: Estimates of the number of hidden units and variation with respect to half-spaces. Neural Netw. **10**(6), 1061–1068 (1997)
17. UCI machine learning repository: heart disease data set. http://archive.ics.uci.edu/ml/datasets/Heart+Disease

Activity Detection Using Time-Delay Embedding in Multi-modal Sensor System

Ferdaus Kawsar[1]([✉]), Md. Kamrul Hasan[1], Tanvir Roushan[1],
Sheikh Iqbal Ahamed[1], William C. Chu[2], and Richard Love[3]

[1] Marquette University, Milwaukee, USA
{ferdaus.kawsar,mdkamrul.hasan,tanvir.roushan,sheikh.ahamed}@mu.edu
[2] Tunghai University, Taichung, Taiwan
cchu@thu.edu.tw
[3] Amader Gram, Dhaka, Bangladesh
richardibcrf@gmail.com

Abstract. About two billion people in this world are using smart devices where significant computational power, storage, connectivity, and built-in sensors are carried by them as part of their life style. In health telematics, smart phone based innovative solutions are motivated by rising health care cost in both the developed and developing countries. In this paper, systems and algorithms are developed for remote monitoring of human activities using smart phone devices. For this work, time-delay embedding with expectation-maximization for Gaussian Mixture Model is explored as a way of developing activity detection system. In this system, we have developed lower computational cost algorithm by reducing the number of sensors.

Keywords: Human activity detection · Remote monitoring · Time delay embedding

1 Introduction

Accurate information regarding human physical activity and ability to access that information in real time has far-reaching significance. Activity information is important to doctors who wants to monitor their patients remotely. This technology can be used for monitoring elderly people who wants to maintain their independence. However, such monitoring systems usually require complex devices and significant involvement from the participants. Complex devices can be expensive whereas intrusive systems greatly discourages the usage in real life. Consequently, we focused on developing monitoring systems using smart phones since smart phones are ideal candidate for numerous innovation. Smart devices has significant computational power, storage and communication capability and is conveniently carried out by mass people. Developing a system centered around smart phones will most likely remove the necessity of carrying other extra devices. Even if it is required to use other sensors, it is possible to

© Springer International Publishing Switzerland 2016
C.K. Chang et al. (Eds.): ICOST 2016, LNCS 9677, pp. 489–499, 2016.
DOI: 10.1007/978-3-319-39601-9_44

connect with those sensors using Bluetooth connectivity. As, by now 2 billion people worldwide are using smart phones, we now have a unique phenomenon where significant computational power, storage, connectivity, and built-in sensors are carried by mass people willingly as part of their life style. This unique phenomenon provides a great opportunity in terms of research and innovation. A realistic smart phone based activity monitoring system can help to reduce the cost of health care. The initial results of these works are illustrated in Kawsar et al. (2015).

2   Background

Gaussian Mixture Model (GMM) provides unique opportunity to analyze time series data from multiple sensors. For this reason, we have used this GMM technique for activity detection with time-delay embedding.

2.1   Time-Delay Embedding with Gaussian Mixture Model

Time-delay embedding theorem gives the conditions under which a chaotic dynamical system can be reconstructed from sequence of observations of the state of dynamical system. The reconstruction preserves the properties of dynamical system that do not change under smooth coordinate changes. Taken's theorem (Takens 1981) provides the conditions under which a smooth attractor can be reconstructed from observations. This theorem essentially provides approaches for reconstructing the essential dynamics of the underlying system using a sequence of observations. The assumption is that the dynamics of the underlying system are significantly different for different activities of a person. In our case, we observed accelerometer data along X and Y axis as well as six pressure sensors from left shoe.

   The parameters of time-delay embedding models are learned using a Gaussian Mixture Model. In our experiments, number of mixture models we used are three. In reality, true dimension of phase space is usually unknown. Based on some trial and error, we used a six dimensional phase space with time lag, $\delta = 5$.

2.2   Gaussian Mixture Model

Gaussian mixture models are extension of k-means models. If random variable X is Gaussian, it has the following probability density function(pdf):

$$N(x|\mu, \sigma^2) = p(x) = \frac{1}{\sigma\sqrt{2\pi}} e^{\frac{-(x-\mu)^2}{2\sigma^2}}$$

   The two parameters are mean, μ and variance, σ^2. $p(x)$ can be conveniently written as $N(x|\mu, \sigma^2)$. If we have independent and identically distributed observations X_1^n from a Gaussian distribution with unknown mean μ, maximum likelihood estimation for μ will be $\frac{1}{N}\sum_i x_i$.

Gaussian mixture model (GMM) is useful for modeling data that comes from one of several groups. The groups may be different from each other. However, data from same group can be modeled using Gaussian distribution. A superposition of K Gaussian densities can be written as

$$p(x) = sum_{k=1}^{K} \pi_k N(x|\mu, \sigma^2)$$

which is called a mixture of Gaussians. Each Gauassian density is called a component of the mixture and has its own mean, μ_k and variance σ. The parameters π_k is called mixing co-efficients. Also, $sum_{k=1}^{K} \pi_k = 1$ and $0 \leq \pi_k \leq 1$ in order to be valid probabilities.

Expectation-maximization (EM) algorithm is an iterative method for finding maximum likelihood estimates of parameters in Gaussian Mixture environment. Maximum likelihood estimation in Gaussian mixture model is the estimation of π_k, μ and σ of the component of Gaussian mixture.

3 Related Works

Shaji et al. designed an innovative BMA classifier in Shaji et al. (2016) that can classify different physical activities: walking, jogging, sitting, standing, climbing upstairs, coming downstairs, and lying down. They having got the accuracy of 96.66 %. The tested results of the BMA classifier is integrated with a complete system where the classification system is able to show the above mentioned task getting data from a context aware system and using their algorithm.

Capela et al. (2016) has developed smartphone-based HAR classifier where accelerometer, magnetometer, and gyroscope data were used from smartphone. The author used orientation correction matrix to all sensor data that can give appropriate information on human movement activities for both able-bodied and stroke populations.

For human physical activity recognition, Kwapisz et al. (2011) used phone-based accelerometers in their research to build human physical recognition system. Twenty-nine users performed daily activities such as walking, jogging, climbing stairs, sitting and standing. Labeled accelerometer data were collected from these users. These data was used as training data to build a predictive model for activity recognition. As users always carry cell phones in their pockets, this work can help to collect information about the habits of millions of users.

They have used accelerometer data from android phone to identify several activities. Android was chosen because the OS is free and open-source, easy to program. This architecture has the advantage of using a device since mass people can keep their mobile phone along with themselves. Authors have used the data to extract six features, namely standard deviation, average absolute difference, average resultant acceleration, time between peaks and binned distribution. Now raw time-series accelerometer data must be transformed into examples since standard classification algorithms cannot be directly applied to it. Three classification techniques - decision trees (J48), logistic regression and multilayer neural network from WEKA data mining suite were used. The system is very unobtrusive as the cell phone carried by users work as data collection system. But it requires the users to carry the phone in a certain location.

Indoor location of a person is estimated in Lee and Mase's (2001) work. The system uses a bi-axial accelerometer, a digital compass and an infrared light detector. This work identifies walking and whether the person is walking in level ground, going up or going down. It also counts the number of steps. The strategy adopted by the researchers is hybrid: dead-reckoning for relative measurements and infrared-based beacon method for absolute measurement. Accumulation of error is common in dead-reckoning system and an infrared-based beacon method that detects signals from a transmitter in a fixed place (stairway) helps to correct those errors. By using conventional peak detection algorithm, the system tries to find the peak values at every sampling. If the values of all four peaks follow some specific conditions, step count is incremented. Another feature called cross-correlation function of $x(t)$ and $z(t)$ is used to improve performance. This feature is helpful for discriminating between level and up/down. The classification results show good performance for level and down behaviors but up behavior detection is not satisfactory. One problem with this work is that the connection to central mobile unit is not wireless.

Yang (2009) developed an activity recognition system using the built-in accelerometers in Nokia N95 phone. Although the study achieved relatively high accuracies of prediction, stair climbing was not considered and the system was trained and tested using data from only four users. Decision tree performed best among the four classifiers evaluated. Other classifiers that were evaluated are Naïve Bayes (NB), k-Nearest Neighbor (kNN) and Support Vector Machine (SVM). As phone's position on a human body varies from person to person, its orientation cannot be fixed. Orientation-independent features extraction was also explored in this study.

Miluzzo et al. (2008) exploits various sensors (such as a microphone, accelerometer, GPS and camera) that are available on commercial smart phones for activity recognition and mobile social networking applications. They collected accelerometer data from ten users to build an activity recognition model for walking, running, sitting and standing. Their applications 'CenceMe', collects sensor data of individuals using off-the-shelf, sensor-enabled mobile phones, analyzes these data, detects the activities and share these information through social networking applications such as Facebook and MySpace. To make the system scalable, classification task was shared between cell phones and back-end servers. They also carried a user study on twenty two people who used CenceMe continuously over a three week period.

Both the Symbian operating system and Java Micro Edition (JME) virtual machine which runs on top of the N95 have been designed to use small amounts of memory and computational resources. Designing and implementing 'CenceMe' application on top of this environment was thus resource-constraining. One of the contributions of the paper is the design of lightweight classifiers, running on mobile phones where classification is split between cell phone and servers. Another contribution is the measurement of the RAM, CPU, and energy performance of the classifiers and the whole 'CenceMe' software suite.

4   Experimental Setup

We have illustrated the experimental setup for smart phone based multimodal activity detection system using plantar pressure sensors in this section. In this work, we have proposed a novel architecture for the unobtrusive detection of human physical activity using accelerometer and gyroscope data from smart phones as well as pressure data from shoes. Our architecture was designed to make the system unobtrusive and robust against various human behavior patterns. We developed a prototype of the activity detection system using smart phones and plantar pressure sensors based on our proposed architecture. We identified the various issues that came up while developing the system alongside the caveats and their origins and possible solutions. We analyzed data from four activities and developed an algorithm based on our analysis. Later we tested how our algorithm performs and achieved very good accuracy for the activities in the data analysis stage. Several modifications of the algorithm and the evaluation of their performances were also discussed.

4.1   Proposed Architecture

In this architecture, pressure sensors are placed inside the shoes. These pressure data are transmitted over Bluetooth to the user's smart phone. If the smart phone is in the range of Bluetooth, the data collection is performed smoothly. Since Bluetooth has a range of 5–30 m, the distance from a shoe to the mobile phone is always within bluetooth range. In this case, we tried to collect pressure data from shoes. Plantar pressure sensor system are used with cell phones for activity detection in this research. In addition, we have also collected accelerometer and gyroscope data from the cell phone. The data collection system collects data from these four sensor systems and stores them in four files in three different folders. We used the data collection system in two ways: learning and recognition stage. Plantar pressure sensor system based on a fabric sensor array shown in Fig. 2 is used in this work.

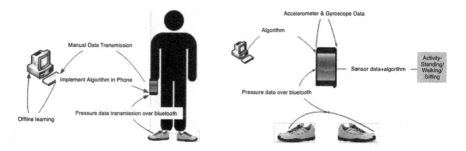

Fig. 1. (a) System architecture for learning stage and (b) system architecture for activity recognition stage.

Fig. 2. Sensor system inside the sole of shoes.

This system was developed by Lin Shu et al. (2010). It has 8 pressure sensors in each shoe. There is also a Bluetooth interface to transfer the pressure data to an Android phone (Fig. 1).

5   Methodology

In this section we have described activity detection using time-delay embedding with Gaussian Mixture Model. The fundamental idea comes from the work of Takens (1981) and Sauer et al. (1991). Their work shows that a time series of observation samples from a system can be used to reconstruct a space topologically equivalent to original system. It is very easy to reconstruct such reconstructive phase space. Time-delay embeddings attempt to reconstruct the state and dynamics of an unknown dynamical from observations of that system taken over time (Frank et al. 2010). Formulating time series algorithm using multi-dimensional phase space is different than developing algorithms using time or frequency domain features (Fig. 3).

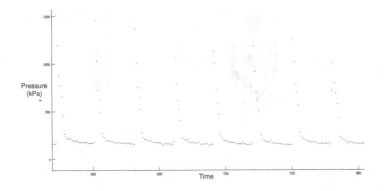

Fig. 3. Data from PS1 for left shoe for running.

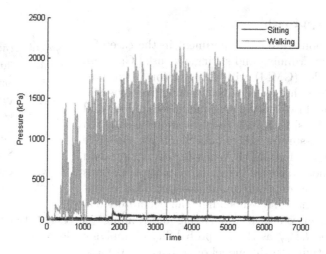

Fig. 4. Data from second pressure sensor (P2) in the left shoe: walking and sitting.

Determining the dimension, d, of reconstructive phase space (i.e. how many measurements have to be considered) and determining τ (at what time the measurements should be taken) is a key problem. A row vector is a point in RPS. d must be greater than two times of the box cutting dimension to be topologically equivalent. In our case, we experimented with the parameter $d = 2$ and $d = 3$. We have presented our findings for these two cases. Following is a plot of a time series for pressure data for pressure sensor 1 (PS1) from left shoe (Fig. 4).

A structure is obvious in Fig. 5 where we made a phase plot in 3 dimension for time lag 5 and 10.

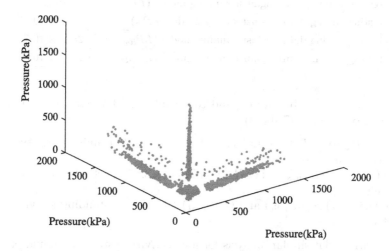

Fig. 5. PhasePlot in 3 dimension with time lag 5 and 10 for running data from pressure sensor 1 of left shoe.

5.1   Our Approach

First we demonstrate our experiment in the case of 2 activities only: running and sitting. We used Gaussian Mixture Model (GMM) with Expectation Maximiza-tion(EM) algorithm for classification of embedding fea-tures. We build two models. One model for running and other one is for sitting. In both cases, we have collected data from pressure sensor data, PS1 of left shoe. We used 5 mixtures for GMM. When tested, sitting data for sitting model showed higher probability; same was true for running data for running model. That means GMM with time delay embedding can accurately dis-tinguish these two activities of sitting and running.

Symbol	Meaning
R	Running
S	Sitting
W	Walking
St	Standing
Sd	Stair down
Su	Stair up
C	Cycling
D	Driving

Fig. 6. Different symbol for various activites

We define LP_{mn} as the log probability of applying data of n activity on the model of activity m. We also define following symbols for 8 activities which shown in Fig. 6. The following table shows the log probabilit for just 1 pressure sensor data, P1 from left shoe. From the above table we see that $LP_{RR} > LP_{sR}$. We also find that $LP_{ss} > LP_{Rs}$. The significance of this numbers is that we can distinguish running and sitting using just 1 pressure sensor P1's data. After a running model is developed from running data and sitting model is made from sitting data, applying running and sitting data on these models show that the probability of running data coming from running model is higher than it coming from sitting model (Table 1).

Table 1. Log probabilities for siting and running activity for P1 from left shoe.

Case	Log probability
Testing running data against running model (LP_{RR})	$-3.0050 \times 10^{+04}$
Testing sitting data against sitting model (LP_{ss})	$-1.7031 \times 10^{+04}$
Testing sitting data against running model (LP_{Rs})	$-4.2674 \times 10^{+04}$
Testing running data against sitting model (LP_{sR})	$-1.1068 \times 10^{+06}$

In the following table, we expand to include standing activity making it a three activity scenario (Table 2).

- Since $(LP_{R\_R}) > (LP_{s\_R})$ and $(LP_{R\_R}) > (LP_{St\_R})$, running activity can be correctly classified.
- Since $(LP_{s\_s}) > (LP_{R\_s}$ and $(LP_{s\_s}) > (LP_{St\_s})$, sitting activity can be correctly classified.
- Since $(LP_{St\_St}) > (LP_{s\_St})$ and $(LP_{St\_St}) > (LP_{R\_St})$, standing activity is cor-rectly classified.

We also carried out similar analysis for four activity system and found out that this approach can correctly classify activities in four activity setting. In our case, these four activities are: sitting, standing, walking and running.

Table 2. Log probabilities for sitting, running and standing activity for P1 from left shoe.

Case	Log probability
Testing running data against running model (LP_{R_R})	$-5.2250 \times 10^{+04}$
Testing sitting data against sitting model (LP_{s_s})	$-3.3829 \times 10^{+04}$
Testing standing data against standing model (LP_{St_St})	$-4.025 \times 10^{+04}$
Testing sitting data against running model (LP_{R_s})	$-1.3754 \times 10^{+05}$
Testing running data against sitting model (LP_{s_R})	$-1.6040 \times 10^{+06}$
Testing standing data against sitting model (LP_{s_St})	$-8.1173 \times 10^{+04}$
Testing sitting data against standing model (LP_{St_s})	$-4.0219 \times 10^{+04}$
Testing standing data against running model (LP_{R_St})	$-1.2025 \times 10^{+05}$
Testing running data against standing model (LP_{St_R})	$-1.1099 \times 10^{+06}$

6   Result

Based on our preliminary experiments, we expanded our system to 8 activity system. These 8 activities are: cycling, running, climbing stairs down, climbing stairs up, walking, sitting and driving.

For each activity, we worked with 3000 samples and we divided the samples in 20 windows making each window with 150 samples. We applied GMM with EM for training. Here we are working with data of single subject. Parameters are as follows:

$$\text{Number of Gaussian Mixture: } 5$$
$$\text{Time Lag}, \tau = 5$$
$$\text{dimension}, d = 6$$

Time Lag, τ and dimension, d were empirically obtained. We adopted a grid search approach and observed the values of τ and d for which activity detection accuracy is best. The following Table 3 shows a confusion matrix derived from applying our approach on accelearation along X-axis. We use the following symbols in the tables: C for cycling, R for running, Sd for downstairs, Su for Upstairs, St for standing, W for walking, Si for sitting and D for driving.

Table 3. Confusion matrix using GMM based on accelerometer data along *X-axis*.

W1	W2	W3	W4	W5	W6	W7	W8	W9	W10	W11	W12	W13	W14	W15	W16	W17	W18	W19	W20	Actual
C	C	C	C	C	C	C	C	C	C	C	C	C	C	C	C	C	C	C	C	C
R	R	R	R	R	R	R	R	R	R	R	R	R	R	R	R	R	R	R	R	R
Sd	Sd	Sd	Sd	Sd	Sd	Sd	Sd	Sd	Sd	Sd	Sd	Su	Sd	Sd	Sd	Sd	Sd	Su	Su	Sd
Su	Su	Su	Su	Su	Su	Su	Su	Su	Su	Su	Su	Su	Su	Su	Su	Su	Su	Su	Su	Su
St	St	St	St	St	St	St	St	St	St	St	St	St	St	St	St	St	St	St	St	St
W	W	W	W	W	W	W	W	W	W	W	W	W	W	Sd	Sd	Sd	Sd	Sd	Sd	W
Si	Si	Si	Si	Si	Si	Si	Si	Si	Si	Si	Si	Si	Si	Si	Si	Si	Si	Si	Si	Si
D	D	D	D	D	D	D	D	D	D	D	D	D	D	C	C	D	D	D	D	D

Table 4. Confusion matrix using GMM based on accelerometer data along *Y-axis*.

W1	W2	W3	W4	W5	W6	W7	W8	W9	W10	W11	W12	W13	W14	W15	W16	W17	W18	W19	W20	Actual
C	C	C	C	C	C	C	C	C	C	C	C	C	C	C	C	C	C	C	C	C
R	R	R	R	R	R	R	R	R	R	R	R	R	R	R	R	R	R	R	R	R
Sd	Sd	Sd	Sd	Sd	Sd	Sd	Sd	Sd	Sd	Sd	Sd	Sd	Sd	Sd	Sd	Sd	Sd	Sd	Sd	Sd
Su	Su	Su	Su	Su	Su	Su	Su	Su	Su	Su	Su	Su	Su	Su	Su	Su	Su	Su	Su	Su
St	St	St	St	St	St	St	St	St	St	St	St	St	St	St	St	St	St	St	St	St
W	W	W	W	W	W	W	W	W	W	W	W	W	W	W	W	W	W	W	W	W
Si	Si	Si	Si	Si	Si	Si	Si	Si	Si	Si	Si	Si	Si	Si	Si	Si	Si	Si	Si	Si
D	D	D	D	D	D	D	D	D	D	D	D	D	D	D	D	D	D	D	D	D

Table 5. Confusion matrix using GMM based on pressure sensor data *P3* of left shoe.

W1	W2	W3	W4	W5	W6	W7	W8	W9	W10	W11	W12	W13	W14	W15	W16	W17	W18	W19	W20	Actual
C	C	C	St	C	Si	C	C	C	C	C	C	C	D	C	C	C	C	C	C	C
R	R	R	R	R	R	R	R	R	R	R	R	R	R	R	R	R	R	R	R	R
Sd	Sd	Sd	Sd	Sd	Sd	Sd	Sd	Sd	Sd	Sd	Sd	Sd	Sd	Sd	Sd	Sd	Sd	Sd	Sd	Sd
Su	Su	Su	Su	Su	Su	Su	Su	Su	Su	Su	Su	Su	Su	Su	Su	Su	Su	Su	Su	Su
St	St	St	St	Si	St	St	St	St	St	St	St	St	St	St	St	St	St	St	St	St
W	W	W	W	W	W	W	W	W	W	W	W	W	W	W	W	W	W	W	W	W
St	St	St	Si	Si	Si	Si	Si	Si	Si	Si	Si	Si	Si	Si	Si	Si	Si	Si	Si	Si
D	D	D	D	D	D	D	D	D	D	D	D	C	D	D	D	D	D	D	C	D

Miss-classifications are shown in red color. Out of $8 \times 20 = 160$ time segments, 11 time segments are misclassified (93.13 % accuracy).

A much better accuracy is achieved by using accelerometer along Y-axis as obvious from the following table (Table 4).

We generated similar confusion matrix based on data from P1, P2, P3, P4, P5, P7. In each case, there are $20 \times 8 = 160$ classifications. For P1, there are 41 miss-classifications. Similarly, for P2, 31; for P3, 9; for P4, 29; for P5, 9; and for P7, there were 12 miss-classifications. As an example of performance of pressure sensors, we show the confusion matrix of P3 (Table 5).

7   Conclusion

Most promising aspect about time-delay embedding with GMM is that significantly good accuracy is obtained just from analysis of small number of sensor data. We have not applied this approach on gyroscope data, neither did we apply on pressure data from right shoe. We are now working to develop a fusion of this approach. For example, we can generate decisions from P1, P2 and P3 sensor and obtain the final decision from fusion of multiple sensor for any time segment. Even with one sensor, we have significant accuracy.

Consequently, it will be possible to reduce computational complexity if we use small number of sensors. As a result, a more energy-saving system can be reality. Such systems can reduce energy cost in two ways. First, as fewer sensor data will be transmitted over Bluetooth, energy can be saved by reducing energy for Bluetooth transmission. Second, as there is less data and consequently, less computation, reduced energy will be needed for computation. Memory and computational saving is significant as it is most likely that activity detection applications will run on resource-constraint smart phones. Most activity system demands real-time detection of accuracy. Reduction in computational cost implies extended battery life. Computational power and battery life, both are scarce resource in cell phones and an algorithm that protects these resources are obviously preferable.

8 Future Works

Our experiment with time-delay embedding shows exciting outcome. This prototype is getting ready to use in Taiwan for elderly care research. Dr. William Chu, the prominent researcher in the field of elderly care, is helping us to setting up the prototype there. In the future, we plan to incorporate multimodal fusion approach with time-delay embedding to improve accuracy further.

References

Capela, N., Lemaire, E., Baddour, N., Rudolf, M., Goljar, N., Burger, H.: Evaluation of a smartphone human activity recognition application with able-bodied and stroke participants. J. NeuroEngineering Rehabil. **13**, 611–622 (2016)

Frank, J., Mannor, S., Precup, D.: Activity and gait recognition with time-delay embeddings. In: AAAI. Citeseer (2010)

Kawsar, F., Hasan, M.K., Love, R., Ahamed, S.I.: A novel activity detection system using plantar pressure sensors andsmartphone. In: 2015 IEEE 39th Annual Computer Software and Applications Conference (COMPSAC), vol. 1, pp. 44–49. IEEE (2015)

Kwapisz, J.R., Weiss, G.M., Moore, S.A.: Activity recognition using cell phone accelerometers. ACM SigKDD Explor. Newslett. **12**(2), 74–82 (2011)

Lee, S.-W., Mase, K.: . Recognition of walking behaviors for pedestrian navigation. In: Proceedings of the 2001 IEEE International Conference on Control Applications 2001, (CCA 2001), pp. 1152–1155. IEEE (2001)

Miluzzo, E., Lane, N.D., Fodor, K., Peterson, R., Lu, H., Musolesi, M., Eisenman, S.B., Zheng, X., Campbell, A.T.: . Sensing meets mobile social networks: the design, implementation and evaluation of the cenceme application. In: Proceedings of the 6th ACM Conference on Embedded Network Sensor Systems, pp. 337–350. ACM (2008)

Sauer, T., Yorke, J.A., Casdagli, M.: Embedology. J. Stat. Phys. **65**(3–4), 579–616 (1991)

Shaji, S., Ramesh, M.V., Menon, V.N.: Real-time processing and analysis for activity classification to enhance wearable wireless ecg. In: Satapathy, S.C., Srujan Raju, K., Mandal, J.K., Bhateja, V. (eds.) Proceedings of the Second International Conference on Computer and Communication Technologies, pp. 21–35. Springer, India (2016)

Shu, L., Hua, T., Wang, Y., Li, Q., Feng, D.D., Tao, X.: In-shoe plantar pressure measurement and analysis system based on fabric pressure sensing array. IEEE Trans. Inf. Technol. Biomed. **14**(3), 767–775 (2010)

Takens, F.: Detecting strange attractors in turbulence. In: Steffens, P. (ed.) EAMT-WS 1993. LNCS, vol. 898. Springer, Heidelberg (1995)

Yang, J.: Toward physical activity diary: motion recognition using simple acceleration features with mobile phones. In: Proceedings of the 1st International Workshop on Interactive Multimedia for Consumer Electronics, pp. 1–10. ACM (2009)

Workshop 2: Smart Rehabilitation Technologies

The Implementation of a Kinect-Based Postural Assessment System

Mu-Chun Su[1(✉)], Sheng-Hung Lin[1], Shu-Fang Lee[2],
Yu-Shiang Huang[2], and Huang-Ren Chen[1]

[1] Department of Computes Science and Information Engineering, National Central University,
Taoyuan City, Taiwan, ROC
muchun@csie.ncu.edu.tw
[2] Department of Rehabilitation, Landseed Hospital, Taoyuan City, Taiwan, ROC

Abstract. In some hospitals, rehabilitation professionals usually adopt the visual assessment incorporated with some posture charts to assess whether a patient has good postures while he or she is standing still or stretching some joints. While the advantages of the visual assessment are its simplicity and no need of expensive equipment, its disadvantages are imprecise, subjective, inefficient, etc. In this paper, we report the implement of a Kinect-based postural assessment system which is able to perform postural assessment and create an analysis report with 62 measurements including 22 angles, 35 distances, and 5 postural rotations. Based on the proposed Kinect-based postural assessment system, rehabilitation specialists are then able to objectively assess the treatment effect after each individual course of treatment. Some experiments were designed to measure the accuracy of the proposed system to verify whether it has the potential of being adopted at hospitals.

Keywords: Postures · Postural assessment · Gaits · Kinect · Therapeutic exercise

1 Introduction

When a patient is admitted at a department of rehabilitation medicine in a hospital, he or she will be assessed by rehabilitation specialists (e.g., rehabilitation doctors, physical therapists, speech therapists, etc.) to devise an appropriate treatment program. According to specific assessment forms, assessment usually involves in body observing (e.g., body, mind, and spirit), recording facts and observations, reporting, monitoring changes, predicting possible outcomes, and making a treatment decision on the needs of the patient.

In many hospitals, especially in some developing and undeveloped countries, the rehabilitation medicine is usually lack of the experience of adopting computerized assessment systems to provide patients with objective measurements and assessments. Most of the rehabilitation professionals usually adopt the visual assessment incorporated with some postural charts so that the assessment will be prone to be imprecise and subjective. Therefore, rehabilitation specialists encounter the problem of being unable to objectively assess the treatment effect after each individual course of treatment.

© Springer International Publishing Switzerland 2016
C.K. Chang et al. (Eds.): ICOST 2016, LNCS 9677, pp. 503–513, 2016.
DOI: 10.1007/978-3-319-39601-9_45

Owing to this problem, it is difficult for rehabilitation specialists to modify their treatment programs to help patients quickly recover from treatment programs and back to normal daily life.

Postures have been considered as an important factor contributing to pains and dysfunction. For example, some researches have shown that posture and equilibrium problems have relations with knee osteoarthritis, neck tension, and back pain [1]. However, postural assessment is still a very challenging task because it tends to be subjective in nature if rehabilitation specialists only adopt simple tools (e.g., goniometer, photographic measurement) to assess postures. The demand for objective postural assessment has become more and more important in these years. A literature review on biomechanical assessment of human posture can be found in [2], where eleven types of technologies (e.g., force plates, photographs, goniometers, sensors, X-ray, Microsoft Kinect sensor, etc.) are discussed. An important issue needs to be solved is the validity and reliability problem. In these years, several measurement technologies have been evaluated based on their validity and reliability [3–9]. An inter-examiner and intra-examiner reliability study was reported in [3]. Souza et al. evaluated the SAPO posture assessment software based on the inter- and intra-examiner reliability of angular measures [4]. Nixon et al. reported the quantitative evaluation of the Kinect sensor for use in an upper extremity virtual rehabilitation environment [5]. Galna et al. established the accuracy of the Kinect in measuring clinically relevant movements in people with Parkinson's disease [6]. Clark et al. established the reliability of the Kinect for the assessment of people following stroke [7]. Cippitelli et al. focused on the validation of a real-time joint extraction algorithm from a side view of a human body [8]. Schmitz et al. provided the measurement of in vivo joint angles during a squat using a single camera markerless motion capture system [9].

The reasons for not adopting computerized assessment systems in some hospitals can be attributed to one or many of the following reasons: (1) some computerized systems are very expensive; (2) there is not yet an system which meets the functional requirements of rehabilitation specialists; (3) rehabilitation specialists are not familiar with the developments of the up-to-date ICT technologies; (4) some assessment systems require long-time training; (5) some assessment systems are not portable; and (6) some hospitals are lack of appropriate assessment environments, etc.

Microsoft Kinect is a viable and low-cost sensing platform capable to provide full-body and limb tracking; therefore, many different approaches have been proposed to utilize the Kinect in rehabilitation and postural assessment [5–8, 10–15]. The evaluation results showed that an average absolute error of angle measurements (e.g., the shoulder joint flexion/extension angle, shoulder joint abduction/adduction angle, and 3-D shoulder joint angle) not exceeding 10.0 % with the comparisons to the Vicon system [5]. Clark et al. stated that although the Kinect my not provide the precision of a multiple camera or body-mounted sensor system, the Kinect provides a more clinically feasible methods on instrumenting gait assessments [7]. Clark et al. reported that the Kinect can be compared to a 3D motion analysis system when assessing anatomical landmark and angular displacement during common postural control tests [11]. All these research results demonstrated that the Kinect is clinically practical.

Although many Kinect-based postural assessment systems have been developed and studied, most of them only provided with measurements of partial regions of the body (e.g., upper extremity [5], movements [6], gait analysis [7, 8], vivo joint angles [9], finger kinematics [12], trunk lean [11, 13], foot posture [14], etc.). This motivated us to implement a Kinect-based postural assessment system which can provide 62 measurements including 22 angles, 35 distances, and 5 postural rotations. Most of the 62 measurements are easy to be computed via the depth information provided by the Kinect; however, since the Kinect is still subjective to inaccurate tracking and skeleton placement, a special algorithm based on the Moore-Penrose generalized Inverse operator is proposed to provide precise measurements about the postural rotations. Some experiments were designed to measure the accuracy of the proposed system to test whether it is clinically practical at hospitals.

The remainder of the paper is organized as follows. We first present the Kinect-based postural assessment system in Sect. 2. In Sect. 3, we give the results obtained by applying the assessment system to assess postures. Finally, Sect. 4 concludes the paper.

2   The Implementation of a Kinect-Based Postural Assessment System

In most hospitals, the execution of the postural assessment is evaluated by a qualified and experienced rehabilitation specialist who adopts the visual assessment and fills the charts with scores. Not surprisingly, these scores are prone to be subjective. Therefore, a computerized posture assessment system which can provide a more objective assessment is required by most rehabilitation specialists in today's evidence-based health care arena. A good computerized postural assessment system should be able to provide precise measurements about postures and output documents of the treatment and progress history. Of course, if the cost of a computerized postural assessment system is low enough but still clinically feasible, then more rehabilitation professionals will be willing to adopt the system for their treatments.

The main goal of this research is to cooperate with the Landseed Hospital in Taiwan to implement a clinically feasible Kinect-based postural assessment system which is able to provide an objective assessment and output an unbiased report of the assessment results. Compared with those existing Kinect-based postural assessment systems which only provided with measurements of partial regions of a participant's body, the system implemented by us can provide 62 measurements including 22 angles, 35 distances, and 5 postural rotations. While the 22 angles (e.g., the horizontal alignment of the head, frontal angle of the right lower limb, vertical alignment of the trunk, left/right hindfoot angle, etc.) was suggested by the protocol of the SAPO software [4] and the 5 postural rotations (e.g., the head, rib cage, and pelvic postural rotation) was measured in [3], the 35 distances (e.g., the distances between the right/left ear and the gravity line, the distance between the anterior superior iliac spines, the distances between the right/left knee and the gravity line, the distances between the right/left shoulder and the gravity line, the length of the right/left foot, etc.) were suggested by a group of experienced rehabilitation professionals at the Landseed Hospital in Taiwan.

To be able to precisely measure 22 angles and 35 distances, total 36 anatomical landmarks are required. One thing should be emphasized is that the placements of the 36 anatomical landmarks play an important role in measuring the angles and distances. The Kinect can provide the 3-D positions of 20 joints but these 20 joints do not all correspond exactly to the positions of the 36 anatomical landmarks, not to mention that we actually need 36 landmarks. Although a markerless postural assessment system is preferred by most of the rehabilitation specialists, we have no choice but require an experienced specialist to place 36 anatomical landmarks on the participant's body.

The procedure for measuring the 22 angles and the 35 distances involves the following four steps.

Step 1. First of all, an experienced specialist place 36 colored balls to serve as the anatomical landmarks on the participant's body as shown in Fig. 1. Basically, we follow the protocol of the SAPO software [4] to locate the 36 anatomical landmarks.

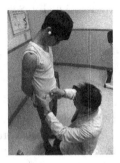

Fig. 1. Participant with anatomical landmarks before static postural assessment.

Step 2. The participant is asked to stand directly facing the Kinect at a distance of 2.5 m. The height of the Kinect is at 1 m above the floor, with the lens perpendicular to the floor and pointing towards the participant. The measurements of the 22 angles and the 35 distances require the 3-D positions of the 36 landmarks and a set of three photographs: anterior view, left lateral view, and posterior view, as shown in Fig. 2.

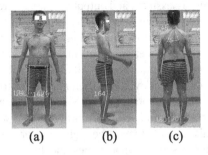

(a)   (b)   (c)

Fig. 2. The 36 anatomical landmarks: (a) anterior view, (b) left lateral view, and (3) posterior view.

Step 3. A colored ball tracking algorithm was developed to locate the 36 colored balls. To reduce the illumination effect, we first transform the RGB color space to the YCbCr color space as follows:

$$\begin{bmatrix} Y \\ Cb \\ Cr \end{bmatrix} = \begin{bmatrix} 0.257 & 0.504 & 0.098 \\ -0.148 & -0.291 & 0.439 \\ 0.439 & -0.368 & -0.071 \end{bmatrix} \begin{bmatrix} R \\ G \\ B \end{bmatrix} + \begin{bmatrix} 16 \\ 128 \\ 128 \end{bmatrix} \qquad (1)$$

where Y, Cb, and Cr represent the luminance, the blue-difference, and red-difference chroma components, respectively. Based on the values of the two chroma components, Cb and Cr, we can quickly locate the 36 colored balls and compute their centroids. In the following, we use the Kinect for Windows SDK v. 18 to determine the 3-D position information for all the located colored balls.

Step 4. Based on the 3-D positions of the 36 landmarks, all the 22 angles and 35 distances can be easily computed. The measurements are then outputted to a report in WORD format.

The aforementioned four-step procedure is for static postural assessment. As for the 5 postural rotations, they involve in dynamic postures. Normand et al. used the PostPrint internet computer system to measure the postures of the head, rib cage, and pelvis as rotations about the Z-axis, Y-axis, and X-axis in degrees and translations in millimeters as displacements from a normal upright stance where they used a right-handed Cartesian coordinate system with X-axis positive to the left, Y-axis positive vertically, and Z-axis positive to the anterior [3]. In total, they measured 9 rotations and 6 translations. In our system, we only measure the five types of the rotations: head rotations about the Z-axis, Y-axis, and X-axis and rib cage rotations about the Z-axis and Y-axis.

The range of motion (ROM) of the head rotation about the Z-axis can be easily computed. First of all, we locate the positions of the forehead and the chin via the use of the face recognition function provided by the Kinect for Windows SDK v. 18. Then the angle between the two vectors connecting the forehead and the chin (as shown in Fig. 3) can be computed via the inner product operator.

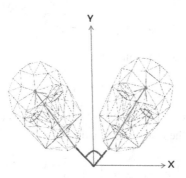

Fig. 3. The ROM of the head about the Z-axis (Rz).

As for the remaining four types of postural rotations, the most important thing needs to solved is the identification of the origin of the rotation axis. First of all, the experienced specialist has to place the colored balls on the participant's chin, ear, center of the chest, and shoulders as shown in Fig. 4. Owing to many disturbing factors (e.g., the displacements during the rotations, the noise, the instability of the Kinect, etc.), the trajectories of the colored balls during rotations may not exhibit a perfect arc as shown in the bottom portion of Fig. 4. If we can't find the right origin of the rotation axis then the computations of the ROM will be wrong.

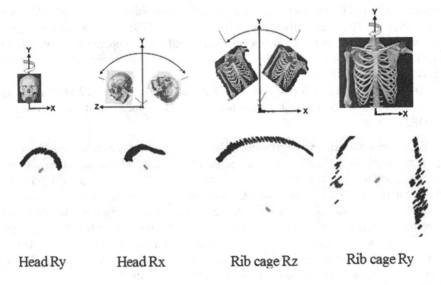

Head Ry   Head Rx   Rib cage Rz   Rib cage Ry

Fig. 4. Four types of postural rotations and their trajectories: head about the Y-axis (Head Ry), head about the X-axis (Head Rx), rib cage about the Z-axis (Rib cage Rz), and rib cage about the Y-axis (Rib cage Ry).

A circle with the center coordinates (a, b) and radius r can be defined by the following equation:

$$(x - a)^2 + (y - b)^2 = r^2 \qquad (2)$$

We may rearrange (2) to be as follows:

$$r^2 - a^2 + b^2 + a(2x) + b(2y) = x^2 + y^2 \qquad (3)$$

Assume we have collected n trajectory points, $(x_1, y_1), \ldots, (x_n, y_n)$, during the rotation procedure. We then have the following equation:

$$\begin{bmatrix} 1 & 2x_1 & 2y_1 \\ 1 & 2x_2 & 2y_2 \\ \vdots & \vdots & \vdots \\ 1 & 2x_n & 2y_n \end{bmatrix} \cdot \begin{bmatrix} r^2 - a^2 - b^2 \\ a \\ b \end{bmatrix} = \begin{bmatrix} x_1^2 + y_1^2 \\ x_2^2 + y_2^2 \\ \vdots \\ x_n^2 + y_n^2 \end{bmatrix} \leftrightarrow W \cdot \vec{p} = \vec{\theta} \qquad (4)$$

where W is an $n \times 3$ matrix, $\vec{p}$ is a 3×1 column vector, and $\vec{\theta}$ is an $n \times 1$ column vector. We may use the Moore-Penrose generalized Inverse operator to compute $\vec{p}$ as follows:

$$\underline{p} = W^+\underline{\theta} = (W^TW)^{-1}W^T \tag{5}$$

After we have computed the $\vec{p}$, we then can find the center coordinates (a, b) and radius r. Based on the computed center coordinates (a, b) and radius r, the ROM can be computed.

3 The Experimental Results

In this section, we present the experimental results for testing the measurement reliability of the Kinect-based postural assessment system. Many aforementioned systems (e.g., [5, 6]) were compared against an infrared camera Vicon system which can be regarded as a gold standard. In addition, most of them reported the reliability in terms of the inter- and intra-class correlation (ICC). In reliability studies, if a method with the value of the ICC higher than a threshold (e.g., 0.7) then it will be claimed to be sufficiently reproducible.

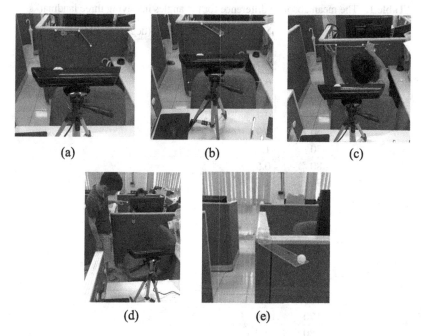

Fig. 5. The ground truth preparing for two types of angles, distance, and rotations. (a) the angles involving three landmarks, (b) the angles involving 2 landmarks and horizontal alignment, (c) the distance between two landmarks, (d) the rotation about the Z-axis, (e) the rotation about the Y-axis.

Although the ICC can serve as a good indicator of reliability, it cannot give clinically relevant information of the true accuracy [3]. In order to demonstrate the Kinect-based postural assessment system implemented by us is clinically feasible, we decided to adopt the mean absolute differences to verify the reliability of the system.

The computations of the 22 angles can be dichotomized into two types: (1) the angles involving three landmarks (e.g., A1, A2, A3, A8, A11, A12, A13, A15, A16, and A18 in [4]) and (2) the angles involving 2 landmarks and horizontal or vertical alignment (e.g., A4, A5, A6, A7, A9, A10, A14, A17, A19, and A20 in [4]). For each type of angles, we created the ground truth for every $10°$ from $10°$ to 180 or $90°$ as shown in Fig. 5(a, b). Then we use the system to measure each angle with ten times. The mean absolute differences are tabulated in Tables 1 and 2. The overall mean absolute difference is no larger than $1.5°$.

The computations of the 35 distances can be dichotomized into two types: (1) the distances between two landmarks and (2) the distance between a landmark and the gravity line. Basically, the accuracy of the measurement of the second type of distance is the same as the first type of distance; therefore, we only verify the accuracy of the first type of distance. First of all, we created the ground truth for every 5 cm from 5 cm to 100 cm as shown in Fig. 5(c). Then we use the system to measure each distance with ten times. The mean absolute differences are tabulated in Table 3. The overall mean absolute difference is no larger than 0.6 cm.

Table 1. The mean absolute difference for the angles involving three landmarks.

Degree	Mean absolute difference (degree)
10	0.5
20	0.7
30	0.6
40	0.6
50	0.7
60	0.9
70	1.3
80	0.5
90	1.6
100	2.9
110	0.7
120	0.7
130	2.0
140	1.1
150	1.6
160	1.2
170	1.6
180	1.2
Average	**1.1**

Table 2. The mean absolute difference for the angles involving 2 landmarks with respect to horizontal alignment.

Degree	Mean absolute difference (degree)
0	0.9
10	0.6
20	0.7
30	2.2
40	2.0
50	1.4
60	2.7
70	2.4
80	0.8
90	1.5
Average	**1.5**

Table 3. The mean absolute difference for the distance between two landmarks.

Distance (cm)	Mean absolute difference (cm)
5	0.2
10	0.5
15	1.2
20	0.4
25	0.9
30	0.7
35	1.0
40	1.1
45	0.7
50	1.1
55	0.3
60	0.3
65	0.9
70	0.4
75	0.2
80	0.4
85	0.4
90	0.5
95	0.4
100	0.5
Average	**0.6**

The computations of the 4 postural rotations shown in Fig. 4 can be dichotomized into three types: (1) rotation about the X-axis, (2) rotation about the Z-axis and (3) rotation about the Y-axis. Basically, the accuracy of the measurement of the first type of distance is the same as the second type of distance; therefore, we only verify the accuracy of the two types of rotations: rotation about the Z-axis and rotation about the Y-axis. First of all, we created the ground truth for every 10° from 10° to 180° as shown in Fig. 5(d, e). Then we use the system to measure each angle with ten times. For the rotation about the Z-axis, if the rotation angle is larger than 50° then the overall mean absolute difference is 1.7°. However, if the rotation angle is smaller than 50° then the overall mean absolute difference is too larger to be acceptable. For the rotation about the Y-axis, if the rotation angle is smaller than 60° then the overall mean absolute difference is too larger to be acceptable. However, if the rotation angle is larger than 60° then the overall mean absolute difference is 5.9°. In our opinion, the large amount of error may be attributed to the inaccuracy and instability of the depth information provided by the Kinect.

4   Conclusions

In this paper, we reported the implementation of a Kinect-based postural assessment system which can create an analysis report with 62 measurements including 22 angles, 35 distances and 5 postural rotations. The experimental results showed that the system could provide acceptable performance in measuring the angles and distances. While the overall mean absolute difference of an angle measurement is either 1.1 or 1.5°, the overall mean absolute difference of a distance measurement is 0.6 cm. Compared with the manual measuring method with the use of simple tools such as goniometer and photographic measurement, this level of errors could be acceptable for many rehabilitation professionals. As for the rotation angles, if the rotation angle is larger than 60° then the system may be acceptable. Otherwise, the error is too large to be acceptable.

Acknowledgements.   This paper was partly supported by Ministry of Science and Technology, Taiwan, R.O.C., under NSC 104-2221-E-008-074-MY2 and NCU-LSH Joint Research Foundation 102-LSH-105-A-004.

References

1. Missaoui, B., Portero, P., Bendaya, S., Hanktie, O., Thoumie, P.: Posture and equilibrium in orthopedic and rheumatologic diseases. Neurophysiologies Clin./Clin. Neurophysiol. **38**(6), 447–457 (2008)
2. Do, J.L., Rosário, P.: Biomechanical assessment of human posture: a literature review. J. Bodywork Mov. Ther. **18**(3), 368–373 (2014)
3. Normand, M.C., Descarreaux, M., Harrison, D.D., Harrison, D.E., Perron, D.L., Ferrantelli, J.R., Janik, T.J.: Three dimensional evaluation of posture in standing with the PosturePrint in an intra- and inter-examiner reliability study. Chiropractic Osteopathy **15**, 15 (2007)
4. Souza, J.A., Pasinato, F., Basso, D., Corrêa, E.C.R., da Silva, A.M.T.: Biophotogrametry: reliability of measurements obtained with an posture assessment software (SAPO). Revista Brasileira de Cineantropometria E Desempenho Humano **13**(4), 299–305 (2011)
5. Nixon, M.E., Howard, A.M., Chen, Y.P.: Quantitative evaluation of the Microsoft Kinect for use in an upper extremity virtual rehabilitation environment. In: 2013 International Conference. Virtual Rehabilitation (ICVR), pp. 222–228 (2013)

6. Galna, B., Barry, G., Jackson, D., Mhiripiri, D., Olivier, P., Rochester, L.: Accuracy of the Microsoft Kinect sensor for measuring movement in people with Parkinson's disease. Gait Posture **39**, 1062–1068 (2014)
7. Clark, R.A., Vernon, S., Mentiplay, B.F., Miller, K.J., McGinley, J.L., Pua, Y.H., Paterson, K., Bower, K.J.: Instrumenting gait assessment using the kinect in people living with stroke: reliability and association with balance tests. J. NeuroEngineering Rehabil. **12**(15) (2015). doi:10.1186/s12984-015-0006-8
8. Cippitelli, E., Gasparrini, S., Spinsante, S., Gambi, E.: Kinect as a tool for gait analysis: validation of a real-time joint extraction algorithm working in side view. Sensors **15**, 1417–1434 (2015)
9. Schmitz, A., Ye, M., Boggess, G., Shapiro, R., Yang, R., Noehren, B.: The measurement of in vivo joint angles during a squat using a single camera markerless motion capture system as compared to a marker based system. Gait Posture **41**, 694–698 (2015)
10. Huang, J.D.: Kinerehab: a kinect-based system for physical rehabilitation — a pilot study for young adults with motor disabilities. In: The 13th International ACM SIGACCESS Conference on Computers and Accessibility, pp. 319–320 (2011)
11. Clark, R., Pua, Y.H., Fortin, K., Ritchie, C., Webster, K.E., Denehy, L., Bryant, A.L.: Validity of the Microsoft Kinect for assessment of postural control. Gait Posture **36**, 372–377 (2012)
12. Metcalf, C.D., Robinson, R., Malpass, A.J., Bogle, T.P., Dell, T.A., Harris, C., Demain, S.H.: Markerless motion capture and measurement of hand kinematics: validation and application to home-based upper limb rehabilitation. IEEE Trans. Biomed. Eng. **60**, 2184–2192 (2013)
13. Clark, R.A., Pua, Y.H., Bryant, A.L., Hunt, M.A.: Validity of the Microsoft Kinect for providing lateral trunk lean feedback during gait retraining. Gait Posture **38**, 1064–1066 (2013)
14. Mentiplay, B.F., Clark, R.A., Mullins, A., Bryant, A.L., Bartold, S., Paterson, K.: Reliability and validity of the Microsoft Kinect for evaluating static foot posture. J. Foot Ankle Res. **6**(14) (2013). doi:10.1186/1757-1146-6-14
15. Su, M.C., Jhang, J.J., Hsieh, Y.Z., Yeh, S.C., Lin, S.C., Lee, S.F., Tseng, K.P.: Depth-sensor-based monitoring of therapeutic exercises. Sensors **15**(10), 25628–25647 (2015)

Author Index

Printed in the United States
By Bookmasters